American Literature

VOLUME

9

OF THE NEW PELICAN GUIDE TO
ENGLISH LITERATURE

EDITED BY BORIS FORD

PENGUIN BOOKS

PENGUIN BOOKS

Published by the Penguin Group
Penguin Books Ltd, 27 Wrights Lane, London W8 5TZ, England
Penguin Putnam Inc., 375 Hudson Street, New York, New York 10014, USA
Penguin Books Australia Ltd, Ringwood, Victoria, Australia
Penguin Books Canada Ltd, 10 Alcorn Avenue, Toronto, Ontario, Canada M4V 3B2
Penguin Books (NZ) Ltd, Private Bag 102902, NSMC, Auckland, New Zealand

Penguin Books Ltd, Registered Offices: Harmondsworth, Middlesex, England

This edition first published in Penguin Books 1967
Published with a revised Further Reading, 1995
3 5 7 9 10 8 6 4

This edition copyright © Penguin Books 1967
Introduction and Notes copyright © G. R. Hibbard, 1967
Further Reading copyright © Michael Taylor, 1995
All rights reserved

Printed in England by Clays Ltd, St Ives plc
Set in Monotype Ehrhardt

CONTENTS

CONTENTS

PART III: THE MODERN AGE

PART IV

PART V: BIBLIOGRAPHY

GENERAL INTRODUCTION

This volume is the last in the series entitled *The New Pelican Guide to English Literature* – not, be it emphasized, a guide to the literature of England, but to literature in English. Thus earlier volumes have included chapters on Scots, Irish, Welsh, Australian and African writers, as well as a whole volume on medieval European literature; and this volume is entirely devoted to American writers. Though American literature is a large and important part of English literature, it is probably the case that much of it is still too little known on the European side of the Atlantic.

The publication of this, as of the earlier volumes of the *Guide*, is something of an act of faith: faith, that is, in the continuing importance of literature at a time when it often seems to be in danger of being submerged beneath the sheer mediocrity of the tens of thousands of books and magazines published each year and the blandishments of a mass entertainment industry. To take one's stand on the 'importance' of literature is not to strike pseudo-religious or socially ameliorative attitudes, but to remind oneself and others that literature, like music and the visual arts, can be a major source of enjoyment and spiritual replenishment. At its best it invokes and fosters a concern for humane values. Moreover, a faith in literature is bound to be a faith in readers, in the continuing potentiality of a 'common' and discriminating reader.

This is not to suggest that it is easy to read serious novels and poetry today. Indeed, it has not been made any the easier and certainly not any the more enjoyable by those waves of 'newer critics' for whom literature appears mainly to provide raw material for dissection, deconstruction, linguistic analysis, and radical historicism. For the very many readers who would enjoy and understand American literature, this volume offers five kinds of related material:

(i) *An introductory account* of colonial literature and society.

(ii) *Surveys of the social context of literature* in the nineteenth and twentieth centuries, providing an account of contemporary society at its points of contact with literature.

(iii) *Two literary surveys*, describing the general characteristics of American literature in such a way as to enable the reader to trace its growth and keep his or her bearings. The aim of these sections is to answer such questions as 'What *kind* of literature was written in this period?', 'Which authors seem to matter most, and why?', 'Where do the main strengths of the period lie?'

(iv) *Detailed studies* of some of the chief writers and themes in each period. Following on the general surveys, these studies aim to convey a sense of what it means to read closely and with perception; and also to suggest how the literature of a given period is best read, i.e. with what assumptions and with what kind of attention. There is also a final chapter which traces the main traditions and continuities and discontinuities in American literature as a whole.

(v) *An appendix of essential facts for reference purposes*, such as authors' and general bibliographies, books for further study, and so on.

The contributors are American and British and British-Canadian. It has seemed right to allow them to retain their American or English spelling.

*

Finally, my very considerable thanks are due to Donald McFarlan of Penguin Books, who with unfailing help and friendliness steered all the eleven volumes of *The New Pelican Guide* through to publication. I also owe a great debt for all the guidance they have offered me in the planning of this volume to Professors Seymour and Sarah Betsky; but for serious illness they would have contributed four chapters to the volume. And lastly, for help of many kinds at the American end of the operation, I would like to thank Celia McGee.

BORIS FORD

The New Pelican Guide to English Literature consists of eleven volumes:

PART I

LITERATURE AND SOCIETY IN
COLONIAL AMERICA

SUSAN MANNING

We must, indeed, all hang together, or most assuredly we shall all hang
separately.

(Benjamin Franklin)

First Reports from the New-found Land

The country is not mountanous nor yet low but such pleasant plaine hils
& fertile valleyes, one prettily crossing another, and watered so conveniently
with their sweete brookes and cristall springs, as if art it selfe had devised
them. By the rivers are many plain marishes containing some 20 some 100
some 200 Acres, some more, some lesse. Other plaines there are fewe, but
only where the *Savages* inhabit: but all overgrowne with trees and weedes
being a plain wildernes as God first made it . . .

(John Smith, *A Map of Virginia*, 1612, p. 3)

Captain John Smith (1580–1631) was an English adventurer who
chronicled the commercial venture which founded the first viable
settlement in the American colonies in Jamestown, Virginia, in 1607.
His account of the land is historical and geographical; it intends to
inform the European reader with the facts of his experience, but the
'sweet brooks and crystal springs', 'as though devised by art', are the
landscape of European pastoral convention; the idyllic area of fertile
plains is an Eden surrounded by a howling wilderness, here peopled
by savages (the indigenous Indians). Order is precariously held in an
environment of chaos. The *Map of Virginia* shows how, from the
beginning, the meaning of America was first projected onto the
land, and then reported back as objective description.

Since Columbus reported his unexpected discovery to Ferdinand
and Isabella of Spain in 1492, European observers and settlers have
confronted the pristine facts of America with a language already
freighted with centuries of tradition and association – *European*
realities. This language 'belonged' in Europe, has its roots and its

3

growth there, and it was applied, fully developed, to a set of circumstances of which it had no intimate knowledge. The complex structures of European thought unavoidably determined not only how the first adventurers viewed America, but what they saw.

The settlers tried to build up a picture intimately derived from concrete realities; American literature is obsessed with catalogues of objects, the observable *facts* of the land. Until European culture confronted the American continent, language had never needed to be innocent, or tried to be so. But when the colonists attempted to bring civilization into the wilderness, to make the facts conform to the pattern they imposed, they found that the wilderness fought back – a settlement was wiped out by savages or swamp-fever; literary models had to be radically revised to accommodate unforeseen but inescapable facts. The first literature of America was propaganda or polemic; it was *purposive* – on a mission to persuade. But it was also distanced from the world it described. From the beginning, American writers exploited a division between the verbal and concrete realities, between language and meaning, between the facts and the way they are described. Their language became self-conscious, no longer guaranteeing meaning, but a double-agent which betrayed the truth it seemed to discover.

The equivocating relationship between language and reality, model and fact, was intensified and given ideological status by the Puritans who arrived in America after 1620 under the double impetus of flight and positive mission. Fleeing from religious oppression by the High Anglicans under Archbishop Laud in England, and driven by the corruption of the English church, they believed themselves to have been divinely chosen to re-establish Christian purity in the unconstrained circumstances of the new land.

Doctrinally, Puritanism was similar to other Reformation theology; its distinctiveness lay in the rigour with which it applied its principles to life, the strong codifying impulse which tended to resolve any complex or ambivalent position into a simpler, polarized one. The Fall was the primary fact of the Puritan consciousness; it marked an irrevocable division into 'before' and 'after'. In it, all mankind was justly damned; God, however, had arbitrarily selected some (the Elect) for salvation through grace. Their fate, like that of the damned or Reprobate, was eternally fixed and unalterable. Salvation, as Luther taught, was by *faith*, through grace, and could not be accomplished by virtuous action. The world was structured as a series of dramatic oppositions: between good and evil, man and God, the Elect and the Reprobate, Faith and Works. The Fall had corrupted man's vision: the Book of Nature, in which he had once been able to perceive God's will directly, now became an enigma, to be interpreted only with the aid of grace and of the other Book, Scripture. The relation between language – the Word – and object was no longer directly descriptive but symbolic: the Fall had introduced to human perception a division between objects and their significance. Without the consciousness of grace meaning was unstable, and every man was shut up inside his own interpretation of the alien world he viewed. The *possibility* of innocent, pristine observation remained, however. The fallen eye was cleansed through the regenerative process of conversion, which was undergone by the Elect as they became conscious of their final salvation. For them, fact would once again be luminous with its own meaning, and the divine pattern would conform to the observed reality.

The Puritan mind was divided between a sense of mission (its reformist, active pole) and a consciousness of alienation (from God, from Nature and from other men). While the mission could be codified as public statement, a declaration of intention, the alienation of the Puritan tended to remain a very private anguish of the soul, a retreat in times of doubt or failed confidence.

The literary consequences of this division did not become immediately apparent. As long as the Puritan settlers in America felt themselves to be fulfilling God's mission, they could believe that the observable fact and its spiritual significance were simultaneously visible to them as a group through God's providential grace. The pre-Reformation church had solved the problem of the corruption of human vision by a combined appeal to papal infallibility and church tradition; the Puritans rejected both, but found an alternative source of authority in the notion of consensus: the joint assent of the community of 'visible saints' (those who could testify to their own conversion and be confident of Election) was taken to be the expression of divine will. The Puritan community therefore exerted a powerful pressure on its members towards consensus and conformity. The presence of dissidents threatened not only social stability, but also the divine authority of the Elect. John Winthrop (1588–1649) declared this sense of communal mission in the sermon 'A Model of Christian Charity' which he preached on board the ship *Arbella* in the mid-Atlantic:

> ... wee must be knitt together in this worke as one man ... allwayes haveing before our eyes our Commission and Community in the worke, our Community as members of the same body, soe shall wee keepe the unitie of the spirit in the bond of peace, the Lord will be our God and delight to dwell among us ... for wee must Consider that wee shall be as a Citty upon a Hill, the eies of all people are uppon vs; soe that if wee shall deale falsely with our god in this worke wee have undertaken, and soe cause him to withdrawe his present help from us, wee shall be made a story and a by-word through the world ...
>
> (Miller and Johnson, eds, *The Puritans*, I, pp. 198–9)

Here the active millennialism which sounds a recurrent note through American history and literature is at a point of high confidence. Before theory has been tried by practice, Winthrop reminds his fellow-passengers of the sacramental nature of their mission, of its importance to the rest of the world, and of the direct support which God has granted them. Sacrifices will be required of them but, most of all, the mission will succeed or fail with the cohesion or otherwise of the community: the perils of dissension are incalculable.

Once they arrived in America, the Puritans engaged in the double activity of reinforcing their symbolic religious mission by accommodating their experiences to an Old Testament idiom in which they were the Jews, God's chosen people, fleeing from oppression in Egypt to a new Canaan, and of adapting this rhetoric to the realities they found. They believed that events in the Old Testament prefigured and were fulfilled in their own experiences; the idea of America, from the beginning, carried a quasi-religious freight. The typological model attempts to re-unite the temporal (the observed fact) with the eternal (its meaning). America was the new Eden. Reality, however, constantly resisted the Puritan pattern. To assimilate the ideal to the harsh actuality of the untamed land peopled with savages which they encountered, they coined oxymorons like 'Wilderness Zion', establishing a fragile verbal consensus or Middle Way between the extremes.

The Puritan enterprise, from the beginning, was a highly self-conscious one, and the settlers commented on their daily labour of taming the wilderness, planting crops and establishing a civil polity in a series of diaries, sermons, poems and histories which derived the ultimate significance of mundane events in the cosmic scheme. Nothing was neutral or random; every fact had to be interrogated for its meaning. There is almost nothing in early colonial literature which could be described as belles lettres: William Bradford (1590–1657), the first governor of the Plymouth colony, believed that in the first landing of the Pilgrims Providence was made visible, God was acting in time. He described this enterprise in his *History of Plimmoth Plantation:*

> Being thus passed the vast ocean, and a sea of troubles before in their preparation ... they had now no freinds to wellcome them, nor inns to entertaine or refresh their weatherbeaten bodys, no houses or much less townes to repaire too, to seeke for succoure. It is recorded in scripture as a mercie to the apostle and his shipwraked company, that the barbarians shewed them no smale kindnes in refreshing them, but these savage barbarians, when they mette with them (as after will appeare) were readier to fill their sides full of arrows then other wise ... Besides, what could they see but a hidious and desolate wildernes, full of wild beasts and willd men? and what multitudes ther might be of them they knew not. Nether could they, as it were, goe up to the top of Pisgah, to vew from this willdernes a more goodly cuntrie to feed their hopes; for which way soever they turnd their eyes (save upward to the heavens) they could have litle solace or content in respect of any outward objects ...
>
> (ed. Adams, 1912, 1968, I, pp. 155–6)

The Puritan combination of mission and alienation is perfectly realized here. From the beginning, the facts failed to fit the model, the individual instance seemed to betray the general promise and outward objects would not conform to inward expectations. An ordered public language confronted a cruel wilderness which refused to obey its rules. Faith sustained the Puritans, however, over the disjunction which threatened their mission, and Bradford tells the quintessential American story of successful enterprise from unpromising beginnings. The colony grows and flourishes under his governance and God's providential guidance, learns how to survive Indian attacks and the undermining activities of traitors, and declines from its original purity:

For now as their stocks increased and the increse vendible, ther was no longer any holding them togeather, but now they must of necessitie goe to their great lots ... the towne, in which they had lived compactly till now, was left very thine and in a short time allmost desolate ... those that had lived so long togeather in Christian and comfortable fellowship must now part and suffer many divissions.

(II, pp. 151–2)

Division not only weakens the community, it is the emblem of moral failure. Cohesion kept a precarious balance in the wilderness; without a corporate faith the model of civility is at the mercy of the lawless facts which desire its destruction.

Puritan New England

The 1630s saw the establishment of a theocratic, Congregational Puritan society in Massachusetts. Attendance at church was compulsory, but church membership was restricted to those who could satisfy the congregation that they were amongst the Elect, and therefore fit to help govern the community. A series of social, religious and political covenants (which would culminate in the Declaration of Independence of 1776) codified the civil arrangements of the society in a legalistic manner that was taken to reflect God's original covenants with the Jews. New England society was not democratic; the consensus which justified and perpetuated the Puritans' mission was carefully monitored and adjusted.

The first generation of settlers managed to achieve a 'consensus' between the covenants of faith and works, to make livable their polarized theology. The Puritan was assured that in practice faith in God and good works were inseparable; a man could not be saved by works alone, but if he were justified by faith, a holy life would follow. Similarly, although the state of a man's soul could not be determined by his outward acts (which was why the testimony of his inward conviction of conversion was necessary), no member of the Elect would lead an unholy life. Thus the demands of theology could be accommodated to worldly needs; a frontier society could not afford sanctimonious idlers amongst its Elect.

An English emigrant became New England's first important poet. Anne Bradstreet (?1612–72), retained the 'European' sensibility which allowed her language to sustain a confident interpenetration of fact and meaning. Her poem 'Upon the burning of our House' lends conviction to its final affirmation of God's providential goodness by not undervaluing the material loss of home, possessions and associations:

> My pleasant things in ashes lye,
> And them behold no more shall I.
> Under thy roof no guest shall sitt,
> Nor at thy Table eat a bitt . . .
>
> Then streight I gin my heart to chide,
> And did thy wealth on earth abide? . . .
>
> Thou hast an house on high erect
> Fram'd by that mighty Architect,
> With glory richly furnished,
> Stand permanent tho' this bee fled.
> Its purchasèd, and paid for too
> By him who hath enough to doe . . .
>
> Ther's wealth enough, I need no more;
> Farewell my Pelf, farewell my Store,
> The world no longer let me Love,
> My hope and Treasure lyes Above.

The mission which bids the Puritan alienate himself from the things of this world is heeded by the poet: the events can be accepted as part of the providential scheme, but there is sufficient real conflict remaining to make the penultimate line a plea rather than a flat assertion. The poignant memory of family suppers eaten in the earthly house which is now ashes gives unassailable currency to the redemptive sacrifice commemorated by the Lord's Supper which promises a heavenly home. Natural facts inevitably brought spiritual facts to mind; the connection does not dismiss the value of the natural, however, but rather enhances it: the world is penetrated by spirit as well as opposed to it. Pattern and fact, the public declaration and the private response, find a single idiom which overcomes their opposition. This was a European voice which was not sustainable for long in colonial America.

The inherent tension in Puritan doctrine between social cohesion and individualism or separatism had troubled colonial society from the beginning. Puritanism tended to make every man's soul the arbiter of his actions and his fate; this was potentially anarchic, and the Puritan authorities insisted that although every man had a duty to work out his own salvation, 'Society in all sorts of humane affaires is better than Solitariness' (*The Puritans*, I, p. 183). Massachusetts in fact forbade solitary living; between 1669 and 1697 the authorities pursued sixty people for living alone. The colony faced its first political crisis during the 1630s, when the Antinomians Roger Williams and Anne Hutchinson challenged in different ways the right of the state to determine matters which they believed belonged only to the soul of the individual. Antinomians took to its logical conclusion the Puritan tenet that the voice of God was heard directly in the Elect soul. In their absolute allegiance to the light within, they anticipated the calls to spiritual experience which would split the New England churches during the Great Awakenings or religious revivals that swept the country a century later.

Just how precarious was the 'middle way' trodden in Massachusetts becomes evident when we understand that it was the sermons of John Cotton (1584–1652), one of the most senior and most respected of colonial ministers, which inspired the thinking of Anne Hutchinson. Their doctrinal positions were almost indistinguishable. The difference was that Cotton, mindful always of human frailty and the dangers of trusting to the natural impulses of fallen man, buttressed his appeal to the soul's response by social consensus and enlightened interpretation of Scripture, and refused to make an absolute distinction between faith and works; while Anne Hutchinson insisted on the individual purity of the heart's responses and renounced the efficacy of works entirely.

She, like Roger Williams, and the Quakers, spoke out not merely for the right to hold their own beliefs, but as a direct challenge to the authorities, which in the end found no alternative to granting them the persecution they so ardently sought. Anne Hutchinson, banished from Massachusetts in 1637, was massacred by Indians in 1642. Roger Williams and his supporters established a new colony, Rhode Island, in 1636, while the Quakers later found a leader in William Penn who secured proprietary rights to Pennsylvania in 1681. The theocracy had no mechanism for compromise; deviants had to be absorbed or ejected. As always in American life, the alternative to assimilation was polarization. The apparently limitless space at the frontiers of society encouraged secession rather than dialogue; dissenters were forced (or chose) to move out rather than engage in compromise. The literary descendants of Roger Williams include Fenimore Cooper's Leatherstocking and Mark Twain's Huck Finn.

New England flourished; it was economically stable, and (after the publication of the 'Cambridge Platform' in 1649) doctrinally established. Common cause and some incipient sense of provincial identity was asserted in the loose associations formed between the colonies. After the Restoration of the monarchy in England in 1660, however, the Puritan mission could no longer be sustained on quite the same terms; the spearhead of reformed religion was stranded high and dry in its city on a hill while the mainstream of English history swept past and beyond.

With the reduced pressure of mission, convincing evidence of Election seemed less forthcoming to individuals, and church membership fell. The children of the original Puritan pilgrims could not demonstrate the same grace given to their parents. Numbers of communicants dropped alarmingly until in 1662 Solomon Stoddard (1643–1729) and others introduced the 'Half-Way Covenant' offering baptism to the children of those who demonstrated their best efforts to lead Christian lives. This was a crucial shift in emphasis between 'faith' and 'works', and blurred the absolute division between the saved and the unregenerate; it introduced doubt where once there had been certainty.

External disasters which beset the colonies were interpreted as God's chastisement of his chosen people for backsliding; the New England ministry made full capital of Indian attacks, fires, and epidemics in a series of 'Jeremiads' – fast-day and Election-day sermons in which the people were exhorted to repent and reform. These Jeremiads were a collective acceptance of responsibility for the evils that beset the community; they reinforced the covenanted relationship of the colonists, and gave reassurance that events were indeed providential rather than random. Once again the literary model was successfully adapted to contain realities which seemed to threaten its adequacy.

The greatest test of the providential mission came in 1692 when Salem Village was afflicted by witchcraft; a massive witch-hunt divided the community and exposed all the inherent tensions of Puritan society. The problem was empirical rather than superstitious: the suffering of those afflicted was observed *fact*, but its interpretation was doubtful. The bewitched declared that they had been tormented by the 'spectres' or visible personifications of the accused; did the appearance of a person's spectre necessarily imply that the individual was a witch or had made a pact with the devil, or could the devil personify someone without that individual's consent? At issue was the Puritans' confidence that they could know God's will directly. Unless the spectre was a sign whose significance could be accurately known, the Puritan was set adrift in a world of inaccessible symbols.

The pressure to achieve consensus was for a while too great, and caution was abandoned in condemning many of those accused. Hysterical fear multiplied the numbers of the afflicted and put pressure on the judges to hasten conviction. By October 1692, fourteen women and five men had been hanged, and one man pressed to death for refusing to plead. Then people began to admit their doubts about the trials; gradually, painfully, the judicial proceedings were dismantled, and the inhabitants of Massachusetts did individual and collective penance for procedures which they had come to recognize as monstrous. In 1690 the colony felt itself very threatened – by England (the English Parliament had revoked its charter in 1684), by Indians, by natural disasters. The witch-hunts seriously weakened the theocratic structure of New England society. Many ministers were publicly discredited, and when the shaken society picked itself up it would never again have quite the same confidence in its ability to discern God's purposes directly from observed events. Failing confidence in their mission had exposed the Puritans to the latent division between events (or words) and their meanings.

Cotton Mather (1663–1728), grandson of John Cotton and of another illustrious Founder, Richard Mather, inherited the full burden of Puritan mission in an era when the promised millennium seemed to be receding. He devoted his life to reinforcing the divine purpose of New England's existence, and to stiffening the moral resolve of its inhabitants. Despite his public and private zeal and his impeccable lineage, Mather's implication in the witch-hunts meant that he never enjoyed the public influence in Massachusetts which he desired and in a sense deserved.

For the active evangelism of the Founders Mather substituted the ordering purposes of the historian. In his *Magnalia Christi Americana* (1702) he attempts to confront the disorders of reality with the structures of language. He exhorts the present to live up to its past, and announces to the rest of the world that New England does indeed belong in the mainstream of history and culture:

I write the *Wonders* of the CHRISTIAN RELIGION, flying from the Depravations of *Europe*, to the *American Strand* ... It may be, 'tis not possible for me to do a greater Service unto the Churches on the *Best Island* of the Universe, than to give a distinct Relation of those *Great Examples*, which have been occurring among Churches of *Exiles*, that were driven out of that *Island*, into an horrible *Wilderness*, meerly for their being Well-willers unto the *Reformation*.

(*Selections from Cotton Mather*, ed. Murdock, 1926, pp. 1, 6)

The literariness of Mather's mission for New England's glory entailed a stylistic alienation from his subject-matter which Bradford's active involvement with history did not incur. He wanted at once to attract a cosmopolitan audience, and to be known as a native American; elaborate displays of erudition established his credentials as a classical historian, while he insisted upon the disadvantages attendant upon his provincial status as 'one poor feeble *American*, overwhelm'd with a thousand other Cares, and capable of touching this Work no otherwise than in a Digression'. Mather's verbal eccentricities anticipate not only Washington Irving's parody *A History of New-York* (1809), but the linguistic exuberance of Melville and the bombastic eloquence of a whole tradition of American orators. They are related to the hoaxing tradition of the tall tale, in which the physical size and abundance of the new continent are thrown against the historical density and greater sophistication of Europe. Sheer power of assertion seeks to overcome provincial narrowness.

In his handbook for ministers, *Manuductio ad Ministerium* (1726), Mather proposes that 'After all, Every Man will have his own *Style*, which will distinguish him as much as his *Gate* [gait]'. He might have found an ally in Edward Taylor (*c.* 1644–1729), the minister of Westfield, Massachusetts, whose poems similarly couch an orthodox theology in a strangely displaced diction. Although he wrote in the age of Dryden and Pope, Taylor's polarized metaphysical modes of perception remained unchanged by time and circumstances. He came to America in 1668 to defend, like other Puritans, the purity of his faith, not to record the facts of the wilderness. Life in an isolated hamlet besieged by Indians gave him new analogies, new 'American' words, but did not modify the Puritan sensibility with which he confronted experience:

> I am a Withred Twig, dri'de fit to bee
> A Chat Cast in thy fire, Writh off by Vice.
> Yet if thy Milke white-Gracious Hand will take mee
> And grafft mee in this golden stock, thou'lt make mee.
>
> (*The Poems of Edward Taylor*, ed. by Donald
> Stanford, New Haven, 1960, p. 47)

Taylor's poetry alternates between such homely diction, the arcane, the abstract, and the crude. There is no central stability in his language; every term is as much – and as little – at home in his verse as the next. Where Donne's paradoxes imply a norm of civilized discourse which can be stretched and startled into new modes of realization, Taylor's best poetry enacts a constant battle between doctrine and assent, word and experience. The language lacks a context of *human* confidence in which to set its faith in the divine:

> Hence glorious, and terrible she stands;   [The City of God]
>   That Converts new
> Seeing her Centinalls of all demand
>   The Word to shew;
> Stand gazing much between two Passions crusht
> Desire, and Feare at once which both wayes thrust.
>
> Thus are they wrackt. Desire doth forward screw
>   To get them in,
> But Feare doth backward thrust, that lies purdue,
>   And slicks that Pin.
> You cannot give the word, Quoth she, which though
> You stumble on't its more than yet you know.
>
> But yet Desires Screw Pin doth not slack:
>   It still holds fast.
> But Fears Screw Pin turns back or Screw doth Crack
>   And breaks at last.
> Hence on they go, and in they enter: where
> Desire converts to joy, joy Conquours Fear.
>
> (*Poems*, p. 455)

The Eighteenth Century: Piety and Progress

While Taylor clung to seventeenth-century ways of articulating the Puritan paradoxes, Mather attempted to move with the times. His *Bonifacius. An Essay upon the Good* (1710) re-stated for the Age of Enlightenment the relationship between faith and works: 'A workless faith is a worthless faith'; the balance of the phrase achieves a pivot between the opposed terms, and the aphoristic form seems to guarantee its stability. But its precariousness had already been demonstrated; the language of transcendence (piety) and the language of action or progress each have a strong pull which tends to disrupt the synthesis. In the eighteenth century these polarities seem most clearly demonstrated by the respective lives and writings of Benjamin Franklin and Jonathan Edwards.

Jonathan Edwards (1703–58) was an apologist for orthodox Puritanism who ended his life quite literally as a lone voice calling in the wilderness. After a period of intense popularity during the Great Awakening, he was ejected from his parish and spent his exile ministering to the Indians in the outpost of Stockbridge, and composing theological treatises on *The Great Christian Doctrine of Original Sin Defended* (1758) and *The Nature of True Virtue* (written 1755–8). Edwards, the grandson of Solomon Stoddard, was appalled by the dilution of Calvinist theory implied in the Half-Way Covenant, and restated an uncompromising if anachronistic Puritanism which emphasized the corruption of human reason and the depravity of will.

The experience of his own conversion convinced Edwards that 'religious affections' – feelings – alone were a reliable guide to the state of the soul; that the awakening of these to a sense of sin and the need for God's mercy was the only true route to salvation. If such a doctrine was obnoxious to many in the age of reason, religious liberalism and worldly prosperity through individual effort, it found an echo of surprising strength in the hearts of others. In 1733, as Edwards noted, 'the *young people* [of his parish] . . . grew observably more *decent* in their attendance on the public worship, and there were more who manifested a *religious concern* than there used to be' (*A Narrative of Surprising Conversions*, 1736). There followed a wave of spectacular 'conversions', beginning in New England, and spreading south and west with the arrival of the English revivalist preacher George Whitefield in 1738. People queued up to reveal their sinfulness, and extravagance and sensationalism inflated the language of depravity until words were superseded entirely by frantic tears, shakings, stampings and fainting fits. There was a strong pull in the Puritan psyche towards emotional release, and the new mood seemed another mark of God's special favour to New England, 'a very *extraordinary* dispensation of providence'.

Edwards, taking advantage of the newly awakened susceptibilities, preached a series of sermons designed to garner in as many souls as possible to what he called his 'harvest' of salvation. At Enfield in 1741 his deadpan delivery of 'Sinners in the Hands of an Angry God' provoked a new wave of hysterical conversions:

> The God that holds you over the pit of hell, much as one holds a spider, or some loathsome insect over the fire, abhors you, and is dreadfully provoked: his wrath towards you burns like fire; . . . The fury of God! the fierceness of Jehovah! Oh, how dreadful must that be! Who can utter or conceive what such expressions carry in them! . . . your punishment will indeed be infinite. Oh, who can express what the state of a soul in such circumstances is! All that we can possibly say about it, gives but a very feeble, faint representation of it; it is inexpressible and inconceivable . . .
> (*Representative Selections*, 1962, pp. 162–9)

This is the rhetoric of sensation, and it is revolting to reason. The middle ground of rational discourse founded in social reality has utterly disappeared; the sinner confronts the wrath of God unmediated and unsupported. Edwards's rhetoric is excessive and without measure; the sheer *abundance* of God's anger is unspeakable. His language has betrayed the communal purpose and delivered up the individual to the terrors of the private imagination.

As the fervour of the Awakenings spiralled out of control, the ministers who had whipped up these emotions increasingly found their role being diminished and their authority questioned. The theocratic consensus was breaking up. Edwards reflected on these events in his *Treatise Concerning Religious Affections* (1746) which makes explicit for the first time the implicit division between the Puritan consciousness and the world. He investigated the relationship between the inward movements of heart in a conversion and the outward signs which accompanied it, and decided that the objective world may well be forever inaccessible to the perceiving consciousness of the 'natural' or unregenerate man. The mind is a bundle of impulses and desires, defined by its responses to sensations which may have no objective source. Fallen Man, distanced from reality, eavesdrops on experience; his mind 'makes use of signs instead of the ideas themselves'. In conversion the relationship between internally and externally generated realities is through grace restored; the regenerate soul has his perceptions cleansed and is assured that what he sees has a true connection with God's natural and supernatural world. But – crucially – Edwards sees this regenerated vision as entirely personal; it does not permit the Elect soul to judge cause from effect in the behaviour of others. There can be no consensus about the nature of external reality even amongst the Elect:

> The true saints have not such a spirit of discerning, that they can certainly determine who are godly, and who are not. For though they know experimentally what true religion is, in the internal exercises of it; yet these are what they can neither feel, nor see, in the heart of another.
>
> (*Religious Affections*, ed. Smith, 1959, p. 181)

If the reality of an experience was entirely *internal*, then language (which – as Edwards understood Locke's analysis in his *Treatise Concerning Human Understanding* (1689) – dealt with sensations on the assumption that they bore a direct relationship to *external* reality) had no tools with which to distinguish the true from the false. Edwards exposed the very American question of whether language *could* contain and express an inner experience. His own writing demonstrates a complete separation between language (such as that of the *Religious Affections*) which attempts to 'explain' religious experience, and that which attempts (as in the sermon) to provoke it.

Edwards shared with his contemporary Benjamin Franklin (1706–90) a thoroughly eighteenth-century desire to reconcile the facts of experience to the structures of belief. Both concede that the visible effect is all that is available for analysis, but where Edwards demonstrates that the nature of an action cannot be judged by its consequences, the resolutely secular and practical Franklin holds that the consequences of the way an individual behaves are the only means available to us to judge the quality of his actions. Whether it be a gadget, a new orthography, a political ideal or a religious belief, the test of its value is whether or not it *works*.

Franklin's activity, physical, intellectual and literary, was prodigious; he spent many years of his life in London and in Paris, first in the process of making his own fortune, then for scientific purposes and finally as an ambassador for his country during the negotiations preceding American independence. His *Autobiography* (commenced 1771) is the greatest masterpiece of American colonial literature, and the richest description of colonial life in the eighteenth century. It is a record of *experience*, in which providence works through the actions of men, and it is one of the few works which is at once distinctively American and completely at home in its social context. It is a work of 'belonging' rather than of alienation; Franklin's mission as the representative American whose personal life reveals the providential design of his country's history sits easily with his resolutely secular emphasis on worldly advancement. The providential and the empirical are not opposed but united.

In his own story, Franklin is at once naïve actor in a world of infinite possibilities, and reflective observer of human limitation. The detachment of the voice gives the incidents a luminous, almost fairy-tale quality, and allows the life to stand free as an 'American' exemplum, unhampered by interpretative sophistication:

> It was about this time that I conceiv'd the bold and arduous Project of arriving at moral Perfection. I wish'd to live without committing any Fault at any time.
>
> (ed. Labaree, 1964, p. 148)

Describing the Puritanical project of his youth, the older Franklin narrates how the rational, ideal world is always liable to be unceremoniously shouldered aside by the 'business' of living, reality. Theory is there to be refined by experience; but although it may sometimes have to be discarded, it is not therefore rendered useless: 'tho' I never arrived at the Perfection I had been so ambitious of obtaining ... yet I was by the Endeavour a better and a happier Man than I otherwise should have been, if I had not attempted it'.

Franklin's Puritan background instilled into him a scepticism about human access to ultimate truths, and a sense of the innate frailty of fallen man. He accepted cheerfully that the mind is a bundle of impulses and desires controlled by reason at only the most superficial level, and turned it wittily to account against his weakly principled younger self:

> ... in my first voyage from Boston, being becalm'd off Block Island, our People set about catching Cod and hawl'd up a great many. Hitherto I had stuck to my Resolution of not eating animal Food; and on this Occasion, I consider'd with my Master Tryon, the taking every Fish as a kind of un-provok'd Murder, since none of them ever had or could do us any Injury that might justify the Slaughter. All this seem'd very reasonable. But I had formerly been a great Lover of Fish, and when this came hot out of the Frying Pan, it smelt admirably well. I balanc'd some time between Principle and Inclination: till I recollected, that when the Fish were opened, I saw smaller Fish taken out of their Stomachs: Then thought I, if you eat one another, I don't see why we mayn't eat you. So I din'd upon Cod very heartily ... So convenient a thing it is to be a *reasonable Creature*, since it enables one to find or make a reason for every thing one has a mind to do.
>
> (pp. 87–8)

Reason is valuable to Franklin, like everything else, in so far as it is *useful*. Such moments of luminous self-awareness come from the return of the rational mind upon its own failures. Unlike Edwards, he does not equate the insufficiencies of reason with corruption and oppose them to sensation or feelings taken to be the reliable arbiters of experience. Franklin's wit provides a continuity of consciousness and language which overcomes the division between what men perceive (divine models or plans) and what they can achieve (the facts of living). His comic consensus of reasonableness re-affirms human worth in the act of exposing its weaknesses.

Independence: Freedom or Alienation?

The American South found its own representatives of the Augustan ideal. Virginia society had developed along different lines from the north; it was controlled not by a Congregational theocracy but by an Anglican 'plantation aristocracy'. These men were literate, cultured and leisured; they did not suffer from the division between public and private, mission and alienation, in quite the same way as the descendants of the New England Puritans, but they none the less made an important contribution to the developing American idiom. Their most famous representative was Thomas Jefferson (1743–1826)

– Virginian, farmer, Enlightenment philosopher and third President of the United States of America. In his *Notes on the State of Virginia* (1784) he took up the challenge of recording the observable facts of his native state, an enterprise begun by John Smith and continued by Virginian patricians such as Robert Beverley (*c*.1673–1722), whose *History and Present State of Virginia* (1705) combined careful observation and scientific curiosity with strongly promotional controlling intentions.

To render the American landscape 'Americanly' Jefferson described it with an 'innocent eye', relying completely on the observable facts which provided the direct data of the senses. The appeal to observation was a means of rescuing man from the corrupt inventions of his own brain. Jefferson was the crucial American exponent of the 'Common Sense' school of Scottish Enlightenment philosophy which exerted a formative influence on the literature and thought of the new democracy. 'Common Sense' distrusted speculative metaphysics and the products of the imagination, and relied instead on the evidences of the senses, 'feelings', as a guide to truth. The 'common sense' of a subject was intuitive, immediate and available to all.

This aversion to metaphysical thinking was supported by the legacy of Puritanism. The Puritans, with their belief in the innate corruption of the postlapsarian mind, had their own reason for distrusting the speculative imagination. To this was added the powerful incentive of 'New World' primitivism: American ideology propounded the virtues of a life of direct contact (through the senses) with Nature. Thus supported, Sensationism held sway over America well beyond the Revolutionary period.

Despite America's predominantly agrarian character, it was the prosperity of its trade and its potential as a market for British goods which first aroused the interest of the English Parliament to colonial affairs, and led to the imposition of a series of taxes and tariffs on American merchants and port authorities. America was to bear a share of the debt England had incurred by the French and Indian war conducted on American soil, which ended in 1763. The colonies bitterly resented what they regarded as unwarranted interference in their trade from a body in which they were not even represented, and began to unite in opposition. Two Continental Congresses in

Philadelphia in 1774 and 1775 brought the colonies together in recognition of their common cause.

The American Revolution was the country's political Great Awakening. Familiar patterns were invoked: the struggle was a means of arresting moral or doctrinal decay; the rhetoric of the Patriots (who supported independence) showed just how revolutionary the language of the Puritan sermon had always been. Satisfying connections were made between the hardships incurred by boycotts of English imports and the need for sacrifices to be made by God's chosen people: 'We may talk and boast of liberty; but after all, the industrious and frugal only will be free' (*Newport Mercury*, 28 February 1774).

Common Sense was the title of the pamphlet which galvanized the American colonists into action in support of their claims against England in 1776. It was written by an Englishman, Thomas Paine (1737–1809), who had arrived in Philadelphia in 1774. The genius of Paine's pamphlet as a catalyst for action was the way in which it combined the plain or 'middle' style of self-evident facts and common sense with a fiercely millennialist rhetoric which derived from his own English radical dissenting background and called up a strong answering echo in these descendants of the Puritans. It made instantaneous and innumerable converts to the cause of American independence.

Five months later, Jefferson drafted the Declaration of Independence at the request of the second Continental Congress; it was amended by Congress, attested by its members and published in July 1776. A common statement of intent was vital at this point to gain foreign support for the colonial cause, so the document had to be acceptable to all the very different sectional interests represented at the Congress. The Declaration was a consensus which papered over the cracks that would open, like the fissure in the walls of Poe's House of Usher, to divide the new nation utterly in civil war. Describing the aims of his Declaration many years later, Jefferson called it 'an appeal to the tribunal of the world . . . for our justification', an attempt 'to place before mankind the common sense of the subject', and 'an expression of the American mind'. These three phrases define the crucial importance of the document to any consideration of American literature and society.

The opening section displays a classic Enlightenment confidence in the adequacy of language to convey truth:

> When, in the course of human events, it becomes necessary for one people to dissolve the political bands which have connected them with another, and to assume among the powers of the earth the separate and equal station to which the laws of nature and of nature's God entitle them, a decent respect to the opinions of mankind requires that they should declare the causes which impel them to the separation.
>
> We hold these truths to be self-evident: that all men are created equal; that they are endowed by their Creator with inherent and inalienable rights; that among these are life, liberty, and the pursuit of happiness; that to secure these rights, governments are instituted among men, deriving their just powers from the consent of the governed ... But when a long train of abuses and usurpations evinces a design to reduce them under absolute despotism, it is their right, it is their duty, to throw off such government, and to provide new guards for their future security. Such has been the patient sufferance of these colonies; and such is now the necessity which constrains them to expunge their former systems of government. The history of the present king of Great Britain is a history of unremitting injuries and usurpations ... To prove this, let facts be submitted to a candid world for the truth of which we pledge a faith yet unsullied by falsehood.
>
> (*Life and Selected Writings of Jefferson*, ed. Koch and Peden, 1944, pp. 22–3)

The languages of law, Newtonian science and religion combine to produce a synthesis which justifies the colonists' actions in the physical, moral and supernatural realms at once. Jefferson appeals to self-evident propositions whose grandeur and simplicity will arouse an immediate assent in the common sense of their audience. No 'other' need be engaged in dialogue, no possible objections foreseen and answered; simple declaration is sufficient. There is a sublime confidence that men are free agents, and that tyranny can be overthrown. The English king and his Parliament have broken the old covenanted relationship between sovereign and subjects and forfeited obedience; the colonists propose a new covenant of American unity to replace the violated colonial relationship: 'we mutually pledge to each other our lives, our fortunes, and our sacred honor'.

The greatest literary works of the Revolutionary as of the colonial society are purposive and public rather than private or belletristic. But as with the earlier works, the 'facts' presented by the Declaration cannot be simple. Intention and idiom interact to produce a vision

of American reality which is not covered by 'self-evident' propositions. The act of separation which brings the new nation into being
is simultaneously a *natural* occurrence, a revolution like the revolution of the spheres, and a profoundly *un-natural* one, which sunders
forcibly the ties of human relationship. The 'natural' language of the
Newtonian universe gives way, as Jefferson reaches his culminating
grievance against the king and Parliament, to a completely different
kind of appeal to the reader:

> They . . . have been deaf to the voice of justice and of consanguinity . . .
> These facts have given the last stab to agonizing affection, and manly spirit
> bids us to renounce forever these unfeeling brethren.

Echoes of the Puritan account of the Fall lie submerged just beneath
the purposive millennialism of the rhetorical surface: the colonists
may seem to be justifying rebellion against legally constituted and
traditionally sanctioned authority. Perhaps theirs is the unlawful
revolt of the child against the father or of brother against brother.

The presence in the defining document of America of this language of sensation, used not affirmatively, but negatively – as of a
violation or a denial of the right of these feelings to exist – is crucial.
Further, in moving from the Newtonian confidence in cause and
effect to the emotionally coercive language of the feelings, Jefferson's
prose changes key entirely. There is, it appears, no continuity between the empirical middle style which appeals to common sense
and self-evident facts, and the sensational language of 'agonizing
affection'. This is not the case in English literature: David Hume
(1711–76), whose *Treatise of Human Nature* (1739) is an important
source of eighteenth-century philosophy's interest in feeling and
sympathy, saw his work as 'An attempt to introduce the Experimental Method of Reasoning into Moral Subjects'; even Sterne,
Jefferson's favourite writer of fiction and the arch-exponent of
Sentiment, was a true Lockian in his mockery of Locke.

When Jefferson moves from the scientific to the moral in his
justification of the American cause, his writing does not register the
continuities established by Hume between the externally and internally directed evidence of the senses. Instead, we are thrust from the
social, daylight world of political necessity into a private realm of
excess and infamy, of things outside the course of nature. The

cumulative toll of grievances becomes a litany of almost infernal
iniquity:

> ... and that this assemblage of horrors might want no fact of distinguished
> die ... he has endeavoured to bring on the inhabitants of our frontiers the
> merciless Indian savages, whose known rule of warfare is an undistinguished
> destruction of all ages, sexes, and conditions of existence ...

This is the realm of the terrorized imagination; in America this
world is peopled by murderous slaves and merciless Indians who
haunt the frontiers of the rational. Jefferson's Declaration of Independence is 'an expression of the American mind' which, stylistically,
establishes that mind as a discontinuous one, divided between an
enlightened, rational optimism and a violated sensibility. Common
sense thought left American literature with a difficulty in finding a
single register in which to render the complete range of human
experience.

In 1782, the year before England finally recognized the independent existence of America, Jefferson's correspondent and admirer
Hector St John de Crèvecoeur (1735–1813) published his *Letters from
an American Farmer*, which deserves to be called the first piece of
American fiction. It is here that Crèvecoeur asks the famous question
'What, then, is the American, this new man?' James (the American
farmer) is a 'simple citizen', the candid man of the Declaration of
Independence, who describes his life in a prelapsarian agricultural
community, 'the most perfect society now existing in the world'.
The peace is shattered by the agonizing war of separation from
Britain which threatens to destroy the boundaries between civili-
zation and the wilderness which encloses it:

> Men mutually support and add to the boldness and confidence of each
> other; the weakness of each is strengthened by the force of the whole ...
> When I consider myself as connected in all these characters, as bound by so
> many cords, all uniting in my heart, I am seized with a fever of the mind ...
> (ed. Stone, 1981, p. 201)

Division, and the loss of the strength of consensus, is as deadly to
the American of the Enlightenment as it was to the settlers of
Plymouth Plantation. In both cases, the other side of liberation is
alienation.

... were his house perpetually filled, as mine is, with miserable victims just escaped from the flames and the scalping knife, telling of barbarities and murders that make human nature tremble, his situation would suspend every political reflection and expel every abstract idea.

(pp. 206–7)

These are the 'merciless Indian savages' of the Declaration, set upon the innocent Americans by their unnatural British brethren, exposing them not only to the 'flames and the scalping knife', but also to the torments of the 'alarmed imagination'. Crèvecoeur's style undergoes the same metamorphosis as Jefferson's as he turns from adequate, social Enlightenment 'facts' to the suggestive, excessive rhetoric of the emotional wilderness. Again, the styles are adjacent, but discontinuous.

Once the overriding pressure towards unity which characterizes the political documents of the Revolution subsided, other voices surfaced, not in dialogue or debate, but dangerously, as repressed opposition. The confident declaration whose structure left no room for another voice found that dissenting 'other' rising from the very depths of itself, to expose the distance between the theoretical adequacy and the actual insufficiency of the enlightened ideal of the 'middle state' or the City on a Hill on which America was founded. The most important novelist of the immediate post-Revolutionary period, Charles Brockden Brown (1771–1810), embodied these contradictions in powerful, inconclusive fictions which had a strong effect on the imaginations of Hawthorne, Melville and Poe. His *Wieland* (1798) propounds an enlightened, democratic ideology within a sensational Gothic plot. It is a novel of radical misunderstandings, in which isolated voices which fail to connect are locked in mutual misapprehension. In *Edgar Huntly* (1799), the enlightened hero pursuing truth finds himself pursued through a nightmare wilderness by ferocious Indians and black panthers. Once again, the rational ideal attempts to control reality, and instead finds itself swamped by a rhetoric of sensation unleashed by the mistaken exercise of principle. Early American fiction discovers that it cannot get away with recognizing only some truths about human nature. It is a short step from here to the terrified fascination of Poe's narrators with the power of the senses to invade and control reason, and his piling up of 'facts' which 'on horror's head horrors accumulate'; or to Melville's Ahab, in whom the rational mind tussles with the lurid imaginings which lie just beneath and which threaten always to pierce its surface; or to Hawthorne's Hester Prynne, whose mind, when deprived of society, ventures too far into the forest and flirts with the spectres of the wilderness.

PART II:
FROM COOPER
TO JAMES

THE SOCIAL AND CULTURAL SETTING

HUGH BROGAN

A New and Anxious Nation

If anyone acquainted with nineteenth-century American literature were asked what was then the chief preoccupation of most American writers, the unhesitating answer would be, 'America itself'. In this the writers were fully representative of a people that was undeviatingly self-concerned. The meaning of America, the destiny of America, the promise of America: so powerful was the spell cast by these topics that visitors from Europe succumbed to it as helplessly as United States citizens themselves. Far too many of these visitors, after making a tour of some weeks or months, felt driven to put their experiences into books with such titles as *Diary in America*, *Domestic Manners of the Americans*, *American Notes* and (most famous of all) *Democracy in America*. It can hardly be supposed that all the dozens of authors involved made money by their publications, but the market for Americana, both within and without the United States, must have been steady, or publishers would have returned the manuscripts. Instead, the flow of European descriptions and commentaries was copious; but it appeared a mere trickle beside the torrent of works from Americans. By the end of the century America (invariably used as a traditional, convenient, but not altogether accurate synonym for the United States) had established itself as a permanent and prominent literary theme, interesting both the highly cultivated few who followed Henry James in his exploration of the interaction between Yankees and Europeans, and the barely literate many, who wallowed in cheap fiction about cowboys and Indians. More than a preoccupation, America had become a legend, something like an obsession, at the very least a mother of myths.

The explanation of this phenomenon is plain enough, but to list all the factors at work would be a lengthy business. So far as the Europeans were concerned, especially in the early part of the century, America was fascinating because it might contain the answer to the problem of the future, which had become urgent since the French Revolution and its attendant wars had swept away the old order of society. America was the only true democracy in the world, and if, as seemed likely, democracy was to be everyone's future, or if, as was certain, it was at least one of the choices now open to humanity, then there was strong reason to study it. The United States had some of the fascination that the Soviet Union was to have in the wake of the Russian Revolution of 1917. And had the publicists of the early nineteenth century guessed in how many other respects the United States was showing the way in which all Western civilization was to evolve, their fascination would have been all the greater.

As it was, they did not entirely understand the phenomenon they were watching. Nor did the Americans. It was clearer, as the decades went on, that they were engaged in the business of nation-building; but exactly what a nation was, and what were its legitimate claims on its citizens, and, above all, how exceedingly common the enterprise was going to become in all continents, were obscure matters indeed. The twentieth century must find this state of mind particularly hard to realize. It has been so clear for so long, not only that the nation-state is the commonest and most durable form of political organization available to us, and nationalism the most powerful force in modern history, but also that the French Revolution itself was nationalistic, as was the reaction against it, that it seems inconceivable that these points were not universally obvious to our ancestors. Nevertheless, the inconceivable was the case.

There was good cause for this short-sightedness. Supra-national forces, such as the alliance between the traditional aristocracies and monarchical dynasties of Europe, and sub-national ones, such as overriding loyalty to your native village or province rather than to a distant government, were still exceedingly strong. And the American experiment itself showed how fragile a thing a new nation was. Again and again the books and journals commented on the anxious passion which Americans put into their patriotic assertions. George Washington had to be semi-divine, the Declaration of Independence and the Constitution had to become sacred texts, the eagle had to scream through hours of bombastic oratory every Fourth of July, because without these things and what they symbolized the American nation was without a tradition, without indeed a reason for existing. Unless the American Revolution had been about something more fundamental than an unpopular tax on tea there had been no sense in quitting the British Empire; and without the belief that the Revolution had been won by the efforts of a united people (rather than by the lucky interposition of a French fleet) there was nothing, it seemed, to hold America together. The diversity of races, tongues, religions and material interests grew greater every year. War and exploration across the Appalachians laid open a continent for the taking: but could one republic effectively govern so vast an empire? Conflict within the country only a few years after the Constitution came into force seemed likely to wreck its institutions; and without them, what chance could there be of forging a nation out of such a heterogeneous accumulation of humanity?

In retrospect it is plain that the forces making for American uni-fication were strong enough for their job, were in fact immensely strong, strong enough to survive a terrible war, helter-skelter social evolution of all kinds, and incessant challenge from all directions. The odds on the success of the American experiment were excellent, far better than those supporting most subsequent experiments of the kind. But the nineteenth century can hardly be blamed for feeling as anxious as it was confident, and for looking for light on its problems all the time and in all corners.

It was a great age of scientific investigation; its various crises hurried on the development of sociological observation and political inquiry. The United States made increasing contributions to the work: by the end of the century Thorstein Veblen had produced *The Theory of the Leisure Class* (1899), and in 1910 Herbert Croly pub-lished *The Promise of American Life*, which applied the principles of Comtean positivism to American life. But most Americans could be forgiven if they could not adopt a coldly scientific attitude to the processes they were so entirely caught up in. It was a matter of desperate importance to them to know what they were doing and where they were going, and the inquiry was so bafflingly large and intricate that they were never satisfied for long with any single set of interpretations, not even those offered by the churches to which they clung fervently. They had feelings to express as well as (in many cases, rather than) minds to satisfy. They wanted to praise or blame their country as well as understand it (some, like James Fenimore Cooper, wanted to do all three). They wanted to explore America, make money out of it, shape it to their own ends. And they wanted to keep their footing in the swirling, never ending rapids of change. The historical crisis which had caught them up was simply too insistent to be ignored for long, especially after it began to display its industrial side. It squeezed the consciousness of all but the most reclusive: among the leading writers only Emily Dickinson seems to have escaped it, and she did so only by methods as heroic as they were unavailable to anyone else.

America, then, was in a crisis of self-creation, but the process was scarcely a linear one. There was no single Big Bang, as at the creation of the universe, to be followed by expansion at a predictable speed. Rather America was like a single star, fuelled by some process resembling nuclear fusion. New centres of energy were constantly bursting into unexpected, unpredictable life. However hard the optimists and pessimists tried to account for it all (the pessimists tried very hard indeed) the reality invariably outstripped their theories. The most adequate reaction, perhaps, was the simple observation that nothing like America, for speed and size, had ever happened before. So it may be that the greatest literary works of the century are those which embody the explosive process itself rather than those which try to analyse it or to moralize it or, still more tamely, to record it.

The sailors at work in the rigging or out astride the spars,
The round masts, the swinging motion of the hulls, the slender serpentine pennants,
The large and small steamers in motion, the pilots in their pilot-houses,
The white wake left by the passage, the quick tremulous whirl of the wheels,
The flags of all nations, the falling of them at sunset,
The scallop-edged waves in the twilight, the ladled cups, the frolicsome crests and glistening,
The stretch afar growing dimmer and dimmer, the grey walls of the granite storehouses by the docks,
On the river the shadowy groups, the big steam-tug closely flank'd on each side by the barges, the hay-boat, the belated lighter,
On the neighboring shore the fires from the foundry chimneys burning high and glaring into the night,

Casting their flicker of black contrasted with wild red and yellow light over
the tops of the houses, and down into the clefts of streets.

(Walt Whitman, 'Crossing Brooklyn Ferry', 1856)

Myths North and South

The American imagination was relatively poor in symbols for its
business of self-interpretation as the nineteenth century began. The
country was in the grip of a ferocious religious revival, which, for
neither the first nor the last time, revivified the imagery of Calvinistic
Protestantism. Some Americans had received a classical education;
many more had access to the English literary tradition. But for
purposes of nation-building these inheritances were not enough. It
was not even enough, in such a profoundly political country (which
makes the commonplace distinction between the social and the
political inapplicable), that Washington Irving, feeling the lack of a
folk-lore, would invent the tale of Rip Van Winkle, or that, a few
decades later, Longfellow would put the earliest days of New England into verse in 'The Courtship of Miles Standish'. What were
needed were authentic, post-Revolutionary, American heroes.
Hence the tradition of semi-fictitious biography, whether Parson
Weems on George Washington or Daniel Boone and Davy Crockett
(ostensibly) on themselves. A myth had to be created of the importance and glory of the Republic as the latest, noblest work of
time. America's sense of separateness, her very sense of inferiority,
of juvenility, could be called in aid: in 1837 Ralph Waldo Emerson
made an otherwise turgid and commonplace commencement address
memorable by proclaiming that now was the time for American
writers to declare their intellectual independence:

We have listened too long to the courtly muses of Europe. The spirit of
the American freeman is already suspected to be timid, imitative, tame ...
We will walk on our own feet; we will work with our own hands; we will
speak our own minds ... A nation of men will for the first time exist,
because each believes himself inspired by the Divine Soul which also inspires
all men.

('The American Scholar')

This sort of thing was repeated over and over again, because
Americans were not only anxious to believe it to be true, but were

determined to make it true. It cannot be denied that to a large extent they succeeded; but they also had a pay a fearful price for attaching themselves to such a programme of virtue.

For the Declaration of Independence and the Constitution left no room for doubt as to what the programme was, and its implications were hammered home, by practical experience, by eloquent politicians, and by the sort of nationalistic strivings just described. Americans were republicans, or rather (for the language of politics changed with the new century) democrats. They believed in the rule of law. They believed in liberty. They believed that all men were created with an equal right to life, liberty and the pursuit of happiness. Thomas Jefferson (1743–1826) had told them that the proposition was self-evident; and indeed it was. Unfortunately they were not living up to their beliefs in one crucial respect.

It is impossible to overstate the importance of slavery as a factor in American life in the ante-bellum period. It poisoned the morning. In the years immediately after the Revolution it was generally agreed that slavery was inconsistent with the basic principles of American republicanism, and there was widespread satisfaction at the thought that economic and political forces were combining to end it in the near future. This expectation was perfectly reasonable: between 1776 and 1804 slavery was abolished in one state after another, until processes of gradual emancipation had been initiated everywhere north of the Mason-Dixon line. In 1808 the Atlantic slave-trade was outlawed, and although this victory for humanity was less noble than it seemed, since some supported it as a means of cutting off immigration from Africa (in this it was the forerunner of many later anti-immigrant laws) and others because it would stimulate the internal slave-trade, still, it was a mark of progress. But progress went no farther. The invention of the Whitney cotton gin, combined with the opening of the new South-West, between the Appalachians and the Mississippi, suddenly made slavery profitable again; as time went on, vastly profitable. And the number of slaves grew, from 1,538,038 in 1820, to 2,487,455 in 1840 and 3,953,760 in 1860. Economic interest, guilt, and fear combined into iron prejudice: the slaveholders were no longer prepared to contemplate emancipation. Even Jefferson, while still counting himself an opponent of slavery, ceased to support any but impracticable schemes for ending it, and denounced

all who looked to more effective means as enemies of public tran-
quillity. But he could not delude himself about the importance of the
question. In his *Notes on the State of Virginia* (1785) he wrote: 'I
tremble for my country when I reflect that God is just; that his
justice cannot sleep for ever' and nearly forty years later, at the time
of the Missouri crisis, he observed that the South had a wolf by the
ears, and that the slavery question would yet destroy the Union.

Jefferson's allusion to God's justice is not only a reminder of how
universal was religious belief in America: it foreshadowed what was
bound to happen to the slavery controversy. Americans who
believed that their political system was the best in the world must
believe that it had the blessing of God upon it; so that if there was an
evil which was patently inconsistent with American institutions it
must also be against the will of God, or so they reasoned. It was not
difficult for them to support their arguments with citations from the
Bible, and dire threats of what would happen at the Second Coming
(which many of them expected hourly) if the Lord found the
nation still wallowing in so black a sin. This was the mental set out
of which abolitionism was born.

It is customary to think of the abolitionists as a group of un-
representative fanatics who achieved very little. But this is to
overlook their impact on the American mind, which in the nineteenth century was very largely the New England mind. For although New England itself dwindled in relative importance in the
Union, Greater New England – the vast North-West, settled from
the North-East in huge numbers between 1790 or thereabouts and
1858 (when Minnesota became a state) – was almost synonymous
with the North which won the Civil War, for it included upstate
New York and western Pennsylvania. It was this region, regularly
toured by preachers and lecturers and by abolitionist agitators who
were something of both, that gave their resonance to the Transcendentalist writers, and to others who are not usually thought of as
Transcendentalists but who were essentially working in the same
tradition. All these writers were more or less abolitionists. Thoreau's
'Civil Disobedience' (1846) sprang out of his refusal, as an abolitionist, to pay taxes which were used to support the pro-slavery war
against Mexico. Longfellow wrote eight anti-slavery poems after
reading a tract by William Channing, a leading Unitarian clergyman

of Boston. Whittier's verse in the same cause fills ninety-eight of the double-columned pages of his *Poetical Works*. Harriet Beecher Stowe, daughter, wife and sister of New England ministers, believed that her *Uncle Tom's Cabin* (1851–2) had in fact been written by God. 'This is actually a little the impression that the novel makes on the reader,' was Edmund Wilson's comment. Abraham Lincoln professed to believe that it had caused the Civil War. But the work coming out of the abolitionist movement which most clearly indicates how anti-slavery had fused Protestantism and republicanism into a new and potent nationalism was the *Battle Hymn of the Republic* (1861) by Julia Ward Howe (it is also noteworthy how much abolitionism contributed to the emancipation of women):

Mine eyes have seen the glory of the coming of the Lord:
He is trampling out the vintage where the grapes of wrath are stored;
He hath loosed the fearful lightning of his terrible swift sword:
    His truth is marching on.

Glory, glory Hallelujah! Sung to the irresistible tune of 'John Brown's Body' (which itself originated in religious camp meetings), the Battle Hymn perfectly expressed that exalted sense of America's destiny which the passionate exhortations of the abolitionists (who, to be sure, had no intention of stirring up a war – William Lloyd Garrison was a pacifist) had instilled into a whole generation of Northerners before 1861. The poets had often enough asserted the divinity of the Union: humanity, according to Longfellow, was hanging breathless on its fate; now as the guns began to fire America *felt* it. The myth had become power.

It derived its strength from many factors besides abolitionism. General Andrew Jackson (President 1829–37), the conqueror of the British at the Battle of New Orleans, had outfaced John C. Calhoun with his challenging toast: 'Our Federal Union: It Must Be Preserved.' This incident gave nationalism a helpful touch of martial glamour; so, and still more, did Jackson's vigorous response to the nullification crisis of 1832–3, when South Carolina declared the federal tariff non-operative within her borders and Jackson, as President, threatened her with military occupation unless she climbed down (which she did). Above all, the migrants moving into the North-West, into Ohio, Indiana, southern Illinois – later on, into

Iowa, Missouri and Kansas – saw the great system of slave plantations not as a distant evil, inconsistent with liberty and Christianity, yet of no immediate concern, but as a rival economic system that had gobbled up the best land in Tennessee, Kentucky, Alabama and Mississippi – land which might otherwise have been farmed by plain people like themselves – and that might yet invade more Western lands, even, who knew, the free states themselves? 'A house divided against itself cannot stand.' They drew the moral, as their spokesman, Lincoln, did; they also feared, as he did, or said he did, that there was a deliberate conspiracy among the leaders of 'the Slave Power' to pull the house down; and they interpreted everything the South did accordingly. That being so, it was natural to turn, as to a last hope, to the federal government for aid and protection, as natural as it was to turn to the new Republican party, which promised, not only an end to slavery extension, but the adoption of the Northern economic programme – protective tariff, a homestead act, a transcontinental railroad, and so on. When the federal government issued its call for help in 1861 it was natural to volunteer for its army. (It was also, as it turned out, natural to want to go home almost at once.)

Every action causes an equal and opposite reaction. As the myth of America gained in strength, the plantation states began to evolve a counter-myth, of Dixie, of the South. It was plagued from the first by fundamental contradictions, of which the most important was that the Southerners were never more American than when they denied their nationality. Their talk was all of rights – the rights of property, states' rights, natural rights – and they could make an immensely plausible case for the view that their decision to secede from the Union, in short, to stage a planters' revolution, was exactly the sort of thing their ancestors had done to the British Empire; they were prepared to argue, at endless length, that slavery was sanctioned by the Bible and secession by the US Constitution; what they could not do so plausibly, though they tried extremely hard, was to show that a tolerable modern society could be built on a foundation of racial slavery. Their inability to make good their rebellion drove the point home. By 1865 Jefferson Davis was ready to free any slave who was willing to fight for the Confederacy; the planters, faced with this, began to wonder if the rebellion any longer made sense; the common soldiers belatedly discovered that it was 'a rich man's war and a poor man's fight'. Under the hammer-blows of the North the Confederacy collapsed; but as it turned out the history of the South was barely beginning.

Meanwhile the Northern cause, the cause of the nation, of the United States of America, had reached its culmination in the work and words of Abraham Lincoln (1809–65). His speeches and letters must rank high in any record of nineteenth-century literature; but his historical importance was that he brought the institutions, ideals and material interests of the Americans into harmony with each other, however briefly. He took up all the themes that had by now merged into the great music of nationalism, and gave them both eloquent words and effective action. He saved the Union, freed the slaves, won the war; he raised the tariff, passed the Homestead Act and signed the Union Pacific Railroad charter, the first federal charter of incorporation issued for nearly fifty years, and a token that America would not be just a republic of farmers much longer; and he invoked the blessing of God on his deeds. At the same time he was too intelligent, too wise, too good a man to act in anything but the humblest spirit. He knew why it was that America had been put to such agony as the Civil War, and it would have been well for his countrymen if they had always remembered it clearly:

If we shall suppose that American Slavery is one of those offences which, in the providence of God, must needs come, but which, having continued through His appointed time, He now wills to remove, and that He gives to both North and South, this terrible war, as the woe due to those by whom the offence came, shall we discern therein any departure from those divine attributes which the believers in a Living God always ascribe to Him? Fondly do we hope – fervently do we pray – that this mighty scourge of war may speedily pass away. Yet, if God wills that it continue, until all the wealth piled by the bond-man's two hundred and fifty years of unrequited toil shall be sunk, and until every drop of blood drawn with the lash, shall be paid by another drawn with the sword, as was said three thousand years ago, so still it must be said 'the judgments of the Lord, are true and righteous altogether'.

(*Second Inaugural Address*, 1865)

This was, in a sense, Lincoln's answer to the challenge of the Contraband Hymn:

When Israel was in Egypt's Land
. *Let my people go!*
Oppressed so hard they could not stand

38

Let my people go!
Go down, Moses! Way down in Egypt's Land!
Tell old Pharaoh, Let My People Go!

Lincoln knew as well as any Bible-reading mother, or any slave, that when Moses came before Pharaoh for the tenth time, and Pharaoh hardened his heart yet again, God slew all the firstborn sons of the Egyptians in the last of the ten plagues; but he submitted, and in the eyes of his countrymen his own death, his martyr's crown, was the final sanctification of the cause to which he had given so much: the preservation of a new nation, 'conceived in Liberty, and dedicated to the proposition that all men are created equal'.

Towns and Frontiers

Discussion of the myth of the nation led inevitably to an evocation of the Civil War, and fittingly too, for the war itself became a great myth, a complex of events giving meaning to history as well as to the millions of lives caught up in it. But not even the Union cause could encompass all the meanings of America, which had continued to develop, in a myriad ways unconnected with the great contest, right through the ante-bellum period and the war.

It was the era of the most spectacular urban growth. Here is a New Yorker of a younger generation than Whitman's:

'. . . At the end of three or four years we'll move. That's the way to live in New York – to move every three or four years. Then you always get the last thing. It's because the city's growing so quick – you've got to keep up with it. It's going straight up town – that's where New York's going. If I wasn't afraid Marian would be lonely, I'd go up there – right up to the top – and wait for it. Only have to wait ten years – they'll all come up after you. But Marian says she wants some neighbors – she doesn't want to be a pioneer. She says that if she's got to be the first settler she had better go out to Minnesota. I guess we'll move up little by little: when we get tired of one street we'll go higher. So you see we'll always have a new house; it's a great advantage to have a new house; you get all the latest improvements. They invent everything all over again about every five years, and it's a great thing to keep up with the new things. I always try and keep up with the new things of every kind. Don't you think that's a good motto for a young couple – to keep "going higher"? What's the name of that piece of poetry – what do they call it? – "Excelsior!"'

(Henry James, *Washington Square*)

The Manhattan type of triviality apparently never alters. But through the vacant chatter of a fool at a dinner-party James fills in the essential background to his story and also catches a historical moment, national in its implications. For although New York was a case apart, going from a population of 152,000 in 1820 to more than a million in 1860 and nearly 3½ million in 1900, the growth of Chicago was in some ways even more extraordinary: founded in 1833, it had become the country's second city (which it remained until the 1980s) in less than sixty years. In 1900 its population was 1,698,575. And the list of the nine largest cities (after New York) testified to the same phenomenon of explosive urban growth, for it was always changing. By 1860 Charleston, Salem, Providence, Richmond, Albany and Norfolk had yielded place to Cincinnati, St Louis, Chicago, Buffalo, Newark and Louisville; by 1900 New Orleans, Newark and Louisville had given way to Cleveland, San Francisco and Pittsburgh. And the total urban population of the United States had risen from 693,000 in 1820 to 30,160,000 in 1900. In that year America was still a predominantly rural nation, but it would not remain so for much longer.

Urban growth was not begun by the industrial revolution; it would be truer to say that the accumulation of capital in America's commercial centres (even Pittsburgh, the coal and steel city, began as a trading settlement at the Forks of the Ohio) began the industrial revolution. But as American industrialism gathered speed, especially after the coming of the railroads, it could not fail to leave its mark. It was felt most of all in old cities like New York, Philadelphia and Boston where memories of the past provided a fixed point against which to measure the rapidity of the changes brought about by trade, internal and external, capitalism, immigration and new technologies. The historian Henry Adams did not always express his astonishment and dread at the new society's dynamism so graciously as might have been wished; but no one was better placed than this grandson and great-grandson of Presidents to discover it. Indeed, he made it the theme of his autobiography. In his lifetime his own city, Boston, from being the capital of American Protestantism, became overwhelmingly Catholic, thanks to the Irish immigration; without, it must be owned, becoming much less provincial and prudish. *The*

Education of Henry Adams (1907) makes sure that posterity has no excuse for overlooking the process.

The new cities bred a new America. Each became a Babel. Even in the eighteenth century Philadelphia had become linguistically and religiously diverse, largely because of German immigration. The nineteenth century intensified and accelerated this, as every other process. When in 1908 Israel Zangwill, an English Jewish writer, brought out his play *The Melting Pot*, the image was gratefully seized on by patriotic Americans who hoped to forge a unity out of diversity; but it was profoundly misleading. There was little melting between language groups. Instead each city became a jumble of nations, classes and creeds; San Francisco's Chinatown and New York's Little Italy were to be only the best-known of many ethnic neighbourhoods; American culture had to change to accommodate these new realities. It was not an easy requirement.

Approximately 32 million immigrants poured into the United States between 1820 and 1914. Only a minority among them spoke English as a mother tongue. When they learned the language it was not as a developing literary medium but as a necessary tool for survival. As for culture, they had their own books, just as they had their own music, churches, eating-places and newspapers. But for those of them who meant to settle in America (not all did) it was necessary to acquire a smattering at least of the native language; and to the extent that they found the good life there, and accepted the country's characteristic institutions, they studied citizenship too, in readiness for the day (which friendly politicians were always happy to hasten) when they would lift their right hands and swear the oath of allegiance. Hence the double function and peculiar atmosphere of the night-schools so hilariously and at the same time so touchingly captured in Leo Rosten's Hyman Kaplan stories.

The immigrants' children picked up English and Americanism much more easily than their parents, in the free public schools which were one of the great nineteenth-century innovations. But even they, when they turned to literary expression, celebrated America with uncritical patriotism:

> Give me your tired, your poor,
> Your huddled masses yearning to breathe free,
> The wretched refuse of your teeming shore.

Send these, the homeless, tempest-tost to me,
I lift my lamp beside the golden door!
(Emma Lazarus, 'The New Colossus')

Even the Irish, the earliest and best adapted of the nineteenth-century immigrant groups, with a strong native tradition of derision, were happiest when celebrating their new home with the zeal of true patriots. Boss Plunkitt sounded almost sincere when he described how patriotically Tammany Hall celebrated the Fourth of July, as required by the constitution of the Tammany Society:

The great hall upstairs is filled with five thousand people, suffocatin' from heat and smoke. Every man Jack of these five thousand knows that down in the basement there's a hundred cases of champagne and two hundred kegs of beer ready to flow when the signal is given. Yet that crowd stick to their seats without turnin' a hair while, for four solid hours, the Declaration of Independence is read, long-winded orators speak, and the glee club sings itself hoarse.

But in Plunkitt's tone we can also hear something of the sardonic note that characterized the voice of Mr Dooley, the immortal Chicago bartender invented by Finley Peter Dunne at the end of the century. Slowly but inexorably a new urban, non-Protestant American culture was advancing as the cities grew. It seemed to promise, or threaten, a transformed country in the twentieth century.

There had always been a violent, rowdy, abandoned life in the ocean and river-ports of America, just as American journalism had always included a scurrilous, vulgar, unscrupulous strain. For that matter, there had always been rich men in America, and they had always wielded great power. But it was the scale of these things, as they developed in the nineteenth century, which began to alarm the old stock. It had been a Jeffersonian axiom that cities were dangerous to the Republic: they bred diseases, they fostered odious class distinctions, they were the home of political corruption. Anti-Catholicism was an even older and more vigorous tradition, and none needed instruction to become alarmed about the huge influx of new stocks, any more than they needed instruction in racial prejudice. Faster and faster, from the 1840s onwards, American life began to take on new contours. And new contours required new myths.

Some still tried to make the old myths serve. The South was pre-eminent in this. Slavery, secession and defeat in the war had made

Dixie a place apart. After 1865 the majority of whites in the section were determined to keep it so. Their success was to carry over into the twentieth century and leave a deep mark on American literature. Something must be said of it.

Mark Twain, himself a child of the ante-bellum South, imputed the folly which brought about the great rebellion to too much reading of Sir Walter Scott. He had a point: the planter class had indeed come to see itself as 'the Chivalry', and plunged into rebellion as if civil war were simply a variant of the Eglinton Tournament. But the insight would be better applied to the post-bellum South. After Lee's surrender to Grant there was a brief moment when the leaders of the former Confederacy might have been induced to surrender intellectually, as it were, and seek a genuine accommodation with the manners and values of the North. But the opportunity, if it existed, was lost, largely because of the murder of Lincoln, and the planter class instead set out, with iron determination and ultimate success, to regain the mastery of the Southern states. The legend of the Old South was an essential part of this counter-offensive. For two generations or more the master-class behaved as if it had made a careful study of *Gone with the Wind*, Margaret Mitchell's celebrated novel, sixty years before it was written. But in fact *Gone with the Wind* was to be merely the most notorious expression of the post-bellum state of mind, and as such well repays reading today, just as D. W. Griffith's hymn to the Ku Klux Klan, his film *The Birth of a Nation*, is well worth viewing. Among other things these works show all too clearly how an addiction to some kinds of myth precludes first-rate literary creation. To realize his genius Mark Twain had to leave the region of his birth.

But if the chief artistic monuments of the period in the South were, literally, monuments – bronze statues of brave young Confederate soldiers, their resolute faces gazing, usually, North – the ground was being prepared for the literary flowering of the region in the twentieth century. All those forces in the South, especially the poorer whites, which had nothing to gain from the myth of the Chivalry, were obliged to find new ways, a new language, newer, or much older, myths to make sense of their lives. Some, surveying the ruined South – ruined much more by a suicidal social order than by the physical effects of the war – might find in defeat a certain dignity, and in the espousal of rural, conservative values a solid vantage point from which to criticize the hurry, excess, cruelty and vulgarity of city life. Others turned to the very opposite – the attempt to build a 'New South', a South which would embrace urbanism and industrialism instead of rejecting them. Others turned to the politics of Populism. The blacks made their own criticism of life, at first in spirituals, then in ragtime and jazz, then in large-scale emigration to the North. The South might seem moribund, but it was quickening.

And even at its nadir it began to find allies. The nineteenth-century American West, even more than the Old South, is a region of legend, and was so even before it became a thing of the past. Horace Greeley's celebrated advice, 'Go West, young man!' would never have become so universally familiar if it had not spoken to a universal instinct. The quest for a new land, a new hope, to the westward was, after all, the very origin of America. Nor was the myth without its own corrupting element. Just as the legend of the South was based on the oppression of Africans, so that of the West was based on the displacement of the American Indians. In a sense, all white settlers in the West were co-conspirators in infamy just as all whites in the South were. But there were important differences. For one thing, the men of the West did not, on the whole, intend to live off the sweat of other men's faces (as Lincoln put it), unlike the planter class. That, indeed, was the nub of their quarrel with the slave power. True, parts of the slave South – Kentucky, Tennessee, the lower Mississippi region, Texas – had been or even at the end of the century still were part of the West; and a great many Southerners found their way to Oregon territory and to California, bringing their racial prejudice and their tradition of lawless violence with them. But the Great West, which stretched from the Appalachians to the Pacific, was too enormous and too varied to be completely contaminated. On the whole its settlers were harmless to anyone, black, white or red.

The line of settlement (commonly called 'the frontier', another phrase heavy with symbolic meaning) moved westward fairly steadily, and was closely followed by the commonplaces of organized life: farms, churches, small towns and tax-collectors. The accidents of history and geography produced enormous variations, which give the process much of its fascination. Thus for years it was believed that a Great American Desert made settlement impossible on the high plains, so the wagon trains crossed it unfalteringly until, beyond South Pass, the trails diverged, one heading north-west to Oregon and the Willamette valley, the other south-west, over even tougher country, to the Sierra Nevada (where more than one party met disaster) and California. This leap-frogging process meant that the West Coast was being rapidly developed while much of the interior was still the domain of untamed Indian tribes. In 1848 gold was discovered in California, which led to the Gold Rush of the following year, a movement which carried along Americans, Chinese, Australians, Mexicans and many others to the territory, though not, in most cases, to fortune. In this way a mining frontier opened in the far West. Mark Train discovered it when, wishing to extricate himself from the Civil War, he arrived in Nevada in 1861. Had his life taken a slightly different course he might have found his way to Texas, as many Southerners were to do after the Civil War, and there met the cattle frontier, where vast herds of longhorns were bred to feed the new cities and provide raw material for the rising canning industry of Chicago.

Instead Twain wrote 'The Jumping Frog' and was soon famous as a humorist in the tradition of Artemus Ward, who, in turn, drew on the tradition of the tall tale. Twain exploited the American passion for newspapers and lectures to make a living. It was partly a yearning for self-improvement and partly a simple need for entertainment in the long quiet of farming and small-town life that produced such phenomena as the Chautauqua Movement, which may be summed up briefly (no easy matter) as a programme of summer schools for the farming masses. Every eminent American could earn good money as a lecturer at Chautauqua or its innumerable imitators, and eminent Europeans also succumbed to the lure of high fees. The atmosphere was cruelly suggested in Max Beerbohm's cartoon, 'The name of Dante Gabriel Rossetti is heard for the first time in the United States of America. Time: 1881. Lecturer: Mr Oscar Wilde'. Matthew Arnold took the bait, fatally undermining his health. Bernard Shaw did not, and lived to the age of ninety-four. But even without Shaw's assistance Chautauqua throve, diffusing some taste of science and high culture among the

many (the practical techniques of farming were better cared for in
the land-grant colleges that were another great nineteenth-century
educational landmark). Chautauqua also helped to forge a new
political culture, and the last challenge of the nineteenth century to
the dominant mode of American nationalism.

This time it was the turn of the North to rebel, or rather, of parts
of it. The states eastward from Illinois were on the whole content to
accept the new America and to vote for the Republican party (now
known as the Grand Old Party or GOP). Challenge to the Republican ascendancy came, in these states, mostly from city Democrats, who, when they did not represent an even more parish-pump
strain in American life than their opponents, spoke for the new
ethnic groups which were so essential a part of the new America.
But west of Chicago the veterans of the Union army were in revolt.
Agricultural production for the world market was becoming ever
more fiercely competitive, as one new region after another was
drawn in; overheads mounted, and the climatic cycle was unkind. A
great revolt against the railroads, and the capitalists who owned
them, and the cities they served, and booze, and immigrants, and
banks, and corrupt two-party politics – in short, against modern
times – swept the prairie West between 1888 and 1896, and much of
the South too. A new party, the People's Party (or Populists) was
formed, determined to dislodge the mighty from their seats, or at
any rate the Democrats and Republicans from Congress. Its leaders
were by no means unintelligent or ill-informed, even if Ignatius
Donnelly, who largely wrote the Populist platform, made himself
ridiculous by asserting that Bacon was Shakespeare (it is a curiosity of the American democracy that its citizens have always been
so attracted by the notion that no mere man of the people could
have written *Hamlet* or *Twelfth Night*). Many of the Populists' proposals were taken up by later reformers and passed into law: for
instance, they demanded that Senators be elected by the people
instead of by the state legislatures. But the Populist revolt was at
heart a recognition, *à contre cœur*, that the unique position of the
farmer in the republic was passing. According to the 1890 census the
frontier was no more, America now being a settled country from
sea to sea, and in 1894, at the Chicago world's fair, young Frederick
Jackson Turner made his name with his elegy, 'The Significance of

the Frontier in American History' – a characteristic Chautauqua performance.

The forces of the old America were waning, so, not surprisingly, the movement dissolved into incoherence. A few demagogues won power in the South, but they stayed within the Democratic party and consolidated their power by race-baiting. The reasonable belief of the Populist leaders that a measure of inflation would help the farmers somehow got transmuted into a crusade for a bi-metallic currency, which in turn aroused the priests of the gold standard. The election of 1896 was fought, ridiculously enough, around this issue, and Republican orthodoxy won, though its Presidential candidate, William McKinley, was, in private, not the truest of believers. More significant was the fact that his opponent, William Jennings Bryan, was a Democrat, not a Populist. The challenge had been absorbed, and the farmers' campaign foundered on the reef of intellectual eccentricity. Bryan's equivalent of the Baconian heresy was his belief in the literal truth of the Bible, a trait that was to be pathetically displayed in the 'monkey trial' of 1925, when he made himself the mouthpiece of those who wanted to drive Darwinism out of the curriculum of the public schools. But the most significantly sad thing about Bryan was that his eloquence, devotion, plain man's Republicanism and faith in the Protestant God were the same traits that had carried Abraham Lincoln to greatness only half a century before. Time had made this not-so-ancient good uncouth.

Innocence and Power

The social and political system that replaced it had far to go in 1896. Big business was still in its infancy: the great names, Rockefeller, Morgan, Carnegie, Harriman, Gould, stood out because there were so few of them. Industrial class conflict was a leading feature of life in the great cities, and was converting such labour leaders as Eugene V. Debs to socialism, and not the Utopian socialism that had led idealistic Americans into the wilderness before the Civil War, but the up-to-date 'scientific' socialism deriving from Karl Marx. Left-wing immigrants had high hopes of America, especially after such incidents as the Haymarket riot of 1886, the Homestead strike and lockout of 1892 and the Pullman strike (led by Debs) in 1894. The developments which would make twentieth-century America so rootedly, almost obsessively, anti-socialist were mostly yet to come. But an assertive nationalism, an insistence that the American way, as received from the great men of the past, was perfect, was certainly one of those developments, and was already potent. It suggests the desirability of closing this essay with some consideration of how America regarded its place in the world of nations as the nineteenth century drew to a close. For nationalism can become imperialism; and both imply an alien context.

Mark Twain first transcended his standing as a mere humorist with *The Innocents Abroad*, which showed that he was a writer of truly original force. It also showed some of the great changes worked on the American people by the rise of industrialism. Previously, American visitors to Europe had been almost entirely of the lowest or the highest economic classes: common sailors and Bostonian *illuminati* such as George Ticknor, one of the founders of Harvard University (as distinct from Harvard College), who made the Grand Tour after the Treaty of Ghent (1814); Herman Melville, a gentleman fallen on hard times, combined the categories by shipping to Liverpool as a cabin boy in 1837. The coming of steamships and the steady rise in the average American income soon put the means for a trip abroad within the reach, or at least the aspirations, of tens of thousands of ordinary middle-class citizens. The age of the great American tourist was beginning; and its first fruits included not only Twain's satirical accounts of his counrymen on their travels but also the many tales and novels of Henry James on the theme of the New World confronting the Old.

It was a tempting theme, and not just because the question of America's role only became pressing (like so much else) after the Civil War. American provincialism, a determination to judge the world rigidly by the standards of Poughkeepsie, was an irresistibly comic topic which yet retained, even after immersion in Jamesian subtleties, a finely simple aspect which suggested that after all there was something to be said for American innocence, as against European worldliness. James saw the pathos as well as the absurdity of his American travellers and stay-at-homes, but his own self-respect was deeply bound up with theirs. He too would remain an innocent abroad.

If so, he was not the only victim of one of the most dangerous American myths. The central affirmation of American politics was that the United States had the best possible system of government and set an example to the world. This belief held its own even after the collapse into civil war should have shattered it for ever. It had its roots in the seventeenth-century religious myth of New England, according to which Massachusetts was as a city on a hill, a beacon of true godliness to a benighted world. The Revolution had transposed the idea into a political key, and American isolation from the rest of the world had done the rest. This isolation was in part the consequence of the British discovery, reached after two expensive wars, that no military action against the United States could be worth what it would cost. The Republic would have little to fear from Britain, and nothing at all from anyone else (the Royal Navy was in the way) until the First World War. This fact, combined with those other facts, the two broad oceans, bred in the people a sense of absolute security. They kept their army, navy and diplomatic establishment to a minimum, and yet were not afraid to 'twist the lion's tail' from time to time. For the rest, they regarded the world chiefly as a field for missionary and commercial endeavour, and seldom doubted that the benefits of American Protestantism and American trade were self-evident to all who encountered them. It was in this spirit that they first began to meddle in the Far East. For the rest, Thomas Jefferson's maxim 'Peace, commerce and honest friendship with all nations, entangling alliances with none' seemed to sum up all the foreign policy they needed.

But it by no means comprised the whole of America's relations with the rest of the world. For one thing the United States was still, culturally, a dependent nation. It was to Europe, above all to Germany, that Americans looked for ideas on education, scholarship and science. The primacy of Italian and French art and music was still acknowledged. English authors were read as avidly in the United States as at home: one of the great scenes of the nineteenth century was the crowd waiting at the New York dockside for the packet that carried the news as to whether Little Nell was dead or not. In none of the arts was there an effective cultural war of independence before the twentieth century, although subjection to the old gods grew steadily more reluctant from the publication of 'The American Scholar' onwards.

Nor did the myth of American uniqueness, innocence and excellence silence all questioning. On the contrary, the mystery of the destiny of the new nation built with such heroism was a pressing problem still, as much for those who looked beyond the country's borders as for those who did not. From first to last the nineteenth century in America was for many an age of anxiety, and the imagination had to serve this, as well as all other states of mind. At first the great questions were confronted more easily in a symbolic than a naturalistic mode, for the novel of manners did not transplant easily to American soil, and the influence of Scott, and indeed of the whole age, drove fiction in a romantic direction. Hence the appeal of the past and of the sea to nineteenth-century writers. Fenimore Cooper, troubled by the rise of a vulgar American democracy which seemed to put in question the achievement of the Revolution, and yet at the same time imaginatively excited by the subduing of the continent, dramatized his preoccupations in the Leatherstocking series. Nathaniel Hawthorne, irked by the rigid demands of the New England conscience, composed *The Scarlet Letter*. Edgar Allan Poe's *Narrative of Arthur Gordon Pym*, drawing on a long tradition of nautical tales, which also generated R. H. Dana's *Two Years Before the Mast* and Joshua Slocum's *Sailing Alone Around the World*, begins as an adventure story about a merchant ship plying out of Nantucket and becomes by the end a fantasy in which Poe can confront, though hardly resolve, the tensions that were driving his native South to shipwreck.

> Lo! Death has reared himself a throne
> In a strange city lying alone
> Far down in the dim West . . .

And finally Herman Melville produced *Moby-Dick*, the greatest of all American works of fiction, which by its very genius and universality transcended even as it embodied the hag-ridden society which gave it birth.

By the last years of the nineteenth century, symbolism had given way to naturalism, as the wilderness had given way to the city. The imagination still served. Henry James perpetually pitted the sensitive and innocent against the cruelties and stupidities of the common human race: it is not only in his avowedly 'international' tales that we may sense again the general American anxiety about the chances of democratic, Protestant, rural virtue in a world growing steadily more alien and oppressive. Behind the ordeals of Isabel Archer and Lambert Strether may be seen the concern of old stock Americans about the rise of the immigrant and the millionaire, just as, behind the narratives' ironical vindication of such virtues as patience, tenderness and courage may be detected a more general American confidence that, whatever the short term might yield, in the long run a great civilization was maturing in America which would carry all before it.

In its own mode of irony the twentieth century was to vindicate this confidence, though the victory of Coca-Cola, blue jeans and chewing gum formed no part of the prognostication. In the short run very different attitudes were to be victorious. As the century ended the United States plunged into war again, first with Spain and then with the Philippines. The consolidated strength of the nation, whether measured in money, men or production, now sought expression not in the pieties of Abraham Lincoln but in the new nationalism of Theodore Roosevelt. The mission of America suddenly seemed to be to go forth and conquer in the name of its superior civilization. It was a formula which was distasteful to many conservatives at the time, and would have horrified most leaders of an earlier era. It was un-American by the standards that had until just the other day seemed unquestionable, and it is not surprising that it was a non-American poet who gave it expression:

> Take up the White Man's burden –
> Have done with childish days –
> The lightly proffered laurel,
> The easy, ungrudged praise.
> Comes now, to search your manhood
> Through all the thankless years,
> Cold-edged with dear-bought wisdom,
> The judgment of your peers!
> (Rudyard Kipling, 1899)

It was an appalling message to those, like William Jennings Bryan, who cherished the old America, and the American people were soon to stop their ears against it. But it was nevertheless an answer to the question of America's destiny, and as the twentieth century brought endless accretions of power and responsibility it began to seem pretty clear that it was no mistake or wrong turning, but the goal to which nineteenth-century nation-building had always tended, whether it knew it or not. America was to be a Superpower; and this fact too the American imagination would have to take into account, one day.

THE LITERARY SCENE

HAROLD BEAVER

The Prophetic Vision

Alexis de Tocqueville had no doubts, in his aristocratic way, what a democratic – that is to say, American – literature implied: a contempt for form; a loose, fantastic style; works speedily, if vigorously, executed at the expense of art:

> Small productions will be more common than bulky books; there will be more wit than erudition, more imagination than profundity; and literary performances will bear marks of an untutored and rude vigour of thought – frequently of great variety and singular fecundity. The object of authors will be to astonish rather than to please, and to stir the passions more than to charm the taste.
>
> *(Democracy in America*, 1840, pt. 2, ch. 23)

Such generalizations were not based on extensive reading. For there was as yet no national literature. When Tocqueville arrived in America in 1831, there was no Poe, no Emerson, no Hawthorne, no Longfellow, no Whitman, nothing as bulky and profound as *Moby-Dick*. His prophecies were based solely on social and political analyses. He had noted the low regard for books in backwoods settlements; their lack of leisure and ready access to English literature. With an unbounded Cartesian confidence he made the following predictions:

First, that the native tongue would fork, as it were, into an English literary (or high) style and a local (or low) vernacular. For 'American authors may truly be said to live more in England than in their own country; since they constantly study the English writers, and take them every day for their models.'

Second, that Americans would become addicted to abstractions and generic terms since such modes of speech seem to enlarge as well as to 'obscure the thoughts they are intended to convey'. This loose blend of the catchpenny and profound, he considered, was due to their isolated and unsettled lives. 'As they never know whether the idea they express today will be appropriate to the new position they may occupy tomorrow, they naturally acquire a liking for abstract terms.'

Third, that the future alone would haunt them: 'in this direction their unbounded imagination grows and dilates beyond all measure'. Though momentarily diverted by the wonders of nature, 'they may be said not to perceive the mighty forests which surround them till they fall beneath the hatchet'. (Thoreau himself could not have put this better.)

Fourth, that America's sole subject would be its unique collective culture, since in democracies, 'where men are all insignificant and very much alike, each man instantly sees all his fellows when he surveys himself'. Heroic poetry, therefore, will be out; 'for an object of slender importance, which is distinctly seen on all sides, will never lend itself to an ideal conception'. Only the national destiny will invite the exercise of poetic power. 'This magnificent image of themselves does not meet the gaze of the Americans at intervals only; it may be said to haunt every one of them in his least as well as in his most important actions, and to be always flitting before his mind.'

Fifth, that in spite of the inconceivably 'petty' and 'insipid' and generally 'paltry' life of men in the United States, all eyes would constantly be raised beyond their nation 'to discern mankind at large'; that the 'I' would expand (as Emerson was to show) until it conceived 'a far broader idea of Providence itself, and its interference in human affairs'. Considering the whole human race, Americans 'easily conceive that its destinies are regulated by the same design; and in the actions of every individual they are led to acknowledge a trace of that universal and eternal plan on which God rules our race'.

Sixth, that in seeking the Oversoul (as Emerson was to call it) of all mankind, Americans would also delve into the innards of each individual man; that the very commonplaces of daily life would force writers (such as Hawthorne and Melville) constantly to search below the external surface which is palpable to the senses, in order to read the inner soul: and nothing lends itself more to the delineation of the Ideal than the scrutiny of the hidden depths in the immaterial nature of man.

Much else, of course, Tocqueville could not envisage. But the grand outline is impressive. Especially for someone who had little to go on beyond the outpourings of Jacksonian oratory. As he coolly noted:

> I have frequently remarked that the Americans, who generally treat of business in clear, plain language, devoid of all ornament, and so extremely simple as to be often coarse, are apt to become inflated as soon as they attempt a more poetical diction. They then vent their pomposity from one end of a harangue to the other; and to hear them lavish imagery on every occasion, one might fancy that they never spoke of anything with simplicity.

Again Tocqueville was right. From at least 1830 to 1860 oratory was the dominant force in American letters. *Moby-Dick* and *Leaves of Grass* are Melville's and Whitman's bravura versions of the great speech. Ahab's soliloquies are incantations to set beside the flamboyant performances of Daniel Webster and John C. Calhoun. 'The imprisoned winds are let loose,' thundered Webster in the Senate in 1850:

> The East, the North, and the stormy South combine to throw the whole sea into commotion, to toss its billows to the skies, and disclose its profoundest depth. I have a part to act, not for my own security or safety, for I am looking out for no fragment upon which to float away from the wreck, if wreck there must be, but for the good of the whole, and the preservation of all.

'Swerve me?' echoed Captain Ahab, like some political rival, one year later:

> ye cannot swerve me, else ye swerve yourselves! man has ye there. Swerve me? The path to my fixed purpose is laid with iron rails, whereon my soul is grooved to run. Over unsounded gorges, through the rifled hearts of mountains, under torrents' beds, unerringly I rush! Naught's an obstacle, naught's an angle to the iron way!
>
> (*Moby-Dick*, ch. 37)

The intensity of vision, the spell-binding gusto, is dizzying. The fate of the whole nation, it seemed, depended on such thunderers. Their aim was to overwhelm the audience and bind it to their will. Until their vision became its vision; their will, its will. As Ahab clinches Ishmael to his oath. As Whitman would clinch us to his side. Brotherhood is all. 'Bear me out in it, thou great democratic God!' cried Ishmael:

who didst not refuse to the swart convict, Bunyan, the pale, poetic pearl; Thou who didst clothe with doubly hammered leaves of finest gold, the stumped and paupered arm of old Cervantes; Thou who didst pick up Andrew Jackson from the pebbles; who didst hurl him upon a war-horse; who didst thunder him higher than a throne! Thou who, in all Thy mighty, earthly marchings, ever cullest Thy selectest champions from the kingly commons; bear me out in it, O God!

(ch. 26)

A single electrifying genius, a single speaker (it seemed) might stave off disastrous disintegration throughout the 1850s: first Webster and Calhoun with their summons to fraternity; then Stephen Douglas and Abraham Lincoln.

Rhetoric was the one, universal literary mode. Everyone studied the triumphs of Jacksonian eloquence. Nearly everyone had a smattering of Cicero. The Lincoln–Douglas debates of 1858 had behind them a century of oratorical development. Funerals, picnics, Fourth of July celebrations called out floods of oratory. The sermon still ranked high as a literary form. Schoolchildren learned orations by heart to declaim on 'elocution days'. Addresses like Henry Clay's 'Evils of War', Edward Everett's 'The Intelligence of the People', Daniel Webster's 'Liberty and Union' and Robert Winthrop's 'Bunker Hill Monument' were included in dozens of school readers. The young Emerson pined for such radiant confidence; and it was Webster, above all, who fulfilled the brief. 'He was there in his Adamitic capacity,' wrote Emerson in 1854, 'as if he alone of all men did not disappoint the eye or the ear, but was a fit figure in the landscape.' It was from Webster and Calhoun and Clay that a whole generation learned the demagogic arts of brilliant speechifying. So Whitman claimed his Websterian right to speak as a 'simple separate person'. 'The United States themselves,' he claimed, were 'essentially the greatest poem'; and of 'all nations the United States with veins full of poetical stuff most need poets and will doubtless have the greatest and use them the greatest.' A distinct corpus of *work* might still be lacking; but for a nation in tumescence – in this state of transcendent erection – Whitman claimed his democratic right to speak.

What Webster and others proclaimed in the public sphere, Whitman overwhelmingly reclaimed for the private:

Walt Whitman, a kosmos, of Manhattan the son,
Turbulent, fleshy, sensual, eating, drinking and breeding,
No sentimentalist, no stander above men and women or apart from them,
No more modest than immodest.

(Leaves of Grass, 1855, section 24)

Conventions that bind the public orator do not restrain him. His rapture is not only meant to entice us. It bursts through all prohibitions to touch and seduce us. This is speech that has cast off all doubts of its own authority to speak. With sublime self-confidence it challenges every taboo, both literary and sexual.

The Literary Market-Place

Such a challenge filled a void. For a familiar argument ran that American writing was hopelessly imitative, that it lacked a proper subject (which implied nobility and ruins). Goethe, it is true, had saluted that very lack in 'Den Vereinigten Staaten' (1827):

> Amerika, du hast es besser
> Als unser Kontinent, das alte,
> Hast keine verfallene Schlösser
> Und keine Basalte.
> Dich stört nicht im Innern,
> Zu lebendiger Zeit,
> Unnützes Erinnern
> Und vergeblicher Streit.

(America, you are better off than our continent, the old one; you have neither ruined castles, nor volcanic rock. You are not inwardly vexed, at this vital hour, by useless memories and vain quarrels.)

But those thudding negations constituted the most worn of all American tropes since Montaigne's eulogy of an American Golden Age. Echoed whimsically by Shakespeare's Gonzalo:

> . . . no kind of traffic
> Would I admit; no name of magistrate;

Letters should not be known; riches, poverty,
And use of service, none; contract, succession,
Bourn, bound of land, tilth, vineyard, none;
No use of metal, corn, or wine, or oil;
No occupation; all men idle, all;
And women too . . .
(The Tempest, 1611–12, II, i)*

To be proudly echoed by Crèvecoeur: 'Here are no aristocratic families, no courts, no kings, no bishops, no ecclesiastical dominion, no invisible power giving to a few a very visible one, no great manufacturers employing thousands, no great refinement of luxury', in his third *Letter from an American Farmer* (1782). To be evasively echoed by Cooper: 'There is no costume for the peasant (there is scarcely a peasant at all), no wig for the judge, no baton for the general, no diadem for the chief magistrate', in *Notions of the Americans* (1828). To be plaintively echoed by Hawthorne:

No author, without a trial, can conceive of the difficulty of writing a romance about a country where there is no shadow, no antiquity, no mystery, no picturesque and gloomy wrong, nor anything but a commonplace prosperity, in broad and simple daylight, as is happily the case with my dear native land,

in his preface to *The Marble Faun* (1860). To be ludicrously multiplied by Henry James:

one might enumerate the items of high civilization, as it exists in other countries, which are absent from the texture of American life, until it should become a wonder to know what was left. No State, in the European sense of the word, and indeed barely a specific national name. No sovereign, no court, no personal loyalty, no aristocracy, no church, no clergy, no army, no diplomatic service, no country gentlemen, no palaces, no castles, nor manors, nor old country-houses, nor parsonages, nor thatched cottages nor ivied ruins; no cathedrals, nor abbeys, nor little Norman churches; no great Universities nor public schools – no Oxford, nor Eton, nor Harrow; no literature, no novels, no museums, no pictures, no political society, no sporting class – no Epsom nor Ascot! Some such list as that might be drawn up of the absent things in American life – especially in the American life of forty years ago, the effect of which, upon an English or a French imagination, would probably as a general thing be appalling,

in *Hawthorne* (1879). What remains, James concludes, undercutting the whole roll-call must be the secret of 'American humour' itself.

For by then the void had already noticeably been filled. The

1850s, in fact, now seem a culminating decade (entitled the 'American Renaissance' by F. O. Matthiessen) to which Hawthorne, Melville, Thoreau and Whitman all made decisive contributions: *The Scarlet Letter* (1850), *Moby-Dick* (1851), *Walden* (1854), *Leaves of Grass* (1855). But a question evaded by Matthiessen is: who bought these books? how big was the book-buying public? Of these four masterpieces only *The Scarlet Letter* was an immediate success, selling 5,000 copies within the first six months. Yet all four authors were dependent, unlike Emerson, on their writing for a livelihood; and this was equally true, after the Civil War, of William Dean Howells, Mark Twain and Henry James. Yet only Twain became a bestseller. Melville made an initial breakthrough with his adventures in the South Seas; James with the mildly scandalous *Daisy Miller*. But their sales soon sagged. Hawthorne, Melville and James each suffered a drastic decline in popularity in mid-career. Howells, in the end, more or less gave up the struggle.

But there *was* a sizable book-buying public emerging in the early nineteenth century. It is nonsense to argue that the American literary community was too small to nourish free-lance writers. Admittedly James Fenimore Cooper's most successful books sold fewer than 10,000 copies within a year of publication; but sixty different editions of *The Sketch Book of Geoffrey Crayon, Gent.* (1820) were available before Washington Irving's death in 1859 and it has been estimated that over half a million copies of his works were sold in the last decade of his life. (Irving, like Emerson and Cooper, was a man of wealth.) Longfellow's sales too are instructive. He was paid only $15 for 'The Village Blacksmith' in 1841, but $1,000 for the poem 'Morituri Salutamus' and $3,000 for 'The Hanging of the Crane'. For his sales were phenomenal. His first collection, *Voices of the Night*, sold 40,000 copies (until absorbed into the *Collected Poems*). *The Song of Hiawatha* (1855) sold 11,000 on publication and a further 10,000 copies a year for the next ten years. The publisher Samuel Goodrich estimated the gross sale of books in the United States in 1820 at $2½ million, in 1850 at $12½ million and in 1860 at $20 million. In the same period the number of titles issued increased more than twenty times.[1]

For this period saw the rise of the great publishing houses – Harper, Putnam, Carey, Thomas, Fields, Cummins and Hilliard –

which dominated the 1840s and 1850s, accompanied by a great burst of magazine and newspaper publishing. By 1860 there were more than six times the number of magazines published than in 1825: that is, 575 magazines, 372 daily newspapers and 271 weeklies, many of which printed stories, essays and verse.[2] In addition there were richly bound, ornamented annuals, gift books and anthologies produced at the rate of some sixty a year. Poe, William Cullen Bryant, Hawthorne, William Gilmore Simms and Nathaniel P. Willis all wrote for them. Rufus Griswold, the best known of these anthologists (now infamous for his slander of Poe), compiled *Poets and Poetry of America* (1842), *Prose Writers of America* (1847) and *Female Poets of America* (1848), all of which sold in thousands. Evert and George Duyckinck's *Cyclopaedia of American Literature* (1855), in two volumes, for the first time familiarized the public with a critical study of American literature.

Poe made his living as a literary editor, moving from Richmond to New York to Philadelphia. Hawthorne's *Twice-Told Tales* (1837) had made their first appearance in *The Token* (a gift book published by Goodrich). Four to five dollars per page seemed to be the going rate. Willis, the most successful bellettrist of the 1850s, received ten dollars per page. The Duyckinck brothers solicited material from young Melville for their *Literary World* (1847–53); and, after the failure of *Pierre* (1852), he entirely relied on anonymous publication in *Putnam's Monthly Magazine*, netting a total income for three years of piecework (1853–5) of around $750.

Melville's failure as a professional writer has by now become legendary: after five years he was deep in debt to his father-in-law, to Harper & Bros in America and to Richard Bentley in England. But he was a difficult author and it seems hardly surprising that *Mardi* (1849) sold only 2,000 copies, *Moby-Dick* (eighteen months after publication) 2,300 and *Pierre* (eight months after publication) 283 copies out of an edition of 2,310. As a result of unearned advances, his accounts were constantly in the red, though *White-Jacket* (1850) was his second most successful book. His earlier books, on the other hand, both did well: *Typee* (1846) reaching sales of around 6,000; and *Omoo* (1847) selling 3,600 on publication. By his brother Allan's reckoning Herman's American income from the first five titles amounted to $3,591; his British receipts to slightly more at $3,775. Adding the British advance of $700 on *Moby-Dick* tots up a grand total of just over $8,000. That is an average annual income of $1,600 over five years, making Herman Melville one of the *best*-paid American authors of his generation.[3]

For a modern estimate we must use a multiplier of (at least) ten. So that by today's reckoning Melville, in his late twenties and early thirties, was earning between $16,000 and $20,000 per year; which seems a decent enough income, seeing that the whole population of the United States in 1850 only amounted to some 23 millions, climbing to 31 millions by 1860. When in late 1866 Melville finally secured a government post as deputy inspector of customs in the city of New York, he earned just four dollars a day: that is, some $1,200 per annum (or between $12,000 and $16,000 in today's terms). With his wife's unearned income he had his 'pittance' at last – far more than he had earned in twenty years of professional authorship. No wonder he had groaned to Hawthorne: 'Dollars damn me. What I feel most moved to write, that is banned, – it will not pay. Yet, altogether, write the *other* way I cannot. So the product is a final hash, and all my books are botches.'

Hawthorne felt much the same way. Only he blamed the 'd—d mob of scribbling women'. Their books, he complained, were selling 'by the 100,000 . . . I should have no chance of success while the public taste is occupied by their trash'. His sole example of this 'trash' was Maria Cummins's *The Lamplighter* (1854), the story of an orphan girl, which sold 40,000 copies in the first eight weeks. But he clearly had a far wider target in mind. Mrs Marion Harland, whose first novel *Alone* (1854) sold 100,000 copies a year for five years, was still being published after the First World War. Mary Jane Holmes averaged a book a year from 1854 (*Tempest and Sunshine*) to 1907. Augusta Jane Evans's *St Elmo* (1866) ranks among the thirty most popular novels ever published in the United States. One of the earliest of these blockbusters was Susan B. Warner's *The Wide, Wide World* (1850), followed by *Queechy* (1852). *The Wide, Wide World* was reprinted thirteen times in two years, to be eventually reprinted sixty-seven times; by the end of the nineteenth century it had sold more than half a million copies. A further trio of novels, published in 1855, sold over 75,000 copies each, netting over $25,000. She was second only to Harriet Beecher Stowe. But the queen of the domestic novel was doubtless Mrs E. D. E. N. Southworth who, after her husband's desertion, wrote *Retribution* (1849), with 200,000 sales, followed by sixty-one more. Her domestic mystery, *The Hidden Hand* (1859), remained in print well into the twentieth century.

No wonder Hawthorne was anxious. In the 1840s and 1850s women's fiction inundated the market. Harriet Beecher Stowe had been writing for eighteen years before her instant fame with the serialization of *Uncle Tom's Cabin* in the *National Era* (1851–2). The first edition of 5,000 sold out in forty-eight hours and for the next two years the presses never caught up with the demand. Total sales in the United States reached a million within seven years and nearly as many again (chiefly in pirated editions) in Britain. It was the first American international bestseller, rapidly translated into more than thirty languages – more than fifty by today. But hers was a polemical text on a politically explosive theme. The run-of-the-mill book was a wholly sentimental affair, concerned mainly with girls confronting the pains and terrors of adolescence. The maternal romances by Catherine Maria Sedgwick ('the American Maria Edgeworth') and Lydia Maria Child of the 1820s and 1830s soon ran into a steady drizzle of tears and prayers. For this huge new market of literate and leisured women needed fiction that spoke to women and dealt with women's problems. An upsurge of women's magazines, like *Godey's Lady's Book*, the *National Magazine* and the *Casket*, was accompanied by a spate of cookbooks and etiquette books and guides to child care. *Godey's* had eighteen regular female contributors; a popular novelist like Mary Agnes Fleming had a $15,000 annual retainer from the *New York Weekly*.

This vast new market, however, was also intensely constricting. Its narrow domestic emphasis served only to enforce a conventional morality. Church and children and chastity were its sole touchstones; and inevitably its values swamped the rest of the literary market-place. That was what Hawthorne was fighting. One by one the older magazines (the *Literary World*, *Putnam's Monthly*, *Graham's*) folded before the Civil War. Those that survived, like *Harper's* (edited by Henry Mills Alden) or the *Atlantic Monthly* (first edited by James Russell Lowell), increasingly became self-conscious arbiters of American taste. All scrupulously avoided giving offence. Thus

Richard Watson Gilder pruned and bowdlerized three pre-publication extracts for the *Century* from *Huckleberry Finn* (1884–5). As he explained to one outraged subscriber:

Mark Twain is not a giber at religion or morality. He is a good citizen and believes in the best things. Nevertheless there is much of his writing that we would not print for a miscellaneous audience. If you should ever carefully compare the chapters of 'Huckleberry Finn', as we printed them, with the same as they appear in the book, you will see the most decided difference. These extracts were carefully edited for a magazine audience with his full consent.

(*Letters*, ed. R. Gilder, 1916, p. 399)

Explaining his blue-pencilling of *Jude the Obscure* for serialization in *Harper's*, Alden told Hardy in 1894:

My objections are based on purism (not mine, but our readers'), which is undoubtedly more rigid here than in England. Our rule is that the MAGA-ZINE must contain nothing which could not be read aloud in any family circle . . . You will see for yourself our difficulty, and we fully appreciate the annoyance you must feel at being called upon to modify work conscientiously done, and which is best as it left your hands, from an artist's point of view.

(J. H. Harper, *The House of Harper*, 1912, p. 530)

William Dean Howells habitually cautioned young writers that it was women, not men, who read books, so it was no use quarrelling with them; there was no appeal from their decision.

If the women's lobby crowded writers at home, British imports crowded them from abroad. Between local squeamishness and foreign prestige native authors felt squeezed. It was England which was deemed to have the literate audience, literary institutions and venerable journals; and the central question, round which emotions swirled, was the problem of copyright. American writers were able to secure copyright merely by residing in Britain. American publishers found pirating English books more profitable than nurturing local talent. Dickens, for one, tirelessly plugged this theme on his American tours. But, as *Uncle Tom's Cabin* proved, piracy was by no means one-sided. Samuel Goodrich estimated that while in 1820 British authors sold twice as many books in the United States as American authors, by 1850 this ratio was exactly reversed. The American Copyright League (supported by such men as Whittier and Twain, Lowell and Oliver Wendell Holmes) stepped up its campaign throughout the 1880s until, with the passage of the International Copyright Law in 1891, things finally changed.

Cultural Independence

But nothing could change the basic fact that now there were *two* independent nations sharing a single language and cultural tradition. As Emerson wrote in *English Traits*, as late as 1856: 'The culture of the day, the thoughts and aims of men, are English thoughts and aims ... The American is only the continuation of the English genius into new conditions, more or less propitious.' The magnet of the 'home', or European, culture continued long after the political revolution. The sensibility of the picturesque early invaded the American landscape. Leading intellectuals like George Ticknor and Edward Everett, historians like Motley and Prescott, literary scholars like Lowell and Longfellow and Francis J. Child (the authority on ballads), all attended continental universities. Many made the Grand Tour, matching mouldering Europe versus commonplace America, like Washington Irving in his *Sketch Book*:

> I longed to wander over the scenes of renowned achievement – to tread, as it were, in the footsteps of antiquity – to loiter about the ruined castle – to meditate on the falling tower – to escape, in short, from the commonplace realities of the present, and lose myself among the shadowy grandeurs of the past.

Cooper stayed for seven years – mostly in Paris or Italy – lamenting the 'poverty of materials' in American life. Emerson left in 1833 to discover his Transcendentalism in Paris and explore the ideas of Wordsworth, Coleridge and Carlyle on their home ground.

But the 1830s, which first introduced the expatriate and international themes (in Cooper's *Homeward Bound* and *Home As Found*, 1838), were also the decade of America's declaration of literary independence. The first chord was struck by William Ellery Channing in his 'Remarks on a National Literature' (1830); the full theme sounded by Emerson's Phi Beta Kappa address, 'The American Scholar' (1837). 'Perhaps the time is already come,' he intoned,

when the sluggard intellect of this continent will look from under its iron lids and fill the postponed expectation of the world with something better than the exertions of mechanical skill. Our day of dependence, our long apprenticeship to the learning of other lands, draws to a close. The millions that around us are rushing into life, cannot always be fed on the sere remains of foreign harvests. Events, actions arise, that must be sung, that will sing themselves.

A battle was already raging in the magazines between the so-called 'Young Americans', who wrote chiefly for the *Democratic Review*, and conservatives, who wrote for the partisan *Whig Review*, *New York Review* and the *Knickerbocker*. Evert Duyckinck was a leading spirit of Young America, preaching 'the New Man in the New Age' animated by democracy. It was he who encouraged the young Melville on his return from the South Seas; that great cry to a 'great democratic God' (quoted above) condenses the very essence of Young Americanism. Thoreau, Hawthorne, Whittier, Bryant and Emerson all contributed to the *Democratic Review*.

To the Whigs, in John Quincy Adams's words, literature 'in its nature must be aristocratic'. How could there be such a thing as 'a democracy of numbers and literature'? Whigs thought of literature in solely aesthetic terms; Young Americans, as a vehicle for *ideas*. Such 'spurious democracy' was denounced as 'perverted'. In some way this polemic is reminiscent of twentieth-century debates pitting art versus commitment. Poe, a decidedly Whig spirit, chose his literary executor, Rufus Griswold, from their ranks. Whitman, his polar opposite, immersed himself in American culture, incarnating its 'geography and national life and rivers and lakes', to 'utter the word Democratic, the word En-Masse'.

By mid-century quite a new self-confidence was in the air, though tense with the threat of Civil War. Washington Irving had still been constantly on the defensive: unsure of the legitimacy of fiction, unsure of his own persona, seeking (he explained) 'only to blow a flute accompaniment in the national concert'. By contrast Emerson and Melville *roared*. They flaunted their national spirit. They ransacked the whole globe. They let their words resound – words which were shaped by three indigenous, or long domesticated forms: the sermon, the essay and the romance.

The sermon, of course, was still universally respected in that oratorical age; its great masters (Henry Ward Beecher, Theodore Parker or Wendell Phillips) drew vast crowds. The discursive, or critical, essay was especially favoured by east coast literati like Lowell, Holmes and, for that matter, Poe. But in its quintessential American guise, the essay had reverted to its origins in Montaigne, hovering somewhere between an (extroverted) lecture and an (introverted) journal, between the public forum and the private form. Keeping journals was Emerson's and Thoreau's main concern. Here they shaped their topics, their epigrams, their oracular style. Essays – even whole books like *Walden* (1854) – were later distilled from them. But first they could be tested live on the great lyceum and Chautauqua circuits.

The tide of nationalism after the Revolution continued to rise. The biggest factor in the spread of American fiction was its role in exploiting the American past and exploring the landscape. Cooper in *The Spy* (1821) incorporated the Indian, the forest, the sea, American history and legend. But he was not unique. The year 1825 alone produced seven novels about the Revolution. The anniversary of the Pilgrims' landing in 1820, the semicentennial celebration of 1826, the start on the Bunker Hill monument, Lafayette's visit to the United States, all helped to stir this mood of undiluted patriotism. Historical romance was the favoured mode; imaginative narrative preferred to documented narrative. Romance, according to Hawthorne, was less concerned with minute fidelity to daily experience than 'the truth of the human heart'. It conceived 'a deeper moral and closer and severer truth' than either Scott or Dickens could provide. As an ideal or 'idealizing' form, 'spiritualizing the grossness of actual life', it allowed American novelists to evade much of the contemporary scene and to continue working the older, emblematic veins of symbolism and of allegory.

'Realism' was not what they were after. The very word was still new, first used for discussing visual arts in the mid-1850s. Hawthorne moaned (in 'The Custom-House') that he could not seize 'the reality of the flitting hour' since he lacked 'the cunning to transcribe it'. Parke Godwin, reviewing Thackeray in 1855, praised the 'reasonable realism' that gave his novels 'the aspect of an actual transcript of the life of society'. The analogy between the camera and the novel became frequent after 1856. Yet Emerson frowned on both Jane Austen's 'pinched and narrow' vision and the Dickensian eye for 'surfaces'. That was not the American way.

The American way was 'ideal', that is full of ideas. It was what we should call a psychological way, intent not so much on life studies as studious vivisection. It was an anatomist's art and clinical talk of 'the spiritual dissecting-knife' was as readily thrown at Hawthorne as at his contemporary, Flaubert. Critics smelt something sadistic in such calculated lancing of festering guilts; and Hawthorne was the first to agree. He was appalled by Roger Chillingworth who 'violated, in cold blood, the sanctity of a human heart' (*The Scarlet Letter*, ch. 17). But he would have resisted Margaret Oliphant's attack, when that English novelist charged him (in *Blackwood's Magazine*, 1855) with misconceiving the very nature of the novel. He never wrote a novel; and if he strained his readers, if he only addressed himself to 'an intellectual audience', as she said, then such was the ambiguous nature of romance. Its art lay precisely in protracted delineation and interpretation.

Melville in 'Hawthorne and His Mosses' (1850) praised him for carrying 'Republican plainness into Literature' and doing away with 'this leaven of literary flunkeyism, towards England'. But it was never as simple as that. Like Emerson and Longfellow before him, Hawthorne too settled in Europe from 1853 to 1860. He too became a passionate pilgrim of sorts. For as only James could recognize, he was trapped; caught between the vacancies of New England and the ambivalences of art; between forebodings of doom and transcendent hope; between puritanism and rationalism; between history and myth; between realism and romance. The very tensions in which he lived and which he unceasingly diagnosed made him the artist he was and the founder of a peculiarly American, self-conscious, ironically embattled, modernist fiction.

International Needs

James, his heir, simply absented himself from America altogether, leaving William Dean Howells in charge of the domestic front. A friend of both James and Twain – of both the eastern and western, the Old World and New World, factions – Howells consistently inveighed against 'literary absenteeism'. Planted centre-stage, he ruled the literary map from the end of the Civil War to the turn of the century. For he was himself a Westerner who had turned East.

Son of a small-town Ohio printer, he took over New England. In 1867 he became an assistant on the *Atlantic Monthly*; by 1871 he had succeeded Lowell as editor-in-chief. He aimed, he said, to 'seek the universal in the individual rather than the social interests'. He was no Dostoevsky, he pointed out, who had been 'led out to be shot, or finally exiled to the rigors of a winter at Duluth'. America was not Russia; American novelists should concern themselves with 'the more smiling aspects of life, which are the more American'.

Such complacency was to be brutally punctured. In May 1886, after police had broken up an Anarcho-Communist meeting in Haymarket Square, Chicago, a bomb exploded, fatally wounding seven policemen and injuring seventy others. That summer eight men were tried for the murders, though there was no evidence linking them to the bomb. But they were known to be radicals; that was enough. Seven were sentenced to death and one to fifteen years in prison. Howells was horrified and threw himself into their cause. His name headed a petition for commutation of sentences. He lobbied without stint to ensure that decency and fairness should prevail. With some apparent success. Nevertheless on 11 November 1887 four of the accused were executed.

This was a turning-point. As Howells wrote, in October 1888, to James:

> I'm not in a very good mood with 'America' myself. It seems to be the most grotesquely illogical thing under the sun; and I suppose I love it less because it won't let me love it more. I should hardly like to trust pen and ink with all the audacity of my social ideas; but after fifty years of optimistic content with 'civilization' and its ability to come out all right in the end, I now abhor it, and feel that it is coming out all wrong in the end, unless it bases itself anew on a real equality. Meantime I wear a fur-lined overcoat, and live in all the luxury my money can buy.
>
> (*Life and Letters*, ed. M. Howells, 1928, vol. 1, p. 417)

He could still wryly cocoon himself and detach himself but his mood had soured. In 1886 he declined an offer to succeed Lowell in the Smith Professorship at Harvard. In 1887 he shifted publishers from Boston to New York. In 1889 he himself physically followed. The move was decisive. It marked the irrevocable shift of cultural power to Manhattan. New York was now the publishing centre (though not the unrivalled literary centre as Boston had been) of the country.

The publication of *A Hazard of New Fortunes* in 1890 marks the transition.

There Howells at last confronted the problems of immigration and untrammelled capitalism. But he also became the channel into America of the new 'naturalism' – the code of Daudet and the Goncourts and Zola. As James had written to Howells in 1884:

> They do the only kind of work, today, that I respect; and in spite of their ferocious pessimism and their handling of unclean things, they are at least serious and honest. The floods of tepid soap and water which under the name of novels are being vomited forth in England, seem to me, by contrast, to do little honour to our race.
>
> (*The Letters*, ed. Percy Lubbock, 1920, vol. 1, pp. 104–5)

For James's ambition was to harness and transcend both French and British and American culture. He aimed to be the Sainte-Beuve of English-speaking letters; he attempted to extend to the novel the principles Matthew Arnold had applied to poetry; and, as an American, he hoped to fulfil the promise held out by Hawthorne. Fluent in French, Italian and German, he aspired to an international role since Americans (he observed at the age of twenty-four) alone could 'pick and choose and assimilate and in short (aesthetically, etc.) claim' their property wherever they found it. James found it mainly in Goethe, Dickens, George Eliot, Balzac, Stendhal and Flaubert.

All his life he agonized over Zola ('worth it if your stomach can stand it'); and he found little to admire in Flaubert after *Madame Bovary*. For 'refinement' and 'awareness' and 'conscious moral purpose' were chiefly what he valued. A novel he broadly defined as 'a personal, a direct impression of life'. The interpenetration was absolute. James's view of art, as of life, was wholly organic. As he asked in a celebrated formula: 'What is character but the determination of incident? What is incident but the illustration of character? What is either a picture or a novel that is *not* of character?' Questions of art, as art, were questions of execution; but the 'essence of moral energy is to survey the whole field'.

His conscience was permanently torn between his moral vision and formalist needs. The solution was never easy. Only when goaded by H. G. Wells did he finally, in a private letter, make the pronouncement: 'It is art that *makes* life, makes interest, makes importance ... and I know of no substitute whatever for the force and beauty of its process.' Art alone makes experience meaningful: Whistler had said as much; so had Wilde. It is the uneasy weight of James's judgement that makes this statement so impressive. It was no flip aesthetic paradox. It was born of long battles with his critical conscience. Form alone was not enough. Documentation was not enough (thus his quarrel with Zola). It is moral awareness – the Arnoldian appeal to the 'amount of felt life' – to which James always returned, whether (at its thinnest) in Hawthorne or (at its fullest) in George Eliot.

Howells became James's henchman in America. His reading was vast. His correspondence was vast. He admired Zola and Giovanni Verga and Pérez Galdós and, above all, Tolstoy. He befriended and encouraged all the most promising youngsters of the next generation: Hamlin Garland, Stephen Crane, Frank Norris, the Yiddish writer Abraham Cahan and the black poet Laurence Dunbar. His role was essential. For by 1900 the cleft between high art and popular art was complete, dividing serious fiction from uplift, or mere fun. Take Horatio Alger. Never had there been such a surefire bestseller. For three decades, from the 1860s to the 1890s, some 110 books with such alliterative titles as *Brave and Bold*, *Sink or Swim*, *Strive and Succeed*, *Strong and Steady*, *Try and Trust*, *Fame and Fortune*, tumbled from the press at the rate of three or four a year. His estimated sales range from 20 to 400 million, beating Mark Twain and Louisa May Alcott – even Dickens – hollow. Yet it was in his generation that the moral certainties of capitalism were first subverted and the summons of 'rags to riches', 'Log Cabin to White House', was thoroughly undermined. The hero of self-improvement, US-style, was shown, for good or ill, to be a mere victim of circumstances and/or his own illusions.

Vernacular Responses

The heroic ideal, though noisily encouraged by dime fiction from Ned Buntline (E. Z. C. Judson) to Zane Grey, had become harder and harder to sustain. For the myth of heroism was dependent on free will. But what Mendel and Ricardo and Marx and Darwin and Freud and Malthus had seemingly taught was that man was trapped; that he was the unsuspecting victim of genetic and economic and political and evolutionary and psychological forces, including an ever-spiralling population growth. The myth of heroism, moreover, depended on a vision of an integrated society with its own economic and sexual hierarchies, its own natural and supernatural controls. But, by the end of the century, the whole universe, it seemed, had disintegrated into a chaos of competing and anarchic forces, receding ever faster to a state of entropic collapse. No counter-attack, however defiant, could be waged by an individual alone.

'We picture the world,' wrote Stephen Crane,

> as thick with conquering and elate humanity, but here, with the bugles of the tempest pealing, it was hard to imagine a peopled earth. One viewed the existence of man then as a marvel, and conceded a glamor of wonder to these lice, which were caused to cling to a whirling, fire-smote, ice-locked, disease-stricken, space-lost bulb. The conceit of man was explained by this storm to be the very engine of life.
>
> ('The Blue Hotel', 1899)

Henry Adams chose to confront the *intellectual* responsibility of opting for anarchy. Crane chose to confront the *moral* responsibility (amid 'the bugles of the tempest pealing') of reeling through the blizzard. For it was as if a blizzard had struck the old American certainties. The new forces of Hegelian idealism and Darwinian biology and economic determinism – of evolution, class warfare and heredity – were peculiarly stacked against the old Jeffersonian belief in personal self-control. Romantic individualism soon soured, in the decades after the Civil War, to a documentary pessimism. Even before 1860 a brilliant minority (that included Hawthorne and Melville) had opted for pessimism. But now there were mass deserters.

How does one plot a meaningful life? How plot a meaningful life in such a meaningless universe? One American response was to ask: 'So what?' 'What, in short,' in the words of William James, 'is the truth's cash value in experimental terms?' (But pragmatism was of little use to men who felt already doomed; for whom both Christianity and the promise of the Greek Revival had failed.) Another was Crane's attempt to reassemble a fragile dignity, a nervous integrity for man. (Within a generation this was reduced to a mere code, a moral shorthand for stoic self-definition and self-control, often called Hemingway's code.) Another was just to drift and to chart that drift in socially upward or downward mobile terms, while desperately groping for self-fulfilment. The site for such chance encounters was now invariably the aggressively commercial and glamorous city. Especially those boom cities of the Gilded Age, New York and Chicago (as in Theodore Dreiser's *Sister Carrie*, 1900). It was in urban anonymity, above all, that the new American woman was to find her ambiguous liberation. A fourth response was simply nostalgia.

For the post-bellum decades were also decades pining for youth, which was the youth of the nation. It was then that America's first great children's books were written: Louisa May Alcott's *Little Women: Or Meg, Jo, Beth and Amy* (1868–9) and *The Adventures of Tom Sawyer* (1876). But the backward glance was also the idyllic glance into every nook of pastoral America (untouched by war) from Kate Chopin's Louisiana tales to Bret Harte's California tales to Harriet Beecher Stowe's New England tales to Joel Chandler Harris's *Uncle Remus* tales. It ranged across the land from the Maine of Sarah Orne Jewett's *The Country of the Pointed Firs* (1896) to the Indiana of Edward Eggleston's *The Hoosier School-Master* (1871) to the New Orleans of George Washington Cable. But this diversity of focus (often called 'local color' fiction) also trained a sharp ear on to the variety of American speech: Cajun voices, Creole voices, New England voices, Indiana (Hoosier) voices, Missouri (Pike County) voices, drawling Southern voices, black voices, Yiddish voices. Twain's *Adventures of Huckleberry Finn* (1884–5) was published at the height of the greatest flood of dialect literature that America has ever known. It glanced both backward in time (to the decade before the Gold Rush) and westward into the heartland of America (from small-town Missouri to rural Arkansas). As Twain boasted in a foreword:

In this book a number of dialects are used, to wit: the Missouri negro dialect; the extremest form of the backwoods South-Western dialect; the ordinary 'Pike-County' dialect; and four modified varieties of this last. The shadings have not been done in a hap-hazard fashion, or by guess-work; but pains-takingly, and with the trustworthy guidance and support of personal familiarity with these several forms of speech.

For he was a master of dialect; and *Huckleberry Finn* is his incontestable masterpiece.

Though settled in the East like Howells, another printer's devil turned novelist, Twain never abandoned his western roots. He remained loyal to the tradition of frontier humour which he had imbibed on the Mississippi and first practised as an apprentice journalist in Nevada and California. It had much to do with shifts of tone between the genteel and the vulgar. In earlier south-western fiction a gentleman always framed the story. Twain revolutionized this tradition by eliminating – or, at least, seeming to eliminate – this double focus. In the opening paragraph of *Huckleberry Finn* the gentlemanly narrator, 'Mr Mark Twain', bows out *in propria persona*. Huck is left centre-stage alone. The achievement of *Huckleberry Finn*, then, can hardly be grasped outside this native tradition. That adolescent voice is both the culmination of one strand of American humour and the origin of a modern American prose style. For it is a voice capable of sustaining a comic dialectic within itself, as Huck had internalized the joker Twain, who had cocooned within himself the gentlemanly Mr Clemens of Hartford, Connecticut.

It is diametrically opposed to such a hierarchically controlled, absolutist style as that developed by James at the turn of the century. Huck resists such luxuriance, such baroque intensities. That is why he could be recovered by Ring Lardner and Sherwood Anderson and Hemingway as a proto-modern. His is a peculiarly American pragmatic and democratic style: a riot of specific and insubordinate units, unenforced by any overarching, syntactically supreme, governing principle. It was a performance so complex that Twain was never able to repeat it himself. Yet it continues to exert an inexhaustible influence on later generations of American prose writers. As T. S. Eliot remarked: 'Twain, at least in *Huckleberry Finn*, reveals himself to be one of those writers of whom there are not a great many in any literature, who have discovered a new way of writing, valid not only for themselves, but for others.'[4]

The discovery of that vernacular voice, in all its complexity, marks a fitting transition to the twentieth century.

NOTES

1. Under the pen-name 'Peter Parley' (first used in 1827) Samuel Goodrich was the most prolific of American children's authors, eventually publishing

some 170 volumes of which seven million had been sold by 1856.

2. By 1900 there were six times as many American newspapers as in the 1860s. Four 'quality' weeklies of 1890, with about 600,000 readers, had expanded by 1910 to twenty weeklies, read by four to five million people.

3. See William Charvat, *Literary Publishing in America* (Philadelphia, 1959), and 'Melville's Income', *American Literature* 15 (1944), pp. 251–61. See also *The Profession of Authorship in America, 1800–1870: The Papers of William Charvat*, ed. Matthew J. Bruccoli (1968).

4. T. S. Eliot, 'American Literature and the American Language', *Washington University Studies in Language and Literature*, new style vol. 23 (1953), pp. 16–17.

FENIMORE COOPER AND THE
LEATHERSTOCKING NOVELS

T. A. BIRRELL

Who is the first American to achieve an international reputation as a professional novelist? James Fenimore Cooper – alas! Temperamentally, Cooper is unlikely to appeal to the modern reader: he stood up for the rights of landlords, he was proud to think of himself as an aristocrat, and he had no faith in one-man-one-vote. As for his novels, they seem to have no sense of form or technique, and no complexity: just rambling adventure stories with no pretence at realism and interspersed with self-indulgent disquisitions on his pet hobby-horses. (We are all environmentalists now, but who would expect to find half a novel – *The Crater* (1847) – devoted to the merits of organic manure?) Like his contemporary, Walter Scott, Cooper does not fit in with any of our preconceptions of what a novel ought to be; and furthermore, he has none of Scott's charm and no desire to be greatly loved by all.

Cooper was born in 1789, the son of a successful land-settlement agent, the legendary Judge William Cooper, founder of Cooperstown in up-state New York, on the shores of Lake Otsego. There was no post-Calvinist angst or Transcendentalist afflatus about the young James Cooper. He spent an idyllic extravert childhood in the small expanding settlement, was thrown out of Yale for horseplay, spent three happy years in the exiguous US navy, married a De-Lancey – one of the old Loyalist families who had lost their fortunes in the Revolutionary war – and settled down to succeed his father as a patriarchal landowner. It was economic necessity – the recession of 1819 and bad financial management – that drove him to novel-writing. His justification for his new occupation was simple and robust: under the guise of light fiction the reader could be informed and instructed.

His first success was *The Spy* (1821), a fictionalized account of the Revolutionary war. The hero, Harvey Birch, is a double-agent in the special personal service of George Washington. What is striking in the novel is Cooper's deliberate injection of a constant moral dilemma: every episode involves the hero in moral judgements that are not easily black or white; the British and the Loyalists are not all villains and the Revolutionaries are not all heroes. Harvey Birch must make his moral judgements by himself, without the support or sanction of 'society' – he is the first of Cooper's many lonely heroes, men-in-the-middle caught between conflicting forces and conflicting allegiances.

Cooper's next novel, *The Pioneers* (1823), set in the year 1793, combines three elements: his own family recollections of the social life of a frontier settlement; a romantic story of star-crossed lovers; and the tragedy of the old hunter, Natty Bumppo (Leatherstocking), and his Indian companion Chingachgook. The characters in the settlement are a microcosm of the American 'melting-pot': a German officer from the Palatinate, a French planter, a freeborn Negro and a Negro slave, an Episcopalian minister, a Yankee doctor, an English sailor, and a garrulous Irishwoman – there is just about one of everything. The settlement is presided over by the patriarchal Judge Templeton, obviously modelled on Cooper's father. Christmastide in the settlement provides plenty of local colour: a dinnerparty, a Christmas Eve service, and a Christmas Day turkey-shoot. But the novel is more than a piece of evocative nostalgia. Natty and Chingachgook provide a challenge to any easy acceptance of the settlement ethic. Chingachgook is an old Indian chieftain, dispossessed and degraded, and Natty, uncouth but white, deplores the destruction of the natural resources of the forest and the lake. Natty stands for the hunter's ethic: to live where he pleases in the forest, irrespective of legal land tenure, and to hunt when and how he pleases to satisfy his immediate necessities. He kills a deer out of season and is condemned by Judge Templeton to a fine, imprisonment and a period in the stocks. The romantic plot makes everything come right in the end, but old Chingachgook dies in a forest fire and Natty leaves the settlement and heads out West.

The son of a land-settlement agent who can see the dilemma of the settlement ethic; an admirer of the Noble Savage who presents us with a 'has-been' Noble Savage; a thirty-four-year-old novelist who can feel the indignities of old age – Cooper reveals in *The Pioneers* that capacity for presenting the contrary states of things which is the hallmark of the creative artist. And although he did not realize it at that moment, it was the mythic figures of Natty and Chingachgook which provided Cooper with the creative focus that he needed.

After a sea-story, *The Pilot* (1823), an imaginary and quite unbelievable episode in the career of John Paul Jones, and *Lionel Lincoln* (1825), a realistic and impartial account of the Battles of Lexington and Bunkers Hill, tacked on to a gothic love-story, Cooper returned to his hero, Natty Bumppo, in *The Last of the Mohicans* (1826): the book established Cooper's international fame and the title became part of our language. Cooper and his family then left for Europe: characteristically, he based himself on Paris rather than on London. He made the Grand Tour, lectured the Europeans on their ignorance of America and wrote three novels to show them what was wrong with their own history and institutions: *The Bravo* (1831), on the corruption of the Venetian republic, *The Heidenmauer* (1832), on the pathos of the Reformation, and *The Headsman* (1833), on the shortcomings of even Swiss democracy.

He returned to America in 1833 and found everything wrong with his own country. The literary lion of Bourbon Paris had difficulty adjusting to democratic New York. He was harried by the Whig press and sought redress in the courts. He retired to his country seat at Otsego Hall – he could now afford to live there – but soon quarrelled with the locals over property rights. His public quarrels did not diminish his literary output, nor did they affect his status as a bestseller, but the constant battle with the American ambience took its toll. The adventure stories were churned out perfunctorily. As for contemporary American society, he said all he really needed to say in a collection of essays, *The American Democrat* (1838). In his first novel of social criticism, *Home As Found* (1838), the effectiveness of the satire is marred by the ineffable gentility of the idealized characters. Three novels – *Satanstoe* (1845), *The Chainbearer* (1845), and *The Redskins* (1846) – were inspired by the current Anti-Rent agitation. The idea of the series was admirable, to illustrate the historical development of land tenure in America from the eighteenth century to his own times, but instead of presenting the social complexities of the situation in a dramatic way, Cooper presents his own case – the landlords' case – in its most extreme form. His last novel, *The Ways of the Hour* (1850), is superficially a mystery story but turns into a diatribe against the jury system – because the juries were always deciding against Cooper himself.

Two novels of Cooper's post-European period stand out in refreshing contrast, and they are the last two Leatherstocking novels: *The Pathfinder* (1840) and *The Deerslayer* (1841). In both novels Cooper looks at nature through Wordsworthian eyes and moralizes on nature with a fundamental Christian piety that he shares with his hero.

In *The Pathfinder* Natty is seeking his path through life. The key to the story is Chapter VII, prefaced by a quotation from Wordsworth's *Yarrow Revisited*. Natty and his companions are moving at night through hostile Indian territory and discuss the sense of the presence of God. Natty cannot find it in church in the garrisons, he can only find it in the forest: 'the woods are the true temple . . . for there the thoughts are free to mount higher even than the clouds'. It is often said that the story of *The Pathfinder* is about Natty in love, but it is obvious from the very outset that the heroine, Mabel, is going to get the handsome young sailor, Jasper. Her father intends her for Natty, it is true, and when he is mortally wounded he entrusts her to Natty in an inordinately long deathbed scene. But the essence of the plot lies in Natty's honourable discharge of his promise to a dying man and in his surrender of Mabel to Jasper. Natty can only preserve his identity, can only maintain his true path in life, so long as he lives in the forest. 'I shall return to the wilderness and my Maker,' he declares, when all is finally settled. *The Pathfinder* is not about marriage versus bachelorhood, or sexuality versus asexuality: it is a Wordsworthian exercise in controlled nostalgia.

The Deerslayer presents Natty as a very young man on his first warpath: indeed, it is largely about the value of human life. The story is set in the pristine beauty of an uncharted lake, the 'Glimmerglass', during the frontier wars of the 1740s: it is the Lake Otsego of Cooper's own childhood. As well as the Wordsworthian influence, the influence of romantic scene painting is also manifest: Cooper repeatedly insists that he is giving us 'pictures' as well as a 'legend'.

Natty, the young and innocent deerslayer, arrives at the lake accompanied by a 'handsome barbarian', Harry March, a strong, brutal trapper (Natty only shoots game, he never uses traps). On the lake stands a log fortress built on piles sunk into a shoal. Here live Tom Hutter, a reputed ex-pirate, and his daughers Judith and Hetty. Harry has come to woo the beautiful Judith; Natty has arranged to meet his boon companion Chingachgook, whose betrothed has been captured by the Hurons who are roaming the lake shores.

When they eventually meet up together, March and Hutter, thinking that the Huron warriors have left their camp unguarded, determine to scalp the defenceless women and children (both the British and the French governments offer money for Indian scalps). Natty refuses to join them, despite their aspersions on his courage. March and Hutter are captured, and in trying to assist them Natty is confronted with the first moral crisis of his life. 'He was entirely alone, thrown on his own resources, and was cheered by no friendly eye, emboldened by no encouraging voice.' He comes up behind an isolated Huron warrior and hesitates to shoot him. The two men engage in conversation and Natty propounds the theory of live and let live: 'the world is large enough for both of us'. They part amicably: the Huron walks towards the woods and Natty towards the shore. The Huron turns and fires his rifle; the bullet grazes Natty who fires back, mortally wounding the Huron. Natty carries the dying warrior to the lakeside to give him water, and assures him he does not want his scalp; they shake hands, and the man dies in his arms. Cooper narrates the episode in great detail and at great length; it is crucial to the book and indeed to his whole concept of the Leatherstocking series.

Natty returns to the fortress and tells Judith and Hetty of the situation. Hetty, who is deeply religious but feeble-minded, slips away and enters the Huron camp to plead for her father. The Indians treat with respect all those that are touched by God (did Dostoevsky read Cooper?). Hetty reads to them from the Bible about turning the other cheek and doing as you would be done by. The Indians 'heard her words with some such surprise as an American of our own times would be apt to betray at a suggestion that the great modern, but vacillating, ruler of things human, public opinion, might be wrong'. Eventually March and Hutter are ransomed with gifts; no sooner are they released but they want to go scalping again.

Natty and Chingachgook succeed in rescuing the latter's betrothed, but Natty himself is now captured. He is released 'on furlough' by the Hurons, on condition that he returns the following day to be tortured and killed. Natty takes a lengthy farewell of his companions and returns to the Huron camp to honour his promise. As he is about to be killed he is rescued, of course, by the British redcoats.

'I shall strive to do a paleface's duty in a redskin society.' Natty is the lonely hunter, striving to live in the wilderness according to a Christian code of conduct derived from, and supported by, a profound consciousness of pristine natural beauty. Fenimore Cooper, beleaguered with lawsuits, at odds with the public opinion of his time, is trying to tell us something about himself. Paradoxically, the mythic adventures of the lonely white Christian hunter and his Indian companion seem to arouse in Cooper a deep moral and religious concern in the day-to-day and hour-to-hour business of living. Cooper's creative sensibility is engaged in the Leatherstocking fiction much more deeply than in the social and political 'issues' which were superficially much closer to his personal interests. Coleridge's judgement, in 1828, was remarkably prescient: 'the further he is from society, the more he seems at home'.

To get some real standard by which to judge any particular novel in Cooper's total oeuvre, we should try to understand what the Leatherstocking tales meant for him, and the novel in which Cooper really establishes the genre is *The Last of the Mohicans*. The immediate inspiration behind the story is to show that America has an ancestral history: a history of violence and slaughter and of human cross-purposes; a history of a precarious civilization built on the ruins of a shattered idyll of the primitive. Cooper's powerful evocation of the pathos of history is created out of virtually nothing: a few bare historical facts, some unreliable missionary narratives, and the vaguest of legends. Cooper had to create his own evidence; every detail depended on his own imaginative powers.

The story in *The Last of the Mohicans* is concerned with an episode in the 'Old French War'. In 1757 a party sets out from Fort Edward to reach Fort William Henry, which is besieged by the French under Montcalm. The party consists of two half-sisters, Alice and Cora

Munro, daughters of the commander of Fort William Henry, who are escorted by Major Duncan Heyward, who is in love with Alice. They are accompanied by Magua, an Indian Huron guide, whose treachery soon becomes obvious, and by David Gamut, a psalm-singing Yankee music teacher. They meet up with Natty Bumppo – here called Hawkeye – and his two Indian friends, Chingachgook and his son Uncas, the last of the Mohicans. After various attacks from hostile Indians they reach Fort William Henry only to find that Colonel Munro has been ordered to surrender to the French. After the surrender the hostile Hurons massacre the defenceless occupants of the fort while Montcalm's troops stand powerlessly by: Alice and Cora are captured by Magua. Heyward, Munro, Hawkeye and his two Indian friends go in search of the girls: after many adventures, Alice is eventually rescued, but Cora and Uncas are killed. Such is the barest outline of the story.

The structure of the book fits perfectly into the exigencies of publication in double volume form. Volume I is concerned with the adventures en route between the two forts and culminates in the massacre at Fort William Henry. Volume II is concerned with the search for the girls, and centres chiefly on adventures in the hostile Huron camp where Alice has been taken, and in the neutral Delaware camp where Cora has been left in safe custody by Magua. After the last chase and battle, Volume II closes with the elaborate ceremonial funeral of Cora and Uncas, which forms an almost operatic grand finale.

All the hard facts, such as they are, are established in Volume I: the geographical background, the historical situation, and the ethnological characteristics of the Indian tribes. In Volume I the characters have to learn to operate within the constraints of that framework, and the experience is painful. In Volume II a second cycle of events begins, in which the characters operate freely: they are 'free' precisely because they have already been conditioned and educated to the exigencies of the historical environment. And it is not only the characters who are conditioned and educated to the historical moment of the American frontier in 1757. We, the readers, as we follow the characters in Volume I, are being conditioned and educated as well. When we come to the events of Volume II we accept, or we are meant to accept, the reality of Cooper's very special imaginative world. A dramatist needs an opening scene, or at most a first act, to establish the terms on which his play is to be understood: Cooper realized that for his own very special artistic problem he needed half a book. The phenomenal success of *The Last of the Mohicans*, in both America and Europe, was a conclusive validation of Cooper's unusual procedure, so that when, fifteen years later, he came to write *The Pathfinder* and *The Deerslayer*, he could assume a conditioned audience, and adopt a unitary structure which enabled him to write with a completely free imaginative flow. He could by then be confident that he had established an acceptable and 'real' world.

The relationship between Volume I and Volume II comes out most strikingly if we consider the development and change in the characters. David Gamut, the hymn-singing Yankee, begins as a comic buffoon (Cooper personally detested the type). But at the end of Volume I Gamut's very foolishness saves him in the massacre: he follows the hostile Indians when they carry off the two girls, and is tolerated by the Indians because they think him mad. In Volume II he meets up with Hawkeye's rescue-party and is instrumental in getting them into the enemy camp. And at the very end of the story, at the funeral ceremonies, when the Delaware maidens have sung their death chants for Cora and Uncas, it is Hawkeye who calls on him to sing a funeral anthem to express 'the Christian fashions'.

Another character who undergoes a radical change is Major Duncan Heyward. In Volume I he is the stiff conventional soldier, whose refusal to duck the enemy bullets earns only the contempt of Hawkeye, who has no patience with such Beau Geste behaviour. But in Volume II Heyward volunteers to be painted as an Indian by Chingachgook and to go into the enemy camp disguised as a madman. And so, led by Gamut the natural fool, Heyward sets off on his dangerous mission. The echoes of *King Lear*, with Edgar as Poor Tom accompanying the Fool, are surely obvious. Cooper is using 'poetic' devices in a way that is quite new. Heyward, demanding to be made to look like a fool, and submitting to having his face painted by Chingachgook, presents us, in all the economy of art, with the confusing ironies of class, profession and race.

Among the Indians, the development in Magua is most striking.

In Volume I he is the stage-villain, rolling his eyes and gnashing his teeth, and exhibiting 'disdain' and 'cold malignancy'. In Volume II, however, he is concerned in rallying his own tribe or in arguing with the neutral Delawares. Here Cooper shows Magua to be as astute, unscrupulous and crooked *as any white politician*. In the debate with Tamenund the Delaware sage, Magua uses a kind of nostalgic evocative 'poetic' prose, whereas Tamenund's speech is rational, not emotive, but imaginatively acceptable as 'foreign' by being couched in the gnomic antithetical sententiousness of a recognizable 'folk' language. It is unfair to Cooper to assume that all his Indians speak in the same way – that is truer of Hemingway's Spaniards.

The themes of sex and race in *The Last of the Mohicans* have occupied so much critical attention that a third, and equally important theme, eschatology, has been almost entirely neglected. Cooper quite simply believed that men's actions on earth were largely determined by their belief in what happened after death, and that was the reason why Indians behave differently from white men and why Hawkeye behaves differently from Gamut and Heyward, with each of whom he has arguments on the subjects of predestination and heavenly bliss. These episodes are clearly a preparation for the final burial scene of Cora and Uncas. The funeral is obviously a 'set-piece', and Cooper has arranged it with formal artistry. Munro stands by the bier of Cora; Chingachgook stands by the bier of Uncas; Alice and Heyward stand together; Hawkeye stands alone; and to complete the pattern, an aide-de-camp of Montcalm appears in the background. As the sun goes down, Tamenund begins the funeral ceremonies, and his words are a cue for the chant by a choir of Delaware maidens. Contrary to what we might have expected, Cooper renders the song of the Delaware maidens in indirect speech. By this device the white mourners are excluded from the full significance of the Indian rites – apart from Hawkeye, who understands the language; and we the readers have also a sense of sharing Hawkeye's secret knowledge. Then comes David Gamut's performance of the Christian obsequies, which forms a striking contrast in artistic effect. Cooper gives Gamut no actual words at all, only a description of the musical quality of his song. By this device the Indians are able, as it were, to 'understand' Gamut and to share his feelings.

And then, when the illusion of sympathetic unity between Indians and whites is at its most profound, Cooper deliberately breaks the spell:

> Munro seemed sensible that the time was come to exert what is, perhaps, the greatest effort of which human nature is capable. He bared his gray locks, and looked around the timid and quiet throng by which he was encircled with a firm and collected countenance. Then motioning with his hand for the scout to listen, he said, –
>
> 'Say to these kind and generous females, that a heartbroken and failing man returns them his thanks. Tell them, that the Being we all worship, under different names, will be mindful of their charity; and that the time shall not be distant when we may assemble around his throne without distinction of sex, or rank, or colour' . . .
>
> 'To tell them this,' said Hawkeye, 'would be to tell them that the snows come not in winter, or that the sun shines fiercest when the trees are stripped of their leaves.'
>
> Then turning to the women, he made such a communication of the other's gratitude as he deemed most suited to the capacity of his listeners.

Hawkeye's reply to Munro, in direct speech, is still poetic and *exalté*, even though its content is negative. It is the subsequent abrupt resumption of the narrative, in polysyllabic prose of a Daniel Websterish orotundity, that brutally and irrevocably shatters the illusion and returns us to a Conradian world of human misunderstandings and cross-purposes. When the exigencies of the novel demand it, there is no doubt that Cooper is capable of using the arts of language for his creative purposes.

Cooper may have thought that he was accepting light fiction, and the narrative of adventure, as a substantive genre, and merely adding to it an instructive element; but in fact he transforms the genre. He was not a literary innocent by any means: he was steeped in Shakespearean drama and had a lively awareness of Romantic poetry. His intensely independent intellectual powers, coupled with his profoundly serious and complex approach to life, had to create a new genre if they were to express themselves in fiction at all. *The Last of the Mohicans* is the first unqualified example in the English language of the novel as dramatic poem.

EMERSON: EXPERIMENTS IN CREATION

JOEL PORTE

'The history of the genesis,' Emerson (1803–82) notes, is the 'old mythology' that

repeats itself in the experience of every child. He too is a demon or god thrown into a particular chaos, where he strives ever to lead things from disorder into order. Each individual soul is such, in virtue of its being a power to translate the world into some particular language of its own.[1]

Emerson's description here of that poetic process whereby each youth attempts to inscribe his own fable of renewal is a fair portrayal of how a lapsed Unitarian minister in 1836 attempted to recuperate his powers by opening a literary discourse with the world. Emerson, Santayana notes, 'was like a young god making experiments in creation'. And *Nature* (1836), accordingly, represents Emerson's initial effort at 'restoring to the world original and eternal beauty' by redeeming and reconstituting his own soul in an imaginative apocalypse.

Stephen Whicher remarks that Emerson's first book 'might have exchanged titles with Poe's *Eureka*'. That, however, is just about all these two odd treatises might be said to share. Poe's 'apocalypse' is the revelation of a cosmos in decline, its stars dead or dying, burning on in paradoxical celebration of their own inevitable fate. Coming at the end of Poe's painful career (1849), it prophesies his own expiration by figuring that of the universe. But Emerson had no intention of singing a sad tale of the Conqueror Worm; *his* worm is mounting 'through all the spires of form' on its triumphant way to becoming human. Emerson meditates on the 'sepulchres of the fathers' in expectation not of joining them but of leaving them behind. We see him, in fact, 'embosomed for a season in nature, whose floods of life stream around and through us', in preparation for spiritual rebirth. 'Infancy is the perpetual Messiah,' he announces, and it is precisely as a newborn bard of the Holy Ghost that he makes his own annunciation.

It is not, however, without its discordant notes, for Emerson saw ruin where he hoped to see paradise. Unitarian Christianity, in his view, was 'corpse-cold', and he believed that theological, philosophical, and literary discourse generally was pervaded with, and vitiated by, 'rotten diction'; words needed to be re-attached to real experience and to a revitalized inner life. Emerson's prime text was nature itself: 'a life in harmony with Nature, the love of truth and virtue,' he insisted, would 'purge the eyes to understand her text'. What Emerson understood by the word 'revelation' was a simple – or radical – purification of both the physical organ of sight and the mind's eye. He felt himself to be an 'immortal pupil', deathless in his vision of the world's loveliness:

> I see the spectacle of morning from the hill-top over against my house, from day-break to sun-rise, with emotions which an angel might share . . . I seem to partake its rapid transformations: the active enchantment reaches my dust, and I dilate and conspire with the morning wind.
>
> (*Essays*, p. 15)

But this 'immortal pupil' dilated most conspicuously and most famously elsewhere, on 'a bare common, in snow puddles, at twilight, under a clouded sky', for example. This *crépuscule* provided a more mysterious, and perhaps more ambiguous, ecstasy than that of Emerson's Assyrian dawn – the *vespertina cognitio*, or 'evening knowledge', appropriate to humans rather than the *matutina cognitio*, or 'morning knowledge', reserved for the divine. Could Emerson really hope to transcend the conditions of mortal being? Under that clouded sky in twilight, he writes, 'I have enjoyed a perfect exhilaration. I am glad to the brink of fear.' We might observe that a *perfect* exhilaration would hardly seem consistent with such a disturbing emotion (and this is the 1849 text; in 1836 Emerson had written 'almost I fear to think how glad I am', presumably realizing – along with Keats – in the course of those crucial thirteen years that gladness is a fragile state of being). So, the word *perfect* shimmers with a hint of its own dissolution, signaling with perhaps an unconscious equivocation that the mark of humankind's fallen state is on our speaker, however lightly, even as he rhapsodically attempts to disown it. In the woods, as opposed to the beclouded common, our death-defying pupil seems to be promised 'perpetual youth' – indeed, 'a thousand years', a millennium, of joy. He does not simply see the truth: he *is* vision as he becomes a 'transparent eye-ball' through which 'the currents of the Universal Being circulate' in apparently so perfect a circle of divine energy that he is 'part or particle of God': 'I feel that nothing can befall me in life, – no disgrace, no calamity, (leaving me my eyes,) which nature cannot repair.'

Emerson had intimated, at the beginning of his book, that he would see 'God and nature face to face'; but he knew of the ancient injunction against such an unmediated vision of the divine. Emerson's fantasy in *Nature* of being taken up into the 'currents of the Universal Being' seems to be tinged with an awareness that Transcendental experience – the ultimate flight into the intense inane – might well entail certain worldly dangers. Five years after the publication of *Nature*, in one of his most orphic addresses, 'The Method of Nature', Emerson would insist that a man capable of exactly obeying the spirit would find himself adopted by it, 'so that he shall not any longer separate it from himself in his thought, he shall seem to be it, he shall be it . . . borne away as with a flood, he becomes careless of his food and of his house, he is the fool of ideas, and leads a heavenly life'. That was even a headier message than the injunction to spiritual regeneration contained in *Nature*, and one delivered not in a book, but in person by the prophet himself. We ought to keep in mind that Emerson's greatest influence in his own time was achieved through his personal appearances. Those who flocked to hear him, Santayana notes, went not so much for the meaning of his words (sufficiently startling, in any case, as we have observed), 'as for the atmosphere of candor, purity, and serenity' that hung about them, 'as about a sacred music. They felt themselves in the presence of a rare and beautiful spirit, who was in communion with a higher world.' Emerson, the erstwhile minister turned Romantic rhapsode, was what he was not only by virtue of his power to translate the world into a particular language of his own, but also by virtue of his *presence* as he delivered that word.

Emerson's greatest addresses, 'The American Scholar' of 1837 and the Divinity School Address' of 1838, are linked by their passionate concern for public speech – 'the speech of man to men'. They exhibit him in the act of forging a new vocation – that of itinerant lecturer committed to expounding his own regenerated self in the idealized forms of Scholar or Preacher or Man of Letters. Emerson would spend his days in his 'private observatory, cataloguing obscure and nebulous stars of the human mind', as he says in 'The American Scholar'. Then he would return to earth, stand on the platform, and sing of what he had seen. He would translate lofty observations into common speech. Emerson's nearly obsessive insistence on action in the address was not only a compensatory response to his own reclusive tendencies; it was also an attempt to argue the more general notion that the world outside the study is the true sounding-board of the self. The tumult of speech – 'in country labors; in town; in . . . trades and manufactures; in frank intercourse with many men and women' – is the necessary source of our vocabulary, the way to wealth for an orator.

As a listener Emerson expects to hear evidence of real experience, otherwise he feels 'defrauded and disconsolate'. This very issue lies, literally, at the center of the Divinity School 'Address', and provides its most humanly effective moment. Emerson recalls a Sunday when he sat in his pew in Concord so bored with the droning tediosities of the minister that he resolved not to go to church again. His eye turns from the pulpit to the windows; it was snowing: 'The snow storm was real; the preacher merely spectral; and the eye felt the sad contrast in looking at him, and then out of the window behind him, into the beautiful meteor of the snow.' *Cold* preaching (that was the term then) makes the snow seem positively hot. By contrast, the Reverend Mr Barzillai Frost (for that was his name) had 'lived in vain':

> He had no one word intimating that he had laughed or wept, was married or in love, had been commended, or cheated, or chagrined. If he had ever lived and acted, we were none the wiser for it. The capital secret of his profession, namely, to convert life into truth, he had not learned . . . not a surmise, a hint, in all the discourse, that he had ever lived at all. Not a line did he draw out of real history.
>
> (*Essays*, pp. 84–5)

The speaker has lived in vain, Emerson argues, if his life fails to inform his speech, if his human nature is not present on the platform.

Emerson wants his divinity to coexist with love and marriage and eating and drinking and ploughing and planting. It was an audacious notion, and the fact that Emerson would say such things to an audience of theological students and their teachers is a measure not only of his determination to shock but also, and more crucially, of his desire to import the language of experience into his own discourse. Speech, Emerson claimed, is symbolic action; but the body's movement is symbolic speech – life speaking through gesture. We get our experience twice then, Emerson implies – from the orator's words and from the physical conviction that accompanies (indeed produces) them. The body is spirit incarnate – moving, and breathing, and giving a local habitation and a name to ideas. It was just such a living model of universal truth that Emerson hoped to be so that he might actually carry with him the feelings of his audience in stating his own belief. He would *stand* for them and thus represent their own dumb yearnings and strivings.

In some ways the 1830s were not a useful apprenticeship for Emerson the would-be essayist, for he had gotten used to the stimulus and excitement of the lecture engagement and found it hard to transfer that lively ambience to the printed page. In his lectures he had hoped, he said, to fire 'the artillery of sympathy & emotion'; being *agitated* himself (his word) he wanted and needed to agitate his audience. But he also needed to compose *for* an audience – to feel the presence of that other to whom he was presumably speaking, to write (as he says) as if writing a letter. 'Every man passes his life in the search after friendship,' Emerson notes in his essay on that subject in the First Series (1841), and he then actually wrote and published the letter which he seemed always to have had in mind: 'Dear Friend, If I was sure of thee, sure of thy capacity, sure to match my mood with thine.' It is an engaging notion: the reader as actual or potential friend. How can we be sure of our readers, Emerson wonders – sure of their abilities and susceptibilities? Who *is* out there? Do we dare confide in our readers? The essayist, of course, must take his chances; but how can one put one's heart into such a chancy business? The answer would appear to be that one cannot – at least not all the time. So in one place Emerson would write, 'I have set my heart on honesty in this chapter,' signaling and assuming an extraordinary degree of confidence in the reader's sympathy and understanding (this is the great essay 'Experience' (1844), the most personal of all his performances). But in another place he would say, 'I am always insincere, as always knowing there are other moods.'

To be sure, for the sake of an argument or an effect, Emerson could carry the whole thing too far and sound wildly irresponsible, even brazen in his refusal to take the measure of his own trustworthiness as a guide:

> Lest I should mislead any when I have my own head and obey my whims, let me remind the reader that I am only an experimenter . . . I unsettle all things. No facts are to me sacred; none are profane; I simply experiment, an endless seeker, with no Past at my back.
>
> (*Essays*, p. 412)

This is really the speech of the devil's child. An authorial voice that explicitly disclaims any authority may seem flatly unworthy of credence unless we pay attention to Emerson's strategy as it unwinds throughout the whole course of 'Circles'. In that frame we come to see that the voice speaking here is not simply affirming its own right to experiment but authorizing ours as well. Emerson's 'shrill tones' are intended to open up *our* eyes and encourage experimentation.

Yet Emerson admits that sometimes he re-reads himself with amazement:

> Our moods do not believe in each other . . . What I write, whilst I write it, seems the most natural thing in the world; but yesterday I saw a dreary vacuity in this direction in which now I see so much; and a month hence, I doubt not, I shall wonder who he was that wrote so many continuous pages. Alas for this infirm faith, this will not be strenuous, this vast ebb of a vast flow! I am God in nature; I am a weed by the wall.
>
> (*Essays*, p. 406)

Emerson seems to have left us high and dry on cloud nine while he collapses like a piece of limp vegetation by the side of the road. 'Nothing is secure but life, transition, the energizing spirit.' Now the energy appears to have flagged and we have to learn to deal with 'vacuity'. Emerson's essays follow these expanding and retracting curves, often in dismayingly rapid cycles. 'In skating over thin ice, our safety is in our speed,' Emerson notes in 'Prudence'. That is explicitly the shrewd Yankee voice of our slippery essayist.

By committing himself to a form so unmoored in its methods, if not in its premises, Emerson agrees in effect to a public display of his own uncertainties:

> He in whom the love of truth predominates will keep himself aloof from all moorings, and afloat. He will abstain from dogmatism, and recognize all the opposite negations, between which, as walls, his being is swung. He submits to the inconvenience of suspense and imperfect opinion, but he is a candidate for truth, as the other is not.
>
> (*Essays*, p. 426)

Emerson the essayist is a dangling man, turning constantly in the turbulent winds of his own shifting doctrine. In particular, we notice that he speaks of the 'walls' between which his being swings as 'opposite negations'. He likes the sayers of no better than the sayers of yes because to deny something requires a certain original energy; affirmation is so easy. He would come back to affirmation when it was a more difficult virtue, as after the death of his son. Now he counsels patience, 'patience, and still patience', believing that he was destined to pass presently 'into some new infinitude, out of this Iceland of negations'. At heart Emerson was a believer who allowed himself, for the sake of argument, frequently to play the devil's advocate. 'Our philosophy is affirmative,' he writes, 'and readily accepts the testimony of negative facts, as every shadow points to the sun.'

That is the Emerson of the First Series of *Essays* (1841). The book is self-assured and almost manically agitated, despite Emerson's fears about producing a 'cold exhibition of dead thoughts'. His stress throughout was on the soul's *activity* – the thinking process that he had argued for so strenuously in 'The American Scholar' – and as a result we see him not so much displaying his thoughts as dancing among them in a wild play of intellectual energy. Emerson's emphasis on the truth of the 'heart' in his first collection of essays may seem surprising coming from such a presumably austere son of the Puritans, but the truth is that the book was completed – to adopt Emerson's own pun – in a highly *cordial* atmosphere. Emerson was working closely with Margaret Fuller (1810–50) on *The Dial*, and between the two of them (as also between Emerson and some other highly attractive and adoring female disciples) shared intellectual passion blossomed into exciting and troubling friendship. Emerson's

Concord circle in this period became a kind of love-feast that helped considerably to warm his cold thoughts as he prepared his book. Emerson believed himself, at heart, to have more passion than he could ever express. Thus he noted in his journal on 11 June 1840:

> I finish this morning transcribing my old Essay on Love, but I see well its inadequateness. I cold [sic] because I am hot – cold at the surface only as a sort of guard & compensation for the fluid tenderness of the core – have much more experience than I have written there, more than I will, more than I can write. In silence we must wrap much of our life, because it is too fine for speech, because also we cannot explain it to others, and because somewhat we cannot yet understand.[2]

Emerson seems perfectly divided between perplexity and reticence in this touching self-appraisal, and his own sense of the inadequateness of his essay as flowing from a fear of giving vent to the hot core at his center certainly helps to explain the curious evasiveness of the piece – the defensive and doctrinaire Platonism that shifts attention from the realities of physical passion to a theory of sublimation. But Emerson was not as completely in control of his feelings as his journal entry and the usual printed text of 'Love' suggest. The original version of the essay on Love began:

> Every soul is a celestial Venus to every other soul. The heart has its sabbaths and jubilees, in which the world appears as a hymeneal feast, and all natural sounds and the circle of the seasons are erotic odes and dances. Love is omnipresent in nature as motive and reward. Love is our highest word, and the synonym of God.

These sentences were excised by the considerably more sober Emerson of 1847 and it is not difficult to see why. This highly colored sexual language makes the heart's sabbath sound rather like a bacchanal, and suggests how aroused, so to speak, Emerson was in 1840–41.

The truth is, though, that Emerson thought of the erotic impulse as the initiating motive behind all creation (he uses such words as *heat*, *passion*, *power*, and *force*), observing that 'men have written good verses under the inspiration of passion who cannot write well under any other circumstances.' Perhaps that also implied that men who ordinarily wrote well enough might do so even more powerfully when nourished by the 'hymeneal feast'. In fact Emerson appears to have entertained a fantasy of himself as being sexually potent enough to wash away his audience in a veritable sea of erotic energy.[3]

'First we eat, then we beget,' Emerson observes; 'first we read, then we write.' These simple equations – reading as eating and writing as begetting – might be said to inform Emerson's major statement about the Transcendental artist, 'The Poet', as do equally his notions about the hidden or subterranean sources of expression. The poet is a *genius* (and Emerson employs the word with the full force of its etymology) who 'repairs the decays of things' by casting out his 'seed', or songs, which 'ascend and leap and pierce into the deeps of infinite time'. He is the creation's 'lover' and the prophet of its 'new religion'. Emerson notes that 'the religions of the world are the ejaculations of a few imaginative men', and he seems to use that curious word with an active sense of its two interchangeable meanings. Emerson conceives of speech and song as a 'necessity', physically (whether male or female; in his journal the word is 'oestrum'), for the poet *must* give vent to his pent-up emotions. Those 'throbs and heart-beatings in the orator, at the door of the assembly', have one end – 'namely that thought may be ejaculated as Logos or Word'. *Thought* here is not so much an intellectual construction as an organic impulse – 'vegetation, the pullulation & universal budding of the plant man', as Emerson puts it in his journal. As Harold Bloom notes, 'the spirit that speaks in and through [Emerson] has the true Pythagorean and Orphic stink . . . The ministerial Emerson . . . is full brother to the Dionysiac adept who may have torn living flesh with his inspired teeth.'

'The Poet' exhibits Emerson soaring into the empyrean of his thought from the shadowy realm of primitive instinct – turning from the shady groves of Bacchus to the sunny fields of Apollo. But he had once again, and more tragically, come to the brink of gladness and over the edge was fear and a darker mood. Between 'The Poet' and 'Experience' falls the shadow of the death of Emerson's first-born, little Waldo, his namesake and brighter self. There can be little doubt that the death of Emerson's son at the age of five – a major influence on the composition of this great meditation – wounded Emerson vitally, making him feel unmanned, less capable of creation than before. Now his dreams have become illusions. The essay begins with the speaker lost on a mysterious staircase, feeling drugged and dopey. Life is a series, like his book of essays, but it has no beginning, no end, and no apparent logic. He has drunk deeply of Lethe and is 'lethargic'. It is noonday, but there seems to be no sun – indeed there is no son. The shadows have deepened: 'Sleep lingers all our lifetime about our eyes, as night hovers all day in the boughs of the fir-tree.' Things swim, his perception is threatened, and he feels like a ghost. Now he lacks 'the affirmative principle' and has 'no superfluity of spirit for new creation'. He has barely enough energy to carry on his spectral existence but not enough 'to impart or to invest'. The question is: how can the artist go on writing in such a mood of deprivation and loss?

Emerson's problem as an artist deprived of his manhood – the hope of his future, the happy memory of his past – appears irremediable. He does indeed seem to be stuck on that ladder which represents the sliding scale of his consciousness, suspended somewhere between heaven and hell – his aspiration and his despair. How can he get moving? The truth is that he has never stopped moving, although he appears to be moving in circles. For the essence of the form Emerson is employing and enlarging is that it keeps on going: the essay is perpetually on-going, a continuous talking with oneself that others are allowed to overhear. It may digress, change its stance and tone, break the monotony or the strangle-hold of one mind by citing others, pause to reflect on its own provisional conclusions and then proceed once more to look for others. It has, precisely, the shape of experience. Though Emerson seems drained of belief, that will not stop him, for the essay is not designed, like a tract, simply to expound a faith. What interests Emerson is not what he or anyone else believes or does not believe; rather, as he says, it is *the universal impulse to believe*. That impulse will keep him and the essay moving. 'Onward and onward!' he exclaims. 'In liberated moments we know that a new picture of life and duty is already possible.' And even here, in the trap of temperament and mood, we may still begin to frame that new picture. 'The elements already exist in many minds around you of a doctrine of life which shall transcend any written record we have.' *That* is Transcendentalism – the irrepressible hope, even from the bottom of the pit, that a new doctrine of life may carry us beyond the present written record, perhaps the very one we are perusing:

The new statement will comprise the skepticisms, as well as the faiths of society, and out of unbeliefs a creed shall be formed. For, skepticisms are not gratuitous or lawless, but are limitations of the affirmative statement, and the new philosophy must take them in, and make affirmations outside of them, just as much as it must include the oldest beliefs.

(*Essays*, p. 487)

Here, then, is the tougher theory of affirmation we were looking for — one that continues, even in the face of discouragement, to work through every negation to the new perspective beyond it. But that will not guarantee a secure place to stand either. We must be prepared still to pack up and move on. 'Every evil and every good thing is a shadow which we cast,' Emerson goes on to say. The shadow then, ultimately, is ourselves, and we can never hope to walk out of that shadow, but must take it with us even as we continue to seek the sun. 'In Flaxman's drawing of the Eumenides of Aeschylus,' Emerson observes, 'Orestes supplicates Apollo, whilst the Furies sleep on the threshold. The face of the god expresses a shade of regret and compassion, but is calm with the conviction of the irreconcilableness of the two spheres.' What a nice touch — the 'shade' on the face of Apollo! Emerson's description of the drawing is an emblem of our condition — suspended somewhere between the Eumenides and Apollo. Though the Furies will continue to sleep on our doorstep we must not give up supplicating the god. Emerson will have nothing to do with the despair which 'prejudges the law by a paltry empiricism'. And once again he counsels patience: what else have we to fall back on?

Patience and patience, we shall win at the last. We must be very suspicious of the deceptions of the element of time. It takes a good deal of time to eat or to sleep, or to earn a hundred dollars, and a very little time to entertain a hope and an insight which becomes the light of our life.

(*Essays*, p. 492)

Note that Emerson is somewhat sly here, for though he says we shall win 'at the last', he does not really mean that we will have to wait, necessarily, until the end of time. It may happen in a flash. In the midst of our loss we may catch sight of a possible gain. That is not a facile optimism but rather a tentative vote of confidence in the spirit's recuperative powers — in its ability to leap to a new quantum level of energy. Here is what Emerson had to say in his journal barely three months after the death of his beloved boy:

... the wealth of the Universe is for me. Every thing is explicable & practicable for me. And yet whilst I adore this ineffable life which is at my heart, it will not condescend to gossip with me, it will not announce to me any particulars of science, it will not enter into the details of my biography, & say to me why I have a son & daughters born to me, or why my son dies in his sixth year of joy. Herein then I have this latent omniscience coexistent with omnignorance. Moreover, whilst this Deity glows at the heart, & by his unlimited presentiments gives me all power, I know that tomorrow will be as this day, I am a dwarf, & I remain a dwarf. That is to say, I believe in Fate. As long as I am weak, I shall talk of Fate; whenever the God fills me with his fulness, I shall see the disappearance of Fate.

I am *Defeated* all the time; yet to Victory I am born.[4]

NOTES

1. Ralph Waldo Emerson, *Essays & Lectures*, ed. Joel Porte, 1983, p. 122. Hereafter cited as *Essays*.
2. *Emerson in His Journals*, ed. Joel Porte, 1982, p. 240.
3. *Emerson in His Journals*, p. 249.
4. *Emerson in His Journals*, p. 283.

NATHANIEL HAWTHORNE,
ARTIST OF PURITANISM

SUSAN MANNING

... art and reflection have never been able to unite perfectly the two elements
of a civilization like ours, that draws its culture from one source and its
religion from another ... This unfortunate separation of experience and its
artistic expression betrayed itself in the inadequacy of what was beautiful and
the barbarism of what was sincere ... We might say, for instance, that the
absence of religion in Shakespeare was a sign of his good sense; that a healthy
instinct kept his attention within the sublunary world; and that he was in that
respect superior to Homer and to Dante. For, while they allowed their
wisdom to clothe itself in fanciful forms, he gave us his in its immediate
truth, so that he embodied what they signified.

(George Santayana, 'The Absence of Religion in Shakespeare', 1896)

Santayana's account of protestant civilization provides the perfect
terms of reference for Hawthorne's work: 'the inadequacy of what
was beautiful and the barbarism of what was sincere' were the very
problems which Hawthorne felt to thwart the integration of art and
life in nineteenth-century America. And yet the writer whom
Herman Melville called 'deep as Dante', and between whom and
Shakespeare he found a difference 'by no means immeasurable', was
able neither to embody life in Shakespearean terms nor to signify its
meaning in Dante's spiritual sense ('Hawthorne and His Mosses',
The Literary World, 1850). Hawthorne himself inherited the Puritan
division between an event and its meaning, or (as it became) between
symbol and significance. His writing cannot tap the range of experience, spiritual or natural, available to the great writers on whom
he models his style; it is never more emptily 'significant' than when
he attempts to evoke an effect through Dantean symbols, or further
removed from reality than when he adopts the pseudo-Shakes-
pearean tones of the common man.

If such direct comparison is not to Hawthorne's advantage, Santayana does furnish a clue to Hawthorne's characteristic concerns as

an American artist and to the qualities which have elevated his reputation amongst modern critics. In the polarized culture which the American Puritans bequeathed to their democratic descendants of the nineteenth century, the problems confronting an artist were an intensified version of what Santayana describes: the choice of allegiance was between the materialist world of progress on the one hand, and the disembodied symbolizing of the Transcendentalists on the other. Hawthorne could align himself with neither.

Puritanism, and the legacy of provincialism it left to America, tended to resolve complex moral positions into an extreme either of righteousness (justification) or of reprobation. It was not only that art and reflection bore a problematic relation to experience, but that experience itself was unstable and liable to division: the phenomenal always called the numinous into question and the spiritual tended to deny the reality of the natural.[1] Hawthorne was sufficiently distanced from the theological centre of his inheritance to allow his imagination to play (like the image of moonlight of which he was so fond) over the surfaces of reality without either resting in experience or annexing it as meaning. His style is a measure of his intellectual detachment from the Puritan vision of life which is his subject matter. As Henry James put it,

The old Puritan moral sense, the consciousness of sin and hell, of the fearful nature of our responsibilities and the savage character of our Taskmaster – these things had been lodged in the mind of a man of Fancy, whose fancy had straightway begun to take liberties and play tricks with them – to judge them (Heaven forgive him!) from the poetic and aesthetic point of view.

(*Hawthorne*, 1879)

As the artist of Puritanism, Hawthorne set himself to understand his inheritance and to create stories which might sustain an illusion of life within the Puritan polarities. In one of his more schematic sketches, 'The May-Pole of Merry Mount' (1836), the opposition of body and spirit is simple, and absolute; their confrontation seems to demand victory of one over the other in terms which admit neither compromise nor complexity. 'Jollity and gloom were contending for an empire' in the guise of a group of revellers from old England and a stern band of New World Puritans:

The future complexion of New England was involved in this important quarrel. Should the grisly saints establish their jurisdiction over the gay sinners, then would their spirits darken all the clime, and make it a land of clouded visages, of hard toil, of sermon and psalm, forever. But should the banner-staff of Merry Mount be fortunate, sunshine would break upon the hills, and flowers would beautify the forest, and late posterity do homage to the May-Pole!

(Twice-Told Tales, p.62²)

But even in this tale, where 'the facts' (as the author's headnote tells us) have 'wrought themselves, almost spontaneously, into a sort of allegory', Hawthorne suggests that resolution lies somewhere between the extremes, in a position not comprehended by their polarities. With a gesture towards a Miltonic 'fortunate Fall', the sketch ends as the bride and bridegroom support each other heavenward, in the 'difficult path' of matrimony.

'Blessed are all simple emotions, be they dark or bright! It is the lurid intermixture of the two that produces the illuminating blaze of the infernal regions,' exclaims the narrator of a later tale, 'Rappaccini's Daughter' (1844). Only simple stories like 'The May-Pole' can be made from 'simple emotions'; the figures in Hawthorne's more complex tales are asked to recognize that (like Melville's tortoise in 'The Encantadas') they are 'both black and bright' (*The Piazza Tales*, 1856). Just as the tortoise, to observation, is *either* black *or* bright, and only understood to be both at once in the synthesizing intellect of the artist, so Hawthorne's tales generate their illusion of life not through observation or experience, but through intuition. He is neither a recorder of life nor a novelist of ideas; in his writing, objects are objects of contemplation, to be investigated in their manifold aspects, but not, finally, to be known. The result is a verbal surface which invites interpretation, but baffles its procedures. Hawthorne's distinctiveness as an artist, his 'Americanness' and his modernity are here: in his tales, formulation precedes, and determines, experience. It is both the source of the peculiarly intense vision of reality he offers us, and of the limitations of this vision.

It is risky to construct an equivalent for an experience which is itself posited rather than known. Because Hawthorne's tales are primarily the product of intensely *imagined* experience, his writing has no apprenticeship, nor does his art progress through recognizable phases of external influence. It seems to have been internally generated to a remarkable extent: the twelve years spent isolate in a room under the eaves of a house in Salem produced some of his most haunting tales of human possibility, both good and ill. (Later he struggled unsucessfully to 'convert' the raw material of his experience as an American in England into fiction, and left behind at his death four turgid and unfinished romances as a poignant testimony of failure.) The intriguing question is how Hawthorne's writing, with its 'inveterate love of allegory' and apparent insubstantiality of conception, *can* implicate the reader as deeply as it does.

Hawthorne's tales often develop from a situation or incident which lies somewhere between fiction and fact; this is a fixed source of contemplation which under intense meditation becomes an image. And this image, reflected like the scarlet letter on the shining breastplate first of the Puritan Endicott ('Endicott and the Red Cross'), and then of Governor Bellingham (*The Scarlet Letter*), reconstructs itself as Hawthorne builds his tale around it, like a hologram: an artefact of apparent solidity which may be viewed in focus from all angles, but which dissolves to the touch into an illusion of light and shade. Or, like the daguerreotype in *The House of the Seven Gables* (1851), it resembles a photographic image which projects reality through artifice to elucidate the relationship between America's Puritan past and the democratic present.

'Wakefield' (1835) shows Hawthorne weaving 'story' from 'fact'. In this tale, unlike the 'spontaneously wrought allegory' of 'The May-Pole', the 'facts' are sufficiently refined to avoid an air of abstraction, but in neither case do they demonstrate their own self-evidence. The truth Hawthorne seeks is neither moralistic, nor absolute. It is rather the less substantial, less inelastic 'truth of the human heart' (*The House of the Seven Gables*, p. 1). Wakefield, upon a whim, leaves his wife without explanation and goes to live 'in the next street' to spy upon his former life. His story may be that of the American artist: the man who distances himself from normal ties, the better to observe and understand them. In so doing, he commits an irrevocable act: 'by stepping aside for a moment, a man exposes himself to a fearful risk of losing his place forever ... he may become, as it were, the Outcast of the Universe'. The artist's stance of detached observation may in fact *preclude* understanding of life, a possibility Hawthorne explored in much greater depth through the figure of Miles Coverdale in *The Blithedale Romance* (1852). Like Coverdale, or the hesitantly emergent narrator of 'Night Sketches' (1838), Wakefield's withdrawal reflects the force of Hawthorne's own ambivalence about experience: 'There is no fate in the world so horrible,' he wrote to Longfellow at the end of his period of self-imposed seclusion,

as to have no share in either its joys or sorrows. For the last ten years I have not lived, but only dreamed of living . . . I have another great difficulty in the lack of materials; for I have seen so little of the world that I have nothing but thin air to concoct my stories of, and it is not easy to give a life-like semblance to such shadowy stuff. Sometimes, through a peephole, I have caught a glimpse of the real world . . .

(Quoted by James, Hawthorne)

What makes 'Wakefield' a tale and not a piece of covert self-exposure on Hawthorne's part is the intensity with which the original incident is refracted upon itself, until event and significance are compositely present to the reader's mind. This 'layering' of reality is quite different from the confidently organic symbolism of Dante, where event, symbol and significance are woven into a single consciousness. Hawthorne's understanding of the Puritan mind provided him with an artistic method which could evoke the mingling of the everyday and the intangible, but (unlike in Dante) at the cost of diminished actuality. For this permeation occurs in his writing in a special area created by the romancer, a 'neutral territory', or realm of art, 'somewhere between the real world and fairy-land, where the Actual and the Imaginary may meet' (*The Scarlet Letter*, 1850, p. 36). This is the realm of the imagination, where the symbol may mediate between the subjective and the objective; it is peculiarly necessary for the American artist, Hawthorne says in the preface to his 'Italian' romance *The Marble Faun* (1860), 'as affording a sort of poetic or fairy precinct, where actualities would not be so terribly insisted upon as they are, and must needs be, in America'.

This neutral territory gives the artist unwilling to engage with 'actualities' ground to explore the grey area at the boundary between the objective and the internally generated perceptions of the human mind:

In the depths of every heart, there is a tomb and a dungeon, though the lights, the music, and revelry above may cause us to forget their existence, and the buried ones, or prisoners whom they hide. But sometimes, and oftenest at midnight, those dark receptacles are flung wide open. In an hour like this, when the mind has a passive sensibility, but no active strength; when the imagination is a mirror, imparting vividness to all ideas, without the power of selecting or controlling them . . . a funeral train comes gliding by your bed, in which Passion and Feeling assume bodily shape, and things of the mind become dim spectres of the eye.

(*Twice-Told Tales*, p.306)

This tale, 'The Haunted Mind', flowers from 'an intermediate space, where the business of life does not intrude'; perspectives are reversed, so that the palpable and the impalpable flow into and out of each other; reality becomes a dream, dreams assume 'bodily shape'. Such scenes as this, or 'The Interior of a Heart' from *The Scarlet Letter*, are not merely further evidence of Hawthorne's self-confessedly weak grasp on the actual, they reveal a potentially fatal disjunction in human perception: the tendency to take one's thoughts *about* something for the reality *in* that thing, as Arthur Dimmesdale would project the enormity of his guilt onto the heavens in the shape of a fiery 'A', or Goodman Brown mistake his darkest suspicions about human nature for the actual depravity of those whom he most reveres. Where reality must first be posited before it can be known, there is a danger that all knowledge will resolve itself into disorders of the mind.

Hawthorne's best tales partake of precisely this interpenetration of perception and actuality, as they examine without succumbing to what Santayana (in a letter to Daniel Cory) called 'the alienation of the intellect from the milieu': a condition which is part disorder of the mind, part the predicament of modern man. 'My Kinsman, Major Molineux' (1832), 'Young Goodman Brown' (1835) and 'Rappaccini's Daughter' revolve about a moment of commitment, which may also be a 'Fall', in which the realities of the mind are brought to the test of an experience beyond themselves. They are not (as they would have been if Hawthorne's allegiance to Puritanism had been religious rather than aesthetic) *allegories* of the Fall, but evocations of the 'fallen' state of mind in which formulation precedes and determines perception. Life in these tales has 'a visionary air, as if a dream had broken forth from some feverish brain, and were sweeping visibly through the midnight streets' ('My Kinsman', *The Snow-Image, and Other Twice-Told Tales*, 1851, p. 228). Thus in the nightmare world of Goodman Brown's journey through the forest, a doubt immediately separates itself from the mind and assumes objectivity: when 'something' fluttered down from a tree, he 'seized it, and beheld a pink ribbon' belonging to his young wife Faith, thereby consigning her to perdition in this *Walpurgisnacht* of the soul (*Mosses from an Old Manse*, 1846, 1854, p. 83).

The climax, in which Goodman Brown is called upon to convert his fancies into a commitment to experience, occurs at a witches' coven in the forest. This meeting may itself be a product of his imagination, but it suggests a moment of truth:

Herein did the Shape of Evil dip his hand, and prepare to lay the mark of baptism upon their foreheads ... What polluted wretches would the next glance shew them to each other, shuddering alike at what they disclosed and what they saw!

(ibid., p.88)

The subsequent moment is hidden, as it must be, from Goodman Brown's consciousness and from the reader's. Sin is not *known*, but *feared*: behind the Miltonic rhetoric, there is a hole at the centre of experience. The peroration of the 'sable form' who is to initiate Goodman Brown into this hell-fired community belongs to Poe's world of exploited sensation rather than to the record of experience:

behold the whole earth one stain of guilt, one mighty blood-spot ... It shall be yours to penetrate, in every bosom, the deep mystery of sin, the fountain of all wicked arts, and which inexhaustibly supplies more evil impulses than human power – than my power, at its utmost! – can make manifest in deeds.

(ibid., p. 87)

There is no 'inside' to an intuition whose verbal surface resonates to the Bible, to Shakespeare, to Milton, but nowhere to an antecedent experience of which it is the expression and the knowledge. Goodman Brown finds that *thinking about* sin has come to replace experience as his only point of contact with the external world. Unlike Dante, who at the beginning of the *Divina Commedia* finds himself 'within a dark wood where the straight way was lost', or the characters in *A Midsummer Night's Dream* or *As You Like It* who go astray in the forest, Goodman Brown does not lose himself in order to re-emerge with a clearer relationship to the truths that lie beyond himself, but to confirm the primacy of mind over substance.

The powerful hold which 'Young Goodman Brown' exerts over the reader's imagination resides rather in the mode of telling than in any substantial 'wisdom' it imparts about sin. The third-person narrative implicates the reader without ever quite involving him: we can neither join Goodman Brown's journey, nor find a stance outside the rampant solipsism of the protagonist's vision. Like Poe, Hawthorne plays on the insecurities of self-consciousness; but unlike Poe's, Hawthorne's writing does not attempt to dissolve the boundaries of identity and coerce the reader into acceptance of the self-generating world as the only reality. There is, as always in Hawthorne's tales, a precise historical base – in this case the Salem witch-hunts of 1692, and the debate over 'spectre evidence': Goodman Brown sees the 'spectres' of the minister and the old dame who taught him his catechism, apparently on their way to participate in the communion of the damned. But was visual personification irrefutable evidence that the person thus projected had *acquiesced* in evil? Is Goodman Brown right to infer truth directly from appearance? Hawthorne's prose always holds to the possibility of a primary reality, although it is only in *The Scarlet Letter* that we may confidently point to its presence.

'Rappaccini's Daughter' also concerns the failure of a young man's faith at the moment of commitment. Giovanni Guasconti, an Italian student, has all the self-confident inexperience of the 'American Adam'; like Melville's Tommo in *Typee* (1846), he is confronted by a complex Eden whose qualities threaten his black-or-white vision. Once again, a story which purports to be told in the third person is in fact generated by the literary expectations of its protagonist, the 'young stranger', who

recollected that one of the ancestors of this family, and perhaps an occupant of this very mansion, had been pictured by Dante as a partaker of the immortal agonies of his Inferno. These reminiscences and associations . . . caused Giovanni to sigh heavily, as he looked around the desolate and ill-furnished apartment.

(*Mosses from an Old Manse*, p.93)

The reader is entitled to suspect anything offered as 'fact' from

Giovanni's reflections; a syntax of doubt modifies everything he observes or imagines, and his decision to remain near Beatrice but not in everyday relationship with her is certain to 'give a kind of substance and reality to the wild vagaries which his imagination ran riot continually in producing'. Giovanni's infatuation with the 'poisonous' Beatrice is divided between a sense of her noxiousness and a perception of her purity. When she seems to shun his touch, he interprets this as her consciousness of her own evil:

> he was startled at the horrible suspicions that rose, monster-like, out of the caverns of his heart, and stared him in the face; his love grew thin and faint as the morning mist; his doubts alone had substance.
>
> (ibid., p. 116)

The confrontation that Giovanni seeks to avoid is with the real nature of his own impulses, the tomb and the dungeon in his own heart. Unable to commit himself to the mingled beauty and corruption of a life lived in the garden with Beatrice, he seeks to 'purify' it of the ambivalence which sustains its being. The final image is violent and destructive: Beatrice dies, poisoned by the 'antidote' Giovanni has smuggled in, but yet more fatally wounded by his venomous words. The literary apotheosis of Beatrice indicts Giovanni's failure (and Hawthorne's refusal) to engage with her reality:

> 'Farewell, Giovanni! Thy words of hatred are like lead within my heart – but they, too, will fall away as I ascend. Oh, was there not, from the first, more poison in thy nature than in mine?'
>
> (ibid., p.127)

In 'My Kinsman, Major Molineux' the hero, equipped like young Benjamin Franklin entering Philadelphia with all the confidence and optimism of the Enlightenment, comes to the city to seek his fortune. He finds a riddling world where no one will give him a straight answer, and wanders the streets in search of his wealthy kinsman before encountering a procession of fire and sword. It belongs to the same internal emblematic framework as young Goodman Brown's satanic sabbath. Robin has 'an indefinite but uncomfortable idea, that he [is] himself to bear a part in the pageantry': as the visionary march draws closer, the observer finds himself infected by its complex emotions. The shock of recognition between Robin and his tarred and feathered kinsman is electric:

They stared at each other in silence, and Robin's knees shook, and his hair bristled, with a mixture of pity and terror. Soon, however . . . a perception of tremendous ridicule in the whole scene, affected him with a sort of mental inebriety . . . The contagion was spreading among the multitude, when, all at once, it seized upon Robin, and he sent forth a shout of laughter that echoed through the street . . .

(*The Snow-Image*, pp. 229–30)

There is no such moment of truth in 'Young Goodman Brown': Robin's laughter is his acceptance of complicity in the anarchic emotions which have degraded his paternal image. Inner impulse and outer action unite not in fear but in assent, before the fiery force sweeps onwards into the night, and Robin is left to construe a future for himself in the light of experience.

The openness of the ending offers a real choice: Robin has life ahead of him where Goodman Brown stands condemned to endless re-enactment of his vision of sin. The 'reality' of 'My Kinsman' is (as the lurid resonances of the procession suggest) no less literary than Goodman Brown's; but where in that tale the internalizing of the distance between formulation and experience generates a portrait of the Calvinist consciousness, in 'My Kinsman' the relationship between the interpretability of the prose and its impenetrability is less easily anchored. The process by which Robin takes his bearings in the world is the reader's: events are significant – but of what? and what is to be Robin's conclusion? This tale leaves the reader like the Surveyor holding the scarlet letter in the Custom-House preface:

[What was] signified by it was a riddle which . . . I saw little hope of solving. And yet it strangely interested me. My eyes fastened themselves upon the old scarlet letter, and would not be turned aside. Certainly, there was some deep meaning in it, most worthy of interpretation, and which, as it were, streamed forth from the mystic symbol, subtly communicating itself to my sensibilities, but evading the analysis of my mind.

(*The Scarlet Letter*, p. 31)

While Hawthorne is willing to concede to his Puritan ancestors that 'some deep meaning' *does* reside in the piece of scarlet cloth, the transformation of the rag into the eponymous romance occurs through an imaginative evocation of possibilities rather than an imposed interpretation; responsibility for the act of elucidation which will release the image finally rests with the reader.

At the heart of *The Scarlet Letter*, Hawthorne's greatest work – where (if it were an English novel) we should expect some central experience – we find a symbol: the scarlet 'A' which Hester Prynne wears on her breast, and whose lurid glow is reflected back from every angle of the fiction. This 'A' is imposed upon Hester by the Puritan community as punishment for adultery committed before the beginning of the narrative; the book is *all* consequence, all effect disjoined from its cause. The reader is in the position of the interpreting Puritan who reasons obsessively backwards from effects, symbols, manifestations in the world to their meanings. Because the event (the act of adultery) is not present in the narrative, the chain of meaning can never be completed. Was the adultery of Hester and Dimmesdale 'an evil deed' which 'invests itself with the character of doom', or did it, as Hester says, have 'a consecration of its own'? The 'deep meaning' discerned by the Surveyor never emerges: the romance enforces the opacity of the symbol, until on the final page it gleams forth as an heraldic device, a symbol only of its own symbolic-ness.

Although the meaning of the original act remains opaque, something *did* take place in the forest: the child Pearl and the scarlet 'A' are its tangible consequences. Hester Prynne is the one figure in Hawthorne's work of whom we may say unequivocally that she has been touched by experience, and brought to recognize a reality beyond herself. Hester's experience is unknowable from the outside, but it is irreducible by the will and uninterpretable by the intellect: 'the infant and the shame were real. Yes! – these were her realities, – all else had vanished!' Accepting these obligations, Hester chooses not, like young Goodman Brown, to wander in 'the passes of the dark, inscrutable forest open to her', but to tame the wildness of her nature in the service of others.

Pearl, her child, and the 'living hieroglyphic' of her sin, is the realm where the Actual and the Imaginary may meet; her reality is both verbal (as the scarlet letter personified in the garments Hester works for her) and has the absolute solidity of the living infant. Pearl's is the innocence of every Romantic child; but if in one sense her questions are guileless, in another they are *more* knowing, more instinctively cognizant of sin and evil than even the obsessively sin-seeking Puritans: 'Why does the minister keep his hand over his heart?' The difference is that all of life is to her *natural*; evil is as much a part of her being as innocence. She exists as an amalgam of adult passions, but without the self-consciousness which is a source of terror to her father. 'Natural' in her illegitimacy, she is the natural product of her parents' passion, and repudiates nothing in herself or in her world, except concealment. Transparent though her motives may be, Pearl retains that 'otherness' denied by the narrative to Chillingworth the wronged husband, to Dimmesdale, and even to Hester; it is not absurd to say of her (as it would be of them) that she is drawn from life. She is, in an important way, a 'real' child, and her 'complex emotions' repudiate the polarized Puritan vision.

Hawthorne evokes the unselfconscious vision of the child through the primary fact in her life – her relationship with her mother – described not as the child herself perceives it (for that is impossible, inarticulacy being built into the integrity of the relationship), but with a sharply focused observation which combines empathy and objectivity. There is a clear source for Pearl in Hawthorne's own observations of his daughter Una, recorded with tender exactness in his American notebooks. Perhaps only the father, standing as he does at an equal distance (but closer than anyone else) from both mother and daughter, has such complete access to – and such complete exclusion from – the complex of feelings which describes their relationship:

> 'Dost thou know thy mother now, child?' asked she, reproachfully, but with a subdued tone. 'Wilt thou come across the brook, and own thy mother, now that she has her shame upon her, – now that she is sad?'
> 'Yes; now I will!' answered the child, bounding across the brook, and clasping Hester in her arms. 'Now thou art my mother indeed! And I am thy little Pearl!'
> In a mood of tenderness that was not usual with her, she drew down her mother's head, and kissed her brow and both her cheeks. But then – by a kind of necessity that always impelled this child to alloy whatever comfort she might chance to give with a throb of anguish – Pearl put up her mouth, and kissed the scarlet letter too!
>
> (*The Scarlet Letter*, pp.211–12)

Detachment is as important as intimacy here. To attempt to explain it would be to be like Chillingworth, the seeker for Truth who violates the sanctity of the human heart. Hawthorne (like his Puritan subjects) worries about his 'distance' from the heart of experience.

To come too close (as an artist must risk doing) is to commit the 'Unpardonable Sin' of Ethan Brand or Chillingworth; to remain outside is, like Coverdale, to be excluded and to cease to know the reality of what one observes. In the relationship between Pearl and Hester, Hawthorne finds a balance where the verbal patterning which accomplishes the intuition (Pearl in kissing Hester's brow and cheeks is re-forming the formulaic 'A') exactly matches an observed experience. There is a perfect moulding of formulation and perception; if the existence of Pearl gives Hester a reality outside herself within the framework of the narrative, it is also what lends her an illusion of life for the reader.

The case is far different with Dimmesdale, the adulterer, who is unable by confessing his guilt to put it outside himself. His life becomes self-consuming; the palpable and the impalpable merge until 'the only truth, that continued to give Mr Dimmesdale a real existence on this earth, was the anguish in his inmost soul, and the undissembled expression of it in his aspect' (*The Scarlet Letter*, p.146). This is the world of young Goodman Brown given a context beyond itself. The narrator stresses not the inevitability but the unnaturalness of the habit of self-projection onto the universe:

. . . it could only be the symptom of a highly disordered mental state, when a man, rendered morbidly self-contemplative by long, intense, and secret pain, had extended his egotism over the whole expanse of nature, until the firmament itself should appear no more than a fitting page for his soul's history and fate.

(*The Scarlet Letter*, p.155)

As Hawthorne pleads for a leaven of experience to temper the self-generating significances of the mind, his analysis of Puritanism makes contact with what he most distrusted about the Emersonian Transcendentalism of his own times:

In my utter impotence to trust the authenticity of the report of my senses, to know whether the impressions they make on me correspond with outlying objects, what difference does it make, whether Orion is up there in heaven, or some god paints the image in the firmament of the soul?

(R. W. Emerson, *Nature*, 1836)

Where Emerson exuberantly espouses Idealism, Hawthorne suggests that it makes a great deal of difference to life whether or not one acknowledges something beyond one's own senses. But in mid-nineteenth-century America, unlike in Dante's Europe, the writer *could not* take the symbolizing route to truth without denying objects, any more than he could (like the scientist Chillingworth) follow the 'Shakespearean' empirical path without denying soul:

> He had begun an investigation, as he imagined, with the severe and equal integrity of a judge, desirous only of truth ... But, as he proceeded, a terrible fascination, a kind of fierce, though still calm, necessity seized the old man within its gripe, and never set him free again, until he had done all its bidding.
>
> (*The Scarlet Letter*, p.129)

This is where Melville seems deeply misguided in his view (in 'Hawthorne and His Mosses') that Hawthorne himself is the man who announces 'I seek for Truth' (*Mosses from an Old Manse,* p.335). *The Scarlet Letter* is not a search for truth: several modes of perception and several 'explanations' remain possible to the end. It is Hawthorne's great achievement that this indefiniteness does not render the book morally void; its ethical stance is taken (as, to an extent, all 'modern' morality must be) *in the presence of* uncertainty. When all knowledge is possibly a product of the mind, and its revelation proceeds by symbols and indirections, how *does* one find a public voice in which to 'open an intercourse with the world'? For Hawthorne, however private his subject-matter, always seeks to address an audience, never himself. In the 'neutral territory' of art he finds an area of reconciliation between the fact and the way it is perceived. Each needs the other to bring it to realization, and they become not opposed but complementary. If Hawthorne's prose neither 'embodies' life nor 'signifies' meaning, it does, at its best, re-establish the *imaginative* relation of observation to belief, and so sustain the complexity of human possibility against the Puritan polarities from which it springs.

NOTES

1. For a fuller account of Puritanism and its implications, see Part One.
2. All references to Hawthorne's works are to the Centenary Edition, edited by William Charvat and others (Columbus, Ohio, 1962–).

EDGAR ALLAN POE:
THE MEANING OF STYLE

R. D. GOODER

Poe has been, notoriously, an embarrassment to American literature. Along with Mark Twain he has been the most popular of all American writers both at home and abroad, and thanks to the interest that the French have taken in him, his influence has reached further than that of any other American writer at all. The French literature on Poe is enormous, and he has been admired by other writers as various as Dostoevsky, Swinburne, G. B. Shaw, Lawrence, Eliot and Auden. Americans, however, have found Poe childish, or unhealthy, or both, and with one or two distinguished exceptions (William Carlos Williams, Allen Tate) have left him to the schoolrooms and to the academies. Poe has been thought to be, on the whole, insufficiently American, and rather unnatural. His solipsistic characters do nothing – except occasionally solving a puzzle – that Americans find admirable, they have no recognizable context, and they establish no relation to ordinary life. Yet, if we stand back from these things, we shall see that they are the very qualities which set Poe's writing close to the centre of American literature.

It is a commonplace that attitudes to nature bear a peculiar and potent charge in earlier American literature. The first American settlers were confronted with a vast and fertile wilderness which on the one hand held the promise of physical and economic salvation, but was on the other hand more threatening than any part of Europe had been from the time the Romans settled it. The threat arose from the sheer scale of the wilderness, from the violent antitheses of topography and climate, and from the savage and increasingly hostile native population. The imaginative possibilities of this landscape were vividly illuminated by the theological preoccupation which the most dedicated and determined group of early settlers, the English Puritans, brought with them. The seductive hostility of nature in the New World provided perfect evidence for a theology so firmly founded on the doctrine of the Fall, at the same time as it supplied a field for the vigorous activities of men and women convinced that their own salvation required them to build a new Jerusalem in the wilderness. Thus did William Bradford describe the safe arrival of the *Mayflower* at Cape Cod in November 1620:

Being thus passed the vast ocean, and a sea of trouble before in their preparation . . . they had now no friends to welcome them nor inns to entertain or refresh their weatherbeaten bodies; no houses or much less towns to repair to, to seek for succour. It is recorded in Scripture as a mercy to the Apostle [Paul] and his shipwrecked company, that the barbarians showed them no small kindness in refreshing them, but these savage barbarians, when they met with them . . . were readier to fill their sides full of arrows than otherwise. And for the season it was winter, and they that know the winters of that country know them to be sharp and violent, and subject to cruel and fierce storms . . . What could they see but a hideous and desolate wilderness, full of wild beasts and wild men . . . What could now sustain them but the Spirit of God and His grace? (William Bradford, *Of Plymouth Plantation*, Book 1, chapter 9)

Two centuries later the wilderness had been partially subdued, and the American imagination overtaken by a more romantic conception of nature. What before had been that from which men had need to be saved, became, in the writings of the Transcendentalists, the very means of salvation.

In the woods, we return to reason and faith. There I feel that nothing can befall me in life, – no disgrace, no calamity (leaving me my eyes), which nature cannot repair. Standing on the bare ground, – my head bathed by the blithe air, and uplifted into infinite space, – all mean egotism vanishes. I become a transparent eye-ball; I am nothing; I see all; the currents of the Universal Being circulate through me; I am part or parcel of God . . . In the wilderness, I find something more dear and connate than in streets or villages. (Emerson, *Nature*)

These two positions, apparently opposite, are yet intimately related: between nature as threat and nature as salvation, nature as malign and nature as benign, imaginative writers of the nineteenth century found their subject.

One consequence of their intense scrutiny of nature is that in American writers the natural world takes on an increasingly subjective character. It is never just disinterestedly present. It may be on the one hand a repository of evil, standing for all that in man which threatens, denies, and destroys his civilized human aspirations; or, on the other hand, it may be a set of signs, directing man to his best and truest self, the self which cannot be expressed within the confines of civilization. But not to be able to fix upon any secure meaning in so elaborate a system of signs as nature offers leaves the writer doubting his ability to discover the truths he set out in search of. Underneath this preoccupation with nature developed a fear of meaninglessness, of inner emptiness. It was out of this fear that Melville and Hawthorne created some of their most brilliant works, tales especially, like 'Bartleby' and 'Young Goodman Brown'. In these tales the protagonists abandon all objective reality and a sense of complete inner insufficiency swallows up consciousness and offers uncertainty as the only available meaning in life.

And yet they do not quite abandon objectivity. In 'Young Goodman Brown', for example, Salem village, the cottage door, Faith's beribboned bonnet, and the path through the forest do have a certain historical and objective *presence*. The story itself is not about them, and in a sense it has nothing to do with them; the story is about something that happens in the mind and soul of Young Goodman Brown. But these circumstantial verisimilitudes provide the nuts, or keys to which Hawthorne's rhetorical skin is attached, and by means of which he draws his writing tight over the hollow resonance of his real subject. Brown, taught to seek in nature for signs of grace, finds only meanings which his own imaginings have put there, and consequently succumbs to despair. But, if Hawthorne's style is something like the skin stretched over a drum, Poe's is rather like something one might use in order to construct a tale *within* the drum. Poe let go all the fixed points which lend fiction a sense of reality, and which his contemporaries feared altogether to abandon, and gave himself over quite consciously to shameless subjectivity, without any pretence of doing something else. As William Carlos Williams wrote:

Hawthorne has no repugnance for handling what Poe purposely avoids, the contamination of the UNFORMED LUMP . . . What Hawthorne loses by his willing closeness to the life of his locality in its vague humors; his lifelike copying of the New England melancholy; his reposeful closeness to the town pump – Poe *gains* by abhorring; flying to the ends of the earth for 'original' material . . .   (*In the American Grain*, 1925)

Hawthorne, despite struggling in the toils of this extreme subjectivity, scarcely recognized himself what he was doing, and remained content to write up the new material in the old way. He continued, in some sense, a realist. But Poe, in recognizing a new subject, took it up in a new manner and a new style. 'By such a simple, logical twist,' Williams says, 'does Poe succeed in being the more American, heeding more the local necessities, the harder structural imperatives – by standing off to SEE instead of forcing himself too close.' As Poe himself said,

That an American should confine himself to American themes, or even prefer them, is rather a political than a literary idea . . . A foreign theme is, in a strictly literary sense, to be preferred. After all, the world at large is the only legitimate stage for the authorial *histrio*. (*The Broadway Journal*, 4 October 1845. *Essays and Reviews*, p. 1076) [1]

Poe saw, as did Hawthorne and Melville, that the real American subject was this consuming subjectivity, wherein the mind loses its way amidst the superabundance of signs, and the consequence of which is terror and moral collapse. Poe's distinction is that he approaches this subject *directly*, refusing to interpose between himself and *it*, or between himself and his style, any easy objective familiarities. Poe's concern is not with the 'spirit of *place*', but with the '*spirit* of place'. The spirit to be analysed is not to be found in the landscape or in the visible manifestations of human habitation and civilized society, but by direct communication with the human mind. And the mind is made up out of material from 'the world at large', or, as Williams says, from 'the ends of the earth'. To address oneself to the ordinary is to miss the chance of treating with the mind isolated from its usual, quotidian context. Hence, Poe's tales occur in such places as 'the most noisome quarter of London', at the edge of 'a dank tarn', in 'an old, decaying city near the Rhine', and in innumerable cellars, or darkened rooms, or fantastically decorated chambers. These are places of the mind, located nowhere, but recognized by every reader. (Poe's tales make poor films, precisely because these places lose their charge as soon as they are assembled for the eye rather than the imagination.) Poe, by extension, recognizes that in artistic matters America might never really have a culture of its own, that its mind would always be constructed from what it made of the rest of the world. In this he is but the predecessor of Henry James in his preoccupation with Europe, or Pound and Eliot in their eclecticism.

Not that Poe was unconscious of the political and social world round him. He was, for example, acutely aware of the way in which the 'mind of the age' not only failed to understand its political and economic spirit, but actually tended to underwrite its vices. Tucked away in a little-known work called 'The Colloquy of Monos and Una' there is a passage of extraordinary synoptic power in which Poe, taking as his *point de départ* the post-lapsarian conceit with which men in the nineteenth century fancied they could understand and control the natural world, launched an attack on the complacent and permissive egotism of his transcendentalizing contemporaries.

> Man, because he could not but acknowledge the majesty of Nature, fell into childish exultation at this acquired and still-increasing dominion over her elements. Even while he stalked a God in his own fancy, an infantine imbecility came over him. As might be supposed from the origins of his disorder, he grew infected with system, and with abstraction. He enwrapped himself in generalities . . . Meantime huge smoking cities arose, innumerable. Green leaves shrank before the hot breath of furnaces. The fair face of Nature was deformed as with the ravages of some loathsome disease.
>
> (*Poetry and Tales*, pp. 450f.)

Such a passage stands as a gloss on all those tales of Hawthorne's, for example, in which the thinker, or man of science, becomes destroyer of nature – 'Rappaccini's Daughter', 'Dr Heidegger's Experiment', 'Ethan Brand', and the like. For Poe this is not merely something to be contemned and corrected; it is endemic to the modern condition. The greater and more particular our interest in nature, the more likely that our researches will end in its destruction. And the more intent our scrutiny after the meaning of nature, the more shall we sink into hopeless and incoherent subjectivity, into – as Poe says – imbecility, system, abstraction, and generalities. Neither a scientific nor a sentimental interest in nature suffices, for the practical effect of the one is a hard and unfeeling pragmatism, and of the other a rhetorical spirituality. In an essay on Poe, D.H. Lawrence said that the real subject of Poe's fiction is the painful separation of the body from the spirit, and that such a separation would be necessary if a real re-birth were to occur in America. He was saying nothing that

Poe would not himself have recognized: the point of 'The Colloquy of Monos and Una' is that the separation between the pragmatic and the spiritual contemplation of nature had gone so far that it could not be retrieved, and that, therefore, man must die and be reborn.

The enormous, unbroken popularity that Poe has enjoyed – in part the consequence of his being a macabre children's classic – has obscured the fact of his being also a thoroughgoing intellectual, the only serious literary critic of his generation, and America's first man of letters. This was remarkable in the 1830s and 1840s. Poe's contemporaries were bent on making money. To be bent on making nothing more substantial than literature was eccentric; to spend time *judging* it, or formulating theories about its creation, was aberrant. But Poe's most famous essays, 'The Philosophy of Composition', 'The Rationale of Verse', and 'The Poetic Principle', grew out of the regular reviewing – much of it hack work – from which he made a living. He was the first to recognize Hawthorne's genius, and early in seeing what made Dickens important; his account of the vices of Macaulay's style anticipated Matthew Arnold's, and he was stimulating and mostly right about those of his contemporaries whom we remember, like Bryant, Lowell, Longfellow and Emerson.

For the rest, we may still enjoy him not for his strictures on forgotten writers, but for what he says in passing about literature. The source of Eliot's famous 'shred of platinum' metaphor in 'Tradition and the Individual Talent' may be found in Poe's essay on N.P. Willis, and in a review of Hazlitt's *Characters of Shakespeare* he anticipated by more than a century the debate about character in Shakespeare initiated by L.C. Knights' *How Many Children Had Lady Macbeth?* Since Poe's first ambition was to be a poet, his criticism – like that of Sidney, Dryden, Coleridge, and T.S. Eliot – was designed to create the taste whereby his own verse was to be judged. It was his misfortune to have a very ignorant audience and little good American writing to work on. No doubt Henry James was right to observe of Poe's criticism that it presented 'probably the most complete and exquisite specimen of *provincialism* ever prepared for the edification of men,' but one may still admire Poe's own attempt to purge American literature of *its* provinciality.

We get up a great hue and cry about the necessity of encouraging native writers of merit – we blindly fancy that we can accomplish this by indiscriminate puffing of good, bad, and indifferent ... We ... thus often find ourselves involved in the gross paradox of liking a stupid book better, because, sure enough, its stupidity is American.

(*Essays and Reviews*, p. 506)

There was hardly any public in America that could have understood what Poe was trying to do. The only serious literary culture was in Boston, where the high-minded Transcendentalism which animated it rendered Poe anathema. Emerson called him 'the jingling man'. But Poe thought literature in danger of corruption when its ends were other than literary, particularly when (as he said in his essay on Longfellow and elsewhere) it fell into the didactic mode. There was no place in Boston, stiff with notions of social and religious reform, for a writer preoccupied with artistic integrity, clarity of effect, and purity of style.

It was the French who were first to see Poe's distinction, and its relevance to their own needs. One of the principal tenets of modernism, the doctrine of artistic purity, urged and consistently re-affirmed by Baudelaire, was lifted from Poe.[2] Indeed, translating Poe proved to be the main literary enterprise of Baudelaire's life. Baudelaire's interest was particularly in Poe's tales, where he found confirmation for his sense of the evil that lies behind the carefully constructed façades of men and society. It was Mallarmé who discovered Poe's poetry, and from that discovery opened the symbolist tradition that has dominated French and to some extent American poetry for the past century. The consuming subjectivity which freed Poe to look 'to the ends of the earth' for 'original material' allowed him also to formulate a theory wherein poetry scarcely needed to acknowledge the facts of the sublunary world:

An immortal instinct deep within the spirit of man is thus, plainly, a sense of the Beautiful. This it is which administers to his delight in the manifold forms, and sounds, and odors, and sentiments, amid which he exists ... But ... mere repetition is not poetry. He who shall simply sing, with however glowing enthusiasm, or with however vivid a truth of description, of the sights, and sounds, and odors, and colors, and sentiments, which greet *him* in common with all mankind – he, I say, has yet failed to prove his divine title. There is still something in the distance which he has been unable to attain. We have still a thirst unquenchable, to allay which he has not shown us the crystal springs. This thirst belongs to the immortality of Man. It is at once a consequence and an indication of his perennial existence. It is the desire of the moth for the star. It is no mere appreciation of the Beauty before us, but a wild effort to reach the Beauty above. Inspired by an ecstatic prescience of the glories beyond the grave, we struggle by multiform combinations among the things, and thoughts of Time to attain a portion of that Loveliness whose very elements, perhaps, appertain to eternity alone. And thus when by Poetry – or when by Music, the most entrancing of the Poetic moods – we find ourselves melted into tears – we weep – through a certain petulant, impatient sorrow at our inability to grasp *now*, wholly, here on earth, at once and forever, those divine and rapturous joys, of which *through* the poem, or *through* the music, we attain to but brief and indeterminate glimpses. (*Essays and Reviews*, pp. 76f.)

Poe, no less than the Puritans and the Transcendentalists, looks inward to discover the paradise above, but lacking any interest in reality, or any interest in morality, he was able to formulate his theory not in terms of description, or of action, but of *style* alone. What validates Poe's theory in a poem is not the accuracy of a description, or the justice of an action, but merely the skill in the collocation of words and their effect upon the mind of the reader, merely, in short, the style. This pre-occupation with style emerges from an almost preternatural self-consciousness which, having lost touch with external reality, has language as its only resource. This language is created not out of fact or experience, but out of linguistic artifacts collected and arranged in such a way that they do not comprehend fact or experience, but taken together are *in themselves* the fact and the experience. Thus is the poem created, or, to put it another way, thus is the subject made object. Such a poem, in theory at any rate, speaks with a special kind of directness, for it is not a metaphorical mediation of common experience, but rather, a direct communication of the meaning of that experience *in a purified form*, or, as Mallarmé wrote, it gives a purer sense to our language – *donner un sens plus pur aux mots de la tribu* ('Le Tombeau d'Edgar Poe').

Poe's most sustained defence of his own poetic practice is to be found in the essay on 'The Philosophy of Composition', which is mainly taken up with an extended account of the composition of what is probably his most famous poem, 'The Raven'. Poe says, at the beginning of this essay,

I prefer commencing with the consideration of an *effect*. Keeping originality *always* in view – for he is false to himself who ventures to dispense with so obvious and so easily obtainable a source of interest – I say to myself, in the first place, 'Of the innumerable effects or impressions of which the heart, the intellect, or (more generally) the soul is susceptible, what one shall I, on the present occasion, select?' Having chosen a novel first, and secondly, a vivid effect, I consider whether it can be best wrought by incident or tone – whether by ordinary incidents and peculiar tone, or the converse, or by peculiarity both of incident and tone – afterwards looking about me (*or rather within*) for such combinations of event or tone as shall best aid me in the construction of the effect. (*Essays and Reviews*, pp. 13f., italics mine)

Poe then analyses 'step by step, the process by which . . . one of his compositions attained its ultimate point of completion'. This analysis of 'The Raven' is detailed, extensive, and precise, and in the end it tells us nothing that we wanted to know. For all the display of precision, for all the elaboration of technical detail, Poe refuses to answer our two most pressing questions: What was the effect he wished to create?, and, What is the meaning or significance of the elements used to bring it about? What is signified by the time of the year or the time of the day, by the bust above the door, by the velvet cushions or the censer or the Seraph who swings it, let alone by the raven itself? All of this is perfectly characteristic of Poe, of course. As in his tales, so even in this critical essay, he fills his void with an extraordinary plethora of detail, giving us a myriad of signs, but no sure clue as to their meaning, or the meaning of the subject which they have been adduced to elucidate. Poe's style is, in his poems, in his tales, even in his criticism at its best, characterized by this detachment, by a neutrality of tone which steadfastly refuses to gratify our taste for rational certainty. It is impossible to determine even whether Poe is being serious or not. In a careful reading of 'The Raven' one finds one's attention stretched between what is clearly hilarious and what is clearly lugubrious, with no clue as to what is intended. The poem may be funny, or it may be melancholy (it has been read either way, and can be read either way by the same reader in different moods), but since it won't declare itself, one's mind hovers intently over the surface of the language. Such tangible impression of the poem as is to be achieved may be measured by the extent to which the mind of the reader becomes one with the language of the poem. Thus extraneous considerations, like the imitation of reality, or the creation of discursive meaning, do not interfere with this direct communication, this language 'purified'.

This is not so far from what is sometimes thought of as Poe's most distinctive achievement, the creation of the detective story. In Poe, Sir Arthur Conan Doyle wrote,

> the secret of the thinness and also of the intensity of the detective story is that the writer is left with only one quality, that of intellectual acuteness, with which to endow his hero. Everything else is outside the picture and weakens the effect.
>
> (Brander Matthews, 'Poe and the Detective Story', in *The Recognition of Edgar Allan Poe*, ed. E.W. Carlson, 1966, p. 90)

What is interesting about Poe's 'tales of ratiocination', that is, 'The Gold Bug', 'The Murders in the Rue Morgue', and 'The Purloined Letter', from the perspective of Poe's more significant tales, is not so much that they turn upon intellectual acuteness, but rather that the intellect involved is successful in solving the problem it confronts. Poe himself thought these detective tales owed their popularity to merely being

> something in a new key. I do not mean to say that they are not ingenious – but people think them more ingenious than they are – on account of their method and *air* of method. In 'The Murders in the Rue Morgue', for instance, where is the ingenuity of unraveling a web which you yourself (the author) have woven for the express purpose of unraveling. The reader is made to confound the ingenuity of the suppositious Dupin with the writer of the story.
>
> (Quoted in Carlson, p. 92)

Yet Poe here indicates the significance of this 'ingenuity': that the hero is not to be distinguished from his creator. Poe the intellectual is in these tales, and they take on, therefore, the character of wish-fulfilments, where the mind of the hero is adequate to the problems he faces.

But of far greater interest than these tales of successful ratiocination are those wherein the problem does not admit of a solution, or where the mind of the hero, or of the narrator, cannot control the conditions under which it is obliged to live. Poe was the most intelligent writer of his generation in America, and the French taste for him stemmed to a degree from the fact that in describing him as 'intelligent' one uses the word rather more in its French than in its English sense. Poe was not 'intelligent about life'. Knowledge of life, and how under ordinary circumstances it is to be lived or endured, forms no part of Poe's fiction beyond the fact that it is frequently interrupted by death. It is, indeed, a sign of this ignorance of life, this unintelligence about it, that Poe's heroes and narrators are themselves such intellectuals. For the essence of Poe's best tales – whether one is speaking of the victim of the Spanish Inquisition who describes his torture at the hands of his captors in 'The Pit and the Pendulum', the restless traveller whose MS is found in a bottle, the husband who immures a black cat with the wife he has murdered, the old man who describes his escape from a maelstrom – is a perfectly conscious clairvoyance in which the intellect controls, or attempts to control, everything. Loss of intellectual control leads to madness or, more frequently, death. Life, therefore, is a matter of will; to remain intellectually conscious is to remain alive. 'Man doth not yield himself to the angels, nor unto death utterly, save only through the weakness of his feeble will,' as Poe quotes Joseph Glanvill in the epigraph to 'Ligeia', Poe's own favourite among his tales.

Poe's tales, then, chronicle the most salient elements of consciousness. I say *salient* elements because consciousness is always under assault from an infinity of variables, and Poe's heroes or narrators are always trying to extract from those variables the one or two elements which will give order amidst the chaos of possibility. The trick is to lay hold of those elements in which real meaning resides, in order to escape the confusion to which consciousness may be reduced in attempting to interpret the infinity of signs with which the external world bombards it. In a late philosophical work called *Eureka* Poe, behaving rather like one of his own heroes, attempted to establish *symmetry* as the key to understanding the inner reality of things. Writing of this work, Paul Valéry said:

The man who attempts to imagine the inner reality of things can do so only by adapting the ordinary categories of his mind. But the more he extends his researches, and, in some degree, the more he increases his power of recording phenomena, the further he travels from what might be called the *optimum* of his perceptions. Determinism is lost among inextricable systems, with billions of variables, where the mind's eye can no longer trace the operation of laws and come to rest on some permanent fact ... Always, like a persistent point, there is some unresolved decimal which brings us back to a feeling of incompleteness, a sense of the inexhaustible.

(Translated from 'A propos d'Eureka', in Carlson, p. 109)

Like Poe, Poe's heroes attempt to reach the optimum of perception, bringing the mind to rest on some permanent fact. In this they do not succeed, the mystery is not unravelled, and the heroes and narrators are lost in the emptiness of insanity or death.

The characteristics of Poe's tales are a fantastical plot, a tone of moral neutrality, a rigorous logical development, all held in a style of brilliant intellectual clarity. Mr Richard Poirier says that the most representative works of American literature 'are designed to make the reader feel that his ordinary world has been acknowledged . . . only to be dispensed with as a source of moral or psychological standards': This is true enough of Hawthorne, or Melville, but not at all of Poe. Poe's tales acknowledge nothing of our world, and are not intended to do so. 'Having conceived with deliberate care, a certain unique or single effect to be wrought out,' Poe says, the writer 'then invents such incidents – he then combines such events as may best aid him in establishing this preconceived effect.' We have to do, then, not with an imitation of reality, but with the imposition of an effect conceived in Poe's own mind, and created out of such incidents, events and observations as his own imagination may supply. The attention of the narrator, and of the reader, is brought to bear on some incomprehensibly attractive element – the great crack running the length of the façade of the house of Usher, the teeth of Berenice, the eyes of Ligeia, the diamond and the dagger in the ragged pocket of the man of the crowd. These things take on, therefore, an immense significance in the minds of the narrators, and consequently in the mind of the reader, but what is never made plain is just exactly what they are significant *of*. The reader is therefore free (or condemned) to attach his own meaning to these elements. Poe's tales operate to create *open* symbols, and the perfect imaginative subjectivity of the author communicates directly with the perfect interpretative subjectivity of the reader.

It is not difficult to see why these tales have attracted such an enormous literature of interpretation. Poe's stories solicit interpretation. Nevertheless, I think it possible that to interpret Poe is in a degree to misread him. Moreover, it is evident that the tales are autobiographical, at least in some sense, and it can and has been shown that the plots are worked up out of Poe's response to contemporary events. But it is equally wrong, I think, to read Poe's tales as elements of his own psychological case history. With Poe we have to do with art of a purer kind than either ingenuity of interpretation or establishment of historical fact allows. These 'salient elements' in Poe's tales are in the end not elements of reality, but elements of style, style at once brilliant and deliberate. The cracks, the teeth, the eyes, the diamonds and the daggers, not to say the tombs, the cells, the black cats, the oblong boxes, the crepuscular light, the garish colours, and all the rest, are so many elements of style which, taken together, go to make up the totality of Poe's 'effect'. What that effect is will depend upon how a reader feels at the moment at which he reads a given tale, and how receptive he is to the style in which it is rendered. This is a technique that has nothing to do with surrealism (though surrealism is one of its distant descendants). For the essence of surrealism lies in its attempt to *abandon* conscious effect, and to strike meaning out of the shattered artifacts of experience. With this kind of randomness, this deliberate pitch at the *un*conscious, Poe has nothing to do. His tales are held together with a tight logic of development, and with a careful and calculated attention to style. The irrationality which is the mark of surrealism is nowhere to be found in Poe. Nor are Poe's tales 'gothic'. Gothic horror suggests that the real world may hold in it, under certain imagined circumstances, such terrors as would strike us with all the reality of a graveyard at midnight, or with a creaking door in a house we thought vacant. But Poe's tales have not that relation to reality. Their effects are of the imagination only, best established in an empty mind, a mind which is for the moment seeking neither enlightenment nor excitement, and is not trying to turn the words on the page into any recognizable simulacrum of reality; a mind, that is, entirely given over to an intense concentration upon nothing so much as the movement of Poe's style. Poe's tales are constructions, often of an extremely elaborate and detailed kind, that can best be erected in a mind alive with nothing so much as a sense of its own darkness.

This is the way in which Poe, at his best, handled the subject which most forcefully presented itself to American writers of the first half of the nineteenth century. The American mind sought for signs in the world which spoke of its relation with a higher reality, what Poe himself called the 'supernal'. Poe simply abandoned the pretence that nature herself could supply a basis for objective certainty, and thus freed his symbols of any responsibility to the ordinary expectations of his readers. What a rainbow is for Emerson, or the frozen surface of Walden Pond for Thoreau, or the song of the mocking bird for Whitman, or Faith's pink ribbon for Hawthorne, or the squeezing of whale sperm for Melville, or a shaft of winter sunlight for Emily Dickinson, so are Berenice's perfect teeth, or a diamond in the pocket, or a black cat, or a cask of Amontillado, for Poe. Save that Poe's symbols have no communication with nature to contaminate the pure subjectivity with which they are to be read. If your interest in external reality is only for signs of God's foot upon the treadle, it scarcely matters whether you fix your attention upon an albino whale, or a set of perfect teeth.

Poe laid down unusually precise canons of art, and in rigorously following them himself he created a handful of tales which are closer to being prose poems than they are to being prose fiction. That intensity of effect which was Poe's principal desideratum may be found in 'The Assignation', 'Berenice', 'Morella', 'Ligeia', 'The Fall of the House of Usher', 'William Wilson', 'The Man of the Crowd', 'A Descent into the Maelstrom', 'Eleonora', 'The Oval Portrait', 'The Masque of the Red Death', 'The Pit and the Pendulum', 'The Tell-Tale Heart', and 'The Black Cat'; and if we were to take them all, regularly, *au grand sérieux*, as the French have done, then we, like them, would begin to feel that there was something *religious* in Poe's writing. But the French have taken too little notice of an aspect of Poe immediately obvious to any English-speaking reader, particularly in respect of those writings which fall short of the intensity of his best work. There is a great deal of writing where a failure of tone betrays Poe into facetiousness, where intensity of consciousness degenerates into dandified self-consciousness. When, as a young man, Henry James reviewed the *Fleurs du Mal*, he held it against Baudelaire that he took Poe too seriously, for 'to take [Poe] with more than a certain degree of seriousness is to lack seriousness oneself'. James did not doubt Poe's distinction, but he saw what the French have not seen: that mixed up in his genius there was a touch of the charlatan. Poe was not unaware of this himself, or at least, there is another group of tales which were written as deliberate hoaxes. Some of these are very good in their way, but they are mere literary tricks, and the question that remains in the mind of an admirer of Poe's is how far this trickery has extended even into his best work.

The tale that most perfectly sums up the problem is 'The Facts in the Case of M. Valdemar'. Here, a narrator with an interest in mesmerism persuades an old friend on his deathbed to allow himself to be mesmerized just before the instant of his decease. Valdemar dies, but is kept in a state of suspended animation for seven months, saying from time to time that he is dead, but giving, otherwise, very little information about the life hereafter. When, at last, he is woken from his trance he in a twinkling rots away to 'a nearly liquid mass of loathsome – of detestable putrescence'. This tale is narrated with all of Poe's most careful attention to detail, and it is certainly possible to argue that in it he addressed himself to those questions about the life beyond this life that so exercised his contemporaries. It is his way of striking through what Ahab calls 'the pasteboard mask' of reality, in order to learn the secrets beyond. But there is no doubt, either, that the tale was written as a hoax, and that the attention to detail was largely for the sake of verisimilitude. So, as with 'The Raven', one scarcely knows whether it is hilarity or solemnity that is the intended effect. The description of M. Valdemar himself provides an example. He is the compiler of a forensic bibliography and the translator into Polish of *Wallenstein* and of *Gargantua*, and he lives in Harlem, New York. But what is most striking about him is

the extreme spareness of his person – his lower limbs much resembling those of John Randolph; and also – the whiteness of his whiskers, in violent contrast to the blackness of his hair – the latter, in consequence, being very generally mistaken for a wig.

(*Poetry and Tales*, p. 833)

This proliferation of detail makes Valdemar not more, but less real, of course, and the touch about white whiskers and black hair is positively silly. There is scarcely any tale of Poe's in which some similar peculiarity could not be found. And yet the concentration which Poe can bring to his subject, the care with which he assembles his materials, and the clarity of his writing, leave the reader content to admire the performance without troubling to question its substance. The hard brilliance of Poe's style reflects the imagination of the reader, and becomes the subject itself. The old adage that style reflects the man – *le style, c'est l'homme* – takes on, in the writings of Poe, a conspicuously American dimension.

NOTES

1. All references to Poe's works are to the two Poe volumes (*Poetry and Tales*, *Essays and Reviews*) in the Library of America series.

2. Cf. Richard Ellman and Charles Feidelson, Jr, ed., *The Modern Tradition*. In this anthology of modernist writing the editors translate, under the title 'The Didactic Heresy', the very passage in Baudelaire's essay on Théophile Gautier (1859) which Baudelaire himself took straight from Poe's essay, 'The Poetic Principle'.

HERMAN MELVILLE:
IN THE WAKE OF THE WHITE WHALE

HAROLD BEAVER

Melville was a major moral and political commentator of his age. Take three of his most celebrated tales: 'Bartleby' (1853), 'Benito Cereno' (1855) and *Billy Budd* (1924). Though differing in structure and narrative technique, they share a single concern. Each centres on innocence of some kind. Each innocent confronts an alien and unimaginable version of himself. Each is trapped in a claustrophobic world. In 'Bartleby' it is the world of Wall Street, controlled by the smuggest form of Christianity. In 'Benito Cereno' it is that of racial war, instigated by whites, but dominated now by the most unscrupulous blacks. In *Billy Budd* it is that of a British man-of-war, undermined by the most devious depravity.

Yet the precise nature of Melville's commentary is never easy to judge. For guile and guilelessness are mutually linked: as Bartleby is linked to the anonymous attorney; the American to the Spanish captain; the Spanish captain to Babo, his slave; and the master-at-arms aboard the *Bellipotent* to its peacemaker, Billy Budd. A point of vantage, or discrimination, belongs to neither. A middleman is needed. But there are no such middlemen, unless it be the self-indulgent intruder, the North American (in 'Benito Cereno') or the fatal father figure, Captain Vere (in *Billy Budd*). All points of view for Melville after *Moby-Dick* (1851) became partial and limited. Thus the need for the readers' constant, watchful discrimination, a kind of double decoding. As Amasa Delano unriddles the mystery of the *San Dominick*, we have to riddle out his text.

What for us becomes a problem of reading was for Melville a problem of writing. Billy Budd (that illiterate with a stutter) is literally an inscrutable and uninscribed blank. So is Bartleby the scrivener who gives up scrivening. So is Moby-Dick, the White Whale himself. 'Benito Cereno' proceeds from the grey murk of its opening to a final court-room revelation. But revelation of what?

All texts for Melville, be they official histories or eyewitness testimonies or myths, were lopsided and capable of being critically undermined. These tales are necessarily commandeered by professional lawyers and naval commanders since their polar opposites, their obsessive doppelgängers (Bartleby, Babo, Budd), remain voids at the centre of the circling exposition in the power of whiteness (the scrivener), or of blackness (the African), or of sexuality (the adolescent sailor).

In his awareness of such shifting perspectives Melville seems peculiarly modern. Yet he fits uncomfortably into the history of modernism. Nor is he usually numbered (like James or Hawthorne) among its predecessors. The one non-American to whose works he is constantly referred, or even assimilated, is that Polish expatriate, Joseph Conrad. (And Conrad, incidentally, could stand neither *Typee*, nor *Omoo*, nor *Moby-Dick*!) Only in an American context do paradigms proliferate: in his relation to Hawthorne, and romance, and autobiography, and sea fiction, and the Calvinist insistence on the 'Great Art of Telling the Truth'. Somehow that leviathan among authors has been consigned to Americanists, to specialists, to a grandiose but isolated cul-de-sac of his own, where (like that skeleton of the 'Bower in the Arsacides') he is ministered to by a priesthood who keep up

an unextinguished aromatic flame, so that the mystic head again sent forth its vapory spout; while, suspended from a bough, the terrific lower jaw vibrated over all the devotees, like the hair-hung sword that so affrighted Damocles.
(*Moby-Dick*, ch. 102)

For the truth is that our contemporary grasp of Melville is partly dependent on our earlier apprenticeship to Baudelaire, say, or Mallarmé, or Joyce, even – as it may sometimes happen – if we have actually read none of those authors at first-hand. And if we are more perceptive than our predecessors half a century ago, it must be because we are their heirs. We do not *use* Joyce to decipher Melville; we simply cannot help reading *Moby-Dick* in the light of *Ulysses*, or even at times of *Finnegans Wake*. I am all for putting ourselves on our guard. Fashion can corset imagination in the oddest ways. But Melville, like Blake and Sterne (to produce at least two supporters whom Melville had read), is, I believe, a large enough author to outlive all our concerns. It is not so much a question of whether he anticipated them as of whether he can accommodate them. His intentions are rarely discernible. His drafts or working notes (bar the uncompleted manuscript of *Billy Budd*) are mostly lost. His famous letters, written in the heat of composition, tell only a partial story. It is the texts themselves in their extraordinary verbal intricacy and hallucinatory cunning – part tall tales, part Yankee cabbala, part *Ancient Mariner* – that continue to exfoliate their meanings.

Melville himself, in a famous metaphor evoking his personal growth, felt that (in writing *Moby-Dick*) he had 'now come to the inmost leaf of the bulb, and that shortly the flower must fall to the mould'; but we refuse to grant him such finality.[1] We prefer to read his texts, in Roland Barthes's phrase, as onions 'whose body contains finally no heart, no kernel, no secret, no irreducible principle, nothing except the infinity of their own envelopes – which envelop nothing other than the unity of their own surfaces'. Such spiralling readings, like the unravellings on cutting into a whale's blubber, can never be wholly premeditated. The reader of *Moby-Dick*, who is summoned physically to his task at the outset ('Call me Ishmael'), is kept to that task by the very sketchy and uncompleted nature of the project: 'For small erections may be finished by their first architects; grand ones, true ones, ever leave the copestone to posterity' (ch. 32).

Melville, that is, demands further generations of readers to complete the structure, to grope for the aspiring meaning, to impose a copestone. Or as he confided in *The Confidence-Man: His Masquerade* (1857), in defending himself from more plausible texts of 'real life':

Experience is the only guide here; but as no man can be coextensive with *what is*, it may be unwise in every case to rest upon it. When the duck-billed beaver of Australia was first brought stuffed to England, the naturalists, appealing to their classifications, maintained that there was, in reality, no such creature; the bill in the specimen must needs be, in some way, artificially stuck on.

Or, taking the argument a step further: 'It is with fiction as with religion: it should present another world, and yet one to which we feel the tie' (chs 14 and 33).

That other world, as H. Bruce Franklin brilliantly exposed in *The Wake of the Gods* (1963), was the world of myth. Like another

Osiris, Ahab is dismembered 'in mid winter' by a leviathan/fish.
Like Osiris, he revives as the sun revives. Dead 'for three days and
nights', Ahab becomes literally a priest-king-god intent on 'supernatural revenge'. As Joyce drew on the oldest European narrative
tradition, Melville drew on Egyptian mythology as the authentic
source (he considered) of Hebrew mythology and so ultimately of
the myth of Christ. It also structured and located his text. As H.
Bruce Franklin commented:

> The Season-on-the-Line forms the chronological and geographical centre
> of *Moby-Dick*. At that time and place the whale for the first and last times
> dismembers Ahab. One Season-on-the-Line passes between these two; pre-
> cisely at this time, Christmas Day, the twice-maimed Ahab begins his fiery
> hunt. Although Ahab's second injury comes shortly before the Season-on-
> the-Line, all three injuries coincide with the various dates given for the
> dismemberment of Osiris, sometimes between the autumnal equinox and the
> winter solstice.
>
> (*The Wake of the Gods*, pp. 83–4)

To transcend the confines of consistent 'realism', Melville, like Joyce,
returned to myth.

Not only to myth, but literally *mythos*, in the sense of speech or
talk. From the start, quite consciously, he was weaving a web of
words. His are texts, in the basic etymological sense, stretched on a
linguistic loom. Treadles and shuttles, the warp and woof of jungle
tendrils, are a constantly recurring theme. 'Loomings', the title of
the very opening chapter of *Moby-Dick*, punningly contains a 'loom';
and an 'Etymology' precedes all, giving the name in thirteen different languages (dead and alive, western and exotic, from Hebrew to
Erromangoan) for 'whale'. The 'whale', it turns out, in Swedish and
Danish 'is named for roundness or rolling'; for *hvalt* means 'arched or
vaulted'. Such root-meanings become almost a principle of composition concealed in the text's cellars and vaults. 'Roll' is the very
first verb used of the whale ('where he rolled his island bulk') just as
it is the last repeated verb of the almost completed text, after the
wreck 600 pages later, when 'the grey shroud of the sea rolled on as
it rolled five thousand years ago'.

That appropriately jokey chapter 'Cetology' (as full of the spurious scholarship of the imagination as any later *apparatus criticus* by a
Borges or Nabokov) first defines the whale as '*a spouting fish with a*

horizontal tail', and then categorizes whales, according to magnitude, into 'three primary BOOKS (subdivisible into CHAPTERS)':

I. The FOLIO WHALE;
II. the OCTAVO WHALE;
III. the DUODECIMO WHALE.

For *The Whale* remained the working title, even by the time Melville signed the contract with Harpers in September 1851. (It was his brother, Allan, who suggested the change.) And if the whale is a whale is a whale, it is also a book (entitled *The Whale*), a self-conscious verbal artefact, moving laterally through its root meanings. For the whole world, like the whale, is round and rolling and arched and vaulted; and the whole *Whale*, as book, is a world to be read with etymological spectacles to trace the overlapping pattern of puns and opposing ranges of double meaning. (As there is a chapter entitled 'Moby-Dick' inside *Moby-Dick*, so there is a White Whale inside *The Whale*.) How those whales slip in and out of their homonyms! The whale turning to a pastoral *vale*, or dirge-like *wail*, or metaphysical *veil*, half-heard in *ale*, that turns to a *wall*. The reader should be alert to such oral shifts as he skims the text. For as the text performs, it insists on our reciprocal and ever vigilant performance. Unlike in the act of whaling itself, in the literary *Whale* it is the unriddling of the circuit alone that matters; it is always the chase, the hunt, and never the capture.

For all his heroic stature we have little to learn, as readers, from Ahab who insists on confrontation, face to face; who is enclosed by a single pun in his despair: 'How can the prisoner reach outside except by thrusting through the wall? To me, the white whale is that wall, shoved near to me' (ch. 36). Language should disclose worlds, not close them. This is what Robert Shulman called 'The Serious Functions of Melville's Phallic Jokes', heard even in those giant 'erections' which he left to the erotic and literary needs of posterity. It is what Barthes called the *jouissance* or bliss of the text. As Shulman more soberly put it: Melville's dislike of closed aesthetic systems is intimately

related to his rejection of the respectable social order, including its economic, political and religious systems. Primal sexual energy is intrinsically subversive of conventional order and of respectable systems . . . His enormous phallic imagery also embodies Melville's belief that the sources of artistic and sexual creation are closely related.

(American Literature, vol. 33, 1961)

Sexual energy apart, in his controlled and ceaselessly patrolled use of language, Melville anticipates that vast late nineteenth-century project which Mallarmé called 'the Orphic explanation of the earth': that is, the project of picturing the whole world not merely *in* language but *as* language. The phallic and bibliographical jokes of 'Cetology' restore the whale (as *'spouting fish'*) back to its etymological roots as a narrative performance. That void, ten chapters on, of 'The Whiteness of the Whale' is also the whiteness of the (FOLIO, OCTAVO, DUODECIMO) text. As Melville expressed it in a dizzying series of oxymorons:

> Or is it, that as in essence whiteness is not so much a color as the visible absence of color, and at the same time the concrete of all colors; is it for these reasons that there is such a dumb blankness, full of meaning, in a wide landscape of snows, a colorless, all-color of atheism from which we shrink?
>
> (ch. 42)

This suggests a speculative absence of the kind that haunts contemporary, French-inspired readings of *all* texts: an infinite regress of meaning among circling signs of all semiological systems. Here we reach the very edge of the textual abyss, the etymological vortex, to which the voyage of the *Pequod* (the name of an extinct tribe of Massachusetts Indians) inevitably drives.

The nature of the journey, then, is from the start self-consciously verbal and etymological and textual. *Moby-Dick* persistently calls attention to itself as fiction. 'Call me Ishmael,' says Ishmael retreating into a fictive world, by choosing the role of teller rather than actor; by turning from those voluminous whales to whales as volumes; by swimming, not through seas, but 'libraries'.[2] His words feed on words and provoke more words. One mode, as in Joyce, is parody. A curious and, at first sight, rather otiose-seeming chapter like 'The Blacksmith' (ch. 112) turns out to play an ironic counterpoint to Longfellow's 'The Village Blacksmith' (1840): the one enfeebled by gin, a suicidal widower, bereft of his children, staggering off at last to sea; the other seated smugly at church among his boys:

> He hears the parson pray and preach,
> He hears his daughter's voice
> Singing in the village choir;
> And it makes his heart rejoice.

The roguish list of 'Extracts' (supplied by a sub-sub-librarian) that precedes the main text makes something of the style, if not the nature, of such parody clear. For if the Osiris myth structures the narrative, Biblical parodies (from the back parts of God to long-haired Jesus-freaks) everywhere inform the structure. *Moby-Dick*'s ultimate and recurring source for parody is the book of Revelation with its dire threat of Armageddon. The whole of Revelation, it becomes clear, underscores Melville's design, turning the Biblical apocalypse to 'leviathanic revelations'.

The book is not only the culmination, the summa, of all pre-Melvillean whaling literature, it exhausts that literature with its speculative irony. Melville insists on a way of reading, a way of double exposure, a way of juxtaposition and compression. For an alternative text is both there and not there. It is both glimpsed and superseded and superimposed. The very act of writing conceals yet further writing. Only a multiple text can respond to the complex simultaneity inherent in all things. Only a multiple reading can respond to the multiple incoherences of a text, the flux and reflux of whose contradictory movements is held in a kind of constant oscillation; whose visible embodiment is a rocking whaleboat; whose most typical trope, the oxymoron (such as 'the coffin life-buoy' of the epilogue). The simultaneity of *The Whale* again and again finds its most obvious expression in the pun. Literally we must learn to 'read about whales through their own spectacles'. We must read, as it were, through eyes situated on either side of our head:

> True, both his eyes, in themselves, must simultaneously act; but is his brain so much more comprehensive, combining, and subtle than man's, that he can at the same moment of time attentively examine two distinct prospects, one on one side of him, and the other in an exactly opposite direction? If he can, then it is as marvellous a thing in him, as if a man were able simultaneously to go through the demonstrations of two distinct problems in Euclid.
>
> (ch. 74)

If reading evokes this two-ply quality, so too, of course does writing. It is the very essence of the Sperm Whale's tail:

The entire member seems a dense webbed bed of welded sinews; but cut into it, and you find that three distinct strata compose it: – upper, middle, and lower. The fibers in the upper and lower layers, are long and horizontal; those of the middle one, very short, and running crosswise between the outside layers. This triune structure, as much as anything else, imparts power to the tail.

(ch.86)

Such is the very nature of this tale, or cross-webbed text. Furthermore such texts, by juggling their constituents, proliferate or extend themselves with a wholly verbal autonomy. Take the Nantucket chapters of *Moby-Dick*, where Melville at the time of writing had never been. The subtext was Obed Macy's *History of Nantucket*; but the text needs only a single image ('a mere hillock, and elbow of sand; all beach, without a background') in order to compose a knot of self-contradictions drawn from Canada to Rome, from Lapland to the Eddystone lighthouse. Or take the Try Pots, recommended as 'one of the best kept hotels in all Nantucket'. The subtext there is from Hosea ('Go, take unto thee a wife of whoredoms and children of whoredoms'), transforming the landlord to one 'Hosea Hussey' and introducing Mrs Hussey 'under a dull red lamp' as literally a hussy wearing a necklace of polished bones. So the Old Testament is linked to Kali, black goddess of death. When Melville's head was flush, every shake of the kaleidoscope could produce new narrative patterns, new chapters that he intercalated into his ever-burgeoning text. Ultimately, like all symbolic ventures, it appears almost autonomous.

Almost, but not quite. Melville's texts, at least before *The Confidence-Man*, are always concerned *with* something, the memory *of* something, the memory of some original violence which has been postponed, or the inscription of that violence (like Ahab's stump or the scars on sperm whales' backs) which has been deferred. That original scene, like Bartleby's mysterious origin, is shrouded in rumour. For Melville's texts work on us rather like rumours: simultaneously presenting a distortion (of something) and a production (of something else) in an indistinguishable amalgam. The need for both reader and writer in their various ways is to sort, to sift this circulation of signs, these rumours (about whales, about Bartleby), these emblems (like the doubloon), these living hieroglyphs (like Queequeg). Such are the exertions of this chase.

For Melville's work is all puzzles. The puzzle of *Typee* is: are they, or are they not, cannibals? The puzzle of *Moby-Dick* is: what, and where, is the White Whale? The puzzle of *The Confidence-Man* is: is he one, or is he many? There may well be an interpreter, either as narrator or protagonist, attempting to unpuzzle the strange case of the lethargic slave-ship ('Benito Cereno'), say, or of the anorexic scrivener ('Bartleby'). Invariably it is a matter of scrutiny and interpretation of signs.

But not all such enigmas, by their very nature, are capable of resolution. They present a crux. They demand some kind of insistent, searching penetration. Which is what Ishmael offers. *His* is the fluid, wayward, spiralling discourse, repeatedly ravelling and unravelling its inquiry, as if spooled on some never-ending shuttle. But there are also obsessional cryptographers, like Ahab, who follow their one fixed code with an unflinching if baffled will, as if

some certain significance lurks in all things, else all things are little worth, and the round world itself but an empty cipher, except to sell by the cartload, as they do hills about Boston, to fill up some morass in the Milky Way.

(ch. 99)

Only one thing is sure: 'on errands of life' (as Bartleby concludes), 'these letters speed to death'. The one inevitability is death-in-life. This very paper is destined to be defaced of every trace. All ends, as it began, in an open whirl, in the blank indeterminacy (of white whale or pallid scrivener) that determines the ceaseless circulation of signs. This Proteus-like instability of the text is reflected in the unceasing, yet hesitant, metamorphoses of the whale as of the text itself. The text reinvents itself from moment to moment, chapter to chapter, by acts of deconstruction (those anatomical examinations of the Blanket, the Tail, the Fountain, the Cassock, the Nut of the whale) which constitute further stages of construction; by an enjoyment of symbols which becomes a further deployment of the text. For Melville's ultimate aspiration, at least in these decades, was some transcendent ecstasy, beyond life and death, in trance.

But that search Melville finally abandoned in *The Confidence-Man*. The novelist, he concluded, was an impostor. On reading

Essays in Criticism he mightily approved Matthew Arnold's quotation from Maurice de Guerin ('The literary career seems to me unreal, both in its essence and in the rewards which one seeks from it, and therefore fatally marred by a secret absurdity'), marginally commenting: 'This is the first verbal statement of a truth which everyone who thinks in these days must have felt.' *The Confidence-Man* in its inconsistency and incoherence presents the novel itself as a self-conscious artefact whose intrusive author manipulates his readers with a series of further incongruous arguments. For what is a novel but 'masquerade'? What is an author but the wiliest of confidence men? Among literary signs the so-called 'natural' and fictive are either indistinguishable or interchangeable. Here all the world is a stage; every actor in drag; every action some kind of transformation. So in *The Confidence-Man* fictions as often as not are told at second or third hand; or further fictions told within fictions. While again and again the narrator intrudes with further digressions or discusses technical matters to underscore the unreality of the narration. But since 'reality' (presumably inhabited by both the narrator and his readers) is similarly presented as a stagy world of disguises and transformations, nothing natural or supernatural, social or artistic, is preserved from the all-devouring circle of fiction. As Edgar A. Dryden put it:

> Plagued by suspicions but led on by such conventional literary clues as puns, complex patterns of imagery, and suggestive allusions to important people, events, and products of human history, the reader is tempted time and again to try to bring to the surface the meaning and order which seem to lie concealed behind the action and words of the novel's characters. But . . . each newly discovered clue, each new operative pattern or allusion, leads not beneath the verbal surface but across it to another mystery or, more often, to an example which subverts the implications of the original pattern.
>
> (*Melville's Thematics of Form*, pp. 151-2)

The very circularity of this procedure is reflected in the first of the author's critical intrusions, with its palindrome-like title: 'Worth the consideration of those to whom it may prove worth considering'. The fatal presence of the confidence man not merely defrauds his victims of their cash but of the very confidence in their own beliefs, their own language, their own roles.

For there is no transcendent, or divine, Truth. (The cosmopolitan, amid yet further echoes from Revelation, finally puts out the solar lamp and brings the novel to its apocalyptic close.) There is no waiting for Godot. There is no supreme, exemplary paradigm, no permanent code or map, as Wellingborough Redburn had discovered as he checked his father's guide-book against his own experience of Liverpool:

> Yes, the thing that had guided the father, could not guide the son . . . And, Wellingborough, as your father's guide-book is no guide for you, neither would yours (could you afford to buy a modern one today) be a true guide to those who come after you. Guide-books, Wellingborough, are the least reliable in all literature; and nearly all literature, in one sense, is made up of guide-books.
>
> *(Redburn: His First Voyage*, 1849, ch. 31)

Nearly all literature! Melville was to add considerably to the saving remnant. As he confided to Hawthorne in 1851:

> And perhaps, after all, there is *no* secret. We incline to think that the Problem of the Universe is like the Freemason's mighty secret, so terrible to all children. It turns out, at last, to consist in a triangle, a mallet, and an apron, – nothing more!

While writing *Moby-Dick* he was still worrying away at the world (or whale) as 'a riddle to unfold', a mystery destined to 'be unsolved to the last' (ch. 110), as indeterminate as the colour white which Melville challenged Champollion himself to read. But what if Queequeg's living hieroglyphs and the whale's 'pyramidical white hump' were a circular language after all? Melville, like Ahab, continued to strip layer from a little lower layer until that pyramidical vastness of riddling meaning was

> found to consist of nothing but surface stratified on surface. To its axis, the world being nothing but superinduced superficies. By vast pains we mine into the pyramid; by horrible gropings we come to the central room; with joy we espy the sarcophagus; but we lift the lid – and no body is there! – appallingly vacant as vast is the soul of a man!
>
> *(Pierre; or, The Ambiguities*, 1852, Bk 21, pt 1)

His sense of the self's instability, of its ability to adopt any role or mask, to become anything precisely because in itself it was nothing, anticipates much of Nietzsche.

On completing *The Confidence-Man* Melville toured the Middle East, visiting both Jerusalem and the pyramids. Then he tried lecturing for a while. But that too failed. The Civil War broke out. At last in 1866 he landed a job as a customs officer of New York City and adopted that role of decent obscurity.

NOTES

1. Letter to Nathaniel Hawthorne (1 June 1851), in *The Letters of Herman Melville*, edited by Merrell R. Davis and William H. Gilman (1960), p. 130. In the six years from 1846 to 1851 five novels had been published. Shipping as a nineteen-year-old merchant seaman to Liverpool had become *Redburn* (1849); escapades on the Marquesas and beachcombing on Moorea, *Typee* (1846) and *Omoo* (1847) and (under dense veils of spiritual and political allegory) *Mardi* (1849); the return home on a US frigate from Honolulu, *White-Jacket* (1850). But the astonishing creative outburst of the first six literary years continued unabated for a second six: *Moby-Dick* marks not the end but the middle of Melville's miraculous span.

2. See Edgar A. Dryden, *Melville's Thematics of Form: The Great Art of Telling the Truth* (1968).

SOME LINES FROM WHITMAN

RANDALL JARRELL

Whitman, Dickinson, and Melville seem to me the best poets of the nineteenth century here in America. Melville's poetry has been grotesquely underestimated, but, of course, it is only in the last four or five years that it has been much read; in the long run, in spite of the awkwardness and amateurishness of so much of it, it will surely be thought well of. (In the short run it will probably be thought entirely too well of. Melville is a great poet only in the prose of *Moby-Dick*.) Dickinson's poetry has been thoroughly read, and well though undifferentiatingly loved – after a few decades or centuries almost everybody will be able to see through Dickinson to her poems. But something odd has happened to the living changing part of Whitman's reputation: nowadays it is people who are not particularly interested in poetry, people who say that they read a poem for what it says, not for how it says it, who admire Whitman most. Whitman is often written about, either approvingly or disapprovingly, as if he were the Thomas Wolfe of nineteenth-century democracy, the hero of a de Mille movie about Walt Whitman. (People even talk about a war in which Walt Whitman and Henry James chose up sides, to begin with, and in which you and I will go on fighting till the day we die.) All this sort of thing, and all the bad poetry that there of course is in Whitman – for any poet has written enough bad poetry to scare away anybody – has helped to scare away from Whitman most 'serious readers of modern poetry'. They do not talk of his poems, as a rule, with any real liking or knowledge. Serious readers, people who are ashamed of not knowing all Hopkins by heart, are not at all ashamed to say, 'I don't really know Whitman very well.' This may harm Whitman in your eyes, they know, but that is a chance that poets have to take. Yet 'their' Hopkins, that good critic and great poet, wrote about Whitman, after seeing five or six of his poems in a newspaper review: 'I may as well say what I should not otherwise have said, that I always knew in my heart Walt Whitman's mind to be more like my own than any other man's living. As he is a very great scoundrel this is not a very pleasant confession.' And Henry James, the leader of 'their' side in that awful imaginary war of which I spoke, once read Whitman to Edith Wharton (much as Mozart used to imitate, on the piano, the organ) with such power and solemnity that both sat shaken and silent; it was after this reading that James expressed his regret at Whitman's 'too extensive acquaintance with the foreign languages'. Almost all the most 'original and advanced' poets and critics and readers of the last part of the nineteenth century thought Whitman as original and advanced as themselves, in manner as well as in matter. Can Whitman really be a sort of Thomas Wolfe or Carl Sandburg or Robinson Jeffers or Henry Miller – or a sort of Balzac of poetry, whose every part is crude but whose whole is somehow great? He is not, nor could he be; a poem, like Pope's spider, 'lives along the line', and all the dead lines in the world will not make one live poem. As Blake says, 'all sublimity is founded on minute discrimination', and it is in these 'minute particulars' of Blake's that any poem has its primary existence.

To show Whitman for what he is one does not need to praise or explain or argue, one needs simply to quote. He himself said, 'I and mine do not convince by arguments, similes, rhymes,/We convince by our presence.' Even a few of his phrases are enough to show us that Whitman was no sweeping rhetorician, but a poet of the greatest and oddest delicacy and originality, and sensitivity, so far as words are concerned. This is, after all, the poet who said, 'Blind loving wrestling touch, sheath'd hooded sharp-tooth'd touch'; who said, 'Smartly attired, countenance smiling, form upright, death under the breast-bones, hell under the skull-bones'; who said, 'Agonies are one of my changes of garments'; who saw grass as the 'flag of my disposition', saw 'the sharp-peak'd farmhouse, with its scallop'd scum and slender shoots from the gutters', heard a plane's 'wild ascending lisp', and saw and heard how at the amputation 'what is removed drops horribly in a pail'. This is the poet for whom the sea was 'howler and scooper of storms', reaching out to us with 'crooked inviting fingers'; who went 'leaping chasms with a pike-pointed staff, clinging to topples of brittle and blue'; who, a runaway slave,

saw how 'my gore dribs, thinn'd with the ooze of my skin'; who
went 'lithographing Kronos . . . buying drafts of Osiris'; who stared
out at the 'little plentiful mannikins skipping around in collars and
tail'd coats,/I am aware who they are, (they are positively not worms
or fleas)'. For he is, at his best, beautifully witty: he says gravely, 'I
find I incorporate gneiss, coals, long-threaded moss, fruits, grain,
esculent roots,/And am stucco'd with quadrupeds and birds all over';
and of these quadrupeds and birds 'not one is respectable or unhappy
over the whole earth'. He calls advice: 'Unscrew the locks from the
doors! Unscrew the doors from their jambs!' He publishes the results
of research: 'Having pried through the strata, analyz'd to a hair,
counsel'd with doctors and calculated close,/I find no sweeter fat
than sticks to my own bones.' Everybody remembers how he told
the Muse to 'cross out please those immensely overpaid accounts,/That matter of Troy and Achilles' wrath, and Aeneas', Ody-
sseus' wanderings', but his account of the arrival of the 'illustrious
emigré' here in the New World is even better: 'Bluff'd not a bit by
drainpipe, gasometer, artificial fertilizers,/Smiling and pleas'd with
palpable intent to stay,/She's here, install'd amid the kitchenware.'
Or he sees, like another Breughel, 'the mechanic's wife with the
babe at her nipple interceding for every person born,/Three scythes
at harvest whizzing in a row from three lusty angels with shirts
bagg'd out at their waists,/The snag-toothed hostler with red hair
redeeming sins past and to come' – the passage has enough wit not
only (in Johnson's phrase) to keep it sweet, but enough to make it
believable. He says:

> I project my hat, sit shame-faced, and beg.
>
> Enough! Enough! Enough!
> Somehow I have been stunn'd. Stand back!
> Give me a little time beyond my cuff'd head, slumbers, dreams, gaping,
> I discover myself on the verge of a usual mistake.

There is in such changes of tone as these the essence of wit. And
Whitman is even more far-fetched than he is witty; he can say about
Doubters, in the most improbable and explosive of juxtapositions: 'I
know every one of you, I know the sea of torment, doubt, despair
and unbelief./How the flukes splash! How they contort rapid as
lightning, with splashes and spouts of blood!' Who else would have

said about God: 'As the hugging and loving bed-fellow sleeps at my side through the night, and withdraws at the break of day with stealthy tread,/Leaving me baskets cover'd with white towels, swelling the house with their plenty'? – the Psalmist himself, his cup running over, would have looked at Whitman with dazzled eyes. (Whitman was persuaded by friends to hide the fact that it was God he was talking about.) He says, 'Flaunt of the sunshine I need not your bask – lie over!' This unusual employment of verbs is usual enough in participle-loving Whitman, who also asks you to 'look in my face while I snuff the sidle of evening', or tells you, 'I effuse my flesh in eddies, and drift it in lacy jags'. Here are some typical beginnings of poems: 'City of orgies, walks, and joys . . . Not heaving from my ribb'd breast only . . . O take my hand Walt Whitman! Such gliding wonders! Such sights and sounds! Such join'd unended links . . .' He says to the objects of the world, 'You have waited, you always wait, you dumb, beautiful ministers'; sees 'the sun and stars that float in the open air,/The apple-shaped earth'; says, 'O suns – O grass of graves – O perpetual transfers and promotions,/If you do not say anything how can I say anything?' Not many poets have written better, in queerer and more convincing and more individual language, about the world's *gliding wonders*: the phrase seems particularly right for Whitman. He speaks of those 'circling rivers the breath', of the 'savage old mother incessantly crying,/To the boy's soul's questions sullenly timing, some drown'd secret hissing' – ends a poems, once, 'We have voided all but freedom and our own joy.' How can one quote enough? If the reader thinks that all this is like Thomas Wolfe he *is* Thomas Wolfe; nothing else could explain it. Poetry like this is as far as possible from the work of any ordinary rhetorician, whose phrases cascade over us like suds of the oldest and most-advertised detergent.

The interesting thing about Whitman's worst language (for, just as few poets have ever written better, few poets have ever written worse) is how unusually absurd, how really ingeniously bad, such language is. I will quote none of the most famous examples; but even a line like *O culpable! I acknowledge. I exposé!* is not anything that you and I could do – only a man with the most extraordinary feel for language, or none whatsoever, could have cooked up Whitman's worst messes. For instance: what other man in all the history of this planet would have said, 'I am a habitan of Vienna'? (One has an immediate vision of him as a sort of French-Canadian half-breed to whom the Viennese are offering, with trepidation, through the bars of a zoological garden, little mounds of whipped cream.) And *enclaircise* – why, it's as bad as *explicate*! We are right to resent his having made up his own horrors, instead of sticking to the ones that we ourselves employ. But when Whitman says, 'I dote on myself, there is that lot of me and all so luscious', we should realize that we are not the only ones who are amused. And the queerly bad and merely queer and and queerly good will often change into one another without warning: 'Hefts of the moving world, at innocent gambols silently rising, freshly exuding,/Scooting obliquely high and low' – not good, but *queer*! – suddenly becomes, 'Something I cannot see puts up libidinous prongs,/Seas of bright juice suffuse heaven', and it is sunrise.

But it is not in individual lines and phrases, but in passages of some length, that Whitman is at his best. In the following quotation Whitman has something difficult to express, something that there are many formulas, all bad, for expressing; he expresses it with complete success, in language of the most dazzling originality:

The orchestra whirls me wider than Uranus flies,
It wrenches such ardors from me I did not know I possess'd them,
It sails me, I dab with bare feet, they are lick'd by the indolent waves,
I am cut by bitter and angry hail, I lose my breath,
Steep'd amid honey'd morphine, my windpipe throttled in fakes of death,
At length let up again to feel the puzzle of puzzles,
And that we call Being.

One hardly knows what to point at – everything works. But *wrenches* and *did not know I possess'd them;* the incredible *it sails me, I dab with bare feet; lick'd by the indolent; steep'd amid honey'd morphine; my windpipe throttled in fakes of death* – no wonder Crane admired Whitman! This originality, as absolute in its way as that of Berlioz' orchestration, is often at Whitman's command:

I am a dance – play up there! the fit is whirling me fast!

I am the ever-laughing – it is new moon and twilight,
I see the hiding of douceurs, I see nimble ghosts whichever way I look,
Cache and cache again deep in the ground and sea, and where it is neither
    ground nor sea.

143

Well do they do their jobs those journeymen divine,
Only from me can they hide nothing, and would not if they could,
I reckon I am their boss and they make me a pet besides,
And surround me and lead me and run ahead when I walk,
To lift their sunning covers to signify me with stretch'd arms, and resume
  the way;
Onward we move, a gay gang of blackguards! with mirth-shouting music
  and wild-flapping pennants of joy!

If you did not believe Hopkins' remark about Whitman, that *gay gang of blackguards* ought to shake you. Whitman shares Hopkins' passion for 'dappled' effects, but he slides in and out of them with ambiguous swiftness. And he has at his command a language of the calmest and most prosaic reality, one that seems to do no more than present:

The little one sleeps in its cradle.
I lift the gauze and look a long time, and silently brush away flies with my
  hand.

The youngster and the red-faced girl turn aside up the bushy hill,
I peeringly view them from the top.

The suicide sprawls on the bloody floor of the bedroom.
I witness the corpse with its dabbled hair, I note where the pistol has
  fallen.

It is like magic: that is, something has been done to us without our knowing how it was done; but if we look at the lines again we see the *gauze, silently, youngster, red-faced, bushy, peeringly, dabbled* – not that this is all we see. 'Present! present!' said James; these are presented, put down side by side to form a little 'view of life', from the cradle to the last bloody floor of the bedroom. Very often the things presented form nothing but a list:

The pure contralto sings in the organ loft,
The carpenter dresses his plank, the tongue of his
  foreplane whistles its wild ascending lisp,
The married and unmarried children ride home to their
  Thanksgiving dinner,
The pilot seizes the king-pin, he heaves down with a
  strong arm,
The mate stands braced in the whale-boat, lance and
  harpoon are ready,
The duck-shooter walks by silent and cautious stretches,
The deacons are ordain'd with cross'd hands at the altar,

> The spinning-girl retreats and advances to the hum of
>   the big wheel,
> The farmer stops by the bars as he walks on a First-day
>   loafe and looks at the oats and rye,
> The lunatic is carried at last to the asylum a confirm'd
>   case,
> (He will never sleep any more as he did in the cot in his
>   mother's bedroom;)
> The jour printer with gray head and gaunt jaws works at his
>   case,
> He turns his quid of tobacco while his eyes blur with
>   the manuscript,
> The malform'd limbs are tied to the surgeon's table,
> What is removed drops horribly in a pail; . . .

It is only a list – but what a list! And how delicately, in what different ways – likeness and opposition and continuation and climax and anticlimax – the transitions are managed, whenever Whitman wants to manage them. Notice them in the next quotation, another 'mere list':

> The bride unrumples her white dress, the minute-hand of the clock
>   moves slowly,
> The opium-eater reclines with rigid head and just-open'd lips,
> The prostitute draggles her shawl, her bonnet bobs on her tipsy and
>   pimpled neck . . .

The first line is joined to the third by *unrumples* and *draggles, white dress* and *shawl*; the second to the third by *rigid head, bobs, tipsy, neck*; the first to the second by *slowly, just-open'd*, and the slowing-down of time in both states. And occasionally one of these lists is metamorphosed into something we have no name for; the man who would call the next quotation a mere list – anybody will feel this – would boil his babies up for soap:

> Ever the hard unsunk ground,
> Ever the eaters and drinkers, ever the upward and downward sun,
>   ever the air and the ceaseless tides,
> Ever myself and my neighbors, refreshing, wicked, real,
> Ever the old inexplicable query, ever that thorned thumb, that breath
>   of itches and thirsts,
> Ever the vexer's hoot! hoot! till we find where the sly one hides and
>   bring him forth,
> Ever love, the sobbing liquid of life,
> Ever the bandage under the chin, ever the trestles of death.

Sometimes Whitman will take what would generally be considered an unpromising subject (in this case, a woman peeping at men bathing naked) and treat it with such tenderness and subtlety and understanding that we are ashamed of ourselves for having thought it unpromising, and murmur that Chekhov himself couldn't have treated it better:

Twenty-eight young men bathe by the shore,
Twenty-eight young men and all so friendly,
Twenty-eight years of womanly life and all so lonesome.

She owns the fine house by the rise of the bank,
She hides handsome and richly drest aft the blinds of the window.

Which of the young men does she like the best?
Ah the homeliest of them is beautiful to her.

Where are you off to, lady? for I see you,
You splash in the water there, yet stay stock still in your room.

Dancing and laughing along the beach came the twenty-ninth bather,
The rest did not see her, but she saw them and loved them.

The beards of the young men glistened with wet, it ran from their
    long hair,
Little streams pass'd all over their bodies.

An unseen hand also pass'd over their bodies,
It descended tremblingly from their temples and ribs.

The young men float on their backs, their white bellies bulge to the
    sun, they do not ask who seizes fast to them,
They do not know who puffs and declines with pendant and bending
    arch,
They do not know whom they souse with spray.

And in the same poem (that 'Song of Myself' in which one finds half his best work) the writer can say of a sea-fight:

Stretched and still lies the midnight,
Two great hulls motionless on the breast of the darkness,
Our vessel riddled and slowly sinking, preparations to pass to the one
    we have conquer'd,
The captain on the quarter-deck coldly giving his orders through a
    countenance white as a sheet,
Near by the corpse of the child that serv'd in the cabin,
The dead face of an old salt with long white hair and carefully curl'd
    whiskers,

The flames spite of all that can be done flickering aloft and below,
The husky voices of the two or three officers yet fit for duty,
Formless stacks of bodies and bodies by themselves, dabs of flesh
    upon the masts and spars,
Cut of cordage, dangle of rigging, slight shock of the soothe of
    waves,
Black and impassive guns, litter of powder-parcels, strong scent,
A few large stars overhead, silent and mournful shining,
Delicate sniffs of sea-breeze, smells of sedgy grass and fields by the
    shore, death-messages given in charge to survivors,
The hiss of the surgeon's knife, the gnawing teeth of his saw,
Wheeze, cluck, swash of falling blood, short wild scream, and long,
    dull, tapering groan,
These so, these irretrievable.

There are faults in this passage, and they *do not matter*: the serious
truth, the complete realization of these last lines make us remember
that few poets have shown more of the tears of things, and the joy of
things, and of the reality beneath either tears or joy. Even Whitman's
most general or political statements sometimes are good: everybody
knows his 'When liberty goes out of a place it is not the first to go,
nor the second or third to go,/It waits for all the rest to go, it is the
last'; these sentences about the United States just before the Civil
War may be less familiar:

Are those really Congressmen? are those the great Judges? is that
    the President?
Then I will sleep awhile yet, for I see that these States sleep, for
    reasons;
(With gathering murk, with muttering thunder and lambent shoots
    we all duly awake,
South, North, East, West, inland and seaboard, we will surely
    awake.)

How well, with what firmness and dignity and command, Whitman
does such passages! And Whitman's doubts that he has done them or
anything else well – ah, there is nothing he does better:

The best I had done seemed to me blank and suspicious,
My great thoughts as I supposed them, were they not in reality
    meagre?
I am he who knew what it was to be evil,
I too knitted the old knot of contrariety . . .
Saw many I loved in the street or ferry-boat or public assembly, yet
    never told them a word,

Lived the same life with the rest, the same old laughing, gnawing,
  sleeping,
Played the part that still looks back on the actor and actress,
The same old role, the role that is what we make it . . .

Whitman says once that the 'look of the bay mare shames silliness
out of me.' This is true – sometimes it is true; but more often the
silliness and affection and cant and exaggeration are there shame-
lessly, the Old Adam that was in Whitman from the beginning and
the awful new one that he created to keep it company. But as he
says, 'I know perfectly well my own egotism,/Know my omni-
vorous lines and must not write any less.' He says over and over that
there are in him good and bad, wise and foolish, anything at all and
its antonym, and he is telling the truth; there is in him almost
everything in the world, so that one responds to him, willingly or
unwillingly, almost as one does to the world, that world which
makes the hairs of one's flesh stand up, which seems both evil beyond
any rejection and wonderful beyond any acceptance. We cannot
help seeing that there is something absurd about any judgement we
make of its whole – for there is no 'point of view' at which we can
stand to make the judgement, and the moral categories that mean
most to us seem no more to apply to its whole than our spatial or
temporal or causal categories seem to apply to its beginning or its
end. (But we need no arguments to make our judgements seem
absurd – we feel their absurdity without argument.) In some like
sense Whitman is a world, a waste with, here and there, systems
blazing at random out of the darkness. Only an innocent and rigidly
methodical mind will reject it for this disorganization, particularly
since there are in it, here and there, little systems as beautifully and
astonishingly organized as the rings and satellites of Saturn:

I understand the large hearts of heroes,
The courage of present times and all times,
How the skipper saw the crowded and rudderless wreck of the
  steam-ship, and Death chasing it up and down the storm,
How he knuckled tight and gave not back an inch, and was faithful
  of days and faithful of nights,
And chalked in large letters on a board, Be of good cheer, we will
  not desert you;
How he follow'd with them and tack'd with them three days and
  would not give it up,

How he saved the drifting company at last,
How the lank loose-gown'd women looked when boated from the
   side of their prepared graves,
How the silent old-faced infants and the lifted sick, and the
   sharp-lipp'd unshaved men;
All this I swallow, it tastes good, I like it well, it becomes mine,
I am the man, I suffered, I was there.

In the last lines of this quotation Whitman has reached – as great writers always reach – a point at which criticism seems not only unnecessary but absurd: these lines are so good that even admiration feels like insolence, and one is ashamed of anything that one can find to say about them. How anyone can dismiss or accept patronizingly the man who wrote them, I do not understand.

The enormous and apparent advantages of form, of omission and selection, of the highest degree of organization, are accompanied by important disadvantages – and there are far greater works than *Leaves of Grass* to make us realize this. But if we compare Whitman with that very beautiful poet Alfred Tennyson, the most skilful of all Whitman's contemporaries, we are at once aware of how limiting Tennyson's forms have been, of how much Tennyson has had to leave out, even in those discursive poems where he is trying to put everything in. Whitman's poems *represent* his world and himself much more satisfactorily than Tennyson's do his. In the past a few poets have both formed and represented, each in the highest degree; but in modern times what controlling, organizing, selecting poet has created a world with as much in it as Whitman's, a world that so plainly *is* the world? Of all modern poets he has, quantitatively speaking, 'the most comprehensive soul' – and, qualitatively, a most comprehensive and comprehending one, with charities and concessions and qualifications that are rare in any time.

'Do I contradict myself? Very well then I contradict myself,' wrote Whitman, as everybody remembers, and this is not naïve, or something he got from Emerson, or a complacent pose. When you organize one of the contradictory elements out of your work of art, you are getting rid not just of it, but of the contradiction of which it was a part; and it is the contradictions in works of art which make them able to represent to us – as logical and methodical generalizations cannot – our world and our selves, which are also full of contradictions. In Whitman we do not get the controlled, compressed, seemingly concordant contradictions of the great lyric poets, of a poem like, say, Hardy's 'During Wind and Rain'; Whitman's contradictions are sometimes announced openly, but are more often scattered at random throughout the poems. For instance: Whitman specializes in ways of saying that there is in some sense (a very Hegelian one, generally) no evil – he says a hundred times that evil is not Real; but he also specializes in making lists of the evil of the world, lists of an unarguable reality. After his minister has recounted 'the rounded catalogue divine complete', Whitman comes home and puts down what has been left out: 'the countless (nineteen-twentieths) low and evil, crude and savage . . . the barren soil, the evil men, the slag and hideous rot'. He ends another such catalogue with the plain unexcusing 'All these – all meanness and agony without end I sitting look out upon,/ See, hear, and am silent'. Whitman offered himself to everybody, and said brilliantly and at length what a good thing he was offering:

> Sure as the most certain sure, plumb in the uprights,
>   well entretied, braced in the beams,
> Stout as a horse, affectionate, haughty, electrical,
> I and this mystery here we stand.

Just for oddness, characteristicalness, differentness, what more could you ask in a letter of recommendation? (Whitman sounds as if he were recommending a house – haunted, but what foundations!) But after a few pages he is oddly different:

> Apart from the pulling and hauling stands what I am,
> Stands amused, complacent, compassionating, idle, unitary,
> Looks down, is erect, or bends an arm on an impalpable
>   certain rest
> Looking with side curved head curious what will come next,
> Both in and out of the game and watching and wondering at it.

Tamburlaine is already beginning to sound like Hamlet: the employer feels uneasily, 'Why, I might as well hire myself . . .' And, a few pages later, Whitman puts down in ordinary-sized type, in the middle of the page, this warning to any *new person drawn toward me:*

Do you think I am trusty and faithful?
Do you see no further than this façade, this smooth and tolerant
  manner of me?
Do you suppose yourself advancing on real ground toward a real
  heroic man?
Have you no thought O dreamer that it may be all maya, illusion?

Having wonderful dreams, telling wonderful lies, was a temptation
Whitman could never resist; but telling the truth was a temptation
he could never resist, either. When you buy him you know what
you are buying. And only an innocent and solemn and systematic
mind will condemn him for his contradictions: Whitman's catalogues of evils represent realities, and his denials of their reality
represent other realities, of feeling and intuition and desire. If he is
faithless to logic, to Reality As It Is – whatever that is – he is faithful
to the feel of things, to reality as it seems; this is all that a poet has to
be faithful to, and philosophers have been known to leave logic and
Reality for it.

Whitman is more coordinate and parallel than anybody, is *the*
poet of parallel present participles, of twenty verbs joined by a single
subject: all this helps to give his work its feeling of raw hypnotic
reality, of being that world which also streams over us joined only
by *ands*, until we supply the subordinating conjunctions; and since as
children we see the *ands* and not the *becauses*, this method helps to
give Whitman some of the freshness of childhood. How inexhaustibly interesting the world is in Whitman! Arnold all his life
kept wishing that he could see the world 'with a plainness as near, as
flashing' as that with which Moses and Rebekah and the Argonauts
saw it. He asked with elegiac nostalgia, 'Who can see the green earth
any more/ As she was by the sources of Time?' – and all the time
there was somebody alive who saw it so, as plain and near and
flashing, and with a kind of calm, pastoral, Biblical dignity and
elegance as well, sometimes. The *thereness* and *suchness* of the world
are incarnate in Whitman as they are in few other writers.

They might have put on his tombstone WALT WHITMAN: HE
HAD HIS NERVE. He is the rashest, the most inexplicable and unlikely
– the most impossible, one wants to say – of poets. He somehow *is*
in a class by himself, so that one compares him with other poets
about as readily as one compares *Alice* with other books. (Even his

free verse has a completely different effect from anybody else's.)
Who would think of comparing him with Tennyson or Browning
or Arnold or Baudelaire? – it is Homer, or the sagas, or something
far away and long ago, that comes to one's mind only to be dismissed;
for sometimes Whitman *is* epic, just as *Moby-Dick* is, and it surprises
us to be able to use truthfully this word that we have misused so
many times. Whitman *is* grand, and elevated, and comprehensive,
and real with an astonishing reality, and many other things – the
critic points at his qualities in despair and wonder, all method failing,
and simply calls them by their names. And the range of these qualities
is the most extraordinary thing of all. We can surely say about him,
'He was a man, take him for all in all. I shall not look upon his like
again' – and wish that people had seen this and not tried to be his
like: one Whitman is miracle enough, and when he comes again it
will be the end of the world.

I have said so little about Whitman's faults because they are so
plain: baby critics who have barely learned to complain of the lack
of ambiguity in *Peter Rabbit* can tell you all that is wrong with
Leaves of Grass. But a good many of my readers must have felt that
it is ridiculous to write an essay about the obvious fact that Whitman
is a great poet. It is ridiculous – just as, in 1851, it would have been
ridiculous for anyone to write an essay about the obvious fact that
Pope was no 'classic of our prose' but a great poet. Critics have to
spend half their time reiterating whatever ridiculously obvious things
their age or the critics of their age have found it necessary to forget:
they say despairingly, at parties, that Wordsworth is a great poet,
and *won't* bore you, and tell Mr Leavis that Milton is a great poet
whose deposition *hasn't* been accomplished with astonishing ease by
a few words from Eliot . . . There is something essentially ridiculous
about critics, anyway: what is good is good without our saying so,
and beneath all our majesty we know this.

Let me finish by mentioning another quality of Whitman's – a
quality, delightful to me, that I have said nothing of. If some day a
tourist notices, among the ruins of New York City, a copy of *Leaves
of Grass*, and stops and picks it up and reads some lines in it, she will
be able to say to herself: 'How very American! If he and his country
had not existed, it would have been impossible to imagine them.'

DEFINING THE SELF:
THE POEMS OF EMILY DICKINSON
L. C. KNIGHTS

Emily Dickinson was born in 1830 in Amherst, in the Connecticut Valley of Massachusetts. Her lawyer father was not only a leading citizen of the town – he was for many years Treasurer of Amherst College – he also played a part in the political life of the State. Her elder brother, Austin, succeeded to his father's role in the town's affairs. Her younger sister, Lavinia, became, as she grew up, the practical housekeeper of the large family house, which had many visitors, political and academic. Emily had four years at primary school, seven years at Amherst Academy, and a year at Mount Holyoke Female Seminary. She was devoted to her home, and from her late twenties showed an increasing reluctance to leave it, or even to be seen by visitors. But if her outward life was uneventful, her inner life was intense and turbulent. She had a succession of – epistolary – love-affairs with men who were a good deal older than herself; and about 1873 there was some question of her marrying the elderly Judge of the Massachusetts Supreme Court, Otis Phillips Lord. It is very doubtful whether she would have relinquished her cherished privacy. Relations within the family, too, were affectionate but anything but straightforward, and towards the end of her life – when Austin, who had settled in a house built in the Dickinson grounds, was increasingly estranged from his wife – they can only be described as tragic.

Her life was in many ways a very full one. She kept up an extensive and varied correspondence, and from her late twenties she was regularly writing poems. A good many of these were enclosed, or included, in her letters. But until near the end of her life those whose professional opinions she respected offered plenty of sympathy but little encouragement to print. As with Hopkins in England, her markedly individual style was well outside the boundaries of current taste, and with the exception of six pieces none of her poems was published until after her death in 1886. The first substantial selection appeared in 1890, soon to be followed by other collections. In 1955 *The Poems of Emily Dickinson*, in three volumes, 'including variant readings critically compared with all known manuscripts', appeared, edited by Thomas H. Johnson, who subsequently brought out a one-volume edition, faithful to the earliest known texts, but without the variants.

The year 1974 saw the publication of *The Life of Emily Dickinson*, in two volumes, by Richard B. Sewall, which is indispensable to the student of the poems. This authoritative work demolishes, finally, the myth of Emily Dickinson as 'the lovable but eccentric genius, the fragile secluded flower'. Her life was, in fact, withdrawn in ways that were, I think, detrimental to her poetry. But it is misleading to emphasize the seclusion too strongly. The figure that Sewall presents is that of 'a perceptive, critical, self-propelling person working hard in the midst of a busy town and a busy family and taking the measure of both'. She had far more for her mind and imagination to work on than her garden and the fields and woods she loved. She kept up with current affairs through the newspapers and through her interest in the public activities of her father and brother. She knew the Bible well enough to use it for familiar reference, quotation, or misquotation. (In her mid-thirties she told a correspondent that she had returned to reading the Bible: 'I had known it as an arid book but looking I saw how infinitely wise and merry it is.') Shakespeare was a life-long companion and stand-by. She read eagerly in current literature – the Brontës, Dickens, Mr and Mrs Browning ... (it is nice to find her, in a letter of October 1879, casually dropping in a quotation from Henry James's *The Europeans*). But the contemporary writer she seems to have admired above all was George Eliot. She was eager for each new work as it appeared, and for particulars of George Eliot's life. Replying to an inquiry from her favourite nieces, she wrote: '"What do I think of *Middlemarch*?" What do I think of glory?' At Amherst Academy and at Mount Holyoke, moreover, the curriculum covered scientific, as well as literary, historical and religious subjects. Geology and botany seem to have had an especial interest for her, and Sewall notes that in her teens her sense of precision 'was already showing itself in ... her herbarium, with its carefully printed Latin names for each item; and she was known among her friends for her detailed knowledge of the flora around Amherst.' Her work was, in many ways, a religious quest, but in a short poem that touches on her aloofness from any of the prevailing orthodoxies it was natural that she should clinch her epigram with a metaphor from science:

> 'Faith' is a fine invention
> When Gentlemen can *see* –
> But *Microscopes* are prudent
> In an Emergency.   (185)[1]

She has little to say directly about the great political and religious issues of the day, but one understands Ted Hughes when, in the fine Introduction to his little volume of Selections, he says that 'The powers that struggled for reconciliation in Emily Dickinson were no less than those which were unmaking and remaking America.'

There is no point in attempting a chronological survey of the poems. Thomas Johnson, who, if anybody, ought to know, declares 1862 'the most crucial and . . . historically eventful year of Emily Dickinson's life', and certainly she wrote more poems in that year – on average, one a day – than in any other. But her work does not fall into recognizable periods or phases, as is the case, for example, with Wordsworth or Yeats. If there is a boisterousness in a few of her early poems this is soon refined into a quite different form of energetic enjoyment. And very early she showed a dislike of public display –

> How dreary – to be – Somebody!
> How public – like a Frog –
> To tell one's name – the livelong June –
> To an admiring Bog!   (288)

– and an unwillingness to make emotional capital out of personal experiences so deep that they could only be touched with circumspection: she complained of those who 'talk of hallowed things aloud, and embarrass my dog'. It is this ingrained reserve or sense of decorum that sharpens her wit and enables her ironies. But whatever caused the formidable output of 1862, her major themes and her manner of coping with them were already established by then.

'Between extremities Man runs his course.' Emily Dickinson

would have understood that line from Yeats. On the one hand was an intense joy in the simple fact of being alive. 'I find ecstasy in living – the mere sense of living is joy enough,' she said to T. W. Higginson on his first visit, and when in a poem she says,

> How mighty 'twas – to be
> A Guest in this stupendous place (304)

there is evidence throughout her work that she meant it. 'Inebriate of Air', she even goes a little drunk to heaven, where

> Seraphs swing their snowy Hats –
> And Saints – to windows run –
> To see the Little Tippler
> Leaning against the – Sun – (214)

But opposed to this was an equally keen awareness of a force, or forces, that could all but overwhelm her. One was an experience that she evokes in the following poem.

> It was not Death, for I stood up,
> And all the Dead, lie down –
> It was not Night, for all the Bells
> Put out their Tongues, for Noon,
>
> . . . .
>
> When everything that ticked – has stopped –
> And Space stares all around –
> Or Grisly frosts – first Autumn morns,
> Repeal the Beating Ground –
>
> But most, like Chaos – Stopless – cool –
> Without a Chance, or Spar –
> Or even a Report of Land –
> To justify – Despair. (510)

This experience of Nothingness, of what Coleridge in a late poem ('Limbo') called 'positive Negation', is, I suppose, at some times and in some degree, known to very many people: two distinguished examples are William James's 'vastation' and Tolstoy's experience at Arzamas, both of them coming, with complete unexpectedness, to men of abounding vitality and creativeness.[2]

That Emily Dickinson was capable of such an experience – and of facing it coolly, even with wit ('the Bells/Put out their Tongues, for

Noon') – helped to make her the poet she was. But more often the
antagonist to Life was, simply, Death. Death was never far from her
attention. There is an especially revealing letter, written when she
was twenty-eight to her loved friends, Dr and Mrs Holland (*Letters*,
II, 341); and even before the Civil War (when 'Sorrow seems more
general than it did') early deaths in Amherst were appallingly
common. 'That *Bareheaded* life – under the grass,' she said, 'worries
one like a Wasp.' But there is no emotional slackness, nothing of
graveyard musings, in her poems on death. Just as her feeling for
Nature is not a vague Romantic indulgence – she knows intimately
what she is talking about – so mortality in her poems is known in
direct physical terms:

> The Cordiality of Death –
> Who drills his Welcome in. (286)

It is this sense of bodily presence, of something immediate and
unique, that gives to such poems their uncanny power, as in the
great 'I heard a Fly buzz – when I died –' (465), or, almost equally
well known,

> A Clock stopped –
> Not the Mantel's –
> Geneva's farthest skill
> Can't put the puppets bowing –
> That just now dangled still –
>
> An awe came on the Trinket!
> The Figures hunched, with pain –
> Then quivered out of Decimals –
> Into Degreeless Noon –
>
> It will not stir for Doctors –
> This Pendulum of snow –
> This Shopman importunes it –
> While cool – concernless No –
>
> Nods from the Gilded pointers –
> Nods from the Seconds slim –
> Decades of Arrogance between
> The Dial life –
> And Him – (287)

What we should notice here is not only the abrupt directness, the
weight borne by homely imagery, the 'Metaphysical' wit, but the

pausing rhythm of that central line when 'the Figures' (ambiguous word) quiver 'Into Degreeless Noon'. As Sewall says, for her, 'Noon became a token of the instantaneous, arrested present which is timelessness, or eternity, or heaven, when all accident or "grossness" is discarded and there is nothing left but essence.'

ⱴ These, then, if we care to put it so, are the terms of her problem: on the one hand an uncommonly heightened enjoyment of the mere experience of being alive, on the other a constant awareness of mortality. As for all poets worth their salt, the problem won't be shuffled off. What distinguishes Emily Dickinson is the single-mindedness with which she confronts this major theme. To hold both terms in a single thought, without avoiding or attenuating either of them, would be to transcend the problem; and the name she used for that transcendence was 'immortality'. Of course, as is usual in speaking of poetry, one gropes for terms. Even to speak of a 'problem', with its suggestion of a 'solution', is to externalize what is essentially an inner process – what Professor Sewall rightly calls her 'restless search for identity and vocation'. To reformulate what I have just been saying: her problem is that of any poet, to find her own integrity and, it is much the same thing, her own unique mode of expression. In a poem (670) she speaks of 'Ourself behind ourself, concealed' as something more awesome than any external terror; but 'The Mind is so near itself,' she said in a letter, 'it cannot see, distinctly.' To find that inner core, at once resistant and creative, all she could do was to labour at what, by the end of her twenties, she knew to be her inescapable vocation.

She was very much alone in her task. Neither the social nor the religious life of Amherst gave her what she needed. The frequent religious revivals left her unmoved, and in her more intimate letters she makes a point of her unorthodoxy. 'Mr S. preached in our church last Sabbath upon "predestination", but I do not respect "doctrines", and did not listen to him.' As a young woman, she confesses in a letter, a sermon upon death and judgement scared her; but she adds, characteristically, of the preacher, 'The subject of perdition seemed to please him, somehow.' In that time and at that place she was, to use her own frequent description, 'a pagan'.

Nor was the literary climate more congenial. When in April 1862 she sent a few poems to the well-known man of letters, T. W.

Higginson, asking him if he could find time to say if her verse 'breathed', she initiated a correspondence that was to continue intermittently throughout her life. Higginson was sympathetic but totally uncomprehending. His first response can be gathered from a subsequent letter from her to him: 'You think my gait "spasmodic" – I am in danger – Sir – You think me "uncontrolled" – I have no Tribunal.' Without a Tribunal, she saw that the only thing for her was to work relentlessly at what she sometimes called her Algebra.

> Bound – a trouble –
> And lives can bear it!
> Limit – how deep a bleeding go!
> So – many – drops – of vital scarlet –
> Deal with the soul
> As with Algebra!
>
> Tell it the Ages – to a cypher –
> And it will ache – contented – on –
> Sing – at its pain – as any Workman –
> Notching the fall of the Even Sun! (269)

Algebraist, workman, or, as she called herself in another poem (488), 'carpenter', she was bound to a craft or science that demanded application, precision and the greatest concentration of which she was capable. It was only by concentrating on her task and its technique that she could find her language for something so intimate as to be bafflingly elusive. 'The Sailor cannot see the North – but knows the Needle can.'

'Language', as I used it at the end of the last paragraph, has more than one meaning. Her primary tools were the common words of the English language, though her vocabulary also takes in geology, geography and exploration. Combining these in deceptively simple verse forms, she achieved concentration both by subtleties of rhythm and rhyme or half-rhyme, and by a frequent use of dashes, instead of conventional punctuation, which has the effect of breaking down grammatical categories with their implication of fixed meanings and relations. The pauses, however slight, allow the implied meanings, the connections and implications, to move into consciousness, with different degrees of presentness and emphasis, subtly controlling the reading voice. Ted Hughes, in the Introduction to his selection of the poems, has a brilliant paragraph on her 'deep, steady focus', 'the pictogram concentration of ideas'. Even the poems that give immediate pleasure expect an uncommonly active response –

> Until the peevish Student
> Acquire the quick of Skill. (545)

– lines that say a lot about education, the imagination, and the ways in which works of art exist in the lives they quicken.

> A word that breathes distinctly
> Has not the power to die. (1651)

Clearly, the reader's active collaboration with the poet's language – idiom, word-play, shifts of tone – is analogous to the creative power of the poet's mind in reciprocal play with all that surrounds it. And it is in that further sense that Emily Dickinson found the language of her deepest intuitions in the world of Nature. To do so was her only way of clarifying a mind 'so near itself' that 'it cannot see, distinctly'.

Not that she set out to create a symbolic language from that world: she began simply by enjoying it, as she continued to do. Just as she kept an herbarium she liked to pin down in words such things as the mushroom in its 'Truffled Hat' (1298), or the way in which hoarfrost transforms a leaf,

> November hung his Granite Hat
> Upon a nail of Plush – (1140)

She catches exactly the zig-zag movement of a bee (319), of a bird hopping and flying (328), of a cat stalking a robin,

> She sights a Bird – she chuckles –
> She flattens – then she crawls –
> She runs without the look of feet ... (507)

And it would be hard to find in verse a better snowscape than the poem that begins,

> It sifts from Leaden Sieves –
> It powders all the Wood.
> It fills with Alabaster Wool
> The Wrinkles of the Road – (311)

But we have only to call to mind her well-known poem on the snake to see that more is involved than observations and enjoyment.

A narrow Fellow in the Grass
Occasionally rides –
You may have met Him – did you not
His notice sudden is –
The Grass divides as with a Comb –
A spotted shaft is seen –
And then it closes at your feet
And opens further on –

He likes a Boggy Acre
A Floor too cool for Corn –
Yet when a Boy, and Barefoot –
I more than once at Noon
Have passed, I thought, a Whip lash
Unbraiding in the Sun
When stooping to secure it
It wrinkled, and was gone –

Several of Nature's People
I know, and they know me –
I feel for them a transport
Of cordiality –

But never met this Fellow
Attended, or alone
Without a tighter breathing
And Zero at the Bone –   (986)

We notice the easy familiarity of 'a narrow Fellow', the precision of 'The Grass divides as with a Comb' and 'a Whip lash/Unbraiding in the Sun', the uncannily effective way in which the verse movement is used in the descriptive section. And the observer's feeling is stated with the same economy, when the jaunty rhythm of the penultimate stanza brings out the stark contrast of the 'tighter breathing' of the close. The snake has not ceased to be a snake, but he is also a representative of the inhuman, the utterly alien, the 'earlier and other creation' invoked in Eliot's 'The Dry Salvages'. It is the familiar, almost affectionate observation that confirms the authenticity of the chillier apprehension: equally, the 'Zero at the Bone' is the correlative – one might almost say the condition – of the 'cordiality'.

But when I said that Emily Dickinson found a language in Nature, or in imagery derived from it, I meant something more than this. It is difficult to define, but in very many of her best poems it is something of her own mind that she finds in the non-human, whether in its joyful or its threatening aspects:

> Nature is what we know –
> Yet have no art to say – (668)

– to say, that is, in familiar conceptual terms. And if her language of joy and free movement is drawn from insects, birds, the movement of wind in trees, and so on, she also has a more sombre language of the weather, as in the superb 'There's a certain Slant of light' (258), of 'geology' – stones, rocks, alabaster, anthracite and volcanoes – and of nineteenth-century science in general. In the famous 'Safe in their Alabaster Chambers' (in the revised version), human death has an implacably cosmic setting.

> Grand go the Years – in the Crescent – above them –
> Worlds scoop their Arcs –
> And Firmaments – row –
> Diadems – drop – and Doges – surrender –
> Soundless as dots – on a Disc of Snow – (216)

Emily Dickinson, then, finds her courage and resolution not in mourning or defying the great implacables, but by assimilating, identifying with, the threatening forces. When these, without losing their actual identity, become part of her inner landscape they evoke and define energies of resistance. This quickening, fortifying activity is, of course, never stated; but it is implicit in what is presented with such stark simplicity.

> Four Trees – upon a solitary Acre –
> Without Design
> Or Order, or Apparent Action –
> Maintain –
>
> The Sun – upon a Morning meets them –
> The Wind –
> No nearer Neighbor – have they –
> But God –
>
> The Acre give them – Place –
> They – Him – Attention of Passer by –
> Of Shadow, or of Squirrel, haply –
> or Boy –

> What Deed is Theirs unto the General Nature –
> What Plan
> They severally – retard – or further –
> Unknown –   (742)

I am convinced that that is a great poem, though it is hard to say why. Perhaps an attempt to give the paraphrasable sense of the difficult third stanza is the best way of finding what is going on in the poem as a whole. We have been told that the trees have no nearer neighbour than God – indeed their solitariness in the landscape has been rather impressively emphasized, also the concentrated attention the poet is giving them. Now the question is implicitly posed: what does the solitary Acre do for them? Well, it gives them 'Place' – place in which to 'Maintain' (maintain themselves? maintain or keep alive something as one maintains a family? maintain or uphold *that* . . .?). Then the mind prepares itself for another implicit question: what do *they* give it? But when the answer comes it is not 'it' but 'Him', presumably God: 'They (give) Him' what is then briefly listed – they attract Attention from a Passer by; they break up the undifferentiated light into Shadow that gives depth and solidity (just as the wind gives them some movement); they bring the attention of a squirrel (there's life there as well as the stir of the wind); perhaps a boy glances at them. That's all: not much, one may say; but the poem is about minimal relationships, and although the mutual gifts are not negligible it is impossible to base on them large statements about God or Nature or the purpose of it all:

> What Deed is theirs unto the General Nature –
> What Plan
> They severally – retard – or further –
> Unknown –

The one-word final line parallels and, across several other muted rhymes, goes back to the one word 'Maintain' that closes the first stanza. The two words balance, not cancel out, each other. The poem is totally agnostic ('Unknown'): but all the same the trees maintain – support – something (squirrels, the poet . . ., though if they 'maintain that . . .' the noun clause doesn't appear).

So what we come back to is not just the trees, but the observer. *She* has maintained, kept up, the steady regard for what is not

especially remarkable – the group of trees – but simply there. The
fact that they *are* there, in their simple undemanding relationship
with other not especially remarkable things or persons, is a mystery
worth contemplating: and in making it a matter for contemplation
– she does a lot with those pondering pauses – she has affirmed,
fairly toughly, her own place in the world.

It is, then, a disturbing but – the paradox seems justified – a
beautifully unruffled poem. The steady focus, the minute details of
phrase or rhythm that convey so much, the recognition that the bare
fact of existence is matter for wonder, and the refusal to go beyond
that, are all signs of a master craftsman who, simply by being true to
her craft, resolved conflicts that were indeed intensely personal, and
yet are common to us all.

There are of course large tracts of experience that Emily Dickinson
takes no account of. But if one sometimes feels that the exclusion is
excessive (as in 'The Soul selects her own Society – /Then – shuts the
Door', 303), one also has to recognize that a condition of her success
was exclusion and concentration. Sometimes, when reading straight
through a number of her poems, we may feel more aware of the
pain of creation – 'Essential Oils', she said, 'are wrung' (675) – than
of any kind of Shakespearean abundance or Blakean 'exuberance'.
But if she is rarely exuberant – and she sometimes is – she had the
resilience that comes from something even more important than 'a
good look at the worst'. Where she found that resilience was,
simultaneously, in 'the self behind the self, concealed' and in the
very world that menaced her: together they produced that *tertium
quid*, neither pure description nor pure introspection, in the few
score of poems that will ensure that she continues to be read.
When she found her concealed self in the objects she so steadfastly
contemplates,

> Either the Darkness alters –
> Or something in the sight
> Adjusts itself to Midnight –
> And Life steps almost straight. (419)

ACKNOWLEDGEMENT

An earlier version of this chapter first appeared in the *Sewanee Review* 91 (Summer 1983). Copyright 1983 by L. C. Knights. Reprinted by permission of the editor.

NOTES

1. Poems are numbered as in the one-volume *Complete Poems of Emily Dickinson*, edited by Thomas H. Johnson.
2. Gay Wilson Allen, *William James: A Biography*, pp. 165–7; Henri Troyat, *Tolstoy*, pp. 316–21.

MARK TWAIN

ERIC MOTTRAM

The thrust of the grotesque in the midst of the apparently normal, exuberant life of Mark Twain (1835–1910) triggered that double of unease and excitement that shaped his strategies of humour. In *Roughing It* (volume 1, 1871), he presents the gold frontier California as 'a wild, free, disorderly, grotesque society! *Men* – only swarming hosts of stalwart *men* – nothing juvenile, nothing feminine, visible anywhere!' But then the female challenges wildness, as it would throughout his career, and violent human demand breaks through human consideration. Moreover, money appears as an ambivalent solvent. When a dress is glimpsed hanging from a wagon, the miners demand to see the rare woman. Her husband protests they have been robbed by Indians and his wife is sick. But he is made to 'fetch her out'. The miners cheer, gaze, touch her dress and collect twenty-five hundred dollars for the couple. In the following chapter, Twain spends in San Francisco as a prospector and stock investor spends, is duly beggared like many others, 'enjoyed my first earthquake', and, twenty chapters later, ends up desperately turning to language for money. In his lectures, 'inferior jokes never fared so royally before'. But they saved him, temporarily. He had enough experience; the grotesque paid.

Two years earlier, the end of *The Innocents Abroad* (1869) had suggested another kind of need when Twain, with considerably high-toned rhetoric, writes of the resistance of the Sphinx to American – indeed, human – aggression in the figure of the 'iconoclast'.[1] The Sphinx epitomizes, in art, a transcendental need which Twain believes to be reflected in its face, a sad and earnest dignity and benignity. This gaze looks '*at* nothing', through Time towards 'the horizon of remote antiquity', the chronicle of departed conflict and power (the subject of Twain's lifelong desire to write of the

166

Middle Ages), and a levelling reminder of inexorable process and judgement:

> It was MEMORY – RETROSPECTION – wrought into visible, tangible form . . . the stony dreamer solitary in the midst of a strange new age, and uncomprehended scenes . . . with its accusing memory of the deeds of all ages, which reveals to one something of what he shall feel when he shall stand at last in the awful presence of God.

But it is still violable by the relic hunter's hammer, the American need to conquer. Twain's notebooks connect this 'iconoclast' with 'the Commissioner of the United States of America to Europe, Asia and Africa', collecting for 'the Smithsonian Institute', an image-breaker, and by 'the laws of Egypt' a criminal. The writing here uses no devices of humour, certainly not irony, the cheaper form social critics employ to boast their superiority, and no dialectical interplay towards some sophistry posing as solution. Twain did not suddenly confront the limits of humour in his later career.

Certainly, after 1889 and *A Connecticut Yankee in King Arthur's Court* his suspicion that the human race was damned intensified. In 1951, in his essay 'Decline and Fall of Mark Twain', Henry Seidel Canby pointed up the more complex circumstances of Twain's career:

> Something was wrong with him, and it is not enough to say that his shift from a confident optimism to a bitter cynicism merely reflects a changed mood in his overconfident country . . . He had undoubtedly shifted with his times from the extravagant optimism of Walt Whitman and his own Colonel Sellers [*The Gilded Age*, 1873] and from Manifest Destiny to the social criticism of the eighties and nineties and the Henry and Brooks Adamses who, like Henry James, believed that America, having over-run a continent, had failed to make a civilization. Thoughtful Americans by the later decades of the century had come to believe that the American dream of a brotherhood of equality had been sold in the market place and was indeed only a dream . . . [But Twain] seems to have had from youth a horrid fascination, like a boy's for gangster pictures, for the depravities of early history. Suetonius was his bedside book, and he revelled in his debauched tyrants who stood for civilization in their day. (ed. A. L. Scott, *Mark Twain – Selected Criticism*, 1955)

Canby sees Twain as 'a neurotic genius . . . a mind of too great sensitivity' in the line of Poe, Hawthorne, Jeffers and Faulkner, and cites events in his early life, his guilts and self-torture, the Civil War legacy. But in fact the neurosis is also in the nation and its behaviour, and Twain responds to that, although no doubt urged into the controls of writing by his own proclivities. At the end of his life, in *The Mysterious Stranger* (1897–1908), Twain has his young hero's sense of sad benignity destroyed by the angelic intelligence of Satan, demystifying any inclination towards a redemptive world of humane alternative ideology. Life may be a dream but it is 'a grotesque and foolish dream'. Where the Sphinx appeared to be gazing in thought on memory in eternity, Satan tells young Theodore Fischer: 'You are but an empty thought, a useless thought, a homeless thought, wandering forlorn among empty eternities!' Fischer's text concludes: 'He vanished and left me appalled, for I knew, and realized, that all he said was true.'

The lecture with jokes in *Roughing It* became a staple of Samuel Clemens' livelihood. Using the joker's powers of deflation and analysis to cause involuntary laughter, itself a cause of the joker's popularity, proved irresistible. But Clemens understood that he needed to isolate and baptize this other half in his schizophrenic life, the duplicitous verbalizer of criticism of his own society. Mark Twain became the instrumentalist confronting the decays of civilization as farce, the form of comedy which contains the most hysteria. But he is the contemporary of Nietzsche (1844–1900), another angel of the annunciation that the god men invented is dead everywhere, leaving the Absurd as the only living space. Operating in the theatre Twain left vacant, Henry Miller writes in *The World of Lawrence* (1932–8):

All the lies and evasions by which man has nourished himself – *civilization* in a word – are the fruits of the creative artist. It is the creative nature of man which has refused to let him lapse back into that unconscious unity with life which characterizes the animal world from which he made his escape.

So civilization is man-made and inescapable – unless you 'light out for the Territory', as the twelve-year-old Huckleberry Finn decides at the conclusion of his *Adventures*. This 'man' originally needed the garden-prison from which he escaped, the myth reports. In America, the West represented a mythic place in which to replay the escape story, which was one of the games the settlers played in puritan New Canaan in the seventeenth century, in the hope of reconstituting a harmonious life within God's Covenant, with the harmonious blacksmith singing at his limited technology. The Territory west that Huck intends to explore has to be carefully dated to the era before territorial rights have been established with barbed wire and windmill, although the gun and the axe had been instrumental for some time. And dated, too, before the wreck of United States unity exposed in 1860 and the Civil War 'secession' from that South Twain was born in, and knew well, as resistance via its slavery and aristocratism. Barbed wire began to enclose the West in 1874, although the Plains were already controlled then by the six-shooter Colt. Such is the history encapsulated in the last words of *The Adventures of Huckleberry Finn* (1885), with their contemptuous misspelling of the key word of American pride:

> Tom's most well now, and got his bullet around his neck on a watch-guard for a watch, and is always seeing what time it is . . . But I reckon I got to light out for the Territory ahead of the rest, because Aunt Sally she's going to adopt me and sivilize me, and I can't stand it, I been there before.

'Time is money', and adoption and civilizing constitute that training for the State, that behaviouristic method, which obsessed Twain. The bullet next to the watch is the crucial conjunction, and it is the gun, the watch and the compass which another youngster, Ike McCaslin, will have to relinquish in his confrontation with the wilderness in order to get at least partly free from civilization in the South (William Faulkner's *Go Down, Moses*, 1942). And Ike has Sam Fathers, of part Indian and part Negro origin, to help him. Huck is Twain's moral imagination at work hoping against knowledge, in 1885, that a white child might contain an aboriginal power to recognize the parental system for what it is: destructive to the point of cannibalism, with Christianity at its malign core. The comedy is to emerge in the hope and constitute at least a minimal reassurance. But as Miller reminds us in his Lawrence book, Nietzsche wrote in the postscript to *The Birth of Tragedy* (1872): 'I appended hopes where there was no ground for hope.' Huck appreciates the grotesque that society has become, but through him Twain coheres something of where the necessities for disobedience initially lie, should a critical adult grow up in opposition to his training. The book deconstructs mainline insistencies in the modern state: the family as nucleus of order and its values, and the father, the parental, the oedipal as its legal basis. The humour emerges from resources which still might challenge these assumed necessities, traditions of authority – Shakespearian infatuation with kings and dukes and such, book-centred obedience (Tom Sawyer's life-style), and slavery embedded in the regulations of the Fugitive Slave Act (the very law Huck has to disobey to maintain his newly discovered human relationship with Jim, the fugitive slave). The laugh for the comedian as social critic inserts trouble into the familiar, brings the audience towards the risking edge. Meanings break. The social has either to re-establish or reform itself.

Mark Twain therefore risked everything, including popularity and the respect of his wife, as Clemens' writing twin in black humour against white tyranny, his crucial technique for depth-sounding the American condition. In his memoir and critique of the South, *Life on the Mississippi* (1883), Twain intimates the source of his self-baptism as a cultural leadsman. The Mississippi riverboat *Paul Jones* nears a dangerous crossing. Clemens, the cub pilot, aged twenty-two, is suddenly in charge. He had admired the skills of the heroic pilot, Horace Bixby, as he listens to the signals of the fathoms beneath the boat and navigates her through. The odds narrow in the 'marks', and 'it was done beautiful', 'a marvellous precision'. Someone remarks, 'By the Shadow of Death, but he's a lightning pilot!' The terms of the fathoming were to penetrate Clemens for ever. The future writer's necessary gift is a hindrance when it comes to his turn to navigate a shoal: 'My imagination began to construct dangers out of nothing, and they multiplied faster than I could keep the run of them.' 'Coward agony' dislocates his confidence. In panic he stops the engines as the leadsman sings out 'Quarter twain! *Mark* twain!' and it looks like the end. But this is Bixby's test. The cub knew 'there was no bottom in that crossing'; he should have kept his confidence in that knowledge.

The other pilot, Mr Brown, suffers from memory – he has not simply the pilot's necessary master-memory of the Mississippi but an automatic storage mechanism, a hindrance to discrimination the future writer will resist: 'a great misfortune . . . its possessor cannot distinguish an interesting circumstance from an uninteresting one. As a talker, he is bound to clog his narrative with tiresome details and make himself an insufferable bore.'

Bixby and Brown haunt Twain's subsequent career, and the duplicities of the twin or twain character obsess his investigations (excellently explored in Justin Kaplan's *Mr Clemens and Mark Twain*, 1966). The *Paul Jones* episode also broaches Twain's fear of loss of control, of being abandoned in a godless – indeed, baseless – world, the controls of which are irresistible. In *The Innocents Abroad*, American pilgrims to the 'Holy Land' on the *Quaker City* (that is, of brotherly love – Philadelphia, the founding city) grow excited for a possible 'little private miracle' on Galilee: 'Never before had I known them to lose their self-possession when a question of expenses was before the tribe.' A slight if indicative episode – but decades later, an American family is abandoned to eternal loss of control on a far from holy sea in 'The Great Dark' (*c.* 1897), in its origins part of the late batch of fictions using the convention of a visitor to human civilization noting its absurd hypocrisies and cruelties – *The Mysterious Stranger* (*c.* 1905), and 'Letters from the Earth' (in Bernard DeVoto's collection of that title, 1963). In these two fictions Twain represents the American venturing into an older territory than his nation's immediacies, and finding exuberant national optimism challenged and finally undermined by fixed existential forces in behaviour. The world becomes as it had been exemplified in Melville's *The Confidence-Man* in 1857, a system of exploitation whose conditions cannot be resolved into comedy beyond satire. Twain became unable to publish a good deal of his writings because they emerged from that entry from Pudd'nhead Wilson's 'Calendar' prefacing the final chapter of his novel: 'October 12. – It was wonderful to find America, but it would have been more wonderful to miss it.'

The Adventures of Huckleberry Finn remains one of the world's great books. But not surprisingly, it has been banned and censored ever since its first publication. Official educationists and simplistic guardians of public morals find the book unacceptable. Some find Twain a racist, although the evidence shows him constantly supporting black Americans, and *The New York Times* published a lately authenticated letter in its issue for 14 March 1985, in which Twain says: 'We have ground the manhood out of them [the black Americans], & the shame is ours, not theirs, & we should pay for it.' But judgements on the book range from 'the most grotesque example of racist trash ever written' (Dr John H. Wallace, Chicago School Board, 1985) to 'one of the most devastating attacks on racism ever written', from Sterling Stuckey, a black professor of history at Northwestern University. One accusation can be immediately scotched: Twain never himself called the escaped slave Jim 'nigger'. The novel is presented as a text in the invented language of a twelve-year-old learning to survive a hostile supremacist South, a drunken and murderous father, a massive river, and human examples of American competitive permission which will stop at nothing in the exploitation of anyone for anything. The word 'nigger' would be a commonplace for the boy and anyone else in the South, as it still is. The turning point indeed comes with Huck's rejection of the lore within the word. His untutored and instinctual humane morality contradicts his training. In chapter 25, the very word 'nigger' is deconstructed by the boy's lonely discovery by experience that his education is wrong. He has just betrayed Jim's confidence and love, and the black American tells him so with pointed dignity:

> It made me feel I could almost kissed *his* foot to get him to take it back. It was fifteen minutes before I could work myself up to go and humble myself to a nigger – but I done it and I warn't sorry for it afterward, neither. I didn't do him no more mean tricks, and I wouldn't done that one if I'd knowed it would make him feel that way.

Training is broken by essential mutuality, and this leads to Huck's breaking of the law. In fact, the brief mutual aid society of freedom on 'a little section of a lumber raft' lasts four short chapters, about thirteen pages or so. The rest is Huck's adventures in the absurd, cruel violences of the South, and the invasion of the hard-won freedom between a middle-aged black and a juvenile white. It is the unbroken and legal education in Tom Sawyer which nearly loses Jim's release in the final essential chapters of the book – a boy trained to obey and arrogantly maintain the parental status quo, and live by unexamined regulation and book-fetishism, willing to sacrifice a man for 'the *adventure* of it'. Huck's adventures partly rectify his 'bringing-up', but the American situation cannot change, nor can Jim's character – and he is certainly not 'freed' by Huck and Tom, but by his owner's testament in deathbed shame.

The narrative is Huck's – his escape from controlling adults, his enterprises, his escape West – and he is officially dead throughout, ready to discover a second identity in order to survive civilization. Both he and Jim are considered by that society in terms of property and money. Jim is a man disguised as a slave; Huck is a boy who goes through multiple disguises as the process of education. Duplicity and violation of law and custom: James M. Cox puts it well in 'Some Remarks on the Sad Initiation of Huckleberry Finn' in *Sewanee Review* (1954):

> Huck's motives, arising from his struggle for survival, allow him to indulge no impracticalities, but he knows the fugitive must rely on magic and superstition to propitiate the inscrutable powers which confront him. The wedding of the practical and the magical gives Huck's character a mobility in the constricting circumstances which envelop him . . . Every living thing becomes a source of danger to the lost boy without a name. (ed. Barry A. Marks, *Mark Twain's Huckleberry Finn*, 1959)

And Cox adds: 'Jim is the conscience of the novel, the spiritual yardstick by which all men are measured.' But it is Tom Sawyer who will inherit and continue the South; and the West, by the time the novel had been written, had long since become the territory of Billy the Kid and the Lincoln County wars.

Twain lived in a curious internal exile, a popular public figure, employed by the government – for instance – to welcome Maxim Gorki, and a disturbed private moralist. When Charles Neider published his edition of Twain's *Autobiography* in 1959, his estate still prohibited the publication of certain sections. Detection of concealed private life is the essence of *The Tragedy of Pudd'nhead Wilson* (1894), Twain's primary use of the most popular form of fiction developed in the nineteenth century, a narrative of sardonically observed strategies of exile and cunning. The initial perpetrator in one plot is black, female and enslaved, defeated by the society she planned to defeat by switching her baby son with the son of her owner, easily managed since her son, like herself, is visibly white. The second plot concerns actual twins rather than apparent ones: Italian aristocrats who enslave a Southern town obsessed with aristocracy. A third plot links them and brings them to the point of change. David Wilson, a young white lawyer from the East, is condemned to twenty-six years' internal exile which prevents him from his profession, after he made a joke to the locals, upon his arrival, natives so witless as to assume Wilson must be daft, a pudd'nhead. Moral for comedians: never make a joke to the stupid; they have a power you have not. Twain knew his paymasters. *Pudd'nhead Wilson* explores the consequences of what Brecht called 'the joke of contradiction' in a passage which can help to explain the need for humour in any competitive and racist society:

> It is not just a matter of art presenting what needs to be learned in an enjoyable form. The contradiction between learning and enjoyment must be clearly grasped and its significance understood – in a period when knowledge is acquired in order to be resold for the highest possible price, and even a high price does not prevent further exploitation by those who pay for it. Only once productivity has been set free can learning be transformed into enjoyment and vice versa.

'To make dialectics into a source of enjoyment', special techniques are required:

> The unexpectedness of logically progressive or zigzag development, the instability of every circumstance, the joke of contradiction and so forth: all these are ways of enjoying the liveliness of men, things and processes, and they heighten our capacity for life and our pleasure in it.
>
> (*Brecht on Theatre*, 1964, pp. 276–80)

Classic comedy dramatizes possible destructions of a social scene but concludes with a new equilibrium of traditional values. Twain discovered that he could never rely on such a recovery, not even in the order of fiction, however grotesque. David Wilson is dubbed fool by a civilization who cannot recognize a joke and operates as fate. He recovers by gaining a then exceptional skill – the classification of fingerprints – signs of absolute individuality which evade all duplicities, whether by black or white, male or female. He wins back his right to profess as a lawyer by detection beyond speculation.

Twain, the critic of American competitiveness, speculated himself to the point of bankruptcy. Money, machines and schemes obsessed him. His letters to his publishers testify to his absorption in the newly profitable market for fiction. The author of *The Gilded Age* and 'The Man That Corrupted Hadleyburg' lived deep in the book trade and its popularity stakes. The newly popular detective story stereotypes seduced him; easy parody and burlesque tempted him. The allegorical speculations of his last texts are a constellation of dreams of disaster whose wit is virtually humour-less. In 'Which Was It?' George Harrison speculates to the point where 'that ghastly sinking at the heart which comes when we realize that the horror which seemed a dream was not a dream but reality . . . is an overwhelming moment, the last perfection of human misery, it is death in life'. Doubleness is intensified in 'In-diantown' through David Grindley, writer of 'fierce and bloody Indian tales':

> . . . there being two of him – the one that God made and another one . . . [one] was a sufficiently indifferent piece of work, but it was at least not a sham – all its parts were genuine; but the other one was all shame; there was not a genuine fibre in it. It was the work of Mrs Gridley . . . [she] put an entirely new outside on David – a shiny new outside, and fine to consider . . . the only one the world knew . . . The real David, the inside David, the hidden David, was of an incurable low tone, and wedded to low ideals; the outside David . . . was of a lofty tone, with ideals which the angels in heaven might envy. The real David had a native affection for all vulgarities, and his natural speech was at home and happy only when it was mephitic with them . . . The real David clothed the truth . . . the sham David turned it loose on the world naked.

The ambiguity of values here is the generative source of Twain's strengths and nervousness, the creative tensions between civilization and its discontents, the fruitful region between society and repression. Analytic wit and humour must contain them, but the grotesque product remains to haunt. *A Double-Barrelled Detective Story* (1902) begins with an epigraph: 'We ought never to do wrong when people are looking.' 'The joke of contradiction' then proceeds from the need to debunk the mystique of superior detective ability. In revenge a Virginian exposes his wife, bound and naked, to his bloodhounds, and leaves her. Years later, her son Archie has become a brilliant tracker-detective in New England, smelling out traces like a dog. His mother says to herself: 'It's a birth-mark! The gift of the blood-hound is in him!' The obverse of this 'grand natural animal talent' minus intellect is Sherlock Holmes, newly invited to Cali-fornia in the 1880s by his weak nephew Fetlock Jones – who promptly exposes him: 'He can't detect a crime except when he plans it all out beforehand and arranges the clues and hires some fellow to commit it according to his instructions.' It is what Harold Rosenberg called 'the tradition of the new', from Godwin and Poe, through Dickens and Conan Doyle to Twain, and on to the repetitive present.

But the most savage detection is self-detection. The reversals in 'The Facts Concerning the Carnival of Crime in Connecticut' (1876) exemplify Twain's extraordinary sense of the security and insecurity of an apparently assured society. As Huck says: 'It don't make no difference whether you do right or wrong, a person's conscience ain't got no sense and just goes for him *anyway*.' He has to refound his conscience. The narrative of 'The Facts . . .' has the jaunty, self-assured tone of a company director who has successfully resisted unwanted morality, the type of the successful businessman, lawyer, police commissioner, state administrator and Mafia man. Confronted in his office by 'a shrivelled, shabby dwarf', 'a nicely adjusted deformity' who bears 'a sort of remote and ill-defined resemblance to himself', except that he is 'covered all over with a fuzzy, greenish mould', he attacks. The dwarf taunts him with a list of dishonest and treacherous acts of power. The creature could be Satan himself, but he is the narrator's own conscience. The director springs at him in 'a blaze of joy and exultation' but the dwarf floats to the ceiling with considerable authority. In a parody of the excessive Puritan conscience, he will force the director to repent *everything* he does. The director accuses him of undermining society. When a momentary twinge of remorse brings the dwarf down, he tears the creature apart and burns 'the bleeding rubbish' – 'My Conscience was dead, I was a free man.'

His divided life over, he engages his pleasure principle in mass murder, swindles and other crimes, including buying up tramps for 'scientific purposes'. The exhilarated prose is the vehicle of release from training, from moral laws which obscure the hedonistic pleasures of self-reliance and free enterprise. After all, where is the defined frontier between the elimination of interference and its murder? Honest competition is still honest. 'The Man That Corrupted Hadleyburg' (1899) probes the semantics of honesty and once again uses revenge as a man's means to retribution. The revenger offers immense wealth to a claimant who is dishonest, and sets the untried town with a reputation for honesty on a course to destruction. It has prayed 'Lead us not into temptation'; the townspeople fear the opportunity for unearned wealth as 'the wages of sin'; one man, Richards, believes that it is blasphemous to refuse it as part of the ordering of Providence. Nineteen principled citizens have been tempted to claim the money with letters from the unknown writer. The town is saved from scandal because Richards' letter has somehow been omitted. The perpetrator writes: 'My idea was to make liars and thieves of nearly half a hundred smirchless men and women who had never in their lives uttered a lie or stolen a penny.' Richards and his wife are to be rewarded, and again they yield to the idea of wealth: 'We couldn't help it, Mary. It – well, it was ordered. *All* things are.' So their consciences 'were quieting down, discouraged'. But trained guilt reasserts itself. They become ill with concealment. On his deathbed Richards confesses. The town changes its name, and changes its motto from *Lead Us Not Into Temptation* to *Lead Us Into Temptation*.

So the questions of Providence and universals are opened and secularized as a release from hypocrisy. With the Civil War, the duplicities of unity between the States ended, and the Mississippi was closed. The jobless Clemens went West to the predatory communities of the mining camps and to the use of his pseudonym for the first time as a reporter on the *Territorial Enterprise* in 1862. Thirty-seven years later the vestiges of practical, exuberant optimism vanish into the controlled hysteria of the exchange between an old and a young man in 'What is Man?'. The former is a materialist Theodore Dreiser would recognize: man is a helpless chemical machine, so controlled by forces that he can have no original ideas or freedom of will. The figure of originating, creativity, willpower and that command over self and not-self which man calls God, does not exist beyond imagination. The young man tries to rescue something: what about Shakespeare? The old man replies: 'Shakespeare invented nothing. He observed, portrayed what had been created, but could create nothing himself: he was a machine, and machines do not create.' When a timid man tries to overcome cowardice, 'it shows the value of training in the right directions . . . training one's self-approbation to elevate its ideals'. In common with the turn of the century behaviourists, Twain believed, as B. F. Skinner will also in the 1960s, that 'training is all there is *to* a man'. His audience was not the sophisticated or 'cultivated' classes. In letters to Andrew Lang in the 1890s, he explained his identification with 'the mighty mass of the uncultivated' which 'has no voice in print' – he 'always hunted for bigger game – the masses'.

The horror of *Pudd'nhead Wilson* is that once the white boy trained as a slave is released, his life is 'terror', 'misery', 'embarrassing'. The black slave is simply sold down the river – that is, into the hell of plantation slavery. The conditioned becomes unconditional. The joke of contradiction ends abruptly. The Christian republic is identical with the terrorism of mechanistic forces. As Wright Morris says in an introduction to the novel, 'we hear Satan, off stage, snickering'. In 'Letters from the Earth', Satan reports back to his employer, God, in his heavenly dictatorship, on the 'Automatic Law' of God-Nature and 'how the Human-Race experiment was coming along'. He concludes – this is Twain in 1908 – 'Human history in all ages is red with blood, and bitter with hate, and stained with cruelties.' If humour is a strategy for exposing the necessarily repressed, 'Letters from the Earth' is a sardonic sarcasm on Pudd'nhead Wilson's *Calendar* text: 'training is everything', the key to a novel which, as Twain observed, 'changed itself from a farce to a tragedy'. According to Justin Kaplan, it 'nearly killed him'. Twain always knew the duplicities – 'Every man is a moon and has a dark side which he never shows to anybody.' Lynch law in Dawson's Landing, Arkansaw, is the public aspect of that darkness exposed in 'To a Person Sitting in Darkness' (1901), a Christian blackness which presumes to 'confer our civilization' on those who are assumed to be pagans. The essay is a damning exposure of the missionary activities of Christian capitalism, to be placed with Melville's *Typee* (1846). Roxy's Tom inherits the Old Testament racist myth of 'the curse of Ham'. And as for law, the Italian twins reach 'the summit of human honor' in the duel, but once they become '*too* popular', they lose the election and become 'in instant danger of being lynched'. The New York *Herald* published Twain's greeting for New Year 1901 addressed to Christendom as a corrupt matron 'full of pious hypocrisies'. In 1907 he published 'Captain Stormfield's Visit to Heaven' (begun in 1868, but delayed partly through his wife's prohibition against printing). The divine domain proves to be a ghastly conventional place, confirming Huck's worst fears – a parody of Earth, but especially American class society. The statement of the captain's guide, Sandy McWilliams, reads somewhat prophetically today (and like an opening salvo in that assault still maintained by Stanley Elkin's novel in the Twain lineage, *The Living End*, 1984):

How are you going to have a republic at all, where the head of the government is absolute, holds his place for ever, and has no parliament, no counsel to meddle or make in his affairs, nobody voted for, nobody elected, nobody asked to take a hand in its matters, and nobody *allowed* to do it? . . . This is Russia – only more so. There's no shadow of a republic about it anywhere. There are ranks here.

In 1903 *Harper's* refused publication of Twain's assault on Mary Baker Eddy (*Christian Science*, 1907) – he called her 'queen of frauds and hypocrites'. He particularly loathed the belief that pain, evil and death do not exist, are mistakes of consciousness. By 1896 he had twice experienced the death of a child, and his wife had been ill all her life after treatment by some quack in her adolescence. The book is a deconstruction of both 'christian' and 'science' for which he had read widely in relevant fields and, as a skilled writer, he understood Eddy's linguistic tactics as 'metaphors gone insane'. And her self-proclaimed divinity was ridiculous to him. But towards the conclusion, Twain broadens his attack:

Our Congresses consist of Christians. In their private life they are true to every obligation of honor; yet in every session they violate them all, and do it without shame; because honor to party is above honor to themselves.

Twain then suggests a 'new literature with romances entitled "How to be an Honest Congressman though a Christian", "How to be a Creditable Citizen though a Christian".' But the Christians win, in alliance with the aristocrats, in *A Connecticut Yankee in King Arthur's Court* (1889). Training to industrial capitalist democracy fails, but goes out apocalyptically. Once again a Twain hero is exiled and reaches for techniques of survival – here the transfer of the lone nineteenth-century engineer to the Middle Ages as exemplary scene of tyranny, slavery, dogma and magic. Into this grotesque location, the American technician is lowered with his skills. Hank Morgan, foreman of the Colt factory in Hartford, Connecticut, centre of America's growing technological strength, becomes the vehicle of a series of jokes of contradiction and anomaly between the alleged past and industrial materialism. 1879 industrial utopian aims fail to transform permanently the feudal structure of Camelot – religion, knights

and Merlin, the power trio Twain clearly believes represent re-
calcitrant human history. Hank does temporarily defeat them and
become Boss of all England in 528, leading the masses from serfdom
to a wage-slave 'colony', 'a Factory'. His 'peaceful revolution'
changes the 'white Indians' into trained competitors. The hilarious
enclosure of Hank in knight's armour is only one kind of imprisonment and 'slow torture'. In fact the joke is countered by panic fear:
'Even after I was frozen solid I could still distinguish that tickling,
just as a corpse does when he is taking electric treatment.'

The Boss puts the populace 'to some useful purpose'. Knights
have to advertise soap or a 'prophylactic tooth brush'. A prisoner
is rescued from Christian priests and, in behaviourist terms, re-
engineered:

> Training is everything; training is all there is *to* a person. We speak of
> nature; it is folly; there is no such thing as nature; what we call by that
> misleading name is merely heredity and training. We have no thoughts of
> our own, no opinions of our own; they are transmitted to us, trained into us
> ... atoms contributed by, and inherited from, a procession of ancestors that
> stretches back a million years to the Adam-clam or grasshopper or monkey
> from whom our race has been so tediously and ostentatiously and un-
> profitably developed.
>
> (ch. 18)

Hank and the Old Man in 'What is Man?' share Twain's beliefs. The
Colt foreman organizes Arthur's Britain just short of the technocracy
of Edward Bellamy's *Looking Backward 2000–1887* published the year
before. But he hurls a homemade bomb at the knights; the hysterical
joking intensifies: 'It resembled a steamboat explosion on the Mississippi; and during the next fifteen minutes we stood under a steady
drizzle of microscopic fragments of knights and hardware and
horseflesh.' Yet it is King Arthur who is accused of being 'full of
ancestral blood that was rotten with ... unconscious brutality,
brought down by inheritance from a long procession of hearts that
had each done its share toward poisoning the stream'. Britain A D
528 reminds Hank of the South and its 'poor whites', 'thirteen
centuries away'. 'Freedom' can only be defined as the freedom to re-
engineer from a fictional belief basis: 'a man *is* a man, at bottom'. So
the lower classes are to be armed with cheap weapons, even if their
subsequent uselessness is converted into a purse-gun with shot-coins.

Civilization is narrowed to weapons versus church and knighthood. The end conflict is a holocaust of 'glass-cylinder torpedoes', thirteen Gatling guns ('a labor-saving device for warfare'), and electrocution of men in armour on barbed wire: '*There* was a groan you could hear! It voiced the death-pang of eleven thousand men.'

Twain's sardonic humour is a state of nerves as he ambivalently resists the church, the army, the class system, free will and his wife's genteel moralism. As Ziffel says in Brecht's *Conversations in Exile* (1948): 'To live in a country without humour is unbearable. But it is also unbearable to live in a country where one needs humour.' Between the initiating of *A Connecticut Yankee* and its completion, Twain's faith in the engineered modern state failed; he told his close friend, the novelist W. D. Howells: 'The change is in *me* – in my vision of the evidence.' In his *Autobiography* he identifies medieval Britain with Leopold of the Belgians' Congo and contemporary Russia. In 1899, he wrote in 'Concerning the Jews':

I am quite sure that (bar one) I have no race prejudices, and I think I have no color prejudices nor caste prejudices nor creed prejudices. Indeed, I know it. I can stand any society. All that I care to know is that a man is a human being – that is enough for me; he can't be any worse.

The exception was the French. In 'King Leopold's Soliloquy' (1906), the tyrant's excuse is that he is human. In *Tom Sawyer Abroad* (1894) the hero believes it is 'religious to go and take land from people that owns it'. The gist of 'Letters from the Earth' is: human existence *is* Hell – there is no need for God to invent another one. Twain had read Jonson's *The Devil is an Ass* in which Satan's agent Pug asserts of human society, 'Hell is a grammar-school to this.' He quotes both this play and *Volpone* to preface *The Gilded Age* (1873), his first extended fiction (written with Charles Dudley Warner).[2] Here, at the outset of his career, he exposes society's crazed speculation in money and land, insane competition and obsessive technology – and its hypocritical refusal to take blame for its behaviour. Colonel Sellars is a Jonsonian epitome of fake buoyancy, a hawker of false panaceas (the centre of false confidence in Melville's *The Confidence-Man* in 1857). When one of the main young characters refuses to edit a newspaper against his principles, he is characteristically advised 'you can't afford a conscience like that'. Washington is given, as it is in Henry Adams's novels of 1880 and 1884, as the centre of national corruption, hub of competition, a 'paradise of speculation'. In volume 2, the later pattern of Twain's work is clearly anticipated: farce turns to catastrophe which humour cannot assuage. Sellars and Washington constitute a state of 'lunacy'. The corrupted heroine's trial for murder becomes a configuration of press, legal and religious hypocrisy. Laura is found guilty and committed to 'the State Hospital for Insane Criminals', but Twain provides an alternative conclusion in which she is freed to 'cheers . . . of popular approval and affection', and seeks to gain a living lecturing on her experiences. Then the novel is twisted again: at her first lecture she is killed by a stone from the mob. The inquest finds she died from 'merely' heart disease.

Thereafter, Twain could only create fictions of the American condition, as a section of the human condition, by skilled strategies of humour, farce and wit – which increasingly broke down into what a later generation of Americans employed as 'black humour', and into direct descriptions of brutality. Twain, the public man, converted rebelliousness into popular humour within the limits of laughter he and the state could tolerate. Although chapter 7 of *The Mysterious Stranger* states 'God has forsaken us', Twain does not develop any further existential philosophy of resilient change; he just notes that man's sense of humour is now 'lying rusting' in the absence of 'sense and courage': 'No sane man can be happy, for to him life is real and he sees what a fearful thing it is. Only the mad can be happy, and not many of those.' Huck's moral survival by 'playing double', entering the jokes of contradiction to destroy as much as he can of the oedipal chaos and risking damnation, turns into happiness only in the brief freedom of the raft between the bordering banks of civilization: 'We said there warn't no home like a raft, after all. Other places do seem so cramped up and smothery, but a raft don't. You feel mighty free and easy and comfortable on a raft.'

The rest is cruel and absurd: a clown-acrobat sheds seventeen suits as his performance. By the time of the later writings published posthumously as *Europe and Elsewhere* (1923), America had become 'the United States of Lynchdom' whose 'supreme trait' is moral cowardice. So concludes a courageous and skilled response to Whitman's 'These States', an astonishing career in abilities to use conventions of humour to balance as long as possible among the erosions of deteriorating confidence. But he knew the truth of chapter 11 of *Huckleberry Finn*: 'they're after us!' – and concealed work which the public and his wife would find objectionable. His authority had to be that of the undertaker in this novel. When a dog barks in the cellar during a funeral, he glides out, whacks the animal silent, returns to the ceremony, and 'in a kind of coarse whisper' tells the preacher, 'He had a rat!', and glides back to his place:

> You could see it was a great satisfaction to the people, because naturally they wanted to know. A little thing like that don't cost nothing, and it's just the little things that makes a man to be looked up to and liked. There warn't no more popular man in town than what that undertaker was.

(ch. 27)

Mark Twain was the kind of man who, when in Oxford to receive an honorary degree towards the end of his life – along with Rodin, Kipling and Saint-Saëns – took the curse off the occasion by replying to why he always carried a cheap cotton umbrella, 'because that's the only kind of umbrella an Englishman won't steal!'

NOTES

1. Ed. F. A. Anderson, etc., Mark Twain's *Notebooks and Journals*, Vol. 1, Berkeley, etc., 1975, p. 450.
2. E. Hudson Long, *Mark Twain Handbook*, New York, 1957, pp. 179–80.

CRANE, NORRIS, AND LONDON

JOHN FRASER

Stephen Crane (1871–1900), Frank Norris (1870–1902), and Jack London (1876–1916) were the first generation of seriously chivalric American fiction writers – the precursors of Hemingway, Fitzgerald, Faulkner, and others.[1] They did not consciously form a school (though Norris and Crane were briefly acquainted as war correspondents in Cuba), and they differed considerably in backgrounds, talents, and achievements. But they had a number of things in common, in addition to their early deaths and their youthful admiration for Kipling. They grew up hungry for life with a capital L in a period of urbanization and narrowing options; they were fascinated with violence and danger; and they explored sympathetically the struggle to break through the shell of habit and affirm the self against the downpullings of guilt and pessimism. Their work is very uneven, especially Norris's and London's. They were writing to make money, they tried a variety of styles, and there are gulfs between their best prose and their worst. Moreover, Norris and London had a good deal of trouble with general ideas in a period that veered between a belief in irresistible social forces and an enthusiasm for the Napoleonic great man. But all three knew what real as opposed to literary-conventional feelings and conduct were like; and when characters, situations, and styles coincided, all were capable of remarkable writing.

Crane was the genius of the three – one of the most gifted, likeable, and admirable of American writers. He was a daring stylistic experimenter who wrote some of the first modernist prose in English and strongly influenced writers like Conrad and Hemingway. But he was also one of the most steadily affirmative of the major American writers, and one of the most enduringly funny – unegotistically funny, like Conrad in *Typhoon*. These qualities were the more striking because the potentials for disaster in him were large. But he coped with his problems in ways that involved considerable intellectual sophistication, and he not only did an extraordinary amount of work during his hectic brief career but moved Conrad to speak later of 'a strain of chivalry [in him] which made him safe to trust with one's life'. Ford Madox Ford called him 'honourable, physically brave, infinitely hopeful, generous, charitable to excess'.[2]

He was the son of Methodists (his father, a minister, died when he was eight), with hell-fire preachers on his mother's side of the family and distinguished soldiers on both sides. And in his slum nouvelle *George's Mother* (1896) he presents a double bind that he obviously knew from the inside. On the one hand, the youth's adoring widowed mother holds up to him the classic American ideal of great virtuousness combined with great authority, so that he dreams of awing people with his 'beauty and wrath'. But on the other, she disapproves of all signs of vanity in him and considers that self-esteem should only manifest itself passively. It is emotionally impossible for him to settle into a routine existence and live with 'the self-pity that comes when the soul is turned back from a road'. But asserting his independence through the drunken camaraderie of the Bowery triggers all his guilt feelings, and he fluctuates wildly between believing the universe adores him and knowing it despises him, with disastrous consequences. Crane himself, however, not only coped successfully with the guilt-instilling processes but avoided the standard American dichotomy of illusionment/disillusionment. As a writer, he does not present us with the kind of ironical pattern in which there is only one route to self-transcendence and that route delusory. Nor does he work in terms of an antithesis between realism and romance.

It was in *Maggie* (1893/6) and *The Red Badge of Courage* (1895) that the principal problem-solving and synthesizing went on.

Crane's approach in *Maggie* is robustly secular and critical. It is a novel of actions, of bodies in action, and there are frequent comedic disjunctions between narrative styles and what those bodies say and do; for example:

> [Pete] was extremely gracious and attentive. He displayed the consideration of a cultured gentleman who knew what was due.
> 'Say, what d'hell? Bring d'lady a big glass.'

But though both the Christian and the chivalric characters come out of it badly, Crane is not engaged in total ideological undercuttings. The hell-fire callousness of Maggie's drunken mother is made worse when she shifts to the language of Christian forgiveness; the abandonment of the ruined Maggie by the swaggering bartender Pete is made worse by the chivalrous terms in which Maggie has perceived him; and Maggie's yearnings for something beyond the squalors of home and sweatshop are presented sympathetically. Nor is there any intimation that slum dwellers are inherently shut out from beauty and heroism. In the famous opening chapter ('A very little boy stood upon a heap of gravel for the honor of Rum Alley'), Maggie's kid brother is indeed fighting with epic valour; and if the melodramas to which Pete takes Maggie are absurd, there is nothing absurd about the theatre itself as a locale in which she can experience greater fullness of being. The social rituals in which the novel abounds – drinking, competing, mourning, etc. – differ from the respectable versions of such things in quality, not kind. And the novel itself, as a manifestation of structured energy, brilliantly resists the realist downpulling that reduces things to a state of enumerative equality. Actions speed up and slow down cinematically. There is no necessary correlation between the seriousness or triviality of a subject (Maggie's suicide, a rambling barroom conversation) and the space it receives. And the linguistic unbalancing that goes on in the discrepancies between styles extends into the finer points of syntax, such as the frequent unexpectedness ('squat, *ignorant* stables', 'a small *pursued* tigress') of the second of a pair of epithets. It is a novel pervaded by discourse.

In *The Red Badge of Courage*, Crane deals frontally with the question of guilt. It is of course the classic phenomenological novel of battle as experienced through a single consciousness. Crane gives us marvellously the fragmentariness, conflicting rumours, and dramatically changing rhythms, the incongruous echoings of ordinary life (soldiers fussily adjusting their cartridge boxes 'as if seven hundred new bonnets were being tried on'), the dramatic departures from it ('It seemed that the dead men must have fallen from some great height to get into such positions'), the kinaesthetic sensitivities ('the flesh over his heart seemed very thin'), and much else. But the novel is also a classic of the divided consciousness and the healing of a split. In it Crane defines the actual immorality of certain kinds of ethical over-intensity and shows that there can be self-affirmation without Nietzschean hardness.

The essential strains in young Henry Fleming prior to battle come from the conflict between his romantic craving for neo-pagan action and the Christian self-abnegation demanded of him by his mother. He is exclusively preoccupied with the impending fighting as a moral test. If he is not totally worthy, then how he behaves will show that he is totally *un*worthy, in terms both of his residual Christianity and of his romantic image of himself. With the entry of his regiment into battle ('One gray dawn, . . . he found himself running down a road-wood . . .'), his self-destructive introspection intensifies. If he is to be tested, it should be under fair conditions; but things increasingly fail to conform to his expectations. The surfacing demonic imagery – serpents, dragons, monsters – indicates how far from innocent and 'Greeklike' the battlefield has become for him; and when the enemy unreasonably returns to the attack after being repulsed, he breaks and runs. During his subsequent wanderings behind the lines, he is tormented by a sense of exclusion and moral transparency: his crime must inescapably be known to *someone*, and is bound to be revealed. And both of his principal attempts to escape from his sense of worthlessness come to nothing. When he invokes the idea of Nature as naturally pacific and thus as endorsing his own flight from violence, the move is blocked when he comes upon a corpse in a chapel-like glade with the ants busily at work upon its face. And his attempt to convert the battle into a machine-like spectacle with no moral claims on him is blocked by the existential awesomeness of the death of his friend Jim Conklin, leaving him overwhelmed with guilt and incapable of the fellow-feeling invited by the tattered soldier who has watched the death with him.

At this point, when it looks as if he has reached a total impasse, life takes over without regard to conventional ideas of crime and punishment. The rout of another regiment shows him that he is far from unique in his fears; he receives his own wound from the swung rifle-butt of one of the fleeing men and becomes a victim rather than a victimizer; and in his dazed and helpless state he is shepherded through the woods to his own regiment by a cheerful,

non-judgemental stranger and received back tenderly by his friend
Wilson. Awakening the following morning free of his supernatural
preoccupations ('The lessons of yesterday had been that retribution
was a laggard and blind'), he feels an affectionate solidarity with his
fellow-soldiers, fights with a single-mindedness that saves them
from disaster, and becomes – in terms much less egotistical than he
had imagined earlier – the hero that he had aspired to be. True, he
has not turned into a story-book paragon; but why should he? And
in comparison with the complex changes in consciousness throughout the novel, it is the mechanical crime-and-retribution model of
morality that looks irreligious.

Rich as it is, however, *The Red Badge* was not one of those novels
like *The Great Gatsby* that leave their authors with essentially nothing
further to write about. Partly Crane continued doing things involving some of the same concerns. The needs that had taken him
on hunting excursions and into low-life areas of New York in search
of experience and journalistic copy now took him to the American
West and Southwest, to Mexico, and to war in Greece and Cuba.
But he would not have continued to see fresh possibilities in situations
without his remarkable mental flexibility (a contemporary reviewer
spoke of his 'quick, nervous, prehensile mind'[3]) and his sophistication
about fictions.

From the outset, Crane was acutely alert to discrepancies between
stereotypes and actualities, and to the possibility of romantic self-
deception. (In 'Virtue in War', some of his soldiers reflect wryly that
'Actually there was not *anything* in the world which turned out to be
as books describe it.') But he detested the smart-aleck knowingness
that diminishes the magnitude of difficulties overcome, and he saw
that the fact that there are conflicting accounts of something does
not mean that all those accounts are necessarily false or that the least
glamorous is necessarily the truest. The denizens of the foetid
Bowery flophouse where a youth passes a night in 'An Experiment
in Misery' may appear comparatively unremarkable in the light of
morning, but that does not make his nighttime sense of their possible
dangerousness absurd, any more than the plainer prose of the later
stories casts doubt on the stylistic fullness of *Maggie* and *The Red
Badge*. And Crane was strongly aware, too, that situations have
game-like rules, the figuring out of which makes it possible to solve

limited problems, whether replacing a wheel on a van, shooting a bear, or wooing a young girl under the nose of her possessive father. Involved in the problem-solving, moreover, is what in 'His New Mittens' he calls 'the enigmatical . . . ideal of form, manner'. If that ideal often makes for humour, including the grim comedy of the flawless 'An Episode of War', whose lieutenant hangs his head and feels that 'he did not know how to be correctly wounded', it is not therefore foolish. Reality for Crane is not something that one arrives at by discarding romance and insisting on the hollowness of conventions.

Reality in Crane's terms is dialectical, and *richer* than it appears at first sight. The details of a new situation – the behaviour of others, the protagonist's feelings, his or her own conduct – may not all fit the stereotypes. The journalist trying to tiptoe away from bandits in 'One Dash – Horses' reflects that 'The man who said that spurs jingled was insane. Spurs have a mellow clash – clash – clash. Walking in spurs – notably Mexican spurs – you remind yourself vaguely of a telegraphic lineman.' But looked at more closely, there are overlappings. And if an individual preserves mental flexibility and takes into account the perceptions of others, he or she may be able to behave creditably. At bottom, all of Crane's best writing involves the drama of categorizing and recategorizing, whether in a statement like, 'We were no longer filibusters. We were men on a ship stuck in the mud,' or a long short story like 'Death and the Child', with its rapid alternation of perspectives on a battle. And the concern to present things as they *do* appear, and not as the mind tells one they ought to appear, is central to his frequent analogy-making (bullets make 'a silken, sliding, tender noise'), his animism, and the expressive use of colour that so irritated some of his contemporaries.

These attitudes can be seen in various combinations in his four best-known shorter fictions. In 'The Blue Hotel' (1896), the Nebraskan locals are at first obstinately non-aggressive, and it is the Swede newcomer himself who turns machismic, accusing the hotel proprietor's son of cheating at cards, and beating him in a fist-fight. But the dime-novel stereotypes are not all fiction, and when the Swede goes on to insult a professional gambler, he achieves the death that he had dreaded. The final disclosure that the son had in fact cheated raises nicely the question of how the Easterner who witnessed it ought to have behaved, and of whether the Swede's response was wholly wrong. In a story nominally undercutting the conventional view of the West, we are brought back to the central Western questions of honour and correct form, as we are in 'The Bride Comes to Yellow Sky' (1898), in which the role-governed code of male bonding both creates violences and permits a peaceful resolution of a conflict. In 'The Open Boat' (1897), as the Crane-like correspondent is well aware, the boat is not a glamorously crowded lifeboat in mid-ocean. It is like a bathtub with four men in it, it is not far from the Florida coast, and trippers are visible on the beach. But the water is real water, and one can still die in it. The four shipwrecked men take things as they come, treat each other civilly, figure out the best way of getting the rowing done, and conceal their private fears. In effect, they behave heroically – and enlarge our sense of that term. Lastly, the nouvelle *The Monster* (1899), the richest of Crane's shorter fictions, is a Chinese puzzle of paradoxes about fictions, role-playing, incongruities (sometimes very funny ones), and responsible action, and leaves us with the question of how the honourable small-town doctor will – and should – behave with respect to the now disfigured and imbecilic black servant who saved his son from a fire but whose continuing presence in town is annihilating his wife's social world.

In the delightful childhood stories of Crane's final year before tuberculosis took him, 'morality' is humanized even further. If their centre is the romantic, hypersensitive consciousness of Crane's boyhood self, a vital presence in them is the doctor-father as he copes with the conflicting claims of justice, sympathy, and humour posed for him by the children's doings. And both he and various other adults behave attractively. In the other major group of later writings, the stories and reports from Cuba, what comes across is Crane's admiration for the stoicism and skill of the regular soldiers, their lack of hatred for the enemy, and their delicacy towards the dead and wounded, such as in the moving story 'The Upturned Face'. Crane had obviously always been conscious of the line of soldiers in his family, and in his own life he had displayed the soldierly virtues. The clearest summation of his position in these later works is to be found in 'War Memories':

There wasn't a high heroic face among them. They were all men intent on business. That was all. It may seem to you that I am trying to make everything a squalor. That would be wrong. I feel that things were often sublime. But they were *differently* sublime. They were not of our shallow and preposterous fictions . . . [I]t was the pageantry of the accomplishment of naked duty, . . . of the common man serenely doing his work, his appointed work.

Frank Norris is a problematic writer who died of peritonitis before the dynamics of his career had had time to work themselves out. As a youth he was obsessed with Froissart and medieval combat. But he had large ambitions and a strong sense of the novel as 'the great expression of modern life', and saw that 'The difficult thing is to get at the [romance of the] life immediately around you, the very life in which you move.' His own predilections are indicated by the statement that

Terrible things must happen to the characters of the naturalistic tale. They must be twisted from the ordinary, wrenched out from the quiet, uneventful round of every-day life, and flung into the throes of a vast and terrible drama that works itself out in unleashed passions, in blood, and in sudden death.[4]

The discrepancy between the Nick–Carraway-like urbanity of his journalism (he was intelligently articulate about the *Realpolitik* of the literary life) and his fascination with the violation of taboos is a bit disquieting. But he too was obviously at work on ongoing problems of intimate concern to him.

His novels (his short stories are insignificant) fall chronologically into three main groups: the deterioration novels (*Vandover and the Brute, McTeague*), the sexual-breakthrough novels (*Moran of the Lady Letty, Blix, A Man's Woman*), and the Epic of the Wheat novels (*The Octopus, The Pit*).

To look at *McTeague* (1899) and *Vandover* (1914) together is to look at the difference between the resolved and the unresolved. The unfinished *Vandover* is the quintessential there-but-for-the-grace-of-God novel. The well-bred young San Francisco artist who goes with whores, contracts syphilis, causes the suicide of a 'decent' girl, and is socially ruined is obviously a Norris surrogate. And in showing whither a lack of moral fibre can lead, Norris writes at times with unsparing realism about his young-men-about-town. The figure of Geary, the Harvard classmate who defrauds Vandover in a business deal and coolly watches him deteriorate, obviously also represents a significant part of Norris's psyche, and the closing pages in which the broken-down Vandover cleans out a filthy working-class house owned by Geary are among the most powerful that Norris wrote. But Norris obviously does not know what to do with the dynamics of Vandover's sexual nausea and will-lessness, and there is a lot of pseudo-explanatory twaddle about atavism. In *McTeague*, however, he does not feel the need to keep explaining his working-class hero. The novel has its flaws: there are stretches of pedestrian surface realism, the principal sub-plot contains some of his most fustian dialogue, and the would-be interconnective gold symbolism has a cartoon-like obviousness. But where McTeague himself is concerned, Norris turns his creative unconscious loose with impressive results.

What he gives us is an extraordinarily powerful study of a marriage, at once individual and representative, in which each partner is both victimizer and victim. With his contentment with small pleasures, his inarticulateness, his inability to cope with social occasions, McTeague is the archetypal hulking American male in need of 'improvement'. And Trina – petite, orderly, hard-working – is the archetypal improving woman. Their deterioration after McTeague loses his right to practise dentistry involves a horrendous development of potentials in both of them – she into compulsive miserliness and lying, he into resentful violence. But because Norris does not feel obliged to moralize everything (and because, too, of his obvious sense of the *strangeness* of marriage), they do not become simply cases. If we sympathize with McTeague in his dumb yearning to return to his lost domestic contentment, we can also sympathize with Trina in her desperate concern to hold on to an area of her identity (her lottery winnings) that stands in danger of being inexorably eroded. Moreover, when she speaks of loving Mac and wanting reassurances that he still loves her, we believe her; throughout, there is an extraordinary erotic charge to their behaviour. And in the chapters after her murder, Norris achieves a remarkable non-judgemental opening-up of the action when McTeague, on the run, is both a man who has committed an unequivocally atrocious murder and also a hunted person craving peace still but fatally doomed not to have it, and half knowing it. The evocation of the mountains, the heat, McTeague's hyper-consciousness of his pursuers, the tricks that his mind plays on him, and the final showdown in the Death Valley furnace is superb.

In themselves the three succeeding novels are negligible. *Blix* (1899), with its wholesome, fun-loving heroine, has an insidious wish-fulfilment charm. But *Moran of the Lady Letty* (1898) is a turning loose of the Beast Within, in which a well-bred San Franciscan teams up with a Nietzschean amazon in conflict with simian Chinese beachcombers, kills his man, masters his woman, and thoroughly enjoys himself. And *A Man's Woman* (1900) reads like a parody designed to confirm every enlightened person's suspicions about turn-of-the-century chivalric romanticism. But in all three novels Norris was obviously trying to figure out how love could be compatible with power. And loathsome as is the strong-man Arctic explorer of *A Man's Woman*, there is some subtlety to how Norris gets two equally strong-willed persons through what at first look like unresolvable emotional difficulties.

Norris's resolution of the marriage question to his satisfaction (and his own successful marriage) obviously made possible the Napoleonic ambitions of the Epic of the Wheat trilogy: *The Octopus* (1901), in which the wheat farmers of the San Joaquin Valley struggle with the monopolistic California railroad; *The Pit* (1903), in which a Chicago financier tries to corner the wheat market; and the un-written third volume, in which the wheat was to have reached the masses overseas. As before, Norris's plotting outran his powers of execution. The mystical parts of *The Octopus* have a saccharine preposterousness, the irony is often mechanical, the attempts to enlist the wheat as an irresistible force in the service of Spencerian optimism fall flat, and in *The Pit* Norris's imaginative energies only become strongly engaged when the climax approaches and he can empathize with his tycoon fighting to stave off financial disaster and hang on to his romantic-minded wife. But *The Octopus* is still an interesting novel. In some ways it is the first wide-screen 'quality' Western in its development of the conflict between the ranchers and the railroad's chief agent, the fat, imperturbably smiling, and absolutely pitiless S. Behrman (never without his initial). But with his characteristic coolness, Norris not only sends the ranchers down to defeat and makes clear that they never had a chance of winning, but tilts things so that Behrman's predatory energies have at least the virtue of single-mindedness, whereas the leading ranchers are compromised by yearning for both the pleasures of wealth and the consciousness of gentility. However, the buoyancy of the doing prevents the novel from being merely depressing, and at times Norris achieves some of those epic effects that he was seeking, especially a feeling of great spaces.

The Octopus and *The Pit* nudge their way towards the line separating the art novel and the quality bestseller, and in terms of the morality-play view of American authorship, Norris, had he lived, would have become rich, fat, and banal. It is possible, though, that he could have carried out with distinction his projected trilogy about Gettysburg. He was fascinated by military doings, had been under fire and seen men slaughtered, understood the excitement of the colossal gamble, and in *The Octopus* handled armed combat convincingly. And he possessed the kind of realism that can sympathize with both sides but knows that when the big battalions are rightly positioned they are going to win, regardless of one's sympathies.

Jack London was the most prolific and popular of the three writers, the author of over a hundred and fifty stories, eighteen novels, and seven books of non-fiction, some of them very widely translated. With his good looks and charm (he was as photogenic as Hemingway), he embodied the best of America for innumerable foreign readers, and was a formative influence for generations of American youth, epitomizing adventure and offering them the pseudo-philosophical wisdom that the British young derived from writers like Hardy, Kipling, and Wells. His traces are apparent in Hemingway, Lawrence, Traven, Orwell, and others. He wrote too much, too carelessly, and in too wide a variety of styles, his work is pervaded by unsynthesized dichotomies, and much of it is of merely period interest. But he was a writer of intense yearnings who knew the awfulnesses that people are capable of and was always conscious of the Nietzschean abyss. And if he is sometimes infuriating, he can also be extraordinarily sympathetic.

In the partly autobiographical *Martin Eden* (1909), London's nearest approach to a conventionally serious novel, there is a painful fascination to the working-class hero's obsession with acquiring culture and becoming a Great Writer. But high culture is personified for him by a middle-class heroine who disapproves of his writing and says things like, 'Every line of the really great poets is filled with beautiful truth, and calls to all that is high and noble in the human.' And though he discovers Herbert Spencer and Nietzsche and takes up with bohemian San Francisco intellectuals, all the reachings after profundity in the novel remain at the level of figurative generality. There is no synthesizing, either by Eden or by the author; success when it comes to Eden is ashen, and he kills himself.

In the forty-odd Yukon stories (1899–1903) with which he first made his name, London was obviously partly trying to define for himself a counter-position with regard to culture. In contrast to spirituality, we have Kiplingesque *doing*: exotic locales, big (that is, money-making) enterprises, cultural pluralism. But except for 'In a Far Country', the stories, especially those with large casts, are un-inspired, over-elaborate, and the most 'literary' of his writings. He did his most personal thinking in the novels immediately following them: *The Call of the Wild* (1903), *The Sea-Wolf* (1904), and *White Fang* (1906). He wrote them around the time of the collapse of his first marriage, and in them he was trying to make his way through the mazes of Nietzschean egoism. In the immensely popular *The Call of the Wild* a civilized dog is cast into the dog-eat-dog world of the frozen North, survives as a sled-dog by discarding the rules of fair play, and eventually finds freedom among his wolf-kin, with a fair amount of editorializing along the way about the primeval beast and the joy of battle. In the insufferable *The Sea-Wolf*, with its cocktail mixture of elements from *Moby-Dick*, *The Blithedale Romance*, and *The Narrative of Arthur Gordon Pym*, a shanghaied bellettrist is exposed to the Nietzschean spoutings of the hell-ship skipper Wolf Larsen (genius, fallen angel, etc.), discovers unexpected strengths within himself, and escapes when the luck of the sea sends him the right kind of woman, a real Mate, and Larsen conveniently goes blind. And in *White Fang* the wolf-dog hero winds up in a good home under a master who respects his wolf identity and to whom he can give complete loyalty.

The three books simplify complicated issues in ways that par-ticularly appeal to the young, and generations of readers must have received from *The Sea-Wolf* and *Martin Eden* the impression that the only philosophical options are a vaporous idealism, a naïve scientism ('Is there anything in the universe that is not subject to the law of evolution?' Martin Eden demands), and a programmatic egoism. But there are important features in the 'wolf' group that became more prominent in London's subsequent work: unblinking accounts of inter-animal violence and human cruelty; impressive presentations of characters enduring the unendurable when the only alternative is death; memorable entries into puzzle-solving processes, such as a wolf-cub finding its bearings in the physical world or a dog figuring out the dynamics of a dog-sled team. London was at his best – and it could be an impressive best – when he was able to project himself in a non-intellectualizing way into the consciousness of individuals absorbed in doing physically dangerous things. In dealing with such situations he was capable of an admirable plain prose, natural-sounding speech, and a non-moralizing awareness of the changes that extreme environments can bring about in people's mental processes, whether the homicidal deterioration of the two tenderfeet in 'In a Far Country' or the conduct of the solitary man in his masterpiece, 'To Build a Fire' (1908). In a cold intense beyond our imaginings, a novice who doesn't fully grasp its dangers makes a series of 'small' mistakes that almost immediately have large consequences. But he carries on methodically without panicking, and when the end draws near, as it soon does, he has no recriminations against the universe, and no self-reproaches.

He pictured the boys finding his body next day. Suddenly he found himself with them, coming along the trail looking for himself. And, still with them, he came around a turn in the trail and found himself lying in the snow. He did not belong with himself any more, for even then he was out of himself, standing with the boys and looking at himself in the snow. It certainly was cold, was his thought.

The same uncomplaining endurance occurs in the moving stories of a successful Northern survival, 'Love of Life', and a lost boxing match, 'A Piece of Meat'. And it bears on London's significance as a socialist writer.

In some respects the term is incongruous. London indeed wrote and lectured on socialism, presented labour unrest sympathetically in two or three weak stories and the good first half of *The Valley of the Moon* (1913), and emphasized capitalist ruthlessness in the futuristic *The Iron Heel* (1907), a novel whose emotional power is confined to the fictitious footnotes. But he was as incapable as Martin Eden of submitting to any collective discipline, and obvious problems are posed by his numerous references to inferior races and the survival of the strong, and his financial extravagances. However, in some of his best prose he shows us working-class individuals memorably asserting themselves in the face of power and authority, like the boxer-revolutionist in 'The Mexican' or the young Jack London who rides the rails and goes to jail with underdog jauntiness in *The Road* (1907), which Orwell rightly called 'a brilliant little book'. And in *The People of the Abyss* (1903) (the other of his two best books) he movingly presents some of the victims of capitalism. Though there are occasional lapses into literariness in it, the best parts are pure Orwell. London had really *listened* to the down-and-outers whom he sought out in the East End and whose speech he convincingly gives us; and his descriptions of processes, such as spending a night in a Whitechapel casual-ward, are exemplary in their unegotistical lucidity.

However, the poise that he displays in such works, and in his happiest book, *The Cruise of the Snark* (1911), was always precarious, and the last cluster of works to be considered here – *Jerry of the Islands* (1917), 'The Red One' (1916), and *Michael, Brother of Jerry* (1917) – shows how far he had moved from it by the time of his death. In the last-named, he says of an escaped convict trying to kick someone to death that 'Everything was against him. His desire to cry was hysterical, and hysteria, in a desperate man, is prone to express itself in terrible savage ways.' There is an undercurrent of hysteria in these disturbing works, with their polarizing of existence into bliss and horror. There had been treacheries and cruelties earlier in a number of his works. But in *Jerry* and 'The Red One' he turns his unconscious loose and gives us a literally man-eat-man world of South Seas horrors. And in chapters 24–34 of *Michael* he laceratingly exposes the atrocities of American performing-animal training – epitomizations of the will to dominate that he had always regarded with mixed feeling.

It has been argued persuasively that London's death was due to a miscalculation about medications, rather than suicide.[5] But by that time his body had been ravaged by alcohol, overwork, ill-health, and toxic medications, and the idea of death as release and rest was obviously not unwelcome to him. However, that is not the note to end on here. Two of his stories seem particularly emblematic of his sense of himself – 'Koolau the Leper', whose leper hero doggedly fights off the forces of law and order and dies a free man in his mountain fastness; and 'The Water Baby', in whose fable-within-a-yarn the young Polynesian diver brings back delicacies from the ocean floor and each time outwits the circling sharks. The sharks got London himself, of course: he lived with wildly conflicting American aspirations and imperatives that tore him apart. But one can say of him, as D. W. Harding said of Scott Fitzgerald, that when he died it was after 'making and spending vastly more money, achieving more fame, and living with more courage than most of us dream of'.[6]

NOTES

1. For an extended discussion of chivalric concerns in turn-of-the-century America, see John Fraser, *America and the Patterns of Chivalry* (Cambridge, 1982).

2. Introduction to Thomas Beer, *Stephen Crane* (New York, 1923), p. 10; *Return to Yesterday* (New York, 1932), p. 36.

3. Unsigned review, *Academy* (1901), reprinted in Richard M. Weatherford, ed., *Stephen Crane: The Critical Heritage* (London, 1973), p. 263.

4. *The Literary Criticism of Frank Norris*, ed. Donald J. Pizer (Austin, 1964), pp. 94, 86, 72.

5. Andrew Sinclair, *Jack: A Biography of Jack London* (New York, 1977), ch. 16.

6. 'Scott Fitzgerald', *Scrutiny*, XVIII (Autumn 1961), p. 166.

THE AMERICAN ADAMS

WAYNE FIELDS

The Adamses loved words. Through four generations they contributed more to American letters than any other family, more not only in volume and longevity but, most impressively, more in variety and scope. Always there was correspondence written with an unflagging commitment to clarity and precision and illuminated by frequent bursts of passion and of humor. There were, from the two presidents (John and John Quincy) and from the congressman/ambassador of the third generation (Charles Francis), speeches and papers of state. There were diaries, treatises on government, and, for John Quincy, the published lectures from his tenure as Harvard's Boylston Professor of Rhetoric and Oratory. And with the fourth generation came a rich harvest of history and historical theory. The literary achievement of the Adams family is remarkable by any standard, a vast commentary on American culture running from the last decades of the eighteenth century through the first decades of the twentieth, and containing works – beginning with the brilliant and irreplaceable correspondence between John Adams and Thomas Jefferson and culminating three generations later in the writings of Henry Adams – that are among the highest accomplishments of American literature.

In the last decade of his life Henry Adams (1838–1918) wrote to his younger brother Brooks, then preparing a biography of John Quincy Adams. The brothers were of different minds concerning their grandfather, Brooks seeing him as an epic figure while Henry found much – at least in the Diary – to reject. 'The warning to me,' Henry wrote,

comes direct from Hell. It tells me never – never – to be didactic. Thank God, I have done little preaching in my life. I have tried to tell stories, and sometimes to found them on a carefully concealed foundation of idea; but I trust I have never tried expressly to improve my fellow-insects . . . I would gladly amuse my world; but I refuse to improve or reprove it.

Like all such claims, the statement is as significant for its untruth as for its truth and, perhaps most of all, for the tension between the two. If Henry's preaching was not of the Puritan variety, the sort that he associated with the 'didactic' grandfather, his lifelong pre-occupation with education suggests he was not completely un-contaminated in this regard. But the old 'uncle', the persona address-ing an indulgent niece in *Mont-Saint-Michel and Chartres* (1913), hoped above all to be amusing and so, clearly, did the witty Henry Adams of the voluminous correspondence. He was, as well, a great storyteller, but when he had completed his brilliant study of the Jefferson and Madison administration – all nine volumes of it – he declared his longing for something more: 'I don't give a damn what happened; what I want to know is why it happened – never could find out – stopped writing history.'

That which drives Adams's writing and generates its capacity to amuse as well as to instruct is always the tension between the 'what' and the 'why', between multiplicity and unity, between the par-ticular – the idiosyncratic – and the desire for an encompassing explanation – for coherence. His historical studies bristle with the detail of multiplicity, and, thoroughly researched, argue for the relevance of every particular, a relevance minimized by the romantic historians in their eagerness to get at a grand American plotline. These details are, in Adams's hands, a source of great pleasure; but the hope, as his lament suggests, was for more, for a principle of coherence in the midst of this multiplicity.

For an Adams, descended from Puritans, the object of study was always the self and, just as surely, America. There was no way to approach the former without confronting the latter, and for an Adams only twenty-three when civil war broke out, the conundrum of how there can be, of the many, one (*E pluribus unum*) is as profoundly a question about the sometimes united states as about the fragmented world of modernity. Thus the appropriateness that one of Adams's first major efforts as an essayist should have been 'The Great Secession Winter of 1860–61', an account of Washington DC during the winter when a nation that had always referred to itself in the plural moved toward official fragmentation even as it gathered itself, militarily, to assert its oneness. And, when the subject was less obviously dramatic, the 1869 Congressional session for instance, the central concern remained the same. What Adams, in 'The Session' would require each of his countrymen to witness is the bewildering 'crash and war of jealous and hostile interests' that rages behind the doors of Congress.

Within the walls of two rooms are forced together in close contact the jealousies of thirty-five millions of people, – jealousies between individuals, between cliques, between industries, between parties, between branches of the Government, between sections of the country, between the nation and its neighbors. As years pass on, the noise and the confusion, the vehemence of this scramble for power or for plunder, the shouting of reckless adventurers, of wearied partisans, and of red-hot zealots in new issues, – the boiling and bubbling of this witches' cauldron, into which we have thrown eye of newt and toe of frog and all the venomous ingredients of corruption, and from which is expected to issue the future and more perfect republic, – in short the conflict and riot of interests, grow more and more overwhelming . . .

There was in this turmoil that which most repelled and, in spite of his protests, most attracted Adams in his country, that which drew him away from the Brahmin culture of Boston and into the tumult of Washington. In 1869 he anticipated a career of covering Congressional sessions, a plan relinquished with his acceptance of a position as professor of history at Harvard and as editor of the *North American Review*. But his enthusiasm for a career of 'sessions' was genuine, its basis the combination of color and energy that, seven years later, brought him back to the Capitol to resume his observing labor. Likewise when the heroine of *Democracy* (1880), the first of Adams's two novels, grows bored with the genteel life of a well-to-do widow, she decides to 'pass the winter in Washington'. 'She wanted to see,' we are told, 'the action of primary forces; to touch with her own hand the massive machinery of society; to measure with her own mind the capacity of the motive power.' The lines speak as much of the author as of their immediate subject, Mrs Lee.

Whether or not it provokes 'preaching', the career as journalist as well as the related vocation of historian were fueled by a reformer's zeal. The Irish gardener who remarked to the child, Henry, 'You'll be thinkin' you'll be President too!', may not have foreseen the profession, but he anticipated the inevitable drive to take up the family burden and to carry it yet another generation. The reformer speaks in all Adams's work, obviously in 'The Session' and even more dramatically in 'The New York Gold Conspiracy' whose inflammatory subject – the 1869 effort of Jay Gould and James Fisk to corner the gold market – made finding a publisher difficult. The gold conspiracy made frighteningly apparent the perilous position of a nation that could fall so completely into the hands of the unscrupulous and avaricious, and Adams's conclusion calls for safeguards to protect popular institutions against corporate villainy. But the genius of Adams's best writing grew not from the familial capacity for sublime indignation but from that indignation combined with a willingness to be amused. Having accepted his own ironic relation to his culture – that of being passionately involved while being effectively detached – he perfected a comic sense that enlivens all his work. The account of the gold conspiracy presents a Republican nightmare, but it is also a comic story of the sort that three years later Mark Twain and Charles Dudley Warner would make up in *The Gilded Age* (1873), and it reads, wonderfully, not only like a carefully researched historical paper but like a tall tale as well.

In *In Defense of Reason*, Yvor Winters, something less than an Adams enthusiast, has declared *The History of the United States During the Administrations of Thomas Jefferson and James Madison* (1889–91) 'the greatest historical work in English, with the probable exception of *The Decline and Fall of the Roman Empire* . . .' If Francis Parkman (1823–93) wrote history in which heroes occupy center stage, generate the energy which drives history, Adams regarded heroes as harder to come by, forcing history, for the most part, to get along without them. Energy comes from other sources – the consequence of multiplicity rather than a hero's singularity: money, population growth, productivity, the conflicts between institutions. The focus on individuals, as Winters suggests, is a focus on 'the play of character', but it is character illustrative of or responsive to energy.

Every critical study of the *History* makes reference to the description of Jefferson both because it is of Jefferson and because it is vintage Adams.

For eight years this tall, loosely built, somewhat stiff figure, in red waistcoat and yarn stockings, slippers down at the heel and clothes that seemed too small for him . . . sitting on one hip, with one shoulder high above the other, talking almost without ceasing to his visitors at the White House. His skin was thin, peeling from his face on exposure to the sun, and giving it a tettered appearance. This sandy face, with hazel eyes and sunny aspect; this loose shambling person; this rambling and often brilliant conversation belonged to the controlling influences of American history, more necessary to the story than three-fourths of the official papers, which only hid the truth.

There is a good deal of America in these lines, an America that is for Adams, any Adams, both brilliant and absurd and from which there would always be some degree of personal estrangement. Such descriptions, realizing more than physical character even while being vivid with physical detail, accompany nearly every individual who enters Adams's narrative, part of an effort both to depict and to interpret. 'Perhaps,' he suggests,

dress could never be considered a trifle. One of the greatest of modern writers first made himself famous by declaring that society was founded upon whole *cloth*; and Jefferson at moments of some interest in his career as President, seemed to regard his peculiar style of dress as a matter of political importance, while the Federalist newspapers never ceased ridiculing the corduroy small-clothes, red-plush waistcoat, and sharp-toed boots with which he expressed his contempt for fashion.

Here, in addition to profound observations about a rhetoric of gesture and costume, is the methodological crux of Adams's work and, inevitably, the source of his greatest frustration: the double movement of searching for 'whole cloth' while attending to an inexhaustible supply of individual threads, the constant use of private perspectives – like those of Senator Maclay in the Jefferson portrait – to supplement, and complicate, the 'official papers', the continual examination – as in the elaborately re-created quarrel over Louisiana that took place in Napoleon's bath – not just of 'the' moment but of those before and after as well.

And treatments of places are like those of persons:

The city of Washington, rising in a solitude on the banks of the Potomac, was a symbol of American nationality in the Southern States. The contrast between the immensity of the task and the paucity of means seemed to challenge suspicion that the nation itself was a magnificent scheme like the federal city, which could show only a few log-cabins and negro quarters where the plan provided for the traffic of London and the elegance of Versailles. When in the summer of 1800 the government was transferred to what was regarded by most persons as a fever-stricken morass, the half-finished

White House stood in a naked field overlooking the Potomac, with two awkward Department buildings near it, a single row of brick houses and a few isolated dwellings within sight, and nothing more; until across a swamp, a mile and a half away, the shapeless, unfinished Capitol was seen, two wings without a body, ambitious enough in design to make more grotesque the nature of its surroundings.

Not only does the passage present the reader with the unfinished Washington of 1800, it also literalizes the morass, the presumption, the shapelessness inherent in American politics, and unconfined to any one period. The winged but bodiless Capitol speaks of more than slowness of construction; it represents a never changing aspect of democracy.

Adams had, early on, committed himself to the notion of scientific history, a 'social physics', Comtian in nature, that would discover laws of history, patterns from the past that could be projected onto the future. Thus the projections offered in 'The Session' as to the increased turmoil that would systematically result from increased population, and the closing assertion of the *History* (after the America of 1817 is compared to that of 1800 – the calculations made and the patterns determined):

[t]he traits of American character were fixed; the rate of physical and economical growth was established; and history, certain that at a given distance of time the Union would contain so many millions of people, with wealth valued at so many millions of dollars, became thenceforward chiefly concerned to know what kind of people these millions were to be.

At first glance this would seem the ideal answer for Adams, all those millions, the glorious variety of their idiosyncrasy preserved, and yet, somehow, a single entity with a character to be observed, but his later lament, that he had not found the 'why' and therefore was done with history, suggests that the resolution at the end of the *History* is a partial one at best. Still he did not quit tending history, nor did he turn away from history that is science, but he approached it in subsequent works from another angle.

During the 1880s while he was at work on the *History*, Adams wrote two novels. The first of these, *Democracy: An American Novel*, like 'The New York Gold Conspiracy', describes the corruption rampant during the Grant administration and warns against the dangers of a politics of self-interest. The second, *Esther* (1884), explores the psychological dislocation resulting from the inability of institutional religion to function with integrity in the modern world. Both have heroines who are paired with – and eventually refuse marriage to – men of energy and power, a senator/cabinet member in *Democracy* and a minister in *Esther*, men who lack the intellectual courage and integrity of the women and who, though seen at one moment as possible centers for reform or reconciliation, prove at last merely to be symptomatic of the problem. Though neither novel represents an altogether successful literary accomplishment, both speak compellingly to dreams of unity more enduring than all others, pathways – different as they may be – through multiplicity. But Esther cries out against her clergyman-suitor: 'It must be that we are in a new world now, for I can see nothing spiritual about the church. It is all personal and selfish.' And at the conclusion of *Democracy* Mrs Lee declares her intention to go abroad, to Egypt: 'democracy has shaken my nerves to pieces. Oh, what rest it would be to live in the Great Pyramid and look out forever at the polar star.'

In the years following the suicide of his wife in 1885, Adams likewise traveled, to Japan, Cuba, the American West, and the Pacific islands; drawing, after his return from the latter, on the stories told him by the royal Teva clan – into which he had been adopted – for the *Memoirs of Marau Taaroa, Last Queen of Tahiti* (1893), a work arguing the superiority of women as forcefully as did *Democracy* and *Esther*. The *History* finished, he wrote poetry, and began conversations with his brother Brooks that would influence the development of a 'dynamic theory of history'.

The eventual products of a lifetime of being an Adams, watching from the margins as economic and political forces swept his country and the world into the twentieth century, the ultimate consequence of a refusal to turn away from familial ideas or personal uncertainties, were two books exciting in their apparent divergence from his previous work but reassuring in their continuation of the old discussion.

In *The Education of Henry Adams* (1918) the quality Henry finds most noteworthy in his father, a person he regards with some ambivalence, is his 'perfectly balanced mind'. 'Charles Francis Adams,' he repeats, was singular for mental poise . . . a balance of mind and temper that neither challenged nor avoided notice, nor admitted questions of superiority or inferiority, or jealousy, of personal motives, from any source, even under great pressure.

This 'balance' or 'poise' is perhaps most remarkable to Henry because it is a trait hardly to be associated with Adams males generally, certainly not the grandfather or great-grandfather, and even more certainly not the son. A similar quality shines forth in the portrait of Albert Gallatin, the Secretary of the Treasury who is, in both the biography and the *History*, the hero of the Jefferson administration. In the Gilbert Stuart painting of the Secretary, reproduced in the original edition of *The Life of Albert Gallatin* (1879), Adams sees 'a sense of repose, an absence of nervous restlessness, mental or physical, unusual in American politicians'. By contrast the Southern 'type' Adams illustrates in his *John Randolph* (1882) is excitable in the extreme, incapable of self-control.

In varying degrees this balance or repose suggests the unity so elusive elsewhere in Adams's experience, the reconciliation that seems beyond hope in the modern world. The grandest masculine emblem of this unity, the baseline for American democracy, is George Washington who, for the entire Adams family, 'stands alone', Mrs Lee's 'Polar Star'. He is the closest thing there is to an American St Michael, composed and resolute. If Grant and Garibaldi were viewed by their countrymen as reincarnations of Washington, to Adams they appear exactly opposite, 'men whose energies were the greater the less they wasted on thought', men 'always needing stimulants, . . .'. Grant, elected because associated with the Union, proves erratic, dangerous because himself unordered. But the unity represented even by Washington is not immediately associated with energy. It was women who, for Adams, were, in their most superb representatives, both energy and unity. Something of this quality can be seen in the sister who confidently whisked Henry through battle lines to get him to Rome, the sister who, dying of lockjaw, somehow remained 'gay and brilliant'. Such too is the character of Marau Taaroa and even more of her grandmother Hinari. Most of all, this is the Virgin of Chartres.

Mont-Saint-Michel and Chartres begins with the church militant, with the church masculine, with Saint Michael de la Mer del Peril.

'Church and state, Soul and Body, God and Man, are all one at Mont-Saint-Michel, and the business of all is to fight, each in his own way, or to stand for each other.' 'We have little logic here, and simple faith, but we have energy.' The excitement of Mont-Saint-Michel comes from the unity of purpose which could thrust up this cathedral out of the living rock, its great triumphal piers erected eight years before the Norman Conquest, its architecture an expression of the same energy that launched the first crusade and that is encountered in *The Song of Roland*. It is the masculine singular and potent. Adams's eleventh century declares the reign of God the Father, 'God the Father as feudal seigneur, [who] absorbs the Trinity, and, what is more significant, absorbs or excludes also the Virgin'. There is little in this of repose, for Adams insists the eleventh century moved 'faster and more furiously' than the nineteenth. But unlike the 'conflict and riot of interests' he sees in his own culture, the eleventh century represents energy generated by unity. 'Barring her family quarrels, Europe was a unity then, in thought, will and object. Christianity was the unit.'

But Michael's cathedral, for all its grandeur, serves as the starting point of a journey that finds its ultimate fulfillment at Chartres, a cathedral that speaks of unity generated by the Virgin and of woman more generally, that is 'a toy-house to please the Queen of Heaven – to please her so much that she would be happy in it – to charm her till she smiled'. To this end architects

needed light and always more light, until they sacrificed safety and common sense in trying to get it. They converted their walls into windows, raised their vaults, diminished their piers, until their churches could no longer stand. You will see the limits at Beauvais; at Chartres we have not got so far, but even here, in places where the Virgin wanted it – as above the high altar – the architect has taken all the light there was to take.

In addition to light the Virgin requires 'space', 'convenience', 'color and decoration to unite and harmonize the whole', for the unity of Chartres is her taste, represents her ascendancy and the consequent pushing aside of the orthodox Trinity for a natural one of father, mother, son, all the while diminishing the role of the heavenly Father and reclaiming the child through his human mother. The values of the church militant give way before the longing for the mother's gifts – 'Love, Charity, Grace'.

Unlike Mont-Saint-Michel, Chartres is elaborate, aesthetically complex, even playful. It is humane. In the twelfth-century political power shifts to the great queens, to Eleanor and her daughters, the *Song of Roland* gives way to *Lancelot, Tristan, Perceval, The Romance of the Rose*. Man serves God through serving woman and hopes for redemption in her mercy rather than in the Father's approval. So in the twelfth century men bow down before women in the church and the state and in art. And the masculine theology of the scholastics, stymied by its own logic, gives way to the mystics, to St Francis and all his little sisters.

The final chapter belongs to Thomas Aquinas, who attempts the grand reconciliation of reason and emotion, of science and theology, of God and man. Here, too, there is an architectural analogy:

> Beginning with the foundation which is God and God's active presence in His Church, Thomas next built God into the walls and towers of His Church, in the Trinity and its creation of mind and matter in time and space; then finally he filled the Church by uniting mind and matter in man, or man's soul, giving to humanity a free will that rose, like the flèche, to heaven.

Thomas's church – like Amiens Cathedral – derives its unity from the fact that 'one idea controlled every line' and Thomas's God is a 'prime motor' supplying 'all energy to the Universe'.

'The real destination of the "Travels",' suggests Ernest Samuels, referring to the 'Travels/France' which Adams had printed under the book's title, 'was of course his own age.' That destination is more directly the subject matter of *The Education of Henry Adams* as its author indicates in 'The Editor's Preface' (written by him but signed – at his insistence – by his former student Henry Cabot Lodge), when he adds to *Mont-Saint-Michel and Chartres* the subtitle 'A Study of Thirteenth-Century Unity' as counterpart to the *Education*'s subtitle, 'A Study of Twentieth-Century Multiplicity'. What his description of the United States in 1800 was to serve in charting the lines of force operative in American history, his depiction of thirteenth-century unity was to provide for Western culture more generally.

If the *Education*, though narrated in the third person, is more obviously personal than any of his earlier works, it benefits from many of the same qualities. His portraits of Lincoln, Grant, Garibaldi, the English politicians of the 1860s, and of his most intimate friends,

Clarence King and John Hay, make available the same penetrating evaluations of character provided by the *History*'s portraits. Quincy, Rome, Berlin, and London are as powerfully portrayed as was Washington DC in the earlier works. Sustained as well is the old capacity for amusement, though largely at his own expense and providing in a book that may yearn to be Augustine's *Confessions*, a frequent touch of Twain's *The Innocents Abroad*. The writing is rich in metaphor and reveals a mastery of syntax, a capacity to hold so many divergent elements together, that an Adams sentence can seem, in itself, a significant victory in the effort to affirm unity in the midst of multiplicity.

But the *Education* is a work divided against itself, or rather separated a little more than halfway through by a missing twenty-year period, a period that contains Adams's marriage, all but the first of his years as a Harvard professor, and the writing of the *History*, a silent chasm, over which one half of his life peers at the other. It is a condition that marks more than chronology. The narrator himself is divided, divided between reflective Quincy and worldly Boston, between eighteenth-century ideals and nineteenth-century realities. He has become, from childhood, accustomed 'to feel that, for him, life was double'. And, as divisions accumulate, more than double.

From cradle to grave this problem of running order through chaos, direction through space, discipline through freedom, unity through multiplicity, has always been, and must always be, the task of education, as it is the moral of religion, philosophy, science, art, politics, and economy . . .

But the first section of Adams's book provides no such education; there is multiplicity but no order, none at least that satisfies him. After college graduation he sails to Germany to study civil law, but apart from a few instances of what he terms 'accidental education', he learns nothing. When hurried off to Rome by his older sister, he finds there 'a gospel of anarchy and vice', as the city places 'conundrum upon conundrum in his educational path'. All explanations fail; no causes explain these effects and even that last refuge, time-sequence, must be relinquished. 'The Forum no more led to the Vatican than the Vatican to the Forum. Rienzi, Garibaldi, Tiberius Gracchus, Aurelian might be mixed up in any relation of time, along with a thousand more, and never lead to a sequence.'

And the principle holds for more than Rome. Even Darwinian biology – in Adams's day the most widely accepted model for order in multiplicity – leads not to evolutionary design but to contradiction in creatures that appear with no apparent ancestry and those that continue, unchanged, through geologic time ('altogether too much uniformity and much too little selection'). That thirty-eight years after the last Adams presidency the office should be held by so primitive a form as Grant was as remarkable as *Terebratula* or *Pteraspis* in biology. The theme of education as elaborated in the first three-fifths of the book is one of failed assumptions, of lessons unlearned rather than learned until, in a chapter entitled 'Chaos', his sister dies – in a Europe torn by an absurd war – an absurd death, the result of a foot bruised in a cab accident.

The second part of the *Education*, though it too contains the anecdotes of autobiography, leads simultaneously toward death and a dynamic view of history. Biology with its 'Evolution that did not evolve', its 'Uniformity that was not Uniform', its 'Selection that did not select' – offers no more helpful a dogma than the Athanasian creed, but physics Adams finds more promising. At the great Chicago Exposition he describes the dynamo, the twentieth-century counterpart to the Virgin as a symbol of energy. In this context a new possibility emerges:

> Thus, unless one mistook the meaning of motion, which might well be, the scientific synthesis commonly called Unity was the scientific analysis commonly called Multiplicity. The two things were the same, all forms being shifting phases of motion. Granted this ocean of colliding atoms, the last hope of humanity, what happened if one dropped the sounder into the abyss – let it go – frankly gave up Unity altogether? What was Unity? Why was one to be forced to affirm it?

The discussion of a scientific understanding of history is incomplete in the *Education*, had already been elaborated in the essays eventually collected in *The Degradation of the Democratic Dogma* (1920), and, for all the emphasis given to the dynamic theory in the *Education*, it is not – in this context – as important for what it is as for what it represents, its use or misuse of science of no particular relevance.

In a manner both perverse and poignant the *Education* parallels *Mont-Saint-Michel and Chartres*. St Michael has his counterpart in the puritanical devotion to duty of the old Adamses, or perhaps in the

Washington of Mount Vernon, figures who called young Henry to the service of the state not as a crusader, but as a secretary, as a student of state documents and of political institutions. The results of his study, like those of the scholastic thinkers under Michael's protective wing, proved self-defeating, leaving the secretary no logical path to follow. Woman, the Virgin, is the absent center of the *Education*, lost in the missing twenty years, though briefly revealed in the dying sister and shadowed in the Saint-Gaudens figure commissioned for his wife's grave. Now, far from Chartres, she yields to energy that does not cohere, that drives apart rather than unifies, that – though ordered perhaps in some grand cosmic scheme – thrusts the particular, the individual, away from any center. But it is energy that can, Adams at last believes, be rendered intellectual, energy that invites, as William Jordy suggests, its Thomas to express it formally. Though the parallel is clear, it mocks as well as excites. Here there is no architectural counterpart, no Amiens, no cathedral of reason and faith with triumphant spire, but violent outward movement, dissolution rationalized.

Wit, taste, and courage justify *The Education of Henry Adams*; these and, ironically, energy, personal energy that survived into old age, energy to travel, to witness, to think, and to compose. The final endeavour, the plunging into yet another form of education, testifies to that vitality more than to any ultimate shape for history. This is energy born of a tension that remained to the end undiminished, pulled on one side by the longing for the one – the mother, who will forgive even an Adams, the pole star that will locate even an American – and, on the other, by the variety of the many, the co-existence of a Jefferson, a Tecumseh, a Burr, a Napoleon. The traditional door for the mystic was barred to Adams, for no matter how he longed for the one, he was too amused by the many to give them up. He wanted, like Whitman, to be both a cosmos and a self but was too inhibited or perhaps too intellectually honest to make Whitman's leap.

The *Education* provided an appropriate end not because it offers a resolution but because it contains all the contradictions inherent in the career, contradictions that satisfy rather than destroy because at some level, whether accepted or not, they simply seem to be in the nature of things. Adams declared every person encountered in the

Education, at last, incomprehensible. And so they are and so is he, and yet he rendered them for us in such a manner that we know them even if we cannot understand them. If in the end Henry presents himself as a failure – a term haunting the critical literature as much as the *Education* – that is only another argument, as he well understood, for his success at what mattered most, his success as an Adams. Of the first seven presidents of the United States, only two failed to be elected to second terms, and both had the same last name, a fact that, even in the fourth generation, rankled and, in true American fashion, reassured.

KATE CHOPIN AND
SARAH ORNE JEWETT

PEARL K. BELL

In the waning years of the nineteenth century, two remarkable women, exact contemporaries living at opposite ends of the immense American diversity, dissented from the cultural shibboleths and popular taste of their time in the way they wrote about the life they knew best. Kate Chopin (1851–1904) was consciously defiant of the decencies and sexual prudery of the 1890s, and sought to uncover the sensuality and discontent of women which the stultifying conventions of the age refused to acknowledge. Sarah Orne Jewett (1849–1909) preferred to look back rather than forward to the emancipated future envisioned by Mrs Chopin; her sensibility and values were deeply anchored in the past of a rural New England that was rapidly disappearing in her lifetime, but she, too, shunned the idealized versions of actuality which a culture dedicated to gentility demanded of its literature.

Immeasurably different though they were as women and as writers, neither Mrs Chopin nor Miss Jewett showed any affinity for the noble morality and complacent optimism represented by the three venerable New Englanders – James Russell Lowell, Oliver Wendell Holmes Sr, and John Greenleaf Whittier – who were still revered as the high priests of American literature. Even so staunch a defender of realism as William Dean Howells could go only so far and no further in accepting writers who dared to concern themselves with the seamier and less benevolent aspects of American society toward the end of the century. In the notorious statement that blighted his reputation for years, Howells urged American novelists to deal with 'the more smiling aspects of life, which are the more American, and seek the universal in the individual rather than the social interests'.

Several notches below this arch conception of literary art, the popular taste of the time was equally uninterested in the depiction of actual life, and the great mass of American readers couldn't get enough of the historical romances churned out by such best-selling novelists as Francis Marion Crawford, who wrote dashing claptrap about aristocratic love and honor in exotic locales; Charles Major (*When Knighthood Was in Flower*); Booth Tarkington (*Monsieur Beaucaire*); and Owen Wister (*The Virginian*). (And still lower down on the literary scale were the successors of the 'damned mob of scribbling women' that Hawthorne had railed against in the 1850s, who flooded the market with their tear-drenched melodramas.) When Crawford scornfully asked, 'What has art to do with truth? Is not truth the imagination's deadly enemy?' he was being exceptionally cynical. Though Mr Lowell and Mr Holmes would not have said it quite so nakedly, Crawford's haughty questions were not all that far removed from what they believed and practiced.

Some few writers of the time thought otherwise. They knew in every fiber of their confidence in themselves that art has everything to do with truth, that the imagination can flourish only when it is fed by the particularity of a writer's experience and judgement. But in the last years of the century such writers as Stephen Crane, Frank Norris, Edward Arlington Robinson, and Theodore Dreiser were either misread, ignored, or denounced because they sought to write more openly about sexual passion and economic corruption than the prevailing culture would tolerate. It was only in a later and different America that the scope and courage of their achievement was recognized. Though they are admittedly lesser figures compared to such towering originals as Norris and Dreiser, Kate Chopin and Sarah Jewett, in their distinctive ways, also rejected the idealization of reality. In their quest for models of the kind of work they hoped to accomplish, they were emboldened by their reading of Flaubert, and sought to enact his axiom that one must write about ordinary life as though it were history. In their dissimilar fashion, they were moved by the same compelling need to trust what they observed and felt as the truth of their literary art.

Kate Chopin (née O'Flaherty) was born a decade before the outbreak of the Civil War in St Louis, Missouri, of an Irish immigrant father and a mother descended from early French pioneers. She grew up equally fluent in English and French, but was always drawn more strongly to French writers than to those of England and her own country. When she discovered Maupassant at an impressionable age, she felt an immediate kinship with a writer who offered 'life, not fiction', because he was 'a man who had escaped from tradition and authority'.

But it was not until she was all of thirty-two, a well-provided-for widow with six children, that this handsome, restless, and ambitious woman began writing sketches and stories about the Creoles, the Cajuns, and the blacks she had known in Louisiana, where she lived during her marriage to Oscar Chopin. The Creoles and the Cajuns who were to figure so prominently in her work were of different stock and rank in Louisiana society. The former were the pure-blooded descendants of French settlers, an aristocracy apart from the Cajuns, who were lower down on the social scale, and were descended from the Acadians expelled from Nova Scotia by the British in the eighteenth century. Sooner than her literary experience warranted, however, she plunged into a novel, *At Fault*, which she published at her own expense in 1890. It deals with a young widow, Thérèse Lafirme, obviously modelled on the author, who takes over the running of a huge plantation after her husband's untimely death. An intelligent, beautiful, independent woman – the first of several such in Mrs Chopin's fiction – Thérèse still clings to a stern moral view of the sanctity of marriage, and she forces the man she loves to remarry the dreary alcoholic he had divorced some years back. Everyone festers in high-minded misery until the awful wife is conveniently disposed of during a violent storm, and the lovers can marry with a clear conscience. For all the charming descriptions of the lush landscape of rural Louisiana, the characters in *At Fault* remain lifeless pawns. The reception of the book was on the whole not unkind, but it soon sank out of sight, and is interesting today mainly as one of the earliest American novels to deal approvingly with the risqué subject of divorce.

Discouraged by the failure of *At Fault*, Kate Chopin began to concentrate on the lively stories about Louisiana that were soon being published in the *Atlantic*, the *Century*, and *Vogue*. Her entire career as a writer was packed into a single, astonishingly prolific decade in which, in addition to three novels, she tossed off some hundred stories, many of them collected in *Bayou Folk* (1894) and *A*

Night in Acadie (1897). The range of these stories is wide, but it is the mettlesome directness she brought to 'forbidden' subjects that now seems so impressive: miscegenation, rocky marriages, rebellious women, even a physically explicit account, in 'The Storm', of a casually adulterous romp that ends with neither guilt nor divine retribution, only the savored afterglow of idle pleasure.

Because Mrs Chopin's stories grew out of her intimate familiarity with the people and customs of New Orleans and rural Louisiana, and she conveys the music of the Cajun and Creole dialects so convincingly, she was regarded by most of her readers as just another local-color writer – a late blooming of the post-Civil War rage for a kind of literary anthropology of regional folkways, in which the dialects and customs of the American provinces were sentimentally depicted as quaint and comic, like hillbillies on television. But Kate Chopin had no interest in such condescending uses of the past, and she resented being identified with such local-color storytellers as George Washington Cable, who also wrote about Louisiana. In the best of her stories the regional peculiarities provide the enriching texture, but her true interest lay beyond that, in the human drama. Though she sometimes reached too quickly for tricky Maupassant-like endings, and often relied on the dubious case of coincidence – she did, after all, want to be published – in the best of her stories she confronted the taboos about sex and marriage with a clear-eyed candor that few writers of the time, male or female, dared to attempt.

Kate Chopin's work contains a smoldering abundance of restless, unhappy wives (and some fretful, dissatisfied husbands, *pour lagniappe*), and in one startling tale, 'The Story of an Hour', written a few years before her masterpiece, *The Awakening*, one can feel the bold design of that novel beginning to take shape in the author's head. In the brief compass of less than three pages, Mrs Chopin described the reaction of a young woman to the news that her husband has been killed in a railway accident. She is stunned, but she finds herself responding to the news not with an outburst of grief but with a whispered 'free, free, free!'

> She saw a long procession of years to come that would belong to her absolutely. And she opened and spread her arms out to them in welcome. There would be no one to live for her during those coming years; she would

live for herself. There would be no powerful will bending hers in that blind persistence with which men and women believe they have a right to impose a private will upon a fellow-creature ... What could love, the unsolved mystery, count for in face of this possession of self-assertion which she suddenly recognized as the strongest impulse of her being!

'Free! Body and soul free!' she kept whispering.

Precisely because 'The Story of an Hour' is almost entirely stripped of any distracting details about setting or character, its meaning is charged with a direct, almost brutal power. The young wife-cum-widow becomes a disembodied voice, not a person, a voice rejoicing in the realization that freedom is no longer unthinkable. Mrs Chopin did make a conciliatory gesture toward the magazine editors of the time by bringing the husband through the door in the last paragraph, whereupon the wife drops dead of 'the joy that kills'. But her irony was unmistakable, and the story was rejected as 'unethical' by the editor of the *Century*. It eventually appeared in *Vogue*, whose editors obviously had a very good idea of the snakes that lurked in their female readers' hearts.

A woman of uncommon urbanity and intelligence, Kate Chopin was appalled by the straitlaced parochialism of American literary culture in the dying century. In breeding, temperament, and taste, she felt much closer to Mme de Staël and George Sand than to any native writers. She smoked cigarettes, liked wine, and saw no reason to play down what a friend described as 'a quality of sex [in her] that is inexplicable'. And she did not hesitate to say exactly what she thought about the suffocating narrowness that dominated the American literary scene. In 1894, after yawning through a conference of the Western Association of Writers (its star was the folksy Hoosier poet James Whitcomb Riley), she denounced the moribund songbirds:

The cry of the dying century has not reached this body of workers, or else it has not been comprehended. There is no doubt in their souls, no unrest ... Among these people are to be found ... a clinging to past and conventional standards ... and a singular ignorance of, or disregard for, the value of the highest art forms. There is a very, very big world lying not wholly in northern Indiana ... It is human existence in its subtle, complex, true meaning, stripped of the veil with which ethical and conventional standards have draped it.

In her view, that veil had been rolled into a noose, strangling the sexual and intellectual independence of American women who foolishly submitted to their husbands' notions. As Mrs Chopin put it in 'The Gentleman from New Orleans', the ideal wife showed 'a certain lack of self-assertion which her husband regarded as the perfection of womanliness'. In story after story she deplored the passive timidity of women – 'self-assertion' was one of her favorite terms – and she delighted in the plucky heroine of 'Athénaïse', who runs away from her husband because 'It's jus' being married that I detes' and despise . . .' As the author wryly commented on the young bride's dilemma, 'The day has not yet come when a young woman might ask the court's permission to return to her mama on the sweeping ground of a constitutional disinclination for marriage.'

After her second collection of stories came out in 1897, Kate Chopin realized that she needed a larger and more sustaining form than the short story to dramatize her vision of female self-fulfillment, and she spent the next year writing her prophetic novel, *The Awakening*, which was published in 1899.

There is no question that she had *Madame Bovary* in mind as she began writing the book: both heroines resent their husbands, neglect their children, take an adulterous lover, and commit suicide. But there are significant differences. Mrs Chopin's Edna Pontillier, married to a wealthy Creole businessman in New Orleans, is not a naïve and restless fool like Emma Bovary, longing to escape from the boredom of provincial bourgeois life. Mrs Pontillier is a sensitive and perceptive woman who put away her girlish fantasies of grand romance when she married. But now, at twenty-eight, the mother of two young sons, she feels strangely haunted by 'an indescribable oppression, which seemed to generate in some unfamiliar part of her consciousness'.

This nameless and perplexing sensation has emerged in the loosening languor of summer, which she is spending with her children on an island in the Gulf of Mexico, and Edna realizes that it has something to do with the dense proximity of the many Creole women whom she ordinarily sees only occasionally at home in New Orleans. In the midst of this Creole and Catholic world, Edna, a Protestant from Kentucky, feels like the odd woman. She had never been at ease with the Creole women's 'entire absence of prudery', and is shocked by the casually uninhibited way they talk about 'unmentionable' intimacies like childbirth. Nor can she understand the free-and-easy flirtatiousness that is never allowed to encroach on their inviolable wifely chastity. When Edna becomes infatuated with Robert Lebrun, a young bachelor on Grand Isle, and begins to take his caressing glances seriously, she has misunderstood the Creole code that finds flirtation amusing but adultery impermissible, a threat to the sanctity of marriage and motherhood.

As Kate Chopin conveys the smell and the look of the tropical island, the rhythmic and dreamy sensuality nourished by the heat of the sun and 'the seductive odor of the sea', it becomes clear that Edna's attraction to Robert is only the outward sign of a profound discontent, and she begins to listen to an unknown part of her inner self that is stirring awake after years of sleep. Without realizing the gravity – and ambiguity – of her words, Edna tells a Creole friend that she would never sacrifice herself for her children: 'I would give up the unessential, I would give up my money, I would give my life for my children, but I wouldn't give myself.' The ominous implications of this confused distinction do not emerge until much later.

As Edna gradually becomes aware of the underlying self that is struggling to declare itself like the howl of a new-born infant, she begins to act out its seditious promptings. When she returns to New Orleans at the end of the summer, she stops being 'at home' on Tuesdays to a stream of visitors who mean nothing to her. She flings off her wedding ring and tries to crush it, and she devotes herself with unaccustomed seriousness to her painting, which until now had been a trifling way of passing the time. In delirious defiance of everything her husband and his society hold sacred, she decides, while the rest of the family is away, to move out of her oppressively opulent house and live alone. In a tiny house of her own, no longer just a decorative part of her husband's property,

she had a feeling of having descended in the social scale, with a corresponding sense of having risen in the spiritual. Every step which she took toward relieving herself of obligations added to her strength and expansion as an individual. She began to look with her own eyes; to see and to apprehend the deeper undercurrents of life. No longer was she content to 'feed upon opinion' when her own soul had invited her.

And yet, when she drifts into an affair with the notorious roué

Alcée Arobin, she feels little joy in this act of her own free will. She wants more than a philanderer can give her, and hopes to find genuine fulfillment with Robert Lebrun. But he cannot bring himself to transgress against the Creole code of chastity, and runs away. With this rejection, Edna's illusion of freedom collapses. She cannot face the negligent life of meaningless affairs that will be her fate – 'Today it is Arobin; tomorrow it will be someone else' – and on a cool spring day she sails over to Grand Isle and plunges naked into the sea that closes over her.

Unlike the many novels about a woman's yearning for self-fulfillment spawned by the feminist movement of our own time, *The Awakening* is almost forbiddingly objective. The nature of Edna's longing has been misunderstood by many of Mrs Chopin's readers, for she never suggests that her heroine's marriage has been sexually inadequate. Edna is awakened not by her need for 'perfect' sex but by her desire for independence, for a life free of the shackles of marriage and children. And Kate Chopin shrewdly perceived the flaw in Edna Pontillier's notion that she would give her life for her children, but wouldn't give 'herself'. Her illusion that the two are separate is part of the more sinister illusion that freedom can be attained through the reckless abandonment of all duties and obligations, especially those imposed by young children. Her unforgivable offense is not adultery but a dream of freedom which threatens the foundations of society not only by rejecting the role it assigns to women, but by rejecting the human burden of obligation. Kate Chopin sympathized with Edna Pontillier's craving for independence, but she also perceived its irresponsibility. She did not subscribe to the moral fallacy of the disconnected life.

In 1899, however, her readers missed the point of her cautionary wisdom, and took *The Awakening* to be a shocking defense of adultery. One reviewer blustered that the novel was 'too strong drink for moral babes, and should be labelled "poison"'. The St Louis libraries quickly acted on the scandal by banning the book from circulation. Kate Chopin was ostracized by polite St Louis society, and blackballed for membership in the Fine Arts Club. She was deeply wounded by the general verdict throughout the country that *The Awakening* was morbid and disgusting, though it does seem odd, given what she knew about the Pecksniffian atmosphere of the time, that she was surprised by the hostile response. When her publisher turned down a new collection of stories without explanation, she felt totally despised and rejected, and in the five years before her death, at the age of fifty-three, she wrote very little. In the new century her name was forgotten, and it was many years before she was newly discovered, by Edmund Wilson, who devoted some appreciative pages to her in *Patriotic Gore* (1962), his study of the literature of the Civil War and its aftermath.

But Kate Chopin came fully into her own when feminist critics, eager to redress the neglect of a pioneer, began reading *The Awakening* in the 1970s. It has by now been widely reprinted, and has become a sacred text. Yet, like many novels that acquire an ideological halo, *The Awakening*, as a work of literary art, is often read too uncritically today. At times Mrs Chopin relied lazily on heavy-handed abstractions that tell rather than show what she wants to say, such as the flaccid apostrophe about Mrs Pontillier's 'position in the universe as a human being' as she begins 'to recognize her relations as an individual to the world within and about her'. This smacks of psycho-babble. But these lapses are minor seen against her powerful evocation of Grand Isle and New Orleans, her psychological astuteness, her use of the sea as the novel's commanding symbol, at once sensual, life-giving, and destructive, and her profound sense of moral complexity. What she might have written if *The Awakening* had not been vilified as poison is impossible to guess, but one can only lament the silence that was not of her own making.

It would be difficult to imagine a woman and a writer who offers a starker contrast to Kate Chopin of St Louis, Missouri, than Sarah Orne Jewett of South Berwick, Maine. They stood at the antipodes of female American experience in the late years of the nineteenth century, and had little in common beyond the regional labels pinned on them by literary historians, and their admiration for Flaubert. Though Kate Chopin, who began writing much later than Sarah Jewett, studied the latter's stories for what they could teach her about style and technique, she could not have found them very useful, for the two women regarded the world in utterly dissimilar ways, and the experience and attitudes they brought to their work were as different as the landscapes of Louisiana and Maine.

Sarah Jewett was born and died in Berwick, and she could not conceive of a life that was not rooted in her rural home town, though she spent part of every winter in Boston and made several trips to Europe. A spinster who seems never even to have toyed with the idea of marriage, she was the daughter of a well-to-do doctor and a mother whose ancestors were sea-captains and ship-builders. Unlike Kate Chopin, who had no interest in the past, Sarah Jewett gave her strongest allegiance to the generations older than her own, for she grew up 'with grandfathers and grand-uncles and aunts for my best playmates'.

But she knew, with a sense of regret that informed every corner of her art, that the world of those grandfathers and grand-uncles was dying in her lifetime. The wharves in the coastal towns of Maine that, before the Civil War, had been thriving centers of shipping, were rotting, the up-country farms were being abandoned as the country moved westward, and the tranquil villages, already trans-formed by textile mills and railroads, were now being invaded by immigrants and summer tourists. As she wrote to Mr Whittier, with a characteristically familial image, 'Nobody has mourned more than I over the forsaken farmhouses which I see everywhere as I drive about the country out of which I grew, and where every bush and tree seem like my cousins.'

It was to the crumbling past that she gave her tenderest loyalty, and her stories are filled with elderly widows and spinsters, with superannuated sea-captains, and aged farmers and fishermen strug-gling to wrest a meager living from the hostile sea and the rocky New England soil. In her childhood she had accompanied her doctor father on his rounds of the isolated farms and coastal villages, and she thoroughly absorbed the speech, the eccentricities, the 'elaborate conventionalities', and the sadness of a pastoral world drifting into anachronism. This loving intimacy became the lifeblood of her urge as a writer to hold that pre-industrial existence alive, in memory, against the corruption of time.

She found her cultural sustenance in the past as well. Her passionate faith in the harmony of man and nature, which meant nothing to the booming industrial life of America after the Civil War, was confirmed and nourished by her devotion to the transcendental themes of Emerson and Thoreau. She knew little about the younger writers of her time, but admired Willa Cather, who became a good friend in the last year of Miss Jewett's life, and it was very much in character that she worried lest Willa Cather, then working in New York on *McClure's* magazine, lose touch with her Nebraska childhood, if she became too involved in 'the "Bohemia" of newspaper and magazine-life'. There was never the slightest danger that Sarah Orne Jewett would lose touch with *her* roots, for they were all of what she was, the strength of her belonging to one place and to a time older than her own. As the lively old countrywoman Mrs Fosdick complains in *The Country of the Pointed Firs* (1896), 'I see so many of these new folks nowadays, that seem to have neither past nor future. Conversation's got to have some root in the past, or else you've got to explain every remark you make, an' it wears a person out.'

Sarah Jewett published over twenty books, the first, *Deephaven*, when she was twenty-eight, and most of the volumes, even those she chose to call novels, are gatherings of sketches and stories that had appeared in the *Atlantic* and, occasionally, elsewhere. She lacked whatever talent it takes to control the lengthy complications of a novel, and when she compelled herself to make the effort, she blundered. Her gift was for place and character, not plot; for the brief glimpse, the small incident that illuminates everything about a person, a family, a house, through the kind of detail and image that become acts of revelation. In 'The Guests of Mrs Timms', a fussy, pretentious woman is described as 'a straight, flat little person, as if, when not in use, she kept herself, silk dress and all, between the leaves of a book'. She could summon up the poignancy of a way of life, at once sustained and imperilled by the sea, with a few spare strokes in the opening of 'By the Morning Boat':

> On the coast of Maine, where many green islands and salt inlets fringe the deep-cut shore line; where balsam firs and bayberry bushes send their fragrance far seaward ... and the tide runs plashing in and out among the weedy ledges ... On the lonely coast of Maine stood a small gray house facing the morning light. All the weather-beaten houses of that region face the sea apprehensively, like the women who live in them.

In Sarah Jewett's great triumph as a writer, *The Country of the Pointed Firs*, published when she was in her late forties, one feels only the faintest premonitory rustlings of the world beyond the village of Dunnet Landing. The life elsewhere, away from this small community facing the sea, seems at first to be entirely absent from the stories which compose this 'novel,' as though these humble old men and women, whose days turn in rhythm with the seasons and the light, are anemones fossilized in amber. But it is soon clear that even though their life seems to be going on in the present, it is the past that Miss Jewett is embracing in an eloquent gesture of farewell. This is never said, of course, since such literalness would violate the art of her elegy. But she succeeded, as we finally realize, in recapturing the past without a trace of false sentiment.

The various stories that unfold in *The Country of the Pointed Firs* are given a tenuous unity by the nameless narrator, a young woman who arrives from the city to spend the summer in this peacefully isolated backwater, and learns to cherish its tranquility along with its idiosyncratic and endearing inhabitants. The summer visitor lodges in the house of a widow, Almira Todd, who dominates the book as the embodiment of man's unity with nature, though she does not appear in each story. A herb gatherer and gardener, she turns her 'rural pharmacopoeia' into soothing remedies that even the local doctor respects. A massive woman of sixty-seven, with 'the look of a huge sibyl', she tells her lodger one day about the man she long ago loved and lost because he was 'far above her'. (This is all we ever learn about class differences in Dunnet Landing.) As she talks, overcome by grief at this painful memory, Mrs Todd acquires a classic majesty in the eyes of her listener: 'She might have been Antigone alone on the Theban plain ... An absolute, archaic grief possessed her, she seemed a renewal of some historic soul, with her sorrows and the remoteness of a daily life busied with rustic simplicities and the scents of primeval herbs.'

Yet Mrs Todd is as down-to-earth as the herbs she grows, and knows everything about everyone in the village; they form the landscape of all her days. She shares them with her lodger: the ancient sea-captain whose memories have slipped a cog, and whose grave face is 'worn into appealing lines, as if he had suffered from loneliness and misapprehension'; the shy fisherman who waits patiently for forty years to marry his beloved shepherdess; the lonely farm-woman who calls herself the Queen's Twin because she and

Victoria were born on the same day. Mrs Todd takes her lodger on a visit to her eighty-seven-year-old mother, a spry little woman who has spent most of her life in contentment on a tiny island across the water. Another day Mrs Todd, her mother, and the visitor take part in a huge family reunion that seems to link the islands and the scattered farms into 'a golden chain of love and dependence', and late in the summer they row out to the barren island where 'poor Joanna', jilted by her lover, hid her sorrow and humiliation in the silent loneliness of an anchorite for the rest of her life.

Yet, though Dunnet Landing has borne its mortal weight of rejection and loss, madness, withered expectations, and eccentricity, it does not remind us of the many rancorous American novels that expose the horrors of small-town life. Sarah Jewett is not Sherwood Anderson, and the people of Dunnet Landing, however odd they may appear, are not grotesques. With the affectionate grace and meticulous observation that shaped her style, Miss Jewett paid tribute to the precious individuality of these country folk, whose modest dignity and natural sense of community had not yet entirely succumbed to an increasingly impersonal industrial age. As one of her bright little old ladies remarks, 'What a lot of queer folks there used to be about here, anyway, when we was young . . . Everybody's just like everybody else now.' In all her work we can feel Sarah Jewett quietly recoiling from the bustling clatter of a modern world that is rapidly destroying the serenity of a life defined by nature. But it could not disappear completely as long as there were writers who understood the imperatives of memory.

It scarcely needs saying that with all her acutely rendered consciousness of the old-fashioned ways, Miss Jewett's Emersonian vision of man in nature neglected a less winning side of the nature of man. As F. O. Matthiessen, the great scholar of the American Renaissance, pointed out in his youthfully florid biography of Miss Jewett, published in 1929 when he was still in his twenties:

She always paints the gentler emotions: blinding hates and jealousies, the fever of lust and the thirst of avarice never throb there . . . There is a stark New England Sarah Jewett does not show, morbid, bleak, and mean of spirit. She looked at nature in its milder moods, and at mankind in its more subdued states of tenderness and regret.

It is so often summertime in her stories, or a benign day in autumn or spring. The crippling severity of the New England winter is rarely mentioned, and although she was by no means blind to poverty in such stories as 'Going to Shrewsbury' and 'The Flight of Betsey Lane', she did not often confront head-on the demeaning squalor and helplessness of the destitute, as she did, for example, in 'The Town Poor'. But even in that chilling story, she took the sting out by ending on a cheerful note of hope. The bitterness and suspicion that Mary Wilkins Freeman, a far less gifted writer of the same generation, revealed in her novels about small towns in New England are not to be found in Miss Jewett's work. As for passion, she ventured no further than the response of an adolescent girl to a dashing sportsman, in 'A White Heron', written a decade before *The Pointed Firs*: 'She had never seen anybody so charming and delightful; the woman's heart, asleep in the child, was vaguely thrilled by a dream of love.' It is not surprising that in reading *Madame Bovary* she was struck not by Emma's sexual romanticism but by her rejection of the natural community to which she belonged.

In her lifetime Sarah Jewett was praised and cosseted as a perfect darling by such titans of literary Boston as Lowell and Holmes. But it was typical of Lowell's lofty astigmatism that he especially approved of her decision, as he put it, 'to work within narrow limitations', and left it at that. As her books appeared, the reviewers almost invariably praised the perfection of her style, the purity of her language, her sweet and ladylike refinement, and her humour. In her own day only Howells seems to have discerned how much she drew from 'the very tint and form of reality', but he did not grasp what that aged reality meant to her, and how thoroughly, however uninsistently, she diverged from the literary givens of the time.

Sarah Jewett's work never suffered the brutal extinction meted out to Kate Chopin, but in the early years of the new century she was read mainly by those whose heads, like hers, were 'full of old women and old houses', and their number was dwindling. Not long after she died, Henry James, in an 'appreciation' so snarled in knots and tangles of circumlocutory wool that the one strand of unembarrassed lucidity can easily be overlooked, wrote that she had 'a sort of elegance of humility'. In the 1930s the influential left-wing critics had as little use for Sarah Orne Jewett as they did for Emily Post. Granville Hicks contemptuously dismissed her as 'merely a New England old maid who believed in piety, progress, and propriety'.

In recent swings of the *Zeitgeist*, Sarah Orne Jewett has, not surprisingly, been largely ignored by feminist critics, perhaps because her aged widows and spinsters are so cheerfully satisfied with their lot, and have nothing to rebel against. In any case, her devotion to the past could hardly endear her to militant crusaders for a liberated future. Perhaps the worst offense, on the part of academic critics, is to pigeonhole Miss Jewett as a regional writer, as though her genius was caged by geography. But neither Sarah Jewett nor Kate Chopin, who has also been labeled 'regional', limited their thoughts or curiosity about human beings to the quaint and the picturesque, as that label implies. Different as they were – the one a modern woman before her time, the other a guardian of the past – they both knew that the truth of art, while necessarily drawing its strength from the writer's experience of a specific place in time, must also transcend it. In this view of literature they were out of step with their own age, but among the novelists of the century that began toward the end of their lives, they would, eventually, be vindicated.

HENRY JAMES:
THE AMBIGUITIES OF CULTURE
ALWYN BERLAND

Many American writers before Henry James (1843–1916) had been concerned with the connections between the United States and an older European culture: one thinks of such figures as Cooper, Hawthorne, Melville, Twain and Howells. But James was to be the first major American writer to become an expatriate, living briefly first in Paris and then – for the larger part of his adult life – in England. There he wrote almost all of his twenty-three novels, a large body of novellas and short stories, several plays, travel books, literary essays, and an autobiography in three volumes, the last of which was unfinished at his death, in England, in 1916.

The reasons for James's expatriation were no doubt complex. He might first have found encouragement in his father's belief that absolute values should not be confused with the parochialisms of a fixed residence. Henry James, Sr, moved his family about a good deal, frequently to Europe. But a more important reason was certainly James's understanding of the kind of culture necessary to him as a writer. His feelings about American culture were complicated; but his sense of its adequacy to the writing of novels is suggested, with some tact, in his early essay on Emerson:

> It would require some ingenuity . . . to trace closely this correspondence between his genius and the frugal, dutiful, happy but decidedly lean Boston of the past, where there was a great deal of will but very little fulcrum – like a ministry without an opposition.
>
> (*Partial Portraits*, 1888, p. 8)

This is likely to recall Matthew Arnold's 'Hebraism': it is a description of Character without Culture.

There is a frequently quoted passage in James's *Notebooks* (which he copied almost word for word in his 1879 study of Hawthorne):

> In a story, someone says – 'Oh yes, the United States – a country without a sovereign, without a court, without a nobility, without an army, without

a church or clergy, without a diplomatic service, without a picturesque peasantry, without palaces or castles, or country seats, or ruins, without a literature, without novels, without an Oxford or a Cambridge, without cathedrals or ivied churches, without latticed cottages or village ale-houses, without political society, without sport, without fox-hunting, or country gentlemen, without an Epsom or an Ascot, an Eton or a Rugby . . .!!'

(p. 14)

One may be amused, as James certainly was, by the note of rhetorical extravagance here, but an essential truth is still involved. Writing to W. D. Howells (in 1880), rather defensively, James said:

. . . it takes an old civilization to set a novelist in motion . . . It is on manners, customs, usages, habits, forms, upon all these things matured and established, that a novelist lives – they are the very stuff his work is made of; and in saying that in the absence of those 'dreary and worn-out paraphernalia' which I enumerate as being wanting in American society, 'we have simply the whole of human life left,' you beg (to my sense) the question.

(*The Letters*, 1920, I, p. 72)

Further, to the sense of an absence of 'high culture' should be added James's conviction (which he shared in various forms with such writers as Twain and Howells) that post-Civil War American society was becoming progressively more industrialized, material-istic, and acquisitive, despite (or perhaps because of) the older Puritan tradition. James's move to Europe, then, has its rationale. Whether he found a society devoid of materialism and acquisition in the civilization of Europe is another matter.

What James sought for in Europe to begin with were the 'accumu-lated monuments and treasures of art', the high culture which through the nineteenth century had been elevated to a new religion by Ruskin, Arnold, and Pater. And because he came to this high culture as an outsider, as an American, he was keenly sensitive to the interplay of traditions which became in his fiction the frequent 'international theme'. From his first major novel, *Roderick Hudson* (1876), to *The Portrait of a Lady* (1881), most of James's fiction deals with Americans who are in tragic or comic collision with the differ-ent traditions and values of Europe.

Roderick Hudson, a young sculptor, is discovered by a discerning American benefactor who takes him to Rome, where there develops a kind of race, romantically depicted, between the flowering of his genius and the growth of an impulsive taste for high living, from which his New England community (and his mother) had earlier protected him. Both Roderick Hudson and Rowland Mallett, his benefactor, are sometimes out of focus dramatically, as though their recent transplanting, like the author's, had confused their characterizations. On the other hand, Christina Light, whose American mother wishes to arrange a brilliant marriage for her, is quite wonderful, enough so that James returned to her for an important role in *The Princess Casamassima*, a Balzac-like convention which James was to use only in her case.

Christopher Newman (in *The American*, 1877), having become a very wealthy businessman (in railroads in the west – shades of the robber barons!) – finds something wanting in his life, and goes to Paris in search of culture and of a cultured wife. He is foiled, somewhat melodramatically, by the young woman's aristocratic French family. While there are some very good characterizations in the novel, and several set pieces that capture well the sense of place so important to the realist tradition, James himself criticized the machinery of his plotting when he came to write the Preface to the New York edition of *The American*. He found much of the story to be 'Romance'.

In *The Europeans* (1878), the locale is reversed and two American expatriates, brother and sister, put themselves under the protection of their New England relatives. Neither the New England family nor their Europeanized relatives can accurately 'read' each other's behavior. The play of manners in this novel, a small comic masterpiece, is exceptionally rich. In contrast to the austere, kindly, rooted moral assurance of Mr Wentworth, the New England patriarch (whom James at one point calls a 'Hebrew Prophet'), we are given his wandering, stereotype-destroying relatives. Eugenia has become a Baroness by way of a morganatic marriage to a Prince (though we are assured that he is only a younger son) of a German principality identified as Silberstadt-Schrekenstein. Her brother, Felix Young, is an aspiring artist, and an exemplary character.

The Baroness, with her grandness of manner, charm, and calculation, hopes to marry a wealthy and well-traveled neighbor of the family. When he hesitates too long she begins a flirtation with the coltish young Wentworth son. Her story is written with sharp ironic observation, the manners of the Petit Trianon let loose in the ambience of a Congregational Meeting House. Felix is quite another matter. He is a young man whose cosmopolitan rearing has made him more worldly than his American relatives, but no less honest and scrupulous. He has a natural gaiety of spirit which – together with the New England tendency to associate Art with Bohemianism – alarms Mr Wentworth. Felix (who clearly has read his Matthew Arnold) reassures him by saying, 'at bottom, I am a terrible Philistine'. His courtship of Gertrude Wentworth, a daughter of New England with an imagination and sensibility dreaming beyond its borders, is portrayed with great sympathy. And indeed, James will always show a particular sensitivity and sympathy for the young, and the innocent, those characters who all too frequently in his fiction are vulnerable to the manipulation or exploitation of the more worldly or unscrupulous. The recurring theme in James is not so much innocence and experience, as innocence and betrayal.

One other work from this early period, again dealing with the 'international theme', merits mention here: the short novel *Daisy Miller* (1879). Criticized by some early readers because the story seemed disrespectful to American Maidenhood, its heroine later became celebrated as an idealization of American Charm. Neither claim is accurate. Daisy Miller is an appealing young American traveling with a well-intentioned, superbly incompetent mother and an amiable spoiled young brother. Mr Miller remains at home, presumably to persevere in the business that provides the means for the acquisition of culture by his family. Daisy's fresh innocence, and the American background which has encouraged her to do what she wishes (while her mother vaguely marvels and frets, both ineffectually), lead her to conduct herself in a manner quite acceptable at home. But she is misunderstood and disapproved of in Europe, especially by the circle of expatriate Americans whom she has met. She dies of a fever caught during an assignation in the Roman Colosseum, an assignation both innocent and foolish – and this tragedy captures well the essential critique which the story suggests about her typically 'American' pursuit of individual freedom: an admirable wish to be free of external restraint, and a relative absence of any more positive substance.

It should be emphasized that James's development of the 'international theme' in these early works involves a good deal more than the competitive interplay of nationalisms or the satirical portrayal of national virtues and vices. James's significant use of this theme was the investigation and measurement of the qualities and characteristics, however associated with different countries, which might together contribute to the making of an ideal civilization. And it is worthy of note that such an idea occurred to him quite early in his career. In 1867 (nine years before the publication of *Roderick Hudson*), we find him writing to an American friend:

> We are Americans born – *il faut en prendre son parti*. I look upon it as a great blessing, and I think that to be an American is an excellent preparation for culture. We have exquisite qualities as a race, and it seems to me that we are ahead of the European races in the fact that, more than either of them, we can deal freely with forms of civilization not our own, can pick and choose and assimilate and in short (aesthetically, etc.) gain our property wherever we find it. To have no national stamp has hitherto been a regret and a drawback, but I think it not unlikely that American writers may yet indicate that a vast intellectual fusion and synthesis of the various national tendencies of the world is the condition of more important achievements than any we have yet seen. We must of course have something of our own – something distinctive and homogeneous – and I take it that we shall find it in our moral consciousness, in our unprecedented spiritual lightness and vigor.
>
> (*Letters*, ed. Leon Edel, 1974, I, p. 77)

James's idea of picking and choosing among forms of civilization, admirable as it sounds, has its own hazards. James felt himself to be healthily cosmopolitan in culture, but he was also cut off from any strong and intimate sense of social community. His work is different, for instance, from that of George Eliot (from whom he learned many other lessons) largely because her novels were rooted in her own experience of an organic community with a specific social history and sense of continuity. As a result, James's novels, while rich in their observation of manners, are frequently silent, or mis-leading, about the actual social context of his characters' behavior. Like his own protagonists, he is open to the charge that he sometimes misreads appearances, and too easily takes outward signs for inward states. Similarly, while James appears to prize a 'sense of the past', his work embodies little genuine understanding of history, so much as it suggests, simply, a sense of the sense of the past.

The major novel of the early period is of course *The Portrait of a Lady* (1881). Since the critics of James have tended to be divided between those who think James's greatest achievements were in his earlier period, and those who argue for the last novels, there is also some division of opinion as to whether *The Portrait of a Lady* is James's finest work. It is certainly one of his best novels, and has proven itself to be one of the accepted classics of the novel in English. In his Preface to the New York edition, James writes that the first *donnée* or seed for the novel came to him as the figure of a young woman 'affronting her destiny'. James admired, above all other English novelists, George Eliot, and her intense psychological and moral realism, especially in her characterizations of women. Much has been written about the influence of George Eliot's *Daniel Deronda* on James's novel and a relationship certainly exists. However, it is also true that there are striking similarities between George Eliot's Gwendolen Harleth and James's Christina Light, in *Roderick Hudson*. But the dates of publication of these two novels are such that any question of a *direct* influence is made irrelevant. What is striking about *The Portrait* is that he places Isabel Archer firmly as the sole dominating center of his work, unsupported by the familiar parallel plot lines common to George Eliot's novels. Isabel Archer (like George Eliot's Dorothea Brooke and Gwendolen Harleth) is both an admirable and a 'limited' heroine. Early in the novel James gives his readers a strikingly detached and critical view of his central figure:

> Altogether, with her meagre knowledge, her inflated ideals, her confidence at once innocent and dogmatic, her temper at once exacting and indulgent, her mixture of curiosity and fastidiousness, of vivacity and indifference, her desire to look very well and to be if possible even better, her determination to see, to try, to know, her combination of the delicate, desultory, flame-like spirit and the eager and personal creature of conditions: she would be an easy victim of scientific criticism if she were not intended to awaken on the reader's part an impulse more tender and more purely expectant.

This particular passage omits mention of Isabel's high intelligence, her charm, and her beauty, all of which are established in her later characterization.

This intriguing young woman is discovered by a wealthy and eccentric aunt, as if by a fairy godmother, who removes her niece from Albany, New York, to the beautiful country house in England which she occasionally shares with her banker-husband, Daniel Touchett, and their son Ralph. Isabel is another in a long line of

James's 'passionate pilgrims' who brings her American 'spiritual lightness and vigor' to the civilization of Europe. The destiny which she
will confront is caught up largely in the question of marriage: she is
courted by an American business tycoon, a distinguished English
lord, and an intensely cultured, but poor, expatriate American who
lives in Italy with his exquisite taste, and his young daughter. It is the
last, Gilbert Osmond, whom she marries, with dire consequences.

Isabel's long journey from innocence to experience, and from
innocence to betrayal, is narrated with superb artistry. By this time,
James had shaped for himself a lofty conception of the novel as a
serious art, as distinct from popular entertainment, or 'loose and
baggy monsters' as he characterized the long rambling episodic
novels of the nineteenth century. His technical masters were the
French realists – most notably perhaps Flaubert – and the expatriate
Russian Turgenev. He placed great emphasis on principles of
composition (frequently the metaphors in James's commentaries on
his novels are architectural). He believed in representation instead of
authorial exposition. In addition, he put great emphasis on the point
of view of his central character, whom he used – with only occasional
departures either to other characters or to his own voice – as a center
of consciousness.

A further point of interest is James's emphasis on intelligence.
Together with the aesthetic appeals of a historical culture, and, James
thought, organically related to them, is the ministering of culture to
inner qualities of sensibility and conduct. Curiosity, the free play of
intelligence and consciousness, the desire to see things as they are
(what Arnold had called 'the scientific passion') – these are ultimate
values for James. Ideally they are combined in the truly cultured
individual with moral vigor and integrity of conduct. And in James's
practice as a novelist, he liked best as leading characters individuals
whose active consciousness and intelligence contribute in a direct
way to their drama. In the Preface to the New York edition of *The
Princess Casamassima* James wrote:

> I never see the *leading* interest of any human hazard but in a consciousness
> (on the part of the moved and moving creature) subject to fine intensification
> and wide enlargement ... the person capable of feeling in the given case
> more than another of what is to be felt for it, and so serving in the highest
> degree to *record* it dramatically and objectively, is the only sort of person on

whom we can count not to betray, to cheapen, or as we say, give away, the beauty of the thing.

Earlier in the same Preface, James wrote of the protagonists who are centers of consciousness for the relating of their tales: 'the power to be finely aware and richly responsible ... *makes* absolutely the intensity of their adventure, gives the maximum of sense to what befalls them'. About *The Portrait* he wrote,

> Place the center of the subject in the young woman's own consciousness ... and you get as interesting and as beautiful a difficulty as you could wish. Stick to *that* – for the center; put the heaviest weight into *that* scale, which will be so largely the scale of her relation to herself.

The best illustration of this principle in the novel is the narrative jump between Books I and II, and the lapse of some four years after Isabel's marriage to Gilbert Osmond. Isabel's friend, Madame Merle – Isabel does not yet know that she has manipulated the marriage – is in colloquy with Osmond. Isabel, entering the room, is made uneasy by the scene. There follows a brilliantly rendered all-night vigil in which Isabel reviews all of the reasons for her unhappiness in her marriage, all of the discoveries she has made about the true character of her husband:

> It was the house of darkness, the house of dumbness, the house of suffocation. Osmond's beautiful mind gave it neither light nor air; Osmond's beautiful mind, indeed, seemed to peep down from a small high window and mock at her ... Under all his culture, his cleverness, his amenity, under his good-nature, his facility, his knowledge of life, his egotism lay hidden like a serpent in a bank of flowers.

And a little later in this 'silent soliloquy', Isabel reflects:

> She was not a daughter of the Puritans, but for all that she believed in such a thing as purity; some of his traditions made her push back her skirts ... It was her scorn of his assumptions – it was that that made him draw himself up. He had plenty of contempt, and it was proper that his wife should be as well furnished; but that she should turn the hot light of her disdain upon his own conception of things – this was a danger he had not allowed for. He believed he should have regulated her emotions before she came to that; and Isabel could easily imagine how his ears scorched when he discovered that he had been too confident. When one had a wife who gave one that sensation there was nothing left but to hate her!

The internalization of this drama gives it a concentration and intensity that more than justifies the narrative break and solicits the reader's sympathy for Isabel, however rash her marriage seems to have been.

The ending of *The Portrait of a Lady* has exercised readers and critics for several generations. Isabel's cousin, Ralph Touchett, whose culture and character is the 'touchstone' for the novel, and who has arranged for the wealth which, ironically, precipitates Isabel's unhappy marriage, is persuaded even on his deathbed that Isabel was meant for happiness. Her American suitor, Goodwood, offers to take her away from her husband and back to America. But Isabel returns to Osmond. Many readers have felt this ending to be unsatisfactory (if not altogether perverse) for different reasons, but principally because it legitimizes a nineteenth-century version of wifely duty far beyond our sense of justice or of reason. She is supremely unhappy in her marriage; she knows that Osmond does not love her; and she knows, further, that she has been manipulated, used, by Madame Merle and Osmond for their own convenience. To go back is to renounce her own happiness. Ralph Touchett puts the question that must speak with some authority for many readers: 'Why should you go back – why should you go through that ghastly form?'

Her renunciation of happiness is motivated in part by her Puritan sense of duty, or her pride, or (what catches up both of these), by a need to preserve her own private sense of identity. James frequently asserted the close relationship of moral sensibility with 'true' culture, and we must accept the thematic point of Isabel's choice of Osmond. One should resist the temptation to allegorize, but Osmond surely represents, however deceptively, the Life of Culture which speaks to Isabel more eloquently than the 'public dynasty' life of Warburton or the 'business dynasty' life of Goodwood. Having made that choice, Isabel will in the end renounce happiness with all the self-justification that a religious code might provide. Isabel, like most of James's protagonists, has no such code, but seems rather to be guided by private imperatives which take the place of more traditional religious or 'public' sanctions. Readers of James will accept such renunciations to the degree that they understand or sympathize with these private conceptions of 'noble conduct'.

To support the primary figures in the novel James deploys a large cast enriched by his ironic social observation. Of Osmond's sister, the notorious Countess Gemini, James writes:

[She] had so mismanaged her improprieties that they had ceased to hang together at all . . . and had become the mere floating fragments of a wrecked renown, incommoding social circulation.

Isabel's friend, the redoubtable American journalist, is 'covering' Rome with a patriotic eye:

Henrietta Stackpole was struck with the fact that ancient Rome had been paved a good deal like New York, and had even found an analogy between the deep chariot-ruts which are traceable in the antique street, and the iron grooves which mark the course of the American horse-car.

The terribly effete American expatriate, Edward Rosier, is most attracted to Osmond's daughter Pansy:

She was such a perfect *jeune fille* . . . A *jeune fille* was what Rosier had always dreamed of – a *jeune fille* who should yet not be French, for he felt that this nationality would complicate the question. He was sure that Pansy had never looked at a newspaper, and that, in the way of novels, if she had read Sir Walter Scott it was the very most. An American *jeune fille*; what would be better than that? She would be frank and gay, and yet would not have walked alone, nor have received letters from men, nor have been taken to the theatre to see the comedy of manners.

Although James's sense of form and of realistic technique might derive from the French, his richness of canvas, his social satire, his feeling for distinctive individuals who are at the same time representative (of class, or country or temperament) still ally him with the English Victorians.

James's next novels followed a period given mainly to short stories and novellas and marked a new phase in his career. The 'international theme' was set aside and he wrote a novel on the post-Emersonian Boston of social reform, *The Bostonians* (1886). This was followed in the same year by *The Princess Casamassima*, which is set in England and deals with anarchist revolution in opposition to a traditional civilization. One sees the shadow of Hawthorne behind the first, and (more faintly) of Turgenev behind the second. These novels are remarkably observant of the social forces which James was portraying, and this has frequently surprised critics and readers who had assumed that James always lived and wrote in an aesthetic remove from the larger social world.

The Bostonians is brilliant as social satire: of the lunatic fringe of post-Emersonian and transcendentalized New England; of popular journalism; of social reforms undertaken in the fervor of moral exaltation; of the self-conscious clash of manners between abolitionist Boston and the unreconstructed South in the years following the Civil War. There is, as well, a superb portrait of the intense Boston lady, Olive Chancellor, whose social and (unrecognized) sexual yearnings for a feminist ideal make her both tragic and appalling. But there is a quality of excess and a strong dose of melodrama in the plot which suggest that James was less than certain about how to deal with his own rich material. This is nowhere more visible than in the last pages of the novel which take on a feverish intensity better suited to the hallucinatory possibilities of Romance.

The Princess Casamassima develops its own version of melodrama; but for all of its 'untypicality' – it is a large, sprawling social novel, somewhat in the manner of Dickens – it seems suited to James's special passions. It involves a young, sensitive, disadvantaged bookbinder, Hyacinth Robinson, who is torn between his discovery of culture and his commitment to a revolutionary movement bent on destroying the entire civilization. The polarity of loyalties basic to the novel is suggested in two quotations. The first is from a letter that James wrote to an American friend, Charles Eliot Norton:

> The condition of that body [the English upper class] seems to me to be in many ways much the same rotten and *collapsable* one as that of the French aristocracy before the revolution – minus cleverness and conversation; or perhaps it's more like the heavy, congested and depraved Roman world upon which the barbarians came down. In England the Huns and Vandals will have to come up – from the black depths of the (in the people) enormous misery ... At all events, much of English life is grossly materialistic and wants blood-letting.
>
> (*Letters* I, p. 125)

James borrowed this passage almost word for word from *The Princess Casamassima*. It establishes a framework of sharp, even radical social criticism that we are more likely to associate with William Morris than with Henry James.

The second quotation comes from a letter that Hyacinth Robinson writes to Christina (whose acquaintance we had made in *Roderick Hudson*), who has become the Princess Casamassima. He has gone to the Continent for the first time, and has fallen in love with the high culture of Europe. From Venice he writes (and I quote only in part):

I've lost sight of the sacred cause almost altogether in my recent adventures. It's not that [the misery of the people] hasn't been there to see, for that perhaps is the clearest result of extending one's horizon – the sense . . . that want and toil and suffering are the constant lot of the immense majority of the human race . . . What strikes me is the great achievements of which man has been capable of in spite of them – the splendid accumulations of the happier few, to which doubtless the miserable many have also in their degree contributed . . . They seem to me inestimably precious and beautiful . . . The monuments and treasures of art, the great palaces and properties, the con-quests of learning and taste, the general fabric of civilization as we know it, based if you will upon all the despotisms, the cruelties, the exclusions, the monopolies and the rapacities of the past, but thanks to which, all the same, the world is less of a 'bloody sell' and life more of a lark . . .

It is perhaps mischievous to suggest that (with notable exceptions) American critics have tended to prefer *The Princess*, and English critics *The Bostonians*. F. R. Leavis, indeed, ranked *The Bostonians* as second only to *The Portrait of a Lady* in James's work. Both novels were serialized in *The Century Magazine* (interestingly enough, *The Bostonians* appeared alongside of Mark Twain's *The Adventures of Huckleberry Finn*). Both of James's novels met with some resistance. 'I have entered upon evil days,' James wrote to his friend W. D. Howells:

I am still staggering a good deal under the mysterious and (to me) in-explicable injury wrought – apparently – upon my situation by my last two novels . . . from which I expected so much and derived so little. They have reduced the desire, and the demand, for my productions to zero.

Another novel, *The Tragic Muse* (1890), attempts a double plot, not altogether successfully. One dramatizes the career of a young actress whose talent is supported by an intense dedication; this story conveys something of James's enthusiasm for the theater – which was centered mainly on the French tradition. The other story deals, rather less convincingly, with a young man torn between a political career which he may pursue with virtually guaranteed distinction and a problematic career as an artist. His chief encouragement in following this second path comes from an artist with a curious, and ambivalently presented, resemblance to the fin de siècle aestheticism of Oscar Wilde.

Perhaps one effect of the dismal response to James's work was a series of short stories and novellas dealing with writers and artists, many of them tinged with bitterness either about the writer's role in his society (as in *The Death of the Lion*), or about lost opportunities (as in *The Middle Years*). Another effect was to turn James from fiction for a period in the 1890s to drama. He wrote four comedies which never reached the stage, and another, *Guy Domville*, which did, but with rather disastrous results. Writing again to W. D. Howells, James sounds desperate: 'I have felt, for a long time past, that I have fallen upon evil days – every sign or symbol of one's being in the least wanted, anywhere or by any one, having so utterly failed.'

In spite of all that, he persisted. Perhaps he recalled the words of Dencombe, the writer in *The Middle Years* (1893), who expresses the profound dedication of his author: 'We work in the dark – we do what we can – we give what we have. Our doubt is our passion and our passion is our task. The rest is the madness of art.'

James turned in the next years to a series of shorter novels, bringing to them what he thought were the lessons he had learned from his work in writing plays. He sketched stories as 'scenarios', and tried for tighter, more dramatic structures. *The Spoils of Poynton* and *What Maisie Knew* (1897), *The Turn of the Screw* (1898), *The Awkward Age* (1899), and *The Sacred Fount* (1901) were among the results. *The Turn of the Screw*, an uncannily powerful short novel, would lead to a history of exhaustive (and exhausting) analysis and controversy, ironically far removed from the neglect which had so affected the author. Perhaps more ironically still, it led to a very successful play (adapted by others), a movie, and an opera by Benjamin Britten. Indeed, James's fiction has lent itself, unexpectedly, to a long series of film and television adaptations which call into question earlier popular views that his refinements and subtleties of substance and of style could never lend themselves to wide appeal.

It was Rebecca West who characterized *The Sacred Fount* as describing

how a week-end visitor spends more intellectual force than Kant can have used on *The Critique of Pure Reason* in an unsuccessful attempt to discover whether there exists between certain of his fellow-guests a relationship not more interesting among these vacuous people than it is among sparrows.

(*Henry James*, 1916, pp. 107–8)

The description is both over-simplified and over-wrought; but it is essentially accurate. It is difficult not to wish that James's celebrations of consciousness and culture were not so frequently indifferent, or even opposed, to the physical and the sensual. James's treatment of romantic love and of sexual imperatives was never distinguished, but in the middle period seems to be particularly pained and finicky.

The best of the novels of this period are *The Awkward Age* and *What Maisie Knew*. Both deal with young heroines caught up in a social milieu in moral crisis. Throughout his career, James's fiction was characterized by its remarkable degree of ethical consciousness. An acute moral sense is manifested both in James's power of evaluating the experience the fiction deals with, and the tendency to choose for his protagonists characters possessing not only a high degree of intelligence and consciousness, but also of moral integrity. The moral awareness of author and of protagonists does not change in these middle-period novels, but its fortunes in the world seem to decline. James may have been convinced by Matthew Arnold's belief that the pursuit of culture leads to the improvement of conduct, but it is a conviction sorely tried by what he saw of contemporary English life. Whether Arnold was wrong (as in part he was), or whether the culture of fin de siècle England was a faulty one, matters less than that James more than ever saw the morally sensitive individual as besieged, no longer supported by the cultural matrix of family or guardians or the larger society. His protagonists tend now to be more passive and suffering, more ineffectual. The title James gave to an 1898 story, 'In the Cage', has its symbolic resonances.

These two best novels are interesting also for their experiments in point of view. James was especially proud of the structure of *The Awkward Age*, which he described (in his Preface) as

a neat figure of a circle consisting of a number of small rounds disposed at equal distance about a central object. The central object was my situation, my subject in itself . . . and the small rounds represented so many distinct lamps, as I liked to call them, the function of each of which would be to light with all due intensity one of its aspects.

This structure he likened to 'the successive Acts of a Play'. The point of view of *What Maisie Knew* is simpler but in some ways more remarkable since he maintains his heroine solidly as the novel's center of consciousness, if not of language, from her early childhood on. The freshness of her consciousness and her moral impregnability make for an especially grim contrast with the self-congratulatory worldliness and moral bankruptcy of most of the adults who impinge upon her.

This contrast is brilliantly suggested by Maisie's habit of repeating words, phrases, whole sentences of her adult guardians with a questioning innocence that exposes their emptiness and undermines the traditional assumption that adults provide children with the moral instruction that may lead them to responsible lives. Indeed, in *What Maisie Knew* the traditional roles of adult and child are reversed, with an effect that is in turn splendidly comical and touching.

James's last period is marked by three novels: *The Ambassadors* (published in 1903, but the first to be completed), *The Wings of the Dove* (1902), and *The Golden Bowl* (1904). These late novels are distinguished by a deeper and deeper probing of human relationships. Character is developed not so much through the traditional focus on the individual as on a creation of character in terms of *others*: we frequently receive a stronger sense of dense relationship than of individuals, though the reader may ultimately remove from the elaborated context of their various relationships the rather fabulous individuals who make up the Jamesian world. The prose is difficult, convolute, analytical. It has become more mannered and more personal than the early style. The demands of narration, exposition, or dialogue may vary, but the late voice is always, and unmistakably, the voice of the master.

Dialogue moves slowly, sometimes tortuously, through the steady intimations of what is never spoken at all. The reader is enticed into a steady collaboration which requires interpretation, inference, anticipation. Single scenes take on enormous powers to hypnotize – or to irritate – as we ravel our way through portentous disclosures, the sense of which may or may not equal the intensity of their representation.

The Ambassadors is in most ways the best constructed of all of James's novels. It has a coherence of form derived in part from the concentration and symmetry of the main story line, in part from

James's most consistent use of a single protagonist as the sole center of consciousness. The somewhat autumnal tone of the novel comes perhaps from its inspiration, which was an account by a friend of W. D. Howells' visit to Paris. James saw in this account something that spoke to him vividly, and brought him back, after many years, to the international theme:

> [A] little idea of the figure of an elderly man who hasn't 'lived', hasn't at all, in the sense of sensations, passions, impulses, pleasures – and to whom, in the presence of some great human spectacle, some great organization for the Immediate, the Agreeable, for curiosity, and experiment and perception, for Enjoyment, in a word, becomes, *sur la fin*, or toward it, sorrowfully aware. He has never really enjoyed – he has lived only for Duty and conscience – his conception of them; for pure appearances and daily tasks – lived for effort, for surrender, abstention, sacrifice.
>
> (*The Notebooks*, pp. 226–7)

Lambert Strether comes from Woollett, Mass., to Paris as an 'ambassador' for Mrs Newsome, whose son Chad has lingered too long in Paris and has presumably fallen into the clutches of a 'bad' woman. Strether's mission is to rescue Chad, and to bring him home to the family business, following which the long-widowed Strether will be allowed to marry the widowed Mrs Newsome. But Strether is overwhelmed by the spell of Paris, which he had visited only once before, as an eager young man. It is Paris that represents what he had once most coveted: curiosity, freedom, the ability to live in the moment, to 'take things as they come', to triumph over what he now calls the 'failure of Woollett': the failure to enjoy.

Strether's sense of a wasted life is touchingly expressed at a Parisian garden party where he speaks to a young expatriate American in whom he sees something of his own youth:

> 'It's not too late for *you*, on any side, and you don't strike me as in danger of missing the train ... All the same, don't forget that you're young – blessedly young; be glad of it, on the contrary, and live up to it. Live all you can; it's a mistake not to. It doesn't so much matter what you do in particular, so long as you have your life. If you haven't had that, what *have* you had? This place and these impressions ... well, have their abundant message for me ... I see it now. I haven't done so enough before – and now I'm old, too old at any rate for what I see ... It's too late. And it's as if the train had fairly waited at the station for me without my having had the gumption to know it was there. Now I hear its faint receding whistle miles and miles down the line. What one loses one loses, make no mistake about that.'

Strether can respond in this late season with wonderful vividness to the aesthetic appeals of Paris, to the splendid surfaces and cultivated manners of Europe. But at the same time he remains loyal to the strong moral consciousness which is also part of his Woollett inheritance, unlike the 'lesser' American pilgrims in James who sometimes surrender their American moral sense for the external trappings of European culture and who consequently end as bad Americans and bad Europeans both. Strether is the closest James ever came to an image of 'the whole man', incorporating the essential best in America and Europe, in character and in culture.

An important contribution to the impression the novel gives of a single formed experience is the way James uses a largish cast of characters not only to further the action, but to provide a scale of discriminations among 'representative' Americans and Europeans. His Americans include, besides Strether, Chad Newsome – young, handsome, polished, but ultimately opportunistic, and overly ready to abandon the woman who has given him so much. For what? For a career in advertising the homely, un-named product of the Woollett manufacture which his mother oversees. We might see him as prophetic of a later type, the Madison Avenue man in a gray flannel suit. Little Bilham, Chad's expatriate friend, has it in him to become another Felix Young or Ralph Touchett, which is what Strether had hoped for Chad. Waymarsh, Strether's old friend, a New England Hebrew prophet (and business success!), claims to hate Paris, and finds 'enjoyment' rather like wrestling with temptation in the desert. Jim Pocock, Chad's brother-in-law, is an amiable vulgarian, happy to float in the Newsome stream. There is a similar shading of women, ranging from the rigid and Woollett-bound Mrs Pocock to Maria Gostrey, the cultivated expatriate American, to Mme de Vionnet, Chad's beautiful and touching mistress. And over-arching all, the redoubtable Mrs Newsome, who never appears in person, but whose felt presence colors everything in the novel.

In the end, Lambert Strether is defeated in his ambassadorial mission and its rewards, but victorious in his achievement of a balanced integrity and wisdom. Whether one regards the novel as tragic or not will depend in some measure on how one ranks these conflicting goals.

If *The Ambassadors* is James's best constructed novel, *The Wings of the Dove* is his most deeply moving. Central to this work is the figure of an eager, engaging young woman of independent means – the 'heiress of the ages' – poised as for flight into the wonders of experience, but doomed by some mysterious and fatal illness. Her model was James's young cousin, Minny Temple, whose early death deeply affected the still young Henry James. This heroine represents again a central theme which appears frequently in James. It was first symbolized in *Roderick Hudson* by the hero's early statue called 'Thirst'. The sculptor says of its subject, 'Why, he's youth, you know; he's innocence, he's health, he's strength, he's curiosity.' Asked if the youth's cup is also symbolic, he replies, 'The cup is knowledge, pleasure, experience. Anything of that kind!' The heroine of *The Wings of the Dove*, Milly Theale, is James's most touching reincarnation of such a figure, deprived as she is of the health and strength that promise a future.

Milly's eagerness for experience becomes inextricably bound to the fortunes of a young Englishwoman and her fiancé, Kate Croy and Merton Densher, who become James's most interesting antagonists. In fact, James builds so carefully and dramatically the 'case' of these two, prepares their temptations and motivations so well that they virtually dislocate the novel's focus. In contrast, while Milly remains a poignant figure, her felt dramatic presence is sometimes shadowy, emblematic rather than real. James was aware of the problem of depicting the course of a fatal illness, and may have wished to 'seek indirection out' for this reason. Further, it may be argued that the central subject of the novel is not so much the story of Milly Theale in herself as in her effect on others. In any case, in this late study of a 'passionate pilgrim' who comes to Europe in pursuit of happiness, and finds instead betrayal, it is the betrayers who command James's most vivid representation.

What is striking about Kate Croy is that she is not at first a deliberately manipulative person, like Madame Merle or Gilbert Osmond, and never becomes a particularly vindictive one. She is motivated by a desperate need to escape the infamy of her father and the despotic control of her aunt (whom James portrays as a quintessence of commercial Britannia), and by her genuine love for Densher. What makes Kate so formidable is not her impulse to villainy, but the sheer force and vigor of her will. This is in sharp contrast to the motivations of her young man. Densher is seen as pleasant, passive, easily manipulated through his love for Kate. He is far from stupid; is in fact regarded as clever. But he finds it easy to avoid attending to the real moral implications of his involvement, at least until he is forced to by the sheer power of Milly's goodness, her dove-like grace. Two forces contend for Densher's soul: the determined will of Kate Croy, the 'lion', and the radiant power of grace in Milly, the 'dove'.

After Milly's death and her remarkable bequest, Densher wishes to force Kate to return to their beginnings, to take each other as they were. And here the tragic power of the novel achieves a fine intensity. The whole course of action has evolved and only at the end, after the fact, do the characters see the long way they have moved, the steep distance of the downward plunge. The disproportion between this vision and their earlier sense of moving only a little, of falling hardly at all, carries with it tremendous dramatic impact. Kate Croy cries out at the end, 'We shall never be again as we were!'

The Golden Bowl is perhaps the most disagreed upon novel in the James canon. This disagreement concerns not only the history of evaluations and appreciation of the novel, but interpretations of the novel's very meaning. The writing is James's most dense, sometimes remarkably evocative and sometimes opaque. The windings and convolutions of sentences at times challenge the artifice of Daedalus. Symbols and images take on a life of their own in length and elaboration. There is an extended comparison of Prince Amerigo to a Palladian church which may strike one as more Baroque than Palladian; and an even more astonishing symbolism of a Pagoda – Maggie Verver's vision of the relationships of the four major characters. These, it is only fair to say, have been much admired. At the same time they seem unduly contrived, unconvincing or even false vehicles for the human values represented.

A problem at least as serious lies in the lack of agreement upon the novel's essential meaning. There is a history of exegesis and criticism which proposes, with roughly equal eloquence, that Adam Verver and his daughter Maggie might be seen as God-the-Father and the Holy Spirit demonstrating the power of compassionate or redemptive love, carrying the erring Prince Amerigo and Charlotte

Stant if not to salvation at least to forgiveness. On the other hand, Adam and Maggie have been seen as vultures of American acquisitiveness, buying up European art and husbands and wives as spoils. If we accept James's intention as ironic, then Adam and Maggie may be seen as the novel's villains. If the novel is straightforward, rather than ironic, then they may be seen as heroic figures. Crucial to our sense of these possibilities is the attitude we are expected to take not only to the characters, but to the Ververs' extreme wealth – its sources and its uses.

Both readings have something to recommend them, but they can scarcely both be true. Neither is conclusive, because the novel is finally obscure, which means that it cannot be understood definitively (in contrast to difficult, where meaning *can* be arrived at, however laboriously). And a key to this obscurity lies in James's ambivalences about the relationships between art and money, culture and acquisition, problems which vex James in most of his later work. The sources of Adam's quite dazzling wealth are never specified, and this vibrates uncomfortably with the picture of Adam as a paragon of mildness and benevolence, and as one of the world's finest connoisseurs. James may not be concerned with this question; he may simply wish the Ververs to have money – frequently he invests his characters with the means that 'liberate' their moral choices from mere contingency, or even from social fact. But elsewhere the issue of acquisition did concern James, especially in relation to culture. The nature of this concern can be seen, most vividly, in his description of Abner Gaw in the unfinished *The Ivory Tower*:

> He was a person without an alternative, and if any had ever been open to him, at an odd hour or two, somewhere in his inner dimness, he had long since closed the gate against it and now revolved in the hard-rimmed circle from which he had not a single issue. You couldn't retire without something or somewhere to retire to, you must have planted a single tree at least for shade or be able to turn a key in some yielding door; but to say that [he] was surrounded by the desert was almost to flatter the void into which he invited one to step ... he had dispossessed himself, if there had even been the slightest selection in the matter, of every faculty but the calculating.

In addition to the ambiguities involving art and money, Adam's relationships with the Prince and, even more, with his wife Charlotte, seem insufferable if they are not merely absurd. Here, as elsewhere in the novel, the reader is so entangled in the sheer complexity of texture – so much of which is splendid – that he scarcely knows where he is in terms of any fundamental or underlying interpretation.

On the other hand, those critics who think the Prince and Charlotte, rather than the Ververs, are the admirable characters in the novel, since they are after all motivated by love rather than by money, are curiously blinded to the way this couple insists on having the best of both possible worlds together. Without the Verver fortune where is their honest passion?

Has Adam Verver bought an elegant objet d'art as a husband for his daughter, and a somewhat less expensive prize as his own wife? Or is he an innocent, a benevolently wealthy American of spiritual lightness and vigor? One quotation from the last pages of the novel might illustrate the ambiguity involved in answering these questions. The four main characters are assembled for a final leave-taking: Adam will take Charlotte back to America, and Maggie will have an undisputed claim on the Prince:

[Maggie] had passed her arm into his [her father's] and the other objects in the room, the other pictures, the sofas, the chairs, the tables, the cabinets, the 'important' pieces, supreme in their way, stood out, round them, consciously, for recognition and applause. Their eyes moved together from piece to piece, taking in the whole nobleness – quite as if for him to measure the wisdom of old ideas. The two noble persons seated, in conversation, at tea, fell thus into the splendid effect and the general harmony: Mrs Verver and the Prince fairly 'placed' themselves, however unwittingly, as high expressions of the kind of human furniture required, aesthetically, by such a scene. The fusion of their presence with the decorative elements, their contribution to the triumph of selection, was complete and admirable; though, to a lingering view, a view more penetrating than the occasion really demanded, they also might have figured as concrete attestations of a rare power of purchase.

To state all of these reservations is not to dismiss *The Golden Bowl* as insignificant. If it is a failure it is a noble one; the novel stays strangely in the minds and imaginations of its readers. James's genius for portraying relationships of some subtlety and complexity is unsurpassed, and the beauty of the writing, for all of its occasional excesses, is admirable. The novel adds to the conviction that reading

James transforms one's whole sense of human relationships; henceforth they will always be seen differently – more sensitively and more richly.

James's last years were given to the writing – after a long visit to the United States – of the fine study *The American Scene* (1907); to the writing of shorter fiction (including a beautiful short story, 'The Bench of Desolation'); to the preparation of the New York edition, commissioned by Scribners, for which he wrote a series of Prefaces which, together, make up an impressive critique on the theory and practice of fiction. He published two volumes of his autobiography; the unfinished third volume was published posthumously. Two novels, both unfinished, but with extensive notes or scenarios – *The Ivory Tower* and *The Sense of the Past* – were also published posthumously. In his last years he joined a public cause for the first time in his life, in aid of the British effort in the First World War. Like Walt Whitman before him, he tended to the wounded. In 1915 he became a British citizen. After so many years abroad as an American this gesture was motivated mainly by his wish to show his solidarity with an England at war, as he thought, to save western civilization. He died in 1916, several months after he was awarded the Order of Merit.

He saw himself as an intensely serious and dedicated professional writer in the tradition of Balzac, about whom he lectured widely during his last visit to America. He was the most prolific of America's major writers, a fact which makes any brief introduction to his work necessarily incomplete. He brought to the novel in English a new seriousness of technique and of a combined moral and aesthetic purpose which has had a great influence on many later writers in America and England. His work embodied much (and discarded much), of the traditional novel, and carried the art of fiction forward toward modernism.

Early in James's career, he wrote an essay, 'The Art of Fiction' (1884), which has become a classic text on the realistic novel. What remains especially striking in this essay for the student of James is perhaps less the defense of realism than James's insistence that the 'experience' from which fiction may be said to spring is as much a matter of consciousness and of sensibility as of mere 'objective' incident or action:

Experience is never limited, and it is never complete; it is an immense sensibility, a kind of huge spider-web of the finest silken threads suspended in the chamber of consciousness, and catching every air-borne particle in its tissue. It is the very atmosphere of the mind; and when the mind is imaginative – much more when it happens to be that of a man of genius – it takes to itself the faintest hints of life, it converts the very pulses of the air into revelations.

Two points might be drawn from this definition: the first is that James's fiction celebrates consciousness as itself an ideal, perhaps in the tradition of Pater's Conclusion to *The Renaissance*. 'Experience' as simply a variety of incidents, actions, places visited, people encountered, matters primarily as these register on, define, and affect the consciousness of his characters. The second point springs from the first: James's fiction may be seen as an important bridge between the nineteenth-century novel, grounded in 'plot', and the modern psychological novel, grounded in consciousness.

Henry James was the celebrator of the cultivated sensibility and of noble conduct. He believed, possibly naïvely, that ethical and aesthetic judgements were, or ultimately should be, the same. He believed ardently that culture was the power that makes this possible, however frequently the forms of culture might be used for exploitation or for misappropriation. He was, perhaps, the last major writer in English to trust in the power of culture, or civilization, not only to enrich human life, but to redeem it. That he was right in these commitments seems to many of us in this besieged age highly problematic. Nevertheless, his work – which is in itself a superb tribute to the achievements of civilization – provides its own living testimony.

THEODORE DREISER:
PROMISING DREAMERS

PHILIP FISHER

Theodore Dreiser (1871–1945) was above all America's great novelist of the will. His career extends from the world of 1900 shocked by Freud's sexual account of the dreaming human imagination to the 1929 collapse of American financial dreamers on Wall Street. Between those years Dreiser wrote five works that are among the greatest of twentieth-century American literature: *Sister Carrie* (1900) and *An American Tragedy* (1925), his two most important novels; *A Gallery of Women* (1929), the single most powerful collection of stories of artistic, bohemian life in American literature, and perhaps its best collection of stories of lives shaped by sexual love; and, finally, *Jennie Gerhardt* (1911) and *The Financier* (1912), two novels in which a more schematic, less incidentally rich structure allowed Dreiser to pose the interwoven patterns of desire and ambition in an extraordinary portrait of business and sexuality in the social landscape of the American city: the new business cities of Chicago, Cleveland, Philadelphia and New York, the centers of muscular capitalism.

The career of Dreiser from *Sister Carrie* to *A Gallery of Women* in 1929 made him the author of a national self-portrait for an America that was urban, capitalist, scaled to opportunity and not to fixed place. It revolved around the self-made woman or man – especially that Dreiserian center, the self-created young woman. These were men and women no longer in search of family life, but linked to others only in the push of competition and the pull of sexual romance. Temporary in all things, provisional as everything must be in a society of invention, Dreiser's is a world of hotels rather than homes, affairs rather than marriages, roles and not identity.

This society of the promising and the unsettled Dreiser celebrates with an enthusiasm that is one of the most strongly marked features of his best work. His is a world of the hopeful and the hopeless, of those who are promising and those who, in the American term, are 'has beens'. Rising and falling, they are women and men for whom having a place, social position, a marriage, or a home adds up to 'being stuck' somewhere in a world where it only counts to be in motion, 'on the move'. The women and men that Dreiser knew best have some of the traits of actresses and actors. They lack a Dickensian uniqueness; their speech is bland, their desires ordinary. One of Dreiser's strongest and most striking claims is the point made implicitly by his style of characterization: unlike England, America is not a society of strongly flavored individuals. American mobility and opportunity produces a self that lacks a 'sentiment of being'. It is labile, externalized, and comes to view the many details of its life as more or less changeable outfits. Houses, relationships, jobs, and social positions count as no more than changes of clothing. At its center are characters like Carrie Meeber or Clyde Griffiths, who not only lack but are indifferent to what we call personal identity. Neither style, nor personal history, neither unique plans, nor strongly felt reactions individualize them. This is a feature of a quick-change society, a society in which being 'available' includes being ready to flee or grab the trappings of identities in a casual way, even where what is fled might include home, family, lovers, work; that is, the many traditional components that gave stability to identity. Seldom does the present stage of a life in Dreiser depend upon the past. Each new opportunity is literally a 'break'.

In the absence of any strong continuity of character or identity, Dreiser locates his women and men, changeable as they are, by means of what does remain fixed within social life: the array of types. Most often a Dreiserian description tells us that the woman or man was 'one of . . .' this or that: one of the new speculators in Chicago, one of those chorus girls looking for a quick break before her youth has passed, one of those formerly rich men who could not adjust to poverty. This is the language of the new sociology in which society is composed of types rather than citizens. A story by Dreiser is the account of the struggle to become an instance of a social type and to be known and seen by others as that type. Identity for Dreiser involves the act that should be called 'looking around to see who I am'. It is an externally referenced identity, both in its location as membership in a type and in its confirmation in the looks of others. In Dreiser there is no self-certainty at all, and it is not felt to be lacking. Uniforms and settings confirm the reality of the self: one of those people that you meet in Hollywood; the type of woman who takes afternoon tea at the Waldorf; the type of businessman who always stays at the second-best hotel. The group to which one belongs is the revealing set. The place in which one is seen or remembered by others gives the revealing setting that expresses the self better than its history or rare acts of morally decisive choice.

Dreiser's poignancy and drama enter through his strategy of coming to know this world through those who never quite belong. Trying to enter as Clyde Griffiths does in *An American Tragedy* or falling out of set and setting as the businessman Hurstwood does in *Sister Carrie*, Dreiser's are stories of candidates for identity or has beens. They slip between worlds as Jennie Gerhardt and her business-man lover Lester Kane do in *Jennie Gerhardt* in which the no longer poor girl is not accepted as part of the stable upper-middle class because she is a mistress and not a wife, while her lover can no longer be accepted by either his family or his associates unless he cast her off because he too no longer matches what his set requires him to be. The Dreiserian character frequently is only permitted to enter settings or social sets at the price of a stain that marks him as not really present. Jennie, as Kane's mistress, can live at the best addresses but will never be visited by her neighbors.

In a mobile society of types, the central Dreiserian woman or man is on the run or on the make; living between worlds; exposed and fragile. They are in the richest sense 'worldless'. That Dreiser's charac-ters are not rebels against a society that marginalizes them, but gives them a chance, or perhaps no more than a hope, provides the energy of his work. His are the as-yet-outside insiders of a society. Perhaps part of the genius of American society has always been to avoid social collision by convincing almost all of its members that they are either insiders or temporarily outside insiders because the door is still slightly open. Rising or falling, the women and men of Dreiser's world have in view that slightly open door.

The language of types and social groups that is given away in that obsessive Dreiser phrase 'one of . . .' is linked to the power of the new sociology in Dreiser's day. Max Weber and Émile Durkheim visualized a social language fixed under the cold stare of the scientist into a system of types. Dreiser's contemporary Veblen, also Chicago-centered in his thinking, invented the comic social classification of America that fixed, as Dreiser would, the reality of patterns over the reality of individual histories of personalities.

Dreiser began as an intellectual interpreter of society, strongly under the influence of the biological vocabulary of Darwinism with its stress on competition, survival, the amoral struggle for existence, and the long-term prospect of extinction. The Darwinian philosophy, taken over crudely as an account of capitalism in the late nineteenth century, was at its core a philosophy of the will, of life understood as force or weakness, of the central power of what came to be called the sexual drive, and of an unsentimental interpretation of motives and outcomes. These were aspects of a new force destined from the start to pose unsolvable problems for the classic Bourgeois culture of the nineteenth century. It is in the struggle between what remained of the family-centered, morally ordered social world that had lost its certainty and the remarkably strong individualism of the artistic will, of the erotic will, and of the will that had economic or political power as its goal that the novels and stories of Joyce, Mann, Dreiser, and Lawrence have a common center.

The American Dreiser had one advantage over his European contemporaries. The setting for his work was one of the most energetic and expansive stages of an as yet incomplete society. The frenzy of building, speculation, and extension both of economic and political power in every imaginable direction during the coming of age of American capitalism between 1880 and 1930 gave to his work a dreamlike setting of hope and collapse, of energy and exhaustion that had no equivalent in a Europe where Empires were in decline and decay.

In tune with an incomplete society, Dreiser captures the condition of 'promising lives' where the future, the possible, the not yet is the focus of the mind rather than the memories or the consequences of the past. His civilization, like his best characters, was essentially hopeful, and it was therefore unsettled. Its future, like the value of land, was bound to be multiples of its present, so it might live in expectation, fantasy, and some slight dread of collapse. One of Dreiser's best images for Chicago is of streetlights turning off and on out in the prairie where no houses or neighborhoods yet exist. The lights burning all night are part of the city's imagination of itself, its confidence that in a few years there will be houses, neighborhoods, streets and traffic where now there is only the sketch of a future in the form of these forlorn lights.

Dreiser knew best the America that, between 1880 and the stock market crash of 1929, was little more than a sketch of its own future, a future towards which it was speeding in the hope of turning out to be what it had willed itself to become. His best characters, like Carrie and the fifteen women of *A Gallery of Women*, are also hopeful and promising figures indifferent to the past and drawn almost sexually towards their own future selves for which their present is merely a rehearsal or a practice. They are characters rich with the kind of anticipation that gives them an attractive glow of incompletely fastened energy. For Dreiser the energy of promise, erotic energy, the energy of the will or of masculine power, and the energy of money which he described in *Sister Carrie* as 'honestly stored energy' were convertible. At some point they converged and were indistinguishable. The play of these energies, especially the complex ways in which, once twined together, they blocked or cancelled one another gave Dreiser the mechanism for his plots.

Dreiser discarded the traditional plot of the social novel, which aimed at conclusions based in socially stable place and marriage, in favor of a pure trajectory of rise and fall. He writes for a civilization whose social space is dangerously vertical. Climbing and plunging, slipping and rising, his characters meet in love affairs where each makes the other's place insecure. Only in time can it be seen which was slipping downward, which up. Each of his plots is the tracing of the libidinal and social economy of one or of a series of love affairs.

The vertigo of the affair has as one of its features a confusion of directions, but only during the first stages of the passion. As the lovers pass out of each other's sight the accelerating fall of one, the dizzying rise of the other fixes each position unambiguously. For the early moments of love the social uniforms of rich and poor, businessman and shop girl, senator and cleaning woman, night club manager and actress are vaporized until at a later stage they return like a prison or, being no longer recoverable, are forfeited along with the world to which they conferred membership and identity. Mobility and self-making are the premises of his plots, but his is a world in which we find, just as often as a self-made man, his counterpart, the self-unmade man, the defector or the fugitive. Dreiser's is a reckless social world. Those on whom he fixes his attention have the addicted appetites of gamblers, and, just as in gambling, most who play, lose. What is most interesting to Dreiser is not the outcome, but motion itself. Both those who rise and those who fall become in the process worldless, anomalous figures, no longer at home anywhere.

Often a Dreiser character has only a temporary address. Shifting from hotel to hotel, as Carrie does at the top of her world of stardom, or as her former lover Hurstwood does in Bowery flophouses at the other end of Broadway, these characters regard residences as little more than a suit of clothing to be discarded when it no longer reflects the up to the minute standing of the self within its world. Many key scenes in Dreiser's works take place within hotels as if the glamorous social promiscuity they make possible, the aliases and short-term hold on status they reflect were clues to the improvised selves and relations of the urban American world. Identity under such emergency conditions has all the features of a performance for which setting, costume, the complementary performances of others, and social life itself are merely paraphernalia of local and temporary value like a city of tents that can be struck in an hour or fled in a minute.

The dizzy, vertical, still unbuilt society that Dreiser takes as his setting gives special place to youth because it is the incomplete stage of the self where possibilities, opportunities, and the hold of its own future over one's self-image make up the very stuff of life. In Dreiser's stories dreaming, yearning, restlessness, and the imagination are almost civic responsibilities. His characters live in a society that invites them to experiment and to grasp themselves, as Emerson would have said, in terms of experimental lives. The actress, the drifter, the small-town Napoleon, and the outsider are each in their different ways aspects of the turbulence of the social surface. They make up those who for whatever personal reason shake up and displace the order that has kept them out or kept them down.

Capitalism produces a kind of wealth distinct from landed wealth because power is easy to gain but impossible to hold and pass on. It is a system of ever new players, new women and new men, new products, and new ways. The railroads that seemed in late-nineteenth-century America to be the essence of wealth and power, holding the country in a stranglehold that could only increase over time, have, a century later, already gone bankrupt. Displaced by the airplane, the trucking industry, the passenger automobile, the long-distance bus, and the interstate highway system, the recently youthful and expansive railroads are, in what is no more than a blink of history, already dinosaurs. The new systems in their turn are also, as Emerson saw, only newer circles waiting to be encircled in their turn.

Dreiser is the only American writer to have grasped, as Emerson did in philosophy, the consequences of this economic system for the self and its improvised relations. The tilt of a permanently re-designable society towards the dreamer, the improvisor, the ex-perimental life, and towards those least damaged by change or flight, those who have become immune to having the ground cut out from under their feet and have therefore come to savor the open and unpredictable, but possibly manageable speed of change: this is a central premise of Dreiser's work. He made a contribution as essential to the American mythography of the self as Walt Whitman's ex-emplary Democratic man captured in the celebratory poet's voice that proclaimed him to be all men and all women. Dreiser's is the exemplary actor, or rather actress, in a world that is economic rather than political. Restless and experimental, his figures dream within a world inviting reconception and expecting each person to imagine a future that builds in a place for his or her self. To situate the self within the world requires altering the structure of the world itself since the past had no such person. This is the psychologically pro-found subjectivization of capitalism as a project of the self that we find in Emerson and Dreiser.

A familiar point is often reached in a Dreiser novel at which his characters are hiding out, concealing themselves from those they used to know, caught between an identity recently fled or tempor-arily suspended, and a new identity not yet real or settled. His married lovers often stall between a wife or family life abandoned but not formally divorced and a mistress joined but not yet married. Abandonment of parents, lovers, wives or husbands is tantalizingly incomplete. Retreat or return seems possible even while it slowly fades. Meanwhile any solid entrance into a new life is blocked. A favorite term of Dreiser's is the word 'drifting'. Those who drift have lost the power of an alert will. They are, as Carrie Meeber's name points out, 'carried' by the events around them. Within an aggressive, business world shaped by the will at its most driven, Dreiser evokes again and again in characters like Lester Kane the nearly sensuous pleasure of passive drifting, of paralysis of the will and indecision. His women are seldom seduced, they drift into affairs. His criminals are seldom decisive: the safe snaps shut and they find themselves with a handful of money.

The central character in each of Dreiser's three most important novels, *Sister Carrie*, *Jennie Gerhardt*, and *An American Tragedy*, is a figure carried forward towards stardom, towards execution, or towards a helpless comfort and estrangement. Each is also carried, or drifts into a terminal worldlessness for which Sing-Sing Prison or the actresses' best suite at the Waldorf are interchangeable symbols. Jennie Gerhardt, Carrie Meeber, and Clyde Griffiths find themselves at last locked in, as Clyde is on Death Row where he awaits execution, to what we call 'solitary confinement'. Each book last pictures its central figure in haunted isolation: Carrie in her rocking chair at the top of the best and newest New York hotel, Clyde in his cell at Sing-Sing, Jennie in the train station watching disappear the coffin containing her last link to any other life than her own. Death Row cell, hotel room, and train station are three perfectly chosen images of temporary and fragile location. Each is a waiting room, a pause within passage and transition. The already condemned murderer pauses here until the execution is prepared. From each of these places one is literally carried by train, elevator, or hearse.

For Dreiser's men the sexual and the social are misaligned. His two great tragedies, that of Hurstwood whose fall complements Carrie's rise in *Sister Carrie*, and that of Clyde Griffiths in *An American Tragedy*, are stories of a shift of weight from one side of life to another in which an inner balance is lost that cannot be recovered. Hurstwood's attachment to Carrie or Clyde's to Roberta involves a fatal misalignment of the parts of a life that breaks the rising pattern of a career. Where in Dreiser there is no advance, there can only be decline.

In *Jennie Gerhardt* Lester Kane pauses, drifts, and stalls, but once he begins to slide, manages to catch himself by accepting the blackmail built into his father's will that cuts him off should he remain with

Jennie. In renouncing her he recaptures not only the inheritance, but every aspect of his wider life: family, marriage, work, money, and social life. The very attachment that misaligns the energies of sexual and ambitious life for Lester Kane, Hurstwood, and Clyde Griffiths was, however, in Carrie Meeber's case aligned parallel and led her to New York, to the theater, and to fame and wealth. Carrie is the one exception to the story that Dreiser tells again and again of the cost of passion incurred by the misdirection of the will in sexual life. Only those like the salesman Drouet in *Sister Carrie*, too easy-going ever genuinely to be attached, are invulnerable.

The word 'attachment' itself, like the word 'drift', can be seen as almost a technical term in Dreiser. While it seems more neutral than love, passion, or desire, the term 'attachment' includes an element of force and a loss of freedom, even an undercurrent of passivity that makes the image of a stalled or drifting will appropriate. One feature of attachment is a torpor, an inactivity, that Dreiser often blames on the age of his male lovers, although Hurstwood and Kane are only near forty. From the outside, the inactivity seems more like a sexual captivity that has drained interest from the world at large. In this, Dreiser follows the hidden puritanism that can be detected in much of Naturalist writing. A no longer moral or social condemnation of sex is staged as an equally devastating account of its destructiveness, now seen in terms of energy instead of sin.

In 'Emanuela', one of the best of his stories in *A Gallery of Women*, Dreiser describes sex as not an idea at all, but an all-pervading state of the self 'like heat or weakness'. These two words trap the physical, pervasive state that Dreiser wants, but at the same time substitute what might be called a hygenic prohibition for the no longer believable moral or social one. Ever since Schopenhauer's pessimistic description of the sexual as nature's trap that tricks even those who have seen the darkness of existence into willing it to continue, Naturalist writers have, as Hardy did in *Tess of the d'Urbervilles* and *Jude the Obscure*, or as Dreiser did in *Jennie Gerhardt* or *An American Tragedy*, made of pregnancy the cruel trick that masters life; and of sexuality, the misaligned force at war with fortune or direction. There are few aspects of Dreiser's work more darkened by Naturalism and its philosophical pessimism than his use of the sexual fall that first enchants, then mystifies, and finally dooms its willing victims.

Only in *A Gallery of Women*, his final major work, did Dreiser release the sexual and make it a subject in its own right. As a book of the twenties these fifteen stories tell of a different and more gritty Jazz Age. On one side they approach the razzle-dazzle fake rich of F. Scott Fitzgerald's Gatsby and Daisy, but on the other they touch ground in the Greenwich Village of rope-sandaled poets, painters off to Paris, and young revolutionaries drawn to an American colony in the Siberia that the Russian Revolution would surely turn into yet another side of Paradise. That future was at first a promise, as Paris was for the young who wanted to paint in the new style of Picasso and Matisse, or as New York City was for every high-energy dreamer too big for small-town life, and on the run from the tedium of life once you 'settled down'. But the promise of all other promises was the erotic itself for which the sex-appeal of money, or politics, or fame, of Greenwich Village or Paris or Hollywood was just an atmospheric setting. In this collection Dreiser wrote a dozen of the greatest stories of lives under the spell of love, sexual passion, and the variability of desire ever written in America. Like his contemporary, D. H. Lawrence, Dreiser designed a new, vitalist narrative in the aftermath of the first Freudian wave. These narratives are timed by the history of the energy of passion which glows incandescent, connects or fails to connect, but inevitably fades. Like the best of Lawrence's stories, these are accounts of lives in which the reality of passion and the reality of the aftermath of passion are the very texture of life history.

It was in the twenties that life in America became noticeably sexy. Money or drinking, whatever their internal value, felt sexy in the stories of F. Scott Fitzgerald. Bullfighting or stoic masculinity became sexy in Hemingway. Twenties communism, bohemianism, the life of painting and writing – even intellectuals were sexy in that great backwash of Freud, Hollywood, and modern advertising that settled in after the First World War. Paris and Greenwich Village were sexiness itself. Hollywood was still too new; it would have to wait until later. The French, of course, had had sex for a long time and were used to it, but for an America that had been making do with sin, transgression, guilt or marriage, the arrival of sex brought with it the effervescence of sexiness, as though once the culture opened this particular bottle it found itself with champagne where it had only expected wine. Dreiser's stories are homage to that moment of cultural sexiness. They share with Hemingway's *The Sun Also Rises* and Fitzgerald's *Tender Is the Night* or *The Last Tycoon* the atmosphere of the intoxicating and dangerous feel for sex. Dreiser's are the richest and deepest cultural trace of this moment in America.

The stories of *A Gallery of Women* are stories for a promiscuous world. Each story has the structure of a meeting with a new and, in the story's perception, intriguing woman. The reader who 'meets' or is 'introduced to' Albertine, Lucia, Ellen, or Esther by the story itself has an experience that Dreiser has designed as a parallel to the stage of getting to know someone through the fascinated gaze of a new affair. The women of these stories remain conspicuously undomesticated. They appear and disappear. Their lives have gaps, other lovers, silences, blank pages. This is the narrative point of view of an affair in an easy-going world of affairs. The sexual fascination is lived through only until it dissipates or turns in another direction. The stories tell of free women, or as they used to be called 'loose' women – a term that should make us see that the alternative would be to be 'tied down' or 'attached'. The French would say that these are the lives of people who are *disponible*, that is, available, ready for this or that new excitement.

At the same time, the women of Dreiser's stories are not opportunists or sensualists so much as young urban dreamers. Dream and the collapse of dreams; love and ruined love; promise and spilled promise: these are the fevers of a speculative time in love with options and risk. Dreiser makes of New York what Dostoevsky did of St Petersburg: a city of dreamers, and of the debris of collapsed dreams.

In his fifteen stories Dreiser made his contribution to that poetry of Manhattan which had had its first harvest in Walt Whitman, and that had in Dreiser's own day begun to make of Greenwich Village a magical location on that American map where Walden Pond, Twain's Mississippi River, the woods of Cooper, the Mississippi towns of Faulkner, and the Arctic of Jack London have displaced mythographically whatever actual locations might be found at those spots. The city itself is a constant character in Dreiser's work, in some ways framing events and persons as a society had done in the past. It is the grid on which reality appears.

Like Joyce's collection *Dubliners* which enacted the hidden forces of Irish cultural life, its stalemates and types, its structures and their personal variations in individual lives, all mapped onto the city of Dublin, Dreiser's stories make of Manhattan a cloud chamber in which the energies and particles of national life gain visibility. The lines of force, the typical figures, the dense social knowledge, the psychology of moments and relationships are all there, beyond the powers of the best Naturalist writing of the earlier generation, and also now freed from mere illustration and shrill politics, and freed as well from the rather cheap pessimism and programmatic attention to victims that had made of early Naturalism an easy target.

The force of the self along with its promise and drive, its sexual hunger and animal vitality work as a potent counterforce to society and nature – those two forces that ground the classic Naturalist victim into the dust so easily. Dreiser, no less than Joyce in *Ulysses*, had found by the 1920s that to tell the story of a modern city, such as Dublin or New York, a matching vitality to the richness of the forces of the city itself was needed. The intellectual inner liveliness of Leopold Bloom plays here the part played by the sexual vitality and ambition of Dreiser's women. Where early Naturalism could only imagine that each must be crushed and defeated without even much of a fight, the later Naturalists saw not only solid and resourceful inner counter-weights, but an outer world of various and often opposed energies.

In both of his major works of the twenties, *An American Tragedy* and *A Gallery of Women*, Dreiser's relation to American experience makes clear his cultural links to his great contemporaries, Joyce, Lawrence, and Mann. All four were writers of massive, central descriptions of their society in a world defined by sexuality and that modern centrality of the will that is our clear inheritance from Nietzsche. Each is also the historian of a problematic economic society in its struggle to accommodate the life of the private will that has its best expression in the artist. The force of the city, of the will, of the sexual and experimental in life are at the core both of early twentieth-century life and of those works of Dreiser that are among its most effective and fascinated depictions.

EDITH WHARTON

MICHAEL MILLGATE

She was born Edith Newbold Jones in New York in 1862. Her
family was rich, aristocratic, absolutely assured of its world and of
its own high place in that world:

> I have heard [wrote Percy Lubbock in his *Portrait of Edith Wharton*] that
> Edith's mother, a high authority on the subject, would count the names of all
> the families, in due order of degree, who composed the world to which her
> daughter was born; and there her world stopped short, it was implied, and
> no mistake about it.

The broad outlines of her upbringing were determined by the conventions of the period and the class to which she belonged, but she
surprised and perhaps alarmed her parents by her intellectual interests
and her devotion to reading, and in 1878, when a volume of her
poems was privately published, she achieved something like eccentricity. Her marriage, in 1885, was conventional enough: her
husband, Edward ('Teddy') Wharton, a family friend thirteen years
older than herself, was a man of few intellectual interests. Edith
Wharton herself, however, in *A Backward Glance*, speaks of his 'good
humour and gaiety', adding: 'he shared my love of animals and out-
door life, and was soon to catch my travel-fever.' The final phrase is
highly significant. Before her marriage she had already spent long
periods in Europe, especially in France, and her enthusiasm for travel
was to remain with her all her life. She was to write books on Italy,
France, and Morocco; Henry James, impressed and a little appalled
by her energetic journeyings to and fro across Europe, the Channel,
the Mediterranean, and the Atlantic, once spoke of her as 'the great
and glorious pendulum'. From an early stage in the marriage
Edward Wharton's health took them to Europe for about four
months of every year, and these were probably the periods when she
was happiest. At the same time, she seems to have found a good deal
of satisfaction in fulfilling her expected social role as a wealthy and

fashionable hostess – although she said in her autobiography that her intelligence tended to frighten her fashionable friends, and her fashionableness to dismay her intellectual ones. She and her husband entertained on a considerable scale, and with a good deal of elegance and flair; she herself devoted much time to the decoration of the various houses in which they lived, and especially of The Mount, in Lenox, Massachusetts, her favourite American home and also her last.

This enthusiasm for interior decoration, then a much neglected field, led Edith Wharton to collaborate with a young architect, Ogden Codman, in a work called *The Decoration of Houses* which was published in 1897. A year previously she had started writing verse again, and had actually had a few poems accepted for publication, but she says in her autobiography that she first learned the art of writing good prose from the advice on the composition of *The Decoration of Houses* given to her by Walter Berry, later to become such an important emotional and intellectual influence in her life. It seems reasonable, therefore, to date the beginning of her literary career from this early work of non-fiction, one which was to enjoy an unexpected and long-lived popularity. In 1899 came her first volume of short stories, *The Greater Inclination*, and this was quickly followed by two more. It was not until 1902, when she was already forty, that she published her first novel, *The Valley of Decision*. As a historical romance, set in eighteenth-century Italy – a period which she also treated in *Italian Villas and Their Gardens* (1904) – *The Valley of Decision* must be considered as an exercise in a genre quite foreign to the main body of her work, even when one makes allowance for the element of historical reconstruction in a novel like *The Age of Innocence*. But with her second novel, *The House of Mirth*, published in 1905, Edith Wharton achieved her fully mature style and manner at the same moment as she discovered her proper subject-matter.

The achievement, indeed, must have been largely dependent upon the discovery. 'Fate had planted me in New York,' she wrote, looking back on the writing of *The House of Mirth*, 'and my instinct as a story-teller counselled me to use the material nearest to hand, and most familiarly my own.' The instinct was sound, and in pursuing it she found her way not only to what she knew best but to the kind of situation which moved her most. Her heroine, Lily Bart, is a beautiful and sensitive girl who is destroyed by the very society whose decorative but inhumane specifications her upbringing had designed her precisely to meet; her hero, Lawrence Selden, is a handsome, intelligent young man who can perceive the falsity of the society's values but who is too weak to rescue Lily Bart from her degradation. These figures were to appear, in modified guises, in many of her subsequent works. And in *The House of Mirth* she first staked out that area of social fiction in which neither Howells, James, nor Dreiser can offer her any serious challenge. As she was to prove in a whole series of novels, her knowledge of upper-class America and of its middle-class fringes, especially in New York in the second half of the nineteenth century, was comprehensive and precise: in dealing with this society she was at once harsher than Howells, more knowledgeable than James, and altogether more sensitive to social behaviour, to manners, than Dreiser, and it is less surprising than may at first appear that such a writer as Sinclair Lewis should have testified to his admiration of her in the dedication of such a novel as *Babbitt*. Deeply indebted as she was to Henry James, disappointing as her novels of the twenties and thirties undoubtedly were, it would be a mistake to think of Edith Wharton as a writer whose best work was already outmoded at the time when it was being produced; the novels of her great period between *The House of Mirth* in 1905 and *The Age of Innocence* in 1920, so nearly contemporary with Dreiser's most productive years, were not made anachronistic by that pioneering achievement for which Dreiser is so often praised. Her social compassion was less profound than Dreiser's, but her perception of social realities was equally acute, and her relevance to the younger writers often thought of as the heirs of Dreiser is indicated not only by Sinclair Lewis's dedication but by the enthusiasm for her work which F. Scott Fitzgerald so often expressed and which in his finest work may be said to have taken the form of emulation.

The House of Mirth is a novel of manners, one of the few distinguished American examples in that kind. As in all of Edith Wharton's fiction, distinctions in social behaviour are firmly drawn; as in all her writing, fiction and non-fiction alike, there is an almost obsessive preoccupation with objects, with houses, furniture, pictures, and with everything which might be said to constitute the décor of life, whether elegant or everyday. But it seems even more important to say of *The House of Mirth* that it is, quite as nakedly as Dreiser's *Sister Carrie*, a novel of class. Edith Wharton's thinking and her political attitudes were never other than conservative, but she knew intimately the society of which she wrote, and she was undazzled by it – which is not to say that she was insensitive to its superficial attractions. Looking back on that society in her old age, she was able to see in it many qualities – above all, a set of basic standards of business and personal probity – which younger generations seemed utterly to have lost sight of. But in *The House of Mirth* she laid bare the construction of that society with all the cold precision of an architectural drawing: she showed just how and where everything fitted together, from the old Dutch and English families which provided the foundations to the newer money-makers who later gained reluctant acceptance. She did so by focusing on Lily Bart, society's victim, and pre-publication versions of the novel now in Yale University Library carry titles – 'A Moment's Ornament' and 'The Year of the Rose' – which point explicitly to the significance of Lily's role. As Lily Bart goes down in the world, too scrupulous to be worldly wise, so Sim Rosedale, the Jewish financier, makes his way slowly to the top, winning social acceptance by a shrewd manipulation of his increasing wealth – in Edith Wharton's own splendid phrase, 'placing Wall Street under obligations which only Fifth Avenue could repay'. After the tough realism of this formulation, one which the whole novel richly documents, we may be less surprised than might otherwise be the case to discover that Edith Wharton's next novel, *The Fruit of the Tree*, is to some extent a 'business' novel, dealing with an attempt to reform conditions in a New England textile mill. As the novel progresses, however, this theme becomes lost in a tangle of other themes – the issue of euthanasia, for example, is raised in a rather arbitrary context – and the novel as a whole, though extremely interesting for its indication of the author's concern with contemporary problems, too obviously lacks firm direction or even convincing characterization to be considered among her most successful works.

In 1907, the year in which *The Fruit of the Tree* was published, Edith Wharton also brought out a short novel – scarcely more than a long short story, what she herself was accustomed to call a nouvelle – called *Madame de Treymes*. It is one of the best of her many masterly achievements in this form, a neatly manipulated contrast between American and European values which loses nothing from the comparison with Henry James's *The American*, to which it seems clearly to be indebted. A few years later, following two collections of short stories, a volume of verse, and a travel book about France, she published *Ethan Frome* (1911), the most famous of her nouvelles and, though one of her least characteristic productions, perhaps still the work by which she is most widely known. In one sense, and by no means the least important, *Ethan Frome* is a formal exercise in the use of the first-person narrator as historian, engaged in the progressive reconstruction of events he himself has not witnessed, collecting evidence from a variety of sources. The technical interest of the book is not, however, the principal source of its fame. What seemed so remarkable to its early readers, what still seems remarkable to anyone familiar with Edith Wharton's other fiction, is the calculated bareness of the New England setting and the harsh fatalism of the action. In its unyielding pessimism, its bleak demonstration of tragic waste, *Ethan Frome* outstrips all its predecessors in the history of American 'realism' – even a book like E. W. Howe's *The Story of a Country Town* – and demands comparison with the late novels of Thomas Hardy. If, at the same time, Edith Wharton lays herself open to those charges of arbitrariness and exaggeration so often levelled against Hardy, her manipulation of the narrative nevertheless achieves considerable emotional intensity, culminating in the appalling revelation of the narrator's eventual encounter with Mattie Silver.

The intensity of *Ethan Frome* is beyond question, yet it could be argued that it is lacking in genuine emotional depth and that its most striking effects are achieved by shock tactics more suited to the ghost story, a variety of fiction at which, in the *Tales of Men and Ghosts* volume of 1910, Edith Wharton had already proved herself an adept. A strong case can be made out, on these and similar grounds, for the superiority of *Summer* (1917), another nouvelle with a New England setting. In *Summer*, as in *Ethan Frome*, Edith Wharton insists on the limited lives, the emotional starvation of the 'hill-people' whose 'aspect, dialect, and mental and moral attitude' she later claimed that she had come to know during her years at Lenox; but in *Summer* the frankness and directness of the presentation of the passionate Charity Royall and the subtle treatment of her relationship with Lawyer Royall, her guardian, make the total effect of the tale more humane than that of *Ethan Frome* and give it a broader range of relevance: there is less intensity, perhaps, but certainly more richness in the development of the central situation.

Another nouvelle, 'The Bunner Sisters,' included in the *Xingu and Other Stories* collection of 1916, must also be reckoned amongst Edith Wharton's most successful achievements. She never wrote more sensitively than in her account of the mingled heroism and pathos of Ann Eliza Bunner's self-sacrifice, and although the tale is set in New York, not in rural New England, it shares with *Ethan Frome* and *Summer* that clear-eyed recognition of the narrowness and misery of so many unknown lives which makes it impossible to speak of Edith Wharton as a novelist simply of the social surface. Even in *The House of Mirth* the final scenes of Lily Bart's social downfall are handled with an unexpected sureness of touch, and in *Ethan Frome* and *Summer* it was apparently part of Edith Wharton's purpose deliberately to challenge the established literary image of the New England countryside. As she wrote in *A Backward Glance*:

> For years I had wanted to draw life as it really was in the derelict mountain villages of New England, a life even in my time, and a thousandfold more a generation earlier, utterly unlike that seen through the rose-coloured spectacles of my predecessors, Mary Wilkins and Sarah Orne Jewett. In those days the snow-bound villages of Western Massachusetts were still grim places, morally and physically: insanity, incest and slow mental and moral starvation were hidden away behind the paintless wooden house-fronts of the long village street, or in the isolated farmhouses on the neighbouring hills; and Emily Brontë would have found as savage tragedies in our remoter valleys as on her Yorkshire moors.

In subsequent pages Edith Wharton goes on to describe how *Ethan Frome* began as an 'exercise' written for a French teacher who was helping her to improve her French – the text of the original composition, now in the Yale University Library, was published in the July 1952 issue of the *Yale University Library Gazette* – and to deny the story that it was Henry James who had persuaded her to return to the abandoned project and complete it in English. But if Henry

James had no influence on the writing of *Ethan Frome* – a quite aggressively non-Jamesian work, apart from its fundamental concern with the problem of point of view – he is a very palpable presence in the novel which Edith Wharton published in 1912, a year after the appearance of her first New England tale.

The Reef is unquestionably the most Jamesian of her major works, and the one, understandably enough, which Henry James himself seems most to have admired. In a letter vibrant with enthusiasm, James praised her for the psychological intensity of the story, for what he called 'the unspeakably *fouillée* nature of the situation between the two principals', and declared: 'The beauty of it is that it is, for all it is worth, a Drama, and almost, as it seems to me, of the psychologic Racinian unity, intensity and gracility.' Later critics have commonly been less certain of the quality of *The Reef*, and some have felt that the persistence of Edith Wharton's exploration of the central situation only succeeds in inflating it beyond all reasonable proportion – that a woman as mature as Anna Leath is supposed to be would not experience quite such perturbation at the discovery that the man she is about to take as her second husband has had an affair with the girl, governess to her young daughter, whom her son intends to marry. Considered in the abstract, the situation may seem too reminiscent of 'the well-made play', all too elaborately contrived; but the real judgement must be of the situation as it is handled in the novel itself, and here the smallness of the central group, and the closeness and multifariousness of the relationships between them, is productive of genuine anguish and of convincing moral tensions. Where Edith Wharton can be criticized is in her attempted resolution of these tensions. She seems not to play entirely fair either with her characters or with her readers, so that we are left with a certain sense of ambiguity about our own, and the author's, feelings towards nearly all the characters, and especially towards Sophy Viner, the governess, whose final actions are splendidly magnanimous but whose strength of personality appears ultimately to be in doubt. Excessively fine though the consciences of its characters may sometimes seem, *The Reef* retains much of that distinction immediately perceived by Henry James, and it must certainly be included in any list of Edith Wharton's four or five best novels.

The action of *The Reef* is set principally in France, where Edith

Wharton had been living permanently since the sale of The Mount in 1910. It was also in 1910 that her husband was at last declared to be in need of continuous treatment and taken to a sanatorium. Three years later she obtained a divorce. In her autobiography she writes with some frankness of Edward Wharton's long struggle 'against the creeping darkness of neurasthenia', but she does not mention the divorce, nor her weariness of the long years shared with a man who – whatever his other qualities – was in intellect so much her inferior and by training so lamentably unsympathetic to everything she valued in the world of art and letters. Also missing from *A Backward Glance* is any direct acknowledgement of her deep attachment to Walter Berry, so long her friend and literary advisor, although her many references to him are couched in terms of evident admiration and gratitude. Berry, a distinguished lawyer, seems only half-heartedly to have reciprocated her affection, and Percy Lubbock speaks of him, with an antagonism he does not attempt to conceal, as a man with 'a deep vault of egotism within,' one whose 'ascendency' cast a 'dry shadow' over the natural freedom and adventurousness of Edith Wharton's mind and imagination.

It is a familiar and curious point of speculation whether the inadequacy, in one way or another, of the men in Edith Wharton's life can be said to have influenced the presentation of her fictional heroes. Certainly the heroes are all, in the final analysis, less than heroic, unable to confront with sufficient strength or resolution the demands of the situations in which they find themselves, incapable of meeting the needs of the women who depend upon them. Lawrence Selden in *The House of Mirth* becomes only the first of a long line of flawed heroes; Amherst in *The Fruit of the Tree* and Darrow in *The Reef* are his early successors, and the tradition continues in *The Custom of the Country* (1913) in the person of Ralph Marvell, the well-meaning but ineffective second husband of the voracious Undine Spragg. *The Custom of the Country* is, in effect, a novel without a hero, or indeed without any character to whom the reader can give full admiration and assent, and it is arguable that the overall impact of the book is therefore somewhat cold and lacking in humanity – two years after the novel's appearance Van Wyck Brooks observed, in *America's Coming-of-Age*, that 'Mrs Wharton's intellectuality positively freezes the fingers with which one turns her page.'

Although *The Custom of the Country* is not a perfect novel it is, in sheer size, scope, and social range, an extremely ambitious one; it is also, with the possible exception of *The Age of Innocence*, Edith Wharton's greatest achievement. The initial theme of social mobility in New York later merges with that of the predatory American abroad, and in thus staking out her ground, thus selecting her material, Edith Wharton was establishing a position of maximum strength. These were precisely the situations which she had most intimately observed and most thoroughly absorbed, the themes with which her natural gifts and acquired techniques best equipped her to deal. Many of these themes and situations, it must be said, were of a kind earlier treated by Henry James; but in *The Custom of the Country*, at least, the differences between Edith Wharton and James become ultimately more impressive than those resemblances which initially command our attention. It is easy to guess that the author of *The Custom of the Country* has read *The American*, *The Europeans*, and other novels and stories by James; almost equally apparent is some kind of indebtedness to William Dean Howells, specifically to such books as *The Rise of Silas Lapham* and *A Hazard of New Fortunes*. But James and Howells did not exhaust the fictional possibilities of the American abroad or of the American *nouveau-riche*, and *The Custom of the Country* suggests very plainly that Edith Wharton differed from her distinguished predecessors in accepting as everyday facts of existence patterns of behaviour and types of motivation which James and Howells would have hesitated, perhaps refused, to contemplate. One registers, quite simply, a toughness about the novel, an unflinching enforcement of social perceptions at once thoroughly informed and thoroughly disenchanted. It is sometimes said that Edith Wharton's obvious hatred of Undine Spragg unbalances the novel and diminishes its credibility. But Undine is not simply a character, she is also the chief vehicle of the book's social and moral criticism; the presentation of her thus becomes a precise index of the author's disgust, and the element of caricature – evident from the moment when we learn her first name and how she came by it – appears, in these terms, not as a failure of characterization but as a calculated emphasis within the overall moral pattern.

The breadth of the social scene in *The Custom of the Country* presented Edith Wharton with a problem she later approached in theoretical terms in *The Writing of Fiction* (1925), asking rhetorically:

If one is undertaking to depict a 'section of life', how avoid a crowded stage? The answer is, by choosing as principal characters figures so typical that each connotes a whole section of the social background.

Clearly, the solution proposed is not without its pitfalls, and in too many of her novels of the twenties and thirties Edith Wharton's attempts to depict representative figures of the contemporary business, social, or literary worlds only revealed just how completely she had lost touch with American life. But in *The Custom of the Country* her sense of the typical, the significant, seems accurate and assured, and even Elmer Moffatt, the immensely forceful Western businessman, is presented with a good deal of conviction and even with a certain amount of sympathy. Edith Wharton wrote best of what she most thoroughly knew, but much of her distinction as a social novelist sprang from her readiness to reach imaginatively to the limits – and even beyond the limits – of her personal experience. Thus although Moffatt is a type, not at all deeply apprehended, she yet persuades us to believe in him as a man with a capacity both for money-making on a vast scale and for some degree of sensitivity in personal relationships, achieving precisely that fusion which we look for in vain among the businessmen created by Dreiser on the one hand or by James on the other.

After *The Custom of the Country* Edith Wharton had no time to publish any other full-length fiction before becoming caught up, to the utmost of her physical and emotional energy, by the outbreak of the First World War. She identified herself from the beginning with the cause of France and played a large part in organizing relief work among French and Belgian refugees. Such writing as she found time for was for the most part directed towards the promotion of the Allied cause. She sought, in *Fighting France: From Dunkerque to Belfort* (1915), to convey what the experience of war had meant to France and to the French people, and in the series of articles subsequently collected as *French Ways and Their Meaning* (1919) she set herself the task of explaining France and the French to American troops crossing the Atlantic to fight on the Western front—a front which she herself had visited when collecting material for *Fighting France*. Two strongly contrasted works make up the bulk of her fiction during these years: *The Marne* (1918), a crudely propagandist nouvelle, and, more surprisingly, *Summer*, which she seems to have begun in a deliberate attempt to escape from the pressures of the war. She later wrote, in *A Backward Glance*:

I began to write a short novel, 'Summer', as remote as possible in setting and subject from the scenes about me; and the work made my other tasks seem lighter. The tale was written at a high pitch of creative joy, but amid a thousand interruptions, and while the rest of my being was steeped in the tragic realities of the war; yet I do not remember ever visualizing with more intensity the inner scene, or the creatures peopling it.

A similar intention, and a like clarity of visualization, seems to have governed the writing of *The Age of Innocence* (1920) in the immediate post-war period. 'I found a momentary escape,' she wrote, 'in going back to my childish memories of a long-vanished America.' It is, specifically, the New York of the 1870s which Edith Wharton re-creates in this most highly finished of all her novels. The re-creation, made marvellously solid by the precise delineation of the social framework and the thoroughly informed selection of visual detail, is of a society on the brink of a dissolution it has scarcely begun even to suspect, a social class complacent in the assurance of inherited wealth and accustomed position and rigid in its refusal to recognize the disruptive forces already appearing in its midst. For Edith Wharton, as she acknowledged, it was a return to her own girlhood, to that narrow world whose constituent families Mrs Jones could recite from memory – a world which had imposed appalling limitations on the individual mind and spirit, but which, in the long retrospect of years and the immediate context of post-war chaos, now began to seem rather saner, more humane, more attractive in its very assurance, than ever it had done before. *The Age of Innocence* rarely sounds those notes of bitterness and satire so strongly audible in *The House of Mirth* and *The Custom of the Country*, which are both set in New York at later moments in its history; instead, Edith Wharton maintains a delicate control over our sympathies, both towards the characters of the novel and towards the society in which they live.

The action of *The Age of Innocence* revolves upon Newland

Archer's attempt to challenge the entrenched social order of wealthy New York. True to the established tradition of Edith Wharton's heroes, Archer ultimately fails, and the representatives of social order succeed in bringing him back into line: he is separated from Ellen Olenska, the woman he loves, and married to May Welland. Although reabsorbed into society, Archer never quite loses the edge of dissatisfaction; far from being actively unhappy, he nevertheless feels that he has somehow been deprived of 'the flower of life' and continues to cherish the image of Ellen Olenska as 'the composite vision of all that he had missed'. As Louis O. Coxe has observed, it is a scarcely less significant aspect of his loss that in giving up Ellen he does not wholly regain May: the important scene between Archer and his son, Dallas, at the very end of the novel clearly reveals that Archer has sadly failed to appreciate the quality of May's life-long love and silent devotion, failed even to suspect that she, too, might be living a 'buried life'.

It is in this final scene that Edith Wharton firmly places the whole story in its full moral and temporal perspective. Dallas Archer, as the brash representative of a younger, more forthright generation, regards with humorous incredulity the scrupulosity, the reserve, the acceptance of social standards, which had been responsible for the 'buried lives' of his father and his father's contemporaries. Here, as throughout the novel, our sympathies are kept nicely in balance. Obviously there is a sense in which Dallas is right. We recognize the element of tragic waste in the lives of Archer, Mary, and Ellen, and we see that waste as in large measure the product of a rigidly repressive society. But we also recognize that the apparently out-dated scrupulosity was not a matter of observing social form for the form's sake alone. The alternation in the novel between impulses towards escape and withdrawals into acceptance is reminiscent, in certain ways, of the controlling pattern of *The Scarlet Letter*, while the issues which exercise Newland Archer and Ellen Olenska are not so very remote from those with which Maggie Tulliver grapples in *The Mill on the Floss*. What faces Newland and Ellen, that is to say, is not a simple question of conforming or not conforming, but a much more difficult problem of fundamental morality; what keeps them apart at those moments when they seem closest to flight is Ellen's clear recognition that happiness cannot be built on the suffering of others.

Archer is further held in check by his own acceptance of the very standards by which his misconduct would be judged, by his own deep contempt for Lawrence Lefferts, the habitual philanderer, whom Edith Wharton skilfully deploys as a minor character; and while we may see this situation as ironic we should not allow that perception to detract from our sympathy with Archer in his agonizing dilemma. It is true that in the opening pages of the book Archer appears to be somewhat satirically presented, but this initial direction is subsequently modified, giving way to an altogether deeper, more serious engagement: the movement, indeed, is somewhat like that in *Middlemarch*, and the analogy may serve to reaffirm the essential moral seriousness of the novel. For we are surely intended to see Archer's dilemma as ultimately insoluble and Archer himself, while less than heroic, as a man conscientiously engaged with the problem of right conduct. He 'gives up' Ellen Olenska, but not wholly from cowardice. Certainly, in the final pages of the novel, his action retains sufficient dignity for his secret cherishing of the remembered Ellen and of the relationship they had once shared to seem adequate justification for his rejection of an opportunity to meet her again after an interval of almost thirty years: to think of her, he feels, is 'more real' than to encounter her as she has become, grown inevitably away from him through the passage of time and the influences of a foreign society.

Edith Wharton's own feelings towards New York and towards America as a whole might perhaps have been defined in somewhat similar terms. She continued to write mainly about America, but the rare successes among her works of the twenties and thirties tend to be set in New York before the turn of the century – one thinks especially of the four nouvelles known collectively as *Old New York* (1924). That she was drawn more often to the contemporary scene seems primarily to have been the result of her growing distress at the directions which modern society seemed to be taking. Unfortunately, living in the quiet elegance of her two French homes, she knew little of that society at first hand; in particular, she became completely out of touch with the society of an America which she seems to have visited only once in the years following the war – in 1924, when she received an honorary doctorate at Yale. It is true that in *Twilight Sleep* (1927) she is reasonably successful in confronting limited aspects of contemporary social issues; and *Hudson River Bracketed* (1929), though badly flawed as a novel, nevertheless presents an extraordinarily interesting treatment – it may be, with some elements of transferred autobiography – of a creative talent making its way, finding its proper paths of development, despite social barriers and personal difficulties of a very formidable kind. But *The Gods Arrive* (1932), the sequel to *Hudson River Bracketed*, is a sadly muddled book, and in none of her other late fiction does Edith Wharton's writing rise at all consistently above the second-rate – although several critics have insisted on the unusual quality of *The Buccaneers* (1938), a novel set in old New York, which she left unfinished at her death in 1937, and in 1934, of course, she published *A Backward Glance*, equal in many respects to the very best of her fiction.

If, however, we must think of Edith Wharton's genuinely creative period as ending with *The Age of Innocence*, we need not too bitterly lament the restriction. During the first two decades of this century she wrote a number of magnificent nouvelles, quite outstanding of their kind, and a series of remarkable novels, the best of which must undoubtedly be placed in the first rank of American fiction produced in that or, indeed, in any period. She also wrote a great many short stories, and while there is no room here to discuss these in detail it can at least be said that although too many of them are effective only in the rather limited terms of plot manipulation, the best display, in even more concentrated form, that precision of observation and characterization which contributes so much to the success of her nouvelles. There are, too, the poems, unrewarding though most of them now appear, and the much more distinguished travel books, in which Edith Wharton continued that rich tradition of American travel writing which Henry James had done so much to sustain – though it was James, ironically enough, who was more in awe than anyone of the range and ambitiousness of her travels as compared with his own: in 1912 we find him writing to Mrs Humphry Ward to report Edith Wharton's return 'from the last of her dazzling, her incessant, braveries of far excursionism'.

A great lady, powerful in personality, spacious in both the scale and the style of her living: that is the impression of Edith Wharton we receive from the recollections of all who knew her. But what is much more important, and will always remain so, is her greatness as a novelist. Because she has so often been regarded merely as a disciple of Henry James, she has too readily been disregarded by literary historians who, in the search for the seeds of future developments, have tended to seize on Theodore Dreiser as the dominating figure of the years when she was doing her most important work. In purely historical terms, the historians may be right, but when her works are judged by standards more absolute it is hard not to allow Edith Wharton a higher place. She is not, of course, with Melville, Hawthorne, James, and Faulkner, the acknowledged giants of American fiction, but she has an assured position among that impressive assembly of secondary figures (it includes Cooper, Howells, Dreiser, Fitzgerald, and Hemingway) which constitutes one of the especial distinctions of American literature.

NOTE

This chapter is slightly abridged from the Introduction to *The Constable Edith Wharton* (4 vols., London, 1966).

PART III:
THE MODERN AGE

THE SOCIAL AND CULTURAL CONTEXT
ALAN TRACHTENBERG

Introduction: Reality and the Writer

'The American writer in the middle of the twentieth century,' novelist Philip Roth observed in 1961, 'has his hands full in trying to understand, and then describe, and then make credible much of the American reality.' A particularly grisly murder in Chicago and its tawdry exploitation in the media occasioned Roth's bleak lamentation in what would become one of the most widely cited literary essays of the period, 'Writing American Fiction'. What the newspapers dish up daily – bizarre murders and mutilations, mindless inanities from public figures, mind-staggering corruption – confronts the writer with an extraordinary predicament: 'the actuality is continually outdoing our talents'. Even the most hideous of actualities come packaged as commodities of entertainment, relishable thrills and re-cyclable fantasies. As the capacity for shock and outrage diminishes, there is a sense that reality itself recedes. The more incredible the real becomes the more elusive, the more remote it seems. Thus what is truly intolerable – a deadening moral insensibility at the heart of daily life – passes unnoticed, unheard, unheeded by the society: 'the fixes, the scandals, the insanities, the treacheries, the idiocies, the lies, the pieties, the noise . . .'

Roth's jeremiad – a rhetorical mode common among disaffected American intellectuals since the days of the Puritan declension in the seventeenth century – echoes a twentieth-century theme. Ezra Pound's 'O helpless few in my country,/O remnant enslaved!' cried out from the refuge of exile to those remaining behind in a philistine America:

> Artists broken against her
> A-stray, lost in the villages,
> Mistrusted, spoken-against,

281

> Lovers of beauty, starved,
> Thwarted with systems,
> Helpless against the control.
> ('The Rest', 1913)

In Roth's version we hear greater urgency, more immediate threats from a culture no longer so much hypocritical as impoverished and incoherent, lost to its own practised values. What place for the serious artist in a society without active standards of decency, decorum and moral intelligence? 'It stupefies, it sickens, it infuriates.' The effect of this alienating condition upon the artist, Roth explains, is loss of role, loss of place, loss of subject:

> For a writer to feel that he does not really live in the country in which he lives – as represented by Life or by what he experiences when he steps out his front door – must certainly seem a serious occupational impediment.

It is a view, of an obdurate social reality, at the base of most serious writing in this century. If the previous century heard accounts of what, to a literary view, was 'missing' in American life – the 'absent things' noted by Henry James, and before him Cooper, Poe, Hawthorne – twentieth-century America has inverted the dilemma: there is too much to take in. In *The American Scene* (1907) James himself inaugurated the new theme; 'features of the human scene' encountered in his visit to the United States in 1904, his first in twenty-five years, proved 'a greater array of items . . . than my own pair of scales would ever weigh'. Facing the new commercial buildings in clangorous downtown Manhattan, he observes:

> . . . in all probability, New York was not going (as it turns such remarks) to produce both the maximum of 'business' spectacle and the maximum of ironic reflections of it. Zola's huge reflector got itself formed, after all, in a far other air; it had hung there, in essence, awaiting the scene that was to play over it, long before the scene really approached it in scale. The reflecting surfaces, of the ironic, of the epic order, suspended in the New York atmosphere, have yet to show symptoms of shining out, and the monstrous phenomena themselves, meanwhile, strike me as having, with their immense momentum, got the start, got ahead of, in proper parlance, any possibility of poetic, of dramatic capture.

Learning that the churchwardens themselves have erected 'the vast money-making structure' that 'overhangs poor old Trinity' results in 'stupefaction'. Altogether the facts of the new American reality 'loom, before the understanding, in too large a mass for a mere mouthful: it is as if the syllables were too numerous to make a legible word'. Thus 'the illegible word . . . hangs in the vast American sky . . . as something fantastic and abracadabrant, belonging to no known language.'

In the early decades of the century, when exile (or in the revealingly American term 'expatriation') lay at hand as one solution, the problem lay in the sheer crudeness and anarchic energy of a rampaging business civilization devoted only to 'vast money-making'. The writer's perception of a bewildering density, a defiant irrationality points to the most severe aspect of the writer's predicament, or, as Henry Adams would put it, the predicament of intelligence itself. Perceptions like James's and Roth's have placed writers and intellectuals outside a popular consensus not merely about the direction and priorities of American life, but about its very reality, an alienation from mainstream values and assumptions remarkably similar to what W. E. B. DuBois describes in *The Souls of Black Folk* (1903) as the inevitable condition, the virtual birthmark, of every black person in the United States:

born with a veil, and gifted with second-sight in this American world, – a world which yields him no true self-consciousness, but only lets him see himself through the revelation of the other world. It is a peculiar sensation, this double-consciousness, this sense of always looking at one's self through the eyes of others, of measuring one's soul by the tape of a world that looks on in amused contempt and pity. One ever feels his twoness – an American, a Negro; two souls, two thoughts, two unreconciled strivings; two warring ideals in one dark body, whose dogged strength alone keeps it from being torn asunder.

'There is,' novelist Ralph Ellison repeated in 1948, 'an argument in progress between black men and white men as to the true nature of American reality.' The coincidence in terms accounts for the frequent appearance in fiction, in Faulkner especially and Ellison himself, of racial difference as a autochthonous symbol, fraught with tragedy and violence, of cultural schism in America, a 'struggle', as Richard Wright put it, over the definition of reality.

Disjuncture between literature and culture already seemed a symptomatic cultural manifestation by the 1920s. In his observations during a visit in 1926 the Dutch historian Johan Huizinga noted (in

'Life and Thought in America') 'a remarkable contrast . . . between the attitude of the nation in general and the tone of its literature'. The culture represented in newspapers, schools, the political arena, the pulpit, the movies, advertisements, was boldly self-confident, 'healthy-minded, positive, and optimistic'. In newspapers, for example, is to be found 'the true expression of the mind of present-day society', the 'real literature' of America:

> The newspaper fulfills in America the cultural function of the drama of Aeschylus. I mean that it is the expression through which a people – a people numbering many millions – becomes aware of its spiritual unity. The millions, as they do their careless reading every day-at breakfast, in the subway, on the train and the elevated, are performing a horrendous and formless ritual. The mirror of their culture is held up to them in their newspapers, with more emphasis and persistence than in any novel.

In serious writing – he speaks mainly of Sinclair Lewis, Dreiser, Mencken, Willa Cather, James Branch Cabell – the picture is one of

> aversion, protest, and accusation . . . Aversion to the all-too-cheap optimism, the national self-overestimation, and the Puritan ideal, a protest against vulgarity and the hollowness of society.

Yet writers like Dreiser and Lewis are not only indulged but read with some avidity and enjoyment, leading Huizinga to wonder if serious literature 'occupies more place than an ornament'. Had dissenting literary views become ornamental, a special kind of distracting entertainment? The new culture's ability to absorb and neutralize even its most acidulous critics seemed part of the same disjunctive phenomenon.

To be sure a goodly number of serious and by no means uncritical writers have achieved popularity and acclaim, as well as sufficient commercial success for a comfortable living by their pen (supplemented in many instances with a teaching post). And of course one thinks at once of exceptions to the rule of the alienated writer, figures like Wharton, Frost, Stevens, Fitzgerald, Bellow and others whose relation to American realities is more complex than the term 'alienation' may signify. Still, the generalization regarding a pervasive contrast and conflict between literary and popular versions of reality holds and serves. Bohemianism, expatriation, commitment to radical political causes and to counter-cultural styles of life are social symptoms of this disjuncture, corresponding to the pessimism, the ironic perspectives, even the complexities and difficulties of modern literary culture: symptoms of dis-ease in the relations between American writers (white and black, male and female) and their country in this troubled century.

Modernity and the Progressive Ethos

The 'immense momentum' James shuddered before on the streets of downtown New York had quite another meaning in the culture at large: 'unprecedented economic growth'. Not that others in the early decades of the century did not share James's shudder and dismay at the concentration of wealth and power in the exploding urban centers – angry farmers and industrial workers, Populists and socialists, small businessmen, anti-monopoly liberals and reformers – but for the society at large the skyscrapers rising at a phenomenal rate in cities across the country inscribed quite legible and unequivocal words: progress, prosperity, abundance. For if the anarchic shape of new city skylines seemed to defy visual interpretation, a statistical reading lay at hand, a set of numbers which signified far-reaching economic and social transformation. The change itself produced a new breed of expert, the economic and financial commentator, who continues to pour forth the figures by which modern Americans have assumed an understanding of that mysterious field of force known as 'the economy'.

The numbers disclose that behind James's 'monstrous phenomena' lay major social changes, a complex of radical transformations in technologies of production and distribution of goods and in the organization of economic power, in the scale and concentration of wealth. The social and economic order put in place in the early decades charts a fundamental pattern of economic and social relations of twentieth-century society, a pattern of steady accumulation of wealth, of population, of industrial power, of rationalization of production and business organization, the emergence of a nation-wide transport-communications system for rapid distribution of goods and the consumer values and ideals accompanying them, and also of visible difference in the distribution of wealth, power and abundance. By 1920 population had increased to almost 106 million from 76 million in 1900. Growth in cities, from internal migration as well as an influx of 14.5 million southern and central European immigrants between 1900 and 1915, surpassed rural population increase by as much as six and a half times. In 1900 40 per cent of the population lived in cities; by 1920 the percentage had risen to more than 50 per cent, and would reach about 80 per cent in the 1960s. National wealth rose from $16 billion in 1860 to $88 billion by 1900, more than doubling per capita income in that period, though within a skewed pattern of distribution. The turn-of-the-century merger and combination movement in business, a major revolution which shattered older Gilded Age forms of individual enterprise to produce a new order of corporate organization and control, intensified the pattern of concentration of wealth. By 1904 less than 1 per cent of the nation's businesses (approximately 2,000 firms) controlled 40 per cent of industrial production. When United States Steel was founded in 1901, combining over 200 manufacturing and transportation companies, its capitalization of 41.4 billion topped the annual budget of the federal government by three times.

Henry Adams's perception of a 'law of acceleration' driving American society relentlessly into modernity seemed confirmed with every release of new economic figures. The rule of the dynamo seemed supreme, and Adams mordantly wondered whether the American mind would catch up with the new energies, whether a requisite 'social mind' would appear in time to take charge of the 'influx of new force'. The new economic and technological forces seemed to hold incalculable consequences, and images of catastrophe contested with images of progress and prosperity; in popular culture, for example, science fiction, including dystopic as well as utopic fantasies, thrived in the turn-of-the-century years. Public concern fastened on those vast, intricate and, to many, mysterious and terrifying creatures known as trusts and corporations which now peopled a new American landscape: what Henry James called 'the new remorseless monopolies'. How to curb their appetite, to limit and regulate their seemingly autonomous power, to penetrate the secrecy which shielded their financial and bureaucratic operations from public scrutiny and accountability: a growing number of educated middle-class Americans in the opening years of the century wrestled with these questions – the same questions which continued to agitate the embattled labor and farmer movements surviving from the turmoil of the 1890s.

Including a number of prominent intellectuals, Progressive reformers now began to address issues of social and economic conflict, and to formulate an activist view of government as a force for the resolution of conflict and the harmonizing of competing interests. Troubled by symptoms of instability in the increasingly complex and inter-dependent economic structure which had evolved under unrestrained private enterprise in the generation since the Civil War – the boom-and-crash business cycle and the rash of industrial strikes marked by violent clashes in the 1890s – the reformers directed their attention to the mutual relations of public and private realms, to the obligations of government toward maintaining both economic well-being and social justice, as well as to protect citizens from excesses of private economic power. The Progressives proposed an active, positive state as an alternative to the laissez-faire outlook of the previous generation.

More properly speaking a wide-ranging set of ideas and principles than a uniform program, Progressivism covered a variety of reform interests and figures, embracing urban reformers like Jane Addams, Robert Hunter, and Frederick Howe, political theorists and social philosophers like Herbert Croly, Walter Lippman, and especially John Dewey, cultural critics like Van Wyck Brooks and Randolph Bourne, and of course a corps of elected and appointed political officials who undertook to institute a program of social and regulative legislation. Although not a coherent and harmonious group – the crisis over Woodrow Wilson's war policy in 1917 would sharply divide intellectuals into a majority pro-war camp and a minority of radical dissenters (Randolph Bourne was especially outspoken, blaming pro-war intellectuals for their 'surrender to the actual') – the medley of Progressive thinkers and planners shaped the first and still the most significant mainstream American response to modernity. They conceived of, and through their legislative program began to lay foundations for, the 'welfare state' which Franklin Delano Roosevelt's New Deal in the 1930s and the John F. Kennedy–Lyndon Johnson Great Society of the 1960s would attempt to build upon.

One version or another of Progressivist vision of a society capable of both social justice and material abundance has served as the basis of consensus in American politic life at least until the Ronald Reagan administration of the 1980s. Many commentators now doubt whether the welfare state (or 'interest-group') liberalism of the 1950s and 1960s will survive the neo-conservative attack of the 1980s, but it is clear that Progressivism set the tone and provided key terms for American public thought in most of the century. And in all likelihood the vision of working capitalism through government intervention and manipulation, a vision which survived two world wars and a world-shaking depression, remains a 'normal' middle-class expectation, even in the face of revived laissez-faire rhetoric in the 1980s. The goal of social harmony through legislative regulation, the assumption of an expanding national product and a more equitably distributed abundance, the commitment to 'welfare', including education and medical care for all the people: these fundamentals of American popular ideology represent the major Progressive legacy.

Against Adams's wise (if dour) 'ignorance' about the outcome of modern society, the middle-class liberal consensus which formed in the opening decades of the century and has remained more or less the major outlook of Americans offered a comforting optimism. Progressivism portrayed the new American world in colors of hope and confidence. President Woodrow Wilson defined its mission in 1913:

> Our duty is to cleanse, to reconsider, to correct the evil without impairing the good, to purify and humanize every process of our common life without weakening or sentimentalizing it.

Evangelical in its fervor to eliminate injustices such as child labor and urban slums, 'scientific' in its preferred methods, Progressivism presumed a synthesis of reason and faith, an alliance of hard statistics and high ideals. No problems seemed beyond the reach of practical solution, given good will and hard work. Only stupidity and willful 'malfeasance' (in Theodore Roosevelt's resounding slap at big business) kept capitalism from working for the benefit of all; certainly, with 'scientific' government intervention through expanding bureaucratic controls and the deployment of 'experts', and the acceptance of 'efficiency' by industrial and business managers, the destructive cycles of boom and crash might be brought to heel. Government properly should take responsibility in these matters, just as benign concern with the welfare of the people bequeathed to the central state responsibility for institutions of social life such as school and family especially.

Some historians have noted a significant paradox in Progressivism. Forward-looking in its explicit goals, its rhetoric often betrayed a retrograde interest, a desire to *restore* as much as to reform. In its appeals to conscience and civic pride, its belief in the power of exposure of wrongdoing (in methods ranging from social surveys to journalistic 'muck-raking') and the efficacy of Christian righteousness, and in its often moralistic defense of the family against the pressures of modernization, Progressivism seems to cling to the past. Its proposals have often seemed an effort to transpose traditional rural values to the big city. Certainly Progressivism has been dogged by contradictions it has found no way of overcoming. Social fragmentation and unbridgeable social divisions represented the Progressivist nightmare. How could it reconcile its underlying conviction in an ideal community, a perfect 'America' (what Herbert Croly called 'the promise of American life'), with the exacerbating hostilities of class, race, gender, religion, ethnic group, which made up the stuff of everyday reality in American cities? Chronic poverty, racial anger and violence, unequal access to political power: these were only the more glaring discrepancies Progressives faced, and to the credit of many of them, honestly recognized as unsettling challenges to the 'promise' of America. Many early Progressive thinkers – Dewey, for example, who proposed a heuristic 'Great Community' (in *The Public and Its Problems*, 1927) as a democratic experiment in resolving conflict and difference – attempted to face up to the paradox of continuing social inequality.

The challenges have grown sharper since, straining the ability of the inherited rhetoric to weather the reality-storms of the twentieth century. The greatest challenges have come from the endemic business cycle, the periodic depressions, recessions, unemployment, cut-backs, and the fears raised by images (not to say realities) of failure and collapse. The Progressive vision presupposes abundance; the fact of chronic poverty and blocked opportunities for education and advancement among blacks and other racial and ethnic groups, has meant that the dominant vision of American progress and prosperity – the stuff of TV commercials and Presidential news conferences – co-exists with its opposite, with a barely admitted sense of crisis, of imminent threat. A heightened sense of contrast between genuine rising levels of prosperity for the white middle class and grim hard times for others also belongs to the Progressive heritage: a dialectic of 'dream' and 'nightmare', of hope and despair which has provided the unhappy stuff of major American writing in this century.

Americanism and the Culture of Abundance

On its hopeful side the Progressive ethos still commands extraordinary loyalty. Seemingly endless supplies and constantly changing varieties (particularly since the micro-chip revolution) of affordable consumer goods, genuinely rising levels of income and living standards – home ownership, medical care, higher education – the real promise of improvement and mobility up the ladder of social status: these tangible accomplishments enjoyed by the majority explain the staying power of the ethos. Of course the images of success circulated by the media across the entire society, and their insinuating, cloying message that success (in job, in love, in pursuit of happiness) is available to all, has churned up discontent, impatience and critique. The century has witnessed not just continuing liberal activism on behalf of the ethos itself – union drives in the 1930s, the campaigns of blacks for fair employment and civil rights, anti-poverty, women's rights and anti-war movements attracting millions of supporters in recent decades, but more radical adversarial groups spinning off from the dominant liberal consensus. Arguing for fundamental changes in the entire system, the Socialist, Communist and New Left movements reached certain peaks of influence and public notice, in the pre-First World War era, the 1930s, and the 1960s respectively, but failed to sustain themselves and win a place within the political culture. Persecution and frequently violent repression of radicals, notably in the 'red scares' which followed the two world wars – arrests, beatings and deportations of suspected 'alien' radicals after 1919, 'loyalty' oaths, blacklists and 'Un-American Activities' investigations in the 1950s – took their toll, but the weakness of leftist movements points chiefly to the tenacious hold of the liberal Progressive consensus, or what came to be known by the 1920s as 'Americanism'.

Attempting to explain what has made America seem exceptionally immune to the class conflicts and revolutionary movements experienced by capitalist societies elsewhere, the non-Communist Marxist Leon Sansom wrote in 1934: 'Every concept in socialism has its substitutive counter-concept in Americanism, and that is why the socialist argument falls so fruitlessly on the American ear.' As a word and an image, Americanism gathered extraordinary power to itself, especially during the period of economic collapse in the 1930s: a decade when the term took on even new force as a rallying-cry for national recovery. The term held together key assumptions of the Progressivist tradition and a popular confidence in the miracle-working potentiality of American technology, couching the synthesis in a language that seemed above parties and classes, equally familiar and relevant to all interests. Combining faith in rationalized technique and economic individualism with a view of humans as acquisitive creatures of desire, craving pleasures of ownership and 'self-improvement', and an ingrained belief in the openness of American democratic society, the absence of rigid class hindrances to self-advancement, Americanism stood for what was different about the United States, the exceptional success of its capitalism. For the philosopher George Santayana that difference – 'the hearty unity and universal hum of America' – was simply the greater allowance enjoyed here by the forces of modernity. Except for its curious gentility in matters of 'culture', Americanism 'is simply modernism – purer in America than elsewhere because less impeded and qualified by survivals of the past'. 'The whole world is being Americanized by the telephone, the trolley car, the department store, and the advertising press.' Americanism is no more than the mechanical production of pleasure – automobiles, radios, cinema, color printing – writ large.

Is Americanism a new type of civilization? The question teased the nervous (as much as nervy) 1920s, persisted through the depression years of the 1930s and the 'affluent society' of the post-war years, turning into a troubled introspection in the aftermath of the 1960s. To be sure, from the beginning of a national consciousness in their country Americans have expressed often a collective unease and insecurity about themselves, about the differences, perhaps making for cultural inferiority, between their 'new world' and the 'old'. Shared by major literary figures like Emerson, Whitman, Hawthorne and Henry James, this popular mode of self-consciousness was a predictable enough reflex (often aggressive-defensive) of newness itself: a struggle with the 'colonial mentality' Santayana identified at the base of the peculiar residue known as the 'genteel tradition'. But in the 1920s the discourse of national self-consciousness reflected upon even more fundamental and disruptive change than the normally fast-paced life of American society had known in the previous century. For if the social philosophy and cultural values Americanism (and its broader grounding in modernity) seemed to triumphant without resistance, certain signs indicated that its hold upon its adherents lacked the settled conviction and loyalty of unquestioned traditional belief-systems.

Resistance to modernity is itself a feature of the culture of modernity: a truism, to be sure, about modern societies everywhere. One of the staunchest patterns in the fabric of twentieth-century American life, anti-modern thought and behavior assumed varied native guises: openly antagonistic in the case of religious fundamentalism, deflected and symbolic in public culture at large, considered and polemical on the part of schools of critical intellectuals. Even within the cornucopian promise of Americanism, the Machine Age burst into a culture in the 1920s still inhabited by what younger critics named 'Puritanism', an older restrictive morality of thrift, self-imposed repression, strict sexual codes, rigid adherence to conventional gender roles, obedience to communal values based on Biblical formulas of behavior. Small-town America was its cherished image: a homogeneous world of industrious white church-going families. It believed in money in the bank, frugal saving over foolish spending.

The old repressive morality may have remained an official doctrine in the age of Calvin Coolidge, but portents of cultural revolution signaled trouble. As early as 1913, the first showing of European modernist abstract, expressionist and surrealist art at the Armory Show in New York provoked shivers of alarm. Nonrepresentational art not only seemed an offense to genteel expectations of art as a vehicle of lofty and up-lifting ideals; it also challenged the conventional American view of the world as a place of solid manipulable things, of forms within which the mind could see its way toward change and reform, toward exploitation and improvement. By the 1920s Freudianism had joined modernism in questioning the autonomy of will and conscious choice; like modern art it evoked images of dark subterranean forces, an 'id' just barely held in check (and why should it be, growing numbers of young people asked?) by a beleaguered ego. The influence of Viennese psychoanalysis sparked a libertarian release, a feeling among many young people in flight from what Sherwood Anderson portrayed in *Winesburg, Ohio* (1919) as the starved emotional life of the repressed American midlands. Many fled to a Bohemian alternative in New York's Greenwich Village before and after the war, where, as Malcolm Cowley describes the scene in *Exile's Return* (1934), their 'liberation' in aesthetic and sexual forms of enjoyment provided a training in the new culture:

Self-expression and paganism encouraged a demand for all sorts of products, modern furniture, beach pajamas, cosmetics, colored bathrooms with toilet paper to match. Living for the moment meant buying an automobile, radio or house, using it now and paying for it tomorrow. Female equality was capable of doubling the consumption of products formerly used by men alone. Even changing place would help stimulate business in the country from which the artist was being expatriated: involuntarily they increased the foreign demand for fountain pens, silk stockings, grapefruit and portable typewriters. They drew after them an invading army of tourists, thus swelling the profits of the steamship lines and travel agencies. Everything fitted into the business picture.

Yet Puritanism failed to die out. The Jazz Age was also the period of the xenophobic 'red scare' in the years just following the First World War, the Scopes Trial over the legality of teaching Darwinism in the public schools of Tennessee, the revival of the Ku Klux Klan (in the North as well as South), of Prohibition. While extremism in defense of the moral foundations of white Anglo-Saxon Christian civilization receded, it would reappear at points of stress in the following decades, and with an unexpected publicist skill in the 'Moral Majority' of the 1980s. What better evidence of the strength of Protestant moralism, a yearning for past simplicities, than the election to the Presidency in successive terms in the 1970s and 1980s of 'born-again Christians'?

The persistence of an evangelical moralism into an age of advertising and consumerism, an age of purchased satisfactions (or the signs of satisfaction) through shopping and spending, has struck observers as an anomaly, one of the 'cultural contradictions of capitalism', in sociologist Daniel Bell's phrase. Historian Warren Susman sees a still unresolved conflict of two cultures, the older producer morality in rearguard battle with the ethos of consumerism. The conflict arises from a change in the social order as damaging to the contours of the older consciousness as a seismic shift: the appearance of a new conglomerate class of white-collar and service workers.

A non-propertied middle class of managers, technicians, engineers, salespeople, and professionals, employees of the large corporate organizations which since the turn of the century ruled a major portion of the private economic sphere, this new predominantly urban and suburban stratum provided an ample market for the flood of consumer goods and cultural products, particularly in the media of print and moving image. They were bearers of a new consciousness about the relation of earning to spending and saving, and new notions of self and identity. Older models of 'character' gave way, or at least began to erode before new notions of 'personality', of self consisting of 'image', of 'impressions' made on others. Terms like influence and manipulation, suggestive of hierarchical social relations within large corporations, and especially appropriate to the burgeoning business of advertising, emerged as prominent themes in social commentary. And underlying the popular talk about 'success', 'getting ahead' and 'adjustment' lay what Huizinga called the 'watchword' of modern American culture: behaviorism. In John B. Watson's *Behaviorism* (1925) Americans learned a new language of selfhood, a view of the self as the locus of stimulus and response, of behavior not as a function of character and will and choice, but of habit: speech as 'laryngeal habit', emotion as 'visceral habit', ideas and decisions as 'verbal habits'. In place of 'I will' Watson proposed a scientific unsentimental exactitude of speech: 'I have had my own laryngeal processes stimulated to work upon this problem from another angle.'

Watson's esotericism in the name of clearing up muddled thinking points to another phenomenon of modernity toward which the culture of Americanism devised certain responses. As knowledge grows increasingly specialized, fragmented and technical, 'popularization' arises, filling the gap between the individual and a too-complex world with easy distillations. Such solutions of the 1920s as the *Reader's Digest* and The Book-of-the-Month Club (founded in 1922 and 1926 respectively) prefigure future directions in the commodification of cultural artifacts and information, and the emergence of what Daniel Boorstin has aptly called 'consumption communities', abstract communities fabricated initially for the sake of sales volume but addressing the genuine need to share, to belong. As new cultural forms, such communities centered on cultural commodities provided a symbolic function: not merely to convey pre-digested knowledge or distribute pre-judged literature (recorded music and reproduction of art-works have since entered the market in similar 'monthly selection' forms), but to distribute, or sell, an idea of belonging to a community of values, however remote and abstract and unreal the community may be. The word 'club' itself enacts a symbolic meaning, a gesture toward a receding world of immediate and autonomous value.

Indeed a quest for community, for a lost connectedness if not a precise future possibility, belongs very much to the spirit as well as the symbolic forms of the popular culture of abundance. The word Americanism itself can be taken as an iconic keyword in this regard: the name of what is held in common, in belief and faith if not in fact, by people lonely for true associations. The same culture which celebrates itself in figures of rising living standards and images of bourgeois fulfillment through consumption also supplies food for what since the 1920s has seemed an insatiable discourse of self-analysis, self-doubt, self-blame, ranging from occasional symposia of intellectuals (another form of popularization) asking 'Whither Mankind', or what has gone wrong in paradise, to astonishingly influential studies (part statistical analysis, part academic theorizing, part sermon) in the mode of social science, from Robert and Helen Lynd's *Middletown* (1929) to David Reisman's *The Lonely Crowd* (1950), C. Wright Mills's *White Collar* (1951), Philip Slater's *Pursuit of Loneliness* (1970), Christopher Lasch's *The Culture of Narcissism* (1979), and countless clones in pop-sociology. The persistence of this mode of social inquiry cum jeremiad – a peculiarly modern blend of academic, moralist, and publicist styles – tells of a nagging uneasiness within the ethos of abundance, an ambivalence at the site of the celebrated success of the American Way.

Dissenting Views

In 1924 the writer and cultural critic Waldo Frank issued a 'declaration of war', 'the war of a new consciousness, against the forms and language of a dying culture' (*Salvos*, 1924). Announcing the death of 'the experiential assumptions that held our culture together' – its pallid religion emptied of mystery, its repressive ethical assumptions, its genteel aestheticism hiding a fear of deep emotion and conflict – Frank lamented the 'misery' in which his generation lived, its spiritual poverty, its emotional and intellectual 'chaos'. A new synthesis, could be attained through the path of art, indeed the same inscrutable art of modernism (Dada, for example) which so offends and bewilders 'the mediocre minds . . . which control our universities and schools and churches, make our laws, rule our states and write almost all our books'. As a vision of being which resists conventionalization, difficult art promises the formative 'Words' required for cultural revolution, 'the new unified experience that will again bind men together in holiness and wholeness'.

Although overt ideological conflicts have rarely disturbed the surface of twentieth-century American political life – even the angry protests and debates over civil rights, urban poverty, and Viet Nam in the 1960s resolved on the whole into questions of national morality – conflicts over values, over rival visions of reality, have continued to trouble intellectual and cultural life. They have tended to remain, however, within the broad terms of a national consensus regarding Americanism, of what belongs and what does not to the repertoire of permissible attitudes and actions. In the 1950s, for example, anticommunism served as a virtual demonology, calling for vigilance against 'disloyalty', 'subversion', 'un-American activities'. In the intimidating atmosphere of that decade the expulsion of various brands and shades of communists and Marxists from universities, government, trade unions, media, pulpit, and the exclusion of Marxism from public discourse, met little resistance. Still, in its own way the rhetoric of liberal consensus continued to encourage dissent, indeed thrived upon it. The promises it offers, of social equality, economic justice, shared prosperity, equal access to happiness, themselves invite an attitude of reform, an expectation that the American polity will consist of continuous debate over methods of realization. Americanism comes equipped, one might say, with its own language of dissent, what some scholars have described as a conventional jeremiad, a consensual vocabulary of protest and an accepted mode of lament over failures. Thus it is not surprising that critics, including Marxists in the 1930s, often framed their dissent as alternative Americanisms. Waldo Frank's utopia of altered collective consciousness, for example, appeared under titles such as *Our America* (1919) and *Rediscovery of America* (1929).

A critique of spiritual poverty, the malaise of a society blindly divided between ritualistic utterance of 'high ideals' and subordinance to the 'catchpenny realities' of business civilization, served as keynote of the first phase of cultural criticism, introduced by Van Wyck Brooks's *America's Coming of Age* (1915) – another revealing title. Brooks's hope for a radical reconstruction to overcome the paralyzing split between 'Highbrow' and 'Lowbrow', between the 'fastidious refinement' of genteel culture and the predatory 'opportunism' of the 'commercialized men', inspired the shortlived but influential journal, *The Seven Arts* (1916–17), which sought to bring forth 'that latent America' trapped within the 'commercial–industrial organization' by exposure to new fiction, poetry, and critical essay. The hope was drowned by the rising drums of war in 1917; for its opposition, led by the young Randolph Bourne, *Seven Arts* was closed down by government order. Bourne's biting essays in these years (he died in the influenza outbreak of 1918, at the age of thirty-four) turned sharply to politics, to scathing criticism of war policy and the instrumentalist outlook underlying it.

Although attacked by younger radical critics in the 1930s and 1940s for what they detected as an attitude more of celebration than in his literary histories of his later phase, the early Brooks remains a vital originator of twentieth-century American criticism of culture. 'If we are dreaming of a "national culture" today,' he repeatedly wrote in his early essays, 'it is because our inherited culture has so utterly failed to meet exigencies of our life, to seize and fertilize its roots.' An active, creative, and efficacious criticism was his goal; evoking Matthew Arnold, he proposed that 'it is the business of criticism to make a situation of which the creative power can profitably avail itself'. In 'The Culture of Industrialism', one of his *Seven Arts* essays, he argued that the 'real work' of American criticism was 'to begin low', to uncover sources for an 'organic native culture' in everyday experience, to encourage a trust in experience, to awaken people to their environment and help them overcome the devitalization of the industrial process. Brooks's hope and confidence represented a unique moment in twentieth-century intellectual life, a moment of absolute conviction in the possibility of a renewed cultural life shared democratically by the entire society:

> We are simply at the beginning of our true national existence . . . As soon as the foundations of our life have been reconstructed and made solid on the basis of our own experience, all these extraneous, ill-regulated forces will rally about their newly found center; they will fit in, each where it belongs, contributing to the essential architecture of our life. Then, and only then, shall we cease to be a blind, selfish, disorderly people; we shall become a luminous people, dwelling in the light and sharing our light.

The evangelical accents of this ringing conclusion to Brooks's essay on 'the culture of industrialism' suggests how deeply was the hold of a positive, progressive vision upon the early generation of cultural critics.

On the whole 'industrialism' rather than 'capitalism' has drawn the fire of dissenting cultural criticism. Lewis Mumford extended his colleague Brooks's concerns into the widest-ranging of oeuvres among the critics of culture, embracing literature, architecture, city and regional planning, utopian thought, and technology. Shall we be the machine's masters or its slaves, he asks throughout his writings, proposing rational controls, the revival of organic community on a regional basis, and a sane balance between technique and value in the solution of urban problems. A keyword for liberal intellectuals who saw in Franklin Roosevelt's programs a possibility of restoring community life, 'regionalism' also served another kind of critique of industrialism in the forceful writings of a group of generally conservative (or anti-liberal) Southern intellectuals known as the Agrarians or Fugitives, including several poets, novelists and critics who would become the prestigious New Critics in literary studies – John Crowe Ransom, Allen Tate, Cleanth Brooks and Robert Penn Warren. The Agrarians' collective statement, *I'll Take My Stand* (1930), reconstructs an admittedly regressive image of Southern agrarian life, based on extended-family and small community values, deference and respect in place of the cash nexus, closeness to the soil, and a true 'defense of the individual' against Northern industrial society, its impersonality, bureaucratic controls, cult of the machine, and worship of money.

Continuity of themes in a dissident perspective – the spiritual poverty of consumerism, the anomie of urban life, cultural fragmentation and loss of central nourishing values, the alienation of factory labor (stressed more often than economic injustices) – proves more telling in retrospect than differences in ideological slant or details of analysis. The post-war years saw an unexpected development, the coming together into a university literary-critical community of urban intellectuals who had dropped or modified their radical Marxist stance of the 1930s – Lionel Trilling, Philip Rahv, Alfred Kazin – and conservative Southerners like Tate, Brooks, Ransom and Warren who took up teaching posts in Northern universities and as New Critics governed taste and the theory of reading for a generation. The movement can be called a withdrawal, necessitated in large part by the impossibilities of steady earnings through writing, but paralleling a growing post-war consensus that structural social problems of poverty and inequality already had been solved or were manipulable by Keynesean economics, that the difficult and vital issues of American capitalist society lay in the realm of culture.

By the 1950s a remarkable post-war prosperity with near full employment and measurable advances in standard of living led many, including former radicals of the 1930s, to embrace Americanism as a successful social order in need only of cultural polish and better values. Abundance, the desire at the heart of Americanism, had earned a delicious renaming as 'affluence', a tonier version of consumer society. And while Harvard economist John Kenneth Galbraith issued a warning about the dangerous neglect of the public sector – inner cities, schools, hospitals and prisons and social services – his *The Affluent Society* (1958) served a function similar to

Reisman's *The Lonely Crowd* in providing convenient tags upon the era, both assuming the paradox of relative social success accompanied cultural troubles.

The troubles seemed deep and unroutable, particularly the retreat to self-enclosed private lives. The closed doors and drawn shades of suburban ranch-style houses joined the 'man in the gray flannel suit' as defining images of the conventional middle-class life against which both Rock and Roll and the Beats, both Elvis Presley and Jack Kerouac, were notable young rebels. In its attractive aura of French existentialism, Oriental inwardness, and voluntary poverty, along with sex, drugs, and avant-garde art, the Beat movement projected an alternative image of communal exchange, of energy devoted to pleasure rather than business, freedom and dissent rather than conformity to family and business norms, experiment rather than convention in art and life. Outward conformity in personal style and political behavior ('commitment' itself aroused suspicion), inward loneliness, loss of bearings, loss of inner-direction and autonomy: Reisman and others diagnosed these as symptoms of the very success of a bureaucratically managed consumer society. The 1920s theme of 'adjustment' once more filled popular discourse, and increased church attendance along with the boom in the trade of psychologists, psycho-analysts and social workers produced another handy pointer for the age: the therapeutic society. Another boom, in 'culture', also focused the scrutiny of criticism, now flowing steadily from university sociology and literature departments, the independent, extra-mural criticism of Brooks and Mumford having since found sanctuary behind college walls. A 'cultural boom' – in sales of paperbacks (the rise in university attendance, by the 1980s reaching over 60 per cent of college-age youth, provided a ready audience), in museum visits and concert attendance – raised worries over quality, superficiality, the deadening effects of formula and popular genre pulp fiction. Yet little in the way of close, exacting and useful analysis of the cultural products of mass culture appeared (Robert Warshow's and Dwight Macdonald's essays in *Partisan Review* and the *New Yorker* are exceptions) until the belated appearance in the 1960s of university study of popular culture studies.

Dissent revived in the 1960s, social guilt released in that decade of civil rights and anti-war protests adding overt political issues to familiar cultural themes: the arrogance of American power abroad, continuing racial and sexual inequalities at home, the persistence of the excluded and neglected 'invisible' poor, as Michael Harrington in *The Other America* (1962) called them, the structurally disadvantaged beyond the reach of an expanding economy. But continuity of theme points up major discontinuities, ruptures in the history of dissenting criticism. The New Left of the 1960s turned against its Old Left parents, former Stalinist and Communist Party faithfuls, as either exhausted radicals or betrayers of an original vision. Herbert Marcuse's *One-Dimensional Man* (1964) its manifesto, the 'counter-culture' which followed upon the activist manifestations of the 1960s viewed itself as a generational rebellion against a stifling and hypocritical middle-class Americanism. And recently the extraordinary assimilation by academic critics in all disciplines of the humanities and social sciences (the distinction itself has begun to erode) of continental theories – the 'post-modernist' (a term more tantalizing than precise) amalgam of structural linguistics, semiotics, psychoanalysis, deconstruction, and Marxist political economy – has introduced concepts and a critical vocabulary which would have grated the ears of the generation of Brooks and Bourne and Mumford. In their analysis of discourses, canons, ideologies, cultural forms and institutions as such, a deeper negative questioning than had yet appeared in modern American thought, dissenting critics now seemed more intent on supplanting precursors – the modernist avant garde itself is not exempt from attack as a bourgeois betrayal – than absorbing them into a continuous tradition, as the generation of Brooks absorbed Emerson and Whitman in their 'little magazine' opposition. Dispersal of dissent, failure of concentration into coherent and continuous sets of ideas and practices with a public range beyond university seminars and endowed journals, a compensation in rhetoric for a disconnection from practical politics: such diversions and divergences have dogged critical social and cultural thought in late twentieth-century America.

The Writer and 'Mass Society'

Brooks's idea of beginning low had in mind a criticism that would find in popular life a restorative vitality for what his generation liked to call 'American letters'. The notion echoed Emerson's 'I explore and sit at the feet of the familiar, the low', an antinomian posture of indifference to European gradations (so cherished among American pretenders to an imported cultivation) of 'high' and 'low', aristocratic and plebian, sacral and vulgar. America would overcome these invidious distinctions, find its own sublimity in 'the meal in the firkin; the milk in the pan; the ballad in the street'. The finding and the making would be the work of the nation's artists; they would teach, in Emerson's words, that though 'the people fancy they hate poetry . . . they are all poets and mystics!' Poets – for Emerson all serious artists were poets – would prove their mettle and their centrality by this mission. The culture would form around them.

Brooks and Frank, and from another quarter Pound, confidently hoped to revive this image of a central poetry, a unified culture. The image has not survived their careers. In an age chronicled by historians as one of affluence, consumerism, conformity, privatism and anxiety, visions of holistic transformation have been driven even further from the centers of cultural and political power than nineteenth-century literary radicals feared themselves to be.

In place of the central, formative art of the two unexampled periods of greatness in American writing, the 'renaissance' of the 1840s and 1850s and the extraordinarily fertile early modernist years of roughly 1912–39, serious writers in the present era aspire at best to an art which, in Kenneth Burke's sane and monitory words in *Counter-Statement* (1931), 'may be of value through preventing a society from becoming too assertively, too hopelessly, itself'. More generously skeptical and secular than Waldo Frank's mystical 'Word', Burke's view expects no more of writers, but no less, than the play of engaged intelligence and imaginative criticism upon a social order they cannot hope to transform, only to correct. It proposes a liberal art, in the fullest, least doctrinaire sense of that abused term: an art of irritation and catharsis, of considered 'modus vivendi', in one of R. P. Blackmur's favorite terms, with the present conduct of life.

But such a role seems unlikely, or at least of low priority, in the university atmosphere of the 1980s. Many observers have remarked upon a turn in academic criticism away from the older idea of a 'function' (in Matthew Arnold's sense of that word) in the public realm, away from a primary (and indeed, in Arnold's view, an ethical) concern with literary creation itself and its contribution to public life. Apparently spellbound with its own procedures and complicities with its traditional object, a literary text under discussion, academic criticism has seemed more devoted to replicating itself than to the improvement of writing and the enhancement of the reading experience. One effect has been a tendency to view novelists as if they were literary critics and theorists, more concerned with linguistic feats and metaphysical acts, with parody and self-deconstruction than with a 'criticism of life'. Brooks's notion of a 'usable past', a critical scrutiny and re-interpretation of past literature for the sake of new literature, now seems quaint.

The severest obstacle lies in the new social conditions of culture. Philip Roth's troubled remark of 1960 that reality surpasses the imagination returns us to the most fundamental cultural fact relevant to American writing in this century: the effort of writers to find and hold on to 'reality' in a society of manufactured emotions, packaged thought, manipulated behavior – a society which has seemed less and less capable of fresh, spontaneous response. A notion of 'mass society', a concept born in Tocqueville's concerns over the fate of intelligence, of independence, and of genuine community in American democracy, lies within Roth's lament, a keening note which sounded in American writing as early as Emerson, Whitman and Melville, but never at the pitch of recent times. Like many sociologists and journalists, writers have testified in poetry and fiction and occasional essays to a new elusive quality in American life, not just the confusion of goals and values of a monied culture (F. Scott Fitzgerald's great theme) or the mad violence and psychic despair of a homeless people (Nathanael West's major insight), but a new quality which escapes easy categorization. 'Mass society' provides an inclusive theory of an atomized dissociated culture, older stable institutions like family and neighborhood dissolving, former assumptions of behavior by class or gender or ethnic identity collapsing, a free-floating amoral consumerism co-existing with certain habitual rituals devoid of serious moral content, the easy conversion by the media of all objects and values into marketable commodities, packaged with the seal of Americanism – thus the manufacture of 'being' along with goods. A world of spectacle, of signs, displaces direct encounters – though 'post-structuralist' critics ridicule the belief in a prior condition of free, unmediated experience as romantic nostalgia.

Actuality poses for serious writers the question not only how to grasp and see such a world steady and whole, but more practically, how to survive as serious within it. For the same processes of economic integration and consolidation which so emphatically have altered the shape of American life since Henry James in 1904 stood shuddering at what a mere ten or twenty story skyscraper portended, have recast drastically the entire field of publishing and produced an image naked and unashamed of the writer as an economic instrument in gigantic money-making empires. What Tocqueville anticipated as a consequence of democracy's suspicion of cultivated elites, that it would 'introduce a trading spirit into literature', has, in its steady accumulation of momentum into the age of incessant corporate expansion, all but converted literature into trade. To say only that business has recast literature as entertainment-commodity is to miss the wider implication, that this development belongs to a process of de-valuation of autonomy and independent intelligence upon which the insatiable appetite of the consumer economy depends. Books are not simply commodities, but artifacts of consciousness, and the logic of publishing, which seeks the greatest returns and thus prefers blockbusters to masterpieces, is coincidental with the ideology of consumer capitalism. What Whitman foresaw as early as the 1860s as a tendency of the new technologies of printing to mass-produce objects 'to amuse, to titillate, to pass away time' has come to pass as an industry of planned distraction. Books are now designed as objects for shelf space at super-outlets, with a pre-ordained shelf life (a month, in the case of one major conglomerate, before consignment to trashing, to conversion as warehouse-heating fuel).

The energy of a market system is simple; it drives out all but the cheapest, most saleable values; it produces with a mechanical inevitability what Whitman called a 'mean flat average'. A prominent forthright publishing executive, who says happily that 'surely it will someday be possible to Dial-A-Book', tells us that

the novel is now ready to compete for the attention of 250,000,000 Americans with pro football, drugs, sex, television, movies, rock and roll, Leonard Bernstein, women's liberation, police corruption ... and life in general.

The size of the markets excites images of rewards beyond belief, of fabulous fortunes and celebrity in wait of the best-selling author; on the other side, a mean income for the bulk of the community of writers well below the poverty line, unless supplemented by other work such as teaching. The situation has only worsened since R. P. Blackmur made this observation in 1945 in 'The Economy of the American Writer':

> The trade of writing is the chief positive obstacle, in our world, to the preservation and creation of the art of literature, and it is an obstacle all the harder to overcome because there is a greater and negative obstacle, which goes with it, in the absence ... of any social, public, or quasi-public institution which consistently and continuously encourages the serious writer to do his best work ... The serious writer has had always to overcome the obstacle of the audience who wanted something less than he could provide and the obstacle of institutions which wanted commitments of him which he could not make and which rejected the commitments he did make. What makes the serious writer think he is worse off today in both respects, is that his readers if he has any, and his institutions if he can find any, both seem to judge him by the standards of the market and neither by the standards of literature nor by those of the whole society. He has therefore rather less to fight either for or against than at previous times.

The absence of a resisting periphery to the 'hot center' of commodity production in literary value compounds the danger to literature itself, to the alternative hypothetical pictures of reality it might proffer as anodynes to the manufactured 'real' by which American society has seemed to live.

An increasingly managed and supervised society – controlled from the top down by invisible agencies – dominated by an instrumental reason which forecloses the free-play and implicit anarchy of both intelligence and spontaneous emotion, of love and beauty: how is the writer to make himself heard let alone credible in such a world? In an electronic age of pervasive corporate control the split between spirit and commerce which repelled the generation of Brooks and Pound seems now an age of innocence. The recurrent search in modern American writing for an appropriate moral style in an age when no value seems immune to appropriation by the devices of mass-produced culture has made the achievement of Hemingway and Faulkner, Frost, Stevens, Williams and Crane all the more deserving and worthy as literary intelligence and cultural capital. No comparable modi vivendi have since appeared in such density of creative accomplishment, and one may wonder whether the terms themselves of the theory of mass society, with its separation of elites and masses, its pre-definition of 'mass' as inert and manipulable, may contribute to the perplexities; it seems to foreclose, for example, moments of resistance and counter-statement from within the mass media themselves, as in certain modes of popular music and film. The survival of serious writing in its market-place competition with the toys of distraction incites the fullest concern. One may venture that the singular perplexities now swarming around the ancient question, What is real? – perplexities not unlike those which provoked the most enduring American works in the past – might prove a resurgent theme in the next phase of wonderment by American writers about where they live.

THE LITERARY SCENE

LILLIAN FEDER

Anglo-American Beginnings

In the early decades of the twentieth century in America, especially in New York City, a growing response to modern painting and sculpture helped to promote experimentation in poetry and drama, but it was in London, largely through the efforts of Ezra Pound (1885–1972), that American writers were first enlisted in the flourishing Continental modernist movement. William Carlos Williams (1883–1963) described the 'great surge of interest in the arts' in New York, which 'came to a head . . . in the famous "Armory Show" of 1913', the excitement aroused by Marcel Duchamp and other avant-garde artists, and the founding of the poetry magazine *Others* by Walter Arensberg and Alfred Kreymborg, whose contributors argued over Cubism and 'the structure of the poem. It seemed daring to omit capitals at the head of each poetic line. Rhyme went by the board. We were, in short, "rebels", and were so treated.' Yet it was in London through Pound's influence that Williams's book of poems *The Tempers* was published by Elkin Matthews in 1913. Williams, the chief exponent of an indigenous American art, objected to Pound's attachment to European and Oriental models, but their long friendship provided one of his major ties to the international avant-garde movement in literature, painting, and music.

For T. S. Eliot (1888–1965) 'the literary scene in America between the beginning of the century and the year 1914' was bleak. Looking back to that time, he could not 'remember the name of a single poet of that period whose work I read', and there was no contemporary English poet from whom he learned anything. It was in England in 1915 that he first heard of Robert Frost, and it was through Pound that he realized that W. B. Yeats was more than 'a minor survivor of

307

the '90s'. Eliot's debt to the French Symbolists, especially Laforgue, is well known, but however close 'The Love Song of J. Alfred Prufrock' may seem to the work of these predecessors, it also reveals that Eliot had early assimilated their influence in creating his own voice, one that is unmistakably modern yet already modulated to the particular tone of psychic alienation that Eliot was to convey in much of his later poetry. Still, from 1911, when he completed 'Prufrock', to 1915, Eliot could find no one who would publish it. Once again Pound, whom he had met the year before in London, came to the rescue, persuading Harriet Monroe, founder and editor of *Poetry, A Magazine of Verse*, to accept it.

Robert Frost (1874–1963) did not meet Pound until after his first book of poems, *A Boy's Will* (London, 1913), had been published, but Pound reviewed it, for the most part favorably, in the English journal *The Freewoman* and in *Poetry* in America, and tried, as he said (*Letters*, 3 June 1913), 'to boom him and get his name stuck about'. But in a short time the two poets were at odds, their differences foreshadowing the long history of critical controversy over whether Frost can be considered modern at all. In 1913 Pound, writing from England to Harriet Monroe (*Letters*, 7 November 1913), expressed his contempt for American 'provincialism' along with the hope that *Poetry* would be the first to create 'a Weltlitteratur [*sic*] standard'. Frost also expected to 'do something to the present state of literature in America' (*Selected Letters*, 6 June 1913). His aim at that time was to impose the intonations of speech on traditional metrical patterns in order to create 'the sound of sense' (*Selected Letters*, 4 July 1913) in his poetry, whereas Pound was determined to disestablish conventional forms and subjects and to become a major force in a revolutionary movement in modern poetry and art. Frost's life and art were rooted in the country; Pound insisted that 'all great art is born of the metropolis (or *in* the metropolis)' (*Letters*, 7 November 1913). Pound had only scorn for the public's response to literature; Frost wanted to attract 'the general reader who buys books in their thousands ... I could never make a merit of being caviare to the crowd the way my quasi-friend Pound does,' he said a few months after meeting him (*Selected Letters*, *c.* 5 November 1913). Frost was convinced that Pound did not understand his poems and had praised them for the wrong reasons. He objected to Pound's view that they are 'simple', insisting, 'If they are they are subtle too.'

It is perhaps only retrospectively that Frost's objections seem worth noting, for Pound's remarks on the simplicity of the poems in *A Boy's Will* were similar to those of British reviewers, and, like theirs, essentially complimentary. But the words 'simplicity' and 'subtlety', and occasionally the two together, were to be used by critics as key terms in evaluating Frost's poetry throughout his career. Antagonistic critics viewed the 'simple' Frost as a traditional poet: pastoral, anachronistic in his technique, and merely a purveyor of homespun verities; whereas those who emphasized his 'subtlety' regarded his stark portraits and ambivalent responses to an indifferent universe as essentially modern.

Even Frost's first book and his second one, *North of Boston*, which was published in London in 1914, evoke both responses. Archaisms, traditional meters and rhymes, and echoes of Romantic and Victorian predecessors can unexpectedly lead to an observation in which a mythical allusion creates the very context of modern alienation from a long tradition of faith and art, a final dependence on one's own resources in the 'vast chaos':

> And yet with neither love nor hate,
> Those stars like some snow-white
> Minerva's snow-white marble eyes
> Without the gift of sight.
>
> ('Stars')

At least four of the poems of *North of Boston* – 'The Death of the Hired Man', 'Home Burial', 'A Servant to Servants', and 'The Fear' – tell of an alienation from family, spouses, the natural world of home and work more commonly associated in modern poetry with an urban environment. The dialogue of 'Home Burial', in which the husband pleads with his wife to 'help' him communicate with her: 'Don't go to someone else this time', and again: 'Don't carry it to someone else this time', makes explicit the pain of aloneness in love that seems at once timeless and contemporary. The speaker in 'A Servant to Servants', the earliest of Frost's deranged women, is a precursor of the many interpreters of their own madness in American poetry of the 1960s and 1970s. Her alienation from her own feelings at the beginning of the poem:

> I can't express my feelings any more
> Than I can raise my voice or want to lift
> My hand (oh, I can lift it when I have to).
>   . . .
> It's got so I don't even know for sure
> Whether I *am* glad, sorry, or anything.
> There's nothing but a voice-like left inside
> That seems to tell me how I ought to feel,
> And would feel if I wasn't all gone wrong.

opens the reader to the suppressed anger beneath the common complaints of a poor farmer's wife about the tedium of her days, her endless, unappreciated work. She defines her madness as 'fancies', and goes on to say, 'it runs in the family'. Explaining, she uses her mad uncle who would 'shout and shout' his rage 'in the night' as a surrogate for her own unexpressed feelings. As usual, she hints at this insight when she tells of her 'half fooling' suggestion that her family place her in the cage that had been built for him: 'It's time I took my place upstairs in jail'. Frost's understanding of the psychic pain expressed in the platitudes of daily life emerges in the homeliest of similes: 'Somehow the change wore out like a prescription' is her comment on a change of scene, 'living by a lake', as a cure for mental anguish.

In 1913 Frost defined 'the sound of sense' as 'the abstract vitality of our speech', and it was through his use of what he called 'pure sound – pure form' (*Selected Letters*, 4 July 1913) that he converted the vernacular of New England into the language of poetry. Even the most traditional of meters to which he clung despite the objections of critics – blank verse – is made new by the voices that break its patterns with idiosyncratic expressions of conflict and loneliness:

It is as simple as this: there are the very regular preestablished accent and measure of blank verse; and there are the very irregular accent and measure of speaking intonation. I am never more pleased than when I can get these into strained relation. I like to drag and break the intonation across the meter as waves first comb and then break stumbling on the shingle.

(*Selected Letters*, 8 July 1914)

The 'strained relation' between the speaking voices and the seeming placidity of their environment are inseparable from the rhythmic effects of their lines. It is a new sound in American poetry.

Frost's desire to distance himself from Pound was motivated not only by his resentment of what he regarded as condescension in Pound's role of patron but also by his irritation at Pound's use of him as a means of attacking American editors. Commenting on Pound's review of *North of Boston* in *Poetry*, he refused to be included in his 'party of American literary refugees in London'. At this time, in early January 1915, Frost feared that England's involvement in the First World War placed his family in danger and was planning to return home. Thus, he was especially eager to dissociate himself from Pound's 'ridiculous row with everybody' in America (*Selected Letters*, 2 January 1915). Frost was antagonistic to the Imagist and vers libre movements; he had little sympathy for or even understanding of Pound's and T. S. Eliot's experimentation with form, their obscurity, and their highly individual use of ancient classical and French Symbolist poetry. Pound's brief interest in his first two books and his friendship with F. S. Flint were Frost's only significant connections with the early Modernist movement in England. The reviews of these books had made him known in the United States and, on his return, he strove to further this success. For some years, many serious readers and critics regarded Frost's increasing popularity, the apparent accessibility of his language and meters, his concentration on rural life, and his lack of interest in the major social and cultural movements of the twentieth century as sufficient reasons for excluding him from the ranks of major modern poets. Yet it was to be the leading New Critics, Cleanth Brooks and Robert Penn Warren, and their younger associate in the Fugitive Group, Randall Jarrell, all of whom were strongly influenced by Eliot, who were to discover a complexity, even as Cleanth Brooks put it, a 'symbolist metaphysical' structure, in Frost's poetry. Jarrell's essays on Frost (reprinted in *Poetry and the Age*, 1953) were chiefly responsible for establishing 'the other Frost', as he calls him, the poet of tragic vision. In these essays, and in others – on Whitman, John Crowe Ransom, William Carlos Williams, and Robert Graves, for example – Jarrell's responses are original, his judgements acute, and his language precise.

Frost's lifelong reliance on the philosophical and literary values of his earliest influences – Emerson, Thoreau, and William James – has been linked to his hostility to the Modernist movement, his conservatism, and the essentially regressive attitudes toward human beings in society that characterized his poetry. In this last respect at least Frost bears some resemblance to the leading Anglo-American Modernists, especially Pound and Eliot. 'From its earliest days,' says Octavio Paz,

modern poetry has been a reaction against the modern era, tugging first in one direction and then another as the manifestations of the modern have changed – the Enlightenment, critical reason, liberalism, positivism, and Marxism ... The modernness of modern poetry seems paradoxical ... In many of its most violent and characteristic works – think of the tradition which runs from the Romantics to the Surrealists – modern literature passionately rejects the modern age.[1]

Intrinsic to Pound's and Eliot's formative influence on the character of American Modernism is a repudiation of bourgeois society and its products – secularism, materialism, and egalitarianism. Their reaction against these manifestations of social change differs in basic respects, however, from the agrarianism of Frost and the Fugitive Group of the early 1920s, which is rooted in American cultural history. Pound's and Eliot's urban cosmopolitanism embraces religious and aesthetic sources ranging from the ancient past of Europe and Asia to their contemporaries in the Continental avant-garde. Their ironic literary allusions and their revisionist approach to contemporary history through recently revitalized myths and rituals produced a curious amalgam of regression and revolution in modern poetry.

By 1915, the year he started working on *Three Cantos*, Pound had been for some time a leading figure in the Modernist movement in London. Fusing Continental Modernist, especially French, aesthetic values and techniques with his unique adaptations of earlier models – classical, Provençal, Oriental, and British – he redefined an international movement for his own aesthetic ends.

As Malcolm Bradbury points out, from its beginnings, Modernism in London combined the native tradition with Continental sources and models. 'T. E. Hulme, for example, so important to the early Imagist climate, looked to French and German sources (especially [Wilhelm] Worringer) but also re-asserted an English tradition of "classicism".' In its 'later stages . . . between 1912 and 1915', Imagism attracted many Americans, but was considerably indebted to French writers:

> It was in part F. S. Flint's magazine reports on the contemporary French movements that produced the notion of having a movement at all, while that movement was itself a synthesis of various Symbolist inheritances from the Anglo-French literary concords of the 1890s with new novelties: Symons, Laforgue, Corbière, Mallarmé, Valéry, but also Bergson, Remy de Gourmont, *Action Française*, and Apollinaire.[2]

Hulme, Flint, and Pound were also drawn to the Japanese haiku, which they viewed as a form of vers libre, the purest example of the principles of Imagism. Pound's study and imitation of the haiku no doubt determined his well-known definition of an image as 'that which presents an intellectual and emotional complex in an instant in time', a conception fundamental to his later development of the ideogrammic method in *The Cantos*. In 1913, when Pound received from Ernest Fenollosa's wife his unpublished manuscripts and notes on Chinese poetry and Japanese drama, he discovered further evidence of linguistic and metrical similarities between Oriental and Imagist poetry. He acknowledged his affinity with the American Orientalist in his introductory paragraphs and his notes to Fenollosa's 'The Chinese Written Character as a Medium for Poetry', which he edited and published along with his own essays in *Instigations* in 1920:

> We have here not a bare philological discussion, but a study of the fundamentals of all aesthetics. In his search through unknown art Fenollosa, coming upon unknown motives and principles unrecognized in the West, was already led into many modes of thought since fruitful in 'new' western painting and poetry. He was a forerunner without knowing it and without being known as such . . . The later movements in art have corroborated his theories.

In notes Pound pointed out similarities between Fenollosa's views on poetry and his own in *The Spirit of Romance* (1910) and 'Vorticism' (1914). Undoubtedly, Fenollosa's emphasis on the primitive origins of language and on movement or 'process' in Chinese characters as opposed to static, abstract substitutes for primal energy, as well as his view that poetry must 'appeal to the emotions with the charm of direct impression', coincide with both Imagist and Vorticist

conceptions, but equally important for Pound and for his influence
on the development of Anglo-American Modernism is Fenollosa's
belief that the Chinese were

great idealists and experimenters in the making of great principles; their
history opens a world of lofty aim and achievement, parallel to that of the
ancient Mediterranean peoples. We need their best ideals to supplement our
own . . .

Pound's translations of Chinese poems in Fenollosa's papers, published in *Cathay* (1915), were the first of many translations of Chinese
poetry in the early decades of the twentieth century that have been
characterized as 'a by-product of the Imagist movement'. But the
conception of Chinese history and art that Pound, inspired by
Fenollosa's posthumous introduction, was to develop would affect
his work more profoundly than these early translations reveal. For
readers of *The Cantos* Fenollosa's exalted view of China's achievement as 'parallel to that of the ancient Mediterranean peoples' can
only evoke Pound's 'Kung and Eleusis', the union of two ancient
models of hierarchical order and ritual observance that he proposes
for the regeneration of modern society. Pound's belief in the vitality
of primitive myth and ritual as basic components of social and
cultural institutions was intrinsic to his view of literary internationalism. His critical role in establishing major aesthetic movements
of the second decade of the twentieth century and in fostering the
work of Yeats, Williams, Eliot, H.D., Wyndham Lewis, James
Joyce, and many others was inextricably connected with the dogmatic eclecticism that increasingly characterized his own poetry and
criticism.

With T. E. Hulme and F. S. Flint, Pound helped to establish
Imagism as a poetic movement to which he soon attracted Amy
Lowell, Williams, Eliot, H.D., and Richard Aldington. By the time
Des Imagistes, an anthology he edited, appeared in 1914, however,
Pound had found the movement too limiting. Leaving Imagism to
the leadership of Amy Lowell, he turned to Vorticism, a movement
established by Wyndham Lewis in 1914, which combined techniques
of Cubism and Futurism and which Pound considered an extension
of the principles of Imagism to other arts. As promulgated in its
journal *Blast*, edited by Lewis, Vorticism supported his own interest

in non-representational art and primitive myth and ritual. Its aim was the abstraction of essential emotion in the formal structure of painting, sculpture, music, and poetry, the medium and the concept being inseparable.

Typically, Pound drew on an odd assortment of examples to arrive at his own definition of what he now regarded as the technical bases of modern art. In the paintings of Lewis, Whistler, Kandinsky, and Picasso, the wood blocks of Edward Wadsworth, and the sculpture of Gaudier-Brzeska he perceived energy and emotion, which are one, expressed in 'pure form'. Adapting Walter Pater's view that 'All arts approach the conditions of music' and his own inclination toward fluidity, metamorphosis, and flux to a vorticist concept of structure, he defines the image as 'a radiant node or cluster; it is what I can, and must perforce, call a VORTEX, from which, and through which, and into which, ideas are constantly rushing'.[3]

In 'Vorticism' and elsewhere Pound expresses strong objections to symbolism. As Boris de Rauchewiltz points out, however, Pound's repudiation

applies only to the use of 'a symbol with an ascribed or intended meaning', whereas he defines symbolism 'in its profoundest sense' as 'a belief in a sort of permanent metaphor' and goes on significantly to explain that this does not necessarily imply 'a belief in a permanent world' but 'a belief in that direction'.[4]

The passages de Rauchewiltz cites first appeared in 'Vorticism' in 1914, evidence that Pound was at this time already forging the language of the 'bust thru from the quotidien [sic] into "divine or permanent world"' that he later says is part of his 'main scheme' in The Cantos.

Pound's early poetry and some of his critical positions – his insistence on organic as opposed to ornamental images and his struggle for objectivity in the creation of 'masks' – no doubt reflect his immersion in the work of Swinburne, Rossetti, Browning, Dowson,[5] and the Aesthetic Movement, the 'movement against rhetoric' of the nineties. Still, if his address to Swinburne as 'High Priest of Iaachus' (A Lume Spento, 1908) sounds like the effusions of a reverential imitator, 'The Tree', published in the same first volume, combines two Ovidian mythical narratives, Daphne and the laurel and Baucis and Philemon, to express a conception of psychic reality inherent in his adaptations of myth throughout his career. These very myths, moreover, were to become part of the unique metamorphic scheme that Pound was to create in *The Cantos*.

His first prose work, *The Spirit of Romance* (1910), also reveals how early he conceived the literary and philosophical foundations of *The Cantos*. Dominant figures of this early book – Richard of St Victor, Arnaut Daniel, Cavalcanti, and especially Dante and Ovid are to recur in *The Cantos* transformed to Pound's belief that 'all ages are contemporaneous' and 'many dead men are our grandchildren's contemporaries'. For Pound nowhere is the basis of this union among generations and cultures more evident than in myth, which he here describes as the vehicle that communicates 'delightful psychic experience'. Ovid, he says, 'walks with the people of myth', and in *The Cantos* he fuses Ovidian metamorphosis with his ideogrammic method to convey his vision of a 'paradiso terrestre'.

Even the briefest survey of Pound's years in London from 1908 to 1915 indicates that the development of his own poetic aims and techniques coincided with major Modernist concerns of this period: the creation of a new idiom and sound in poetry suited to the contemporary world, the interpretation of classic texts as contemporaneous, the assimilation of primitive, classical, Oriental, and Continental models in a new internationalism, the incorporation in art of anthropological and psychological discoveries regarding myth, ritual, and other non-rational forms of communication, the expression of a modern consciousness simultaneously abstracting and rejecting the environment that energizes it. These elements all converge in Pound's *Three Cantos* (1917) on which he began work in 1915 and which he was to revise extensively.

The profound effect that Pound and Eliot had on each other's work from the beginning of their acquaintance is an integral part of the literary history of the modern period. The facsimile edition of the original drafts of *The Waste Land* with Pound's annotations, published in 1971, is the most dramatic evidence of the critical influence of one modern poet on another, but Eliot had also served as Pound's critic, suggesting revisions in *Three Cantos* and *Hugh Selwyn Mauberley*. As important as particular revisions these poets made in each other's work was the similarity of their feelings about what Eliot called a writer's 'own contemporaneity'. Their poetry expresses this response not only through the Modernist techniques mentioned above, conveyed in a fragmented structure and verse free yet disciplined enough to depersonalize the consciousness of its creator, but finally through their conversion of traditional sources to a quest for direction in the chaos of modern life. For Pound this was to lie in his own blend of Neoplatonic idealism, Eleusinian ritual, and Confucian order; for Eliot in the orthodoxy of Anglo-Catholicism.

In Eliot's view, Pound's work can be judged only as a totality: 'his poetry *and* his criticism *and* his influence on men and on events at a turning point in literature'. The same could be said of Eliot. In fact for many years after the publication of *The Waste Land* it was Eliot's poetry and criticism that had the greater impact on American literature. Soon after its appearance in the early twenties *The Waste Land* became a standard against which the poetry of decades would be measured. Both its detractors and admirers reacted intensely. There were objections to its obscurity, allusiveness, erudition, its tone and language. But to most of its readers the language and structure of the poem expressed the despair, anxiety, and yearnings of post-war society internalized in the consciousness of the speaker, in which all the characters merge. Through adaptations of myth and ritual, bearing their current anthropological authority via James Frazer and Jessie Weston, combined with scenes from contemporary high and low life and the multiple associations of literary echoes, the poem identified a personal sense of fragmentation with cultural and social upheaval.

Writing about the reception of *The Waste Land* almost a decade after its appearance, Eliot objected to the view of 'some of the more approving critics' that he 'had expressed "the disillusionment of a generation" . . . I may have expressed for them their own illusion of being disillusioned,' he says, 'but that did not form part of my intention.' 'Disillusionment' is indeed the wrong word, for it denotes too conscious and deliberate a reaction. What the poem does convey is unconscious conflict emerging in images of sexual impotence which reflect the sterility of a society that debases its artistic and religious heritage. Pagan myth, Christian symbols, and ironic allusions to literature merge to express a consciousness of inner conflict never resolved but merely diverted to a ritual quest for meaning. The very openness of Eliot's form, the freedom of association – to the Bible, the Tarot pack, Ovid, Dante, Shakespeare, Webster, Baudelaire, Verlaine, to name but some – and the easy equation of disparate historical and religious symbols connect what Eliot was later to call his 'personal and wholly insignificant grouse against life' with cultural history.

Even as he adapts current rational approaches to myth and rite – Frazer's revelation of primitive patterns of thought persisting beneath the surface of modern society and (despite his objections to Freudian psychology) interpretations of myth as the language of the unconscious – Eliot teases the imagination with an ancient promise of spiritual regeneration through ritual observance tainted but not quite extinguished. It is easy enough to understand why a post-war generation of readers could feel that this was the uncompromising aesthetic form that could channel their anarchic feelings. Albert Corde, the hero of Saul Bellow's *The Dean's December* (1982), represents many an American intellectual who, feeling like an anachronism in the present, has still not 'detached' himself from his youth in the thirties when *The Waste Land*, along with 'Shakespeare and Plato, ... "The Gardens of Proserpine" and "Lapis Lazuli"', formed a canon of values now seemingly abandoned.

There were, of course, dissenters, even among those who recognized Eliot's genius. A famous passage in William Carlos Williams's *Autobiography* (1951) describes 'the appearance of ... *The Waste Land*' as 'the great catastrophe to our letters'. Eliot had given 'the poem back to the academics'. Williams goes so far as to call *The Waste Land* 'an atom bomb' that destroyed the impulse of his own group, which included Alfred Kreymborg, Mina Loy, Marianne Moore, Kay Boyle, and Louise Bogan, to create a type of modern poetry rooted in America. As for himself, he 'felt at once that it had set [him] back twenty years'. Paul Mariani discounts Williams's appraisal, suggesting that he wrote it 'with a failing memory and the hindsight that thirty years of the English and American academy had provided to reinforce his judgement'. The fact is, he says, the literary scene in America in 1922 was 'itself a wasteland'; many writers had left the country for the more stimulating atmosphere of post-war

Europe, and those who remained had no common group or purpose. He points to Williams's 'By the Road to the Contagious Hospital' and Hart Crane's early work on *The Bridge* as responses to *The Waste Land*. Crane himself considered his poem 'For the Marriage of Faustus and Helen' an answer to Eliot's pessimism.

Williams's remarks may contain some retrospective insight, but they also confirm his earlier reservations about Eliot's effect on contemporary poetry. Writing on 'Prufrock' in *Kora in Hell* (1920), he called Eliot 'a subtle conformist', and he may well have foreseen that for Eliot revolutionary techniques would ultimately be the means of renewing traditional sources and values.

Eliot's criticism had prepared the way for and continued to reinforce his role as the dominant American literary figure of the first half of the twentieth century. In *Axel's Castle*, first published in 1931, Edmund Wilson describes the 'extent of Eliot's influence' on American literary and academic life as 'amazing':

> With the ascendancy of T. S. Eliot, the Elizabethan dramatists have come back into fashion, and the nineteenth-century poets have gone out, Milton's poetic reputation has sunk, and Dryden's and Pope's have risen. It is as much as one's life is worth nowadays, among young people, to say an approving word for Shelley or a dubious one about Donne. And for the enthusiasm for Dante – to paraphrase the man in Hemingway's novel, there's been nothing like it since the Fratellinis![6]

This influence was only to increase during the next thirty years, but there were opposing voices, Williams's, Hart Crane's, and Wallace Stevens's the most enduring among them. In fact, at the height of Eliot's critical authority, Williams attracted far more followers among younger poets: Louis Zukofsky, Karl Shapiro, Charles Olson, Allen Ginsberg, and Robert Duncan.

A Contemporary American Consciousness

In the huge body of prose and poetry that Williams produced in every conceivable form, he is explicit in his aim: to create a voice simultaneously his own and that of modern America. From early works, such as *Kora in Hell* and *The Great American Novel* (1923), to the last book of *Paterson* (1958) and *Pictures from Breughel and Other Poems* (1963), he wrote as a 'United Stateser' (admitting, in *The*

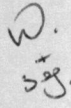

Great American Novel, 'Yes it's ugly, there is no word to say it better'.) For him this meant using language as it is spoken by Americans and thus liberating 'the world of fact from the impositions of "art"'. It is the imagination revitalizing words, he believed, that charges writer and reader with a new consciousness of factual reality: 'poetry does not tamper with the world, but moves it'. Composing the essays of *In the American Grain* (1925), Williams sought 'the spirit, the ghost of the land' in its history, which he wished to incorporate in the texture of his writing.

Williams has said that his career as a physician was fundamental to his writing, and it is evident that his continual exposure to the medical and domestic intimacies of his patients, the abrupt rhythms of his days as he treated chronic and sudden illness, accounts for the matter-of-fact tenderness toward human and external nature that permeates his work. Medicine, according to Williams, 'gained [him] entrance to the secret gardens of the self':

> I was permitted by my medical badge to follow the poor, defeated body into those gulfs and grottoes. And the astonishing thing is that at such times and in such places – foul as they may be with the stinking ischiorectal abscesses of our comings and goings – just there, the thing, in all its greatest beauty, may for a moment be freed to fly for a moment guiltily about the room. (*Autobiography*, pp. 288–9)

It is this experience of the self through an apprehension of the physical reality of people in their intrinsic locality that forms his language.

Throughout his poetry, novels, and essays, Williams writes of his struggle to discover the form that could capture the immediacy and complexity of this experience. His attraction to the Imagist movement is evident in his early poetry, but he soon rejected its principles along with free verse. Continually experimenting with new forms, he was influenced by Dadaism, he says, in writing *Spring and All* (1923) and *A Novelette* (1932). With Louis Zukofsky, Charles Reznikoff, and George Oppen, he fashioned the Objectivist theory of the poem as an object that, like a 'symphony or cubist painting', expresses its meaning through its form. The poet's words, they believed, must create a new reality, that is, 'an object consonant with his day'. In the last chapter of his *Autobiography*, as he reflects on *Paterson* he thinks of Whitman, who claimed that he 'had broken the dominance of the iambic pentameter in English prosody' but 'had only begun his theme'. Now, he believes, it is up to his generation 'in the new dialect, to continue it by a new construction upon the syllables'. In the process of writing *Paterson* II, he discovered the 'variable foot', and, a few years later, he found his answer to the quest for a 'measure' that reflects the 'relative order' of modern life in the 'relatively stable foot'.

Williams's theories on writing are often idiosyncratic versions of common avant-garde ideas and techniques. Incorporated in his fiction or poetry, they take on its vitality, becoming part of its very subject and idiom. His repeated injunction 'no ideas but in things' is inseparable from the poetry of *Paterson* (1946–58):

> – Say it, no ideas but in things –
> nothing but the blank faces of the houses
> and cylindrical trees
> bent, forked by preconception and accident –
> split, furrowed, creased, mottled, stained –
> secret – into the body of the light!

just as the 'identity' of Mr Paterson is his internalization of the city. In this 'interpenetration, both ways', mind and body, word and fact, man and city are one.

Inevitably, *Paterson* has been compared to *The Waste Land* and *The Cantos* as an interpretation of modern life. There are, of course, obvious differences: Eliot's and Pound's breadth of reference to diverse cultures and their nostalgia for a nobler past as opposed to Williams's concentration on the local as representative and his rejection of traditional artistic 'objects', which he views as outworn by time. More basic, however, is the emotional atmosphere that, despite structural variations and disjunctions, creates the dominant tone of each of these poems. One clue to their differences lies in the fundamental issue of love, which, expressed or denied, determines this pervading quality.

For all three poets love between individuals follows the course of Eros, the universal principle of fertility and creation operating in nature and society. In the sterile atmosphere of *The Waste Land* desire is thwarted by impotence or expressed in sordid coupling. Pound evokes many mythical figures and deities in *The Cantos* who represent love and fertility – Helen, Eros, Aphrodite, Demeter,

Persephone, Priapus, Pomona, Dionysus, Silenus – to create his own mythicized version of history, which is juxtaposed against the corruption of the present. Personal love is absent from the poem except perhaps as a memory trace, the 'true heritage' that offers comfort in the *Pisan Cantos*. Pound's avowals of love, which he identifies with light and creation in *The Cantos*, and his explicit statement in the last one, 'If love be not in the house there is nothing', are counteracted and ultimately refuted by the hatred and contempt directed throughout the poem at historical figures, living and dead, Jews, and the social and economic manifestations of *'Democracies electing their sewage'* (italics his).

Although the emotional range of *Paterson* is broad, the dominant tone of the poem is determined by Williams's characteristic manner of approaching the 'whole knowable world' as charged with eroticism. Landscapes, urban scenes, even the river stained with industrial pollution, animals, human beings in their beauty and ugliness, and sometimes both at once, are all invested with the erotic energy that assures the continuity of life. Sexuality can be brutal and lonely, but its very manifestation is a sign of the endless fertility of nature. The lines:

> Beautiful thing, your
> vulgarity of beauty surpasses all their
> perfections!

celebrate the vitality of the ordinary whose limits exceed the power of the art contained in the Library to energize the imagination, but these lines are also a comment on the nature of his own myth-making.

Williams seems to have misunderstood the generous appraisal made by Wallace Stevens (1879–1955) of his position among contemporary poets in the famous preface he wrote for Williams's *Collected Poems, 1921–1931*. Irritated by Stevens's remarks on his 'passion for the anti-poetic', Williams failed to see how great a compliment his friend was paying him. In defining Williams's 'essential poetry' as 'the result of the conjunction of the unreal and the real', Stevens discerns a struggle similar to his own, to apprehend 'that truth, that reality to which all of us are forever fleeing'. In a later essay he considers Williams 'a writer to whom writing is the grinding of a glass, the polishing of a lens by which he hopes to be able to see clearly. His delineations are trials. They are rubbings of reality.' Again it seems clear that Stevens was also writing about himself, particularly in describing the 'modern world' as resulting from 'such activity on a grand scale', evident not only in literature but in the visual arts, revolutionary politics, and 'everything'. No modern poet has expressed more urgently than Stevens 'the need to see, to understand' that exists 'beneath the chaos of life today and at the bottom of all the disintegrations'. This need, he says, 'springs from the belief that we have only our own intelligence on which to rely'. For Williams reality, affirmed by the imagination, is an end-product, a 'new object'; for Stevens it is process, subject, and method. Stevens's early and most persistent subject is the relationship between the external world and the mind's imaginative conception of reality. His capacity to re-create in poetry the very processes by which the imagination, mediating between the two, produces 'insight of a special kind into reality' may account for the fact that, though his work was neglected at the height of Pound's and Eliot's influence, Stevens now seems the most contemporary of the modern poets.

Like Pound and Eliot, Stevens was influenced by Laforgue and Baudelaire in his early poetry, but, as several critics have observed, Stevens's sense of the comic modifies the ironic tone he imitates.[7] The work of his major contemporaries had little effect on his development. Although he accepted Williams's revisions of some of his early poems which were published in *Others*, their differences on the basic issues of form and point of view were lasting. A few rhythmic echoes of Eliot in his early poems do not invalidate Stevens's repudiation of Eliot's influence: 'Eliot and I are dead opposites and I have been doing about everything that he would not be likely to do.' Pound, who misinterpreted Stevens's independence as a lack of seriousness, none the less needed nine question marks in one sentence on this subject to express an uncharacteristic perplexity: 'Stevens?????? the amateur approach, the gentle decline to take responsibility of being a writer???' What Pound did not perceive was that Stevens's unwillingness to ally himself with Modernist movements reflected a life-long commitment to creation as discovery, which for him was solitary and individual. He belonged to no group. 'The essential fault of surrealism,' he says, 'is that it invents without discovering.' Believing that 'Form has no significance except in relation to the reality that is being revealed', he pursued that 'supreme fiction' which only his explorations of reality could produce.

From 'Sunday Morning' (1915), 'The Comedian as the Letter C' (1922), and other poems of *Harmonium* (1923) to what may be his last poem, 'A Mythology Reflects Its Region' (1955), Stevens tracks the mind apprehending and creating the reality of the external world, the self, and the language that mediates between them. The devious ways of self-creation are conveyed in the disguises and evasions of his various personae, but none of them, not Crispin or the man with the blue guitar or Peter Quince, is merely autobiographical as they enact the internalization and symbolic transformation of the reality of the modern world. The 'mind,' Stevens says, 'is the most terrible force in the world principally in this, that it is the only force that can defend us against itself. The modern world is based on this pensée.' In exploring the mind's defenses, Stevens is always conscious of its vulnerability to necessity, change, and death.

The modern mind, he believes, rejects the lofty projection of traditional myth: 'Phoebus is dead, ephebe,' and indeed, 'The death of one god is the death of all.' Stevens rarely alludes to conventional mythical figures and narratives, and even when he occasionally does so, it is continuity and change in the mythmaking process that concern him. He himself is one of the great modern inventors of myth.

In 'The Comedian as the Letter C', Crispin, valet and buffoon in service to bourgeois society, transforms himself into the modern poet as prototypical quester. An 'introspective voyager', he has relinquished his former 'mythology of self,/ Blotched out beyond unblotching', to discover 'some starker, barer self / In a starker, barer world', the reality that the mythology of his earlier adaptations had evaded. In the jungle of Yucatan, at an early stage of his quest, he finds relief 'in the fables that he scrawled / With his own quill', which require 'an aesthetic' appropriate to 'Green barbarism turning paradigm'. Here he feels prophetic, sensing 'an elemental fate,/ And elemental potencies and pangs,/ And beautiful barenesses as yet unseen . . .' Crispin's response to the fabulous and his subsequent experience of a thunderstorm as 'the quintessential fact, the note / Of

Vulcan that a valet seeks to own' lead to a freedom of mind he had not known before, 'a self possessing him,/That was not in him in the crusty town/From which he sailed'. The fabulous in relation to reality from which it emerges is his initiation into further adventures of the spirit – the lunar imagination in the Carolinas, the conception of a colony whose 'soil' would produce 'a new intelligence', the life of a philosophical hermit, and finally the return to his home and the satisfactions and limits of marriage and fatherhood, his own 'ele- mental fate' foreseen in the jungle of Yucatan. The quotidian is his destiny, but the poet who returns can no longer 'be content with counterfeit,/With masquerade of thought . . .'.

A later poem, 'The Owl in the Sarcophagus' (1947), is concerned with 'the mythology of modern death', the means by which the mind accepts the ultimate reality of extinction through myths that betray their origin and purpose. In this poem Stevens invents three mythical 'forms' that 'move among the dead': 'high sleep', 'high peace', and 'she that says/Goodby in the darkness, speaking quietly there,/To those that cannot say good-by themselves'. The third form mediates between the other two and the dying, for she is 'a self that knew, an inner thing', the individual's unconscious knowledge of mortality.

Both conscious and unconscious processes invent these mythical forms: 'the eye that needs,/Needs out of the whole necessity of sight' and 'the ear' that 'repeats/Without a voice, inventions of farewell'. They arise out of need, which Stevens, like Freud, mythi- cizes as Ananke, a principle of reality in 'the Greenest Continent' (*Owl's Clover*, 1936). Here, 'Fatal' and 'fateful Ananke' is 'the common god' and 'the final god' who exposes the nature of godhood as the 'necessitous', unheeded 'cry' of human limitation incorporated in the creation of a supreme fiction.

Helen Vendler traces Stevens's response to the 'preeminent ques- tion' of 'whether the sublime was livable' in modern America from his interpretation of this ancient concept as 'The empty spirit/In vacant space' in 'The American Sublime' (1935) through his later realization that the experience of the sublime is 'like/A new know- ledge of reality' in 'Not Ideas About the Thing but the Thing Itself'[8] (1954). The reverse is also true for Stevens: to discover reality through the exploration and invention of its fictive forms is to experience the sublime in its most elemental inner manifestation. Like other modern poets, for example, W. H. Auden, Conrad Aiken, Edwin Muir, and W. S. Merwin, he returns the gods, those 'personae of a peremptory elevation and glory' in ancient society, to the human mind that conceived them.

The exploration of consciousness in the modern world takes various other mythical forms in twentieth-century American poetry. By 1930 Hart Crane (1899–1932) assumed that modern poetry had 'long since passed the crest of its rebellion against many of the so-called classical strictures', and that its more permanent concern was

based not on Evolution of the idea of progress but on the articulation of the contemporary human consciousness *sub specie aeternitatis*, and inclusive of all readjustments incident to science and other shifting factors related to consciousness.

The most immediate of those factors was the rapid industrialization of America, 'machinery', which, he believed, could 'not act creatively' in the 'lives' of modern poets 'until, like the unconscious nervous responses of our bodies, its connotations emanate from within – forming as spontaneous a terminology of poetic references as the bucolic world of pasture, plow, and barn'. *The Bridge* is his paramount representation of that contemporary consciousness forming a pervasive myth that unites America's historical and cultural past – Columbus, Pocahontas, Captain John Smith, Rip Van Winkle, Edgar Allan Poe, and above all Walt Whitman – with its present and future. Following in the tradition of Whitman, 'Our Meistersinger', and calling upon the Brooklyn Bridge to be 'our Myth, whereof I sing', Crane links its symbolic and actual functions; it is 'harp and altar, of the fury fused', and it is also 'steeled Cognizance', a structure produced by modern technology invested with the perception of the poet. Ultimately it is divine love that transforms 'granite and steel' into an 'intrinsic Myth' of human ingenuity and aspiration.

Conrad Aiken's response to the challenge of new discoveries and values is also aesthetic, but it is entirely secular. In a preface written in 1965 for a new printing of *Preludes for Memnon* (1931) and *Time in the Rock* (1936), he looks back to what he calls the 'psychological predicament' of the poet of the 1920s and 1930s:

... the preludes were planned to be an all-out effort at a probing of the self-in-relation-to-the-world, the formulation of a new *Weltanschauung*. For where was one to go, or what stand upon, now that Freud, on the one hand, and Einstein on the other, with the shadow of Darwin and Nietzsche behind them, had suddenly turned our neat little religious or philosophic systems into something that looked rather alarmingly like pure mathematics?

The two volumes of *Preludes*, which Aiken (1899–1973) regarded as 'one unit', are central to his poetic development. They are his most direct expression of the psychic reality inherent in mythical distortions. Influenced chiefly by William James and Freud, he employs classical myths as instruments for probing the human 'consciousness' (a term he uses frequently) of vulnerability to inner and external forces of destruction.

Aiken's view of human aloneness in the universe is optimistic, even exultant. God is finally reduced to 'Lord Zero', and in the nothingness that remains human beings are offered the possibility of achieving godhood by accepting the realities of limitation and death. One is reminded of Stevens's aphorism: 'God is in me or else is not at all (does not exist).' If 'Lord Zero' is Aiken's mythical construct of the consciousness of a universe without order and purpose, it is also a representation of intellectual freedom and of creation out of void.

The Novels of the 1920s and 1930s

Implicit in the tone and atmosphere of some of the greatest poems of the post-war period, such as *Mauberley* (1920) and *The Waste Land*, is the assumption that the spiritual and cultural values of Western civilization have been irreparably damaged. Poems IV and V of *Mauberley* connect the corruption inherent in that civilization with the war and its aftermath:

> There died a myriad,
> And of the best, among them,
> For an old bitch gone in the teeth,
> For a botched civilization . . .

Those who survive come 'home to old lies and new infamy'. But it is the novelists – especially F. Scott Fitzgerald (1896–1940), John Dos Passos (1896–1970), E. E. Cummings (1894–1962), Ernest

Hemingway (1899–1961), and William Faulkner (1897–1962) – who explore the effects of the war on individual lives which expose the social realities masked by the Great Crusade.

Although Fitzgerald's *This Side of Paradise* (1920) does not deal directly with the war, it was the first of the American novels to convey the disillusionment and consequent rebelliousness of post-war American youth – the members of the so-called Jazz Age – their rejection of established standards of conduct and their seemingly reckless insistence on defining themselves in accordance with their own desires and values. The war has taught Amory Blaine, Fitzgerald's central character, and his generation that there are no heroes. 'We *want* to believe,' he says, but neither politics nor literature offers any models:

> How'll I fit in? What am I for? To propagate the race? According to the American novels we are led to believe the 'healthy American boy' from nineteen to twenty-five is an entirely sexless animal. As a matter of fact, the healthier he is the less that's true. The only alternative to letting it out of you is some violent interest.

By the end of the novel, he feels he has 'every reason to throw my mind and my pen in with the radicals'. Despite its sentimentality, the shallowness of its emotional content, and its adolescent grandiosity, *This Side of Paradise*, which became a best seller, seemed to speak for a generation whose excesses dramatized its alienation from post-war national goals: the restoration of 'normalcy' under Harding and the industrial expansion of the boom years under Coolidge.

The actual experience of the war and its devastating effects are graphically communicated in Dos Passos's *Three Soldiers* (1921), especially in the figure of John Andrews, a gifted young musician whose talents are submerged and whose individuality is reduced to ineffectual gestures by the machinery of war and bureaucracy. Both Dos Passos and Cummings served in the Norton-Harjes Ambulance Corps, which Alfred Kazin has called 'the most distinguished of all the lost generation's finishing schools'. *The Enormous Room* (1922), Cummings's account of his months in a French prison, 'wrote itself', he says, when he 'was observing a negligible portion of something more distant than any sun; something more unimaginably huge than the most prodigious of all universes –'. This, he goes on to say, is 'The individual'. The narrator of *The Enormous Room* conceives of his prison experience as a psychological pilgrim's progress, an internalization of the hypocrisy and brutality of war. Dos Passos wrote an enthusiastic review of *The Enormous Room* in *The Dial*, comparing Cummings with Defoe in his directness, but most reviewers were shocked by its unconventional form, at once autobiography and fiction, its mocking tone, its surrealist revelations of internalized reality, its use of obscenity, and its unsparing disclosures of dehumanized cruelty.

In *A Moveable Feast*, which he wrote between 1957 and 1960, Hemingway looked back to the 1920s when he, Dos Passos, Cummings, Pound, and other young writers and artists became part of the group of American expatriates living in Paris. He tells of his initial irritation at Gertrude Stein's phrase 'a lost generation', yet he quoted it as one of two epigraphs to his first novel, *The Sun Also Rises* (1926), using the passage from Ecclesiastes beginning, 'One generation passeth away, and another generation cometh . . .' to 'balance it' and to supply his title. The major characters of this novel, its narrator, Jake Barnes, and Lady Brett Ashley, soon became prototypes of a generation of expatriates acting out the despair of post-war disillusionment in drink, in desperate efforts at pleasure and love, and in adherence to a personal code which demands a constant vigilance against the fraudulent. They recognize each other instantly: 'He's one of us . . . Oh quite. No doubt. One can always tell.'

The code is implicit in Jake's narrative style – Hemingway's famous 'simple declarative sentence' and plain diction; his prose expresses an individual ethic that counters the traditional and deceptive heroic code of allegiance to social and political institutions. It is the language of post-war contempt for grandiose promises and lying slogans. Jake's and Brett's understatements convey avoidance of sentimentality and a distrust of language itself, whether it solicits a stock response or threatens to evoke suppressed emotion. Jake's thoughts about the wound that rendered him impotent dwell on its absurdity: 'I suppose it was funny.' And tears are his only release from these words in which his thoughts are formed to control his feelings. Later, when Jake expresses his love to Brett, her response is, 'Let's not talk. Talking's all bilge.'

Fundamental to the code is an apprehension of nothingness, the residue of the chaos and violence of war, an emptiness in the self and society. Cultural impositions of value have been revealed as expediencies. Not only in *The Sun Also Rises* but throughout Hemingway's novels and stories, what remains is a self-imposed system of values: loyalty to the few who enact defeat in a style that defies its meaning, acceptance of violence and death, and acknowledgement of these natural realities in ritual contests – bullfighting, hunting, fishing – or simply in the inevitable contest between love and death.

In this last contest, the plot of *A Farewell to Arms* (1929), all that one can salvage from inevitable defeat is personal courage. Like all of Hemingway's heroes, Frederic Henry despises cant: the abstractions of war, 'such as glory, honor, courage, or hallow were obscene beside the concrete names of villages, the numbers of roads, the names of rivers, the numbers of regiments and the dates'. Yet he and Catherine are very much concerned with the courage they must maintain in their alliance against the rest of the world. It is the basis of their code.

If people bring so much courage to this world the world has to kill them to break them, so of course it kills them. The world breaks everyone and afterward many are strong at the broken places. But those that will not break it kills.

The lieutenant-colonel demanding, 'If you are going to shoot me, please shoot me at once without further questioning. The questioning is stupid,' makes an individual comment on the war that condemns the 'beautiful detachment' of those responsible for its consequences. The brief appearance of this 'old man with his hat off' and the shots Frederic hears tell more about what the war meant to a generation of writers and readers than does the romantic fantasy of the doomed lovers. The lieutenant-colonel's terse replies to his questioners and his final command convey the art of the code in prose that both defines and exemplifies it. Both the art and the code were to produce a generation of imitators in popular and serious fiction.

Turning from Hemingway's international settings – France, Italy, Switzerland – back to the American scene of Faulkner's first novel *Soldier's Pay* (1926), one finds no code that can counter, even temporarily, the dreadful reality of the war which has imposed on a provincial town in Georgia the demands of a world beyond its comprehension. The illusions of heroism that sent young men to battle have ended in the figure of the 'War Hero', Donald Mahon, wounded, gradually going blind, and waiting to die. Mahon's passivity, his total alienation from his family, his fiancée, and his society, is reflected in the consciousness of the other characters, who are defined by their relationship to him, a technique Faulkner was to use with greater subtlety in his later novels.

By 1925 Fitzgerald had developed into a mature novelist. In *The Great Gatsby*, which appeared in that year, he produced a new type of American fiction which recalls Henry James's consciousness of class as a formative element of character and morality and simultaneously depicts the breakdown of such stratifications during the post-war years. Jay Gatsby incorporates the grand fantasies of the twenties along with the shoddy bargains that were struck in efforts to realize them. Without any support from family or friends, he is a product of the nation itself, compounded of a 'corruption' that could never quite submerge its 'incorruptible dream'.

In Fitzgerald's portrait of the twenties that dream of limitless possibility – of a grace and freedom that can be wrested from the self and the soil – has become the inherited property of the ruling class. Tom and Daisy Buchanan, who manipulate its promise as their elders have managed the banks, the railroads, and the stock exchange, have come to represent the dream and are its destroyers. Their wealth and power are manifested in clothes, cars, manners, smiles, even in Daisy's voice, which Gatsby says 'is full of money', but in their ease and carelessness, Tom and Daisy are as ruthless in manipulating human lives as is Meyer Wolfsheim, the racketeer who claims to have 'made' Gatsby. Gatsby's dream, however tawdry, is beyond Wolfsheim's or the Buchanans' comprehension. As Nick Carraway realizes, it is rooted in the discovery of America itself, the very 'presence of this continent' which once held 'something commensurate' to the human 'capacity for wonder'. The list of those who came to Gatsby's parties, and the descriptions of their financial and social connections along with brief anecdotes, ironically evoke the Homeric Catalogue of the warriors who came to fight at Troy. It seems likely that Fitzgerald – or Carraway – intends the ironic association, especially as he concludes the list with an echo of the Homeric summary of the Catalogue of the Greek leaders, 'These were the chiefs of the Danaans and their rulers,' in the sentence, 'All these people came to Gatsby's house in the summer.' In the catalogue of those Gatsby summoned to enact a parody of his vision, Carraway seems to catch momentarily that 'elusive rhythm, a fragment of lost words, that I heard somewhere a long time ago', which he feels is present 'through all [Gatsby] said, even through his appalling sentimentality'. It is, he believes, 'incommunicable forever', yet he does transmit its bitter echo in an epic convention applied to the chiefs and leaders of American industry, politics, and the movies, their relations and 'girls', who have reduced the American dream to the pursuit of success and finally leave Gatsby, their product and their scapegoat, 'standing . . . in the moonlight – watching over nothing'.

Fitzgerald portrays America as the internalized image of a few individuals, expressed in their aspirations and ultimate defeat. They appropriate and misuse the nation's vast resources, denying its limits as a defense against their own. He views this fantasy as part of their heritage:

the illusion of eternal strength and health, and of the essential goodness of people – they were the illusions of a nation, the lies of a generation of frontier mothers who had to croon falsely that there were no wolves outside the cabin door.

This oversimplified view of the psychological roots of self-deception operating in American society has a certain validity applied to Gatsby and Carraway, but in the later novel in which this passage appears, *Tender is the Night* (1934), it seems a rather trivial basis for the conduct of Dick Diver, the psychiatrist who cannot cure himself. Fitzgerald's portrayal of the glamorous and blighted lives of American exiles in that novel resembles Hollywood films of the period (indeed, the events of Book II, 'Rosemary's Angle', are told from the point of view of a Hollywood star), diverting the audience from the real illnesses of their society: the effects of rapid industrialization, the loss of foreign markets, the impoverishment of farmers, and the unrestrained financial speculation which led to the stock market crash and the great depression. It was John Dos Passos who invented a fictional form that encompassed these crucial events in American history.

Although Dos Passos's sympathy for the working class and outrage at social injustice briefly attracted him to communism, his lifelong commitment to individualism and his contempt for power structures of any kind soon made him skeptical of all political systems. Furthermore, the tension between his abhorrence of modern industrialized society and his stylistic adaptations of its idiom and rhythms, his use of collage and impressionist association, place him in the mainstream of the literary modernists whom he greatly admired. *Manhattan Transfer* (1925), his exploration of life in post-war New York City, was praised by early critics for its innovative cinematic and journalistic techniques, which captured the reality of contemporary urban life.

In the three novels that comprise the trilogy *USA* (1938) – *The 42nd Parallel* (1930), *1919* (1932), and *The Big Money* (1936) – American economic, social, and political history, from the beginnings of the twentieth century to the stock market crash, is intimately connected to ordinary human experience: love affairs, hunger, boredom, strikes, the books people read, their hopes, and their disillusionment. Dos Passos discloses the ambivalent relationship between American social institutions and the individuals simultaneously formed by and alienated from them. 'The Newsreel' provides the historical setting, dehumanized and often brutal, and 'The Camera Eye' a personal, impressionistic response to the multitudinous events, characters, and historical figures of this trilogy.

In the opening chapter of his last novel, *Century's Ebb* (1970), Dos Passos addresses Walt Whitman, the American poet he most admired, asking him: 'Here, now, today, if you came back to us, Walt Whitman, what would you say?' The question, implicit throughout Dos Passos's work as it is in much of William Carlos Williams's and Hart Crane's, is a standard by which modern industrialized America is judged and found wanting. Like Whitman, Dos Passos is a *'Singer of occupations'* (*Century's Ebb*, italics his). The characters of *USA*, whose interior lives are not examined, emerge in work or other action, but in their struggle to achieve a measure of individual choice and fulfillment – the traditional promise of America – they are isolated and ultimately defeated.

A grimmer view of the isolation of human beings in American society of this period emerges in Nathanael West's novels, especially

Miss Lonelyhearts (1933), set in New York, and *The Day of the Locust* (1939), in Hollywood. Lacking the energy of protest that Dos Passos's protagonists manifest, West's characters seem to internalize the national mood of depression and act out their hopelessness in melodramatic gestures that mock their very intention. It is by now a commonplace that West was influenced by the Symbolists, Freud, Dostoevsky, and William James. Reading his novels, however, one is struck by the ease with which he assimilates these sources to his own vision of the grotesque and the violent inherent in ordinary life. Like the letters in *Miss Lonelyhearts*, West's novels portray a milieu in which problems have no solutions, questions no authentic answers, and the bizarre thought or act becomes a desperate method of mediating between the self and a hostile world.

Observing a man who seems to be dying 'stagger into a movie theater that was showing a picture called *Blond Beauty*' and a woman 'with an enormous goiter pick a love story magazine out of a garbage can', Miss Lonelyhearts muses: 'Men have always fought their misery with dreams.' Yet, in the America of the thirties, even dreams have been debased, 'made puerile by the movies, radio and newspapers. Among many betrayals, this one is the worst,' and Lonelyhearts includes his own dream among them. West's fiction has been more highly regarded by recent critics and novelists than it was by his contemporaries. Flannery O'Connor and John Hawkes have referred to his influence on their writing, and his grotesque characters and parodic method seem to have foreshadowed 'post-modern' relativism and non-referential fragmentation.

The profoundest narrative of the blight on the American dream conceived in this period springs not from the metropolis but from small-town rural life in Northern Mississippi, the setting of William Faulkner's tragic legend of the nation's past and contemporary history. As Robert Penn Warren has demonstrated, Faulkner 'writes of two Souths: he reports one South and he creates another'. In fifteen novels and a great many short stories his legendary Yoknapatawpha County, rooted in actual history, emerges as the locus of the national consciousness bearing unexpiated guilt, which is delineated in a body of legendary materials, like the mythical backgrounds of ancient tragedy. Past and present history, the state and the family, are inextricably bound by an inherited curse on the land and its inhabitants.

In Faulkner's fiction the violations which have laid this curse on generations are the abuse of the land and the enslavement of fellow human beings. As in ancient tragedy, rape, incest, and murder are never merely individual acts; they exemplify the fate – or portion – assigned to individuals acting out inherited roles.

In *Sartoris* (1929), the first of the novels set in Yoknapatawpha County, traditional Southern values no longer sustain individuals such as Bayard Sartoris, who re-enacts his family's history only in the violent death he compulsively seeks. His wife, Narcissa, looking at a miniature of Bayard's twin brother, John, painted when he was eight, seeing the 'warm radiance' of the child who grew up to be killed in the war, 'realized as she never had before the blind tragedy of human events'.

The Sound and the Fury (1929), Faulkner's greatest novel, is a more complex treatment of a Southern household's role in the historical process of change, decline, and endurance. Employing four different points of view, he merges past and present internalized in unresolved conflict in the minds of individual characters. One of Faulker's most daring techniques in this experimental novel – the stream of consciousness that is the idiot Benjy's perception – discloses a sensuous and emotional apprehension of relationships within the Compson household. With this elemental response are contrasted Quentin's unyielding fixation on the past, in the second section, and Jason's squalid adaptation to the modern world in the third. Faulkner is expert at creating the inner voice, not only Benjy's and other human ones, but 'an inaudible tune out of the dead void' which Luster's fingers 'teased out of the slain wood' of a chair back, a 'soundless and involved arpeggio', the voice of nature inherent in its products. As the Yoknapatawpha legend continues in thirteen more novels, from *As I Lay Dying* (1930) to *The Reivers* (1962), and in many short stories, other voices mingle with those of the Compsons and the Sartorises, lamenting or justifying the exploitation of the land and its people, most of them, whether the Snopeses's or Gavin Stevens's, conveying the end of traditional expectations and values. Like Isaac McCaslin, some of the blacks, especially Dilsey, Sam Fathers, and Lucas Beauchamp, Faulkner's symbols of endurance, seem to incorporate an intrinsic courage and dignity unaffected by loss and change. These portrayals have been lauded as enlightened and attacked as ultimately racist. Lee Jenkins, for instance, has written that 'the black race, as depicted by Faulkner . . . relinquishes the will to the greater animating power of the life-force, however blind, however blundering, in its always inexorable, and ultimately triumphant, ascendancy'. This judgement seems valid applied to black characters as individual victims of white oppression. But the blacks of the Yoknapatawpha legend, like the Sartorises, the Compsons, and the McCaslins, are also involved in what Faulkner called 'the blind tragedy of human events'. For the Sartorises this means violent death; for the Compsons, inevitable decay and corruption; for the McCaslins, the integrity of renunciation; for the blacks, not only the inherent capacity to struggle and endure but the heuristic role of survivor.

In the early 1940s few critics appreciated Faulkner's highly original adaptations of modernist techniques to extend the implications of regional conflict to contemporary American and European society. By the time the *Portable William Faulkner*, edited by Malcolm Cowley, first appeared in 1946, most of Faulkner's books were out of print. This volume of selections from his work, and especially Cowley's introduction, established his reputation.

Faulkner is the leading figure in what has come to be called the Southern Renaissance, a cultural movement predominantly but not exclusively literary. Its beginnings can be traced to the group of poets and critics who published the magazine *The Fugitive* (1922–5) in Nashville, Tennessee. In 1930 several of its contributors – John Crowe Ransom, Robert Penn Warren, Allen Tate, and Donald Davidson – were among the twelve Southerners whose manifesto *I'll Take My Stand* defended the agrarian life of the ante-bellum South against what they regarded as the dehumanization of modern American society by science, technology, and capitalist materialism. As they developed into distinguished novelists, poets, and founders of the New Criticism, these writers deviated in varying degrees from this regressive and narrow regionalism, but throughout their work the relation between past and present, tradition and individuality, is a pervading theme.

Warren, who was an early admirer of Faulkner, objected to interpretations of his fiction 'as merely Southern apologetics'. Regarding 'respect for the human' as 'the central fact of Faulkner's 'work', Warren perceives the major conflict in his novels and stories as between this heritage and the forces of modernity – the 'abstraction', 'mechanism', and 'irresponsible power' that are 'the enemy of the human'. In this respect, as in his concern with the impact of a complex heritage of traditional values in conflict with unexpiated guilt, Warren's work reflects Faulkner's influence. This is evident not only in *All the King's Men* (1946), Warren's best-known novel, but in his long poem *Brother to Dragons* (1953), which deals with a historical episode that Warren treats as 'a human constant'. Like Faulkner, he mythicizes Southern history, but in designating 'no place' and 'any time' as the setting for a dialogue among the poet, Thomas Jefferson, members of his family, and their slaves, he projects past events into the present and future. Essentially the poem is about self-creation, which is as much a historical as an individual process. Other writers clearly influenced by Faulkner are William Styron and William Goyen, especially in their early novels, and Reynolds Price.

Developments in Drama

The modernist movement in American drama began in the second decade of the twentieth century in small enterprises such as the Washington Square Players, the Provincetown Theater, and the Neighborhood Playhouse. These groups produced Ibsen and Shaw as well as original plays that reflected their influence, combined with a new conception of individual and family conflict based on popular versions of Freudian psychoanalytic theory.

Eugene O'Neill (1888–1953), the greatest playwright to emerge from this period, adapted expressionist techniques to native realism in such dramas as *The Emperor Jones* (1920), *The Hairy Ape* (1922), *The Great God Brown* (1926), and *Lazarus Laughed* (1927). The most important dramatic affinity that O'Neill acknowledged was with Strindberg. In writing modern tragedy, O'Neill enlarged Strindberg's view of irresolvable human conflict through the Freudian tragic conception of illumination as both the price and the reward of acknowledging unconscious drives. Although in his trilogy *Mourning Becomes Electra* (1931) O'Neill's modern versions of Aeschylus's characters in the *Oresteia* often seem to be neither archetypes nor individuals but something in-between, naturalistic reductions of more vivid ancestors, they are affecting as they struggle in the trap of their psychic inheritance.

His last and greatest plays, *Long Day's Journey into Night* (written 1939, first produced 1956) and *The Iceman Cometh* (written 1939–41, first produced 1946), reveal a deeper insight into the unconscious processes that determine human behavior. O'Neill transforms his own painful experience into the prototypical emotional crises of modern human beings sustained by neither religious nor social bonds and left only with an awareness of emptiness that somehow must be filled. The isolation of the characters in *Long Day's Journey*, O'Neill's tragedy of his own family life, is the 'curse' that drives them to drink, drugs, and grandiose fantasies, substitutes for the selves they cannot acknowledge and the love they can neither give nor receive. Each time they approach or are confronted with authentic feelings, they return to the illusions that feed and destroy them. If they express what they feel, they instantly retract the trenchant remark, the impulsive gesture, love and hate cancelling each other out to nothingness.

Although the plot and characters of *The Iceman Cometh* are obviously related to those of Maxim Gorki's *The Lower Depths*, O'Neill's portrayal of the intrusion of reality on the fragile defenses of delusion is more subtle and complex. No scene in modern drama is more effective in its revelation of the cost of psychic ambivalence than the one in which Hickey, the salesman of pipe dreams, hears his own voice crying out to the dead wife he loved and hated, killed and mourns: 'Well, you know what you can do with your pipe dream, you damned bitch!' Only Samuel Beckett has dramatized the ineffectual struggle against nothingness as poignantly.

The two major playwrights of the post-Second World War period, Tennessee Williams (1914–82) and Arthur Miller (1915–   ) differ as much from O'Neill as they do from each other in their dramatic material and techniques. Whereas Williams generally portrays psychological aberration intensified by a decadent Southern culture, Miller is concerned with broader social and economic issues which determine the private agony of individual human beings. Like O'Neill, Williams and Miller are rooted in the tradition of realism, which they modify with expressionist techniques, but each made of this blend a style uniquely his own. In his first successful play, *The Glass Menagerie* (1945), Williams is explicit about his use of nonrealistic techniques: His 'scene is memory', he says, and Tom Wingfield as narrator, the 'screen device' (generally omitted from performances but indicated in the published version), the recurring melody of 'The Glass Menagerie', and the lighting are all used to dramatize the past merging with the domestic life of the present and determining the inevitable guilt, loss, and sorrow of the protagonists. *The Glass Menagerie* and *A Streetcar Named Desire* (1947), Williams's most acclaimed drama, portray the sordidness of lower-class life as present reality measured against the lost aristocratic traditions of the Old South. Both ways of life are parodies – the dream and the reality simultaneously divulging the pathos of human beings trapped by desires which they cannot acknowledge or which they act out in obsessive need.

In *Streetcar* Williams is at his best in juxtaposing the bizarre detail, the sensational episode, with the fragility of human feelings and dreams. Blanche Du Bois transcends her role as a faded Southern belle turned nymphomaniac as she struggles to disguise her vulnerability as pride, her loneliness as choice. Sexual frustration and aberration, the individual isolated in a society without tradition or values, are recurrent themes of Williams's later plays. Increasingly, if less successfully, he dealt with psychological platitudes – the effects of a loveless childhood and sexual repression in *Cat on a Hot Tin Roof* (1955) or sensational material – murder and cannibalism in *Suddenly Last Summer* (1958) and castration in *Sweet Bird of Youth* (1959). Yet, even in these plays, he is able to transmit the 'organic' quality of 'truth, life, or reality' through light, sound, bizarre characters, symbolic objects, and authentic dialogue, which locate the brutal events of his plots somewhere between external and inner reality. Except for O'Neill no other modern American playwright has so successfully given shape to this amorphous area, though many have tried, among them Arthur Miller.

Beginning with his novel *Focus* (1945), which deals with anti-Semitism, Miller has consistently written from a position that he calls 'deeply social'. His first successful play, *All My Sons* (1947), obviously owes much to Ibsen, a debt Miller acknowledges at some length in his Introduction to his *Collected Plays* (1957). Another important influence was the Group Theater, which no longer existed when he began *All My Sons* but to which Miller traces his belief in 'prophetic theater':

> Perhaps it signifies a theater, a play, which is meant to become part of the lives of its audience – a play seriously meant for people of common sense, and relevant to both their domestic lives and their daily work, but an experience which widens their awareness of connection . . .

Moving from the linear realism of *All My Sons* to an expressionist mode in *Death of a Salesman* (1949), Miller creates 'the process of Willy Loman's way of mind' enacting his past assumptions and values in the present. Through entirely or partly transparent settings, the music of a flute, Willy's imaginary conversations with the Woman with whom he had an affair in Boston and with his dead brother Ben, Miller conveys the breakdown of the psychic defenses that have formed the symbolic salesman's version of the American dream of success. Willy is a more likable and more realistic example of this peculiarly American breed than is O'Neill's Hickey, yet it is Hickey who reveals the tragic personal and social implications of his role as seller of dreams. Willy remains rooted in his time and place, a moving domestic figure who is never quite at home in the expressionistic structure meant to enlarge him. Miller's desire to create modern tragic drama, a common aim in America and Europe of the forties and fifties, is not realized either in *The Crucible* (1953) or *A View from the Bridge* (1955, revised 1956), which do convey his talent for social realism. Although these plays suggest historical correspondences between past and present, their action depends too heavily on the limitations of a single character intended as representative but too naturalistically drawn to assume that stature.

Among the younger playwrights of the fifties and sixties Edward Albee (1928–) seemed the most promising. *The Zoo Story* (1959), *The American Dream* (1961), and *Who's Afraid of Virginia Woolf?* (1962) were among the first American plays to incorporate techniques of the Theater of the Absurd, which Albee adapted to an American idiom. In *The American Dream*, Albee does not deal with the degradation of a lost ideal, as do Crane, Fitzgerald, Dos Passos, Nathanael West, and other modern writers; his play is a devastating comment on the very notion that the American dream is anything but a lifeless image of shoddy materialism produced by the banalities of advertising. Like Ionesco, Albee is concerned with the ways in which language fragments and thus controls perceptions of reality. In this play the American family, the principal subject of modern American drama, is reduced to a stereotype of impotence and greed; in *Who's Afraid of Virginia Woolf?*, Albee's best-known drama, it is a desperate connection between a husband and wife who communicate primarily through contempt and cruelty. Here, as in *Tiny Alice* (1964), history is a mockery, motivation an illusion. Albee's nihilism, relieved only by shocking wit and the tension of impending violence, seems to have defeated not only his protagonists but the playwright himself, whose more recent dramas, for example *A Delicate Balance* (1966) and *Seascape* (1975), have not had the impact of his earlier work.

Other New Voices of the 1950s and 1960s

By the late forties and the beginnings of the fifties, the early American Modernists – Pound, Eliot, William Carlos Williams, Stevens, Hemingway, Dos Passos, and Faulkner – had produced their best and most influential work. In *Across the River and into the Trees* (1950) and *The Old Man and the Sea* (1952) Hemingway seemed to be imitating his earlier fiction. Faulkner's late Yoknapatawpha novels continue but do not enlarge his Southern fable. In the novel entitled *A Fable* (1954) his effort to extend his tragic view of human limitation and endurance through Christian symbolism is counteracted by rhetorical flourishes that at times seem to mock his vision. As Dos Passos moved to the political right, his fiction became increasingly polemical. After *Four Quartets* (1943) Eliot published chiefly criticism and drama. In the Cantos Pound wrote in St Elizabeth's Hospital, to which he was committed from 1945 to 1958, and those he continued to write after his release, he relied chiefly on techniques he had devised earlier, collage, abrupt shifts in tone and allusion, and references to classical, Oriental, and medieval models for his conception of an authoritarian 'paradiso terrestre'. Only for Williams and Stevens was this the period of the fullest development of their genius.

In the decade after the Second World War the influence of all these writers appeared in varieties of experimental naturalism and realism in fiction and eclectic neoclassicism in poetry, even as new voices contested their authority. Saul Bellow has said that in his early books he 'was afraid to let [himself] go ... In writing *The Victim* I accepted a Flaubertian standard.' *The Adventures of Augie March* (1953) is the first of his novels in which he was 'emancipated' from 'a borrowed sensibility'. Bellow's ambivalent connection with models prized by the Modernists, which is apparent in his earliest novels, *Dangling Man* (1944) and *The Victim* (1947), and which emerges with more authority in *Augie March*, has been fundamental to the development of one of the most original voices in modern fiction. The protagonists of Bellow's novels suffer from the characteristic modern alienation from society and from their own sense of self but, Jew or Gentile – Tommy Wilhelm or E. H. Henderson or Moses Herzog – they seize the day. Like Wilhelm, the poorest imaginable businessman, they know that within their own being 'the business of life, the real business – to carry [one's] peculiar burden, to feel shame and impotence, to taste these quelled tears – the only important business, the highest business' is 'being done'.

These characters counter their estrangement from wives, parents, lovers, the sights, sounds, and values of modern urban society, with an emotional and cultural history of their own, which draws as much on European literary and philosophical traditions as it does on Bellow's Jewish background. He is the least self-conscious, the most cosmopolitan, of American Jewish writers. If even Henderson, the millionaire rain king, is a Jew in Protestant disguise, as has been suggested, 'the disturbance in [his] heart', the recurrent voice saying '*I want, I want, I want,*' is by no means exclusively Jewish; it is the voice of modern man, desiring sustenance beyond the satisfaction of his appetites and fantasies. Returning from his symbolic voyage into his primal self in Africa, Henderson recalls that he either wrote in a letter to his wife or merely thought: 'I had a voice that said, I want! *I* want? I? It should have told me *she* wants, *they* want. And moreover, it's love that makes reality reality. The opposite makes the opposite.' Henderson is one of Bellow's many characters 'burdened', as Alfred Kazin says, 'by a speculative quest, a need to understand their particular destiny within the general problem of human destiny'. The conflict between this need for private contemplation and assessment of reality and its actual demands, most clearly defined in *Herzog* (1964), is resolved in Bellow's *The Dean's December* (1982), for the love that Henderson imagined has become the later novel's action.

No two modern novelists more clearly differ from each other than Bellow, the persistent creator of the contemplative hero, whose anger and pain are turned chiefly on himself, and Norman Mailer (1923–), consistent in only one respect: his lifelong preoccupation with sexuality and violence outwardly directed. Mailer's *The Naked and the Dead* (1948), the most acclaimed American novel of the Second World War, portrays a battle for a Pacific island as symbolic of the violence endemic to individual and social history, a technique that contrasts with the descriptive portraits and flashbacks of its conventional structure. Obviously influenced by the naturalism of Hemingway and Dos Passos, Mailer conceives of war as the ultimate weapon of a mechanistic society against which individual resistance is fruitless. Throughout the years of the Cold War and the social and political upheavals of the sixties, Mailer, in fiction and non-fiction, and in his fusions of the two, became known as the creator of that most characteristic product of American advertising, the image, in his case the image of the writer whose life enacts the contemporary political, cultural, sexual, and literary scene. The very title of *Advertisements for Myself* (1959) announces that the self has become an image.

Mailer's greatest strength lies in his use of this image as an instrument to combat what he regards as organized power and corruption. *The Armies of the Night* (1968), for all its narcissism, reveals the intensity of personal involvement in the anti-Vietnam war protest movement. He is also aware of its weaknesses: the 'comedy of the New Left, its Achilles' heel, black as tar', the division between middle-class whites and the new movement for black power. The image projected through his fiction, however, and most clearly revealed in *An American Dream* (1965), has assimilated the worst excesses of infantilism and cruelty increasingly exploited by the popular media. Even in *Why Are We in Vietnam?* (1967), a far better novel, we hear Mailer's voice through the disc jockey's, indulging in his familiar associations of the waste and agony of war with impersonal sex and gratuitous violence.

The American novel that had the greatest impact on the generation of the sixties was Joseph Heller's *Catch-22* (1961), which projects

343

events of the Second World War into the political and economic atmosphere of the years of disillusionment that followed: the Cold War and the military and industrial expansion of the fifties. As critics have pointed out, Heller (1923–) borrowed from sources as diverse as Kafka, Dostoevsky, Céline, Nathanael West, the Marx Brothers, and S. J. Perelman in his creation of grotesque and wildly comic characters and episodes, but no model can account for Heller's invention of a new concept of conscientious objection, which contrasts strongly with Mailer's strident identification with the very strategies he opposes. What Robert Brustein calls Heller's 'new morality of refusal' questions the validity of all institutions and the deepest assumptions of Western society: normality, logic, the relation of language to reality. Yossarian, Heller's hero, madly reverses all accepted standards of conduct in order to preserve the ultimate source of reality, the self. The comic imagination of this mad Assyrian is the only defense against dehumanized bureaucracy and the 'clinging, overpowering conviction of death' that is its product.

The work of Heller, Kurt Vonnegut, Thomas Pynchon, John Gardner, James Baldwin, Philip Roth, Robert Coover, William Burroughs, and Jack Kerouac exemplifies the shift to the experimental novel of protest of the late fifties and early sixties. Although they all emerge from a period of social upheaval in America, these writers do not constitute a homogeneous group. In fact, the variety of their motivations for and style of protest reflects the spontaneity of the period.

James Baldwin (1924–87) began by distancing himself from earlier black protest literature, especially Native Son (1940), by Richard Wright (1908–60), in which, Baldwin believed, the black was portrayed as white society's stereotype of primitive hate and rage. Baldwin's oversimplified assessment of this great novel was an early expression of his own ambivalence toward the role of the black writer as separate from the mainstream of American literature. Yet, in The Fire Next Time (1963) and later essays, Baldwin's eloquent indictments of the injustice inflicted on American blacks express an anger and a bitterness that question the possibility of integration. Although he has been criticized for concentrating on his own deprivations rather than on the political, social, and economic oppression of black people, Baldwin's essays and his best novel, Go

Tell It on the Mountain (1953), transcend personal revelation in their depiction of the complex ways in which the particular traumas of growing up black in America are basic to self-definition. It is by no means a new theme in black literature. In *Native Son* Bigger Thomas attempts to forge an identity out of the rage and hatred with which he counters the stereotype of himself as 'black, unequal, and despised' that he has internalized. Near the end of his life, glimpsing the possibility of emerging from the isolation of hatred through union with other people, he is so frightened by this new vision that he asks: 'Was not his old hate a better defense than this agonized uncertainty?' It is a question that Baldwin, Ralph Ellison, and other black novelists continued to raise.

As social protest the Beat movement seems trivial compared with the movements for civil rights, integration, and black nationalism. Yet, as an expression of individual opposition to social conformity, it drew on a long American tradition from Thoreau and Whitman to Paul Bowles and Henry Miller. The leading figures of this movement, William Burroughs (1914–), Jack Kerouac (1922–69), and Allen Ginsberg (1926–), appalled by the growing regimentation of American political and cultural life in the late forties and early fifties and the paranoiac suppression of dissent, viewed themselves as outsiders who found avenues of personal and aesthetic realization in exile, drugs, and sexual non-conformity.

Burroughs's best-known novel, *Naked Lunch* (Paris, 1959; New York, 1962), was written chiefly in Tangier, where he was befriended by Paul Bowles, an earlier exile. There are similarities in Bowles's and Burroughs's use of bizarre sexual adventures, cruelty, and pain to convey heightened states of consciousness in fiction, but a more profound influence on Burroughs, Kerouac, and Ginsberg, as well as on Mailer, Philip Roth, and other writers of the fifties and sixties, was Henry Miller (1891–1980). Although much of Miller's work was banned in the United States until 1961 because of his graphic depictions of sexual encounters, French editions of his novels circulated in the years immediately following the Second World War. To a generation coming to maturity in the fifties, Miller's bohemianism and his plotless narratives of sexual adventurism, which he promulgated as a means to freedom and self-fulfillment, were a welcome antidote to the general aesthetic and social conformity of the period. In *Tropic of Cancer* (Paris, 1934; United States, 1961), *Tropic of Capricorn* (Paris, 1939; United States, 1962), and other works of Miller, the writer's sensuous response to reality is a form of social criticism and political rebellion. Miller was to be justly attacked by feminist critics of the 1970s for his depiction of women as mere sexual objects, but his celebration of depersonalized sexuality, with its shallow feelings beneath the surface excitement, should also be regarded as an assault on the self of men as well. His seemingly exalted conception of the self as a sexual and literary manifestation prepares the way for Burroughs's and Kerouac's experiments in transcending the limits of autonomy, their goal being the dissolution of the self through sadomasochism, drug addiction to the point of courting death, and the act of writing.

The language and subjects of Beat poetry were as shocking to the literary sensibility of the fifties as were those of its fiction. The appearance of Allen Ginsberg's *Howl and Other Poems* in 1956, the year before Kerouac's *On the Road*, seemed a revolt against prevailing standards, particularly those of the New Criticism, which still dominated leading literary journals, such as the *Partisan*, *Kenyon*, and *Sewanee* reviews. In the very first line of 'Howl', 'I saw the best minds of my generation destroyed by madness, starving hysterical naked. . .', Ginsberg challenges the genteel persona of the poetry of the early fifties and opts for a Whitmanesque public role. One hears also his affinity with William Carlos Williams in the communication of ideas through the painful 'things' of daily existence and with Burroughs and Kerouac in the representation of madness, produced by despair or drugs or both, as simultaneously a product of and revolt against the heartlessness of contemporary American society. By the early sixties, Ginsberg turned from drugs to yoga meditation as a way of achieving oneness with the processes of life, which include death. Although the means are different, the aim is the same: the creation of a poetry that reflects a heightened personal and social consciousness.

Among the Beat poets associated with Ginsberg – Gary Snyder, Gregory Corso, Lawrence Ferlinghetti, Philip Whalen, and others – Snyder (1930–) remains the most interesting. In his *Myths and Texts* (1960), *The Back Country* (1968), as well as in his later poetry, Snyder combines a serious understanding of Buddhist philosophy with Amerindian myth. His work reveals the influence of Kenneth Rexroth, Pound, and William Carlos Williams, but he is highly original in his engagement with human and external nature as both archaic and modern, particular and universal.

During a visit to San Francisco in 1957 Robert Lowell (1917–77) became aware that the style of the few poems he had written were 'distant, symbol-ridden and willfully difficult'. He had already been moving away from the influence of Hopkins, Eliot, and Tate to the new confessional mode that would result in *Life Studies* (1959). Writing prose, and particularly his autobiography, he had come to believe that 'the best style for poetry was . . . something like the prose of Chekhov or Flaubert'. Additional and perhaps more important new models were the poetry of Elizabeth Bishop and William Carlos Williams.

Lowell's use of direct and colloquial language in *Life Studies*, his 'tricks with meter and the avoidance of meter', his new freedom with rhyme and his adaptations of the rhythms of speech were techniques he developed for self-discovery in poetry. The poems of *Life Studies* evoke the past of his parents' youth 'when the unemancipated woman/still had her Freudian papá and maids!' ('During Fever') exerting its emotional demands on the son. As the relationship between past and present unfolds, American history and case history mingle in bits of dialogue or brief incidents to disclose personal frustration, suffering, and madness. In his later work, Lowell sometimes returned to the strict meters and mythical images he abandoned in *Life Studies*. He was to write in a variety of styles from sonnets to free verse, but his work as a whole is consistent in at least one respect; as he said, 'the thread that strings it together is my autobiography'.

From the 1950s through the 1970s, many American poets – Hayden Carruth, John Berryman, Theodore Roethke, Sylvia Plath, Anne Sexton, as well as Ginsberg and Lowell – expressed the most extreme condition of modern alienation in autobiographical accounts of the dissolution of the self in madness. This recent preoccupation with madness differs in fundamental respects from that of the surrealists, who believed that the products of psychic automatism, however mad, served to unite the poet with others in a revolutionary consciousness at once social and aesthetic. Although the approaches to madness of modern American poets vary greatly, from the controlled wit of Lowell, recording his observations in the asylum in 'Waking in the Blue' to the hallucinatory images of Plath, from Ginsberg's identification of his symptoms with those he attributes to America ('America') to Roethke's exclusion of any but personal concerns as he merges with external nature, all of them convey extreme isolation in society and a simultaneous fear of and fascination with their own psychic dissolution, the 'abyss' of the self.

In an interview Sylvia Plath (1932–63) told of her excitement over Robert Lowell's *Life Studies*, especially his poems about his experience in a mental hospital. She was drawn to such 'peculiar private and taboo subjects . . . explored in recent American poetry', especially the poems of Anne Sexton (1928–74), 'who writes also about her experiences as a mother; as a mother who's had a nervous breakdown, as an extremely emotional and feeling young woman'. The central preoccupation of both Plath and Sexton in their poetry was suicide as a mythical construct of transcendent power. For both death was ultimately mother, father, lover, beloved friend, and threatening enemy, all of whom merged in a self-created god within their beings. As Sexton puts it:

> But suicides have a special language.
> Like carpenters they want to know *which* tools.
> They never ask *why* build.
>
> Twice I have so simply declared myself,
> have possessed the enemy, eaten the enemy,
> have taken on his craft, his magic.
> ('Wanting to Die', *Live or Die*)

Like Sexton, Plath describes herself as rising from the dead to 'eat men like air', a 'Lady Lazarus' who incorporates the enemy and thus possesses his power. No other poet, not even Sexton, so thoroughly perfected the 'special language' of irresolvable conflict enacted in suicide. In poems written in the last months of her life, realistic details of illness, parts of faces and bodies, odors and sounds emerge as dream and hallucinatory images, 'the voice of nothing', seeking identity in language.

Plath's impression that a 'taboo' had been lifted in contemporary American treatments of madness was valid. What was new in this period was the revelation of autobiographical facts and intimate details of sexual and domestic life, as well as a post-Freudian sophistication regarding mental illness. Explicit treatments of madness in literature were but one of many manifestations of the general breakdown of taboos, the new personal and sexual freedom demanded as part of their political rebellion by the generation that came to maturity in the sixties. Poets who protested against the Vietnam war, such as Ginsberg, Lowell, and Denise Levertov, or were involved in the feminist movement, such as Adrienne Rich, wrote highly personal poetry. In addition, the sense that the individual no longer had a stable role in society, that the very existence of the autonomous self was in doubt, was expressed in revelations of private experience, however atypical or bizarre. In 1974 Allen Ginsberg, looking back on his vision of expanded consciousness as an instrument of social amelioration, views himself as

> Solitary in worlds full of insects & singing birds all solitary
> – who had no subject but himself in many disguises . . .
>
> ('Ego Confession')

Contemporaries

Many contemporary writers have continued to develop the modes they devised in the sixties. Adrienne Rich's (1929–) recent poetry, for example, increasingly reflects her involvement in radical feminism and her assertion of her identity as a lesbian. Her efforts to achieve political and personal integration in her art have produced a style that blends oblique, partly conscious associations with explicit statements of her position. Rich has written of her admiration for the poetry of Eleanor Ross Taylor (1920–), whose first book, *Wilderness of Ladies* (1960), contained two poems that Rich 'carried about with [her] for a decade as a kind of secret knowledge: "Woman as Artist" and "Sister".' Rich refers to this affinity in a review of Taylor's *Welcome Eumenides* (1972), in which she discusses Taylor's revelations of 'the underground life of women, the Southern white Protestant woman in particular, the woman-writer, the woman in the family . . .'. Taylor is indeed an extremely gifted and subtle poet whose work has not been sufficiently appreciated. In the title poem of *Welcome Eumenides* the speaker, Florence Nightingale, juxtaposes the life of nineteenth-century upper-class British women with the 'wards at Scutari' where she tends the men wounded in the Crimean War. The intricate connections between Florence Nightingale's memories and dreams and her responses to the suffering of the wounded create a brilliant portrait of a woman countering the violence of history with fortitude and compassion.

Poets and novelists such as Nikki Giovanni, Toni Morrison, Toni Cade Bambara, Lucille Clifton, and Alice Walker view women's issues as related to the special concerns of blacks. Although in 'Nikki-Rosa' (1968), Giovanni (1943–) expresses the hope that 'no white person ever has cause to write about me/because they never understand Black love is Black wealth . . .', she and other contemporary black women writers reach beyond black experience in portraying the effects of discrimination and poverty. Morrison (1931–), for example, depicting the black woman's struggle for identity and personal freedom in *Sula* (1973), discloses psychological resources on which both black and white women have drawn in maintaining an 'underground life'.

The best-known black male writers – Robert Hayden, Imamu Amiri Baraka (LeRoi Jones), Ishmael Reed, Charles Wright, and Michael Harper – incorporate their heritage in their work in various ways. Whereas Baraka, the most militant, has separated himself from mainstream American society and its literary traditions, Hayden and Wright have adapted Modernist techniques in their poems on both black and more general subjects. Hayden's (1913–80) portraits, for example, of a fraudulent preacher mesmerizing his congregation ('Witch Doctor', 1962) or of the poet's father expressing love in the only ways he allows himself, by rising early to warm the home and polish his son's shoes ('Those Winter Sundays', 1962), create scenes of American life that transcend a particular environment.

Black writers have generally connected self-definition with the identity of their people as a whole. When, at the end of *The Color Purple* (1982), Alice Walker (1944–) thanks 'everyone in this book for coming' and identifies herself as 'A. W., author and medium', she suggests that she is a spokesman as well as an individual voice. A more common tendency in contemporary fiction, however, is a turning inward, characters or narrators concentrating on the self as grandiose or abnegated, as sexual performer or writer or both. One of the most amusing, and to some critics irritating, portrayals of this self-absorption is Philip Roth's (1933–   ) Nathan Zuckerman who, having written the notorious novel *Carnovsky* (obviously *Portnoy's Complaint*, 1969), devotes years to its defense. In the three novels that, with an Epilogue, comprise the trilogy *Zuckerman Bound* (1985), Zuckerman is obsessed with his identity as a Jew and a male, and it is his revelations in his fiction of his ambivalence toward the one and his assertion of the other that are his deepest concern. This trilogy, a counterattack on moralistic criticisms of Zuckerman's (and Roth's) revolt against traditional Jewish moral values, is essentially a caricature of the Jewish–American writer's efforts to define his role in contemporary America.

Roth's conception of the writer in *Zuckerman Unbound, My Life As a Man* (1974), and elsewhere is a bizarre version of a conventional theme: the struggle of the artist to assert his individuality even as he remains bound to the very influences he contests – family, tradition, and society. 'Post-modern' novelists, whose major subject is the act of writing, would question the validity of such a struggle, since the reality it supposedly mirrors is itself a fiction. From the sixties to the present, John Barth, Robert Coover, Ronald Sukenick, Donald Barthelme, Gilbert Sorrentino, and Raymond Federman have responded to what Barth called 'the felt ultimacies of our own time', the view that traditional subjects and forms of fiction were exhausted, by rejecting the linear structure and realistic characters of conventional fiction and its use of language to reify experience. Mingling the techniques of popular and high art, adapting the language of technology and the slogans of advertising, these novelists produce 'images of images'.[9] Yet their acceptance of the contingency of factual reality results in a fiction that more often reflects than repudiates the dominant cultural atmosphere of contemporary American society.

This abandonment of the long struggle to discover the 'supreme fiction' that both incorporates and creates reality through the medium of language constitutes a major break with the modernist tradition. But this is only one tendency in recent fiction and poetry. Many novelists and poets experiment with forms that respond to the continuous challenge of Stevens's view of the 'possible':

It must be that in time
The real will from its crude compoundings come,

Seeming, at first, a beast disgorged, unlike,
Warmed by a desperate milk. To find the real,
To be stripped of every fiction except one,

The fiction of an absolute – Angel,
Be silent in your luminous cloud and hear
The luminous melody of proper sound.

('Notes Toward a Supreme Fiction', VII)

In *Gravity's Rainbow* (1973) Thomas Pynchon's (1937–)
metamorphic effects, the merging of various eras, and the clashes
between dehumanized technology and human desire demand that
the reader discover for himself a vestige of reality as a defense against
anarchy. Walter Abish's (1931–) *How German Is It* (1980) insists
on the power of history as memory. Repressed, denied, it is never
entirely obliterated. Emerging as corpses of concentration camp
victims buried beneath a recently constructed modern city, memory
imposes the past on the city built to revise it. Abish's style, like his
title, merges question with statement. His spare sentences convey
processes of the mind suppressing but finally unable to avoid
fragments of memory, perceptions, feelings, and facts – the materials
with which it creates reality.

Among contemporary poets, John Ashbery (1927–) most
strikingly, in Marjorie Perloff's words, 'turns the Stevens mode on
its head by cutting off the referential dimension'. He adapts techniques of surrealist and abstract expressionist painting to suggest the
impossibility of apprehending a fragmented reality. In his poetry the
self is amorphous, existence is meaningless. His chief subject is the
activity of the individual consciousness creating forms for its seemingly haphazard associations. In contrast, Galway Kinnell (1927–)
embraces external reality, investing himself in political and social
conflict in his work as in his life. Kinnell, as intense as Ashbery is
tentative, celebrates the wonder of birth and the depth of his
attachment to the physical world, and faces the actuality of death.
Ashbery and Kinnell, in their opposing views of the poet's ability 'to
find the real', exemplify, as do the other contemporary poets and
novelists mentioned in this chapter, the variety of current responses
to a continuous cultural issue.

NOTES

1. *Children of the Mire: Modern Poetry from Romanticism to the Avant-Garde* (Cambridge, Mass., 1974), pp. vi and 32.

2. *Modernism 1890–1930*, ed. Malcolm Bradbury and James McFarlane (Harmondsworth, 1976), p. 176.

3. Quotations are from 'Affirmations, As for Imagisme', *The New Age* (28 January 1915), reprinted in *Ezra Pound: Selected Prose 1909–1965*, ed. William Cookson (New York, 1972), pp. 374–7; and from 'Vorticism' (1914), reprinted in *Gaudier-Brzeska: A Memoir* (New York, 1970), pp. 81–94.

4. 'Pagan and Magic Elements in Ezra Pound's Works', *New Approaches to Ezra Pound*, ed. Eva Hesse (Berkeley, 1969), p. 174.

5. Recent scholars have demonstrated how deeply Pound and other modern poets were indebted to the Romantics and the Victorians. See, for example, Carlos Baker, *The Echoing Green: Romanticism, Modernism, and the Phenomena of Transference in Poetry* (Princeton, 1984), and Carol T. Christ, *Victorian and Modern Poetics* (Chicago, 1985).

6. *Axel's Castle: A Study in the Imaginative Literature of 1870–1930* (New York, 1931), pp. 116–17.

7. See, for example, Michael Benamou, 'Jules Laforgue and Wallace Stevens', *The Romantic Review* L, 2 (April 1959), and Robert Buttel, *Wallace Stevens: The Making of Harmonium* (Princeton, 1967), Chapter VII.

8. 'Wallace Stevens: The False and True Sublime' (1971); reprinted in *Part of Nature, Part of Us: Modern American Poets* (Cambridge, Mass., 1980), pp. 1–11.

9. The phrase is from David Antin's analysis of paintings by Andy Warhol quoted in Leo Steinberg, *Other Criteria: Confrontations with Twentieth-Century Art* (New York, 1972), p. 91. Several of Steinberg's comments on 'post-Modernist painting' are applicable to post-modern literature.

THE DESIGNS OF ROBERT FROST

WILLIAM H. PRITCHARD

> You are not going to make the mistake that Pound makes of assuming that
> my simplicity is that of the untutored child. I am not undesigning.
>
> (Frost to Thomas B. Mosher, 17 July 1913)

Both in his letters and his poetry, the assertions of Robert Frost
(1874–1963) have a way of performing what it is they promise, and
the above one, written home from England to a Maine publisher
and collector, is typical. In it the writer proves that his supposed
'simplicity' – Frost's first book of poems, *A Boy's Will*, was being
praised at the time by Pound and others for just that quality – is
really not so simple. Yet he proves it not by insisting that, in fact, he
is full of design (one of his best poems is titled 'Design') but rather
that he is 'not undesigning'. The subtle difference between a positive
assertion and one made with a double negative is what Frost's poetry,
and indeed his writing generally, demands that a good reader hear.
One of his most important formulations, made in a letter from
about the same period to his American friend and ex-student John
Bartlett, puts a case for the centrality of listening to poetry:

> It is so and not otherwise that we get the variety that makes it fun to write
> and read. *The ear does it.* The ear is the only true writer and the only true
> reader. I have known people who could read without hearing the sentence
> sounds and they were the fastest readers. Eye readers we call them. They can
> get the meaning by glances. But they are bad readers because they miss the
> best part of what a good writer puts into his work.
>
> (22 February 1914)

He does not just say, dutifully, that in the activity of reading poetry
both eye and ear are important; rather that 'The ear is the *only* [my
italics] true writer and . . . reader'. There is a priority here that is crucial
to Frost's artistic career, as well as to his life outside the poems.

It is also the belief on which he staked his identity as a poet who would speak to a wider audience than could ever be spoken to by his contemporaries – Pound or Eliot or Stevens. Frost had no desire to be what he termed 'caviare to the crowd', saying in another letter home that 'there is a kind of success called "of esteem" and it butters no parsnips'. From the very beginning of his publishing career in England in 1913–14 he was determined, he said, to 'reach out' to 'the general reader who buys books in their thousands'. By way of accomplishing this, he proceeded not by setting himself up as a purveyor of this or that idea about life (although the rural nature of his material proved attractive to readers) but by writing as if there were people out there ready to hear what he had to say. Or they could be 'made' to hear it by their being entertained and delighted with exactly rendered tones of speech, with something they had heard somewhere before – with what he called, most tellingly, the 'sound of sense'.

He defined this sound of sense, the 'living part of a poem' (as he put it in January 1914) as 'intonation entangled somehow in the syntax idiom and meaning of a sentence', and as 'only there for those who have heard it previously in conversation'. By so defining things he placed himself in corrective opposition to the brilliant practices of poets like Tennyson and Swinburne whose great successes, Frost insisted, were a matter of harmonized consonants and vowels, of 'effects in assonation':

> But they were on the wrong track or at any rate on a short track. They went the length of it. Any one else who goes that way must go after them. And that's where most of them are going. I alone of English writers have consciously set myself to make music out of what I may call the sound of sense.
>
> (4 July 1913)

No matter that at the time Frost wrote these sentences, contemporaries of his such as Hardy and Yeats were doing something very much like making 'music' out of the 'sound of sense' (Hardy's *Satires of Circumstance* and Yeats's *Responsibilities* were both published in 1914). Frost needed to imagine himself as engaged in a heroic enterprise and as doing it on his own, even doing it in another country than his own.

He had come to England with his wife Elinor and their four children after some years on a farm in Derry, New Hampshire.

There, while raising chickens without notable success or undue energy, he became interested in the talk of his neighbors, turning round in his head the voices that would fill many of his poems. Most of his first three published books of poetry were written in some form or other during this time at the Derry farm, and in retrospect Frost saw the often lonely, isolated life he lived there as a preparation for a wider, public, and above all a poetic life:

> I kept farm, so to speak, for nearly ten years, but less as a farmer than as a fugitive from the world that seemed to me to 'disallow' me. It was all instinctive, but I can see now that I went away to save myself and fix myself before I measured my strength against all creation.
>
> (22 March 1915)

Such measuring began modestly, as he moved back toward the world by accepting jobs as English teacher in private academies in New England, but more grandly when in 1911 he sold the farm and moved to England for purposes of nothing less than seeking his poetic fortune. Although he knew no one in the mother country, through his own enterprise and good luck, and through the interested efforts of contemporaries he met there like F. S. Flint and Ezra Pound, he had – by the time the war forced him to return to America in the winter of 1915 – published two volumes (*A Boy's Will*, 1913, and *North of Boston*, 1914) with a third one (*Mountain Interval*, 1916) virtually ready for the press. He had also made a number of interesting and useful alliances, with the Georgian poets and especially with Edward Thomas (whose vocation as a poet Frost first encouraged), and he had accomplished the strong beginnings of a reputation that was only to grow in the years to come.

Thomas proved to be the most perceptive critic of Frost's early work. Reviewers of *A Boy's Will*, while well-disposed toward the American poet ('He is without sham and without affectation,' said Pound) were content to praise the poems for their simplicity. Yet the term is inadequate to characterize the artful complication of Frost's style in his first book. Consider the octet from a sonnet, 'The Vantage Point':

> If tired of trees I seek again mankind,
>   Well I know where to hie me – in the dawn,
>   To a slope where the cattle keep the lawn.
> There amid lolling juniper reclined,

> Myself unseen, I see in white defined
>   Far off the homes of men, and farther still,
>   The graves of men on an opposing hill,
> Living or dead, whichever are to mind.

The rhyme pattern is 'not undesigning', nor is the sound of sense in the accent that must be given to 'Well' (it is of course an adverb, not an interjection), nor is the suspended, quite elaborate syntax of the eight-line sentence with its aptly pointed dash in line two or its ease of commas in lines five and eight. This is a poem which toys with the idea that the 'I' can do anything, turn whichever way he pleases, contemplate what or whomever he chooses to contemplate, as the spirit moves him. Its tone is mild and unboastful, as if this were merely the way things are, and as if we were being vouchsafed no more than the facts:

> And if by noon I have too much of these,
>   I have but to turn on my arm, and lo,
>   The sunburned hillside sets my face aglow,
> My breathing shakes the bluet like a breeze,
>   I smell the earth, I smell the bruisèd plant,
>   I look into the crater of the ant.

The sestet is a different kind of sentence, to be delivered in one breath, as the series of declarative assertions with strong, simple, sometimes repeated verbs ('sets', 'shakes', 'smell', 'look') render the up-close inspection of natural things provided by this new vantage point. 'Never if you can do it,' Frost wrote to Bartlett, 'write a sentence which does not posture specially.' The difference between the first and second parts of 'The Vantage Point' is registered by the reader as something heard, by the way the rhythm of the sentence plays itself off against the metrical grid: 'The possibilities for tune from the dramatic tones of meaning struck across the rigidity of a limited meter are endless,' Frost was to write in 'The Figure a Poem Makes' (1938).

Looked at historically, particularly with reference to nineteenth-century American poetry, Frost's practice was a refreshing and a revolutionary subverting of what passed for the Grand Style in all too many post-Civil War writers. As may be noted by browsing through Bliss Carman's *Oxford Book of American Verse* (1928), the strutting dignity with which those poems set forth their noble sentiments is matched only by their rhythmic inertness ('I do not know beneath what sky / Nor on what seas shall be thy fate; / I only know it shall be high, / I only know it shall be great' – Richard Hovey). It was Frost's distinction to banish such inertness by writing lines like the following (from another early poem, 'Storm Fear') where a man voices his uncertainties in the face of a winter storm:

> I count our strength,
> Two and a child,
> Those of us not asleep subdued to mark
> How the cold creeps as the fire dies at length –
> How drifts are piled,
> Dooryard and road ungraded,
> Till even the comforting barn grows far away,
> And my heart owns a doubt
> Whether 'tis in us to arise with day
> And save ourselves unaided.

One partly understands why the poem from which these concluding lines are taken was thought of as 'simple'. There are only three words of more than two syllables. The named circumstances, the feeling of helplessness and fear, are easily available ones, as familiar – even as comforting – as the barn used to be until the snow made it seem far away.

But almost immediately we notice how the disposition of words and line lengths and rhymes is anything but simple. The poem's overall pace is attractive partly through the variations in line-lengths: 'Two and a child' *looks* like feeble protection when compared with 'How the cold creeps as the fire dies at length', which takes as long to say as it did to feel the creeping cold and dying fire. At the same time the rhymes make for continuity and suppleness of movement by never quite coming when you expect them, by having the last word of 'Those of us not asleep subdued to mark' rhyme with the ends of lines much earlier in the poem; by having the key word 'doubt' in the third from final line go back to an early line ('Come out! Come out!'); by deferring over the course of five lines the unobvious rhyming pair of 'ungraded' and 'unaided'. And 'simplicity' is hardly the name for the effect gained by using the surprising word 'subdued', placed as it is quite daringly after 'asleep', by way of subtly naming a state of acute yet feeble awareness. Nor are we simply dealing with a bad snowstorm; it is not just that the people may need to be plowed out, but that this situation inspires a tremor of metaphysical worry, no more nor less than that, as real and perhaps as transient as the storm itself, or the poem. Such a movement from the level of sense to that of spirit is unpretentious and unobtrusive, but from the very beginning it lay at the heart of Frost's enterprise as a poet, and there was nothing simple about it.

A Boy's Will also contained a number of poems in which Frost revealed his affiliations with, rather than his divergences from, the Tennysonian–Swinburnian 'track', poems in which 'effects of assonation' are both noticeable and artful. But the more original work – the poems just mentioned, plus 'October', 'The Tuft of Flowers', and 'Mowing' – was first payment on his witty boast to Bartlett (4 July 1913) that 'To be perfectly frank with you I am one of the most notable craftsmen of my time. That will transpire presently.' He was also shrewd enough to have ready a second book whose style and subject was quite distinct from that of A Boy's Will. North of Boston, originally billed in his publisher David Nutt's catalogue as 'Farm Servants and Other People', capitalized on Frost's perception that he was thought of as somebody who did the 'farm' thing in poetry. This 'book of people', as his dedication to his wife called it, consisted of some fifteen longer poems, and although an 'I' occasionally appears (notably in 'Mending Wall', 'After Apple-Picking' and 'The Wood-Pile') the focus is not mainly on the subjective presence that pervaded A Boy's Will. Nor is there heard the bittersweet lyric voice from that first volume, with its appealing combination of wistfulness, regret, quiet irony, and gentle protest. In its place we hear voices in conflict with and correction of one another, 'characters' who are not to be identified with someone named Robert Frost. So the most dramatic of the poems in North of Boston begins this way:

> He saw her from the bottom of the stairs
> Before she saw him. She was starting down,
> Looking back over her shoulder at some fear.
> She took a doubtful step and then undid it
> To raise herself and look again. He spoke
> Advancing toward her: 'What is it you see
> From up there always – for I want to know.'

> She turned and sank upon her skirts at that,
> And her face changed from terrified to dull.
> He said to gain time: 'What is it you see?'
> Mounting until she cowered under him.
> 'I will find out now — you must tell me, dear.'

As 'Home Burial' develops and the woman begins to talk back to her husband, the narrator pretty much disappears, forbears the making of characterizing, explanatory comment about the accusations and resentments his protagonists express to each other. And the poem's excitement comes wholly from their play of voices.

Frost claimed that for a time, in his years of 'isolation' on the Derry farm, he preferred 'stocks and stones to people', but that before long he was listening to the way they talked:

> I like the actuality of gossip, the intimacy of it. Say what you will effects of actuality and intimacy are the greatest aim an artist can have. The sense of intimacy gives the thrill of sincerity. A story must always release a meaning more readily to those who read than life itself as it ever goes releases meaning.
>
> (22 March 1915)

This 'releasing' was to be effected, however, not by a narrator who at a certain moment stopped the music and laid out the correct understanding of what was happening, but through nothing more than whatever the voices in conflict added up to — and the reader had to do the adding up. Concurrently Frost lowered the diction of these poems 'to a level even Wordsworth stayed above', as he wittily put it. This was a risky decision in so far as, judged by individual lines of poems, the work did not look much like 'poetry', at least as many readers in 1914 expected poetry to look and sound. The effort was toward realism, toward achieving 'the thrill of sincerity' which could come from human speech artfully imagined so as to give the impression that no one was running the show, that these people had just begun to talk and that we were privileged to overhear them.

At the same time, poems such as 'Home Burial', 'The Death of the Hired Man' (which achieved anthology popularity), 'The Black Cottage', 'A Servant to Servants' and others, were no mere exercises in technical craftsmanship detached from moral and human concerns. In one of his highly perceptive reviews of the volume (he reviewed it no less than three times!) Edward Thomas boldly spoke of *North of Boston* as containing 'masterpieces of deep and mysterious tenderness'. And a contemporary critic, Margery Sabin, has put saliently the larger motive out of which these poems derived their energies and resonance:

Frost in 1914 wanted to believe – and wrote poems out of that belief – that human vitality takes on a suprapersonal existence in the established intonations of speech, intonations which the individual may draw on for personal expression and, perhaps even more important, for the reassuring recognition that his single life is connected to other lives. What Frost calls 'the abstract vitality of our speech' gives reassurance that the life within us is not eccentric or monstrous. It ceases to be monstrous once it participates in the verbal forms through which other people also enact their lives.

('The Fate of the Frost Speaker', *Raritan*, Fall 1982)

One of the loveliest demonstrations of such 'reassurance' comes at the end of 'The Black Cottage' and may serve also to suggest how, even though Frost claimed to be writing in a 'low' style, the poems show moments of heightened awareness and imagination in which characters are led, as if by a power outside them, into an eloquence of utterance that is 'poetic' even by the traditional standard.

In 'The Black Cottage' the narrator and his friend, a minister, stop on their walk to visit an abandoned house where an old woman lived whose husband and sons had died in the Civil War and whom the minister knew as a long-time member of his congregation. In reminiscing, he is led to speculate about the passing of time, the changing and eroding of all things, and in reaction he suddenly begins to imagine through language a 'desert land' of which he would be the monarch, this land dedicated to permanence – 'to the truths we keep coming back and back to':

> 'So desert it would have to be, so walled
> By mountain ranges half in summer snow,
> No one would covet it or think it worth
> The pains of conquering to force change on.
> Scattered oases where men dwelt, but mostly
> Sand dunes held loosely in tamarisk
> Blown over and over themselves in idleness.
> Sand grains should sugar in the natal dew
> The babe born to the desert, the sandstorm
> Retard mid-waste my cowering caravans –

'There are bees in this wall.' He struck the clapboards,
Fierce heads looked out; small bodies pivoted.
We rose to go. Sunset blazed on the windows.

Edward Thomas observed that most of the poems in *North of Boston*
were written in 'the good old English idiom of blank verse', but this
verse, anything but homely, is of great richness and convolution,
marked by a propulsive forward movement and a diction ('Scattered', 'idleness', 'retard') as 'high' as its visionary subject requires.
Yet that there are impulses other than the visionary (the minister is
really indulging his own version of a boy's will) is acknowledged by
the end of the poem, when suddenly the bees make themselves felt
and the syntax shortens into terse declaratives, subject and verb and
object. Ezra Pound remarked in his review of *North of Boston* that
'The Black Cottage' is 'very clearly stated'. Clarity of statement,
however, is not a sufficient term to suggest the dramatic and
compositional force of the poem.

It might be argued – and indeed it has been by more than one
critic of Frost – that *North of Boston* is his most original book of
poems and that he was never to write another one as distinctive.
And it is true that, as a narrative poet, he began to rely more on the
performing resources of a central speaker–entertainer who sounded
much like Frost himself – the Frost, that is, who upon his return to
America early in 1915 became increasingly a public figure, a great
success as a reader of his poetry in colleges and clubs, a humorous
entertainer who could be depended upon to put on a show as
spellbinding as Dickens's or Mark Twain's. It is worth insisting also
on the increasing importance of Frost's role as a teacher, not just or
even mainly in the classroom. Beginning in 1917, when Alexander
Meiklejohn hired him at Amherst College, he maintained to the end
of his life academic affiliations of various sorts with Amherst, the
University of Michigan, Harvard and Dartmouth. But he liked to
refer to himself as a 'symbolic teacher', just as – while he continued
to be a farmer ('I always have a farm in my backyard,' he would
say) – it was a symbolic rather than 'real' farming in which he
engaged. Frost's teaching went on less in the classroom course than
from the public lecture podium and in the countless conversations
(often of a monologue sort) he conducted with undergraduates,

teachers, and ordinary 'lay' readers ('I want to reach out to all sorts and kinds') who were convinced they had some special relationship to this extraordinary person.

As he became more successful, more in demand, more of an entertainer, he risked – and did not always avoid – declining into a predictable act, the distinctness of his poetry lost in what Randall Jarrell called 'the public figure's relishing consciousness of himself'. Yet despite that figure's sometimes blotting out the very private genius of Frost's art, the heartening fact is that, although he never wrote another book like *North of Boston*, he continued to write poems for almost fifty years until his death in 1963, and up through the publication of *Steeple Bush* (in 1947, when he was over seventy) wrote them on a fairly regular basis. Some of his finest efforts may be found in the first fifteen poems of *A Witness Tree*, a volume published in 1942 at the end of a decade in which he endured the death of his favorite daughter, the death of his wife, and the suicide of his son. Earlier, *Mountain Interval* (1916) and *New Hampshire* (1923, which won him the first of his four Pulitzer prizes) not only contained some of the best poems he was ever to write (a short list would include 'An Old Man's Winter Night', 'Birches', 'A Star in a Stone-Boat', '"Out, Out –"', 'To Earthward', 'Two Look at Two', 'Stopping by Woods on a Snowy Evening', and 'The Road Not Taken') but showed a fusion in many of the poems between lyric and narrative impulses. While *A Boy's Will* was predominantly a 'subjective' book of lyrics, and *North of Boston* an 'objective' book of narratives, stories with people in them, it now became more difficult to classify many poems which had elements of both.

For example, 'An Old Man's Winter Night' (from *Mountain Interval*) tells the story of how an aged man 'keeps' his house and farm as the darkness of the night and his attendant old age press in upon him. In the early lines of the poem, Frost's manner is de-signedly 'awkward' so as to present the man's situation in verse no more elegant or eloquent than its subject – a diminished life:

> What kept his eyes from giving back the gaze
> Was the lamp tilted near them in his hand.
> What kept him from remembering what it was
> That brought him to that creaking room was age.

Yet as 'An Old Man's Winter Night' moves to its conclusion, and as the man prepares to retire for the night, its manner mixes lyric, 'poetical' pathos with an ironic, more prose-like understanding and acceptance:

> He consigned to the moon – such as she was,
> So late-arising – to the broken moon,
> As better than the sun in any case
> For such a charge, his snow upon the roof,
> His icicles along the wall to keep;
> And slept. The log that shifted with a jolt
> Once in the stove, disturbed him and he shifted,
> And eased his heavy breathing, but still slept.
> One aged man – one man – can't keep a house,
> A farm, a countryside, or if he can,
> It's thus he does it of a winter night.

This is poetry which invites us to sympathize with, to feel for the pathetic old man alone, close to insensibility, whose gesture to the moon ('broken' itself) is the rueful one so beautifully presented in the word 'consigned'. Yet as the situation invites pity, a studied wryness in the narrative treatment makes pity impossible (the moon is 'in any case' better than the sun, at least as far as looking after icicles and snow goes). With the words 'One aged man – one man – can't keep a house/A farm, a countryside' we seem to be moving out toward some large cosmic statement about human loneliness, of how our circumstances and surroundings always outmatch us, especially as age and isolation come on apace. Yet just before such a statement is attained, and in the middle of the penultimate line, Frost turns back on it: '. . . or if he can,/It's thus he does it of a winter night.' In 'Mowing', the mysterious key assertion is that 'The fact is the sweetest dream that labor knows'. 'An Old Man's Winter Night' is a poem, finally, that respects the fact of a life, of man's existence, rather than how that life can be used to illustrate cosmic or moral meanings. Whether he can or can't 'keep' a farm, a house, or a countryside, is not as important as to respect the fact of what he is, to see what he has done and is still doing: 'It's thus he does it of a winter night.'

The playfulness that permeates Frost's poetry is partly a matter of its dependence on such largely unspecified words as 'thus' or 'keep' or 'does'. 'Something there is that doesn't love a wall', 'Mending Wall' begins, and along with the poem's speaker we are brought up against 'something' in the poem that organizes our attention in a fresh way. At the end of 'Two Look at Two' (from *New Hampshire*) a pair of lovers have been climbing a mountain and, almost at the point of turning back, first see a doe looking at them, then later a buck who eyes them quizzically. These confrontations are presented with delicacy and lightness of touch; but the end of the poem moves into something beyond lightness, as the buck breaks the spell by passing 'unscared' along the wall which separates animal from human:

> Two had seen two, whichever side you spoke from.
> 'This *must* be all.' It was all. Still they stood,
> A great wave from it going over them,
> As if the earth in one unlooked-for favor
> Had made them certain earth returned their love.

Frost's poetry is filled with such 'as if' moments, in which what his essay 'The Figure a Poem Makes' called 'a momentary stay against confusion' is enacted by the poem. The 'great wave' which goes over the couple at the end of 'Two Look at Two' is testimony that human beings can feel about 'the earth', can imagine 'as if' moments in ways the earth itself, for all its solidity, cannot. Frost's generosity and boldness toward our human ways of making significance of life have not been remarked on enough.

If, after *North of Boston*, his narratives are as a rule less dramatic, more relaxed, even garrulous in their pace, and usually spoken by Frost-the-bard (who makes his longest and most wisecracking appearance in the long poem 'New Hampshire'), his lyric poetry up through the 1942 *Witness Tree* reveals riches only hinted at by the poems in *A Boy's Will*. Randall Jarrell's wonderful essay 'To the Laodiceans' is the best introduction to this body of work which calls forth all the lively responsiveness a reader can bring to it. A short list of poems may suggest how variously expressive they are in range of style and tone. In addition to ones previously mentioned, consider 'Spring Pools', 'Acquainted with the Night', 'The Onset', 'Nothing Gold Can Stay', 'The Need of Being Versed in Country Things', 'Neither Out Far Nor In Deep', 'Provide, Provide', 'Design', 'The

Silken Tent', 'I Could Give All to Time', 'The Most of It', and 'Never Again Would Birds' Song Be the Same'. This is to choose only twelve titles from a group which, without much lowering the overall quality of writing, could be expanded to double, even triple the size. In these poems Frost writes as a post-Romantic (or post-post-Romantic) poet, both acknowledging the visionary impulses that found expression in Wordsworth and Shelley (and closer to home in Emerson and Thoreau) while subjecting those impulses to ironic, frequently humorous treatment.

Most often the impulse in the poem is toward some permanence, toward something more than a *momentary* stay against confusion, as is represented, say, by the desert paradise of the minister's imaginings in 'The Black Cottage'. Typically a Frost lyric presents the attractive temptation to stop or to rest in a notion of fixity; or, alternatively, to give in to the flux, 'to go with the drift of things' (as in the early 'Reluctance'). Then, at a crucial point in the lyric, this impulse is countered by a contrary one, a 'backward motion' (in the language of 'West-Running Brook', Frost's most metaphysical poem) in which our human will expresses itself. The gesture of refusal – or of self-preservation – may on occasion be a lofty one, as it is in 'West-Running Brook': 'Not just a swerving, but a throwing back,/As if regret were in it and were sacred.' Or it may be accomplished with the lovely and humorous grace of these final lines from 'Come In', a little poem in which the speaker is powerfully affected by the music of a thrush singing from within a wood. The man hears the thrush's sound as like 'a call to come in/To the dark and lament': yet he politely declines the invitation:

> But no, I was out for stars:
> I would not come in.
> I meant not even if asked,
> And I hadn't been.

The extra bonus of that final line is the sort of payment readers come to expect from a good Frost poem which, like the man himself, is not undesigning.

Like that of his great predecessor Ralph Waldo Emerson, Frost's work has never been sufficiently appreciated in England (though, paradoxically, England gave him his start), perhaps in part by way of a reaction to the rather promiscuous admiration he has inspired from so many sorts of American readers, many of whom have no time for T. S. Eliot or Wallace Stevens. But Frost's poetry is as difficult and as rewarding as that of his distinguished contemporaries. If, for some American readers, the homely nature of his materials – cows and apples and stone walls – predispose them to like the poetry because it is made out of them, they are no more simpleminded than 'cosmopolitan' readers who feel easy with mythical allusions in Eliot but disdain cows and apple trees as a fit vehicle for serious poetry. We would do well to heed Frost's own dictum to an American friend in 1914, when he told Sidney Cox that the true poet's pleasure lay in making 'his own words as he goes' rather than depending upon words whose meanings were fixed:

> We write of things we see and we write in accents we hear. Thus we gather both our material and our technique with the imagination from life; and our technique becomes as much material as material itself.

It was this principle that Pound saluted in Frost when in his review of *North of Boston* he said, conclusively, 'I know more of farm life than I did before I had read his poems. That means I know more of "life".'

ELIOT, WILLIAMS AND POUND IN
THE TWENTIES
DONALD DAVIE

Harold Monro, writing in the London *Chapbook* in February 1923, observed of T. S. Eliot's (1888–1965) *The Waste Land* that 'in England it was treated chiefly with indignation or contempt', whereas in America *The Dial* had awarded the author its annual prize of $2,000. But the implied contrast is misleading. Allowing for the conventions of sedate amenity that governed American reviewing (as for the most part they still do), one can detect in the American reviewers of Eliot's *Poems* (1920) and of *The Waste Land* (1922) the same recalcitrance that the British reviewers expressed more cheekily. Louis Untermeyer, Robert Frost's correspondent who was to be an influential anthologist, wrote of *Poems* (*The Freeman*, 30 June 1920) that 'Eliot cares less for his art than he does for his attitudes'; and that 'the exaltation which is the very breath of poetry – that combination of tenderness and toughness – is scarcely ever present in Eliot's lines.' When *The Waste Land* appeared, Untermeyer had become more irate: 'The *Dial*'s award to Mr T. S. Eliot and the subsequent book-publication of his *The Waste Land* have occasioned a display of some of the most enthusiastically naive superlatives that have ever issued from publicly sophisticated iconoclasts.' The poem itself he found 'a pompous parade of erudition', and he decided that 'were it not for the Laforgue mechanism, Mr Eliot's poetic variations on the theme of a super-refined futility would be increasingly thin and incredibly second rate' (*The Freeman*, 17 January 1923). Obviously a writer who is happy with 'super-refined' (elsewhere he says that Eliot's 'Portrait of a Lady' is 'extraordinarily sensitized') is not a critic worth pausing on for long; and yet when Untermeyer cites all too patent imitations of Eliot's 'Sweeney Among the Nightingales' in quatrains by Osbert Sitwell and Herbert Read and Robert Nichols, one can see good reason for him to think that Eliot's reputation, achieved so fast on such a slender body of work, was no more than modish. And indeed it asks no great exertion of the historical imagination to recognize that, at a time when 'the Sitwells' were taken to be 'modernists' equal with Eliot and Pound (1885–1972), modish was just what Eliot's reputation was. The achievement was quite otherwise; but it would be several years before that could be perceived, and the perception validated.

For this no one in America deserves more credit than Edmund Wilson. He wrote, in *The Dial* for December 1922, the most emphatically welcoming and apparently influential review of *The Waste Land*, and although this reads a little quaintly now because Wilson took very seriously Eliot's supposed debt to Jessie L. Weston's *From Ritual to Romance* (which later criticism has taken lightly), his piece had the great virtue of conceding valid points to the opposition:

> It is true his poems seem the products of a constricted emotional experience and that he appears to have drawn rather heavily on books for the heat he could not derive from life. There is a certain grudging margin, to be sure, about all that Mr Eliot writes – as if he were compensating himself for his limitations by a peevish assumption of superiority. But it is the very acuteness of his suffering from this starvation which gives such poignancy to his art.

However, it was more than three years later (*The New Republic*, March 1926) that Wilson brought Eliot's poetry home to the bosoms of his countrymen. He did so, having 'The Hollow Men' before him, by insisting on the extent to which Eliot was indelibly American:

> Mr Eliot has lived abroad so long that we rarely think of him as an American and he is never written about from the point of view of his relation to other American authors. Yet one suspects that his real significance is less that of a prophet of European disintegration than of a poet of the American Puritan temperament. Compare him with Hawthorne, Henry James, E. A. Robinson and Edith Wharton: all these writers have their Waste Land, which is the aesthetic and emotional waste land of the Puritan character and their chief force lies in the intensity with which they communicate emotions of deprivation and chagrin.

It is not at all incongruous that Wilson, who thus insisted on Eliot's Americanness, should a few years later, in his pioneering classic *Axel's Castle* (1931), insist on Eliot's Frenchness, thus giving substance and weight to Untermeyer's too glib acknowledgement of 'the Laforgue mechanism'. By taking seriously Eliot's debt to the

French *symbolistes* (as before him only Allen Tate had done, in *The New Republic*, 30 June 1926), Wilson was still stressing Eliot's Americanness by showing at any rate how un-British he was. Not surprisingly, though deplorably, British and also many American readers continued to ignore Eliot's French affinities, following instead the hints that Eliot had dropped for their benefit in his criticism, implying his kinship with such solidly English writers as Donne and Webster. As Tate remarked austerely, 'His Elizabethanism has indubitably been too ingenuously appraised by some critics.'

If we chronicle not how Eliot's reputation was advanced, but how Eliot's poetry (and all modern poetry) came to be understood, the part played by Allen Tate bulks very large and honourably. He was among the first to champion Eliot. Already as a young man of twenty-four he had pressed Eliot's claims upon his seniors, John Crowe Ransom and Donald Davidson, in the circle of the Nashville 'fugitives'; and this initially provincial dispute was played out on a national stage as early as 1923 when, in the *New York Evening Post Literary Review*, Ransom, with the courtly composure that was to be his hallmark, tried to promote Robert Graves before Eliot, only to be taken to task in the same columns by his younger associate. The exchange shows neither Ransom nor Tate at his best. But both were themselves poets, and by that token were concerned more urgently than other commentators, even Edmund Wilson. From 1927 onwards, as the consequences of Eliot's baptism into the Anglican church showed up in the imagery of 'Journey of the Magi', 'A Song for Simeon', 'Animula', and most conspicuously 'Ash-Wednesday' (1930), Tate, open to the solicitations of Christian belief, took up the running on Eliot's behalf from the non-believer Wilson.

It was not easy. Tate, an ambitious poet whose few irreplaceable poems were yet to come, was by 1927 in animated correspondence with two poets, Yvor Winters (1900–1968) and Hart Crane (1899–1932), who were at one, if in little else, in their certainty that Eliot's fame and Eliot's precedent were bad news for American poetry. Already in 1926 (*The New Republic*, 30 June) Tate was obliged – faced with the aridity in diction and imagery of 'The Hollow Men' – to concede that 'It is possible that he has nothing more to say in poetry.' Yet this admission was not so grievous for Tate as it would have been for others. For Tate's very distinguished criticism, then and afterwards, was always more concerned with the socio-cultural conditions for poetry than with poetry itself. And so it was not with any special disappointment that Tate envisaged how Eliot's message, his distinctively American apprehension of Europe, might thereafter be conveyed less in poems than in his conduct of *The Criterion*, the magazine he had begun to edit in 1923:

> Going home to Europe, Mr Eliot has had to understand Europe; he could not quite sufficiently be the European simply to feel that he was there; he has been forced to envisage it with a reminiscent philosophy. And it is not insignificant that the quarterly of which he is the editor is the first British journal which has attempted to relate the British mind to the total European mind; that has attempted a rational synthesis of the traditions of Roman culture; that has, in a word, contemplated order.

And Tate proceeded to cite, with equanimity and approval, some of the non-English writers whom Eliot had solicited for *The Criterion*, or else had approved there: Charles Maurras, Paul Valéry, Henri Massis, Oswald Spengler – several of whom would not unjustly, though with the benefit of hindsight, be condemned later as fascist or proto-fascist.[1]

But in any case there was a grave difficulty. For if Eliot's debt to the French poets went beyond an easy charting of 'influences', or the neat and better than neat adaptation of French lines (for instance, from Laforgue) into English, it could only have meant an elimination from poetry of any notion of 'message'. 'Message' was precisely what French poetry, at least since Mallarmé if not before, had set its face against. But like in the British and the American traditions the expectation that the poet would have a message was so ingrained that even by those readers most alert to and informed about Eliot's French connections *The Waste Land* was still thought to deliver an urgent signal – usually about the bankruptcy of the European, or the Western, cultural and civic traditions.

In this dilemma, Eliot was less than helpful to his apologists. The editor of *The Criterion*, from 1923 and more insistently from 1926, revealed himself as a writer with indeed a message, of a very bleak and uncompromising sort, affronting at almost every point the suppositions of secular liberalism. And it was asking too much of readers that they should insulate Eliot the editor and editorialist from Eliot the poet; so that they should read 'Ash-Wednesday' without feeling that they were being nudged into the Roman Catholic or the Anglo-Catholic church –

> At the first turning of the second stair
> I turned and saw below
> The same shape twisted on the banister
> Under the vapour in the fetid air
> Struggling with the devil of the stairs who wears
> The deceitful face of hope and of despair.
>
> At the second turning of the second stair
> I left them twisting, turning below;
> There were no more faces and the stair was dark,
> Damp, jaggèd, like an old man's mouth drivelling, beyond repair.
> Or the toothed gullet of an agèd shark.
>
> At the first turning of the third stair
> Was a slotted window bellied like the fig's fruit
> And beyond the hawthorn blossom and a pasture scene
> The broadbacked figure drest in blue and green
> Enchanted the maytime with an antique flute.
> Blown hair is sweet, brown hair over the mouth blown,
> Lilac and brown hair;
> Distraction, music of the flute, stops and steps of the mind
>   over the third stair,
>
> Fading, fading; strength beyond hope and despair
> Climbing the third stair.
>
> Lord, I am not worthy
> Lord, I am not worthy
>   but speak the word only.

It is perfectly true that there is nothing conclusively in the poem to make us identify the first stair with Dante's *Inferno*, the second with his *Purgatorio*, the third with *Paradiso*; as there is not (a more piercing uncertainty) anything to determine for us whether 'the broadbacked figure drest in blue and green', with his 'music of the flute', is an image of what must be renounced in order to achieve Paradise, or else an image of how terrestrial life can most nearly attain the paradisal. But no one will seriously maintain that the verses do not have a design upon us; that they do not promulgate a message – the message that all secular explanations of human life are vain and inadequate. That the alternative religious explanation should still not know what value to put on 'music of the flute' – this will be experienced by some as a cruel disappointment, by others as a welcome acknowledgement that dogmatic certainty on the large scale can comprehend uncertainties on the small. But in either or any case these verses must surely confound the French theorists: the poem as a construction of words must be – at least when the words come from such a charged area of human experience as these do – a construction also of sentiments and ideas. The poem does convey a message, though the message cannot be at every point decoded.

Allen Tate rose to this challenge. His essay on 'Ash-Wednesday' (*The Hound and Horn*, January–March 1931) has been anthologized many times, and rightly. It is a masterpiece of literary criticism, precisely by being much more than that; under its surface is the furious rejection by Tate, now consciously an alienated Southerner and impenitent Confederate, of the scientific humanism of Yankee America. Tate saw clearly the point at issue: 'Mr Eliot's critics are a little less able each year to see the poetry for Westminster Abbey; the wood is all trees.' And his retort, masterfully bold though disingenuous, is that 'in a discussion of Mr Eliot's poetry, his doctrine has little to command interest in itself'. Of 'Ash-Wednesday' Tate said, among much else that was penetrating:

These six poems are a brief moment of religious experience in an age that believes religion to be a kind of defeatism and puts its hope for man in finding the right secular order. The mixed realism and symbolism of 'The Waste Land' issued in irony. The direct and lyrical method of the new poems creates the simpler aesthetic quality of humility. The latter quality comes directly out of the former, and there is a nice continuity in Mr Eliot's work.

Before he is through, Tate is claiming that 'Ash-Wednesday' represents 'probably . . . the only valid religious poetry we have', and he isolates two features of the writing which lead him to think this. One, which need not concern us, has to do with imagery. The other emerges when he remarks in the opening lines 'the regular yet halting rhythm, the smooth uncertainty of movement which may either proceed to greater regularity or fall away into improvisation'. This perception is picked up later, more than once, as Tate moves through the poem: 'subtly and imperceptibly the rhythm has changed . . .', 'there is constant and sudden change of rhythm . . .', 'a broken and distracted rhythm'. If we read 'Ash-Wednesday' through with Tate's commentary at our elbow, we see at any given point what he means: he has a good ear, as we might expect from his own poems (which are however metrical, as 'Ash-Wednesday' isn't). And we may agree that what binds together the six parts of 'Ash-Wednesday' is in large part something rhythmical. It remains true that in Tate's criticism and since (for no advance has been made in this quarter) 'rhythm' and 'movement' are wholly impressionistic – you hear what the critic is talking about, or else you don't. This is one area where modern criticism has notably failed. To be sure, the vocabulary for defining such rhythmical effects is yet to seek; but should not critics apply themselves to seeking and finding that vocabulary, instead of pursuing semantic and allusive niceties? In all the many thousands of words that have been expended on Eliot's achievements, this crucial matter – his alertness to, and exploiting of, the rhythms of the English verse-line – remains a vacuum, occupied only by unsupported and insupportable appeals to 'the ear'.

In 1927 Tate's correspondents Winters and Crane had been discussing between themselves not Eliot but William Carlos Williams (1883–1963). On 19 March that year Crane told Winters that 'Williams probably means less to me than to you', and then proceeded to a hesitant account of how he felt about this one of their older contemporaries:

There is no doubt of the charm of almost all of W's work. I except the Paterson and Struggle of Wings lately published in the Dial. I think them both highly disorganized. But in most of Williams' work I feel the kind of observations being 'made' . . . seem to me too casual, however delightfully phrased, to be especially interesting . . .[2]

Later in the letter, considering apparently a different sort of poem written by Williams, Hart Crane confesses:

Personally I often delight in some of these excursions of W's – but I won't 'approve' of them. They are too precious, insulate to all but – at least I fancy – a few 'choice spirits', and even then rather toylike. I don't mean that I'm a democrat. But I don't believe in encouraging the fancy – as long as there is imagination.

It is impossible to recognize in the poet thus characterized – 'precious', 'insulate', 'toylike' – the William Carlos Williams whom American opinion over the last thirty years has promoted as a respectable, and better than respectable, counterweight to Eliot. For one thing, the poet thus extolled has been presented as above all poetically 'a democrat'. Yet Crane's assessment of Williams still has its validity, as is apparent if we consider (wearily, for it is the instance always cited) Williams's 'The Red Wheelbarrow'. The British poet Charles Tomlinson has cited this piece to enforce his contention that 'There is no occasion too small for the poet's celebration.' But is this, in any case, true? Commonsense, not without distinguished endorsement from past centuries, thinks as Hart Crane did that it is not true at all; that on the contrary there are occasions too trivial, too lacking in dignity or resonance, to deserve the ceremoniousness that, as Tomlinson perceived, verse-writing always brings with it. The unfortunate effect in such cases is portentousness; and 'The Red Wheelbarrow' is surely in this way *portentous*:

> so much depends
> upon
>
> a red wheel
> barrow
>
> glazed with rain
> water
>
> beside the white
> chickens.

'So much depends,' says the little squib (for it is nothing more), on the wheelbarrow, the glaze of rain, the chickens. But just how much *does* depend? The momentousness of the sparsely furnished scene is blankly asserted, not proved. Or rather it *is* proved – by sleight of hand; for if the little scene is not momentous, how did it come to be framed, in all its sparsity, by so much white paper? The reverential hush is thus not only demanded, but enforced. The poet cannot lose; whatever claims he makes for the momentousness of his subject-matter are vindicated simply by the way those claims are made.

Such poetry is invulnerable, existing in a self-sealed and self-justifying realm called 'aesthetic', from which no appeal is allowed, or can be made, to other realms like the ethical or the civic. The literary histories invite us to associate such a belief in the unbreachable autonomy of art with haughty and disdainful decadents of the 1880s and 1890s. The achievement of Williams, of his followers and admirers, has been to show that the most secure haven for such doctrines is on the contrary in an ideology that is aggressively egalitarian, and also secular. For the belief that 'there is no occasion too small' is naturally at home in a society that resists any ranking of certain human and civic occasions below or above certain others. And thus it seems that liberal social democracy cossets and protects the aesthete as no other form of society does. Williams's 'It all depends' asserts and takes for granted the absence of any agreed hierarchies, hence the freedom of any individual to establish and assert his own hierarchy, without fear of challenge. 'Spring and All', a more substantial and widely praised poem, follows the same procedure as 'The Red Wheelbarrow' with the added spice of *faux-naïf* cuteness (announced in the very title, and taken up in epithets like 'twiggy'). One hopes that that is not what Crane had in mind when he credited Williams's poems with 'charm'.

Williams had certainly written better poems than these, and doubtless Yvor Winters had those others in mind when, in *Poetry* for May 1928, he wrote of 'the most magnificent master of English and of human emotions since Thomas Hardy, William Carlos Williams'. Significantly, this was in a review mostly concerned to deplore Eliot's influence on poetic style. At that time hardly anyone but Winters would have named Williams in the same breath as Eliot, and it is characteristic of Winters's perversity (or his independence) that thirty years later, when it had become usual to set Williams up against Eliot, Winters's opinion of Williams had long been much less favourable. However, he never ceased to admire a poem like 'The Widow's Lament in Springtime':

> Sorrow is my own yard
> where the new grass
> flames as it has flamed
> often before but not
> with the cold fire
> that closes round me this year.
> Thirtyfive years
> I lived with my husband.
> The plumtree is white today
> with masses of flowers.
> Masses of flowers

> load the cherry branches
> and color some bushes
> yellow and some red
> but the grief in my heart
> is stronger than they
> for though they were my joy
> formerly, today I notice them
> and turned away forgetting.
> Today my son told me
> that in the meadows
> at the edge of the heavy woods
> in the distance, he saw
> trees of white flowers.
> I feel that I would like
> to go there
> and fall into those flowers
> and sink into the marsh near them.

This must be the sort of writing that Crane had in mind when he applauded Williams (still rather grudgingly, however) for sometimes attaining 'the classic manner of the old Chinese poets'. Certainly the deliberate naïveté here is not in the least false, but has the limpid directness of some of the Chinese poems that Pound had marvellously transfigured in *Cathay* (1915). And so it was reasonable for Crane and Winters, who in the twenties was reaching for this style in his own poems, to call such writing 'imagist'. (Williams however in such a poem beautifully weaves the syntax of the sentence into and over his verse-lines – which is not a resource that most imagists were aware of.) Certainly this limpidity is not within Eliot's reach even when he is trying to be limpid, as in 'Ash-Wednesday'; and of course the experience of a simple person enduring a commonplace and unavoidable sorrow is such as Eliot could never manage, early or late. It has to be pointed out, to those who are sure that Eliot is a great poet, what vast tracts of human experience are never touched on in his poetry.

Williams himself had entered the lists against Eliot, saying of Eliot's early poetry (and Pound's also):

It is the latest touch from the literary cuisine, it adds to the pleasant outlook from the club window. If to do this, if to be a Whistler at best, in the art of poetry, is to reach the height of poetic expression, then Ezra and Eliot have approached it and *tant pis* for the rest of us.

And Williams jeered:

> I do not overlook De Gourmont's plea for a meeting of the nations but I do believe that when they meet Paris will be more than slightly abashed to find parodies of the middle ages, Dante and Langue D'Oc foisted upon it as the best in United States poetry.

This was in *The Little Review* for May 1919, where Williams was taking issue with praise of Eliot by one of Pound's British friends, Edgar Jepson; but Williams's hostility to British culture ran deeper than that, and was to be a permanent feature of his outlook. His malevolence towards Pound, his friend since their college days in Philadelphia, is extraordinary; and when in 1920 he amplified this piece in the prologue to his *Kora in Hell*, Williams compounded the offence by quoting selectively from a private letter that Pound had written him. Astonishingly, Pound did not break off relations. Instead he was provoked, in a letter, into one of the most illuminating and betraying comments that he ever made, on Eliot, Williams and himself:

> There is a blood poison in America; you can idealize the place (easier now that Europe is so damd shaky) all you like, but you haven't a drop of the cursed blood in you, and you don't need to fight the disease day and night; you never have had to. Eliot has it perhaps worse than I have – poor devil.
>
> You have the advantage of arriving in the milieu with a fresh flood of Europe in your veins, Spanish, French, English, Danish. You had not the thin milk of New York and New England from the pap; and you can therefore keep the environment outside you, and decently objective.
>
> (*Selected Letters*, ed. D. D. Paige, p. 158)

Pound here anticipates, and paints in a blacker hue, Edmund Wilson's recognition that Eliot is 'a poet of the American Puritan temperament', and Pound claims to be tarred with the same brush himself. One must mind one's manners (and one's metaphors – tarring with brushes, for instance!) when venturing on to the territory that Pound opens up with his reflections on the ethnic mix of the American population, and the distinction that he makes between the older stock (Eliots and Pounds) and the relatively late-come immigrants (Williams's stock on both sides). Moreover Pound's antisemitism, later so notorious, certainly casts a sinister light on his readiness to broach these issues. Yet these matters, it has been suggested, lie deep

– indeed, *unutterably* deep – in every American psyche; and it is good that from time to time the unutterable be uttered – it is, one might say, one of the things that we look to poets for. There can be little doubt for instance that the doubtfulness or downright hostility felt towards Eliot by some Americans, particularly in recent decades, derives from the *sort* of American Eliot was – and remained, long after he had taken British citizenship. Eliot hailed from St Louis, but the Eliots there seem to have regarded themselves as Bostonian and Unitarian missionaries to that mid-western Philistia. The poet did not share this sense, he actively disliked it, but he could not escape – not even in Europe – from what he saw as the balefulness of that inheritance. He was what we have learned to call a WASP, and his lifetime coincided with the process, not yet quite completed, by which that caste – white Anglo-Saxon protestants of the north-east – was supplanted from the position of privilege that they had enjoyed from the first days of the Republic. That privilege, and the airs and presumption that went with it, are still resented; and some of the resentment has rubbed off on the poet.

Pound's case is by no means so clear-cut. At least one of his grandparents had made a career on the frontier; and in *The Cantos* this forbear, Thaddeus Coleman Pound, makes several entries, always with an encouraging flourish on the drums. It is the more remarkable that Pound in his letter to Williams should diagnose himself as suffering from a milder form of Eliot's disease; most of the time, alike in his life and his poetry, he seems to be denying it by strenuously over-compensating. Only once, late in life when he made as much of an excuse as he would ever make for his antisemitism, did Pound ever again enter the plea for himself that he suffered from the cultural anaemia of growing up in a suburb of an Eastern seaboard city. As for Williams, who had an English father, it would be easy to explain away his hostility to England; but the sorrier likelihood is that he saw quite justly the baleful mixture of timidity and arrogance which characterized literary London in his lifetime. However, Pound's diagnosis of Williams's condition was surely perceptive: Williams could abide American reality (where Pound and Eliot had to flee from it) because, as in the admirable 'To Elsie' ('The pure products of America/go crazy'), he remained the immigrant, the outsider looking in on the behaviour of the nation that he had been, by the sheerest accident, born to.

Yvor Winters, eschewing lurid and unstable metaphors of blood-poisoning and leukaemia, applied the discipline of intellectual history to isolate the virus that for him too disabled American literature of the north-east. It was, he decided, Emersonianism – a disease (if that is what it is) which is certainly no less rife now than it was when Winters made his diagnosis fifty years ago. This investigation was part of the wholesale scrutiny and revaluation that Winters was shocked into by the suicide of Hart Crane in 1932. In that revaluation, whereas Pound held his modest but respectable place, Williams was drastically demoted without Eliot's rising in the scale against him. Winters in California perhaps thought himself securely distant from the seat of the infection; he never visited Europe, still less was he tempted to expatriate himself.

Pound's forbearance towards Williams remains astonishing, the more when we realize that Williams's challenge to him came when he was remarkably uncertain and at sea about his own talents and the direction in which he should go. Bowled over by the originality and assurance of Joyce's *Ulysses*, which was being sent to him by the author in typescript section by section, Pound was between 1920 and 1922 dismantling the several hundred lines of *The Cantos* that he had written and published, and recasting them radically, using some of the same material but trying for a less personalized presentation. Moreover Pound had reached Williams's conclusion about literary London, and in 1920 left for Paris, whence in 1924 he moved to Rapallo. His acrid and accusing farewell to London was *Hugh Selwyn Mauberley* (1920). But the poem of his that he most needed reassurance about was *Homage to Sextus Propertius* (1919), and for that he had to wait a long time. When Eliot in 1928, loyally reciprocating services rendered, edited Pound's *Selected Poems*, he insisted on excluding the Propertius poem, and it was not until 1932 that Basil Bunting wrote, already retrospectively, 'In my considered opinion, 'Propertius' was the most important poem of our times, surpassing alike "Mauberley" and "The Waste Land".' This was in *The New English Weekly*, a London journal of very limited circulation; there appears to have been no comparable acknowledgement in the poet's native land. Bunting, who respected Eliot, applied himself first to rebutting the reasons which Eliot gave, in his Introduction to *Selected Poems*, for omitting this long and elaborate poem:

> It is impossible to understand why Eliot should have excluded the 'Propertius' from his selection of Pound's work. The plea of its difficulty will not hold, for as a consummation is always simpler than a beginning, the 'Propertius' is certainly much simpler than some of Pound's shorter earlier works whose content is sometimes elusive, tenuous, evanescent . . .
>
> . . . The question of the relation of Pound's poem with the book of Propertius's elegies does not arise, except for the literary historian. There is no claim that this is a translation. The correspondence, the interpenetration of ancient and modern, is Pound's, not Propertius's . . .[3]

Half a century later, such commentary as there is on Pound's poem is still for the most part concerned with this question that for Bunting 'does not arise'. When he goes on to justify his high estimate of the poem, Bunting specifies:

> The beautiful step of the verse, the cogent movement of thought and feeling throughout, the sensitive perception of the little balanced in the great and their mutual dependence, the extraordinary directness, here and there quite naked, achieved in spite of the complexity of the whole conception; . . .

Some of these claims can be considered, and either allowed or disallowed, only by looking at the work as a whole; others can be at least understood after reading only a few lines:

> My cellar does not date from Numa Pompilius,
> Nor bristle with wine jars,
> Nor is it equipped with a frigidaire patent;
> Yet the companions of the Muses
>   will keep their collective nose in my books,
> And weary with historical data, they will turn to my dance tune.
>
> Happy who are mentioned in my pamphlets,
>   the songs shall be a fine tomb-stone over their beauty.
>   But against this?
> Neither expensive pyramids scraping the stars in their route,
> Nor houses modelled upon that of Jove in East Elis,
> Nor the monumental effigies of Mausolus,
>   are a complete elucidation of death.
>
> Flame burns, rain sinks into the cracks
> And they all go to rack ruin beneath the thud of the years.
> Stands genius a deathless adornment,
>   a name not to be worn out with the years.

Noting in passing how conclusively the 'frigidaire patent' rules out any notion of a translation of Propertius (unless it were translation in the sense of a raucous travesty or 'put-down' – and indeed some academic latinists did misconceive Pound's poem in that way), some early readers were understandably disconcerted by the inversions of conversational or prosaic word-order – 'Happy who', 'Stands genius' – especially from a poet who some years before had seemed to polemicize for just that rule about word-order which he here flouted. But these inversions were quite different in purpose and effect from those that Pound had practised indiscriminately in his earliest collections, and thereafter castigated; these were not poeticisms, but indications that he was addressing a sophisticated urban intelligentsia, that of Great War London, just as Propertius had addressed the sophisticates of Augustan Rome. The clue is in the diction, which gives 'are a complete elucidation of', for 'clears up' or 'makes clear'. The poet writes for, and gives a voice to, people whose privileged education has closed off for them the possibility of speaking as limpidly and directly as the speaker of 'The Widow's Lament in Springtime'. A special pathos is achieved when the poetry acts out the predicament of people whose all too expert command of language debars them (paradoxically) from expressing a common human sorrow – mortality, the fear of it, and its conclusiveness – as limpidly as could Williams's 'widow'. In the end the speaker of *Homage to Sextus Propertius* wins through to articulating that common plight as memorably as Williams's speaker does – with, as Bunting says, 'extraordinary directness . . . quite naked'. But Pound's speaker, so far from naïve, has had to struggle through to that desired but unfamiliar nakedness; and Pound's verse enacts the struggle.

It may seem that when Bunting speaks of 'the beautiful step of the verse', he is gesturing into a void not much less than Allen Tate when he wrote of the 'rhythm' and the 'movement' of Eliot's 'Ash-Wednesday'. But in fact the metaphor 'step', implying tread, implies also volition and direction. More important, since Pound's use of indentations conveys visually the effect of the verse-lines being 'stepped' down the page, to speak of 'step' shifts attention from what rhythmically happens between the start and end of a line to how the poet manages the turn from one line to another. (And 'verse', from *versus*, means precisely 'turn'.) To be sure, this is still rudimentary and indefinite. But certain writings by Pound, Bunting and a couple of others can take us a little further. What all of them contend is that the auditory effect of *all* English-language verse can only in a schematic and starveling fashion be pin-pointed by applying the only two measurements that traditional scansion recognizes: on the one hand the number of syllables, on the other the number of occurrences of *ictus* or 'stress'. One feature of English verse that is scanted by this method, or can be acknowledged only incidentally, is one that every careful reader knows from his or her experience: *tempo*, the speeding up or slowing down of enunciation, and therefore of apprehension, as we read through a line or through several lines in sequence.

This seems to be intimately connected with another principle, which is more radical and therefore more important: that of *quantity*, of syllables as being, in relation to their contiguous syllables, either long or short. The variation between English-language speakers about what syllables, in effect what vowels, they treat as long or short, is so great that there can be no question of imposing on English verse a quantitative metre such as was used for ancient Latin (doubtless with some strain for those who spoke classical Latin with dialectal variations as to quantity). This granted, it remains true, as anyone's experience of his own and others' speech-habits will confirm, that some English vowels are experienced and expressed as relatively long, others as relatively short. Not just unmetrical poets like Pound (for the most part) and Bunting, but also a strictly metrical poet like the later Yvor Winters, came to think that the finest auditory effects in English-language verse were attained by those poets who attended to the quantitative element in British or American speech as an incalculable dimension super-added to the recognized and calculable dimensions of syllable-count and stress-count. Quantity in this sense, *duration*, is what musicians and musical composers are continally concerned with; and so it is not surprising that poets of this way of thinking, like Pound and Bunting, show themselves avidly interested in poetry which has been, not at a level of theory but as a fact of performance, intimately associated with music: poetry that has been set, or has been written in the hope of being set, to music. It is notable that it was Bunting, in his generation the only British emulator of Pound, who was most confident and insistent that in these matters Pound's immediate master was American, the Walt Whitman of 'Out of the Ocean Endlessly Rocking'. It is in any case certain that for years before *Homage to Sextus Propertius* Pound had been studying, not for their content chiefly but as models of musical form, the poems in quantitative metre of ancient Greece. (His British predecessor in such technical study had been Thomas Hardy; but that is another, and difficult, topic.)

These matters are important because they explain how Pound and Eliot, who had campaigned as a team and would help each other for many years to come, radically differed not just in themes and attitudes (of which something will be said hereafter) but at this deep level, in the not altogether conscious interstices of their craft. Fortunately Eliot declared himself unequivocally, in an essay, 'Reflections on *Vers Libre*: '. . . the ghost of some simple metre should lurk behind the arras in even the "freest" verse; to advance menacingly as we doze, and withdraw as we arouse.' This is what Pound could never have said. When, infrequently, he wanted to write in 'some simple metre', he did so; but when more often he wanted to get away from standard metres, he left them behind altogether, no ghost of them lurking behind his arras. The difference between the two poets corresponds (not quite exactly, because the nature and history of French verse differs so greatly from English) to the distinction that the French make between *vers libre* and *vers libéré*; between, we may say, free verse and freed verse. Eliot's practice, as his remarks just quoted make clear, was always 'freed' verse: verse freed indeed from the constraints of traditional prosody, yet rather constantly recalling to the reader's ear one of the traditional patterns it was departing from. (Hence, notably in 'Gerontion', Eliot's ability to approximate and even conform to Jacobean blank verse, yet to depart from it smoothly when he pleased.) Pound's verse on the contrary was, at least after *Homage to Sextus Propertius*, free, not 'freed': the rhythms that he sought and attained either had never appeared before in the language, or else had not appeared there for many centuries. His departure was much more radical. And yet he was not doctrinaire about it, having declared on the contrary (as early as 1917, significantly in a review of Eliot's *Prufrock and Other Observations*):

Unless a man can put some thematic invention into *vers libre*, he would perhaps do well to stick to 'regular' metres, which have certain chances of being musical from their form, and certain other chances of being musical through his failure in fitting the form.

The one who *was* doctrinaire was Williams, who regarded the iambic measure as a chief curse of the English legacy from which American poetry must free itself if it was ever to stand on its own. However, Winters was to decide that Williams was 'wholly incapable of coherent thought', and when Williams tried to explain his own rhythmical procedures he invented 'the variable foot' – which is, as has been remarked, the equivalent of a rubber inch. Williams had a good ear, and since his death some of his admirers have made more sense of his procedures than he could ever make for himself, but the lamentable effect of his example has been to lead poets to trust their ear implicitly, thus discrediting the very notion of *measure*.

The closeness of Pound's and Eliot's collaboration when they were young did not become clear until 1972. In that year comparisons of Eliot with Pound were stimulated, and exacerbated, by the publication of what were called the 'drafts and transcripts' of *The Waste Land*; that is to say, the heterogeneous packet of typescripts and manuscripts which Eliot had dumped on Pound in Paris, out of which Pound had helped Eliot to extricate the poem that for forty years had been known under that title. In most ways this book reflected great credit on both poets, and was affecting evidence of their mutual trust, of how their common dedication to the poetic calling had precluded any taint of rivalry or wounded *amour-propre*. On the other hand the material which Eliot had put into Pound's hands turned out to be so inchoate that many readers were led to wonder how far the poem as they had had it all these years was in any authentic sense Eliot's at all. To be fair to him, he had repeatedly hinted that, when the evidence was in, it would show that Pound's contribution went far beyond the mere passing of judgement on particular passages; and indeed it turned out that the very structure of the poem had been extricated by Pound, rather than conceived and composed by the poet whose name appeared on the title-page. This was disconcerting, to say the least. It was not easy to think of a precedent, and one could be forgiven for concluding that the notorious obscurity of the poem came about not by the author's design but accidentally, because the work was the product not of one mind but of two. The poem, we might say, is in two minds about itself and its own meaning.

But that is not the whole story. For Pound undoubtedly made the poem more obscure by asking for the excision of some transitional and bridging passages where the language was not at full pressure, but on the other hand he caused to be removed some extended sections which, being plainly extraneous, could only have added to readers' bafflement. Moreover in some important respects Pound was more old-fashioned than Eliot. As his later disastrous interventions in politics would make clear, he was a realist in quite a simple-minded sense, one who was concerned for public life, and believed (like activists of the Left) that a poet had the right and the duty to act in and upon that life quite directly; whereas the oddly distant weariness of Eliot's political pronouncements, even when he was most *engagé* as editor of *The Criterion*, revealed a man for whom the psychological reality of private torments took priority over any reality which announced itself as social and public. Thus Pound was quite ready, and became eager, to deliver a message, though with more obliquities and delays than the impatiently moralistic reader could see reason for; whereas Eliot, true to his inheritance from French *symbolisme*, was sceptical and chary of conveying in poetry any message at all. (Pound had studied some of the same French poets, notably Laforgue and Rimbaud, but he had profited by them in a quite different way from Eliot, and he was averse to the central thrust of the *symboliste* endeavour, to which indeed the imagist or *imagiste* movement which he had sponsored had been intended as a challenging alternative.)

This difference between the two of them showed up in *The Waste Land* drafts. For among the rather few objections by Pound that Eliot paid no attention to were one or two which would have required him to make consistent, in terms of locality and historical period, some of his references to London life. Eliot seems to have ignored these suggestions because for him the physical and social landscape of London was no more than a screen on which to project a phantasmagoria that expressed his own personal disorders and desperations (partly sexual, as one might expect, and as the drafts make clear); whereas Pound seems to have supposed that the subject of the poem was London in all its historical and geographical actuality, much as the city of Dublin was from one point of view the subject of Joyce's *Ulysses*. Quite independent of Pound, most admiring commentators have read the poem more nearly as Pound read it than as Eliot intended. They could always have maintained of course that, whatever the poet's intentions, the poem as an achieved entity answered to their interpretations. But critics of the twenties, knowing nothing of Pound's part in the poem, and ignorant also of Eliot's private sufferings through his wretched first marriage, saw no need to go so far around, to support their conviction or assumption that *The Waste Land* was a poem with a message.

What was known about Pound's association with Eliot did Pound's reputation no good at all. The insufferable Untermeyer in 1923 castigated the texture of *The Waste Land* as 'that formless plasma which Mr Ezra Pound likes to call a Sordelloform'; and in the same year in London, Clive Bell, the voice of 'Bloomsbury', said of Eliot that 'no aesthetic theory can explain his indiscreet boosting of ... the lamentable Ezra Pound.' But the most vicious discrimination had come in the previous year, from Edmund Wilson, who applauded the structure of *The Waste Land* by contrasting it to 'the extremely ill-focussed Eight Cantos of his imitator Mr Ezra Pound, who presents only a bewildering mosaic with no central emotion to provide a key'. Eliot, distressed, wrote to Wilson and to another of his champions, Gilbert Seldes, protesting that he did not want to be praised at Pound's expense since he was indebted to Pound (as indeed his dedication to Pound as *il miglior fabbro* had elegantly acknowledged). Eliot told Wilson and Seldes that 'I sincerely consider Ezra Pound the most important living poet in the English language.'[4] But the damage had been done, and Wilson's elevation of Eliot at Pound's expense was to be echoed time and again for at least thirty years, and indeed is still to be heard even today. Pound suffered immediately, in his pocket-book. Always short of money, Pound in the twenties found one outlet after another closed to him and had great difficulty making ends meet. He seems not to have whined, and his only complaint, posthumously recorded by Bunting in his obituary of Pound, is drily judicious: he 'said in the Thirties that Eliot had got stuck because he could not understand Propertius [i.e. Pound's *Homage*] and all the rest had got stuck a few books earlier still.'

How early Pound came by this perception is not clear, but certainly he had no illusions from the first that his *Cantos*, building as they did on the rhythmical and thematic procedures of *Homage to Sextus Propertius*, would be found readily acceptable. In 1922 he explained in a letter:

> Perhaps, as the poem goes on I shall be able to make various things clearer. Having the crust to attempt a poem in 100 or 120 cantos long after all mankind has been commanded never again to attempt a poem of any length, I have to stagger as I can.
>
> The first 11 cantos are preparation of the palette. I *have to* get down all the colours or elements I want for the poem. Some perhaps too enigmatically and abbreviatedly. I hope, heaven help me, to bring them into some sort of design and architecture later.
>
> (*Selected Letters*, p. 180)

Excusably perhaps, neither Edmund Wilson nor any one else could understand, or could credit, the scale on which Pound was working: 120 cantos, and by the time Pound died in 1972, the poem had fallen only just short of that. In a poem designed on such a scale (and this evidence of 'design' on such a scale from the first is astonishing) it was obviously illegitimate to look, as Edmund Wilson did, for emotional or affective unity in each or any Canto in isolation. As Pound confessed in another letter in 1933: 'Most Cantos have in them "binding matter", i.e. lines holding them into the whole poem and these passages don't much help the reader of an isolated fragment . . . More likely to confuse than help.' Pound was in all seriousness embarked on an epic poem (which he defined, following of all unlikely authorities Rudyard Kipling, as 'the tale of the tribe'); he could not and did not expect understanding from readers who supposed that the epic poem had died in the seventeenth century if not before, whose expectations therefore were conditioned by their experience of the brief or else extended lyric. There are lyrical passages or interludes in *The Cantos*, as in any epic poem, but to excerpt these for applause while deploring their context is to fudge the issue, and evade the challenge of the poem as a whole. The scale on which Pound was working was not clear even to the poet himself;

so that the eleven cantos which he originally designated as 'preparation of the palette' are now by responsible commentators considerably extended – to the extent that the first thirty cantos, which are all that the twenties knew of the poem (*A Draft of XVI Cantos* (Paris, June 1925); *A Draft of the Cantos 17–27* (100 copies, September 1928); and *A Draft of XXX Cantos* (210 copies, August 1930)), are now often regarded as laying out on the painter's palette the hues that only in subsequent cantos would be combined to polemical and imaginative purpose. Certainly only in the next batch of cantos (post-1930), which began with extended excerpts from the founding fathers of the Republic, would the scale or enormity of the poem become apparent, also its topicality and its Americanness. Of the first thirty cantos by themselves, no account is more plausible than that of a writer in the *New York Herald Tribune Books* for 9 January 1927, who decided: 'Mr Pound is avowedly writing a history of the Mediterranean basin.'⁵ The writer was Ford Madox Ford, who was among the most loyal as he had been among the first of Pound's friends; in the twenties he was as penurious and as out of fashion as Pound.

It is easy to cheat when quoting from these early cantos: either by imposing a seeming self-closure on passages that are in fact open at both ends, or (and as well) by presenting a lyrically appealing passage as typical of the whole. Any quotation must in any case be extensive:

> So that the Xarites bent over tovarisch.
> And these are the labours of tovarisch,
> That tovarisch lay in the earth,
> And rose, and wrecked the house of the tyrants,
> And that tovarisch lay then in the earth
>   And the Xarites bent over tovarisch.
>
> These are the labours of tovarisch,
> That tovarisch wrecked the house of the tyrants,
> And rose, and talked folly on folly,
> And walked forth and lay in the earth
>   And the Xarites bent over tovarisch.
>
> And that tovarisch cursed and blessed without aim,
>   These are the labours of tovarisch,
> Saying:
>   'Me Cadmus sowed in the earth

And with the thirtieth autumn
I return to the earth that made me.
Let the five last build the wall;

I neither build nor reap.
That he came with the gold ships, Cadmus,
That he fought with the wisdom,
Cadmus, of the gilded prows. Nothing I build
And I reap
Nothing; with the thirtieth autumn
I sleep, I sleep not, I rot
And I build no wall.
   Where was the wall of Eblis
At Ventadour, there now are the bees,
And in that court, wild grass for their pleasure
That they carry back to the crevice
Where loose stone hangs upon stone.
I sailed never with Cadmus,
   lifted never stone above stone.'

'Baked and eaten tovarisch!
'Baked and eaten, tovarisch, my boy,
'That is your story. And up again,
'Up and at 'em. Laid never stone upon stone.'

'The air burst into leaf.'
'Hung there flowered acanthus,
'Can you tell the down from the up?'

As 'tovarisch' quite raucously announces, Pound here in Canto 27 reflects on the October Revolution in Russia in 1917. And not only the Xaritès (or Charitès, the Greek Graces) bend with some solicitude over the unnamed revolutionary comrade, so does the poet – for indeed in 1930 Pound's desire for an authoritarian leader in politics was as ready to fix on Lenin as on Mussolini. Rather plainly the poem decides, as others have decided before and since, that the revolution's humble heroes, revolution once accomplished, did not know what to do with the liberation they had achieved. One needs Ford Madox Ford's emphasis on 'the Mediterranean basin' to understand that 'tovarisch' is being dignified by having his exploits measured against the myths of ancient Greece – for instance, that of Cadmus, founder of Thebes, who sowed dragon's teeth from which sprang warriors which fought among themselves until only five remained. Pound has no recourse to that staple of anti-Russian propaganda in every generation (some of it was being aired in these years in Eliot's *Criterion*) according to which the Russian is 'asiatic', outside the confines of Europe. What will disconcert readers who come to Pound after Eliot, what they will find either refreshing or exasperating, is the literalness of Pound's imagination. When he has tovarisch say, 'Nothing I build', this is to be understood not allegorically but literally: working of stone, either architecturally or sculpturally, was for Pound at all times the register of culture – a conviction which he shared in his lifetime with few except the British art-critic whom he knew and esteemed, Adrian Stokes. Thus the reference to the ruined walls of Eblis, in Aquitaine, is not gratuitous; and we know from other passages that Pound's refusal in the last resort to take seriously Russia's contribution to European culture was grounded in his notion that Russia had never produced an indigenous tradition of stone architecture.

On the other hand, when in the ruined court of Eblis the bees find 'wild grass for their pleasure', that is good too. For human building (art) and the processes of germination (nature) are not in this vision opposed, as alternatives we must choose between. The one mirrors the other, and is nourished by the other. To build is as natural as to procreate. Accordingly tovarisch condemns himself not only because 'nothing I build', but also because 'I reap/Nothing'; the failure in the one capacity implies a failure in the other. The identity of the two activities is asserted, with a succinctness that only the build-up has made possible, in 'flowered acanthus' (*acanthus*, a classical motif of architectural sculpture, is also the stylized representation of specific foliage), and also in 'Can you tell the down from the up?' (for there is no way of deciding whether 'nature' is the 'up' and 'art' the 'down', or vice-versa). This sanguine trust in the unity and coherence of the universe is as far as possible from 'the American Puritan temperament', as Eliot suffered it and articulated it. And nearly half a century later, when *The Cantos* would tail off (not discreditably) in 'Drafts and Fragments', Pound would still be purveying the same message, in terms of 'the gardens of Proserpine', the mineral and metallic gardens that Proserpine according to the myth created in the underworld, to duplicate as 'art' the springing herbage that she inspired in spring and summer through her six months in the overworld.

No one in the twenties could have divined this over-arching design, nor did Pound suppose that anyone would.

How any of this was relevant to twentieth-century America was precisely the question that Williams had raised when he jeered at 'parodies of the middle ages, Dante and Langue D'Oc' being presented as 'the best in United States poetry'. And it is true that Williams was aware of creative work in American photography and painting, as Pound in his self-exile could not be. But Pound with his invaluable naïveté really believed that the United States was 'a land of opportunity'; that his nation's glory was all in the future, and would be achieved if only Americans would sort out those achievements of European culture (and of non-European cultures also) which were worth their emulating and trying to surpass.

NOTES

1. See C. K. Stead, *Pound, Yeats, Eliot and the Modernist Movement* (1986), pp. 203–4.

2. Thomas Parkinson (ed.), *Hart Crane and Yvor Winters. Their Literary Correspondence* (1978), pp. 69–70.

3. Carroll F. Terrell (ed.), *Basil Bunting. Man and Poet* (Orono, Maine, 1981), pp. 253–4.

4. Noel Stock, *The Life of Ezra Pound* (1970), 249–50; quoted by Michael Grant in *T. S. Eliot. The Critical Heritage* (1982), I, p. 20.

5. Brita Lindberg-Seyersted (ed.), *Pound/Ford. The Story of a Literary Friendship* (1982), p. 86.

WALLACE STEVENS AND THE POETRY OF SCEPTICISM

CHARLES TOMLINSON

When in 1943 Yvor Winters (1900–1968), in *The Anatomy of Nonsense*, commented on the poetry of Wallace Stevens, he referred to 'a combination of calm and terror' that 'will be found in only one other poet in English, in Shakespeare as one finds him in a few lines of the more metaphysical sonnets'. With the appearance in the fifties of *Selected Poems*, one discovers Winters' high estimate being endorsed by Donald Davie in a review entitled 'Essential Gaudiness': 'He is indeed a poet to be mentioned in the same breath as Eliot and Yeats and Pound.' Winters' piece had had for its title 'Wallace Stevens, or the Hedonist's Progress', containing reservations about that 'essential gaudiness' which Davie was to go on to salute. Davie himself, when he reprinted his own essay in *The Poet in the Imaginary Museum* (1977), registered in a footnote: 'I should now probably be more captious about Stevens than I was when I wrote this.' This wavering on the part of two of our most interesting critics is a measure, perhaps, of the difficulty of being fair to Stevens and of seeing his quirkiness and gaudiness in relation to that soberer 'middle style' which marks his later poems of meditation in *Transport to a Summer* (1947), *The Auroras of Autumn* (1950) and *The Rock* (1955). 'Middle style' for Stevens, it must be understood, usually implies rather more elevation than for most other poets.

Like Eliot, Yeats and Pound, Stevens was writing his earliest poetry at a time when the poetic idiom stood in need of renewal. Unlike them, he was often content to take over Victorian modes and, simply by the audacity of his use of such modes, to turn them to his own purposes. His subject-matter stands frequently close to accepted poetic conventions and themes, in spite of the whimsical titles, like 'Le Monocle de Mon Oncle' or 'The Comedian as Letter

393

C' from his first volume, *Harmonium*, of 1923. After these, one is a little surprised at the old-fashioned romantic excess in some of the actual writing:

> The dark shadows of the funereal magnolias
> Are full of the songs of Jamanda and Carlotta
> – The son and the daughter who come to the darkness
> He for her burning breast, and she for his arms.

– written so close in time to the composition of Pound's *Hugh Selwyn Mauberley* and Eliot's *The Waste Land*. Poor vintage Keats, Meredith, Browning are the origins of such passages, and the Shakespearian note is reach-me-down Elizabethanizing like 'the unconscionable treachery of fate'. As for Stevens's themes, one of the most important in *Harmonium* had been run ragged by romantics and decadents alike – namely the alliance of Death and Beauty. 'Peter Quince at the Clavier', for all the chic of its title, is a set of variations on this theme, where Stevens wins the day by his sheer imaginative panache and his witty reversal of the traditional Christianizing commonplaces:

> Beauty is momentary in the mind –
> The fitful tracing of a portal;
> But in the flesh it is immortal.
> The body dies; the body's beauty lives.
> So evenings die, in their green going,
> A wave interminably flowing . . .
> Susanna's music touched the bawdy strings
> Of those white elders; but, escaping,
> Left only Death's ironic scraping.

Stevens, at forty-four (the age when he published *Harmonium*), is self-conscious about his themes in a way romantics and decadents were not. Hence, to a point, the jokes of his titles, establishing (uneasily at times) an ironic attitude to the subject-matter which follows. Thus, in 'Le Monocle de Mon Oncle', Stevens inspects, presumably through his uncle's monocle, the kind of middle-aged romantic poetry his uncle might have written. He considers the theme of spring – 'Shall I uncrumple this much-crumpled thing?' he asks. Both Winters and Davie seize upon this section of the poem which, venturing beyond Keats, Browning and Meredith, results in something that is recognizably Stevens's own:

A red bird flies across the golden floor.
It is a red bird that seeks out his choir
Among the choirs of wind and wet and wing.
A torrent will fall from him when he finds.
Shall I uncrumple this much-crumpled thing?
I am a man of fortune greeting heirs;
For it has come that thus I greet the spring.
These choirs of welcome choir for me farewell.
No spring can follow past meridian.
Yet you persist with anecdotal bliss
To make believe a starry *connaissance*.

To the apparently stale topic and into the apparently unusable idiom Stevens brings new life, an awareness of nature that is fresh and individual in this evocation of wet woods, the sounding of bird-song through wind and rain, and the song of the one bird whose 'torrent' is at once a joyful rediscovery of his kind and a release. Perhaps one of the most poignant touches throughout Stevens's oeuvre is his feeling for the way human and animal awareness sometimes overlaps and yet differs (see, for example, 'A Rabbit as King of the Ghosts' and 'Song of Fixed Accord').

Intimations of freshness also impinge through the nostalgia of another early sequence in *Harmonium*, 'Sunday Morning'. A woman is meditating on the fact of death:

She says, 'I am content when wakened birds
Before they fly, test the reality
Of misty fields by their sweet questionings;
But when the birds are gone, and their warm fields
Return no more, where, then is paradise?

The phrase 'test the reality/Of misty fields by their sweet questionings' establishes with beautiful implicitness the felt space at the back of bird-song and the sense of the surrounding continuum of nature now no longer clearly seen because of the mist. This power of sensuous evocation, rather than the sensuous particularizing of shapes and substances of the kind one finds in (say) Hopkins, shows itself both in the poems in traditional blank verse and those of a more recognizably modern cut like 'Thirteen Ways of Looking at a Blackbird', also from *Harmonium*, but evidently of a later date than 'Le Monocle' and 'Sunday Morning'. 'Thirteen Ways' strips perception of all imaginative excess:

IV

Icicles filled the long window
With barbaric glass.
The shadow of the blackbird
Crossed it, to and fro.
The mood
Traced in the shadow
An indecipherable cause.

XIII

It was evening all afternoon.
It was snowing
And it was going to snow.
The blackbird sat
In the cedar limbs.

The sharpness of Stevens's evocations of his sensations of the natural scene, and of the loneliness he feels before that scene, recur again and again. Stevens is a poet whose imagination warms to the cold. He wanted to write a 'poetry of earth' and to be the poet of 'a physical universe', praising 'total satisfaction, the moment of total summer'. Yet 'total summer' seems to yield little but rhetoric to Stevens's wintry temperament. True, there are poems of joy in spring and autumn, but the snowscape remains one of his favourite genres, from the desolate compactness of his early and famous 'The Snowman' to the extended meditations of his penultimate collection, *The Auroras of Autumn* (1950):

> The season changes. A cold wind chills the beach.
> The long lines of it grow larger, emptier,
> A darkness gathers though it does not fall
>
> And the whiteness grows less vivid on the wall.
> The man who is walking turns blankly on the sand.
> He observes how the north is always enlarging the change,
>
> With its frigid brilliances, its blue-red sweeps
> And gusts of great enkindlings, its polar green,
> The color of ice and fire and solitude.

This late poetry of the aurora borealis still harks back in a chastened manner to the organ-note effects of the earlier pieces: 'The color of ice and fire and solitude' has a kind of lonely gusto that sorts well with the New England stoicism that watches out winter through yet another March snow storm.

Stevens's conviction that 'The great poem of earth remains to be written' does not quite carry him sufficiently far to write it. He sometimes watches out winter with an answering, icy grandeur. At others, he tries to involve us in a celebration of the physical universe at which he is both priest and organist, the organist's skill in opulent improvisation making up for the priest's uneasy faith when, after moments of reconciliation or truce between mind and matter, the going gets difficult. And, yet, again, and perhaps most acceptably, a Stevens of the middle-style finds a way of telling us that the fiction of the poem, by clearing a space for meaning and fresh apprehension, can reconcile us to a world of fact in a way that the fictions of religion no longer can, as in 'Notes Towards a Supreme Fiction':

> The death of one god is the death of all . . .
> Phoebus is dead, ephebe. But Phoebus was
> A name for something that never could be named

and

> The poem refreshes life so that we share,
> For a moment, the first idea . . . It satisfies
> Belief in an immaculate beginning
>
> And sends us, winged by an unconscious will,
> To an immaculate end. We move between these points:
> From that ever-early candor to its late plural . . .

Here, Stevens is following out the implications of one of his earliest poems, 'A High-Toned Old Christian Woman' from *Harmonium*, where the notion 'Poetry is the supreme fiction' first appears and where he tells her that now the church has failed our imaginations, poetry must do the job for us. If the idea that 'Poetry is the supreme fiction' is a frank extension of the ideas of a Victorian like Matthew Arnold in his *Literature and Dogma*, the ideological background to 'Sunday Morning' is also Victorian and a response to conflicts that the Victorians were the first to make explicit. 'Sunday Morning' sets out one of the basic themes of all Stevens's work and this theme was already Tennyson's in *In Memoriam* namely, the difficulty of Christian faith in a universe where accidental causes seem to nullify the possibility of belief in God. In the opening of the

sequence we listen to the meditations of a woman as she reflects on
'the dark / Encroachment of that old catastrophe' which is the death
of Christ. She meditates in a setting where the painterly colour of
oranges, 'the green freedom' of a cockatoo and a certain leisurely
sensuousness are impinged upon by the thought of death and particularly by the death of Christ. Stevens registered this impingement
which, one might suggest, underlay his entire dialectic, with a marvellously sure touch:

> Complacencies of the peignoir, and late
> Coffee and oranges in a sunny chair,
> And the green freedom of a cockatoo
> Upon a rug mingle to dissipate
> The holy hush of ancient sacrifice.
> She dreams a little, and she feels the dark
> Encroachment of that old catastrophe,
> As a calm darkens among water-lights.
> The pungent oranges and bright, green wings
> Seem things in some procession of the dead,
> Winding across wide water, without sound.
> The day is like wide water, without sound,
> Stilled for the passing of her dreaming feet
> Over the seas, to silent Palestine,
> Dominion of the blood and sepulchre.

Yvor Winters, in the above-mentioned article, has written well of
the passage when he comments, 'The language has the greatest possible dignity and subtlety, combined with a perfect precision. The
imminence of absolute tragedy is felt and recorded, but the integrity
of the feeling mind is maintained . . . The calm clarity of tone would
be impossible were the terror emphasized for a moment at any
point . . .' This same 'calm clarity of tone' governs the superb last
lines of the poem where pigeons make

> Ambiguous undulations as they sink,
> Downward to darkness, on extended wings.

When Harriet Monroe first printed the poem in *Poetry* (*Chicago*),
she was troubled by the unappeasing tragedy of these final lines,
and moved into final position the penultimate section, one where
Stevens's tone is less sure, but where there is a brassy triumphalism
which might carry the anxious reader over what is actually being
said:

> Supple and turbulent, a ring of men
> Shall chant in orgy on a summer morn
> . Their boisterous devotion to the sun,
> Not as a god, but as a god might be,
> Naked among them, like a savage source . . .

In 'Shakespeare and the Stoicism of Seneca', T. S. Eliot complains about the stoical habit of 'cheering [oneself] up' in the face of absolute tragedy. Stevens's vision of boisterous pagans, or perhaps a future race of supermen worshipping the sun, has a rhetoric which is going to be characteristic of his more willed attempts to 'save the appearances'. The elation soon fades, however, into poetic plangency:

> And whence they come and whither they shall go,
> The dew upon their feet shall manifest.

The lift of the diction in this is banished by the last section and its more subdued stoicism:

> We live in an old chaos of the sun
> Or old dependency of day and night . . .

This world drifts on, with no divinely sanctioned purpose, through space, an 'island solitude', and the poem with its 'casual flocks of pigeons' enacts the movement 'downward to darkness' and annihilation.

If there is a loneliness in Stevens's poetry which places him close to the European scepticism of Nietzsche – a disbelief that found its most lasting poetic embodiment in the *Duino Elegies* of Rainer Maria Rilke – a certain bourgeois common sense and a taste for the good things of the passing moment kept him back from the frank despair hidden away in Nietzsche's diary entries: 'How have I borne life? By creating.' This might well have been the epitaph of the German poet Gottfried Benn, whose aesthetic nihilism, for which Nietzsche's example was crucial, often reads like a reductio ad absurdum of Stevens's 'belief' in 'the supreme fiction':

> A word, a phrase –: from cyphers rise
> Life recognised, a sudden sense,
> The sun stands still, mute are the skies,
> And all compacts it, stark and dense.

A word – a gleam, a flight, a spark,
A thrust of flames, a stellar trace –,
And then again – immense – the dark
Round world and I in empty space.
(Trans. Richard Exner)

Benn, one feels, sets the poetic act too far apart from other daily human acts of endeavour, negotiation and ordering, so that the light struck off it illuminates only itself and the waste land spread around it. In Germany, after the Nazi débâcle and the collapse of one practical attempt to create the Superman, no doubt it felt like that to be a poet. But if we are to interpret the world only in terms of 'feeling like that', poetry would soon be in danger of becoming merely an art of mood, hardening into a frigid stoicism. Stevens's 'American Sublime' suggests an American version of something of this kind, but the difference is at once apparent in the play of Stevens's humour:

. . . when General Jackson
Posed for his statue
He knew how one feels.
Shall a man go barefoot
Blinking and blank?
. . . And the sublime comes down
To the spirit itself,

The spirit and space,
The empty spirit
In vacant space.
What wine does one drink?
What bread does one eat?

Moreover Stevens hankers back to the images of Christian sacrament. So the intellectual and emotional need which resulted in his deathbed conversion to Catholicism was always present. At the time of *Ideas of Order* (1935) in which 'The American Sublime' appeared, it was the empty air rather than the sacraments that held the centre of his imagination, as in 'Evening Without Angels' from the same volume. In such a universe, nature reflects back at man the order his imagination has projected on it:

Sad men made angels of the sun, and of
The moon they made their own attendant ghosts . . .

This poet, whose ultimate conversion came as such a surprise to his admirers, had once reserved for the art of poetry the resolution of disbelief and the task of ordering:

> The epic of disbelief
> Blares oftener and soon, will soon be constant.

> Some harmonious skeptic in a skeptical music
> Will unite these figures of men and their shapes
> Will glisten again with motion . . .

Stevens can pursue his main theme, without the strenuosities implied here in 'Sad Strains of a Gay Waltz', in such pieces as 'A Postcard from the Volcano' (also from *Ideas of Order*), a poem where a hint of historical perspective enlarges the point of view:

> Children picking up our bones
> Will never know that these were once
> As quick as foxes on the hill;

> And that in autumn, when the grapes
> Made sharp air sharper by their smell
> These had a being, breathing frost;

> And least will guess that with our bones
> We left much more, left what still is
> The look of things, left what we felt

> At what we saw. The spring clouds blow
> Above the shuttered mansion-house
> Beyond our gate, and the windy sky

> Cries out a literate despair.
> We knew for long the mansion's look
> And what we said of it became

> A part of what it is . . . Children,
> Still weaving budded aureoles,
> Will speak our speech and never know,

> Will say of the mansion that it seems
> As if he that lived there left behind
> A spirit storming in blank walls,

> A dirty house in a gutted world,
> A tatter of shadows peaked to white,
> Smeared with the gold of the opulent sun.

Motifs first established in *Harmonium*, which are to be reintroduced

again and again for development and variation, are clearly present
here. They begin with the title. Why 'A Postcard from the Volcano'? The poem itself is the postcard, the necessarily arbitrary
snapshot of reality (there *could* be thirteen!) from a given angle. A
frame is being placed round the chaos of nature. An order results
from the angle at which the picture is taken. The volcano represents the unordered chaos, the material to be shaped by the
intervening human mind. The threat of the sky is there as usual.
The opulent sun the ring of men chant their devotion to in
'Sunday Morning' takes its place, as throughout Stevens's verse, as
the symbol of renewal and hope of a fresh beginning. The action
of the imagination, Stevens's recurrent theme, is present in the
suggestions that, though men die, they not only leave behind them
their bones, but also transmit their way of looking at things. Even
the sky 'cries out a literate despair' because of the poetic faculty
of the imagination to imprint itself on it. Similarly with the
mansion,

> We knew for long the mansion's look
> And what we said of it became
> A part of what it is . . .

That other allied theme of Stevens, that the house the imagination
builds out of the rubble of reality must fall into decay and return to
the primal chaos, thence to be rebuilt by a fresh act of intuitive
construction, is embodied in the fate of the shut mansion that
becomes 'a dirty house in a gutted world', then – with the possibility
of new life and coherence appearing through old decay –

> A tatter of shadows peaked to white,
> Smeared with the gold of the opulent sun.

In many poems of a similar scale, one feels that Stevens found the
best outlet for his talents, where the lightness of touch revolves a
theme that is treated humanly, delicately and with a nice balance of
tone: the postcard, the poet's fiction, restores a freshness to the
world we live in, though the moments of order are provisional and
threatened by time and the death of both individuals and cultures.
Humour and the play and inventiveness of language can keep these
moments bright in the mind, moments that serve to open up the

mind, 'The way, when we climb a mountain,/Vermont throws itself together.'

'The Idea of Order at Key West', another poem from the same volume, shows us once more the less wintry side of Stevens's imagination. This mid-period Stevens has a woman singing by 'the ever-hooded, tragic gestured sea', and the sound of her voice confronts 'the meaningless plungings of water and wind', so that a kind of ordering seems to take place as song measures its own ambience:

> It was her voice that made
> The sky acutest at its vanishing.
> She measured to the hour its solitude.
> She was the single artificer of the world
> In which she sang. And when she sang, the sea,
> Whatever self it had, became the self
> That was her song, for she was the maker. Then we
> As we beheld her striding there alone,
> Knew that there never was a world for her
> Except the one she sang and singing, made.

Even when the speaker of the poem and his companion, Ramon Fernandez, have turned towards the town, and the singing has ended, an 'idea of order' seems to have spread out from it to all they see:

> . . . The lights in the fishing boats at anchor there,
> As night descended, tilting in the air,
> Mastered the night and portioned out the sea
> Fixing emblazoned zones and fiery poles,
> Arranging, deepening, enchanting night.

'The Idea of Order at Key West' tells us much about one aspect of Stevens's imagination – an aspect Helen Vendler acutely, even harshly characterizes in *On Extended Wings. Wallace Stevens' Longer Poems* (1969), when she writes, 'Stevens' self seems to have presented him with a world excessively interior, in which the senses, with the exception of the eye, are atrophied or impoverished . . .' It is less the impoverishment than the interiority which strikes one in the poem under discussion:

> And when she sang, the sea,
> Whatever self it had, became the self
> That was her song, for she was the maker.

'She was the maker'. So in some sense, the singer is the poet and what she does he does. His words, like her notes, spilling out over nature or 'reality', annex it to human needs. Here her music virtually compels it into ordered significance. Yet, curiously, Stevens himself stands apart with 'pale Ramon', as if he cannot quite believe in the woman's opulent solipsism. ('The American Sublime', placed next in the book, even seems calculated to take the wind out of her sail.) Frank Doggett, in *Stevens' Poetry of Thought* (1966), introduces into a discussion of the poem a passage from Schopenhauer's *The World as Will and Idea* on the nature of the lyric: 'Schopenhauer says of the singer or pure lyrist "the subjective disposition, the affecting of the will, imparts its own hue to the perceived surroundings, and conversely, the surroundings communicate the reflex of their colour to the will".' In this act of absorption and expression Schopenhauer sees nature, through human consciousness, speaking to itself. Perhaps the most extreme example of this notion is the Wagnerian one when Isolde, in her final Liebestod, so imparts the hue of the lovers' situation to the conclusion of the opera that, as 'pure lyrist', she converts all elements to her own 'subjective disposition' and, indeed, knows

> that there never was a world for her
> Except the one she sang and, singing, made.

Wagner's other protagonists here virtually faded away beyond the veil of Maya by the final bars of Isolde's outpouring. Stevens, however, both in the poem and elsewhere, notes a recalcitrance in the situation – that which refuses to be wholly dissolved away into the conceptions of the mind keeps moving in from the peripheries to challenge the lyric accord. Thus in *The Rock* (1955), the last poem in this last gathering of poems is entitled 'Not Ideas About the Thing but the Thing Itself' and that 'world excessively interior', of which Vendler speaks, is once more beset from beyond itself:

> At the earliest ending of winter,
> In March, a scrawny cry from outside
> Seemed like a sound in his mind . . .
>
> That scrawny cry – it was
> A chorister whose c preceded the choir.
> It was part of the colossal sun,

> Surrounded by its choral rings,
> Still far away. It was like
> A new knowledge of reality.

'A new knowledge' implies a new person. Thus if there is something waiting to get into us, there is also something waiting to get out of us, 'the auroral creature musing in the mind', and the two are enabled to interact because, as Stevens says, 'Two things of opposite natures seem to depend on one another, the imagined and the real.' 'The auroral creature' finds release as 'the imagination pressing back against the pressure of reality' ('The Noble Rider and the Sound of Words').

So Stevens concludes *The Rock* by a variation on one of his earliest poems, 'Le Monocle de Mon Oncle', his listening outwards remembering back to the red bird 'that seeks out his choir'. This seeking out of the choir demands a continual poetic readjustment, a readjustment that Stevens in a note *On Poetic Truth*, possibly written in 1954, sees as a guarantee of novelty. His transition from this thought to the role of modern theology is at once unforeseen and yet characteristic of Stevens's leanings towards religion:

> Novelty must be inspired. But there must be novelty. This crisis is most evident in religion. The theologians whose thought is most astir today do make articulate a supreme need, ... the need to infuse into the ages of enlightenment an awareness of reality adequate to their achievements and such as will not be attenuated by them. There is one most welcome and authentic note; it is the insistence on a reality that forces itself upon our consciousness and refuses to be managed and mastered.

This presumably was what Stevens meant when he declared, of the supreme fiction, that 'it must change'. His hope was that it was a mask of the real. But so often the real seemed illusively distant and difficult to situate within the body of the universe.

I have said that Stevens is a poet of evocations rather than patterned inscapes. He hovers above and about his subjects rather than entering into their life co-extensive with his own. 'The American Sublime' may complain of 'The empty spirit / In vacant space', yet no square inch of American space is really empty or unpatterned. Desert or forest will both give back to the eye enough particulars to nourish and sustain if the demands of subjectivity are not exorbitant. The singer in 'The Idea of Order at Key West', in singing beside the sea, does not explore, say, her relation as a woman to the sea through the lunar cycle, or meditate on the fact that 'human tears' as the scientist tells us, 'are a re-creation of the primordial ocean which, in the first stages of evolution, bathed the first eyes' (R. L. Gregory, *Eye and Brain*). Hugh Kenner (*A Homemade World*, 1975), contrasting Stevens with William Carlos Williams, argues that the latter, unlike Stevens, 'was untroubled by any sense of [Nature's] remote exteriority because he sensed his own biological kinship with processes of struggle and growth':

> Compose. (No ideas
> but in things) Invent!
> Saxifrage is my flower that splits
> the rocks.

And Kenner goes on: 'A way to be part of the world is to consider that through the world as through yourself moves the energy of a cellular dance.' He quotes Williams's prolonged meditation on the unfolding of a flower, *The Crimson Cyclamen*, and concludes:

> Helped out by experiences Wordsworth couldn't have – time-lapse films of opening flowers, and a biology of dynamics, not of classifications – this kind of writing about natural processes belongs to a new phase in the history of poetry. To a reader of professional books on nutrition and mitosis, 'Nature' meant something both intimate and thrusting.

Stevens's sensibility was formed in a previous era and from sources other than these. For all the differences, his was a sensibility far closer to Wordsworth's than to time-lapse photography. Yet Stevens, too, relishes the idea of the dance. It was this that drew him towards the end of his life to write his introduction to a translation of Paul Valéry's *Dance and the Soul*. Why was Stevens drawn to Valéry's conception of the dance and in what way does it differ from the cellular dance of which Kenner speaks? To try to answer these questions reveals further evidence of Stevens's persisting inheritance from the nineteenth century. *The Rock*, the final section of *Collected Poems*, appeared in 1955. To this late phase belong also his two Valéry prefaces – the one already mentioned and another to *Eupalinos*. In some of the poems of this phase Stevens often seems to be content with the pleasures of simply not knowing, of being unsure. And this acceptance produces some of his most quietly impressive poems – 'Long and Sluggish Lines', 'To an Old Philosopher in Rome', 'Song of Fixed Accord', 'The River of Rivers in Connecticut', 'The World as Meditation'. *The Rock* itself is more austere than these, swept clean of all gaudiness. The Valéry prefaces seem almost to have stepped back in time from these works towards a more aggressively aphoristic stance.

At the end of his preface to Valéry's dialogue *Dance and the Soul*, 'Man,' says Stevens somewhat unexpectedly, 'has many ways to attain the divine and the way of Eupalinos [namely the architect, the supreme constructor, in the dialogue of that name] and the way of Athikte [the dancer in the other dialogue] and the various ways of Paul Valéry are a few of them.' One wonders if Stevens meant something just as vague here by 'the divine' as Valéry by 'the soul' in his title *Dance and the Soul*. The way of Eupalinos was the knowledge of his craft – architecture, and, by analogy, poetic construction. What of the way of Athikte, the dancer who gives herself to the pattern of the dance as the stylist gives himself to his style? In Valéry's dialogue, Socrates, who is present at her performance, exclaims, 'Is not the dance, O my friends, that deliverance of our body entirely possessed by the spirit of falsehood, and of music which is falsehood, and drunk with the denial of null reality? – look at that body, which leaps as flame replaces flame, look how it spurns and betramples what is true.' This conception of the dance recalls one aspect of Stevens's conception of poetry as the supreme fiction, and of style as a fine excess, the panache that makes life bearable as against 'the sorry verities' that trouble 'the weeping burgher', in the poem of that name. Valéry's 'null reality' and Stevens's 'sorry verities' seem closely related. So Athikte's dance, in the face of all that, is scarcely a dance of biological kinship with a cellular universe but rather a drunken solipsism. This is, of course, Paul Valéry speaking and not Wallace Stevens. Yet this Nietzschean metaphysic of the self-expressive and self-consuming flame that dances before a meaningless universe must have appealed to Stevens in certain moods – why else this late tribute to Valéry's prose? There had even been a touch of Valéry's ninetyish bravado in Stevens's use of the word 'exquisite', when he had once written: 'The final belief is to believe in a fiction, which you know to be a fiction, there being nothing else. The exquisite truth is to know that it is a fiction and that you believe in it willingly.' A more persuasive formulation of Stevens runs, 'We accept the unknown even when we are most skeptical' ('The Irrational Element in Poetry').

But poetry qualifies in subtle ways such declarative utterances about the supreme fiction and *The Rock* goes on to qualify much that Stevens had said in prose. (By the same token, the prose Valéry is not the great poet of *Le Cimetière Marin*.) If, in *The Rock*, 'The World as Meditation' is 'about' the supreme fiction, it is also 'about' an attitude of mind that is content to repose within its own uncertainty – one close to that 'negative capability' Keats admired, 'when a man is capable of being in uncertainties, mysteries, doubts, without any irritable reaching after fact and reason'. This is a scepticism that nourishes rather than undermines. In the poem, in Penelope's meditation, the world has gone on renewing its promise and she has awaited its revelation. Her waiting could as well be that of a religious discipline as of a meditation on that supreme fiction which can be approached only by way of 'notes towards', but is never to be finally apprehended:

> Is it Ulysses that approaches from the east,
> The interminable adventurer? The trees are mended.
> That winter is washed away. Someone is moving
> On the horizon and lifting himself up above it.
> A form of fire approaches . . .

'*Je vis un rêve permanent, qui ne s'arrête ni nuit ni jour,*' is the epigraph this poem carries from the violinist and composer, Georges Enesco. Penelope has lived this dream out of a kind of animal faith, in a world that exceeds her and yet promises more than its exhaustible present:

> The trees had been mended, as an essential exercise
> In an inhuman meditation, larger than her own.

For Stevens, the world itself must be expressed with the image of an interiority, as if he remembered from his reading of Schopenhauer that notion of nature speaking to itself, and meditating through the human consciousness. But such philosophic notions are provisional, and so are all 'final' certainties:

> But was it Ulysses? Or was it only the warmth of the sun
> On her pillow? The thought kept beating in her like her heart.

The two kept beating together. It was only day.

It was Ulysses and it was not. Yet they had met,
Friend and dear friend and a planet's encouragement . . .

The phrase 'It was only day' seems a massive and miraculous understatement, massive and miraculous enough to sustain that pulse beat of her heart and imagination:

She would talk a little to herself as she combed her hair,
Repeating his name with its patient syllables,
Never forgetting him that kept coming constantly so near.

If, to borrow Winters' word, the woman in the peignoir amid coffee and oranges in 'Sunday Morning' is a hedonist, Penelope, in her patience, is a stoic but not of the inhuman kind. As she takes cognizance of a world that exceeds the human, she feels within herself a 'barbarous strength' that 'would never fail'. Stevens, too, lived out his last days, from all accounts, in exemplary and stoic calm, through the final stages of the stomach cancer which an operation had failed to remove. He had imagined a self to meet that, also, in his meditation on the last days of one of his chief mentors, George Santayana, 'To an Old Philosopher in Rome':

It is a kind of total grandeur at the end,
With every visible thing enlarged and yet
No more than a bed, a chair and moving nuns,
The immensest theatre, the pillared porch,
The look of candles in your ambered room . . .

This final variation on that early theme of Stevens, 'Downwards to darkness on extended wings' allows the wings to extend with a convincingly majestic sweep. What is contemplated here is not the image of a solipsist dancing on the brink of the void, but

The human end in the spirit's greatest reach,
The extreme of the known in the presence of the extreme
Of the unknown . . .

This poem also is a late triumph of Stevens's middle style which seems to have survived that hedonist's progress Winters once lamented. So do many of the fine late poems that appeared after his death in *Opus Posthumus*.

WILLA CATHER AND
'A WAY OF REMEMBERING YOUTH'
BLANCHE H. GELFANT

'To fulfill the dreams of one's youth' – that, says Father Vaillant in *Death Comes for the Archbishop* (1927), is 'the best that can happen to a man.' That was also the best that could have happened to a woman like Willa Cather (1873–1947), who believed that youth was a time of aspiration, passion, and desire – a vitalizing time for those who possessed 'the treasure of creative power'. In *The Song of the Lark* (1915), Cather's autobiographical heroine Thea Kronberg possesses this treasure, and she knows that her art – that all art – is 'a way of remembering youth'. In time, Cather would become famous for her evocations of youth, the early striving years of a man or woman that, at best, coincided with the founding years of a country. In lyrical tones that modulated from celebration to lament, Cather called forth memories of America as a young land, 'not a country at all', *My Ántonia* (1918) notes, 'but the material out of which countries are made'. The prairies of the Midwest are still pristine in *O Pioneers!* (1913) and *My Ántonia*, their red grass swaying; and the Southwest's red sand-hills in *Death Comes for the Archbishop* are still peopled with Indians and Catholic missionary priests on horseback. In *Shadows on the Rock* (1931), Cather turned her retrospective gaze upon Quebec and saw, as if centuries had not elapsed, the 'proud' rock upon which French settlers had yet to transplant their Old World traditions. Places as inhospitable to humans as rock, desert, or treeless prairies had existed in the past as potentiality, Cather thought, imbuing them with the essential quality of youth; such places needed to fulfill their historic destinies as urgently as a young woman like Thea Kronberg needed to fulfill herself as an artist. Remembering the dreams of youth, Cather turned to the historic past for her settings, recovering unforgettable images of a country in the process of beginning and then, as it grew older, in various stages of loss. Youth and decline, a patterned movement in Cather's fiction, modulated the mood of her novels from celebration to nostalgia or regret.

In her last published novel, *Sapphira and the Slave Girl* (1940), Cather recorded her earliest memories, those of her childhood years in Virginia, where she lived in her grandparents' home Willowshade until she was nine. Although some critics consider this work attenuated, it merits close examination because it reveals synoptically all of the elements of Cather's art; indeed, it permits a succinct review of her art while providing also an introduction. First of all, it testifies to Cather's extraordinary power to recall the past. Though she visited Virginia in 1938 in preparation for writing, her memory needed no refreshing, for she remembered Willowshade exactly as it had been, with its nearby creek and its mill, its back wing and portico. In the novel she reproduced the parlor with its Wilton carpet of 'pink roses and green leaves', its sofas fastened with 'tidies' and heavy chairs fitted with 'fat horsehair chair-bottoms'. She rendered exactly the fields and trees of Willowshade and its profusion of flowers: syringa, scentless dogwood, jonquils, lilacs, morning-glories, wild honeysuckle with 'long, trembling stamens which made each blossom look like a brilliant insect caught in flight'. Such intimate and particularizing details give all of Cather's novels a compelling sense of immediacy, of life in the very process of being lived; consequently, her books never seem to be 'something invented' but rather – to use a self-reflexive phrase from *A Lost Lady* (1923) – 'living creatures, caught in the very behavior of living'.

Cather's re-creation of the past, her way of remembering, always involved ambiguities. Though she wished to separate art, which she believed should illuminate timeless universal truths, from timely social issues, inevitably these issues entered her novels and remained there in a state of irresolution. The slave-trade was obviously nefarious in *Sapphira and the Slave Girl*, but the experience of the captured Jezebel aboard a slave-ship and on a slave-block shows that survival is possible. Indeed, Jezebel may be said to prevail; at the end of her long life she is cared for by Sapphira, who remembers to bring the dying old woman her favorite flowers. Moreover, the slave Samson refuses the freedom offered by his master, and young Nancy, sexually pursued and harassed, almost turns away from the chance to escape. If mistress serves slave in *Sapphira and the Slave Girl* (though she also beats her with a wooden hair brush), and slave refuses freedom, then the moral issues the novel raises become murky. Only Rachel Blake is unequivocal in her view that '*owning people was wrong*'. The ambiguities that reveal and conceal the social tensions in *Sapphira and the Slave Girl* are epitomized in Cather's description of Mill House (drawn from Willowshade): 'All was orderly in front . . . Behind the house lay another world; a helter-skelter scattering . . .'. Like other Cather novels, *Sapphira and the Slave Girl* ends with an epilogue. Set twenty-five years after Nancy's escape from Mill House, the epilogue restores the order that had been shattered by sexual jealousy and the violence of slavery. It describes Nancy's reunion with her now aged mother, a scene witnessed by Sapphira's granddaughter, who is Cather herself being remembered as a child of five.

When she was nine, Cather's life in Virginia ended abruptly as her family moved to the vast empty prairies of Nebraska. In one of the most widely quoted moments in *My Ántonia*, Cather re-creates her own feelings as a child coming into a prairie land where, as her character Jim Burden says, 'there seemed to be nothing to see; no fences, no creeks or trees, no hills or fields'. The loss of a familiar landscape, of the hills of Virginia with its creeks, trees, fields and fences, made one lose one's sense of self. Like Jim, who felt himself 'erased, blotted out', Cather experienced in Nebraska's prairies 'a kind of erasure of personality'. That was her phrase in a 1913 interview; in 1921, she said simply that the new country had made her feel 'little and homesick and lonely'. However, by 1921 the novels Cather had written celebrated childhood on the Nebraska prairies as 'the best days', those that in *My Ántonia* flee fast but leave memories that 'are better than anything that can ever happen to one again'.

Cather's first eighteen months in Nebraska were spent on her grandparents' farm on the Divide, a stretch of high plains that she loved to explore. If her sense of self had been erased, it was now being restored as her mind absorbed rich and lasting images of an extraordinary landscape that seemed alive and in motion, as if, she wrote in *My Ántonia*, 'the shaggy grass were a sort of loose hide, and underneath it herds of wild buffalo were galloping, galloping . . .'. For Cather, landscape was an emotion as well as a place, even more, a living entity which she described as sentient and changing, involved in an intense life of its own. Wherever she was, this life excited her creative imagination, not only by providing delicately particularized settings for her stories, but also by inspiring plots consonant with the inner drama of a place. The Divide was dramatic in its vastness and volatility, its rapidly changing seasons producing radical changes in weather and way of life. These were closely reproduced in Cather's Nebraska novels as the pioneer farmers of *O Pioneers!* and *My Ántonia* accommodated to the seasons, to their regularity and their vagaries – the sudden hail storms, heat waves, blizzards, and droughts that made life on the prairies seem unpredictable and unprotected. In *A Lost Lady*, a later Nebraska novel set in a later time, the seasons determine the Forresters' comings and goings until finally, the victims of financial failure, the Captain and his lady become the prisoners of winter.

Though all three Nebraska novels are episodic, fragmented in structure, their time sequence fractured as years elapse or are elided, they create an illusion of coherence, even of inevitability, as they describe the prairie seasons succeeding each other in their irrefrangible pattern. *My Ántonia* begins in 'glorious autumn', moves to winter, when the snow 'spilled out of heaven', describes spring as sheer ecstasy – 'the throb of it . . . the vital essence of its everywhere' – and with summer resolves the year and its own form. Creating art out of her intimate sense of Nebraska, a place that had left American writers uninspired, Cather could say of herself what Virgil is imagined by Jim Burden as saying when he wrote of his 'little rural neighborhood': 'I was the first to bring the Muse into my country.'

In 1884 when her family moved to the small nearby town of Red Cloud, Cather discovered another indigenous place to which she would bring a rather skeptical muse. Red Cloud appears in her works under a variety of names: Black Hawk, Sweet Water, Hanover, Moonstone, Frankfort, Haverford. In 'The Sculptòr's Funeral', an early and much-anthologized story, Cather depicted the Midwest small town as 'a borderland between ruffianism and civilization', a marginal place that stifled its aspiring young artists, who had to leave it to survive. 'Old Mrs Harris', a late story and one of Cather's most touching, portrays a young woman's desire to escape from her small town with the ambivalence and complexity of vision that characterize Cather's best fiction. Vicki Templeton, the young protagonist, represents Cather as she remembers herself in Red Cloud, centered upon her own needs and ambitions. While the story justifies Vicki's desire for a college education, it shows how youth and desire blind the girl to the problems of her mother and grandmother. Both women are displaced persons whose Southern manners cause them to be misunderstood or rebuffed by the Midwest community. Both are following 'the long road that leads through things unguessed at and unforeseeable', a woman's road that Vicki will someday travel. Cather's own road would lead her ultimately to write this beautiful, perceptive, and self-forgiving story of her young days in Red Cloud, but first, like her young heroine, she had to leave her family and small town and seek a new life.

That new life began in the early fall of 1890 when Cather left Red Cloud for Lincoln, the capital of Nebraska and site of the state university from which Cather was graduated in 1895. Though Cather condensed and romanticized her university years in the 'Lena Lingard' section of *My Ántonia*, she re-created its essential meaning to her when she described the mood of the college and of her character Jim Burden as a student. Remembering the University of Nebraska, barely twenty years old at the time, she wrote in *My Ántonia*: 'There was an atmosphere of endeavor, of expectancy and bright hopefulness about the young college that had lifted its head from the prairie only a few years ago.' In this new and expectant atmosphere, Jim Burden was introduced to 'the world of ideas', experiencing 'that time of mental awakening as one of the happiest' in his life. Highly active in Lincoln, Cather became a reporter for the city newspaper, reviewing plays, operas, and books at a prodigious rate. Constantly confronting works of art, she began to formulate the aesthetic principles that would shape her career. She was at the same time writing and publishing her first stories, but under the necessity of earning a living, she had to subordinate her fiction to journalism and reviewing. Her activities in Lincoln prepared her thus for an editorial career that took her to Pittsburgh and subsequently to New York, her home for forty years.

In New York, rather remarkably, Cather became editor for the famous 'muck-raking' magazine *McClure's*. Although she was uninterested in social reform and described reformers as dreary or fanatical, she successfully edited *McClure's Magazine* for six years, deploring the time it demanded but finding the opportunities for travel it afforded ultimately crucial to her writing. For while on assignment in Boston in 1908, she met Sara Orne Jewett, the author of *The Country of the Pointed Firs* and of stories set in a Maine landscape that Jewett knew as intimately as Cather knew Nebraska's prairies. Jewett urged Cather to describe the country she had internalized as her memory of the past. In a statement that was to be widely quoted, she wrote Cather: 'The thing that teases the mind over and over for years, and at last gets itself down rightly on paper – whether little or great, it belongs to Literature.' Jewett's advice was prescient, for the first novel Cather had published in 1912, *Alexander's Bridge*, was imitative and contrived; set in sophisticated London and Boston, it lacked the aesthetic authenticity Cather would achieve in her prairie novel *O Pioneers!*, the work in which, she said, she finally found her own voice.

While *O Pioneers!* celebrated the striving years when a country and a heroic young woman grew to maturity, it sounded dissonant antiphonal voices through its multiple plots. The life that comes to fruition in the main plot, as Alexandra Bergson's dream of a great nurturing farmland is realized, contrasts with the precipitately violent death that in the subplot strikes Alexandra's adored brother and the woman he loves; inevitably in Cather's novels sex proves dangerous if not deadly. Cather's ambivalence extended to the new land, as much the novel's protagonist as its heroine, Alexandra Bergson. Like many of Cather's characters, the land presents a divided self. On the one hand, it is 'a wild thing that had its ugly moods' and showed them to man; the 'absence' on it of 'human landmarks' was 'depressing and disheartening'. On the other hand, there was 'something frank and joyous and young in the open face of the country': its atmosphere was 'tonic', reflecting its 'strength and resoluteness'. These are the qualities Alexandra personifies: 'a tall, strong girl, . . . [who] walked rapidly and resolutely, as if she knew exactly where she was going and what she was going to do next'. Alexandra and the land were both moving towards the future, which the novel celebrates in the earth's rich harvests and the farmers' prosperity. *O Pioneers!* describes the success of human effort, but it implies that without a recognition of the wide world that lies beyond the prairies, the striving of its immigrant pioneers is diminished, their struggle limited in meaning. As Alexandra says: 'If the world were no wider than my cornfields, if there were not something beside this, I wouldn't feel that it was much worth while to work.' Life on the prairies, Alexandra knows, could be 'just the same thing over and over'; 'it's what goes on in the world that reconciles' her to the intrinsic monotony of that which she values, the synchronization of human rhythm with the steady rhythm of the seasons. Beyond both monotony and excitement, beyond human life on the prairies or in the vast cities, an eternal order prevails, which Alexandra, like many Cather characters, sees symbolized in the stars.

In 1912, Cather had made the first of several visits to the Southwest, where she encountered a startling desert landscape scattered with traces of a pre-Columbian Indian art and culture that she found inspiring, the relics of an old time renewing her artistic vision. In *The Song of the Lark*, she attributed to her heroine her own sense of spiritual upsurge and rededication in Arizona; she has Thea return home as she did, determined to give her life entirely to her work. Some years later, New Mexico inspired 'Tom Outland's Story' in *The Professor's House* (1925), an interpolated tale that tells how young Outland discovered an abandoned stone city created by Pueblo Indians in an age long past. The story represents a consummation of Cather's descriptive powers. Her style is easy, lambent, and translucently beautiful as she describes air, sun, water – the elements of life – with unmatched purity and passion. The desert landscape also inspired a late work that some critics consider her best, *Death Comes for the Archbishop*. She said she knew she must write this historical romance as soon as she saw the Cathedral of St Francis in Santa Fe. She turned the story of its construction into a spiritual apotheosis for her Father Latour, who with his faithful vicar – both based on historical priests – brought God's word to the desert wilderness.

Though Cather's prairie novels brought her fortune and fame, and her war novel, *One of Ours* (1922), won her the Pulitzer Prize, her critical reception has had its vicissitudes. In the 1930s, critics concerned with immediate social issues found love stories like *Lucy Gayheart* (1935) vapidly irrelevant, and historical novels like *Shadows on the Rock* (1931) inexcusably escapist. (As a Romantic, Cather valued escape as the purpose of literature.) Subsequently, however, critics began to discern beneath the apparent simplicity and artlessness of Cather's writing an art that was involuted, complex, elusive, and rich. Some found significant mythic analogues for earth mothers like Alexandra of *O Pioneers!* and Ántonia of *My Ántonia*, and others, significant literary parallels for characters like Myra Henshawe of *My Mortal Enemy* (1926) and Marion Forrester of *A Lost Lady*. Currently, feminist critics are discovering that Cather portrays women possessed of great strength – driving, creative, and successful women as different as Alexandra Bergson, Ántonia Shimerda, and Thea Kronberg. They discern also Cather's awareness of women's victimization, shown not only in stories that blatantly dramatize a woman's plight, like 'A Wagner Matinee', but also in self-subverting depictions of such ostensibly privileged women as Marion Forrester or Sapphira Dodderidge, who suffer because of the restrictive and yet demanding roles assigned to them by society.

As with many American writers, Cather's ideas required her art, for stripped of her language they seem merely conventionalized expressions of antagonism towards a mechanical age and of romantic longings for a lost golden time. That time is usually revealed as one's own childhood, when one lives the 'realest' life as one's 'original, unmodified' self. These are the words of Godfrey St Peter in *The Professor's House*, a character at the height of his career who discovers that career, wife, family 'were not his life at all, but a chain of events that had happened to him'. His real and inviolable self was the solitary boy he had been and whom he could recover through memory or, more ominously, through death. For Cather, remembering constituted a supreme creative act. She returned to the historic past and to her childhood in order to create romantic visions of what had been and had been lost. However, she often subverted her own romances by portraying the violence that had existed in the past and the dangers of fixation upon the past in characters who, like St Peter, found the present 'bloomless' and 'without joy'. Perhaps her characters feared a joyless life because they had experienced happiness so deeply and completely that life lived without ecstasy seemed to them not merely dull but dismal. No one wrote with such immediacy of happiness as Cather – happiness simply in breathing the air, or placing a hand on a tree, or tracing the clouds in the sky. The emotions Cather evoked in her stories, rather than their ideas, give them the universality that she believed belonged to art. Anywhere in the world one can understand the happiness Jim Burden felt when he lay with his back against the sun-warmed pumpkins:

'I was entirely happy. Perhaps we feel like it when we die and become a part of something entire, whether it is sun and air, or goodness and knowledge. At any rate, that is happiness; to be dissolved into something complete and great.'

This last sentence is Willa Cather's epitaph, inscribed on her tombstone in Jaffrey, New Hampshire. She died quietly in her home in New York in 1947, having remained faithful in her art to her way of remembering.

'THE FLIGHT OF THE ROCKET' and
'THE LAST GOOD COUNTRY':
FITZGERALD AND HEMINGWAY IN THE 1920s

WARNER BERTHOFF

The upper Middle West of the United States, Fitzgerald's and Hemingway's home territory, is the hardest of American regions to characterize culturally and historically, though conceivably the easiest to be surprised by. During these writers' early life it had been substantially settled and occupied for barely two generations. As a developed, English-speaking society it was not older than Texas or California, and while American industrialization rolled forward in the later nineteenth century it was, if anything, more volatile, more continuously self-transforming. French-built St Louis apart, the chief midwestern cities had been, as late as 1850, not much more than accidental commercial villages and frontier trading posts. In the decades following they had come to dominate the productive economy of the country and coincidentally to nurture, in their booming growth, a main share of post-Civil War popular mythology. The inventors Edison and Kettering were midwesterners, as were the illustrious generals who had salvaged victory in the war and, after 1870, most of the presidents who were absentmindedly overseeing America's surge to world power. So too, by birth or adoption, were Rockefeller and McCormick, Clement Studebaker (model for Dreiser's Archibald Kane), Orville and Wilbur Wright, Henry Ford and the founders (Armour, Swift) of Chicago's meatpacking fortunes and, equal to any, the indisputably fabulous James J. Hill who, coming at eighteen to 1859s St Paul five years after Fitzgerald's embarrassingly self-made and Irish-born grandfather, built the St Paul Pacific and Great Northern Railroads and in alliance with the New Yorker J. P. Morgan outgeneraled E. H. Harriman himself in the gigantic merger battles of 1901.

At all levels men of this era built their lives in the upper Middle West on the jagged cusp between the original frontier and runaway modernization. Like Hemingway's doctor-father they might forge a solid professional practice in a prosperous new Chicago suburb, supporting in comfort wives and children anxious for both social rank and individual notice of some undefined sort, and yet return as often as they could to the ruggedness of frontier conditions, as to the near wilderness of northern Michigan where as a boy Hemingway discovered his lifelong passion for shooting and fishing and the tactical mastery of difficult terrain.

Far more than in later decades the chief midwestern cities during this expansive half-century also took the lead in cultural innovation. Not for nothing was Chicago selected as the site of the World's Columbian Exposition of 1893. It was from a base in Chicago that the economist Veblen mockingly dissected the twin systems of modern business enterprise and modern leisure-class self-gratification; it was in Chicago that Louis Sullivan and Frank Lloyd Wright set about revolutionizing American architectural practice. It was in newspaper offices in Chicago and other midwestern cities that Dreiser gained his earliest national reputation, as did, after him, the mordantly innovative vernacular satirists George Ade and Ring Lardner. And it was in Chicago first of all that American literary modernism began to stabilize its voice and outlook, with the founding of Harriet Monroe's *Poetry* in 1912 and Margaret Anderson's *Little Review* in 1913. More or less inevitably it was to Chicago that the autodidact midwestern modernist Sherwood Anderson, who appeared in both journals and would leave his narrative stamp on early stories of both Hemingway (1898–1961) and Fitzgerald (1896–1940), came to begin re-creating himself as an autochthonous American artist.

In the Midwest after 1900 the rules for art as for the whole conduct of life were there to be remade. An American from the Midwest – in a detail of popular mythology picked up by the east-coast narrator of Edmund Wilson's *I Thought of Daisy* (1929) – 'might turn into anything'. So he might, at twenty-five, brashly set about competing as an equal with the recognized masters of his trade and begin at once, as Fitzgerald wrote Max Perkins in 1922, to create in his own fashion 'something *new* – something extraordinary and beautiful and simple and intricately patterned'. At the same time the midwestern temper was, rather to its own chagrin, self-consciously provincial, looking east and to Europe for ultimate approval.

Confident of being at 'the warm center of the world' – the words are Nick Carraway's in *The Great Gatsby* – it was also wary of being exposed, especially following its excited excursion eastward into the Great War, as only at 'the ragged edge' of a newly formed and still forming universe. It was securely planted yet indefinably restless and unsettled, producing after 1910 and 1920 both the monumental complacency that made *Main Street* and *Babbitt* period bywords and young ambitions ready to capitalize without constraint on a new era's superflux of fresh creative opportunity.

For Fitzgerald and Hemingway as writers the particular form of opportunity was determined by the onrush of Anglo-European modernism, that liberation of individual talent in all the arts in which Americans like Eliot, Pound, and Gertrude Stein were already formative influences. It was the modernist renaissance, and the new openness of judgement and behavior generally, that drew them as writers to Paris in the early 1920s, as it was the emergent critical consensus supporting modernism that, greeting with discriminating approval what they themselves considered their best work, helped each establish an authorial identity he could not subsequently live down. Inevitably they met in Paris in the mid-twenties, as they might well not have done living and working only in the United States. (It was the period, Gertrude Stein remarked, when 'everybody was twenty-six'.) From that point forward their careers and reputations closely shadowed each other, not least in their own competitive self-scrutiny. Sharp differences in temperament, in popularity and fortune, and of course in compositional signature only heighten for us, half a century later, impressions of a fundamental resemblance.

Each of them, for example, came early and all at once into his distinctive mastery. Each accomplished, before reaching thirty, work he would not afterwards surpass or even quite match, except fragmentarily. Each achieved that limited yet intense originality of style which sooner or later attracts bluff parody but which no one else can betray into parody as they themselves did – styles capable of single passages as poignant and memorable as great lyric poetry, startling readers into recognition of things massively felt but not yet distilled into precise awareness.

Each of them too, it may finally be said, found one central story to tell and one story only, establishing it early and returning to it again and again. Each strikes us, even at his best, as writing from a condition of intense imaginative arrest, a condition which nevertheless furnishes an attentive steadiness and conviction able at times to counterfeit the most complex imaginative control. Each in his most durable work projected morally compromised narrator-participants a few important years older than himself, making them party at critical moments in the story to the worst corruption narrationally on offer. Each, that is, spoke through a narrating voice of a certain fixed kind, one looking back without relief to some catastrophic turning point that cannot be reversed or, concurrently, to some lost and mourned alternative. Fitzgerald mainly elects to give us the flash and wide flare that forerun the predestined catastrophe. He gives us, to use his own figure, the upward 'flight of the rocket' – provisional title for *The Beautiful and Damned*, his first fully calculated major undertaking. Hemingway pivots his relentless narratives of disaster and defeat around ironic recollections of lost primal circumstance, symbolized in particular by the vision of some 'last good country' – title of the latest and longest of his autobiographic Nick Adams stories. But the cohering fictional and interpretive logic driving each man's story forward seems much the same, born from the same explosive convergence of historical occasion and native circumstance.

Fitzgerald, three years senior, was sooner off the mark. Exposed at an eastern school and at Princeton to at least headline notions of modern literary seriousness and favored by the attention of a few extraordinary undergraduate friends (Edmund Wilson and John Bishop first of all), he aimed high from the start, if only in transferring reveries of being one of 'the big men' of his time from the context of college athletics and theatricals to that of high literary achievement. When at twenty-one he began constructing a novel his head was overrun with competing models of up-to-date excellence. The project's original title was *The Romantic Egotist*, a pairing of lecture-hall categorizations that suggests the particular character of its normal enough first-novel factitiousness. It may also suggest something essential to genuineness of achievement at any level: on the one hand a sense, however limited its first expression, of what affective focus the writer's central intuitions are most responsive to, and on the other, in that first title's loosely oxymoronic form, of the need to balance self-projection with undeceived self-judgement. At the core of all Fitzgerald's writing is a surprisingly resourceful intuition of the logistics as well as the pathos of modern egoism, the glamor to itself but equally the self-destructiveness. But his very soundness of conception on this ground too often allowed him to be careless and uncertain in devising a structure for what he knew to say.

In purpose and design *This Side of Paradise* (1920) spills all over the place, though it has the beguiling impudence to try to make aesthetic capital of its own disorderliness. Its remarkable public success assured Fitzgerald that he was on a composite track worth following. An exercise in a displaced bourgeois-suburban version of the coming-of-age format that in English fiction traces back through Compton Mackenzie's *Sinister Street* to *The Ordeal of Richard Feverel*, *This Side of Paradise* aims at being as well a frontline history of contemporary morals and of an epoch-marking revolution in popular manners. It also aims at assessing the uncharted social and historical transformations that furnish its episodic matrix. The transparently autobiographical protagonist is someone who, as we hear in the last chapter's Shavian dialogue with a 'big man' from the world of corporate power, has read Walter Lippmann on drift and mastery and Henry Adams on modern historical acceleration as well as Shaw himself; the theme-codifying prefaces to Shaw's plays are an obvious model for the division into short titled sections that ratchets the story forward and covers for its shortfall of dramatic interest.

Shaw's epigrammatic conciseness and the hyperbolic American equivalent to be found *c.* 1920 in H. L. Mencken's commentaries were valuable antidotes to *Sinister Street*, a doubly bad precedent with its 800-plus pages about youthful self-centeredness facing a compromised world and its Edwardian mix of neo-Gothic sensationalism and modern disenchantment ('a voice insinuating, softly metallic ... fingers that touched his wrist as lightly as silk ... a horrible sense of publicity ... of money hard and round and powerful'). But Fitzgerald – that one among the younger writers, Gertrude Stein said, 'who wrote naturally in sentences' – trusted too much to phrase-making, to the forced adjective, the offhand analytic generalization, the snap of a moralizing summary. What is intended as shrewdly penetrating comes off as mere knowingness ('She had that curious mixture of the social and the artistic temperaments found often in two classes, society women and actresses'). To any reader for whom, after *The Great Gatsby*, Long Island will forever be 'that slender riotous island which extends itself due east from New York', the sprinkling of words like 'riotous' all around the early fiction – the Princeton Triangle show as 'a riotous mystery' and so forth – is a performative embarrassment.

Fitzgerald's overdrawn second novel, *The Beautiful and Damned* (1922), was even more of a patchup, yet stands as a more ambitious attempt at full-dress psychological portraiture and at a representative chapter of contemporary moral history. Neither the title nor the airy knowingness of the opening sentence – 'In 1913, when Anthony Patch was twenty-five, two years were already gone since irony, the Holy Ghost of this later day, had, theoretically at least, descended upon him' – are encouraging portents. But in charting the marriage and life-progress of two children of American wealth reared to take unquestioningly for their own all that pleased them in life and seeking in every crisis only to be 'comfortable and safe' in some recovered simulacrum of childhood protectedness, the novel takes on more affective momentum than, on any page, its self-preening swagger would seem to permit. It has the ambiguous pressure of Fitzgerald's own moral vanity behind it, source of both his worst lapses and his truest apprehensions. (It has also his rising ambivalence about his own hectically glamorous marriage and career.) In its basically simple design the book bears an odd resemblance to Dreiser's powerful *Sister Carrie* (1900), most of all when the draining away of the male protagonist's moral strength is set against the still ascending curve of the 'almost masculine' heroine's self-possession, though in the end she does *not* succeed as an actress and he regresses into infantilism and the company of Ivy League dullards and wastrels. It may be seen as a version of *Sister Carrie* (whose author Fitzgerald considered, along with Mencken, 'the most important man in the country') composed by someone who has found out about Flaubert's *Sentimental Education*. It is also, in clear outline, a mock-up of *Tender Is the Night*, Fitzgerald's short-circuited masterwork of the 1930s.

Interestingly this novel's best moments are perhaps its most surrealistic, when Fitzgerald's trademark blend of excitability and apprehensiveness precipitates directly in something random and phantasmagoric – like the moment on the eve of Anthony Patch's marriage when the noise of a woman's demented laughter comes to him across an alleyway as the noise of life itself: 'Life was that sound out there, that ghastly reiterated female sound.' It is possible to think that the best of the short stories Fitzgerald was pouring out and successfully marketing alongside his first two novels are those most open to the same fantastication.

These early stories, one after another set out along some pattern of vaulting hopefulness and remorseless disillusion, have been praised for their social acuity, their control over the complex stratifications of American behavior. But the farther in time we stand from them, the more narrowly angled seems their grasp on any actual society. This is not simply a matter of their absorption in the rituals of wealth and near-wealth. What they know, what Fitzgerald himself knew, is an affective reality independent of the particulars of actual social encounter but also possibly – and this is its strength – anterior to them: the reality, that is, of socially expressed envy and humiliation, of unappeasable restlessness and raw unfocused desiring. Over and over these stories tell how, faced with everything unanticipatable in modern life, the imagination takes refuge in alternating fantasies of domination and ruin, magical conquest and equally magical, or demonic, frustration and bafflement.

In plotting his stories Fitzgerald depended on contrivances and interventions as manipulative as those patented by O. Henry, still the master spirit of the popular magazine market. As good a later story as 'Babylon Revisited', with its compounded representation of loss and regret and ambiguous self-accounting, pivots on a single arbitrary shock of intrusion. Not even 'Absolution', prospecting the ground from which Fitzgerald would draw forth a year later the history of Jay Gatsby, escapes a sense of narrative forcing. Only when the matter of the story becomes at every turn a function of the consciousness of the central agent, making the general dream-vision his dream, does it effectively overcome – and 'Winter Dreams' is as good an instance as any – this hovering artificiality.

Or when the fantastication that underpins the whole comes directly to the surface and begins to compose the whole narrational circumstance. This further release into extravagance is what brings off a jokey entertainment like 'Rags Martin-Jones and the Pr-nce of Wales'. The major achievement of this kind is surely 'The Diamond as Big as the Ritz' (1922). In this long story, virtually a novella, a superbuccaneering Gilded Age family named Washington has built up over three generations a murderous, slave-holding fortress and pleasure palace on top of a diamond mountain and stands prepared in its 'monstrous condescension' to fight off any threat from outside and to bring on general holocaust if other strategies fail. 'The Diamond' qualifies, in its self-delighting preposterousness, as the ultimate America-as-Eldorado story; it stands solidly between Fenimore Cooper's prophetic allegory of the fortunes of the Republic in *The Crater* (1847) and the rocket-flight apocalypse of Pynchon's *Gravity's Rainbow* (1973). And more than anything Fitzgerald had yet published it anticipates the extraordinary convergence of personal and national mythologizing that he famously achieved in *The Great Gatsby* (1925).

One other factor in the unlikely success of 'The Diamond' is the split perspective gained by its presentation through the eyes of an outsider, a young man from some bypassed town in the American heartland. Indeed, as a final patch of dialogue hints, the entire fantasy may be its two young survivors' own mid-American dream. ('"It *was* a dream," said John quietly. "Everybody's youth is a dream, a sort of chemical madness."') In *The Great Gatsby* the same split perspective is all-important. Gatsby's self-propelled rocket flight to grandeur and squalid oblivion provides the central coordinates for the narrative text itself, which enacts – in the first-person voice – Nick Carraway's double education into moral reality and into the contradictory covenants at the center of American history.

This simplest of compositional shifts, from third-person to first-person narration, proved both stabilizing and re-empowering to Fitzgerald's repertory of performative tricks. It gives context to his insistent phrase-making; accepting Nick's throwaway ironies about the 'usually plagiaristic' intimacies of young men or about wanting 'no more riotous excursions with privileged glimpses into the human heart', we are, by the second page, ready to acquiesce in his claiming for his protagonist 'a romantic readiness such as I have never found in any other person' and his assurance that the cause of his own overpowering disillusionment is not anything Gatsby has been or done but what has preyed on Gatsby, 'what foul dust floated in the wake of his dreams. . . .' The book's judgemental lines of force could not be more precisely drawn. Nick's intervention makes a space, too, for the expert mimicry of a whole subordinate range of self-betraying American voices – Catherine Wilson's whispered 'Neither of them can stand the person they're married to', the racketeer Wolfshiem's valedictory 'such a mad act as that man did should make us all think', or a drunken party-guest's confidential explanation why he was so slow getting out of the car he has smashed into a ditch: 'At first I din' notice we'd stopped.' More important, the first-person refractions cover over, or nearly do, the parts of the story – Gatsby's actual business life, or, as Fitzgerald wrote to Edmund Wilson, 'the emotional relations between Gatsby and Daisy from the time of their reunion to the catastrophe' – that Fitzgerald admitted he had no clear feeling about or knowledge of. What he hadn't himself imagined thus merges convincingly enough with what Nick Carraway finds barely conceivable and responds to as mysterious, fantastic.

Above all, Nick's confessional narrative suffuses the improbabilities of Gatsby's history with the pathos and conviction of his own encounters with contemporary reality. A showcase instance would be the famous listing in Chapter IV of all those who came to Gatsby's parties the summer of the story, 'gray names' on a 'disintegrating' time-table which is nevertheless hardly two years old (a detail in that poetry of time that is one of the book's deftest achievements). A simpler one is the brief run of paragraphs in Chapter II laying out the novel's metropolitan theater of action, force-field for both its excitements and its conspiratorial exclusions:

I began to like New York, the racy, adventurous feel of it at night, and the satisfactions that the constant flicker of men and women and machines gives to the restless eye. I liked to walk up Fifth Avenue and pick out romantic women from the crowd and imagine that in a few minutes I was going to enter into their lives, and no one would ever know or disapprove . . . Again at eight o'clock, when the dark lanes of the Forties were lined five deep with throbbing taxicabs, bound for the theater district, I felt a sinking in my heart. Forms leaned together in the taxis as they waited, and voices sang, and there was laughter from unheard jokes, and lighted cigarettes made unintelligible circles inside.

The Great Gatsby is not flawless. Undergraduate smartiness pushes back in; the weak gag about Gatsby's identifying San Francisco as in the Middle West (to confirm the 'something a little sinister' Nick senses about him?) is totally implausible, and the charged lines early in Chapter VI defining the protagonist as 'a son of God' – 'a phrase which, if it means anything, means just that' – come off as patchwork bluster. More than once the set of balancing acts the narrative advances by seems ready to topple. But all such shifts and dodges are eternally forgiven in the beauty and precision of the last pages, when the unloving Buchanans' 'money or . . . vast carelessness, or whatever it was that kept them together' is set in place as the unyielding nemesis of the whole affair, and Gatsby's absurd dream recedes into 'that vast obscurity beyond the city, where the dark fields of the republic rolled on under the night'.[1]

The book's achievement, unequivocally praised by judges as authoritative as Edith Wharton and T. S. Eliot, haunted Fitzgerald. With *Tender Is the Night* (1934), much delayed and never structurally resolved, he returned in Book One (as originally printed) to a version of the narrative refraction used in *Gatsby*; but once his Hollywood starlet has performed her function in building up the elusive attractiveness of the main couple, she becomes only a plot device. The book stands as a more elegant and sustained re-enactment of *The Beautiful and Damned* with, as it progresses, a corresponding attenuation. (Yet there is a fine recovery in the short last chapter, at least for readers knowing something of the forlorn geography of western New York State.) Some Fitzgerald partisans find evidence of a return to mastery in *The Last Tycoon*, posthumous and unfinished, but the ineffectiveness of filtering key impressions through the sensibility of a young woman infatuated with the movie-producer hero, and the triviality of studio episodes meant to display his magnetism and romantic integrity, suggest otherwise. The 'unassuming dignity' that Anthony Powell remembered about Fitzgerald's personal presence in 1930s Hollywood, and certainly the graciousness and good humor, register better perhaps in his abundant correspondence and in the personal, and confessional, essays Edmund Wilson collected after his death in *The Crack-Up*.

*

Fitzgerald's strongest work in the 1920s is built on a fundamental disproportion between the tawdry excitements and miseries of the given story and the vast moral and historical importance that in one way or another attaches to them. To his midwestern adaptability and the broad stimulus of modernism, the era of his coming of age added one other shaping influence, the sustained national self-audit occupying American writers and thinkers after 1917.[2] The same instinct for discovering in the marginal affairs of a few persons the temper and direction of a whole society and era enters into Hemingway's brilliantly precocious narratives from the start. With a first handful of laconic one- and two-paragraph sketches of scenes of war and the bull ring – sketches that became the numbered interchapters of *In Our Time* (1925) – Hemingway stepped directly, at twenty-four, into the company of Pound and Ford, Joyce and Gertrude Stein. After two novels and a second collection of stories he was, at thirty, *chef d'école* for a whole rising American and European generation in prose fiction. The force of his presence reached beyond the contagiousness of his remarkable style. 'More than any other writer,' V. S. Pritchett would write in 1941, 'he has defined for us the personality of our own time.'

His own formalized accounts of that style are not fully reliable as guides to its effectiveness. In the familiar passage at the beginning of *Death in the Afternoon* (1932) describing his early motives and purposes, the stress is on fidelity of primary emotion ('knowing what you really felt, rather than what you were supposed to feel, and had been taught to feel') and on unobstructed facticity ('what really happened in action; what the actual things were which produced the emotion that you experienced'). The passage in *A Farewell to Arms* (1929) at the beginning of the masterfully drama-tized Caporetto débâcle, about the obscenity of words like sacred, glorious, hallow and in vain alongside 'the concrete names of villages, the numbers of roads, the names of rivers, the numbers of regiments and the dates', bears the same minimalist emphasis. But the expert opening sentence of *A Farewell* is nothing if not abstract and generalized. 'In the late summer of that year we lived in a house in a village that looked across the river and the plain to the moun-tains' – what in fact this immediately establishes are two literally spell-binding tonalities: an intimacy of address (*that* year, *we* lived) coercing us into becoming accomplices in the narrator's tensely precise act of valedictory recollection, and the constrained watchfulness or apprehensiveness drawing observation out from house and village over a neutral space of river and plain – the prepositions and single conjunction taking on the force of verbs – to the foreboding mountains from which, sooner or later, the trouble is coming.

The power of that simple, paratactic style to project or recover felt experience overwhelmed its early hearers. Cyril Connolly, speaking as 'Palinurus', bears witness: 'The greatness of Hemingway is that he alone of living writers has saturated his books with the memory of physical pleasure, with sunshine and salt water, with food, wine and making love, and with the remorse which is the shadow of that sun.' But this, too, a little misrepresents the scope and solidity of observation in the early writing. It fits well enough the memorable set-piece midway into *The Sun Also Rises* (1926) on the fishing trip into the hills beyond Burguete, through beech woods and shaded grass to cold, clear, white-water streams – one more representation of the purged and restorative 'good country' of Hemingway's repetitive mythmaking. It doesn't, however, do full justice to the calculated impact of quite casual descriptions, as of the car ride bringing Jake Barnes, the book's narrator, up from Bayonne toward the Spanish frontier, a passage lightly evoking the occupational integrity of a whole alternative society and so beginning to make firm the moral dynamic, between integrity and corruption, outflowing release and sterility, the main action of the novel will turn on:

We passed some lovely gardens and had a good look back at the town, and then we were out in the country, green and rolling, and the road climbing all the time. We passed lots of Basques with oxen, or cattle, hauling carts along the road, and nice farmhouses, low roofs, and all white-plastered. In the Basque country the land all looks very rich and green and the houses and villages look well-off and clean. Every village had a pelota court and on some of them the kids were playing in the hot sun. There were signs on the walls of the churches saying it was forbidden to play pelota against them, and the houses in the villages had red tiled roofs, and then the road turned off and commenced to climb . . .

Green pastoral hills and travel-poster villages, to be sure, but also – carefully noted – flourishing gardens, well-kept houses and fields, men and animals at work; a society, in brief, with firm rules and customs, ceremonial institutions and licensed departures, that will prove capable of effectively resisting and assimilating foreign profanation.

The secret of these effects is not simply in the spare vocabulary and syntax – Hemingway, when he wanted to, could uncoil sentences as overloaded as Faulkner's – but in attaching what is registered to some active sequence of reimagined experience. Two early sentences in the nostalgia-drenched late memoir, *A Moveable Feast*, show how this narrative style works at its simplest and how easily it collapses into mannerism. In the book's first paragraph: 'We would have to shut the windows in the night against the rain and the cold wind would strip the leaves from the trees in the Place Contrescarpe.' 'In the night', rather than 'at night', shifts us from generalized summary to a particular remembered moment, and the action of the wind is what would in fact be observed from an about-to-be-shut window. In the first paragraph of the chapter following, the basic structure of statement is repeated and with an extra touch of explanatory concreteness – 'We burned *boulets* which were molded, egg-shaped lumps of coal dust, on the wood fire, and on the streets the winter light was beautiful' – but without the jog of a specific remembered instance, the effect is willful and self-parodying. Interestingly the difference matches an evident difference in the two recollections. The first is of an event that in however small a way was forced on the observing consciousness; the pleasurable impression is salvaged from something initially discomforting. The second is of circumstances calculatingly (and self-approvingly) created. Its very inconsequence calls attention to something intrusive in the passage: a determination first of all to establish credentials, to be known for fine taste – slightly esoteric but thoroughly naturalized – and discriminating sensory judgement. (The difference offers a microinstance of the falsifications that overtook Hemingway's later writing and mar even as well-managed a construct as *For Whom the Bell Tolls*, his most determinedly ambitious novel. When he built his narratives on the recollection of events and actions that he had had no choice not to undergo and absorb, that had come to him – like those of boyhood and young manhood – under their own impulsion, that peculiarly studious and attentive habit of mind which to Malcolm

Cowley marked him off from the rest of the young expatriate talents in the mid-twenties could operate without interference. When later on, living more and more inside a self-fabricated personal myth, he began making books out of activities and places he had elected for the sake of the pleasure anticipated from them – Africa and the Caribbean, fishing and big-game hunting – there is a palpable loss of control.)

The famous style, with its projection of a corresponding ethic and a whole measured strategy for maintaining balance against the on-slaught of temporal experience, is nowhere more efficient than in passages of dialogue. Both the short stories and the novels depend heavily on dialogue: on otherwise unspecified shifts of tone between speakers, alternations of intimacy and formality, or on sudden silences – like the silence and then aggressive sharpness of speech overtaking the punched-up prizefighter in the beautifully accom-plished early story, 'The Battler'. The dramatic range of this practice of dialogue is distinctly limited. With young women characters, most of all the protagonists' accommodating girl friends, it is nearly always at the edge (or well over it) of factitiousness. But no one has ever done better at entering into the conspiracies of male com-radeship; the solidity of secondary characterizations like the army doctor Rinaldi in *A Farewell to Arms* and indeed of a dozen and more supernumerary soldiers, priests, hotel and customs and police personnel, is all in their overheard voices. Friends who knew Hemingway well remembered in particular, according to Carlos Baker, a 'special clairvoyance' in social contacts (along with an appalling gift for bullying); the American diplomat Ellis Briggs thought him the most perceptive man he had ever met in sensing nuances of interpersonal feeling. 'In a group of people, if two of them were antagonistic to each other, Ernest felt it at once . . .'

That atmosphere of antagonism, real or impending, is Hem-ingway's surest fictive invention, and it is made more intensely affecting by the dream of happiness and escape it breaks in upon. In all his writing, figures move between a world of violence where every life is at risk and the apprehension of another kind of world, one that is the purified image of their desiring. In *The Sun Also Rises* it is the fishing episode, and the austerity in general of Spanish manners and the Spanish landscape, that offsets the grasping personal betrayals of the main story, the '[too] much wine . . . ignored tension, and . . . feeling of things coming that you could not prevent happening'. In *A Farewell to Arms* the brief fantasy early in Book One about going up into the Abruzzi – 'where the roads were frozen and hard as iron, where it was clear cold and dry and the snow was dry and powdery and hare-tracks in the snow and the peasants took off their hats and called you Lord and there was good hunting' – gives us an alternative world never quite lost sight of in the conflict and agony that follow.[3] In *For Whom the Bell Tolls*, Spain itself, as realized in particular in what Edmund Wilson accurately described as the 'social romance' of the isolated guerilla band, becomes the 'good country' being ravaged and betrayed in the amoral violence of war. Even with the posthumous compilation *Islands in the Stream*, where Hemingway's increasingly aggressive fears and fantasies run more and more out of control, that art of placing the action along some tense boundary between everything desirable and secure and something menacing in life which can never be propitiated gives us one more precise and urgent opening description:

The house was built on the highest part of the narrow tongue of land between the harbor and the open sea. It had lasted through three hurricanes and it was built solid as a ship. It was shaded by tall coconut palms that were bent by the trade wind and on the ocean side you could walk out of the door and down the bluff across the white sand and into the Gulf Stream. The water of the Stream was usually a dark blue when you looked out at it when there was no wind. But when you walked out into it there was just the green light of the water over that floury white sand and you could see the shadow of any big fish a long time before he could ever come in close to the beach.

It was a safe and fine place to bathe in the day but it was no place to swim at night. At night the sharks came in close to the beach, hunting in the edge of the Stream, and from the upper porch of the house on quiet nights you could hear the splashing of the fish they hunted and if you went down to the beach you could see the phosphorescent wakes they made in the water. At night the sharks had no fear and everything else feared them. But in the day they stayed out away from the clear white sand and if they did come in you could see their shadows a long way away.

The body of Hemingway's writing is not large. Most of his novels have the concentration and compactness of novellas – even *For Whom the Bell Tolls*, as some first reviews recognized, may work best as a sequence of stories – and the short stories he valued enough to keep in print make up, even with the whole of *In Our Time*, a single volume. The range of behavioral observation is correspondingly narrow. Its strength and integrity at its best, however, remain undeniable, and almost invariably turn on some version of the dialectic of menace and escape, nightmarish violence and the dream of a sanctuary elsewhere. A final instance is that late addition to the Nick Adams cycle, written the year following the phenomenal popular (more than critical) success of *The Old Man and the Sea* (1952), which Hemingway provisionally titled *The Last Good Country*. Here Nick, earlier seen as a small boy and then as a young man out of school and off to and back from the war, is the age of his great prototype, Huck Finn himself, and is on the run from game wardens out to punish him for out-of-season poaching. Not a little of the dialogue between Nick and his fiercely loyal kid sister (called 'Littless'!) is in the late vein of stiff-lipped sentimentality, but as Nick goes on deeper into untracked woods and waters where no one has walked since Indian days, all that relish and precision in sizing up battle terrain that Hemingway's Second War associates reported of him come back into play, and the narrative gathers to itself, once more, the old excitement and conviction. It is another American tale of lighting out, *in extremis*, for 'the territory', and as with Mark Twain, greatest of all mid-American fabulists, once Hemingway reached that point in it he could not imagine any sequel. The story, three times as long as even 'Big Two-Hearted River', is one he never finished.

NOTES

1. A confirmation of Fitzgerald's attentive respect for Dreiser is his adaptation, in writing out Nick's visionary final musings, of the passage that closes the last sketch in *Twelve Men* (1919).

2. These were the years of *The Seven Arts* and *The Dial*, Mencken's *American Language*, Santayana's *Character and Opinion in the United States*, Van Wyck Brooks's diagnostic studies of Twain and James, Harold Stearns's symposium *Civilization in the United States*, Williams's *In the American Grain*, Hart Crane's *The Bridge*, and of mass-circulation scholarly works like Parrington's *Main Currents in American Thought* and the Beards' *Rise of American Civilization*.

3. The power and shock of the ending of *The Snows of Kilimanjaro* (1936) spring, on the other hand, from our realization that the place 'wide as all the world, great, high, and unbelievably white in the sun' – the snowy mountain top itself – is the place of death.

JOHN DOS PASSOS AND
NATHANAEL WEST:
SATIRISTS OF THE AMERICAN SCENE

TOWNSEND LUDINGTON

A typical perception of the literature of the 1930s in the United States is that it is proletarian writing portraying workers, labor strife, and left-wing politics. While authors who had established themselves earlier – Hemingway, Fitzgerald, and O'Neill, for example – continued their work and were not thought to be 'proletarian', the era has been perceived to be a time when political novelists such as Mike Gold, Jack Conroy, and Robert Cantwell, and dramatists such as Clifford Odets and John Howard Lawson, extolled the virtues of the working class while excoriating the excesses of capitalism. The decade ended with the appearance of one of the most popular novels ever to be published, John Steinbeck's *The Grapes of Wrath* (1939). That it is less political than often thought does not matter; it was read as a proletarian epic summing up the era of the Great Depression.

What is skewed about this view of the literary history of the 1930s is how it overlooks the fact that the decade was a time of literary innovation. The writings of the likes of Gold, Conroy, and Lawson are forgotten except as footnotes to the period; what endures in addition to the work of writers such as Hemingway and Fitzgerald who carried into and beyond the era is that of writers who consolidated modernism with a broader social concern. Two of the best examples are John Dos Passos (1896–1970) and Nathanael West (1903–40).

One does not usually place them together, yet several reasons make it logical to do so. Both were modernists who in their different ways attempted to cope with a world bereft of old systems of order. Both considered themselves outsiders and turned to satire – of very different sorts – as their way of seeing not only the United States but the human condition. And both wrote their most important fiction in the 1930s. In addition, both were innovative, Dos Passos with the form of his major trilogy *USA* (1938); West with the absurdist nature of his literary vision.

That both felt themselves outsiders and during their young lives went so far as to change their names reflects an ambiguity toward themselves which resulted in a satiric bent. They partly scorned the groups from which they felt excluded, yet partly yearned for acceptance. In Dos Passos's case, he was born John R. Madison, the illegitimate son of a southern gentlewoman and a New York corporation lawyer. After a lonely time abroad – what he much later termed a 'hotel childhood' – he matriculated at a New England preparatory school, Choate, in 1907. Only after leaving there and before entering Harvard University in 1912 did he take the name Dos Passos, his parents having married in 1910. He grew up seeing himself not separate from a bourgeois life-style, but apart from the family, friendships, and sense of place that created the comfort of upper-middle-class life in America. Living mostly on the Continent and in England until he went to Choate, he thought himself an outsider peering in at the nation, the United States, he wanted to make his own, his *Chosen Country* he termed it in the autobiographical novel published in 1951. Coupled with what he gained from his exposure to 'the New' in the arts while at Harvard and from the ideas filling journals such as *The New Republic, The Masses*, or the more literary *Seven Arts*, his 'outsidedness' produced a rebellious mood even before he shipped abroad in June 1917, as a volunteer ambulance driver on the Western Front. Of what he soon found there he wrote in anguish, 'Horror is so piled on horror that there can be no more.' The world seemed shattered by the general conflagration of the First World War, and he burst out in his journal:

My God what a time – All the cant and hypocrisy, all the damnable survivals, all the vestiges of old truths now putrid and false infect the air, choke you worse than German gas – The ministers from their damn smug pulpits, the business men – the heroics about war – my country right or wrong – oh infinities of them!

(*The Fourteenth Chronicle*, ed. T. Ludington, p. 90)

Someone who perceives himself an outsider and who has observed an event as cataclysmic as the First World War does not necessarily become a satirist. Dos Passos did because with bitterness he noted the vast divide between man's stated ideals – often bombastically expressed – and reality. Steeped in writers such as Thackeray, Fielding, Hardy, Flaubert, and the Spaniards Antonio Machado and Pio Baroja, Dos Passos as a socially engaged author saw his role to be like that of 'the doctor who comes in with his sharp and sterile instruments to lance the focusses of dead matter that continually impede the growth of intelligence'. Before solving 'the ugly and the savage and the incongruous aspects of society', man had to reveal them 'as brutally and nakedly as possible'. He made these comments about the satiric artist George Grosz in 1936; they could as well have been about himself, because from his college days on he had written satire in his attempt to explode the sham and cant that too nearly filled the world he saw.

Throughout his career he battled against the organizations he perceived to be stifling individual freedom; his fiction railed against oppressive monoliths: the military in *One Man's Initiation – 1917* (1920) and *Three Soldiers* (1921); the city in *Manhattan Transfer* (1925); capitalism in the three novels constituting the *USA* trilogy: *The 42nd Parallel* (1930), *1919* (1932), and *The Big Money* (1936); the Communists in *Adventures of a Young Man* (1939), *Most Likely to Succeed* (1954), and portions of numerous other works; big government of various forms in *Number One* (1943), *The Grand Design* (1949), *The Great Days* (1957), and *Century's Ebb* (1975); and labor unions in *Midcentury* (1961). Cataloging Dos Passos's work and the objects of his satire simplifies matters; *Midcentury*, for example, attacks not only the labor unions in the United States but also big government, the Communists, and what he had earlier termed monopoly capitalism, while it celebrates free enterprise. His fiction might best be described as satiric chronicles of the twentieth-century United States. For him the ideal narrative was one that combined fiction and history, and it might be said about his fictional canon that in it he was trying to swallow America whole. For the reader, Dos Passos's many offerings are likely to be too bitter to be imbibed during one long sitting.

The West canon is no less vitriolic. If anything it is harsher; but it is briefer, consisting of four short novels: *The Dream Life of Balso Snell* (1931); *Miss Lonelyhearts* (1933); *A Cool Million* (1934); and *The Day of the Locust* (1939). Although the movie industry, the

subject of his last novel, was topical, most of West's work appears
less so than Dos Passos's fiction, which is grounded in specific details
from the time in which it is set. Yet West's satires touch upon the
modern condition, and *Miss Lonelyhearts* and *A Cool Million* in
addition to *The Day of the Locust* are set in the United States. More
significantly, the books are about a nation in despair. Robert Emmet
Long, among other critics, has seen 'the theme of thwarted identity
in West's work' and has noted 'his attraction to dwarfs, freaks and
deformed characters, who, in his view, are symptomatic of man's
condition'. Long continued:

> Perhaps no writer of the thirties was so thoroughly pessimistic as West.
> No sense of community exists in his fiction, and institutional life and all the
> communal legacies of the past are voided. Most of all, there is no sense or
> possibility of love in his novels. Love is reduced always to sexuality . . .
>
> (*Nathanael West*, p. 21)

While Dos Passos's early years gave him a reason to think himself
a child without a country, West need not have felt alienated from
his home, yet apparently he did. He was born Nathan Weinstein in
1903 in New York City to parents who had immigrated to the
country relatively recently. Jewish, they sought to 'Americanize'
their family quickly and to a great extent separated themselves from
the Jewish community while doing little or nothing to educate West
about his religious heritage, which surely contributed to a sense of
uncertainty about himself. When he changed his name in 1926, the
act was a kind of affirmation of what Long termed 'a deeply
ambiguous identity'. 'Nathanael' implied New England and 'a secure
place within an established cultural order'; the family name West
implied California and 'dreams of newly-monied "success"'. Certainly West recognized the conflict between these two cultural styles,
but he was too perceptive not to realize that in the old New England
order lay the materialistic instincts which spawned the Golden West.
Thus in *A Cool Million* a former President of the United States,
Shagpole Whipple, is as avaricious as are all the other characters
enthralled by the American dream of success, and it is that myth,
fundamental to the American mind, which is satirized rather than
one or another geographical region.

As a child West lived in a world apart, one of books and solitude where his idiosyncratic vision of humanity could develop undisturbed. His inventiveness extended to his academic career. He managed to forge a transcript of his high-school record so that he was accepted at Tufts College in 1921. Expelled for bad grades one semester later, he applied to Brown University and was accepted by substituting for his own the transcript of another Nathan Weinstein at Tufts. Because that Weinstein was a good student, West received a substantial number of credits and was able to graduate from Brown after two and a half years. He enjoyed his time there, where his eccentricities amused his fellow students. He liked being among 'the establishment', yet deeply resented being excluded from social groups such as fraternities because he was Jewish, even if somewhat masochistically he visited them frequently. The experience was all grist for his fictional mill, as was the time he spent in Paris after graduation. Life there was appealing, but what most interested him were the avant-garde movements in art, Dadaism and surrealism in particular, although they were not entirely new to him. Along with wide reading and an already decided inclination toward satire, Dadaism and surrealism were the ingredients that produced West's first short novel, *The Dream Life of Balso Snell*, a parody of modernist styles and themes in which the hero while walking near the city of Troy comes upon the Trojan horse, enters it through its anus and wanders through its intestines where he encounters various grotesques.

The episodes in this fantasy West apparently dreamed while working as a night manager in a cheap hotel, the Kenmore Hall, between 1927 and 1929, then in one somewhat better, the Sutton, from 1930 to 1932. More important for his literary career, Long noted, the hotels fed West's imagination, especially the Sutton, whose tenants 'came to seem a microcosm of the displaced and the "unsuccessful" in American society. Noting their attempts to present a genteel façade, and sensing the desperation beneath it, he became fascinated by their inner lives.' He occasionally would even steam open their mail, not just to be able to mock them, but to understand the deep misery that is the subject of each novel, whether it be a psychological study of alienation, sexual frustration, and loneliness (*Miss Lonelyhearts*); a caricature of the Horatio Alger myth of success (*A Cool Million*); or a mockery of California and Hollywood (*The*

Day of the Locust) where a crowd made 'savage and bitter, especially the middle-aged and the old, . . . by boredom and disappointment', went beserk and in its frenzy ripped and tore itself apart.

For both authors Hollywood was the epitome of a United States gone awry. Dos Passos, the older of the two, had already written important works about the country by the time he did a short and unhappy stint in California as a screenwriter in 1934. 'People you meet out here greet you with a nasty leer like the damned in Dante's Inferno . . .,' he wrote Ernest Hemingway shortly after arriving in Hollywood in late July 1934. Two months later he retreated from the scene, but by then he had absorbed enough of it so that in *The Big Money*, his chronicle of 1920s America, it became a narrative about the opportunistic actress Margo Dowling, a key symbol of the frenetic, hollow life-style Dos Passos satirized.

West was much more familiar with Hollywood than Dos Passos ever was because he moved there to be a scriptwriter in 1933 and remained most of the rest of his life. His masterpiece, *The Day of the Locust*, was directly influenced by Hollywood; was set there, in fact, and portrayed the film capital as an 'American dream machine' whose unrealities tantalized a population grown surly because of constantly disappointed expectations. In West's Hollywood nothing was as it seemed: film studios were a jumble of glitter and rubble and of fake piled on fake. At one point Tod Hackett, the novel's weak hero, set out across a studio lot in search of Faye Greener, the would-be starlet after whom he lusted. As he started, 'a platoon of cuirassiers, big men mounted on gigantic horses', galloped by. The sun was hot, so Tod sought shade and rested for a moment,

under an ocean liner made of painted canvas with real lifeboats hanging from its davits. He stood in its narrow shadow for a while, then went on toward a great forty-foot papier mâché sphinx that loomed up in the distance. He had to cross a desert to reach it, a desert that was continually being made larger by a fleet of trucks dumping white sand. He had gone only a few feet when a man with a megaphone ordered him off.

Tod's marvelously bizarre journey continued as he came to a pond in which floated some 'large celluloid swans'; a bridge with a sign 'To Kamp Komfit' led to 'a Greek Temple dedicated to Eros', where a statue of that god lay 'face downward in a pile of old newspapers and bottles'. He then pushed his way through more of the detritus of this dream world until he ended his remarkable journey, Faye forgotten, when a fake Mont St Jean collapsed around French and British armies of actors refighting the Battle of Waterloo. Both sides retreated crying *'Sauve qui peut!'*, or rather, West added, 'Scram!'

His comments about Tod's thoughts reveal a great deal about the author's vision of the world. Tod, he noted, 'had lately begun to think not only of Goya and Daumier but also of certain Italian artists of the seventeenth and eighteenth centuries, of Salvator Rosa, Francesco Guardi and Monsu Desiderio, the painters of Decay and Mystery.' And a moment later, when Tod came on a large, desolate dumping ground, he 'thought of Janvier's Sargasso Sea. Just as that imaginary body of water was a history of civilization in the form of a marine junkyard, the studio lot was one in the form of a dream dump. A Sargasso of the imagination!' (*Complete Works*, pp. 350–56).

For both West and Dos Passos, the United States of the depression years had become a vast dumping ground of dreams and history. Most of the population had not achieved the American dream of success; in their scramble after that elusive myth they had abandoned history – for West to do so was part of the human condition; for Dos Passos, it was a matter of the nation in its greed having forgotten its ideals. One of Dos Passos's heroes was Walt Whitman, not the exuberant poet of 'Song of Myself' who celebrated the pre-Civil War United States, but the author of *Democratic Vistas*, the pained nationalist who feared that the 'fervid and tremendous *Idea*' which had created a storybook democracy was mired in 'solid things' . . . 'science, ships, politics, cities, factories', during the years of 'unprecedented material advancement'. Dos Passos wrote thus of Whitman in his last work of chronicle fiction, *Century's Ebb* (p. 13). But Whitman's concern had always been his and was the overriding theme of the *USA* trilogy: the nation in its greed had forgotten that its roots historically were in freedom and open competition. When the critic Malcolm Cowley wrote Dos Passos after the publication of *1919* to ask about the 'general trend' of the work, Dos Passos responded:

. . . gosh that is a poser . . . I don't know if there's any solution . . . I think also – if I manage to pull it off – the later part of the book shows a certain crystalization (call it monopoly capitalism?) of society that didn't exist in the

early part of 42nd Parallel (call it competitive capitalism?) – but as for the
note of hope – gosh who knows?

(Fourteenth Chronicle, pp. 403–4)

So it is that in 'Camera Eye (49)', the third-to-last segment of the
narrative device through which Dos Passos rendered his autobiography impressionistically, he wrote about his involvement in the
defense of the condemned Italian anarchists Sacco and Vanzetti.
Believing them victims of repression during the 'Red Scare' of
1919–20 and convinced of their innocence, he had worked to free
them in 1926–7 and had traveled to Plymouth, Massachusetts, to
speak to local people who knew them (Plymouth is a symbol of
freedom as the site of the Pilgrims' landing in 1621). In *The Big
Money* he wrote:

this is where the immigrants landed the roundheads the sackers of castles
the kingkillers haters of oppression this is where they stood in a cluster after
landing from the crowded ship that stank of bilge on the beach that belonged
to no one . . .

how can I make them feel how our fathers our uncles haters of oppression
came to this coast how say Don't let them scare you make them feel who
are your oppressors America

rebuild the ruined words worn slimy in the mouths of lawyers districtattorneys collegepresidents judges without the old words the immigrant
haters of oppression brought to Plymouth how can you know who are your
betrayers America

or that this fishpeddler you have in Charlestown Jail is one of your founders
Massachusetts? [1]

Here Dos Passos recaptured his feelings during the last days of the
long effort to free the two Italians. A subsequent 'Newsreel', number
LXVI, another narrative device by which he chronicled the events of
the period 1900–1930, informs us that 'SACCO AND VANZETTI
MUST DIE'. Dos Passos's response in 'Camera Eye (50)' was outrage:

they have clubbed us off the streets they are stronger they are rich they
hire and fire the politicians the newspapereditors the old judges the small
men with reputations the collegepresidents the wardheelers . . .

America our nation has been beaten by strangers who have turned our
language inside out who have taken the clean words our fathers spoke and
made them slimy and foul . . .

they have built the electricchair and hired the executioner to throw the switch

all right we are two nations

(pp. 413–14)

and he closed the piece, 'we stand defeated America'.

Individuals defeated by the massive forces of industry, wealth, corruption – one can think of a dozen similar terms – are the constant subject of both writers. In *Three Soldiers* Dos Passos's three central figures are beaten down by the military; in *Manhattan Transfer*, Jimmy Herf wanders out of the city past 'dumping grounds full of smoking rubbish-piles'. 'How fur ye goin?' asks a truck driver from whom Herf begs a ride. 'I dunno,' is the answer, 'pretty far.' Alienated, lost, defeated: so it goes in every work with the exception of *Chosen Country*, where Dos Passos's autobiographical hero and his new wife find a separate peace, and happiness, *apart* from the rest of society. It is no different for West; Miss Lonelyhearts is killed as he tries to reach out, Christ-like, to the crippled grotesque, Peter Doyle. Lemuel Pitkin of *A Cool Million* is literally dismantled – he has lost an eye, his teeth, one leg, a part of a hand, and his scalp before he is assassinated while addressing a crowd on behalf of the 'Leather Shirts', a Fascist organization. And Tod Hackett, maimed by a rioting crowd at the end of *The Day of the Locust*, is carried off screaming in a police car.

While both authors were 'Depression novelists', they were, more broadly speaking, modernists; Dos Passos first with *Manhattan Transfer*, West with all four of his published works. In his modernist city novel, Dos Passos strove to assert his creative will through the form he imposed upon his material. 'I had done a lot of reading knocking about the warwracked world,' he commented much later:

> Some of the poets who went along with the cubism of the painters of the School of Paris talked of simultaneity. There was something about Rimbaud's poetry that tended to stand up off the page. Imagism. Direct snapshots of life. Rapportage was a great slogan. The artist must record the fleeting world the way the motion picture film recorded it. By contrast, juxtaposition he could build reality into his own vision: montage.
>
> New York was the first thing that hit me when I got back home [from traveling abroad in the early 1920s]. I started rapportage on New York ...

443

The narrative must stand up off the page. Fragmentation. Contrast. Montage.
The result was Manhattan Transfer.

(Unpublished ms., University of Virginia Library, pp. 3–4)

Few if any of Dos Passos's statements express precisely the point
that the form of *Manhattan Transfer* is an affirmation of the author's
self; yet it is. Such a conscious ordering of materials, such stylizing,
cannot but be that. Like the artists who had influenced him, the
variety of what he *showed* as well as the multiple perspectives, the
devices of fragmentation and montage, and the effort to create an
impression of simultaneity were the imposition of his creativity
upon what he termed in the same statement 'the panorama of history
that roared past my ears'. For him, as for visual artists, there was no
longer a single, simple, linear (or photographic) reality. Form and
content were, as he observed in 1928 about the poet e. e. cummings's
avant-garde play *Him*, the means 'to generate feelings and put them
immediately up to the understanding, . . . to express sensations rather
than tell about them'. Dos Passos explained that 'narrative exposition
style [which I take to mean not only telling, as opposed to showing,
but a semblance of objective realism] does not give us the satisfaction
it once did. We want to recreate the event more immediately.' [2] To
do that meant amassing the raw materials of a time and place and
shaping them in stylized fashion on the page. Thus, *Manhattan
Transfer* begins with an impressionistic passage that tries to convey
the sights, sounds, and smells of a ferry slip; it is immediately
followed by two narrative sequences. And a short while later, in the
second chapter entitled 'Metropolis', Dos Passos inserted fragments
from a newspaper. The result has the effect of a collage, a fragmented, multi-perspective, but finally partial vision of a modern
city in which none of the characters gains perception or a sense of
order.

This modernist novel by an author rebelling against the past is
what he later termed a 'chronicle of the present'; [3] it would take the
shock of the executions of Sacco and Vanzetti to turn him toward
history for an answer to the modernist search for meaning. They died
in 1927; after an extended trip to Russia, from which Dos Passos
returned unconvinced that communism was the solution to the ills
of monopoly capitalism, he set out in the *USA* trilogy to chronicle
the first three decades of the twentieth century. Rebuilding the

foundations – the language – of democratic government ruined by 'lawyers districtattorneys collegepresidents judges' would, he hoped, enable Americans to make sense of the present. The first step was to understand the past, and so, using multiple narrative devices such as he had in *Manhattan Transfer* but adding more, he began a work that would present a collage of the USA as many layered, or angled, as he could make it.

Dos Passos can serve as one model of the American writer who came to modernism, a writer who, while discarding many of the old truths, in some ways like the philosopher William James before him willed himself to believe in the possibility of order, although to discern what this might be was an arduous, perhaps impossible task. He was too much the economic determinist to believe that the individual might find refuge on some island in the stream of events, or to be satisfied with a private existence in the present, natural world. He hoped to find answers by sorting through the nation's language, which was its history.

West was equally the modernist, not because of the form of his work but because of his vision, a dark one in which there was no heroism, nor were there alternatives to a world of cruel violence. 'In America violence is idiomatic,' he wrote in 1932:

> Read our newspapers. To make the front page a murderer has to use his imagination, he also has to use a particularly hideous instrument. Take this morning's paper: *Father cuts son's throat in baseball argument*. It appears on an inside page. To make the first page, he should have killed three sons and with a baseball bat instead of a knife.
> ('Some Notes on Violence', *Nathanael West: A Collection of Critical Essays*, ed. Jay Martin, 1971, p. 50)

'Whether they are housewives or whores, Mexicans or cowboys, Alger boys struggling upward, journalists or would-be actors,' wrote his friend, the author Josephine Herbst, 'the people in West's novels are all bit players in a violent modern drama of impersonal collective forces.' No one wins, she pointed out; 'the only valid currency is suffering'; and she noted, 'If there is a vision of love it is etched in the acid of what love is not. If there is courage it is no more than the persistence of human beings to endure in spite of all.'[4] Scarcely popular in the 1930s, West now seems ahead of his time, a writer who from a very particular perspective was summarizing his age. If

John Dos Passos was attempting the great collective novel in *USA*, so too was West in *The Day of the Locust*. Los Angeles is the United States in miniature. Readers at the time the novel was published for the most part missed this; now we have no trouble in understanding that California – or a part thereof – is a microcosm of the nation. Put another way, what happens there soon happens elsewhere; West saw that and in *The Day of the Locust* painted a satirist's terrifying picture of a society where fear, anomie, and violence reign.

Because his last novel presents such a bizarre world, we tend not to understand how rich in actual detail it is. Like Dos Passos in *USA*, West was declaring, 'These are the facts; this is American life.' The novel, one knowledgeable person asserted, 'was not fantasy imagined, but fantasy seen', and Jay Martin has observed that 'the geography of streets and canyons in the novel can be mapped, and both are accurately described.' The architectural mélange and the uses of language – colloquialisms as well as affectations – are accurate too. What is remarkable is their prophetic quality. If in the 1930s it was only in Hollywood where one might find an adobe hacienda next to a French chateau, today such is the case in any suburban housing development, whose names – Timberlyne, Falconbridge, Buena Vista – are designed to evoke in prospective home owners emotions such as robust manliness, snobbishness, or the sense of exotic lands. Both West and Dos Passos understood the implications of the new American landscape, and what finally makes their best work enduring is not topical politics, but their statements about mankind in the modern world. In that sense, they are the most serious sort of political novelists.

NOTES

1. *USA: The Big Money* (Boston, 1946), pp. 390–91. References are to this edition published by Houghton Mifflin, which because of being reset and including drawings by Reginald Marsh was considered new.
2. 'Mr Dos Passos on "Him"', *New York Times*, 22 April 1928, sec. 9, p. 2.
3. 'Contemporary Chronicles', *Carleton Miscellany*, X (Spring, 1961), p. 25.
4. 'Nathanael West', in Martin, ed., *Nathanael West: A Collection of Critical Essays*, p. 13.

EUGENE O'NEILL AND REAL REALISM

JEAN CHOTHIA

In 1933, Eugene O'Neill summed up his achievement to date. He recorded in his notebook, 'Grand total 29 long plays, 24 one acters', as if recognizing that he had reached a watershed in his writing life. His most recent play, *Days Without End*, had ended with the hero crying, 'Life laughs with God's love again. Life laughs with love,' but, despite that affirmatory claim, it had been completed only with great difficulty and the following year's notebook entry reads, 'Near breakdown from overwork . . . six months compulsory rest.' Although, to all appearances, O'Neill was flourishing, with successful productions of his two mammoth plays, *Strange Interlude* and *Mourning Becomes Electra*, attracting attention in Europe and the accolade of the Nobel Prize still to come in 1936, no new play would be produced after *Days Without End* until *The Iceman Cometh* in 1946.

Revivals continued, particularly after the creation in 1935 of the Federal Theatre Project which performed them throughout America, but it became increasingly evident that O'Neill had retreated from the theatre he had led for nearly two decades in which more than thirty of his plays had been produced. While no single dramatist appeared to replace him, the want was supplied during the 1930s by a range of work very different from his own: Maxwell Anderson's historical verse plays; Hecht and MacArthur's hardboiled New York comedies; Clifford Odets' urban protest plays for the Group Theatre; the Federal Theatre's Living Newspapers. O'Neill, his stature acknowledged, began to seem a figure of the past.

He, meanwhile, living in seclusion, struggled with a huge cycle of history plays which would demonstrate the spiritual failure and materialism of America, traced through events within a single family between the American Revolution and the present and, like many of his earlier plays, would include fictionalized versions of O'Neill's own private relationships.[1]

Since this Cycle, 'A Tale of Possessors, Self-Dispossessed', was eventually destroyed, unpublished, in 1944 and 1952–3, it is impossible to know whether it could have been completed had O'Neill not succumbed to a terrible physical paralysis. But references to the Cycle work throughout the thirties imply that there was, as well as commitment and detailed planning, a continual struggle with material that frequently proved intractable. Even in his early enthusiasm, there had been signs of floundering and confusion, as when he wrote to a friend, in July 1935:

Each play will be concentrated around the final fate of one member of the family but will also carry on the story of the family as a whole . . . In short it is a broadening of the Electra idea – but, of course, not based on any classical theme. It will be less realistic than Electra in method, probably – more poetical in general, I hope – more of The Great God Brown over and undertones, more symbolical and complicated (in that it will have to deal with intermingling relationships) – and deeper probing. There is a general spiritual undertheme for the whole Cycle and the separate plays make this manifest in different aspects.

(to Robert Sisk)

Later, he found himself 'hoping for a surge of creative energy', unable to 'figure out an ending', recording that the new play was 'psychologically too complicated', and, in 1939, writing to Lawrence Langer:

I made myself put it aside for the past seven months. Had gone terribly stale, as I told you when we talked on the phone, and did not start the fifth play beyond getting it ready to start. Since then I have been working on other things.

These 'other things', were The Iceman Cometh and the scenario of Long Day's Journey into Night, which two plays, he would claim, gave him 'greater satisfaction' than anything he had ever done. With A Touch of the Poet, detached from the Cycle in 1942 and completely rewritten, A Moon for the Misbegotten and the short two-hander, Hughie, all written between 1939 and 1943 in a remarkable burst of creative energy, they constitute the final phase of O'Neill's writing life. They draw more directly on O'Neill's personal life than anything he had previously written but, wholly dramatic, flexible in their dialogue, fully achieved in their form, they succeed in moving beyond the private to convey the essence of American – indeed, Western – experience in our time: the restlessness of the mobile society, the tensions within the nuclear family, the isolation and inarticulacy of the individual, the way in which the past shapes and haunts the present. These had been O'Neill's themes throughout his writing life but had never before been realized so powerfully, leading T. S. Eliot, for one, to place O'Neill's work 'very high indeed' and describe *Long Day's Journey into Night* as 'one of the most moving plays' he had ever seen.

It is as if the seclusion and the long struggle with the Cycle material had freed O'Neill to face his own past much more directly and, with time, had enabled a simpler but more achieved form to emerge from the experiments, excesses and discoveries of the earlier work. O'Neill's writing up to 1934, which was widely recognized at the time as initiating an American drama, can now be seen as a long apprenticeship in which, rarely satisfied with his own achievement, O'Neill explored the possibilities of theatre.

By the second decade of this century, new ventures in publishing, tours by European companies, the founding of theatre magazines like Craig's *The Mask*, had resulted in an influx into America of plays and of ideas about theatre practice that had been fermenting in Europe since the early 1880s. Naturalism, symbolism, expressionism, arrived almost simultaneously in America and, for the first time, the drama began to interest serious young writers and thinkers. This led to the founding of various independent theatre companies eager, like the Provincetown Players for whom O'Neill wrote, to discover new American dramatists or, like the Neighbourhood Playhouse and the Theatre Guild, which produced his work from 1928 onwards, to provide a forum for the new European drama.

The Provincetown Players (founded 1915), produced works by Dreiser, Wallace Stevens, John Reed and Djuna Barnes, among others. Elmer Rice adapted German expressionist techniques to an exposé of the business world (*The Adding Machine*, 1923), Sidney Howard wrote daringly about sexual passion in rural New England (*They Knew What They Wanted*, 1923), but O'Neill outstripped all the writers of his time in the seriousness of his engagement with ideas and his persistent theatrical inventiveness.

For nearly two decades, following the production in 1916 on the wharf at Provincetown of his one-act play *Bound East for Cardiff*, O'Neill absorbed ideas from Europe. He was hailed in 1918 by George Jean Nathan as America's 'first really important dramatist', widely acclaimed in the press after the success, in 1920, of his full-length play, *Beyond the Horizon*, called by Thomas Wolfe 'the beaconlight in our own drama today'. Lionel Trilling, who was a Provincetown Players subscriber, later recalled the excitement generated:

> To the audience of the Twenties however, it was O'Neill's style rather than the content of his plays that was of first importance. Style, indeed, was sufficient content: the language of *Anna Christie*, the crude color, the drumbeats and the phantasmagoria of *The Emperor Jones*, the engine rhythms, the masks, the ballet movements of *The Hairy Ape*, all constituted a denial of the neat proprieties, all spoke of a life more colorful and terrible than the American theater had ever thought of representing. It was at first the mere mechanical inventiveness of Eugene O'Neill, his daring subjects and language which caught the public imagination.
>
> (Introduction, *The Hairy Ape* etc., 1937)

But, although he was clearly excited by theatrical innovation, it was not 'of first importance' to O'Neill. The experimentation is part of a search for verbal and scenic analogues of experience.

The half-light and phantasmagoric visions, the syncopated sound of *The Emperor Jones* (1920) evoke the forest and the panic fear of the man who flees through it. They lead the audience into the recesses of Jones's mind by enacting sequences from his personal, racial and atavistic past. The excessively cramped space and red furnace-light of the stokehole in *The Hairy Ape* (1922) where men move like zombies, shovelling coal in unison, and the Fifth Avenue populated by marionette-like figures in evening dress, masked and talking in toneless voices, represent stages in Yank Smith's search for a meaningful sense of self. The terrifying walk Jim and Ella must take between opposed lines of blacks and whites in *All God's Chillun Got Wings* (1924), offers a striking scenic image for society's hostility to mixed marriage, while the reduction of the acting space as the stage walls are moved inwards, scene by scene, suggests the growing emotional claustrophobia of the relationship. The removable walls of *Desire Under the Elms* (1924) are used to create a poignant image of isolation when the harsh old man, Ephraim, fails in his attempt to confide in his young wife whose attention, we perceive, is passionately concentrated on her stepson, silent and restless in the adjoining room. As O'Neill put it in a letter to the critic Arthur Hobson Quinn:

> To be called a 'sordid realist' one day, a 'grim pessimistic Naturalist' the next, a 'lying Moral Romanticist' the next, is quite perplexing . . . I've tried to make myself a melting pot for all these methods seeing some virtues for my ends in each type of them, and, thereby, if there is any real fire in me, boil down to my own technique.
>
> (A. H. Quinn, *History of American Drama*, p. 199)

O'Neill is attracted to expressionist and symbolist methods, to the use of abstraction in set, gesture and dialogue but these are constantly brought into conjunction with his concern to express not the remote and metaphysical but the familiar and the human, not the immediately observable surfaces but the 'behind life'. As he wrote of his play *Welded* (1923):

> I want to write a play that is truly realistic. That term is used loosely on the stage, where most of the so-called realistic plays deal only with the appearance of things, while a truly realistic play deals with what might be called the soul of the character. It deals with a thing that makes the character that person and no other. Strindberg's *Dance of Death* is an example of that real realism.
>
> (Quoted A. and B. Gelb, *O'Neill*, p. 520)

The development of a lively and flexible verbal language was crucial to the achievement of such expressive realism.

Whereas Twain had introduced vernacular narrative into the novel, specifically American speech forms had been used only for occasional comic figures in the nineteenth-century theatre. In overturning this convention, O'Neill made a claim for a more authentic dialogue and extended the possible range of language. Many of the characters in his early plays speak one or another American vernacular mode – Bronx, New England rural, New York Negro, immigrant accented or, as in the S. S. *Glencairn* sea plays and *The Hairy Ape*, a mixture of all of these. A multitude of variant voices are intercut with each other, offering a shadowy image of America and its restless, mobile population and, since O'Neill, successive American dramatists have used various immigrant or regional dialects or city slang as their linguistic medium. These characters suffer loss, know despair or joy, fear the future and tremble at the past in dialect, and O'Neill gains access to the colour of slang and vernacular phrases and to different rhythmic patterns from those of General American (Standard Middle Class American English), and gains a various linguistic texture for the drama. Contending with inarticulacy, he discovered polyphony but, at the same time, made the inarticulacy evident in certain repetitive, limited or stereotypical phrases the characters use which imply that the origins have become petrified, the characters circumscribed by the limitations of their speech.

This double effect is evident in the opening of *Desire Under the Elms*, one of the most accomplished plays of the early years. After Eben has appeared and responded to a magnificent stage sunset with the bare, 'God! Purty!', his brothers enter, also gazing at the sunset, and this is what we hear:

SIM. Purty.

PETER. Ay-eh.

SIM. Eighteen year ago.

PETER. What?

SIM. Jenn. My woman. She died.

PETER. I'd fergot.

SIM. I rec'lect — now an' agin. Makes it lonesome. She'd hair long's a hoss's tail — an' yaller like gold!

PETER. Waal — she's gone. They's gold in the West, Sim.

SIM. In the sky?

PETER. Waal — in a manner o' speakin' — thar's the promise. Gold in the sky — in the west — Golden Gate — Californi-a! — Golden West! — fields o' gold!

SIM. Fortunes layin' just atop o' the ground waitin' t' be picked! Solomon's mines, they says!

PETER. Here — it's stones atop o' the ground — stones atop o' stones — makin' stone walls — year atop o' year — him 'n' yew 'n' me 'n' then Eben — makin' stone walls fur him to fence us in!

SIM. We've wuked. Give our strength. Give our years. Ploughed 'em under the ground — rottin' — makin' soil for his crops! Waal — the farm pays good for hereabouts.

PETER. If we ploughed in Californi-a, they'd be lumps o' gold in the furrow!

(I, i)

We believe in the poverty of the characters' speech because of devices like the repeated 'purty', the halting expression of loss in, 'Jenn. My woman. She died' and the recurrent use of 'stalling words', 'waal', 'ayeh', even when other parts of the dialogue are more expansive. In this sequence, the pace quickens when the word 'gold' generates a series of thought associations until interrupted by a second word, 'stones'. Throughout the play these words, usually opposed to each other, reverberate, off-setting dream against reality as the sons re-enact the possessive greed and attempted escape of their father until the end of the play when, his world collapsed about him, Ephraim turns finally to the stones saying:

'Mebbe they's easy gold in the West, but it hain't God's gold. It hain't fur me . . . Waal – what d'ye want? God's lonesome, hain't He? God's hard an' lonesome.'

(III, iv)

In the late twenties, O'Neill tends to the grandiose: to huge crowds, multiple scene changes, elaborate mask schemes and, in an effort to extend the linguistic range from what he had come to think of as 'the dodge question of dialect', to a quasi-poetic prose or a loose General American that lacked the rigorous shaping of the dialect usage. If the 'soul of the character' frequently seems buried under theatrical spectacle and Nietzschean philosophizing in plays such as *Lazarus Laughed* (1927) or *Dynamo* (1929), the attempt to find images of the human self does continue, sometimes clumsily, as in the removable masks which differentiate the real and superficial self in *The Great God Brown* (1926); sometimes ponderously, as in the interior monologues spoken while the other characters freeze in *Strange Interlude* (1928); occasionally with striking succcess, as in the reverie scenes and the conclusion of *Mourning Becomes Electra* (1931) where, learning from experience, O'Neill abandoned masks and interior monologue in favour of echoes and recurrent key words in dialogue that is interactive with telling gesture.

O'Neill sets *The Iceman Cometh* and *Long Day's Journey into Night* in 1912. Both plays present a group of people isolated together from the world and, in both, he draws on autobiographical material now remarkably transformed so that our attention remains with the play and its characters and we are only retrospectively aware of the author's private sufferings which had been intrusively evident in numerous rebel-poet and failing-mother characters in the earlier years. But these two plays are antithetical in several important ways, each developing one of the dominant strains in the earlier work, as their settings indicate: settings which, it should be said, will recur in subsequent American drama.

The Iceman Cometh is set in a New York city bar. Characterized as:

the No Chance Saloon, ... Bedrock Bar; the End of the Line Cafe; the Bottom of the Sea Rathskeller ... no one here has to worry about where they're going next, because there is no farther they can go.

(I)

– it is the quintessence of those settings, tramp steamers, bars, cheap hotels, where, in the earlier plays, isolated individuals gather to work, eat, sleep, their more intimate personal relationships lost in the past and glimpsed only through transforming memory and where O'Neill exposes the fragility of the society these individuals have constructed for themselves. *Long Day's Journey into Night* is, by contrast, set, like *Desire Under the Elms*, *Welded* and *Mourning Becomes Electra*, in a small-town family home. Its four characters belong to a nuclear family and O'Neill explores, more intently than ever before, the nature of their bondage to it and to each other. In both plays, the audience is aware that chaos and isolation lie threateningly behind the action but, whereas in *The Iceman Cometh*, Larry Slade, the one character who perceives this fully, is continually moved to the periphery of the action, as a choric commentator, all four characters of *Long Day's Journey into Night* move steadily closer to such recognition.

The dramatic effect of *The Iceman Cometh* derives, firstly, from the success with which O'Neill, in a subtler and more complex version of the polyphony and group action of the early sea plays and *The Hairy Ape*, differentiates all seventeen characters in Hope's Bar so that, even when it images torpor, the stage teems with life; and from the way he so varies and interweaves their words that the activity of each at any given point, besides characterizing that figure, contributes to the ongoing action of the play. The shadowy image of America is much more clearly focused now.

Not only national origin but former occupation, class, education and, therefore, degrees of articulacy are indicated through speech.

General American with a slight colouring of national accent is spoken by four characters, Larry (Irish), Jimmy (Scottish), Lewis (English) and Oban (American, upper class), who have access to a range of syntactical transformations. Hickey and Parritt also use General American but with occasional colloquial solecisms and more simple sentences. Pronunciation and confusions of word order and grammar ('Always there is blood . . .', 'Vit mine rifle I shoot damn fool Limey officers py the dozen') indicate that English is the second language of Hugo (Central European) and Piet (Afrikaans), while the remaining characters all have low colloquial speech, that of Harry, Mosher and Macgloin being coloured by slang vocabulary, Macgloin's with additional Irish turns of phrase and that of the bartenders, whores and Joe with notably substandard syntax, to which Joe has added a few specific Negro markers. The intrusive argot of each man's abandoned occupation demonstrates that the past still possesses him, although atrophied now. We can identify in Hope's bar a one-time confidence trickster ('rube', 'short change'), a policeman ('sugar galore'), a journalist ('bitter sorrows', 'losing the woman one loves by the hand of death'), a salesman ('honesty is the best policy', 'don't look at me as if I was trying to sell you a gold brick. Nothing up my sleeve'), and a whole range of others.

The Iceman Cometh, like Ibsen's *The Wild Duck*, takes the convenient or sustaining life-lie as its subject but, like its other notable source, Gorki's *The Lower Depths*, centres not on an individual but on this group of down-and-outs, versions of unaccommodated man. In Act I, they play verbal games, spin fantasies about the past and future, spar and tease each other, passing the time, waiting for Hickey. He comes, not to bring the anticipated life of free-flowing rot-gut whiskey, but to save them from themselves by making them encounter and, thereby, vanquish their life-lies, or pipedreams. In Act II, the characters veer between mutual affection and hostility, settling, in Act III, into harsh discord and self-concern, demonstrating how delicate a construct the society had been. By the beginning of the fourth act, the life we witnessed in the first has completely vanished. As their now inert speech indicates, they are left with no inner resources, recognizing themselves as empty shells. Only with the final removal of Hickey can they, at first tentatively and then with hedonistic gusto, reconstruct their former existence, return to their former verbal flourishes and gather once more into a cohesive group.

The spiritual resurgence is measured in the linguistic resurgence as Harry Hope, returning to his earlier robust speech mode and his habitual oath, 'Bejees', leads the others back to life in a rhythmically patterned speech that touches on many of their shared concerns:

> Bejees, fellers, I'm feeling the old kick, or I'm a liar! It's putting life back in me! Bejees, if all I've lapped up begins to hit me, I'll be paralysed before I know it! It was Hickey kept me from –. Bejees, I know that sounds crazy, but he was crazy, and he'd got all of us as bughouse as he was. Bejees, it does queer things to you having to listen to a lunatic's pipedreams . . . Bejees, it's good to hear someone laugh again! All the time that bas— poor old Hickey was here, I didn't have the heart – Bejees, I'm getting drunk and glad of it! [*He cackles and reaches for the bottle.*] Come on, fellers. It's on the house.

Although we have seen the artifice of the construct, we cannot help but respond to the renewed vigour but, unlike the hedonistic group, we must also be conscious of Larry, at the side of the stage, unable now to reintegrate into the group, without hope because without illusions; so that we, unlike the group, hear desperation as well as relief, fear as well as joy, in the communal shout which emerges from the chaos of conflicting songs which ends the play.

The endings of many of the early plays were their weakest part because the action didn't draw to a convincing or genuinely searching conclusion. Here, O'Neill creates a powerful scenic image that, compelling in itself, grows from and gives significant shape to the action and language of the foregoing play.

O'Neill is fully articulate, too, in the complementary play, *Long Day's Journey into Night*, his story of mutual attachment and recrimination within intimate human relationships. Although the fictional time span of the play is limited to a day and a night, it is expanded to include the recent and distant past of the characters because they search their memories for moments when they had optimistic belief in the future, for the disappointments and catastrophes that have diminished them or for the never-to-be-located point where things went wrong, but also because we, as audience, gradually become attuned through repeated gestures and echoic and patterned words to the play of past experience within present existence.

Certain gestures (tidying hair, striking a histrionic pose) are repeated; certain references recur (to Shakespeare, to music, to the Virgin Mary, to the dead baby, to cheap doctors); but also patterns of language usage are established whereby each character, as well as the General American they all speak, can adopt other speech modes that derive from their reading or life-style. This is a crucial new departure because it brings colour to the dialogue without the limitations or stereotyping apparent when a character speaks only a low colloquial form and without the embarrassment of authorial attempt at poetic rhythms. Mary, under influence of the drug, uses a gushing girlish speech ('her eyes look right into your heart', 'I was so mad at myself'); Tyrone quotes Shakespeare sententiously; Jamie parodies his father with distorted readings of Shakespeare lines and apposite stage directions, quotes melancholic fin de siècle poetry or, more harshly, falls into coarse Broadway slang, while Edmund echoes the others' quotation; uses parodic versions of his brother's slang and, occasionally, budding poet, attempts to express his mystic experience in poetic prose, which is always self-consciously placed by him ('I couldn't touch what I tried to tell you just now'). Such linguistic elements allow O'Neill to vary the surface of the play while creating a dense texture of implication. More than that, the shifts between them enable some of the most poignant moments as when the hurt inflicted by Edmund's mockery of Jamie's slang:

> They never come back! Everything is in the bag! It's all a frame-up! We're all fall guys and suckers and we can't beat the game! . . . Christ, if I felt the way you do —!
>
> (II)

is measured in Jamie's simple reply, 'I thought you did.'

O'Neill compels audience belief in the relationship between the four fictional Tyrones by creating what might be called a 'family rhythm' in the dialogue that seems to root the characters in a shared past of the kind we have ourselves experienced in comparable relationships. They address each other familiarly, teasing about personal matters – snoring, slimming, digesting. They laugh at the same jokes and the laughter is deflected in evidently habitual reproach. Quarrels flare out of nothing, and as quickly subside; allegiances shift and each character interjects his or her word in a way only possible among people with a history of such interactions. More obviously, we catch echoes of one character's speech in that of another. Edmund, for example, engaging in reverie, adopts words habitual to his mother's drug-influenced speech, 'fog', 'alone', 'lost', 'hide', 'ghost'; and Jamie, shortly afterwards, comments drunkenly on his own quotation of Wilde's 'The Harlot's House', 'not strictly accurate. If my love was with me I didn't notice it. She must have been a ghost.' Without making anything explicit, O'Neill allows the audience to perceive the unconscious irony of Jamie's words and to recognize the part his relationship with his mother has played in warping his life.

There are areas of reticence between these people to which we also become sensitive. They use euphemisms, hiding from Edmund's TB by calling it a 'summer cold', referring to morphine as 'the poison', 'her curse', so that O'Neill can raise the dramatic tension by breaking the taboo, as when Edmund cries, 'Mama it isn't a summer cold, I've got consumption'; can compound the effect when Mary, unlike the audience, fails to respond at all to the cry, and then disarm the audience's hostility to the unfeeling mother, after Edmund has stumbled miserably away, in her sudden bare recognition, 'Oh, James, I'm so frightened. I know he's going to die.' We, as audience, gradually come to know from such tormenting exchanges that the time will never be ripe, opportunities will always be missed, precisely because the cruellest denials are summoned by the most heartfelt attempts at mutual confidence.

Attention is continually shifted from facts and events to their emotional significance and the audience slowly becomes attuned to the texture of the dialogue, able to leap the gaps and understand the shared assumptions, because O'Neill has confronted us with our own familiar patterns of conversation. Much of the emotional intensity of the play, indeed, derives from the way O'Neill, after appearing to satisfy, continually frustrates the audience's impulse to sympathize with one character above the others, to have a secure viewpoint on the action. At any given moment, one of the four dominates the action revealing his or her thoughts, delight, disappointment, engaging our sympathy until the same character acts or speaks cruelly, thoughtlessly, and the sympathy is alienated, the place at the centre of our attention taken by another character. We must hold the claims of all four characters and delay judgement on the accusation and counter-accusation we hear.

At the end of *Long Day's Journey into Night*, Mary stands left front of the stage and speaks quietly to herself while her three men sit in silence, stage centre. Her words contain no deep thought, no great poetry, and yet they are almost unbearably moving. The effect could only be achieved in the drama where the verbal and visual combine in scenic images; where we can hear one character while watching others who listen silently, tormented by the words, and where a word, a gesture, even a position on the stage can activate our memory of other moments that have prepared, and can now extend, the immediate image. A chandelier is flashed on, a Chopin waltz played on the piano, and Mary enters, the hair she has continually neatened in her nervous tension is now let down and she carries her wedding dress, retrieved from the old trunk in the attic. Things which through repeated naming have become emblems of family mythology are now present on the stage, forming a powerful scenic image. The various speech resources of the characters, quotation from Shakespeare, from fin de siècle poetry, Mary's gushing schoolgirl register, are newly potent at this moment when the characters are, at last, all together and all apart in the night of the title, to which the whole play has been inexorably moving, when Mary will have fully succumbed to the drug.

O'Neill, who used a haunting Creole lament in an early sea play, gradually quickening drumbeats in *The Emperor Jones*, patterned singing of 'Shenandoah' in *Mourning Becomes Electra*, here appeals to the auditory imagination with verse whose rhyme and metric allows it to linger in the mind after it has been uttered. Three stanzas of Swinburne's 'A Leavetaking', spoken by Jamie, are interwoven with dialogue in which each man, in turn, makes a brief and futile attempt to impinge on Mary's reverie. At once sonorous, impersonal and dreadfully appropriate here, the poem offers the minimal comfort of artistic ordering: an elegy, spoken by the son for whom the least comfort is possible. The impact of Jamie's quotation, 'there is no help for all these things are so', set against the naïve trusting words of Mary's final monologue, 'I know she heard my prayer and would always love me and see no harm ever came to me', are hardly bearable to the stage listeners and the audience watching them; the more so because, as Mary's present tense ('I *know* she heard my prayer') indicates, she speaks as if she had, indeed, escaped into the optimistic world of her schoolgirl past while we must share the perspective of the on-stage listeners. In the quiet ending of her speech and of the play, the verb tense changes treacherously:

That *was* in the winter of senior year. Then in the spring something happened to me. Yes, I remember. I fell in love with James Tyrone and was so happy for a time.

And she becomes, once more, the middle-aged woman remembering her past self in a present from which there is no escape for any of the four Tyrones. There is no finality in such a play; no satisfaction in poetic justice meted out. Life continues without solutions; not purged of suffering at all.

In these late plays, O'Neill finds fully expressive scenic and linguistic means to explore those themes of alienation, inarticulacy and dispossession, experienced by people striving for something more, which had occupied him since his early sea plays. Using an unusually extensive, although always realistically motivated, range of registers and speech forms, he dramatizes the human search for identity and for faith that life has purpose and shows this search to be both sustaining and tormenting. In this achieved voicing of the experience of being human in America, in the post-Freudian, post-Christian world of Western capitalism, lies O'Neill's claim to be the first significant American dramatist.

NOTE

1. The Cycle material is described in Travis Bogard's excellent critical biography of O'Neill, *Contour in Time* (1972), pp. 268–75. *More Stately Mansions* (London, 1964), ed. Karl Gierow and Donald Gallup, reconstructs this Cycle play from more than six hours' playing time of surviving material. The progress of the Cycle is charted in letters to B. H. Clark, Kenneth Macgowan and Robert Sisk, throughout the 1930s.

CASTING A LONG SHADOW:
FAULKNER AND SOUTHERN
LITERATURE

FRED HOBSON

If it is a critical commonplace that the American South has produced some of the most important literature written in English in the twentieth century, it is equally true that the South produced very little of merit before that time. For H. L. Mencken was not far off when he wrote in 1920 that the South was the 'Sahara of the Bozart' – a cultural and literary desert. Virtually no writers of national, not to mention international, reputation had emerged from the Southern states in the nation's first century and a half. Of major American writers, only Edgar Allan Poe was unquestionably a Southerner; whether Mark Twain of Missouri was or was not is still being debated.

That is not to say that the South lacked for writers; it was rather that most of the work they produced was of exceedingly poor quality. The reasons for the inadequacy of imaginative literature are many: the region was rural, isolated, under-educated; it was not given to the life of the mind (the Southerner 'had no mind', Henry Adams wrote in the *Education*; 'he had temperament'); those Southerners who did think deeply concentrated not on belles lettres but on politics, in particular – before 1861 – on a defense of the South's peculiar institution, chattel slavery, and – after 1885 – on an equally strong defense of racial segregation. Thus much of the fiction and poetry of the nineteenth-century South assumed a patriotic duty: its highest purpose was to defend the Southern way of life.

Just what happened in the 1920s to change Southern writing is debatable. The renascence of Southern literature – or its nascence – might be attributed in part to the opening up of the South after the First World War, the coming of industry to the region, the critical distance achieved by young, aspiring writers who had fought in France or worked in New York, and, finally, as Allen Tate explained it, a 'backward glance' taken by Southern writers as they moved from a traditional agrarian world into an uncertain New South. Although these factors may account for the Southern Renascence historically and sociologically, the Renascence remains a phenomenon that defies easy explanation. What is certain, however, is that there arose in the South in the 1920s and 1930s a group of writers the stature of which had not been seen in any one American region since New England in its flowering nearly a century before. The South was *still* rural, isolated, under-educated; but the most benighted state of all, Mississippi, produced William Faulkner.

Faulkner (1897–1962) was not the first Southern writer of the twenties to produce genuinely important work. Shortly before 1920 a group of young teachers and students at Vanderbilt University in Tennessee began to meet to read and criticize each other's poetry. Led by John Crowe Ransom, a Tennessean educated at Oxford, the young poets in 1922 founded a magazine, *The Fugitive*, to serve as an outlet for their verse. Within three years the Fugitive poets – including Ransom, Donald Davidson, Allen Tate, and Robert Penn Warren – had made their marks with a new kind of Southern poetry characterized by wit, irony, restraint, and formal precision – a poetry which, they announced, fled from 'nothing faster than from the high-caste Brahmins of the Old South'. Having left the traditional South, however, the Fugitives in the late 1920s returned to it. In 1930 Ransom, Davidson, Tate, Warren, and eight other Southerners produced *I'll Take My Stand; The South and the Agrarian Tradition*, a work nearly Thoreauvian in its indictment of industrialism and progress. In their essays they responded to a spirit engendered by the liberal mainstream of Southern writers of the 1920s including Thomas Wolfe, who produced in *Look Homeward, Angel* (1929) an autobiographical work both romantic and satiric which demonstrated little affection for the traditional South.

William Faulkner, too, produced his first notable work in 1929 – the novels *Sartoris* and *The Sound and the Fury* – although at first he received less attention than Wolfe. The reason, in part, was that Faulkner wrote *The Sound and the Fury* in a stream of consciousness that was difficult for readers accustomed to the well-made stories of Sinclair Lewis, Fitzgerald, and Hemingway. The novel, which Faulkner called his 'most splendid failure', is a tragedy, nearly Greek in its power and intensity, on the perils of pride and the failure of love. It is also the story of the decline and fall of a once-powerful family. There is neither love of father for mother, nor father or mother for son, nor brother for brother – only the acute need of the idiot Benjy for his sister Caddy, the possessiveness of another brother Quentin for Caddy, and the desperate attempts of Caddy to find love through sexual promiscuity. The father – detached, ironic, cynical – takes refuge in drink, the mother – neurotic and ineffectual – in self-pity. But Quentin is the character most complex and, finally, most defeated. Driven by a rage for order and a need to arrest time, he succeeds in neither pursuit. The first of Faulkner's 'puritans', obsessed with family honor, afraid of his own sexuality, and wanting nothing more than the childhood innocence he had shared with Caddy, he commits suicide at Harvard, stopping time in the only manner he can.

Sartoris and *The Sound and the Fury* are the first novels of the Yoknapatawpha series that center around the fictional town of Jefferson and county of Yoknapatawpha in northern Mississippi. Indeed, by the time he had completed the Yoknapatawpha novels in 1962, Faulkner had written a historical chronicle of his section of the South covering nearly a century and a half, from the early nineteenth century through the mid twentieth. But Faulkner was not a historical novelist in the sense that he was principally concerned with historical forces and the significance of great events. One may read *The Sound and the Fury* as a commentary on the decline of the old Southern ruling order, represented by the aristocratic Compsons, ante-bellum planters who cannot cope with the modern world. But that was hardly Faulkner's primary intent. He was concerned, rather, with telling the story of a particular family, with the innocence of children who cannot adjust to adulthood, with the elusiveness of objective truth. When Wolfe wrote *Look Homeward, Angel* and *Of Time and the River* (1935) he was highly conscious of that geographical entity called 'the South'; and T. S. Stribling – a writer who dealt with much of Faulkner's material, who, in a very real sense, got there first – could not create believable flesh-and-blood people, so intent was he on depicting 'representative' Southern types. Faulkner's characters – Quentin Compson, Dilsey, and later Thomas Sutpen, Flem Snopes, and Lucas Beauchamp – may also be seen as 'types' of Southerners, but only by readers and critics after the fact, after these characters became part of Southern mythology. Faulkner, at least in the early part of his career, was concerned with the concrete, the particular, not the abstract. Indeed, if anything, *The Sound and the Fury* suffers from a lack of social and historical context. The story of Faulkner's 'children' – his 'heart's darling' Caddy and her lost brothers – was the story he was compelled to tell.

There was, especially in the early Faulkner, a certain self-indulgence, a refusal to compromise with popular taste (except, to some extent, in his potboiler *Sanctuary*). If *The Sound and the Fury* was nearly a *tour de force*, his next novel *As I Lay Dying* (1930) was altogether that. Its fifty-nine interior monologues tell the story of the Bundrens' absurd six-day journey to Jefferson for the purpose of burying the wife and mother, Addie – although, as we see later, her husband Anse wants to reach Jefferson to acquire a new wife and new teeth, and her daughter Dewey Dell wants to find a way to abort her pregnancy. Unlike his contemporaries Stribling and Erskine Caldwell, whose method was satire and whose characters were little other than rural clowns, Faulkner's method was tragedy, albeit tragicomedy at times; epic, albeit mock-epic. Certain of his characters – no matter how absurd and grotesque their attempt to drag a decaying corpse through fire and flood to burial – possess an inherent dignity. The story he tells, in certain respects, is not unlike *The Sound and the Fury*: a story of family fragmentation and, particularly, the responses of the sons to a woman (in this case, Addie) and the eventual descent into madness of the most insightful and sensitive of those sons (Darl). Addie articulates Faulkner's own rage against abstraction:

> That was when I learned that words are no good; that words dont ever fit even when they are trying to say it. When [Cash] was born I knew that motherhood was invented by someone who had to have a word for it because the ones that had the children didn't care whether there was a word for it or not.
>
> (*As I Lay Dying*, Vintage Books, pp. 163–4)

After the publication of *The Sound and the Fury* and *As I Lay Dying* – and particularly, the next year, the sensational *Sanctuary* – Faulkner began to gather a certain critical and popular attention, although he was most often misplaced in the camp of those Southerners who were shattering the romantic Southern image and helping to create a new image of a savage, benighted South. In fact, not only did Faulkner have a deep allegiance to certain elements of the Southern past but he was also, in some ways, within a Southern literary tradition, although he turned that tradition on itself. The Southern writer had long been known, to his discredit, for his love of language, his noble sentiments and rhetorical flourishes, all stemming from the Southern fondness for preaching and political oratory. Faulkner too was given to long, flowing sentences and excessive adjectives, but he brought a control, a discipline, and a concreteness to his writing that his predecessors had lacked.

If in his first four Yoknapatawpha novels Faulkner was seen as a dispenser of Southern Gothic, chronicler of a primitive and frightening South, his other two great tragedies, *Light in August* (1932) and *Absalom, Absalom!* (1936), enhanced that reputation. They were also, among other things, further statements against abstraction on the author's part, statements against a life lived according to a design. The Southern rage against abstraction was well-established before Faulkner began to write; ante-bellum Southerners had complained of the penchant for abstraction on the part of the New England transcendentalists and various other social reformers, and just as Faulkner was beginning his career the Nashville Fugitive-Agrarians were issuing indictments of abstraction and of those, such as social scientists, whose premises, they believed, rested on abstractions rather than on observable truth. There was always a certain irony in the Southern fury against abstraction, since Southern society from the late nineteenth century had rested on an abstraction, racial segregation, which viewed humans not as individuals but as types. None the less, Faulkner joined his Southern predecessors who had written harshly of those who would impose a system of values which violated the integrity of the individual experience.

Thus both *Light in August* and *Absalom, Absalom!* can be seen as tragedies of abstraction. Joanna Burden and Gail Hightower, two social pariahs in *Light in August*, and Thomas Sutpen, the tragic protagonist of *Absalom, Absalom!*, are all creatures of abstraction, characters whose lives and whose plans for others are based on designs. The two novels, as well, reveal a breadth of vision, a social dimension and historical sense, that *The Sound and the Fury* and, to some extent, *As I Lay Dying* had lacked. Faulkner's picture of Jefferson and Yoknapatawpha is fuller, more inclusive. The majority of characters are neither decadent aristocrats, as in *The Sound and the Fury*, nor poor whites, as in *As I Lay Dying*. Rather Faulkner deals to a much greater extent with the Southern plain people – people economically deprived but possessing a basic honor, a sense of responsibility.

Light in August can perhaps best be understood in light of the work of Sherwood Anderson, Faulkner's early mentor, who in *Winesburg, Ohio* (1919) created characters he called 'grotesques', lonely people who lived their lives according to a single 'truth', or part of life, which became an obsession. *Light in August* has indeed a galaxy of grotesques: Hightower, the cast-out Presbyterian minister who lives in the heroic past, obsessed by the absurd Civil War death charge of his grandfather; Miss Burden, possessed of a mission to shape, reform, and redeem the Negro race; Joe Christmas, the wanderer and sufferer whose life-long search for his racial identity ends with his murdering Joanna Burden and, nine days later, his own death; Doc Hines, the racial fanatic, and McEachern, the religious fanatic, who combine to warp Christmas; and Percy Grimm, the white supremacist and pre-Nazi who murders and castrates Christmas. Against this cast of grotesques are two characters who are sometimes taken as norms in the novel: Lena Grove, the pregnant wanderer who responds viscerally and concretely to life and is taken in by the community; and Byron Bunch, the plain white laborer who is himself in partial exile from the human community until he is brought into it through his love for Lena. Those who have contended that Faulkner's women characters are less sensitively drawn than his men might find evidence in *Light in August*. We have Joanna Burden and we have Lena, the one pure abstraction, the other pure concreteness: the reformer and the earth mother.

Absalom, Absalom! is perhaps Faulkner's greatest novel, one of the most notable of the century, combining the internal drama and the family tragedy of *The Sound and the Fury* with a social and historical richness that earlier novels had lacked. Here the author brings back Quentin Compson, and has Quentin, at Harvard in the year before his suicide, ponder the story of Thomas Sutpen, the Virginian of low birth who created a magnificent plantation out of the Mississippi wilderness of the 1830s and 1840s. This story, like *The Sound and the Fury*, is told from multiple points of view: those of Quentin; his father, the same cynical, defeated philosopher of *The Sound and the Fury*; Rosa Coldfield, whose sister Sutpen had married seventy years before and who herself had been exploited, insulted, and outraged by Sutpen; and Shreve McCannon, Quentin's Canadian roommate who is detached not only from the faraway and exotic South but also from New England and its fervent neo-abolitionist views toward Dixie.

As several scholars have noted, *Absalom, Absalom!* is a detective story, and what the narrators attempt to discover is the true nature of Thomas Sutpen, his relationship with his sons, and — finally — precisely why his younger son, the puritan Henry, killed the older, the mixed-blood hedonist Charles Bon. Sutpen is a giant, a man of exalted ambition and determination and, finally, tragic stature, historically accurate yet transcending time and place. Just how historically sound Faulkner is might be suggested by comparing Sutpen with the 'generic Southerner' of W. J. Cash's later classic work, *The Mind of the South* (1941). In his book Cash was concerned with revealing the truth about the origins of the ante-bellum Southern aristocrat, the cotton planter, who often claimed to have come from gentry but in fact usually rose from yeomanry. He was rough and crude, he started with nothing except energy, determination, and a capacity for hard work. From the beginning, Cash maintained, his primary characteristics were 'innocence', simplicity and a 'most intense individualism'. He came into the new land, made his way on the frontier where shrewdness was more important than refinement (where refinement was, in fact, a handicap), where the admired qualities were 'great personal courage, unusual physical prowess, the ability to drink a quart of whiskey'. He acquired land and slaves, grew cotton, took a wife, soon became wealthy, and eventually built a big house which some called a mansion. And he dreamed. Though uneducated and unacquainted with formal culture, he aped Tidewater manners and made himself an 'aristocrat'. He wanted education and culture and good marriages for his sons and daughters. He wanted, that is, to found a dynasty.

This is very nearly Faulkner's Sutpen, although Faulkner adds a certain ruthlessness and mythic proportions to his character. Sutpen, too, was an upland cotton planter, a shrewd, strong, courageous, ambitious man who started with nothing, worked hard, acquired wealth and position, built a big house, aped Tidewater manners when he chose, wanted education, culture, and good marriages for his son and daughter – and wanted to found a dynasty. What else was Thomas Sutpen but the embodiment of the extreme individualism Cash described, himself a man of terrible fury? And did he too not dream, and was not his problem also 'innocence'? That was precisely his tragic flaw, as Mr Compson explained it to Quentin: an innocence, first, of social distinction, of the ways of society; and, later, a more profound innocence, which he never overcame, of the knowledge that all human designs do not work out, that courage and shrewdness are not enough.

If Thomas Sutpen's problem was innocence, so in a different manner was Quentin Compson's, and Quentin's claim to the role of leading protagonist in *Absalom, Absalom!* is perhaps greater than Sutpen's. Sutpen is remote, nearly a half-century dead as the story takes place, but Quentin is always present – first out at Rosa Coldfield's house, in September 1909, just before he leaves for Harvard, listening to her story of that 'demon' Sutpen and how he had wanted to marry her, *but only if she would give him a male heir*; then back at his father's home, listening to Mr Compson's stories of Sutpen, handed down from *his* father who had known Sutpen well: and finally, in the second half of the book, in January 1910 in the tomblike chill of his room in Cambridge, Massachusetts, trying to reconstruct Sutpen's story with his roommate Shreve. The Canadian's approach to Sutpen's story and to the American South is an intellectual approach, first one of great curiosity, then of incredulity: 'Jesus, the South is fine, isn't it. It's better than the theatre, isn't it? It's better than Ben Hur, isn't it?' But Quentin approaches Sutpen's story in a manner that is understandable if we consider his mental state in *The Sound and the Fury*. Haunted by the Southern past as much as he is drawn to it, Quentin tells his story not with intellectual detachment but with a visceral commitment to the importance of what he is telling. Both blessed and cursed with an excess of consciousness, he agonizes over the larger meaning of Sutpen's story, over the significance of what had happened in the South during the century just past. If Quentin hoped to escape his past by pouring it out, in fact in the telling he is only drawn in more deeply. He returns, in his mind, to the burden of the Southern past, of Southern values, of Southern myths, of himself and his family as Southerners: for how different, three-quarters of a century back, were the origins of the Compson dynasty from the origins of Sutpen's? Five months after he told his story to Shreve – five months after he answered Shreve's question 'Why do you hate the South?' by protesting, 'I dont hate it . . . *I dont. I dont!* ' – he committed suicide.

Quentin was hardly the only Faulkner character finding the burden of Southern history too heavy to bear. In *Go Down, Moses* (1942), particularly its most notable section, 'The Bear', Faulkner creates in Isaac McCaslin a character who feels more keenly than any other the racial sins of his fathers and tries to make amends for them. Isaac discovers at age sixteen in the plantation ledgers that his grand-father had fathered a daughter by one of his slaves, and then had fathered another child by that daughter. Unable to come to terms not so much with miscegenation and incest but rather with his grandfather's callous *use* of his slaves, Isaac renounces his title to the McCaslin plantation and chooses the life of a simple carpenter. Intertwined with the tainted McCaslin family history is the story of young Isaac McCaslin's love of the wilderness, particularly the hunt each November for a legendary bear, Old Ben. Ike is a child of the forest, having served an apprenticeship to the ageless Sam Fathers, part-Indian, part-black, who presides as a sort of priest over forest rituals. The bear is killed when Ike is sixteen, and the story ends two years later with Faulkner's description of the mechanically inept Boon Hogganbeck sitting under a tree full of squirrels, trying fran-tically to put his gun back together, shouting, 'Don't touch them! Don't touch a one of them! They're mine!' Faulkner's final scene serves as a metaphor for 'The Bear', indeed for all the stories in *Go Down, Moses*. It is a commentary on the madness to which greed of ownership – possession and exploitation of land, resources, and other humans – will drive men.

Faulkner was to return to racial themes frequently in the latter half of his career, most notably in *Intruder in the Dust* (1948), but in mid-career he came to rely increasingly on his comic sense. For Faulkner, more than any other twentieth-century American author, is the heir of two parallel American literary traditions. He is the most notable twentieth-century descendant of that American tradition of darkness, of sin and guilt and the soul in conflict with itself, that 'house of tragedy' first inhabited by the Puritans and, in the nineteenth century, by Nathaniel Hawthorne. But he followed as well in the tradition of frontier humor, that legacy of tall tales of the Old Southwest which reached its highest form in the work of Mark Twain. 'Old Man', a section of *The Wild Palms* (1939) which tells the story of a beleaguered convict battling for survival and dignity in the great Mississippi flood of 1927, is a tale rich in mythology and archetypes; but it is also a deeply humorous story, full of the comedy of situation and dialogue. A comic spirit of the ludicrous and the absurd also characterized *As I Lay Dying* and parts of *Light in August*. But it was in the Snopes Trilogy – *The Hamlet* (1940), *The Town* (1957), and *The Mansion* (1959) – that Faulkner's comic sense achieved its finest results.

Faulkner had conceived the Snopes stories in the late 1920s. The Snopeses are his classic poor whites – and, since 'poor white' to Faulkner referred not to economic status so much as moral integrity or a lack thereof, Flem Snopes remains a poor white even after he ascends to the presidency of the Jefferson bank and occupies an antebellum mansion. Flem's rise from sharecropper's son to general store clerk to restaurant owner to bank president could, on its surface, be a story in the Horatio Alger tradition of American success fiction. Flem follows the formula: he is shrewd, he works hard, marries the boss's daughter, makes the right contacts, seizes opportunities as they arise, and gains wealth and position. This is a version of the story of Thomas Sutpen or, indeed, of Fitzgerald's Jay Gatsby. But the comparison breaks down completely because Flem Snopes is a man devoid of passion, of the *dream* which drives Sutpen and Gatsby. He is, rather, a creature of moral and emotional emptiness. He represents to Faulkner that rootless, traditionless, amoral Southerner who came to power in the new chaotic South created by the Civil War. And he is successful because he is not bound by older codes of honor by which Faulkner's ante-bellum aristocrats, the Compsons and Sartorises, presumed to control their affairs.

Of the three Snopes novels, *The Hamlet* illustrates best Faulkner's denunciation of Snopesism – and his comic method as well. His supreme comic creation, it is set in Frenchman's Bend, a community in Yoknapatawpha County populated by plain whites, devoid both of aristocrats and blacks. In this novel Faulkner combines several stories he had earlier written and brings back certain of his earlier characters, not only Flem but the woman he marries, Eula Varner (as sensual and fecund as Flem is sterile), as well as the sewing machine salesman Ratliff, a common man of uncommon sense and decency, yet a victim of Flem Snopes in the end. *The Hamlet* is clearly an episodic novel, and the finest of the episodes is the section which had appeared earlier as the story 'Spotted Horses' (1931). Here, as elsewhere, we discover just how closely Faulkner followed in the tradition of those yarn-spinners of the nineteenth-century Southwest. Among the identifying marks of Southwest humor were the presence of wild animals of great strength, a plot in which one character outwits or cheats others, and, finally, a physical cruelty and suffering which, in context, appears comic if not ludicrous. 'Spotted Horses' indeed involves such animals – the wild horses Flem brings back from Texas – and people are injured, families torn asunder by the raging horses. Behind and above all the chaos stands Flem Snopes, always detached, often not even present, but shrewdly managing the entire affair. When one of the aggrieved, Mrs Armstid, approaches Flem after the rampage has subsided, asking for the money that is due her, he refuses, but rather gives her a mere pittance, a five-cent piece of candy for her son. After cheating her, he makes her feel grateful. 'By God, you can't beat him,' cries an admiring Lump Snopes.

Neither of the succeeding novels, *The Town* and *The Mansion*, demonstrates the virtuosity of *The Hamlet*. For virtually all of Faulkner's best fiction had been written by the early 1940s. Neither *Intruder in the Dust* nor *A Fable* (1954) was artistically successful, and *The Reivers* (1962), a light-hearted reminiscence, possesses little of the power of his earlier work. Thus, in little more than a decade, from the late 1920s to about 1940, Faulkner had created a body of fiction unparalleled in its richness and variety by that of any other American writer save perhaps Melville or James. He had achieved for the American South what Hawthorne, nearly a century earlier, had achieved for New England: he had confronted its past, its historical burden, had dealt with the sin and guilt, the pride and shame of men like his own ancestors, and out of his imagination had made Gothic romance, historical chronicle, and, finally, tragedy. He had created a world out of 'his own little postage stamp of native soil' in northern Mississippi.

It is only partly true, as critics sometimes claim, that the primary task of the Southern writer over the past four decades has been to escape the shadow of William Faulkner. In fact, Faulkner's shadow did not loom so large in his own time, and his acknowledged stature in his own country had to await the publication of Malcolm Cowley's *Portable Faulkner* (1946) and the awarding of the Nobel Prize for Literature in 1950. In the 1930s his contemporary Wolfe (1900–1938) was better known, though Wolfe's career was already in decline. An heir to the tradition of Southern rhetoric, Wolfe could not, like Faulkner, control and discipline his language. His second novel, *Of Time and the River*, was published only after his editor Maxwell Perkins had reshaped it, and his final two novels, *The Web and the Rock* (1939) and *You Can't Go Home Again* (1940), were reconstructed and completed by editor Edward Aswell after the novelist's death in 1938. Wolfe was a writer in the tradition of the poet Walt Whitman, a tradition which held that the function of the artist was lyrical, often excessive, self-expression. His reputation suffered in the mid-1930s in part because he pleased neither the Marxists, with their emphasis on social issues and economic determinism, nor the New Critics with their emphasis on form, restraint, and artistic precision. But Wolfe himself was primarily responsible for his decline. The verdict Bernard DeVoto pronounced on him in 1936 seems sound today: 'Genius is not enough.'

Faulkner's other contemporaries, the Fugitive-Agrarians, after early careers as poets and, briefly, self-conscious Southern social commentators, became in the 1930s national men of letters – poets, New Critics, and, in the cases of Tate and Warren, novelists as well. Tate (1899–1979) continued to affirm in his poetry the value of tradition and to demonstrate the perils of self-consciousness that had informed his greatest poem, 'Ode to the Confederate Dead' (1927). There Tate's persona, a Prufrock-like figure of locked-in ego, stands at a cemetery gate and ponders but cannot identify with the slain Confederates. His introspection and rationalism damn him, and he is left with only the grave, the decomposing wall, and 'the gentle serpent, green in the mulberry bush'. In his novel, *The Fathers* (1938), however, Tate demonstrated that tradition alone was not sufficient. To Major Buchan, Tate's representative of ordered ante-bellum Virginia, ritual, decorum, and tradition are all; to his reckless son-in-law George Posey, they are nothing. Posey is an 1860s version of modern man – energy and motion without direction – but he fares little worse in Tate's novel than the Major. Here Tate acknowledges that the ante-bellum South was seriously flawed. The sins of the Buchan family – an insistence on honor, outdated codes of conduct, and an overweening pride in family – were in large measure those of the older South.

Warren (1905–) wrote with greater power than Tate. Both his poems – vital, often colloquial, and demonstrating a narrative gift Tate lacked – and his fiction are overwhelmingly concerned with human guilt and responsibility, with the 'awful responsibility of Time'. Warren is a philosophical novelist, and his greatest work, *All the King's Men* (1946), poses against each other two philosophical positions: the pragmatism of Willie Stark, the low-born, demagogic governor of Warren's Deep South state, and the Emersonian idealism (later modified) of Jack Burden, the young man of privilege who becomes Stark's press aide and serves as the narrator of Warren's novel. Placed against each other as well are two views of history: a historical determinism which presupposes that forces control man and an antithetical view which holds that man cannot escape his role in history. A modern, alienated man anticipating Walker Percy's protagonists, Burden considers the assassination of Willie Stark, the suicide of the man he learns is his father, and his own misdeeds, and comes reluctantly to accept the view that ideas and actions indeed have consequences.

Although Warren portrays the South as a corrupt, violent land, he was overshadowed in his portrait of Southern benightedness by several other writers at mid-century. Richard Wright (1908–60), Carson McCullers (1917–67), and Flannery O'Connor (1925–64) all contributed in various ways to the image of a savage South. McCullers' *The Heart Is a Lonely Hunter* (1940) describes the wasteland of a small Southern city inhabited by Andersonian grotesques, characters cut off from family and tradition whose groping efforts to communicate are usually futile. All the grotesques revolve around Singer, a deaf-mute who smiles and nods but does not comprehend, and who in the end, desperately lonely himself, commits suicide. O'Connor's version of Southern Gothic is vastly different from McCullers' but even more chilling. Indeed, there may be no Southern writer before 1960 so given to violence in fiction as O'Connor. An avowedly religious writer, a Roman Catholic in the midst of a fundamentalist Protestant South, she maintained that violence was necessary to shock modern man out of his secular complacency and into an awareness of good and evil, salvation and damnation. Her novels *Wise Blood* (1952) and *The Violent Bear It Away* (1960) as well as numerous short stories depict characters haunted by God – Old Testament monomaniacs in the midst of the twentieth-century South. Hazel Motes, a Christian *malgré lui*, stalks the streets of the secular city in flight from the 'ragged figure' who haunts his mind, embraces the animal and the material and founds a Church Without Christ before finally succumbing to his fate, torturing and blinding himself and dying, renouncing the world. Another backwoods prophet, Francis Marion Tarwater, cannot escape his mission to baptize his nephew, even if drowning becomes the means of baptism. O'Connor is another of those Southern writers with a fury against abstraction, against rationalism and scientific fact. Her portrait of Rayber, the rationalist schoolteacher, is one of the most scathing indictments of modern man ever drawn.

Richard Wright, the black Mississippian, writes still another version of Southern Gothic – and when Wright writes Southern Gothic, he writes autobiography. Wright, indeed, is one Southerner who, up until the late 1960s, might not have been included in a discussion of Southern literature at all. For it was often assumed in such discussions that Southern literature was white literature. In truth, the Southern black and white experiences have a great deal in common, and black and white writers share a common heritage – one characterized by a distinct sense of place and an abiding awareness of the burden of the past, one which held family and religion at its center, and held a distinct preference for the concrete to the abstract. This is not to say that Wright himself shared all these values, for Wright's early life – extreme poverty and humiliation, family discord, an exposure to fear and violence that went beyond that of most black Southerners – was far less stable and more fragmented than the lives of most black Southern writers. And it is out of his own experience that Wright created *Uncle Tom's Children* (1938), *Native Son* (1940, a novel set outside the South), and his painful autobiography *Black Boy* (1945). In these works Wright documents the American racial nightmare, from the lynchings of rural Mississippi to the degradation of segregated Chicago. As he writes in his introduction to *Native Son*, in response to the contention that the American experience did not engender a rich tragic sense:

We do have in the Negro the embodiment of a past tragic enough to appease the spiritual hunger of even a James; and we have in the oppression of the Negro a shadow athwart our national life dense and heavy enough to satisfy even the gloomy broodings of a Hawthorne. And if Poe were alive, he would not have to invent horror; horror would invent him.

(Perennial Library, p. xxxiv)

Eudora Welty (1909–   ) of Mississippi grew up in the same state as Wright at essentially the same time, and like him she grounded her fiction in the life she observed around her. No writer of Southern Gothic, however, she presents a South which is eccentric and often backward, but hardly savage. She is, indeed, the supreme comic writer of the modern South, but she also writes with a deep understanding of the frustrated desires and thwarted ambitions of her characters. Her novels, particularly *The Robber Bridegroom* (1942), *Delta Wedding* (1946), and *Losing Battles* (1970), are eloquent reflections on time, change, and the threat of the outside world to an insular, protected tradition. In these novels and in her collection of stories *The Golden Apples* (1949) Welty demonstrates a breadth of vision foreign to O'Connor and McCullers, deep but narrow writers. Here she fuses myth with reality, keen social observation with fantasy. As short story writer she is brilliant. Stories such as 'Why I Live at the P.O.', the comic description of a young woman's chosen separation from her family, and 'The Worn Path', the moving story of an aged black woman's fortitude and endurance, demonstrate her humanity and her versatility.

In many respects, Welty is the last of those great Southern writers whose work began to appear before 1945. Those Southerners who came of age in the 1930s and 1940s and began to publish in the years after the Second World War seem often to be dealing with a vastly different South. The novels of William Styron (1925–) and Walker Percy (1916–) are illustrative. The earlier Southern fiction had been set in the rural South; that of Styron and Percy largely in cities and suburbs, Styron's often in locales far removed from the rural South, Percy's in New Orleans and in any number of New South cities. Yet the work of both writers is rooted in the Southern literary tradition. One can find in Styron's first novel, *Lie Down in Darkness* (1951), the pervasive influence of *The Sound and the Fury*. Like Faulkner, he writes a family tragedy culminating in the suicide, in a Northeastern city, of a favored child who is obsessed with time and confused about love. The family includes, besides that child, a weak father, a puritanical mother, and a mentally retarded child. The suicide of Peyton Loftis, like that of Quentin, is preceded by a lengthy interior monologue. And Styron's later novel *Sophie's Choice* (1979) resembles the autobiographical fiction of Thomas Wolfe: the story of a self-conscious young Southerner living in Brooklyn, attempting to write the Great American Novel and to make sense of the world around him.

Percy's debt to past Southern writers is less obvious, but his grounding in Southern cultural and literary tradition is no less firm. The cousin and adoptive son of William Alexander Percy, author of the Southern classic *Lanterns on the Levee* (1941), Walker Percy came to reject the stoicism and racial paternalism of his kinsman, yet in his fiction returns to the central question of Will Percy: what happens to a Southerner of sensitive nature and good breeding when he encounters a crass, materialistic New South? Percy is a curious combination of social satirist and Christian existentialist, and his first two novels, *The Moviegoer* (1961) and *The Last Gentleman* (1967), suggest both his social and philosophical concerns. In the former novel Binx Bolling escapes from the malaise – takes the Kierkegaardian leap from the aesthetic to the religious – by making a commitment of self and marrying his cousin Kate. In the latter novel we follow the wanderings of Will Barrett, another genteel Southerner overly given to abstraction and afflicted by acute self-consciousness, from New York to Alabama to the American Southwest. Both novels, but particularly the latter, show Percy to be what his later novels have confirmed: among writers of fiction, the sanest, most penetrating observer of the contemporary South.

Were there space one could discuss the work of other post-war Southerners: the poetry of James Dickey and A. R. Ammons, the fiction of Ralph Ellison and John Barth, as well as the more recent work of Ernest Gaines, Alice Walker, Cormac McCarthy, and Barry Hannah. McCarthy and Hannah, among other novelists, write a sort of neo-Southern Gothic, and McCarthy's *Child of God* (1973), a tale of murder and necrophilia more lurid than anything Faulkner or Erskine Caldwell ever invented – or, in a more contemporary vein, Hannah's *Ray* (1980) – assure us that a savage South still lives in imaginative literature. The problem for the neo-Gothic novelist is that Southern social reality, broad and representative reality, no longer supports his fiction. Not only is verisimilitude sacrificed, but a certain urgency, a rage to be heard, may have left that writer's voice. Indeed, the danger for the Southern writer is that what to Faulkner and Warren and Welty was original and organic may become, in a different age, ritualized, stylized, stale. The promise of Southern literature, then, lies in a different direction, and a writer like Walker Percy, keenly observing city and suburb but always aware of what came before, has pointed it well. The Southern writer must observe *his* contemporary South – not Faulkner's – and that South, despite the influx of outsiders, a new prosperity, and Sun Belt optimism, is still distinctive.

FORM AND MEANING IN
AMERICAN LITERARY CRITICISM

RICHARD RULAND

Criticism and philosophy have always been closely allied. Our taste, our sense of what is good and beautiful, is inextricably bound to our sense of reality, our ideas about the nature of the world and the life we find ourselves living in it. The story of criticism is in many ways the story of epistemology, that study of our efforts to know the world. What we think we 'know', and how we attempt to validate our knowledge – how insistent our 'sense of things' is – will bear directly on the questions we ask of an artist's work.

These matters have inescapably influenced the literary critic in the practice of his craft. Edgar Allan Poe urged a distinction between Beauty and Truth in a deliberate effort to escape traditional assumptions that basic truths of reality are readily available to us, while Ralph Waldo Emerson insisted that a critic should judge literary work wholly by its success in leading its reader to transcendent truth. Formalist critics from Henry James to Eliot, Blackmur and Wimsatt, have emphasized 'this poem which is a poem and nothing more – this poem written solely for the poem's sake', as Poe put it. But such apparent emphasis on art's 'intrinsic' worth is actually a bold defense of a special way of knowing, an insistence on the unique insights into the nature of reality that art provides and scientific positivism can only, as Wordsworth complained, 'murder to dissect'. From Poe's sonnet, 'To Science' (1829), to John Crowe Ransom's *The World's Body* (1938), the theorist of Formalism has celebrated the 'dream beneath the tamarind tree', the realities and values we can never test but can imagine and embody only in symbolic constructs of language.

But if critical reading and discourse about literature has always rested on the philosophical views of its practitioners, whether acknowledged or not, the last two decades have provided a veritable explosion in our acceptance of the fact. This is an 'Age of Theory'.

Every critical assertion of the past or present is being subjected to close analytic scrutiny to determine the worldview which has shaped it. Einsteinian relativity in physics described an indeterminate world at the very moment that the coherent views of traditional theism and Arnoldian humanism apparently failed the test of war and holocaust. Writers like William James, Eliseo Vivas, Ernst Cassirer and Wallace Stevens tell us that we live in a world of symbol systems, that we are the artists of our own realities, builders of 'fictions' valued as more or less 'adequate', never quite 'supreme'. Much of the modern world has apparently accepted these views of a pluralistic, perceiver-shaped reality; their impact on literary criticism has been immense. Elder Olson's formulation is in itself witness to this epistemological ferment: 'The number of possible critical positions is relative to the number of possible philosophic positions.' If its substance applies to the entire history of literary criticism, the confidence of its assertion marks a new awareness among today's students of literature.

In his essay of 1888, 'The Art of Fiction', Henry James recalled that 'only a short time ago' the novel hardly seemed a subject for serious discussion. 'It had no air of having a theory,' James complained, 'a conviction, a consciousness of itself behind it – of being the expression of an artistic faith, the result of choice and comparison.' This is James's apposite way of telling us what he means by theory, that 'latent core of conviction' that helps us understand what an art 'thinks of itself'.

During the period I have alluded to there was a comfortable, good-humored feeling abroad that a novel is a novel, as a pudding is a pudding, and that our only business with it could be to swallow it. But within a year or two, for some reason or other, there have been signs of returning animation – the era of discussion would appear to have been to a certain extent opened.

No one with any interest in American literature can be unaware that the Age of Criticism so warmly welcomed at mid-century has been propelled during the 1970s and 1980s into a startling 'era of discussion' – some have found it a seething jungle of contradiction and futile speculation. But James would surely have been pleased and amused for, as he says, literary criticism, like the art it considers, 'lives upon discussion, upon experiment, upon curiosity, upon variety of attempt, upon the exchange of views and the comparison of standpoints.' James suggests that any 'genuine' artistic success must rest upon such an exchange of views, that although such success is always delightful to behold, 'theory too is interesting'.

Until recently, there has been no such climate of theoretical discussion in America, a fact that goes a long way to explain the eccentric nature of much of the best writing done before the present century. Americans wanted very much to have a literature of their own. They were certain that a new land, a new theory of government, a new 'nation of nations' could not define and express itself by imitating the art of Britain. But what their literature was to look like and what the materials of its composition would be were questions that rarely escaped the reductive simplifications of everyday journalism. The direct result has been a literature that rarely seems to know what it has set itself to do.

American writing from the seventeenth century to the present can be seen as an unreflective assimilation of disparate, unexamined theories of literature, from the 'plaine style' of Puritan New England ('God's Altar needs not our Polishings') through reliance first on the rationales of Pope, Addison and Goldsmith, then on those of Wordsworth and Scott, Flaubert and Zola, Yeats and Joyce. Such a simplification emphasizes the role literary criticism plays in identifying the assumptions about the nature and function of their art that such imitated writers have made. Where these assumptions are widely recognized, discussion of the kind James describes is possible, as is the growth he associates with it. In such an intellectual climate we can speak of a critical tradition, an on-going discourse on questions of literary form, the 'rules' of genre, the relation of a fictive world to the historical world of social relations we call 'real', and responsibilities literature may or may not have to such vexed matters as 'meaning' and 'truth'.

Poe and the Centrality of Form

The earliest discussions of literature in the United States are remarkable for their aversion to such theoretical speculation. But one of the best professional reviewers challenged both the theoretical naïveté and superficial nationalism of his fellows. Edgar Allan Poe

(1809–49) wondered whether the question of a national literature was not more political than literary; his insistence on distinguishing the two anticipates critical debates that haunt us still. In his own time it contributed to his ostracism from the literary establishment. Poe believed that literature had laws and concerns of its own, and he set himself to explore them in his essays and reviews. As W. H. Auden has remarked, much of Poe's best criticism 'will never be read widely because it lies buried in reviews of totally uninteresting authors' and titles like *Sacred Philosophy of the Seasons*, *The Christian Florist*, and *The History of Texas*. 'One is astounded,' Auden observes, 'that he managed to remain a rational critic at all, let alone such a good one.'

Poe *was* a good critic, a remarkably good one, not so much in the separate practical judgements so often colored by envy and delusions of persecution, but in his attention to the premises on which such judgements rest; he anticipated the New Critical Formalism of a few decades ago and the various critical movements which have succeeded it. But only in France, through Baudelaire and the Symbolists, has Poe had his due. 'Poe was the first,' Paul Valéry remarked in 1929, 'the first to think of giving a pure theoretical basis to literary works.' Writing for Poe was a craft, a discipline of 'ratiocination' exercised in the pursuit of specific purpose.

In the whole composition there should be no word written of which the tendency, direct or indirect, is not to the one pre-established design. And by such means, with such care and skill, a picture is at length painted which leaves in the mind of him who contemplates it with a kindred art, a sense of the fullest satisfaction.

The 'kindred art' is the art of criticism, and its 'sense of the fullest satisfaction' is an aesthetic response dependent on the successful exercise of craft; it is the experience of Beauty.

As critic, Poe set himself against his age and invited a century of neglect by challenging the most firmly held tenet of his contemporaries: he decried as the 'heresy of *The Didactic*' the assumption that art exists primarily to teach or reinforce currently accepted moral truths. In a direct borrowing from Coleridge's *Biographia Literaria*, he insisted that the '*immediate* object' of the writer's efforts is 'pleasure, not truth'.

We would define in brief the Poetry of words as the *Rhythmical Creation of Beauty*. Beyond the limits of Beauty its province does not extend. Its sole arbiter is Taste. With the Intellect or with the Conscience it has only collateral relations. It has no dependence, unless incidentally, upon either Duty or *Truth*.

Poe's separation of literature from the conventional values of his time and the demonstrable truths of science forced him into what now appears an unnecessarily extreme choice between Truth and Beauty. As the Symbolists and later New Critics were to insist, the symbol which is the literary work can provide experience, knowledge, a truth of a fundamentally different kind than that available to the Lockean positivism of sense data. They found reasons to celebrate art that Poe seemed to anticipate only vaguely, but they have honored, by echo and allusion, his insistence that 'there neither exists nor *can* exist any work more thoroughly dignified – more supremely noble than this very poem – this poem *per se* – this poem which is a poem and nothing more – this poem written solely for the poem's sake'.

If we remember that a critic's sense of the nature and purpose of literature rests on his image of the world, we will understand why Poe reminds us so frequently of Mallarmé, of T. S. Eliot's criticism and Brooks' and Warren's *Understanding Poetry*. As Paul Valéry noticed, the universe pictured in Poe's long prose-poem *Eureka* in 1848 anticipates remarkably that of Einstein.

It would not be exaggerating its importance to recognize, in his theory of consistency, a fairly definite attempt to decribe the universe by its *intrinsic properties* . . .

That its tendency approaches recent conceptions becomes evident when one discovers, in the poem under discussion, an affirmation of the *symmetrical* and reciprocal relationship of matter, time, space, gravity, and light.

Poe, that is, saw the work of art as a self-supporting universe analogous to the one that sustains the sphere we live upon.

Poe's innovative departure from the established critical approaches of his age can be appreciated by comparing him to James Russell Lowell (1819–91), the nation's most popular critic before William Dean Howells (1837–1920). Lowell and the younger men who followed him agreed in their respect for the Greek humanism advocated by Matthew Arnold. But Arnold's faith in great literature as a viable substitute for waning religious certitude became for them almost entirely an ethical preoccupation with art's responsibility to teach men how to behave in society. Lowell was committed to the normative aesthetic of Alexander Pope, to the insistence that poetry had serious public responsibility to teach while pleasing, to capture verbally 'what oft was thought but n'er so well expressed'; such convictions kept the work of Bryant and Longfellow on every parlor table and consigned that of Poe and Walt Whitman – sometimes literally – to the flames.

As the world changed after the Civil War, so did the way men understood art and the truths it confidently bequeathed. Lowell and the 'Genteel Tradition' that his followers nourished during the final years of the century were supplanted by the powerful philosophic currents of Romanticism and Realism as the conviction grew that literary theory and practice borrowed from an England of an earlier time had little to offer to the art of America – and that that little had been soon exhausted.

A man of brilliant gifts, Lowell's writing reflects at every turn his theoretical aimlessness, the high price paid by those who cannot settle upon the purpose of what they do or how to accomplish it. As his Neo-Humanist descendants would illustrate in the early decades of the next century, criticism based on traditional moral value was unable to grasp, let alone nourish, the literature of Modernism.

Form as Meaning: James, Eliot, and the New Criticism

To the extent that Modern and Post-Modern American literature has concerned itself with epistemology, the mystery of knowing, it has built on the critical theory and practice of the mature Henry James (1843–1916). Recognition of James's success in describing his art of formal skill and psychological subtlety came slowly, perhaps because, like Poe, his insistence that literature rendered life in complex ways all its own ran counter to the nativist, vernacular social realism of Twain and Howells. The popular conviction that the good writer concerned himself with the workaday world of property, social interaction and manners – the world of the traditional English novel transmuted by egalitarian democracy – dominated American criticism until the late 1930s.

Henry James, possibly the most influential literary theorist America has produced, believed theoretical criticism vital to the health of his chosen art. His 'The Art of Fiction' (1888) was an early effort to define the goals and methods of the novelist that continued into the prefaces he wrote for the New York edition of his novels and tales (1907–9) – commentaries that he hoped, he wrote Howells, would serve as a 'sort of comprehensive manual or *vade-mecum* for aspirants in our arduous profession'. James's Prefaces guided writers and critics alike during the succeeding years, for they set the example and provided the vocabulary for the close textual analysis of prose fiction practiced by a generation of New Critical Formalists. Like Poe, James insisted that 'Questions of art are questions (in the widest sense) of execution.' This indeed is his prerequisite for critical engagement: 'We must grant the artist his subject, his idea, his *donnée*: our criticism is applied only to what he makes of it. Naturally I do not mean that we are bound to like it or find it interesting: in case we do not our course is perfectly simple – to let it alone.' James the artist and James the critic engaged equally in what he called 'the search for form', and he too rejected Poe's Heresy of the Didactic, Lowell's literature of comfortable truths that tied the value of art to its skill in virtuous instruction. He turned instead to the careful social description of the French, of Balzac, Flaubert and de Maupassant. For a time he accepted the honest availability of the world they assumed and concentrated his attention on the lessons of execution they offered.

James wished to be just such a careful craftsman. Scattered throughout his criticism we find pleas for a 'science of control', a 'science of composition . . . architecture, distribution, proportion'. 'It will strike you perhaps that I speak as if we all, as if you all, without exception were novelists, haunting the back shop, the laboratory . . .' This is indeed the way James habitually spoke. He called *The Golden Bowl* a 'feat of engineering', and he once described drama with an analogy that comes close to a literal picture of his standard for any artist:

The successful writer must combine and arrange, interpolate and eliminate, play the joiner with the most attentive skill; and yet at the end effectually bury his tools and his sawdust, and invest the elaborate skeleton with the smoothest and most polished integument . . . The five-act drama . . . is like a box of fixed dimensions and inelastic material, into which a mass of precious things are to be packed away. It is a problem in ingenuity and a problem of the most interesting kind. The precious things in question seem out of proportion to the compass of the receptacle; but the artist has an assurance that with patience and skill a place may be made for each, and that nothing need be clipped or crumpled, squeezed or damaged . . . At last [he] rises in triumph, having packed his coffer in the one way that is mathematically right. It closes perfectly, and the lock turns with a click; between one object and another you cannot insert the point of a penknife.

Recalling this commitment to formal mastery, Leon Edel remarked that James had 'taken the novel-machine apart in a very American way and given it a technology it had not possessed'.

But formal craft alone is not solely what James came to mean by the truthfulness of art, the interest it provides through its 'personal', 'direct impression of life'. Art must concern itself with 'all experience', its province is 'all life, all feeling, all observation, all vision' – its ultimate goal is 'to render the look of things, the look that conveys their meaning'. James eventually decided that the French Realists 'are a queer lot, and intellectually very remote from my own sympathies. They are extremely narrow . . .' He dismissed their views as 'mandarin' and concluded that they

are not getting hold of that larger humanity which is alone eternally interesting . . . they have almost nothing to show us in the way of the operation of character, the possibilities of conduct, the part played in the world by the *idea* . . .; man, for them, is the simple sport of fate, with suffering for his main sign – either suffering or one particular satisfaction, always the same.

Surface description for its own sake, in short, tended toward the determinism of Naturalism. For James, the sharply observed detail was valuable for what it could be made to suggest, the moral interest beneath the surface that he so admired in Hawthorne. A prime example is the 'one particular satisfaction' just referred to. James argued strenuously for freer treatment of sex in the British and American novel; to overlook it was to falsify life. But 'sexual passion', he insisted, is 'poetically interesting' only 'for what it represents . . . it finds its extension and consummation only in the rest of life . . . What the participants do with their agitation, in short, or even what it does with them, *that* is the stuff of poetry . . .' Anything else, he adds with one of his most damning epithets, 'is the open door to the trivial.' The ultimate issue was not craft after all, or not craft alone. In turning to the inner world of consciousness as the source of 'interest', as the place where meaning is shaped and morality is determined by the self that perceives, James drew near to the thought of his brother William and the formulations of American Pragmatism – and thereby assured himself a place in literary history as the first great dramatist of perception.

But neither Henry James nor Poe affected the dominant tradition of literary criticism during the early decades of the present century; criticism remained broad in concern and weak in theory. 'What had criticism in America usually been if not predominantly social, even political in its thinking,' Alfred Kazin (1915–) noted in 1942:

From Emerson and Thoreau to Mencken and [Van Wyck] Brooks, criticism had been the great American lay philosophy, the intellectual conscience and intellectual carryall. It had been a study of literature inherently concerned with ideals of citizenship, and often less a study of literary texts than a search for some new and imperative moral order within which American writing could live and grow . . . It had always been more a form of moral propaganda than a study in esthetic problems . . . Just as the main tradition of American letters for a century and more had been the effort to create a truly national literature, a literature of broad democratic reality, so criticism had usually sought . . . to unite American writers in the service of one imperative ideal or another.

Journalistic critics like H. L. Mencken and Stuart Pratt Sherman argued strenuously and often entertainingly about the didactic purpose of literature unaware that the world each saw and wanted portrayed differed profoundly. Until the New Critical revolution signalled by *Understanding Poetry* (Cleanth Brooks and Robert Penn Warren, 1938) and *Theory of Literature* (René Wellek and Austin Warren, 1949), the ethical Neo-Humanism of Irving Babbitt and Paul Elmer More – through disciples like Sherman, Norman Foerster and many others at universities – had much success in shaping American literary education along Arnoldian lines.

The tradition of wide public discourse described by Kazin was continued by critics as dissimilar as Edmund Wilson (1895–1972), Lionel Trilling (1905–75), Irving Howe (1915–), and Kazin himself. Though their social and political philosophies might differ, most of them saw literature as a means to an end – an informed citizen in a just, comprehensible social world. They frequently attributed the cultural ills of the day to the hegemony of scientific positivism, and yet often they assumed a reality that could be known as they understood science to know it, a reality that remained stable in the pages of history and was reflected clearly and directly in the writings of the authors they favored.

In such a climate, the suggestion that art offered an alternate way of knowing could be found only in the fringe publications of the avant-garde. For T. S. Eliot (1888–1965), the criteria of mainstream criticism ignored what made art what it is and thus failed to see clearly how it participated in and helped us know the world we live in. He agreed with his friend Irving Babbitt that the greatness of literature could not be judged solely in literary terms, but he had learned from Ezra Pound and the French Symbolists, from Poe and Henry James, that whether or not a text was literature at all could be determined *only* in literary terms. By the mid-1920s the political and ethical concerns of Neo-Humanism and Anglican Christianity were leading Eliot far from the aesthetic preoccupations recorded in *The Sacred Wood* (1920), but for decades his insistence on 'the poem itself' was the rallying cry of the first total revolution in the history of American literary criticism.

Like many revolutions, this one had philosophical roots which have too rarely been understood. Eliot's literary ideas owed a good deal to the theoretical training he received at Harvard University from 1906 to 1914. The eminent philosopher of Pragmatism, William James, had retired in 1907, but his influence remained powerful on a faculty that included Josiah Royce and two of Eliot's mentors, Irving Babbitt and George Santayana. (A. N. Whitehead came to Harvard in 1924.) In addition to studying Elizabethan and Jacobean drama and the poetry of Donne and Dante, the young Eliot read deeply in social anthropology and philosophy. During a brief period before moving to London he taught in the philosophy program, and by 1916 he had completed his doctoral dissertation on the Oxford idealist, F. H. Bradley.

There are sufficient elements here to indicate the general direction of Eliot's life and career. His later choice of Christian conservatism would occur in a world he had been taught to see was his for the shaping: 'The letter giveth life.' And he had been taught as well, by Santayana, that beauty is a species of value ... If we approach a work of art scientifically, for the sake of its historical connexions or proper classification, we do not approach it aesthetically. The discovery of its date or of its author may be otherwise interesting; it only remotely affects our aesthetic appreciation.

The distinction anticipates the fundamental New Critical discrimination between the 'extrinsic' approach to the literary text — the approach of traditional academic scholarship and other critical schools (biographical, psychological, socio-economic, mythic) – and the 'intrinsic' emphasis of Formalist New Criticism.

In 1936, when John Crowe Ransom (1888–1974) wished to distinguish his literary position from the ethical imperatives of the New Humanists, he admitted that he too was a 'dogmatical critic', but he insisted that 'there are categories of beauty to be discussed, and techniques of beauty; for beauty is comparatively rare, and probably it is achieved and maintained often with heroic pains. It has the same right to its connoisseurs that moral character has.' In *God Without Thunder* (1930) and *The World's Body* (1938), Ransom's complaints parallel Poe's assault on science for robbing us of our necessary dream beneath the tamarind tree, the beliefs we need to give our life meaning, and he insisted that poetry alone can supply the lack. We need, he argued in *The New Criticism* (1941), an ontological criticism. With its debts to Poe, James, and Eliot, such a criticism was already abuilding, and it took its name from Ransom's volume. Like Ransom, Allen Tate (1899–1979) was an admirer of Eliot, and with Donald Davidson, Robert Penn Warren, Cleanth Brooks and W. K. Wimsatt, he and the others fashioned an approach that captured first the arena of published criticism and then that of the nation's classrooms. They were followed eventually by a host of practitioners, some of them markedly narrower in vision and imaginative reach. But they influenced as well most of the period's major critics, from Yvor Winters and F. O. Matthiessen to R. P. Blackmur, Kenneth Burke, and the Chicago Aristotelians.

The New Criticism seemed new in America because it embraced an ontological idea of art that had largely gone unnoticed in Poe, James, and Joel Spingarn's Crocean aestheticism. Reinforced by Symbolist thought introduced by Arthur Symons in *The Symbolist Movement in Literature* (1899) and Eliot's admiration for Jules Laforgue and other French poets, the New Critics insisted on what they called the 'autonomy' of the work of art – that it was *sui generis*, with laws peculiar to itself. The position led to a great deal of misunderstanding, as the fifth edition of *Understanding Poetry* (1950) acknowledges. Twelve years had passed since the influential textbook's appearance, and Brooks and Warren speak with justifiable pride of their success: 'Today the critical attitude has entered into hundreds of classrooms.' But they fear their emphasis of 1938 has been misconstrued:

A decade ago the chief need was for a sharp focus on the poem itself. At that time it seemed expedient to provide that focus, and to leave to implication the relation of the poem to its historical background, to its place in the context of the poet's work, and to biographical and historical study generally.

And so in the new edition, 'though we continue to insist upon the need for a sharp focus upon the poem itself', various aspects of a poem's context also receive attention. But no intelligent teacher, the new preface chides,

has ever presented poetry in a vacuum ... On the contrary, he brings every resource he possesses to bear upon the poem ... *to see how history, literary and general, may be related to poetic meaning.*

The insistent italics appear in the text, but they have not protected its authors or their fellow critics from dismissal by more recent writers who have sought to move 'beyond the New Criticism'. As we shall see, developments of the past two decades that clearly rest upon the work of Eliot, Ransom, and their colleagues are often separated from it in what has come to seem a ritual killing of the fathers.

Despite the view of recent ahistorical commentators, 'autonomy' for the first New Critics did not mean placing poetry 'in a vacuum'. It meant only that they sought, as Malcolm Cowley observed about the entire Formalist tradition, 'to establish literature as an independent country, with a history and geography of its own'. Allen Tate made the case every Formalist from Poe to the present would urge against those whose readings of literary works center on the implications of their paraphrasable contents. Paul Elmer More 'is primarily a moralist, which is a worthy and serious thing to be,' Tate observed. But 'his failure to understand the significance of style is a failure to understand most of the literature he has read.'

The New Critics' insistence that the literary work represents an autonomous entity, linked to the workaday world in its genesis and materials but separable for purposes of interpretation, led to the method of critical explication presented in *Understanding Poetry* and its innumerable successors. Following the lead of Eliot and traditional rhetorical analysis – drawing, that is, on some of the same legacy adopted by Chicago neo-Aristotelians like R. S. Crane, Richard McKeon, Elder Olson, Norman Maclean and Wayne Booth – Brooks and Warren demonstrated a fine-toothed verbal analysis of individual poems. The works treated are usually short, often by Eliot's favorites, the English Metaphysicals. In the rhetorical ironies of Donne's densely packed lines, the rich resources of verbal play create mutually limiting tensions that the critic examines and describes as a universe unto itself. For the second generation of New Critics in the 1950s, the method could become tediously mechanical and bloodless, but when used by what came to be called 'good readers', the poetry being scrutinized yielded wonders of implication; the whole emerged as richly superior to the sum of its parts, and easy separation of content and form disappeared as varied elements fused into meaning.

New Criticism, it is now a commonplace to observe, taught Americans how to read. Like all philosophical positions, the ontology which prompted the method of explication continues to be controversial, but the subtlety and care of the analytic techniques can and do exist independently. Interest in rhetoric had once been a staple component of American popular culture; with the New Critics the subject returned to classroom and critic's study. The lasting legacy of the movement is the presumption that any reader must read as closely as the New Critics urged, no matter what ultimate uses he has for his inquiry. As F. O. Matthiessen (1902–50), one of the most distinguished scholar-critics to learn from New Criticism, remarked in *The Responsibilities of the Critic* (1952), 'If we are to have adequate cultural history, we must begin by respecting the texts themselves.'

Criticism and the Problem of Knowledge

In 1919, Eliot concluded his seminal discussion of 'Tradition and the Individual Talent' by halting 'at the frontier of metaphysics'. What the genteel platitudes of Lowell's day and the superficial wranglings of the present century gradually made clear is that fundamental philosophical issues could be avoided no longer. Americans have historically shown little appetite for the systematic questioning common abroad. The interest Poe and James took in literary theory was not typically American and hence received little attention from their contemporaries. But it was very American of them to look to Europe for the discussions they missed at home. Eliot too fed his appetite for theoretical discernment at foreign tables, but he found gifted compatriots equally eager to explore fundamental issues; the result was a shift in critical methodology and taste unmatched in American literary history that continues to make itself felt in the criticism of all the arts. Eliot, James and Poe represent a native tradition richly receptive to foreign influence; to the extent that New Criticism canonized their views, American literature and criticism of the present century have become ever more international in flavor.

The philosophical revolution that generated the current age of theory played its part in shaping the developments we sometimes label Modernism. Unlike its manifestations overseas, however, Modernism in America was almost entirely aesthetic, with few social or political ramifications. It might therefore have been difficult to predict that among the major beneficiaries of this fundamental questioning in the United States have been the sociological and political approaches to literary criticism, particularly those influenced by Karl Marx. In place of a theory of history which predicted the disintegration of western capitalism – and led to naïve reduction as literature was tested by its sensitivity to and participation in History's inevitable march – modern Marxist critics can assume that the social and political world they question is man-made. Since it reflects the values of its builders and serves to confirm those values, the entire western world can be seen as the result of 'false consciousness', the product of circular reading and reinforcement of a reality shaped by short-sighted self-interest. Such a reality is in no way absolute. It can be questioned at its sources in human consciousness and identified in the works of literary tradition. By suggesting that an author can free his 'reality' from the assumptions of his flawed culture only through heroic effort, if at all, the new Marxist critic has fashioned a permanent place for himself as a literary nay-sayer. Since, as Terry Eagleton remarks of *The Waste Land*, fertility rites will never redeem our class-ridden civilization, the Marxist socio-political critic seems unlikely ever to encounter a literary product of his culture that he will be wholly able to approve.

The case is not as extreme for critics whose primary loyalty is to minority liberation. Champions of women, blacks, Chicanos and Native Americans hope to supplant 'false consciousness' with 'consciousness raising', perhaps because their vision is not of a re-created world but rather one brought into more equitable balance. They too point to unstated assumptions of value in the works they discuss, but usually with the implication that in America identifying an injustice can and eventually will lead to its redress. For all critics who see literature as cultural symptom and instrument, the new epistemological awareness has opened fresh channels of literary discourse. Most of them now accept, with greater or lesser optimism, a reality that is perceiver-shaped, a language, as Fredric Jameson argues, that holds us prisoner of the very instrument we would use to fashion our escape.

For students of myth and the work of Carl Jung, however, literature leads less to the assumptions of social organization than to the shared shape of human experience, perhaps to the Collective Unconscious itself. Frazer's *Golden Bough*, Jane Harrison's *Prolegomena to the Study of Greek Religion*, the work of Jung and Jessie Weston describe patterns in myth, in the unconscious shaping of dreams, that link literature with some vast narrative system constitutive of human history. For Northrop Frye (1912–   ), literature is composed of archetypes, not necessarily of the Jungian sort but rather counters, conventions that it inherits from earlier literature: poems are made from other poems. Myth, in Frye's ambitious *Anatomy of Criticism* (1957), is less a story than a method, a process of what would later be called intertextuality. Art is about art in an 'autonomous verbal structure' that yet contains 'life and reality in a system of verbal relationships'. Frye's response to the limits of positivistic description attacked by Formalist New Critics is an elaborate taxonomy of genres that he calls Aristotelean. Moving rapidly from individual works to their classes, Frye treats the enormous universe of literary history as the only human history we can know; he thus extends Arnold's faith in literature's power to replace religious certitude far beyond anything Arnold could have imagined. All the world's literature taken together constitutes man's figural embodiment in language of the reality he has assimilated, the ways in which he has found meaning in his world. For Frye, this enormous universe of symbolic discourse is a scriptural resource; the study of its inner relationships and underlying archetypal motifs reveals truths heretofore available only through divine revelation.

Frye's work at the University of Toronto has coincided significantly with the rise of Structuralism in Europe, where once again the erosion of epistemological absolutes has played its part. The linguistic work of Gottlob Frege, Ferdinand de Saussure and Roman Jakobson – who eventually moved to Harvard – successfully challenged theories of language which linked words directly with the material world. Language for the Structuralist is a system of signs arbitrarily employed in signification. Any declarative statement draws on the relations of its terms to others in the system and to the auditor's conversance with the total language, or 'langue', being employed. As with Frye's archetypes, meaning is purely a matter of convention, our grasp of the part in what might be called the ecology of the whole. Application of these structured perspectives has been reinforced by the cultural pluralism of anthropology, especially the work of Claude Lévi-Strauss – who collaborated with Jakobson in a meticulous and influential reading of 'Les Chats de Baudelaire' (L'Homme, 1962).

In 1966 Geoffrey Hartman welcomed Structuralism as 'a new kind of criticism which could view literature as an institution with its own laws or structural principles, yet relate these to both local traditions and the societal as such'. The emphasis here is very close to Frye's: Hartman (1929–) sees an escape from what seems the narrow and closed world of Formalism into time and the sweep of history. But from the artist's point of view, the price has been high, for structuralist critics, like those who adopt the perspectives of Frye, are primarily concerned with the network of relationships between the parts composing the whole, either the langue or the collective myth that is the ultimate focus of their study. The individual work of the individual writer is a single star in a vast galaxy; what the poet thinks of as his poem is no more than the result of his inescapable programing, the flowing through his being of pre-fabricated perceptions and verbal formulae. As an actor in the drama of literary creation, the author – and Roland Barthes' (1915–80) remark became a slogan – was dead.

Those like Robert Scholes who turned the insights of Structuralist systems analysis to the less cosmic questions of literary art have become known as Semiologists. Literary works are of course complex formal patterns of words. How these words bring their meanings, their significations, from the constitutive relationships of the langue into the writer's discourse, how these relationships acquire added meanings from the new system of the individual written work – these are the concerns of the semiologist. It is through Semiology that the linguistic and philosophical currents of the Continent have had the greatest impact on literary criticism in the United States. Two native traditions help explain this impact. The first is the Formalist legacy which buttressed the New Criticism of mid-century. The second is the heritage of Pragmatism. In the thought of C. S. Peirce, William James, and C. I. Lewis, Americans have an intellectual tradition reaching back to Emerson which regards the universe as a system of signs drawing its meaning, to a greater or lesser degree, from the relation of its parts as grasped through the intentions of its human perceiver. Like his brother Henry, for William James the 'Truth' is the successful connection of perceiver and world, 'successful' when the perceiver can thereby function to his ultimate well-being. James's way of 'reading' the material world parallels the Semiologist's approach to the formal verbal system called a poem. A successful reading is one in which the complex relations of the poem's details are apprehended to render the fullest possible awareness of the total work.

Semiology thus strikes many Americans as New Criticism moved from a symbolist to a pragmatic epistemological base. But the shift has been wholly unacceptable to a large segment of the literary community. When the New Critical methods for finding meaning captured in the intricacies of literary symbol systems are wed to a world-view of Absolute Truth, a Truth closely linked, for many of the New Critics, with the revelations of their personal religious traditions, the modern epistemological revolution which American Pragmatism has nourished seems – to recall Andrews Norton on Emerson's Transcendentalism – 'the latest form of infidelity'. At issue, as it was in the Biblical criticism of the previous century, has been the 'ontological status' of the literary work's meaning. Is it single and fixed, placed in the language of the text by its author and available to the humble and careful seeker like treasure in a chest? Or does a poem's meaning reside elsewhere, perhaps in the relationship of an individual reader to his awareness of the systematic arrangements that are the text? Is there only *one* system present *to* be read, or is any linguistic discourse a Byzantine over-lay and virtually indecipherable scramble of coherent but competing systems? In the America of the 1980s there is a wide gulf between many New Critical Formalists and younger critics attracted to Post-Modern conceptions of meaning. M. H. Abrams (1912–   ), an eminent example, labors through scholarship and carefully refined taste to read literary works as he believes they were devised by their authors to be read, while readers like J. Hillis Miller (1928–   ) object on basic philosophical ground to Abrams' quest for single and correct interpretations.

Critics as dissimilar as Hillis Miller, Paul de Man (1919–83), Harold Bloom (1930–   ) and Stanley Fish (1938–   ) have demonstrated repeatedly how Formalist methods of literary analysis can be continued and enhanced by awareness of semiological theory. But they insist as well that the revolution in thought that has moved this century from a world of determinable truth to one of multiple, often conflicting interpretations has totally and irrevocably altered how we think of – and teach – works of literature and the reading appropriate to them. This generational friction is gradually being recognized for what it is, a philosophical debate, and since the epistemological certainties of earlier centuries seem at present to have a shrinking number of serious defenders, we can assume that the newer assumptions will gradually transform many of the literary and educational practices of the nation.

One of the earliest discussions of these antipathetic views and their far-reaching implications was E. D. Hirsch's *Validity in Interpretation* (1967). The title suggests two foci of critical discussion during the past twenty years. As Jane P. Tompkins argues in her excellent survey, *Reader-Response Criticism: From Formalism to Post-Structuralism* (1980), the common ground of twentieth-century criticism distinguishes it from that of earlier centuries: most of it focuses on the interpretation of literary texts. Hence the recent flurry of theoretical activity, by frequently pursuing the same ends, allies itself more than its often ahistorical proponents are willing to admit with the interpretive goals of mid-century Formalism. Hirsch (1928–) chooses the word hermeneutics to describe this concern, and he draws on the long tradition of Biblical exegesis to explore what a text might be taken to be and what we might mean by interpreting it. The notion of 'validity', however, marks the chasm where New Critics and their successors part company. As we have seen, if the critic's presumption is that a single textual interpretation can be isolated as somehow the 'right' one, he is implicitly affirming an epistemological authority – or, as is now commonly said, he is ·'privileging' one reading over another. Hirsch's resolution of the dilemma is to use 'meaning' for the recoverable intent of the original creative act and 'significance' for the varied interpretations subsequent generations of readers have found 'valid'.

It would take us far afield to explore how central to the present century this division has been. The debates over Tradition prompted by Eliot's *The Waste Land* (1922) and 'Tradition and the Individual Talent' (1919) signaled a crisis in the theory of history – our inability to establish whether the past has absolute value in itself or whether, like any other text, the past concerns us only as we variously read and interpret it from the multiple perspectives of today. Our loss of confident faith in any of the scriptures and traditions we have inherited has deprived us not only of the well-springs of explanation and value but also of the very means of establishing the 'validity' of our individual readings of reality. A world without absolute, unchallengeable norms, without epistemological certainty, is a world of ultimate Protestantism: every man becomes his own philosopher, his own arbiter of the true and the real.

In literary criticism, analogous concerns have led to intense debate over the role of the reader in discovering – or determining – the meaning or meanings any text may be said to have. Earlier critical discourse had addressed the relation of the author to his work (biographical and psychological criticism), the inter-dependence of work and world (socio-political criticism and the determining conventions of literary history and myth), and the shaping internal tensions operative in the work itself (Formalism, Structuralism and Semiotics). Recent inquiry has turned to the neglected participants in the entire process; if a text may be said to speak, its discourse has come to be seen as less a monologue than a dialogue. For many recent theorists, a text exists only through the participating perception of its reader; some go so far as to affirm that a literary work – like any other event – has as many meanings as it has readers. As in the larger philosophic universe, so in the more modest realm of literary criticism: the decay of interpretive certainty has made each individual consciousness – each reader – an active partner in creating the meaning of the object perceived.

Varying degrees of centrality have been granted to the reader-perceiver in creating the meaning of a literary work. The phenomenology of Georges Poulet and the early Hillis Miller concerns itself with a passive, almost erotic subjection of reader to the author's presence in the text, while for Michael Riffaterre (1924–) and Jacques Derrida (1930–), the human agent's role in establishing meaning is limited by the shaping power of structural and semiological codes – those 'systems of intelligibility', as Jane P. Tompkins puts it, 'that operate through individuals' and determine their observations. Following in the footsteps of William James and I. A. Richards (1893–1979), the psycho-analytic critic Norman Holland (1927–) has argued that 'interpretation is a function of identity', that all our experience is 'creative and relational', and that we treat a work of literature just as we do anything we encounter: we acknowledge what we can use, interpret it, and assimilate it to maintain our stability and sense of identity. Like Emerson before him, Holland affirms the separateness of the self and the otherness of the object, but all knowing is reciprocal and – in the tradition of Richards – healing. The early work of Stanley Fish posits something like a Structuralist reader, asking – the words are Jonathan Culler's – 'what must an ideal reader know implicitly in order to read and interpret works in ways which we consider acceptable?' But more recently Fish has concluded that conventions are important only in the use we make of them and that readers actually create the works they read – meaning and meaningful existence is not on the printed page but is the experience we have while reading. A poem is thus not simply a formal object in space but an experience in time; its meaning is what happens as the reader negotiates its lines.

Walter Benn Michaels has seen most clearly how much this Post-Modernist thinking in America owes to the Pragmatists, especially C. S. Peirce (1839–1914). To an extent new to history, the individual human self is made constitutive of reality, and so for Michaels Descartes' separation of subject and object or the New Critics' separation of reader and text can be ignored because both the self and the world it knows are cultural, historical constructions. In this view, *any* meaning – of text or world – is relative, time-bound and inescapably self-interested.

It is perhaps not a large step from this individual creation of meaning to denial that anything at all is meaningful – or has value that is related to meaning. The most extreme version of these views has become known as Deconstructionism, an aggressive impressionism that places reader-response at the center of any quest for meaning in the literary experience. Victor B. Leitch suggests that the deconstructive approach begins when 'Nietzsche, Freud and Heidegger call into question and destroy the metaphysical concepts of being, truth, consciousness, self, identity, and presence.' Since the post-structural Deconstructionist recognizes no referential connection between linguistic signs and any truth outside them, a literary text becomes in effect a cognitive playground. As Jonathan Culler notes,

> Although Derrida's writings all involve close engagement with various texts, they seldom involve interpretations as traditionally conceived. There is no deference to the integrity of the text, no search for a unifying purpose that would assign each part its appropriate role. Derrida characteristically concentrates on elements which others find marginal, seeking not to elucidate what a text says but to reveal an uncanny logic that operates in and across texts, whatever they say.

The logic 'revealed' is controlled only by the deconstructive critic's ingenuity, and so the improvisational opportunities of the approach resemble, as many have noticed, the creative independence assumed by the jazz musician in his elaborations on a composer's melodic text. The results make creative claims of their own, but they rarely contribute to reader comprehension of the text in hand.

Deconstruction in the United States can be traced to Derrida's paper, 'Structure, Sign, and Play in the Discourse of the Human Sciences', delivered in 1966 at Johns Hopkins University. The consequent work of Paul de Man, J. Hillis Miller, and most notably, Geoffrey Hartman, has forced current American criticism to accommodate a powerful neo-romantic impulse that argues through example – as H. L. Mencken and Leslie Fiedler had some years earlier – that criticism is a performative art, that the critic is in important ways a creative artist. Firmly based at Yale University – ironically the center of New Criticism decades before – the major Deconstructionists are often grouped with a more independent Yale professor, Harold Bloom, in their dismissal of what has come to seem the Lockean positivism of the New Critics' isolation of meaning in the individual literary text. Bloom calls his *The Anxiety of Influence* (1973) a poem, and although his romantic humanism stops short of what he calls the 'serene linguistic nihilism of Deconstructionism', he would doubtless accept Hartman's praise of his fellow interpretive improvisors as 'the unacknowledged poets of our time'.

Some Critical Issues

In 'The Critic Who Does Not Exist' (1928), Edmund Wilson expressed regret

that some of our most important writers . . . should work, as they apparently do, in almost complete isolation, receiving from the outside but little intelligent criticism and developing, in their solitary labors, little capacity for supplying it themselves.

The absence of an 'atmosphere of debate' is 'a sign of the rudimentary condition of our literature in general'. Unlike the energetic theoretical discussion of the French, criticism in America lacks

the interest of the intelligence fully awakened to the implications of what the artist is doing . . . There is one language which all French writers, no matter how divergent their aims, always possess in common: the language of criticism.

Wilson's complaint has been sounded frequently in America, and yet the nation has long ignored both the rich theoretical tradition of fundamental questioning pursued by the Formalist heirs of Edgar Allan Poe and the creative formulations of Jamesean Pragmatism. Like the Symbolist movement of the last century, current epistemological speculation has traveled from afar to encounter warm welcome on native ground well prepared to receive it. The result has been a flurry of intense critical discussion that has often surprised the continental thinkers apparently responsible for it. The Pax Romana of New Criticism spanned a quarter century, but it has yielded in the past two decades to debate of sufficient vigor to recall H. L. Mencken's zestful report on the 1920s:

> Ears are bitten off. Noses are bloodied. There are wallops both above and below the belt . . . [that] melodramatize the business of the critic, and so convince thousands of bystanders, otherwise quite inert, that criticism is an amusing and instructive art.

Unfortunately for inert bystanders and serious artists, however, today's discourse – in reaching beyond the metaphysical frontiers Eliot and his contemporaries were reluctant to cross – is often couched in a language of abstractions only the most persistent can follow and enjoy.

There is no reigning theory of literature in America as the century draws to a close. And consequently there is no dominant theory of criticism or agreement on a canonical literary tradition. As realization grows that all criticism rests on philosophical assumptions, the epistemological pluralism of our age multiplies theories of art. These in turn generate revisions of the literary canon, anthologies which embody them, and continuing debate over who the significant American writers are and how they should be read and taught. This ferment, this grudging agreement to disagree, characterizes contemporary critical discourse in America. It has fueled new interest in the history of criticism, in its issues, dialogues, persistent questions and time-bound answers. Perhaps the only incontestable conclusion at the moment is that few appear willing any longer to accept traditional visions of unmediated reality. The result can only be continuing efforts to discover the fundamental meaning and value of literature for the life of man and the universe he creates.

HENRY MILLER AND NORMAN MAILER

JOHN W. ALDRIDGE

In 1976, Norman Mailer (1923–   ) somehow found the time while working on his massive historical novel, *Ancient Evenings* (1983), to bring together, and prepare critical introductions for, various selections from what he believed to be the best of the writings of Henry Miller (1891–1980), published as *Genius and Lust* (1976). Until the early 1960s several of Miller's books – most notably, *Tropic of Cancer* (1934; 1961), *Black Spring* (1936; 1963), and *Tropic of Capricorn* (1939; 1961) – were banned on the ground of obscenity from publication in the United States, although they had long enjoyed wide circulation abroad and among American connoisseurs of dirty books.

Mailer's first motive in offering the new collection was to take advantage of the relaxed vigilance of the courts and reprint portions of some of those hitherto contraband books as well as others in the hope that, since they no longer needed to be read in the febrile atmosphere of the salacious, they might have a chance of being appreciated for the qualities he perceived in them. He also wanted to argue his case for Miller as one of the major, albeit neglected writers of his literary generation.

There is attractive filial devotion in all this on the part of a younger writer who owes his elder a very large debt of influence and who resembles him in some rather remarkable ways. Mailer may be forgiven for having claimed considerably more for Miller than most of us would be disposed to support without considerably hedging our assent. Yet it is perfectly true that Miller's reputation after all the years of his notoriety is still by no means securely established and that he has remained a mysterious, vaguely appealing, but somehow unenviable quantity in American literature. This is not, however, at all the same as saying that Miller has continued to suffer neglect. He survived the extremely protracted period of his obscurity to see all his books become lawfully available and sources of comfortable income. Since the early 1960s at least a half-dozen book-length studies and two substantial volumes of critical essays about him have been published. Still, it must be admitted that as Miller's books have ceased to be controversial, they have not gained in interest, and the scholars, in assimilating him into the canon of standard modern authors, may in fact only have made him eligible for admission to the hallowed vaults of scholarly entombment.

In any event, it may be possible now to separate the excellent from the dreadful in his work (and there is a great abundance of both) and to arrive at some understanding of the factors that have helped to create the anomaly of his position at this time. First, it should be said that Miller was a writer whose literary quality was at any moment largely determined by the nature and intensity of his feelings about a particular subject. There was very little, if any, separation in him between the man who suffered or hated, lusted, or loved and the mind which created. Thus, when he felt extravagantly and positively, he tended to give way to gush, sentimentality, and pontification – elements that flawed his otherwise quite magnificent book on Greece, *The Colossus of Maroussi*. When, on the other hand, he felt little or negatively, he could be detached, derisive, as cuttingly heartless as a suicidal court jester, and at such moments he was capable of writing like the best who ever wrote.

This is probably why some of his most successful and authentic work is about sex and the Brooklyn world of his childhood. Toward the former he seems to have felt a tremendous cruel hilarity in the face of the grisly horniness of it all, and toward the latter an at times overpowering repugnance which was mitigated, however, by his sense of the pathos of the life led by and foisted upon him by his grim German-Lutheran parents. In portions of *Black Spring* and in the incomparable memoir 'Sunday After the War' (1944), Miller describes these people 'who . . . never once had . . . opened the door which leads to the soul, never once did . . . dream of taking a blind leap into the dark', and who helped to create him in the rabidly adversary role which he defended from then on with a puritan rectitude at least equal to theirs.

Like so many American writers of his generation Miller formed his artistic premises in the matrix of the subversive, on a fanatical commitment to a doctrine of total personal freedom and the most unsettling honesty about himself and his emotions – whatever, in fact, represented an engagement of life antithetical to the hypocrisies of official society. At a time when, for the provincial American, raw experience in and for itself seemed equivalent to ascension to God-head, Miller became a supreme cultist and chronicler of the rawest experience conceivable. Miller dedicated himself to becoming the world's first artistically serious writer of pornographic novels at a time when reason and repression were still the mandatory features of established culture, treating the sex act as if it were a triumphant dance on the grave of the righteous.

But what is perhaps most striking about Miller is that, in the service of his nihilism, he was able to reduce himself back to a state of total infantile irresponsibility without the slightest twinge of con-science. This more than anything may well be what helped estrange him from American readers, for he tended to play far too cheerfully and guiltlessly the complete bastard for us to love him very much. It would seem that we can accept such a man only so long as we have reason to suspect that in some as yet unpolluted part of himself he is conscious of violating principles he knows to be right. The quite honorable French tradition of the *flâneur* is alien to us, and par-ticularly odious is one who is a professional idler in everything except copulation and the writing of filthy books. Miller saw the sex act as one of the funniest routines in the human vaudeville, and he also saw it, in the form of its usual practice in the bohemian world he knew, as one of the most obvious symptoms of the emotional illness of modern culture, which had evolved from a state of miserable re-pressiveness to a state of moral anesthesia without ever attaining to a genuine revolution of feeling. It is true that he was himself in some large degree a sufferer from the same disability. Mailer correctly observed in one of his critical introductions that Miller could not write about sex with love, for love was something felt for an ideal woman, a virginal image one worshipped in fantasy, while one copulated with whores who were all other women.

Yet Miller in his best work was always able to transcend the sordidness implicit in this view. What saved him was his power to find high pleasure in the sexual comedy and positively to revel in the detritus thrown off by the process of the world's dissolution. Miller delighted in the ugliness of the bodily functions because it was for him an affirmation of the vitality of life at a time when the forces of technology were hard at work regimenting, purifying, and intellectualizing life out of existence.

It is fitting that Mailer in particular should have chosen to reintroduce Miller through his admirable collection to an audience which had not previously responded to him with very much enthusiasm. Mailer and Miller resemble each other in several important ways — in their outrage at the totalitarianism of modern machine society, the displacement of instinct by scientific methodology, spontaneous emotion by the calculated determinations of the will, unique individuality by the mass standardizations of the modern egalitarian state. They are also closely similar in their common desire — expressed in formal ideological terms by Mailer, through textual implication in Miller — to foment rebellion against these deadly processes and, partly through the deliberate cultivation of obscenity, to do what they can to restore the integrity and vitality of the subliminal self.

In fact, for at least the first twenty years of his writing career, Mailer made a determined effort to exploit all the resources of literary and social outrageousness in order to bring about a revolution in the consciousness of his time. This fight caused deep erosion of his ego, even at the moments when his ego was most insufferably in evidence; and inevitably it provoked him to follies and excesses that did him and his work serious harm. For one thing, it led him to antagonize large sectors of the reading public. For another, it gave almost everything he wrote during the decade following the appearance of his first novel, *The Naked and the Dead* (1948), a curiously strained, claustrophobic quality that seemed to speak of the existence of creative ambitions too intense for his creative grasp. One could sense in both *Barbary Shore* (1951) and *The Deer Park* (1955) that the main current of his energy was trying to go elsewhere, trying to engage certain crucial ideas that were beginning to take shape in his mind, but was being balked by some recalcitrance in his material or some limitation in his language. Deep within those books one felt the pressure of something big growing, a vision or prophecy or simply a hatred that was perhaps too radical and disturbing to find embodiment in the conventional forms of the novel, perhaps too radical and disturbing for Mailer himself. For a long time Mailer was driven to seek easy and sensational shortcuts to the fulfillment he appeared unable to find in his work. He tried to gain attention through self-advertisement, challenges of the law, attempts to pass himself off as a New York mayorality candidate, as the only man with guts enough to defy Sonny Liston to his face, as the man mainly responsible for John Kennedy's election to the Presidency. The essays, furthermore, in which he put forth these claims seemed to be the only writing he was able to do, and this struck many people as an open admission that he had at last decided he could not make it in an important way as a novelist and was trying to salvage what was left of his career by peddling his megalomania to *Esquire*.

It was hard to say whether prevailing opinion was right or wrong, whether these were indeed the antics of a man sick for publicity at any price, or the honestly frustrated responses of a writer who for some reason could not mediate successfully between his ambitions and the restrictive literary circumstances of his time. Undoubtedly, they were a little of both. But certain clues like those to be found in the autobiographical passages of *Advertisements for Myself* (1959) seemed to suggest that although he was indeed sick for publicity, he was not sick for it at any price. If he behaved irresponsibly, he did so for naïve but wholly honorable reasons: because he suffered from a deep-lying dissatisfaction with his position as a serious novelist and was trying in all the wrong ways to break out of an impasse. It only made his dissatisfaction seem more poignant to recognize, as of course he could not, that it was based on a sadly inflated idea of the kind of position a serious novelist can expect in our day to enjoy. Very early in his career Mailer fell victim to the notion that large popular success was the fit and natural reward for significant achievement in the novel. Thus, Ernest Hemingway, for example, was both great and world-famous and so, in more modest degree, were F. Scott Fitzgerald, John Steinbeck, and Thomas Wolfe. Mailer of course reacted powerfully and personally to the good fortune of these men and from it abstracted a formula for success with which he proceeded, characteristically, to prove himself a failure. It seemed to him that if a novelist were serious enough and good enough, he would inevitably be widely read and widely praised. If he were not widely read and widely praised, that could only mean that he was not good enough. In fact, he could consider himself a total loss unless his books made the bestseller lists and stayed on them a certain generous number of weeks.

It apparently never occurred to Mailer that the times in which he himself became a novelist were very different from the 1920s and 1930s, and the whole relationship between the novelist and the reading public had profoundly changed – and changed, according to his own logic, for much the worse. Among the writers with whom he could consider himself in direct competition, only J. D. Salinger (1919–   ) enjoyed anything like the status of the younger Hemingway or Fitzgerald, and there was much in Salinger's work and reputation at which Mailer might legitimately have sneered. Most of his other contemporaries, furthermore, appeared to have resigned themselves to being more praised or criticized than read, and to have a certain limited status in the literary world while remaining virtually unknown to the general reading public. But Mailer took it for granted that his really decisive competition was not with his contemporaries, for whom, on the whole, he had little respect, but with the most distinguished of his predecessors. Thus, one found him in *Advertisements for Myself* brooding over Hemingway's career and trying to discover the secret of the master's 'strategy', or admiring, among others, Truman Capote (1924–84) because Capote had managed to parlay his pretty eccentricities into a campy kind of celebrity. From the beginning the emphasis for Mailer was all on the image a writer might, with care and cunning, project. Hemingway's career had been exemplary in this regard. For years, according to Mailer, Hemingway had written nothing 'which would bother an eight-year-old or one's grandmother', and yet his reputation was firm because 'he knew in advance, with a fine sense of timing, that he would have to campaign for himself, that the best tactic to hide the lockjaw of his shrinking genius was to become the personality of our time'. Hence, it followed with a perfect twisted consistency that Mailer, the present sufferer from lockjaw, had only to become a comparable personality in order to achieve a reputation of comparable firmness.

The point seemed to be that Mailer was convinced that it can be 'fatal to one's talent not to have a public with a clear . . . recognition of one's size'. Just how the public could be expected to achieve such a recognition without being provided with work of size, he did not explain. He simply needed to think extremely well of himself in order to write even half well, and the trouble was that every time he would manage to begin thinking well of himself something would happen to make him think badly.

The autobiographical sections of *Advertisements for Myself* were very largely a record of the forces that conspired to deprive Mailer of his self-esteem. First *Barbary Shore*, then *The Deer Park* failed to win the approval he so desperately required. The former did not make the bestseller lists at all; the latter made them for a tantalizing week or two, then slipped off, if not quite into oblivion, into the next worst thing: middling, lukewarm notoriety. After the failure of *Barbary Shore* he was plagued by the intuition that he was working his way toward saying something unforgivable, not something badly or opaquely said but something unforgivable. The trouble, it seemed, was that the book was simply too powerfully and painfully honest for human consumption. Thus, he rationalized, and thus he agonized over his failure to achieve a success that he would probably have despised if he had achieved it.

His difficulties finding a publisher for *The Deer Park* had been another blow to his self-esteem. 'For the vitality of my work in the future,' he said, 'and yes, even the quality of my work, I needed a success and I needed it badly if I was to shed the fatigue I had been carrying since *Barbary Shore*.' If *The Deer Park* had managed to be

a powerful best seller . . . I would then have won. I would be the first serious writer of my generation to have a best seller twice, and so it would not matter what was said about the book . . . a serious writer is certain to be considered major if he is also a best seller.

And to be *considered* major by virtue of one's sales figures was not only the same as *being* major; it was essential to one's *continuing* to be major.

The implications of such statements are so appalling that one is shocked by them out of almost all understanding of the truth they conceal. Yet the truth, however ugly, is undeniable. Success, even of the most blatantly commercial kind, *can* very often make the difference between being critically recognized and being ignored. It is a matter, as Mailer himself once put it, of 'relaxing the bite of the snob to the point where he or she can open the mouth and sup upon the message'. Bestsellerdom has often been known in our day to create a large, if temporary reputation on the strength of very little evidence, just as it has been known to rescue from obscurity a reputation that deserved to be large. For a writer of Mailer's competitive temperament and particularly his early experience of success with *The Naked and the Dead*, it is easy to see how continued success could become a psychological necessity on which the quality of his subsequent performance might very well depend. The fact that he happened to have become a kind of writer who could no longer please a large public did not diminish his need for the benefits to be derived from having pleased. It simply deepened his confusion and frustration.

The whole trouble was that the huge success of his first novel had infected him with the values, if not the skills, of a petty politician. He had pleased his constituents and been elected to office. He may, as he said, have been running for President ever since 1948, but his politics had altered radically in the interval and so apparently had the character of his constituents. He could hardly expect to charm them with his bright promise of 1948. He could not go on writing *The Naked and the Dead* over and over. Yet the books he had written seemed necessarily unpleasant, and those he wanted to write seemed destined to grow more unpleasant the more he hoped that by some miracle their unpleasantness would win him the election.

His frustration was such that he appeared to be on the verge of doing almost anything to bring that miracle about except the thing that his needs, as he stated them, made logically imperative: to write quite cynically what the public wanted to read. Since that was unthinkable, the politician in him turned ugly and began to campaign against him. By the time he started writing the fateful *Village Voice* columns (1954–7), he had acquired the suicidally belligerent habits of a man who understood his own value so little that he felt compelled to seek his image in the outrage of others (I offend; therefore, I am). He began to court hostility with as much vigor as he had previously courted popularity. And it became apparent that he needed to be hated in order to start loving himself once again and resume the lone, aggressively outlaw role that he sensed was his natural one. He now began for the first time since *The Naked and the Dead* to be honest with himself, not with his work, but with himself. For the first time he admitted that what he wanted more than success was to provoke, incite, and if possible, revolutionize – to do, in short, what he had all along been trying to do without wanting to accept the consequences. Ironically, it was from this time on that he began to show signs of becoming the major writer he had been asking the public to take him for, notably in the sections of *Advertisements for Myself* in which he lamented most bitterly his lost battle to be accepted as major. There and in the essays he soon began to publish in *Esquire* and later collected in *The Presidential Papers* (1963) – the essays that so many people saw as evidence of his creative failure – he produced by far the best writing he had ever done. In particular, at some moment in that bleak period of foiled prospects and compensatory bluster and brag, he seemed to have discovered a style, his true style, one entirely unlike any to be found in his earlier novels. Both *Barbary Shore* and *The Deer Park* had suffered badly from verbal constipation. The clean, hard, yet flexible language of *The Naked and the Dead* had given way in those books to something choked and flat, without flexibility or ease, heavy, toneless, and very dead. It is clear now that Mailer was quite simply never a novelist in the true sense after *The Naked and the Dead*, and that book, like most war novels by young men, was as much an accident of experience as it was a creative achievement, although indeed it was that. But after it Mailer began to have real difficulty projecting his feelings and ideas into an objective dramatic situation. The necessity to create characters and relate them meaningfully to one another obviously forced him to be concerned with problems that did not really interest him. His natural subject was not, it seemed, other people but himself. He did not want to invent; he wanted to confess, to display *himself* as the sole recorder and protagonist of significant contemporary experience.

So it was that when he came to write *Advertisements for Myself* and the *Esquire* essays, Mailer experienced an immense release of inhibitions and was able for the first time to confront his feelings and ideas in their full complexity, to make complete use of his resources not only as a highly skilled worker in language but as an intuitive thinker of an at times almost superhuman sensitivity to the psychic and social realities of his time. And he expressed this sensitivity in a style that combined the mean talk of the hipster and the edgy rhetoric of psychiatry into a prose instrument as lethal as a switchblade.

Advertisements for Myself was thus for two crucial reasons an extremely important transitional work in Mailer's career: in it he found his true relation to the prose medium, and through the new freedom afforded him by that relation he discovered his most complex and vital subject — Norman Mailer seen as combined victim, adversary, hero, and fool being simultaneously humiliated and aggrandized as he engages the ogres and windmills of contemporary history. By 1959 his remarkable sensitivity to the intricate telegraphies of status had already taught him this much: that to be taken seriously as a man and writer you do not *demand* the approval of the public, for this puts you in the position of appearing to feel arrogantly superior to them. The far better way is to make the public feel superior to you by demonstrating just how pathetic you have become in trying to win their approval. If, as Leslie Fiedler once remarked, nothing succeeds for Americans like failure, it is equally true that confession of failure is not only cleansing to the soul but absolutely wonderful for one's public image.

Having apparently learned all this by 1959, Mailer went on to learn something even more essential to his future prosperity: how to make himself into the kind of writer who would finally neutralize through his work some of the mistrust and hostility he had generated through his public behavior. First, he began making much more direct use in his fiction of his own well-publicized obsessions and aberrations — his interest in the mystical properties of the orgasm in *The Time of Her Time* (1959), the spiritually regenerative effects of wife-murder in *An American Dream* (1965), the cathartic possibilities of the scatalogical in *Why Are We in Vietnam?* (1967). This had the effect of dissociating these ideas from his public self and from the essays and interviews in which he had first presented them as shockingly offensive personal interests, and giving them the safely general and objective quality of fictional themes. As such, they might still seem offensive. But at least they would be identified with his imaginary characters and no longer be taken as quite such literal evidence of his own moral corruption.

At the same time he was also discovering how to project in his work – primarily in the meta-journalism he began to write in the late sixties – a self-image which became steadily more attractive, because a new note of humor gave it an air of ironic detachment and ambiguity that was both appealing and enormously effective as a tranquilizer of enemies. He was no longer the victim of his bludgeoning first-person delivery. Instead, Mailer became his own most derisive critic as he observed his various personae – aging, hungover activist in Washington, 'the reporter' in Miami and Chicago, Aquarius in Cape Kennedy and Houston – pass through the postures of acute embarrassment, ineptitude, braggadocio, affectation, and occasional wisdom, hamming it up for the gallery or putting down a rival, but always finally being put down hardest by himself. The writer in him had now found a way of using these familiar traits as material, and in the process he turned his worst vices into almost lovable virtues.

In achieving these realignments Mailer can hardly be accused of cynicism. He seems rather to have passed into a new phase of personal and creative development in which he was able to engage himself and his material in fresh terms. By the late sixties he had gained in wisdom as well as age. But also it was highly fortunate that he began just then to offer in his journalism a kind of material singularly appropriate to the historical moment. It had been obvious for years to others, if not to Mailer, that if he expected, as he claimed, to have a revolutionary influence on the consciousness of the age, he would be unlikely to do so through the novel. Moreover, the form itself seemed inadequate to satisfy the needs of a younger generation who had grown to believe that the social realities of this world are far more important than imaginative fictions, and who were trying to relate to issues as the generation before them had tried to relate to ideas. Perhaps even as far back as *The Naked and the Dead* it had been evident that Mailer's particular powers found their most intense stimulus in moments of social and political crisis, in apocalyptic confrontations between individuals and the massive forces of historical and institutional change. The march on the Pentagon, the riots in Chicago, the Presidential conventions of 1968 were as beautifully suited to Mailer's temperament and style as if he had invented them himself – which, in fact, he might have done – and it so happened that all the seismic instruments agreed that these occasions demanded expression in precisely the form he and he alone could give them.

If he had come to envision himself as a symptomatic consciousness mediating between his personal micro-hells and the major disasters of his age, he now had an audience desperately in need of someone on whom they could project their own more incoherent sense of being both agents and dupes of history. What they found in Mailer was a spokesman who could bring forcefully into focus the contradictory elements of this feeling, and, above all, a human being whom they could accept − as they had accepted no one since John Kennedy − for a hero because he epitomized in his humanness the ambiguities necessary to an acceptable heroism at that time. He was tough, brash, defiantly irreverent, a taker of unbelievable risks. But he was also − and openly admitted to being − vulnerable, uncertain, fearful of the impression he was making on others.

Yet that exactly was the secret of Mailer's appeal, for he was guts at war with all his unmastered contradictions and fears, and he monitored them in battle with that deadly obsessiveness of the general who has never quite grown up to the courage of his command, brooding over the corpses of real men when he should have been figuring the cold statistics of killed and wounded. Mailer was like the early characters of Hemingway, and of course he would like to have thought that he was more than a little like Hemingway himself. He was all blustering defense mechanism, the hairy fist clutching the fragile rose, bravery earned at the expense of panic, a mass of insecurities constantly in need of the challenge that would force him into at least the appearance of strength. He thus dramatized the antithetical impulses that underlay the protest movement and the psychology of the young. He expressed their strong mistrust of the pieties of the establishment at the same time that he forced them to confront their own even more pompous pieties. He embodied their sense of self-importance and of insignificance, their faith and their cynicism, their desire to make the grand gesture and their intuition that the grand gesture would probably have slight effect on anyone, least of all the blind course of history.

But these same qualities that made Mailer so attractive to the younger readers of his journalism also helped to ingratiate him with older readers and even former enemies. That developing note of self-derisiveness which came to characterize his treatment of his various personae was accompanied by an increasing tendency to equivocate about issues and people he at one time most probably would have demolished. Practically every portrait he drew of public events and personalities could be seen to have a dimension of meliorating ambiguity. If he put down liberals, one also noticed that he put down conservatives. He might show irritation over the fact that Ralph Abernathy had kept the press waiting forty minutes in Miami. He might even use the occasion to deliver one of his most agonized and eloquent perorations on the whole oppressive phenomenon of Negro rights:

... he [Mailer] was so heartily sick of listening to the tyranny of soul music, so bored with Negroes triumphantly late for appointments, so depressed with Black inhumanity to Black in Biafra, so weary of being sounded in the subway by Black eyes, so despairing of the smell of booze and pot and used-up hope in the blood-shot eyes of Negroes bombed at noon ...

He might even acknowledge the presence in 'some secret part of his flesh [of] a closet Republican', yet the confession clearly costs him something in 'dread and woe'. Its impact is softened if not canceled by his so evident guilt, and that, it turns out, is not his loss but his gain, for he put into words our most vicious buried hatreds but purged himself and us with the detergents of self-disgust.

In the same manner one also saw him in *Armies of the Night* (1968) open an attack on his peers, yet with a sure instinct for the right one to destroy – Paul Goodman, lost to him anyway, but not Robert Lowell, or Dwight Macdonald, who at that moment was known to be at work on a review of *Why Are We in Vietnam?* for *The New Yorker*. Again, it would be unfair to suggest that what has really happened to Mailer is that he has become a politician: his vision has simply grown more dialectical. What now often *appears* to be circumspection has worked powerfully to his advantage. He now knows how little real profit there is in the self-indulgence of the direct attack, and how much potential risk. To allow oneself the exhilaration of trying with a single blow to kill off all one's literary competitors – as he very nearly succeeded in doing in the two critical essays, 'The Talent in the Room' (1959) and 'Some Children of the Goddess' (1966) – is to take the chance of undermining one's whole campaign for the championship. Mailer did not dare to afford such luxuries now that he saw he had become the caretaker of a possibly major reputation and a talent for winning the large-scale approval he had fought for throughout his literary life.

During the 1970s and now well through the 1980s his career has proven him correct. He has become widely recognized as the possessor of a major reputation, and he has won large-scale approval because he is now finally appreciated as a major literary talent. He has gone on to produce more remarkable journalism in *The Executioner's Song* (1979), what he has called a 'real-life novel' about the Utah murderer, Gary Gilmore, and in 1983 he brought out *Ancient Evenings*, his huge historical novel set in ancient Egypt, which was widely and respectfully, if somewhat perplexedly, reviewed.

Mailer is now clearly a prominent elder statesman and the foremost celebrity of American letters, the recipient of prizes and honors which even his former enemies agree, however reluctantly, he entirely deserves. It may be that he has not succeeded in revolutionizing the consciousness of his age. But he has decidedly enlarged it. And if he has not yet become the great novelist he has so long endeavored to be, he has become a powerful creative force and intelligence, surely the most courageous, energetic, and aggressively adventurous American writer of these largely undistinguished years.

SAUL BELLOW'S ENIGMATIC IRONIES

FRANK WHITEHEAD

Bellow's modestly prolific output (nine novels and two volumes of short stories between 1944 and 1984) has evoked a remarkably variegated outpouring of commentary and assessment, ranging from brusque dismissal as 'a minor comic novelist' to comprehensive bibliographies recording 'the kind of world-wide recognition given only to great writers'.

Where judgements differ so widely, it seems sensible to start with the short novel which displays Bellow's distinctive talent in its most unflawed and undiluted form. *Seize the Day* (1956) covers, at most, eight hours in a single day in the life of Tommy Wilhelm, an out-of-work sales executive in his mid-forties, who is emotionally and financially in extremis; but this brief period is captured for us with a riveting immediacy. This is partly a matter of the vivid physical evocation of the New York setting – the Upper Broadway hotel where Wilhelm starts his day, together with its immediate environs. Relevant too, as Wilhelm swiftly takes on for us a living presence, is the ease with which Bellow's descriptive touch moves almost unnoticed from an objective third-person viewpoint, to Wilhelm's own rueful self-perception, and then to another character's vision of him (his elderly father's fastidiously disapproving scrutiny). As in all his successful fiction, however, Bellow's narrative technique is rooted essentially in the persuasively authentic idiom which he has forged for his protagonist's consciousness, a consciousness through which we view not only the events of this particular day, but also, via a sequence of excoriating flashbacks in memory, the salient episodes in his past life which have brought him to his present impasse. From these elements the novelist has created a 'dramatic poem' with an organic coherence whose closely knit verbal texture eludes any attempt at brief quotation.

Wilhelm gave up his position with the Rojax Corporation out of pique because they wanted him to share his territory; he has left his wife who vindictively duns him for money and refuses to divorce him; and his finances are in crisis because under the influence of the bizarre and enigmatic Dr Tamkin he has plunged his last $700 on a speculation in the commodities market which is turning out badly. These are only the latest in a long series of misjudgements reaching back to his college days, when he went to Hollywood on the grudging recommendation of a disreputable talent scout and wasted seven years there trying to become an actor.

After much thought and hesitation and debate he invariably took the course he had rejected innumerable times. Ten such decisions made up the history of his life. He had decided that it would be a bad mistake to go to Hollywood, and then he went. He had made up his mind not to marry his wife, but ran off and got married. He had resolved not to invest any money with Tamkin, and then had given him a check.

In the space of a few pages this central theme has thus been laid out for us with admirable economy.

No less succinct is the presentation, this time in dramatic form, of another recurrent theme, Wilhelm's ambivalent relationship with his handsome and distinguished old doctor father. Though 'deeply hurt' at his wealthy father's blandly affable resistance to a plea for help, Wilhelm understands the self-preoccupation which underlies it ('Old people . . . have hard things to think about. They must prepare for where they are going. . .'); and when they meet at the breakfast table he starts out with the intention of restraining himself and avoiding further appeals. Inevitably the intention breaks down as his highly charged feelings are further inflamed by his father's unsympathetic cross-questioning and advice; and there is an unerring precision, at once comic and agonizing, in Bellow's step-by-step charting of the angry confrontation which ensues and which leaves Wilhelm with 'the salt odor of tears in his nose' as he inwardly curses himself with the ludicrous animal names he reserves for such occasions.

But at the same time, since there were depths in Wilhelm not unsuspected by himself, he received a suggestion from some remote element in his thought that the business of life, the real business – to carry his peculiar burden, to feel shame and impotence, to taste these quelled tears – the only important business, the highest business was being done. Maybe the making of mistakes expressed the very purpose of his life and the essence of his being here.

It is insight into this compulsive masochistic drive in Wilhelm that gives Tamkin much of his hold over him:

'... Now Wilhelm, I'm trying to do you some good. I want to tell you, don't marry suffering. Some people do. They get married to it, and sleep and eat together, just as husband and wife. If they go with joy they think it's adultery.'

When Wilhelm heard this he had, in spite of himself, to admit that there was a great deal in Tamkin's words. Yes, thought Wilhelm, suffering is the only kind of life they are sure they can have, and if they quit suffering they're afraid they'll have nothing. He knows it. This time the faker knows what he's talking about.

At once comic and slightly sinister, Tamkin himself is superbly realized, an obvious charlatan yet with something unfathomable in his grotesqueness. As Wilhelm listens, wavering uneasily between fascination and incredulity, to the self-styled psychologist's ready flow of talk, a weird mixture of pseudo-scientific gibberish and unbelievable tall stories intermingled with patches of shrewd good sense, we can see that the themes have here been wholly absorbed into the novelistic medium – inextricably embodied in the verbal patterns of dialogue, interior monologue and characterization through which the fiction comes alive for us.

Wilhelm's 'day of reckoning' proves catastrophic indeed, as his commodity holding is wiped out by a further fall in the price of lard, Tamkin is nowhere to be found, and a final anguished appeal to his father to pay his hotel bill is angrily rejected. By the concluding page not only are we left guessing what will become of Wilhelm next, we are also left with an unresolved complexity in our own attitude towards him. The sardonic comedy which alternately tempers and heightens the realism of the narrative has undercut the temptation to identify unreservedly with his self-pity; having watched his nervous tics and twitches, observed him dropping his pinched-out cigarette-butts into his jacket-pocket from which he later secretly and repeatedly extracts first a sedative and then a pep-pill, seen him in the telephone-booth frenziedly trying to tear the apparatus from the wall after his wife has hung up on his angry reproaches, we can admit the justice of his father's irate description of him as 'you slob'. At the same time the authorial empathy which has generated such strong involvement in his predicament has been reinforced by a recurrent strand of 'water' imagery which underscores Wilhelm's insistent feeling that he is drowning under his troubles. At the end, walking distractedly among the Broadway crowds, Wilhelm thinks he catches sight of Tamkin, and in pursuit of him he is carried along inside a funeral chapel and into the slow line moving past the coffin. At the sight of the dead man he dissolves into an increasingly uncontrollable paroxysm of grief – tears shed partly for the inescapable human fate, but above all for himself and his own plight.

> He, alone, of all the people in the chapel was sobbing. No one knew who he was . . .
> . . . The flowers and lights fused ecstatically in Wilhelm's blind, wet eyes; the heavy sea-like music came up to his ears. It poured into him where he had hidden himself in the center of a crowd by the great and happy oblivion of tears. He heard it and sank deeper than sorrow, through torn sobs and cries toward the consummation of his heart's ultimate need.

Though some critics have managed to detect an affirmative note in this conclusion, a careful reading can surely leave no doubt that the 'heart's ultimate need' refers back to Wilhelm's dimly recognized conception of the self-castigating 'peculiar burden' which is for him the 'real business' of his life. But where the novelist stands, in any final balancing of attitudes, in relation to this compulsive drive in Wilhelm is certainly enigmatic, possibly (we may feel) evasive.

The success of *Seize the Day* owes much to the novelist's ability to distance himself from a protagonist who is superficially, at least, very unlike himself. In *Herzog* (1964) this distance has dwindled almost to vanishing-point, so that it is hard to see the eponymous hero, middle-aged, twice-married, highly educated, a sometime professor of English, as much more than a shadowy stalking-horse from behind which Bellow can vent some embittered personal grievances and at the same time indulge a penchant for high-sounding disquisitions upon civilization's current malaise. For given the exiguous nature of the plot it is inevitably the innumerable letters which Herzog writes but doesn't send (to friends, relatives, past colleagues, a miscellany of famous writers living and dead) that form the residue left in our mind by the novel. At one point the respect which Bellow accords to Herzog's philosophizing is encapsulated in a reference to 'the unbearable intensity of these ideas'; but the trouble is that the 'ideas' as presented turn out to be irredeemably banal and platitudinous, even when portentously decked-out with almost every conceivable cultural allusion from Aristotle to Zarathustra. Intelligent though he is as a novelist, Bellow seems to have singularly little capacity for discursive thought, a deficiency confirmed in his only non-fiction book *To Jerusalem and Back* (1976), where the fresh and vividly funny cameo of the first five pages, a novelist's account of a real-life plane journey from Heathrow to Israel in the company of two hundred fervent Hasidim, contrasts so conspicuously with the cliché-ridden argumentation of the remaining 177 pages. It is as if for him the fictional mode is a necessary condition for any genuinely creative thinking, and in *Herzog*, where his main energies have been diverted into a false channel, the narrative structure has become troublingly incoherent and arbitrary.

What cannot be doubted, however, is the remarkable variety that has quite rightly been ascribed to his oeuvre. Bellow has said that in *The Adventures of Augie March* (1953) he took off many of the restraints, associated with the acceptance of 'a Flaubertian standard', which he felt had disabled him in his first two novels from finding a form in which he felt comfortable. The result is a long, sprawling, episodic first-person narrative told in straightforward time-sequence and an almost ostentatiously American idiom, the flavour of which is well conveyed by the often-quoted opening sentences:

> I am an American, Chicago born – Chicago, that somber city – and go at things as I have taught myself, free-style, and will make the record in my own way: first to knock, first admitted; sometimes an innocent knock, sometimes a not so innocent. But a man's character is his fate, says Heraclitus ...

The authenticity of Augie's distinctive blend of Yiddish intonation, syntax and humour has been vouched for by those competent to judge;[1] and even his frequent recourse to cultural name-dropping, surprising at first sight from someone with so little formal education, can be justified by the fact that he is a voracious and wide-ranging reader, and by reference to a tradition in Yiddish literature which derives in turn from a tradition in Yiddish conversation. (Saul Bellow has been quoted as saying that Yiddish conversation is 'full of the grandest historical, mythological and religious allusions. The Creation, the Fall, the Flood, Egypt, Alexander, Titus, Napoleon, the Rothschilds, the sages and the Laws may get into the discussion of an egg, a clothes line or a pair of pants.') The engaging linguistic surface cannot, however, conceal a disconcerting heterogeneity within Augie's innumerable adventures, a disparateness of tone and narrative mode that makes it difficult at times to hold together the different episodes in any significant relationship to each other. How for instance do we reconcile the impressively detailed realism of the lengthy opening Chicago section with the vividly pictured but flamboyantly fantastic account of the Mexican expedition designed to train an eagle to hunt giant lizards, or with the highly entertaining but surely self-indulgent episode of Augie's wartime ordeal in an open boat on the Atlantic ocean in company with a crazed biophysicist who does not want to be rescued?

Even so, a loose-limbed structure does gradually emerge, casting doubt on the adequacy of the label 'picaresque' which has often been fastened on to this novel. The account of Augie's impoverished Chicago upbringing needed its expansive length and meticulous detail in order to give due weight to 'all the influences . . . lined up waiting . . .' to form him; since as he grows into adulthood he discovers that he has '*opposition* in him', 'a great desire to offer resistance and to say "No!"' to other people's plans for him. This self-protective caution is thrown to the winds, not perhaps wholly convincingly, during his passionate affair with Thea, the beautiful upper-class eccentric who takes him off with her eagle in pursuit of confirmation for her obsessive conviction that 'there must be something better than what people call reality'. After the lizard-hunting founders on the eagle's 'cowardice' and Augie's clumsy horsemanship, Augie bums his way through a directionless series of adventures in an obstinate unfulfilled search for the 'axial lines' which he feels would give purpose to his life.

However, the essential theme of the book is Augie's resilience, his ability to pick himself up in face of repeated disappointments, in face even of his own acceptance of the truth encapsulated in Kayo Obermark's pessimistic dictum: 'Everyone has bitterness in his chosen thing', a pessimism echoed in both the experience and the utterances of so many of the novel's subsidiary characters. Eventually the war temporarily gives Augie a sense of direction and provides the context for an impulsive marriage entered into with high hopes. But in our final glimpse of him he is reduced to travelling around post-war Europe arranging black-market deals, his eyes opened to his wife's deviousness and duplicity, wryly conscious of the 'fate' implicit in his 'character', yet still 'a person of hope', still capable of giving free rein to the *animal ridens* in himself – the laughing creature, for ever rising up. Some critics have objected to an unconvincingly forced note in what they see, surely simplistically, as the 'optimism' of this ending. It would seem to be more in keeping both with the author's other endings and with what has gone before in this overlong, wayward but frequently absorbing mélange to find in its closing pages a deliberate inconclusiveness, an intentionally enigmatic irony. But even those readers who require a novel to do more than simply pose questions must concede that *Augie March* enabled its author to give exploratory utterance to themes which he would later develop with fuller cogency.

In *Henderson the Rain King* (1959) the central character, though again an American, is not Jewish but Gentile – a fifty-five-year-old WASP millionaire from an old and distinguished family who nevertheless behaves, as he says himself, like a drunken bum. (Paradoxically, perhaps, in 1964 Bellow selected as the one among his characters most like himself 'Henderson – the absurd seeker of high qualities'.) In a comically varied colloquial style designedly very different from that of Augie March, Henderson tells his own story of his trip to the African interior, a trip motivated by despair at the insistent voice within himself continually demanding: 'I want, I want, I want!' It should be stressed that for all the vividness of the description of the terrain and the plausibly circumstantial detail about the customs of the two remote tribes he encounters, the Africa he penetrates to is unashamedly symbolic, a mental construct not to be taken in any 'factualist' sense. Bellow recounts that Professor Herskovits, with whom he had studied African ethnography many years earlier, scolded him over *Henderson*, saying that 'the subject was much too serious for such fooling'.

It is indeed the case that *Henderson* is frequently very funny indeed, but the joke is mostly at the expense of Henderson himself and the rash ebullience with which he repeatedly launches himself, Quixote-like, into situations he hasn't sufficiently understood. This trait cannot but bring to mind the *schlemiel*, the comic figure of Yiddish literature and Yiddish folk-tradition whose chronic ill-luck is due to his own ineptness. Bellow's only overt use of the term relates to Augie March, whose worldly-minded elder brother thinks him 'hasty, too enthusiastic, or in a few words, something of a *schlemiel*'; but the concept has unquestionably been at work, consciously or otherwise, in the shaping of many of his protagonists, Wilhelm and Herzog included, and has, indeed, provided, in memorably compressed form, the title of his second volume of short stories, *Him with His Foot in His Mouth* (1984).[2] Strangely, however (perhaps in some way it is part of the joke?), the Gentile Henderson is the most unremittingly *schlemiel*-like of all Bellow's heroes – 'doomed always to bungle', as he says of himself after he has 'goofed' in his project to relieve the Arnewi, a charming and gentle matriarchy whose cattle are dying of drought. His plan goes disastrously astray when his improvised bomb destroys the dam-wall as well as the water-polluting frogs; and he has to move on ignominiously to put himself at the mercy of a very different culture, that of the warlike and ruthless Wariri. Here his impetuous participation in their rain-making ceremonies turns him even more disastrously into their Sungo or Rain King, and thereby the putative successor to young King Dahfu and his exacting marital obligations to his numerous wives.

Henderson's eventful compulsorily prolonged stay with the Wariri is recounted with a compelling narrative verve which is continually enlivened by the stunning panache of the narrator's linguistic style and only occasionally dimmed by our mystification as to how seriously we are to take Dahfu's curiously hybrid philosophizing. Henderson is completely won over by Dahfu's personal magnetism, seeing him as 'that marvelous guy'; but he is less certain about his ideas, even though he falls in with them to the extent of repeatedly accompanying him into the lion's cage and trying with a disabling lack of conviction to change his own personality by exercises in leonine roaring. Nevertheless it *is* a changed man who returns to America determined to rebuild his loving relationship with his wife Lily and to make a reality, even at his advanced age, of his long-deferred yearning to qualify as a doctor; and this change he attributes to his African experiences as a whole and his contacts with Dahfu in particular.

What can we glean about the nature of this wisdom he has gained? Speaking retrospectively, Bellow saw the novel's intention as focused upon Henderson's search for 'a remedy to the anxiety over death', and certainly this topic plays a part in his final conversation with Dahfu shortly before the king's death. However, if we trust the tale rather than the teller, we find that more weight attaches to the concluding sentences of Henderson's attempt to explain to Lily what Dahfu's ideas were:

'I had a voice that said, I want! *I* want? I? It should have told me *she* wants, *he* wants, *they* want. And, moreover, it's love that makes reality reality. The opposite makes the opposite.'

The impact of this, in the context of the novel as a whole, is not diminished by the information that Henderson is here reconstructing what he *thinks* he said in those last few pages of a letter which his native guide Romilayu later lost and which were in any case written when he 'had had quite a lot to drink' – a device characteristic of the varied procedures whereby, formally at least, Bellow dissociates himself in a number of his novels from his characters' philosophic statements. Moreover the complexity of Henderson's interaction with his African mentors embraces several other strands: Dahfu's perception of Henderson's 'monstrous pride' in his capacity for suffering; the contrast Henderson draws between 'Be-ers' such as Dahfu, and 'Become-ers' who, like himself, 'are very unlucky'; Henderson's very pertinent recollection that 'a service ideal exists in our family, though sometimes in a setting of mad habit'. Even if we feel that in the end the attempted integration of these diverse elements is confused rather than coherently enigmatic, *Henderson* is certainly the most sheerly enjoyable of Bellow's novels; while at the same time its bizarrely exotic fantasy touches (evasively, perhaps) on depths which justify the author's feeling, in defensive response to Professor Herskovits, that his 'fooling' had been 'fairly serious'.

Mr Sammler's Planet (1970), in sombrely realistic mood, returns us to the vast American city, in this case New York, observed with bleak detachment by a septuagenarian Polish–Oxonian survivor from the Nazi holocaust who retains contrasting memories of his years in Bloomsbury in the twenties and thirties when he and his wife enjoyed 'the cultural best of England'. On one level Sammler's disillusionment is with America ('advertised throughout the universe as *the* most desirable, most exemplary of all nations') and its modish sixties abandonment of hitherto-accepted values: '. . . disintegrated assurances . . . people justifying idleness, silliness, shallowness, distemper, lust – turning former respectability inside out'. This moral somersault has its most trenchant symbol in the elegant Negro pickpocket whom Sammler observes at work on his regular late-afternoon bus, at first by chance, later with an imprudent fascination which leads the thief to track him to his apartment building and in a corner of the lobby silently exhibit to him his huge penis as a 'serenely masterful' warning. The specifically American dimension is further represented by Sammler's great-niece Angela Gruner whose sexual excesses are imprinted in her 'fucked-out eyes' (her father's brutal expression) which never lose 'their look of erotic experience', and by the ludicrous escapades of her impulse-driven brother Wallace (in his father's judgement 'a high-IQ moron').

But Sammler's weary disenchantment has a wider remit than these examples might suggest. More than from any other source his problems stem from the activities of his 'wacky' forty-year-old daughter Shula and her estranged husband, the violent and irresponsible Eisen; and for each of them their 'madness' relates to an earlier European dislocation – for Shula her wartime years sheltered from the Nazis in a Polish convent, for Eisen his wartime wounds at Stalingrad and his subsequent motiveless mutilation. Add to this the appalling catalogue, gradually revealed to us, of the experiences of Mr Sammler himself from the time when he was trapped in Poland in 1939 to his rescue by his nephew from a DP camp in 1947, and we can see that for Sammler, as for Bellow, it is not America but the whole of humanity that is in the dock. Indeed so formidable is the indictment that we can understand Sammler's wryly favourable reaction to the idea of colonizing the moon, as proposed in detail by

the Indian biophysicist Dr Lal in the manuscript which Shula has
covertly and crazily purloined for her father to read:

... 'How long,' went the first sentence, 'will this earth remain the only
home of Man?'
  How long? Oh, Lord, you bet! Wasn't it the time – the very hour to go?
For every purpose under heaven ... To blow this great blue, white, green
planet, or to be blown from it.

Clearly the novel's strange and arresting title was chosen with
deliberation.

In its narrative structure *Sammler* is mainly a reprise, in a different
key, of that employed in *Seize the Day* – the events of a brief period,
in this case a couple of days, are seen through Sammler's eyes while
at the same time his memories gradually fill in for us the background
necessary for understanding. But in contrast to the ready flow of
recollection powered by Wilhelm's compulsive self-flagellation,
Sammler's memories, particularly those from the more distant past,
emerge fitfully and fragmentarily as if forcing themselves upward
into a consciousness which would prefer to keep them under. Thus
only slowly, and usually only when triggered by some painful
current stimulus, do we learn the full extent of the horrors he
somehow survived during the Second World War, horrors such
that it was only after an interval of some ten or twelve years that he
began to feel himself a living human being again.

Throughout the few days of New York spring which we experience via Mr Sammler's one remaining 'good' eye, his preoccupations
centre round his nephew Dr Elya Gruner who is in hospital awaiting
death from an inoperable brain aneurysm: understandably therefore
his mind reverts repeatedly to his own near-death in Poland, to the
mass-grave he had helped to dig and from which, 'strangely exceptional', he somehow clawed his way out. Bellow has succeeded
admirably in creating a wholly distinctive voice for this civilized
meditative survivor who has been brought back to grapple for a
second time with the problem of how to confront one's own death.
Regrettably, however, this voice is not maintained consistently
throughout: despite his expressed preference for what Sidney Smith
termed 'short views', Mr Sammler is allowed at times, both in his
internal monologues and in a prolonged discussion with Dr Lal, to

extend his ruminations to an excessive length and in a manner which strongly suggests an adulteration of the created character with the voice and views of his creator. The weakness which undermined *Herzog* reappears here, in fact, though fortunately only as a relatively minor blemish.

At first seemingly haphazard, the experiences of Mr Sammler's two days, some commonplace, some bizarre, prove in the end to have a compelling inner logic as well as a significant thematic relevance. His visits to the hospital convince him that the 'gimmick' in Elya Gruner's throat cannot postpone death for long, that his nephew knows this, and that his ostentatious determination to be a 'good patient' is his way of encountering what Sammler thinks of as his 'moment of honor'. But his desire to affirm human solidarity with Elya in his time of need is interrupted and diverted, firstly by Shula's capers with the stolen manuscript and then by Wallace Gruner's lunatic search for his father's hidden Mafia money, as a result of which Sammler finds himself stranded next morning in Gruner's flooded New Rochelle mansion. His eventual journey to the hospital is further delayed by an encounter with a streetside brawl occasioned by his indiscretion in talking too freely about the pickpocket, and when he finally reaches the hospital he makes an enemy of Angela Gruner by over-zealously urging her to a deathbed reconciliation with her father, so jeopardizing his own and Shula's future material prospects (pointlessly since Gruner, taken downstairs for so-called 'tests', has in fact already died).

While we may sense in all this that Sammler, too, has a touch of the *schlemiel* in him, the intricate sequence of events reaches a genuinely moving close as the old man has to face an uncertain future not only bereft of Elya's financial support but also 'deprived of one more thing, stripped of one more creature . . . one more reason to live'. But Sammler's most bitter regret is at his failure to reach his dying nephew in time to talk with him again, however trivially, for *Mr Sammler's Planet* seldom strays far from its central concern with the problem of how a man can 'make sober decent terms with death'. Intentionally or not, Bellow's answer is inconclusive, and for all its imaginative power the novel's final effect on the reader is disturbing and comfortless.

It will be evident that the extreme diversity of the novels discussed so far arises very largely from the variedness of their male central characters. By contrast minor characters are inclined to fall into certain types which, with repetition, become almost stereotypes: an obvious example is that of the elder brother (Simon March, Will Herzog) who has made a material success of his life in the business world, but remains protectively fond of his more intellectual and unworldly sibling. This stereotyping is even more noticeable in Bellow's women, who are too often relegated to one of two categories: on the one hand the domineering and persecuting wife or ex-wife; on the other the glamorously attractive mistress, the sex-object of male fantasy who is required to be not only beautiful but also skilled in erotic technique (Ramona for instance, whom Herzog describes with self-congratulatory satisfaction as 'a true sack artist'). In his later work, however, his portrayal of women becomes less markedly one-dimensional, with characters such as Margotte, the widowed niece, good-hearted, sloppy, cheerful, maladroit, earnestly and tediously talkative, in whose apartment Sammler has a room.

More significant than the recurrence of character-types and type-situations is Bellow's repeated harking-back to a small number of themes which have almost the status of obsessions. Notice, for instance, the number of his characters who pride themselves upon having 'a talent for suffering'. Even more central is his characters' preoccupation with the difficulty of coming to terms with the prospect of death, a concern whose impact is undoubtedly heightened by the author's fascination with the more gruesome aspects of modern high-technology medicine. But in what is essentially a secular context (for despite the high proportion of Jewish characters there is a notable absence of reference to synagogues or to rabbis) it is clearly the finality of death which is hard to take.

This, allied to a dissatisfaction with the predominantly materialist-empiricist cast of twentieth-century thinking, seems to lead Bellow to a never wholly explicit yearning for some substitute for religious belief which might muffle the anguish of mortality by offering hope of survival after death in some form, however attenuated. When Sammler, despite his former agnosticism, moves in his seventies towards 'God adumbrations' and 'strong impressions of eternity', the terms of his new-found mysticism are sufficiently nebulous for Bellow to feel no obligation to dissociate himself from them. More commonly, however, such intimations are presented in a distinctly eccentric way-out form (in *Henderson* the Wariri beliefs about transmigration of souls, in *Humboldt's Gift* (1975) the ideas of Rudolf Steiner) which enables Bellow to float them with an apparent hint of seriousness and yet avoid any commitment to them.

Associated with this restless quest for 'something beyond' (Thea's 'something better than what people call reality'?) is Bellow's developing critique of the values which regulate people's behaviour towards each other in everyday life. From Tommy Wilhelm's simplistic indignation at the way people 'adore money' and are 'feeble-minded about everything except money', this has over the years steadily extended its scope until it has become in *Mr Sammler* a far-reaching denunciation of the dominant values of American civilization, and, consequently, of the whole of the Western world, since, as Dr Lal observes, 'Of course in a sense the whole world is now US.'

Nevertheless one cannot help feeling that this critique is less thoroughgoing than Bellow supposes it to be, and that, more than he is aware, he has remained in certain respects imprisoned in the assumptions of his own culture – in his attitudes towards women, for instance; in his implicit acceptance, even if qualified, of the individual competitiveness which is the driving-force in almost all his American male characters; in a certain machismo element, however muted, which goes along with this; and (perhaps most culpable of all) in a surprisingly tolerant acceptance of the power wielded by gangsterdom in all walks of American life – a tolerance which is not made less shocking by the fact that some of his hoodlums are comically incompetent. There may perhaps be truth in the complaint that, in his concentration on the individual, Bellow has neglected to provide any structural analysis of the social and political power-relations which shape and constrain the individual's experience; in short, to borrow the American critic Mark Schechner's way of putting it, 'there is no real politics anywhere in Bellow's writing'.

Against this background Bellow's latest novel, *The Dean's December* (1982), has a special interest. Corde, a middle-aged Huguenot-Irish Midwesterner, Dean of an unnamed Chicago college, finds himself 'shut up in an old-fashioned apartment' in Bucharest, giving support to his Rumanian wife whose mother, a one-time Party member and former Minister of Health, is dying in hospital of a stroke. Once again everything is experienced through the medium of the protagonist's consciousness; but although the current narrative, for all but the last thirty pages, is located in Bucharest (tussles with the bureaucracy, visits to the hospital, arrangements for the funeral), Corde's backward reflections focus almost entirely on Chicago, where he has had to leave his affairs in acute crisis.

The verbal texture created to convey this consciousness is a remarkable achievement – quite unlike that of any previous novel and accurately attuned to the personality it identifies. Corde describes himself as 'temperamentally an image man', someone moreover who obstinately continues to uphold the importance of poetry in sustaining our capacity for living.[3] On the one hand his instinct for 'particularity', for the details through which alone the 'actualities' of the human scene can be grasped, endows his perceptions of people, places and situations with a peculiarly luminous realism. On the other, his natural gift for metaphor bubbles up time and again, to illuminate their inner as well as their surface reality. Here, for instance, he is remembering a thought which came to him during a sticky interview with his objectionable student-nephew:

> You had to study Mason to find the humanity in him. It was as hard to see as the thin line of mercury in some thermometers. But if you turned your thermometer in the light and found the lucky angle, you'd be sure to get a reading.

This dual approach pays off best in the characterization of individuals: Corde's wife Minna, an internationally distinguished astrophysicist, the most subtly and sensitively portrayed of all Bellow's women; her elderly aunt Gigi, struggling to take over as head of a family in which she has always been the younger sister; even the repulsive Dewey Spangler, once a high school friend of Corde's, now a high-powered globe-trotting journalist who maliciously uses his syndicated column ('dependable expository prose for the busy reader') to destroy the Dean as an academic.

It works less well when the author is offering to delineate a whole society, since the perceptive eye can see only what its owner chooses to look at. Corde assures the American ambassador that he is well up in the dissident literature; and not unnaturally the picture we get of Bucharest is a fairly standard Cold War stereotype of an East

European capital, enlivened and lent credibility by a limited range of vivid personally observed detail. The bonus from this is that, having summarily despatched the backwardness, poverty and tyranny of a Communist regime, Bellow seems to have felt freer than ever before to launch a no-holds-barred account of his native Chicago, with full weight given to the contrast between the 'Malignant Mammonism of the Magnificent Mile' (epitomized in a lavish birthday party given for a bored Great Dane) and the squalid desolation of the inner-city slums, home of the 'black underclass'. Corde, tired of the distortions of generalized opinion, has set out to see for himself, and the resulting articles in *Harper's* have excited an outraged reaction which is the major ground for his college Provost's determination to get rid of him as Dean. The content of the offending journalism comes to us almost entirely through Corde's recollections of his legwork in quest of material; in their graphic particularity these 'images' have the merit of making real for us a kind of poverty and wretchedness almost entirely absent from Bellow's normal predominantly middle-class milieu.

But in this case too the impressionistic approach has its limitations, perhaps even dangers. Himself become a 'whirling soul . . . lifted up, caught up, spinning, streaming with passions, compulsive protests, inspirations', Corde can see hope only in a moral revolution in which his readers, confronted with these 'actualities', would join with him in 'reconstituting' themselves. He finds two outstanding black examples of the 'moral initiative' he desiderates, one a former drug addict who has set up a detoxification centre in a decayed South Side wilderness, the other a former director of County Jail, victimized for his Herculean attempt to clean up the (mainly black) rackets inside the prison. The two are brought alive for us with superb verbal artistry. The danger, not wholly avoided, is that, in the nature of Corde's approach, they come over too much as exceptional cases, leaving an overall impression of the 'black underclass' as dangerous, brutal, criminalized; while, despite some hints here and there, the novel includes no serious analysis of the power groups (mainly white) really responsible for the city's running and for its corruption.

These reservations about one facet of *The Dean's December* must not be taken as calling into question the stature of this fine and complex novel, which in its totality (and it skilfully interweaves many narrative strands necessarily unmentioned here) is certainly one of its author's most impressive successes. In its concluding pages, moreover, Bellow directs a steadier and less equivocal gaze at that 'anxiety over death' which has been an insistent preoccupation in so much of his fiction. The death of Minna's mother has throughout been close to the emotional centre of the novel, both in its devastating effect on Minna herself (brought fully up against 'the blank of death' for the first time), and more subtly but no less convincingly in its impact on Corde. As he accompanies his still-convalescent wife to her postponed session with the Mount Palomar telescope, the vast and bitterly cold observatory dome 'inevitably' carries Corde back to the 'killing cold' of the domed crematorium in Bucharest. But in the context of this 'look at astral space' with 'its power to cancel everything merely human', the idea of death is experienced in a different key – one which recalls and gives a cosmic dimension to Corde's earlier speculative intuition, when looking out over Lake Michigan from his sixteenth-storey porch, that death might be '. . . like being poured out to the horizon, like a great expansion . . . the soul finding an exit'. At the open top of the Mount Palomar dome Corde feels 'the living heavens looked as if they would take you in . . . as if you were being informed that what was spread over you had to do with your existence, down to the very blood and the crystal forms inside your bones'.

Bellow's earlier gropings towards an invocation of the numinous as an aid to making 'decent terms with death' had always seemed over-explicit or over-schematized in ways which the author himself felt uneasy about, so that there had to be an awkward element of legerdemain about their presentation. In the sober but finely modulated prose of these final pages he has achieved a near-poetic resolution of this deeply felt conflict by relating it to an inconceivably vast non-human setting. 'Everything overhead was in equilibrium, kept in place by mutual tensions. What was it that kept *his* tensions in place?' There is an unforced integrity of feeling in this which reminds us of (and perhaps owes something to) Wordsworth's 'Rolled round in earth's diurnal force'. In this ending, at least, enigmatic irony has been transcended.

In *Mr Sammler's Planet* there occur several bizarre incidents which in an earlier Bellow novel would surely have seemed comic but which, refracted through Sammler's consciousness, strike one only as unedifyingly ludicrous. There are no such incidents in *The Dean's December* where the tone throughout is one of responsible realism, lightened only by the occasional flash of Corde's pungent wit. By contrast Bellow's most recent story 'Cousins' (published in 1984 and included in *Him with His Foot in His Mouth*) returns us to a world of fantastic characters and incidents presented now with deeply serious intent but in a tone of mordant farce. It suggests a fitting close to this chapter for two reasons: firstly, the narrator Ijah Brodsky in 'a moment of impotent indignation' provides a succinct and penetrating rundown on the relation between the 'four-mansion crooks' who are 'in the rackets' and those in outwardly respectable 'business', the 'top executives, the lawyers at the nucleus of power' — precisely what was noted as missing in *The Dean's December*; secondly Ijah is gradually led beyond the exclusivity of the cousinship links to which he has devoted so much of his life's energy to an acknowledgement of the higher claims of a world-wide solidarity, led there moreover by a meeting at once funny and touching with the most brilliant and eccentric of all his blood-cousins.

Over his writing career as a whole Bellow has gained a well-deserved reputation for 'amazing variety', since each new novel has conveyed a sense of being radically different from its predecessor in style, setting, incident and structure, and of representing for its author a new beginning, a commendably fresh attempt to grapple both with his own personal conflicts and at the same time with issues currently dominant in the problematic modern world around him. It is surely a remarkable testimony both to his vitality and to his stature that this is more than ever true of the fiction he has produced in his seventh decade.

NOTES

1. See, for instance, Michael Allen, 'Idiomatic Language in Two Novels by Saul Bellow', *Journal of American Studies*, 1 (1967), 275–80.

2. For a fuller treatment see Sanford Pinsker, *The Schlemiel as Metaphor* (Carbondale and London, 1971), especially the chapter entitled 'The Psychological Schlemiels of Saul Bellow'.

3. For a developed exposition of this aspect of the novel see Seymour Betsky, 'In Defence of Literature: Saul Bellow's *The Dean's December*', *Universities Quarterly*, 39 (1984/5), 59–84.

ROBERT LOWELL, THEODORE ROETHKE, AND SYLVIA PLATH

DAVID HOLBROOK

There are common qualities in the poetry of three American poets who came to prominence in the sixties and seventies, Robert Lowell (1917–77), Theodore Roethke (1908–63) and Sylvia Plath (1932–63). They came from the university world, Lowell and Roethke were friends, and Plath was Lowell's pupil at one stage. A deeper similarity between them appears, as one grapples with trying to understand them. One can't understand them, and certainly can't discriminate between their best work and their worst, without exploring what the psychoanalysts call 'unconscious material'. One cannot simply enjoy their poems as works 'on the page', and this is so because at times they threaten us. Lowell writes idolizations of destructive behaviour, and some of his intimate revelations are evidently written in a spirit of cruel offence to those close to him. Roethke often seems on the verge of madness, as does Plath, who idolizes suicide and even matricide. So, we are obliged to enter into the kind of territory explored by R. D. Laing in *The Divided Self*, and to employ phenomenological disciplines, in the interpretation of symbols. This takes one inevitably into the complexities of their lives, and so into characteristic strains in Western consciousness – of the kind, say, that are examined by Rollo May, the Existentialist psychotherapist, in books such as his *Love and Will*.

There seem to be two extremes to the ranges of this symbolism of inner disturbance. At one end of the scale there is a language and mode of anger and hate: 'Daddy, you bastard, I'm through!' (Sylvia Plath, 'Daddy'), 'You are a bastard, Michael, aren't you. *Nein!* . . .' (Lowell, *Lord Weary's Castle* – the connection between these moments is made by Ian Hamilton, Lowell's biographer). In each of these poets there are moments when the writer seems to be raving to himself or herself, seething with hate. At the other extreme, there is another common feature, a recognition of a deeply immature self, a child, a puppy, or an infant which seems as if it has never been born, and which seeks to begin *to be*. In this we may find the expression of a deep-seated predicament of the Western soul, as expressed by Sylvia Plath in the phrase, 'I have a self to recover': the sense that the full potentialities of the self have never been found, at the level of being, and so life seems to lack meaning. Sylvia Plath's 'Bee' poems seem to be about the verb 'to be'. Roethke's poems *The Lost Son* and others in that mode seem to be about being uncertain who or what one is, and wanting to be:

> Has the dark a door
> I'm somewhere else, –
> I insist!
> I am.

In response to this need, 'society' treated them in various ways, from using strait-waistcoats on them, or electro-convulsive therapy, or drugs; while they sought a transformation through alcohol abuse, sexual adventures, or suicide, and the struggle led to various forms of mental breakdown. Roethke, Randall Jarrell, Plath, and Lowell all had periods of mental illness, while Plath and Anne Sexton – another pupil of Lowell's – committed suicide, as did Jarrell himself; John Berryman leapt from a bridge and Lowell's death seemed to have been a consequence of some death wish, as Hamilton suggests. Lowell used to try to strangle his women and often treated them cruelly; Plath reveals in her Journals how much she hated her mother, her husband, and how much she feared turning this on herself; while in biographical accounts Lowell's behaviour at drinking parties is frightening, ending with the police restraining him, and leading him away to be treated with thorozine and lithium, as he raved about Hitler.

I introduce these poets in this way, because there is a prevalent view in our literary world that these problems do not exist, or at least that literary criticism should not allow itself to deal with such issues. The critic Al Alvarez, who was a friend of Lowell and Plath, urged that the artist's best work is done by 'cultivating his psychosis'. Each of the poets of which he approved was 'salvaging his work from the edge of some kind of personal abyss'. But it is not true that the work escapes even if the personal self goes under. The double-faced nature of the work itself requires our discrimination. On the one hand there is the genuine reco|;nition of vulnerability, of, one can say, humanness. On the other there are false postures, as when, as critics record, Lowell descends to a 'merciless masculinity' and 'bullshit eloquence', sometimes incomprehensible or tedious, in a 'private mumble'. Unravelling these distinctions can help lead us into the most radical problems of the contemporary sensibility and of our general culture.

Given such life-problems, it is not surprising that these poets often failed. But with each there are poems in which the art triumphs successfully, and justifies the attention given to these writers – for, even at their worst, because they write with such vividness, they offer us material which makes the predicament of the present-day consciousness manifest.

The poem of Roethke's I find most satisfactory is 'Meditation at Oyster River' in *The Far Field* (1964). It has two representative characteristics: it is written in retreat, where nature is contemplated by the poet alone, trying to find meaning in the world: and it seeks a sense of 'being' in a regression to infancy. In both spheres it is an attempt to recapture 'intentionality', that element of the creative consciousness which is so disastrously lacking in the modern scene. It begins:

> Over the low, barnacled, elephant-colored rocks,
> Come the fat tide-ripples, moving, almost without sound, toward me,
> Running along the narrow furrows of the shore, the rows of dead
>   clam-shells;
> Then a runnel behind me, creeping closer,
> Alive with tiny striped fish, and young crabs climbing in and out of
>   the water.

In the long lines of the opening is enacted the coming in of the tide: it is slightly menacing ('a runnel behind me, creeping closer') and it speaks of an immense power – yet there is 'No violence'. The noise of the gulls ('child-whimpering'), the dabbling of his toes in the brackish foam, and the twilight wind 'light as a child's breath' all evoke a feeling of going back to the simple sense of at-one-ness with the rhythms of the world such as we can experience on a sea-shore. There is a widening perspective of time:

> A fish raven turns on its perch (a dead tree in the rivermouth),
> Its wings catching a last glint of the reflected sunlight.

In this scene, with the long wave-ripples of the tide coming in, and the sense of the gentle progress of time, he contemplates the self in being-unto-death:

> The self persists like a dying star,
> In sleep, afraid. Death's face rises afresh,
> Among the shy beasts, the deer at the salt-lick,
> The doe with its sloped shoulders loping along the highway,
> The young snake, poised in green leaves, waiting for its fly,
> The hummingbird, whirring from quince-blossom to morning-glory
> With these I would be.

He wants to be an animal, though recognizing their mortality, because of their intentionality – they are doing something, going somewhere: he wants *to be* with them, although they are being-to-death.

> And with water: the waves coming forward without cessation . . .
> The tongues of water, creeping in, quietly,

He throws projections of himself into the scene, and in section 3 becomes the sandpiper, the hummingbird, the kingfisher:

> In this hour,
> In this first heaven of knowing,
> The flesh takes on the pure poise of the spirit,
> Acquires, for a time, the sandpiper's insouciance,
> The hummingbird's surety, the kingfisher's cunning . . .

He wants to be-in-the-world as these bird creatures are, who have such 'pure purpose' in their environment.

So, thinking of them, he remembers the great bursting of the waters that characterizes the spring in Michigan. First, a waterfall beginning in spring, yielding a small rainbow that can be 'taken in, embraced, by two arms' – a symbol of the child's entrancement by mysterious phenomena, and the adult's fascination with them. And then the breaking of the ice:

> Or the Tittebawasee, in the time between winter and spring,
> When the ice melts along the edges in early afternoon.
> And the midchannel begins cracking and heaving from the pressure beneath,
> The ice piling high against the iron-bound spiles . . .
> And I long for the blast of dynamite,
> The sudden sucking roar as the culvert loosens its debris of branches and sticks,

> Welter of tin cans, pails, old birds nests, a child's shoe riding a log,
> As the piled ice breaks away from the battered spiles,
> And the whole river begins to move forward, its bridges shaking.

It is a powerful sustained image, symbolic of a new beginning sweeping away all the accretion of the ordinary, caught up in the obstructive paralysis of the ice. Obviously, it has a symbolic significance − and it is this that the poet hopes to gain, by his peaceful meditation − a shift of spirit, a new flow.

The child's shoe in the rubbish of the river is significant: somewhere in the debris of childhood is the reason for the dammed-up sense of the inauthentic. So, now, as the light wanes, he regresses further:

> I rock with the motion of morning;
> In the cradle of all that is,
> I'm lulled into half-sleep
> By the lapping of water . . .

The 'lapping' is in a sense a going back to the (mother's) lap to find 'Water's my will and my way . . .' What he seeks is to flow again, into the future with a sense of meaning.

> And the spirit runs, intermittently,
> In and out of the small waves,
> Runs with the intrepid shorebirds −
> How graceful the small before danger!
>
> In the first of the moon,
> All's a scattering,
> A shining.

The last lines echo the great reparative moment in *The Ancient Mariner*, where the influence of the moon-mother's light redeems the world blighted by the Mariner's destructiveness. It is the same moonlight that we have at the end of 'Frost at Midnight' and in Mahler's *Das Lied von der Erde* − 'O wild delicious world!'. It conveys a sense of feeling that the world is vastly benign and imbued with love. By projecting himself into the small '*intrepid*' birds which busy themselves in their 'pure' purpose between the great tides, Roethke finds here a profound sense of at-one-ness, and a sense of joy and beauty, and so meaning, which is rare in modern poetry.

I was interested to learn from Ian Hamilton's biography that 'For the Union Dead' (originally published in *Life Studies: Selected Poems*) was a poem on which Robert Lowell 'worked' more than he worked on any other. It still seems to me the most successful of Lowell's poems, perhaps because it is a step into the public world, a step which prevents Lowell sinking into mere personal rumination and into his egocentric confusion. At the same time it seems to be perhaps the deepest poem about his predicament – and that of Western consciousness: it can find nothing to believe in except the self and, at the heart of the self, finds vacancy. At the same time, there is the presence of the challenging eye of the self that was once a boy, aware of the potentialities in existence.

The poem opens by referring to two losses – the decline of the traditional community and its culture: the aquarium which represented both cod-fishing and the study of marine life is decrepit. The other loss is of the keen expectancy of childhood:

> The bronze weathervane cod has lost half its scales.
> The airy tanks are dry.
> Once my nose crawled like a snail on the glass:
> My hand tingled
> to burst the bubbles
> drifting from the noses of the cowed, compliant fish.

The child saw the zooified fish as brought from the wild sea into a human environment, and so, cowed and compliant. The child used to look at them and see in them a magic with which he would like to interfere, as by bursting the bubbles that rose from them.

From this vision of childhood excited by the world and the boy's desire to intervene in it, he reverts to himself, here and now, looking at the centre of Boston. As a boy he sighed for the mysterious primitive world: today he looks on a different kind of life –'dinosaur steam-shovels':

> as they cropped up tons of mud and grass
> to gouge their underworld garage.

What flourishes in this world is *spaces*:

> Parking spaces luxuriate like civic
> Sand piles in the heart of Boston.

The only remaining symbol of traditional meanings seems to be that the girders holding up the old statehouse are merely *painted* pumpkin colour. The statehouse is shaking over the excavations – and this image is a universal one for the Western world, where we wonder how long our significant institutions can survive the march of 'development' that is impatient with them.

Opposite the statehouse is the bas-relief frieze sculpted by St Gaudens, of Colonel Shaw and his Negro infantry, to celebrate the ending of the Civil War: 'Propped by a plank splint against the garage's earthquake . . .' The alliteration and the sounds of 'plank splint', create the construction noises that rock the foundations of these monuments: what intrinsic value do these have, among the march of space? The events celebrated were terrible enough:

> Two months after marching through Boston,
> half the regiment was dead;
> at the dedication,
> William James could almost hear the bronze Negroes breathe.

No doubt that was what William James said, that excellent psychologist, but his remark raises subtly the problem of 'being-unto-death' – the Negro soldiers have been dead long ago, and even when the monument was unveiled it was nothing but metal. The 'life' is only in the idea, in consciousness; but is it 'in' the modern consciousness, and can it be restored to it?

Lowell is aware that such monuments are an embarrassment to the modern world. And while he himself cannot embrace the virtues and qualities for which Colonel Shaw stands, he admires him. The ambivalence he feels is characteristic of the liberal democrat who can no longer endorse the traditional virtues; while, at the same time, no more adequate source of value appears:

> Their monument sticks like a fishbone
> in the city's throat.
> Its Colonel is as lean
> as a compass-needle.
>
> He has an angry wrenlike vigilance,
> a greyhound's gentle tautness;
> he seems to wince at pleasure,
> and suffocate for privacy.
>
> He is out of bounds now.

'Out of bounds' is a wry joke – the figure of the Colonel is behind the builder's barriers: but he is 'beyond the pale' in contemporary attitudes to history, valour, endeavour. There was a time when men with certain values were prepared to die for them, but today this is felt to belong to a rigidity that is outmoded and dangerous:

> He rejoices in man's lovely,
> peculiar power to choose life and die –
> when he leads his black soldiers to death,
> he cannot bend his back.

The dry irony of the voice comes from one who is appalled by the Vietnam war, and the use of black soldiers in it – for what values? And the question is stretched back to the Civil War and the fight against the Confederate South. There is a tradition of triumph over slavery, not least in New England:

> On a thousand small towns New England greens,
> the old white churches hold their air
> of sparse, sincere rebellion; frayed flags
> quilt the graveyards of the Grand Army of the Republic . . .

But today? The stone statues of an idealized Union Soldier are eroded by the rain. Shaw's father wanted no monument except the ditch, where his son's body was thrown with his 'niggers'. But what are today the fruits of the heroism? 'The ditch is nearer . . .'. And here 'the ditch' simply becomes one of the 'spaces' which triumph in today's world, which has become ironic about heroism. We have experienced the First World War, which put paid to heroism in its mud: and the Second World War which brought the atom bomb:

> There are no statues for the last war here;
> On Boylston Street, a commercial photograph
> shows Hiroshima boiling
> over a Mosler safe, the 'Rock of Ages'
> that survived the blast.

Lowell is obviously appalled that a photograph showing the atom blast that killed tens of thousands should be used for advertising purposes – not least a safe blasphemously named after the 'Rock of Ages'. The ironic implication of the tone is that all symbols are being reduced, massively, to nothing – this is another triumph of 'space', of emptiness.

'Space is nearer': the social problem was not solved by the Civil War – the blacks are still underprivileged, although now their predicament is a feature of television attention. There is, presumably, some idealism here, and the 'bubble' of the devotion to a cause:

> Colonel Shaw
> is riding on his bubble,
> he waits
> for the blessèd break.

But, the tone suggests, there will be no 'break'.

All we have is subservience, cowed and compliant, as if the cars were fish in the big space of the civil works, subdued and deprived of their vitality.

> The Aquarium is gone. Everywhere, giant finned cars
> nose forward like fish; a savage servility
> slides by on grease . . .

The servility and the grease isolate modern man from the keen and purposeful engagement with 'being' which Shaw exemplifies. Yet we can no longer believe in his kind of values. What then? Lowell merely stands in a state of paralysed perplexity, before the encroaching emptiness of the modern world. Yet in its perplexity, and its record of the troubled consciousness, the poem makes a gesture towards the restoration of the intentionality which has been lost.

A parallel engagement with an existential problem – though very different in its subject and manner – may be represented by what seems to me the most remarkable of Sylvia Plath's poems, 'The Night Dances' (*Ariel*, p. 27). Because she was such a schizoid individual, Plath was able to have uncanny insights into what the Existentialists call *Sorge*, the 'dread' that lurks behind ordinary existence. Most of us settle for what Martin Heidegger called *Verfallensein*, 'forfeiture': we can't always live in sole concentration on the authentic, in open-eyed contemplation of the awfulness, conscience and destiny of our existence (*Angst, Gewissen, Schicksal*). Sylvia Plath at certain moments experiences a genuine terror of being alive and of being-unto-death, '*das Sein zum Tode*'.

In 'The Night Dances' she is aware that in the twizzling movements of her baby there is a meaning. In the baby, the smile (as F. J.

J. Buytendijk put it) is 'the miming of mind' – when the infant first smiles, it is as if a great gulf has been passed, between non-being and being, in the recognition of 'being for'. The baby's smile fills us with an intense happiness, for a piece of protoplasm, an 'other' created out of our own bodies, asserts its human sympathy and response across the gulf. Without that response (as in the autistic child) there would be no life of being. Yet there is always the dreadful possibility that the gulf will not be bridged, and the gesture lost for ever.

> A smile fell on the grass.
> Irretrievable!

So, the meaning of the cot-dances (important manifestations of the immature creature's freedom) may be lost for ever:

> And how well your night dances lose
> themselves. In mathematics?
>
> Such pure leaps and spirals –
> Surely they travel
>
> The world forever . . .

This mathematical emanation is like the Cartesian universe, a theoretical structure. What place does she have in this mathematical abstraction which the infant spins? She is aware that, though she cannot 'receive' or 'possess' the meaning of the child's body language, she does take in a richness from the gifts it offers her:

> I shall not entirely
> Sit emptied of beauties, the gift
> Of your small breath, the drenched grass
> Smell of your sleeps, lilies, lilies.

Her experiences of her baby are like lilies to her, beautiful and symbols of fresh growth.

But the flesh of the lilies bears no relation to the baby's: and does not have to bear the problem of *relationship*. The lilies become tiger lilies or calla lilies – they do not have to complete the mysterious processes whereby the human being becomes conscious and autonomous, through creative intersubjectivity. When we think of this,

> The comets
> Have such a space to cross,

> Such coldness, forgetfulness,
> So your gestures flake off –

Because she is a schizoid individual, unsure about the substantiality of her 'inner contents', she fears that the baby's self or being will bleed away by loss, even as it strives to cross the gulf to her. After all, what is there 'in' those gestures that *can* cross such a gulf?

> So your gestures flake off –
> warm and human, then their pink light
> Bleeding and peeling
> Through the black amnesias of heaven.

On her part, can she receive them?

> Why am I given
> These lamps, these planets
> Falling like blessings, like flakes
> Six-sided, white
> On my eyes, my lips, my hair
> Touching and melting.

The infant's 'messages' fall on the outside of her tegument as a being: she can see they are beautiful, but (like Coleridge) she cannot *feel* they are, or that they are really penetrating and enriching her. So the last line is the awful

> Nowhere . . .

Yet, the poem itself conveys well enough that she knows that she is not *entirely* bereft of 'blessings': the message, even if not understood, gets through. And the poem has courageously looked at the fundamental human problem, of whether we can ever really cross the great gulfs between ourselves and other beings. Difficult though this poem is, it is outward-looking and universal – it explores a problem of existence which we all, from time to time, confront.

There is yet another mode in these poets, which reveals more truly the nature of the problem behind the troubled consciousness. This is especially evident in the strange mad-dream poetry of Roethke such as the *Lost Son* sequence, and in Sylvia Plath's poem, written in a psychiatric hospital, 'Poem for a Birthday'. In this poetry, indeed, it is a *birth* that is sought – birth into a new being is the aim of the yearning.

In this mode of poetry, there remain many problems for the reader, as to what exactly the poetry is about: who is speaking, to whom, and what is the topic? In a poem by Roethke such as 'The Shape of the Fire', who is the 'nameless stranger'? Who is saying 'Mother me out of here'? Who is 'the flat-headed man'? What is being done to whom? If we read this poem and then turn to Sylvia Plath's 'Poem for a Birthday' some of the mythology seems to have become hers – 'Have you come to unhinge my shadow?' could be a line of hers, and Roethke's world seems, like hers, a world in which sinister shadowy people do stranger things to the self, which yearns for 'being for'. The mythological mother is there, yearned for desperately:

> Mother, you are the one mouth
> I would be tongue to – Mother of otherness
> Eat me.
>
> > (Plath)

> My meat eats me. Who waits at the gate?
> Mother of quartz, your words writhe into my ear.
> Renew the light, lend whisper.
>
> > (Roethke)

Addressing Roethke after his death, Lowell writes

> You honored nature, helpless, elemental
> creature, and touched the waters of the offing
> You left them quickened with your name: Ted Roethke . . .
> Omnipresent, the Mother made you nonexistent,
> you, the ocean's anchor, our high tide.
>
> > ('For Theodore Roethke', in *Notebook*)

And Lowell addresses his own mother:

> Mother, Mother!
> as a gemlike undergraduate,
> part criminal and yet a Phi Beta,
> I used to barge home late.
> Always by the bannister
> my milk-tooth mug of milk
> was waiting for me on a plate of triskets.
> Often with unadulterated joy:
> Mother, we bent by the fire
> rehashing Father's character . . .

Mother and father have a mythopoeic significance in each of these poets.

At the heart of the problem we find expressed as 'unborn' feeling such as Roethke's 'mad' poems explore – those poems from which Sylvia Plath took much of her 'voice' and manner, to explore the same problem. Childhood is recalled as a time when being seemed to be called forth:

> Snail, snail, glister me forward.
> Bird, soft-sigh me home,
> Worm, be with me.
> This is my hard time.
>
> Fished in an old wound,
> The soft pond of repose:
> Nothing nibbled my line,
> Not even the minnows came.

There is a powerful theme in American literature, not only to return to nature, as in *Walden*, but return to the primeval state of relationship to Nature, Mother Nature, as with Huckleberry Finn, living in a cave or on a raft, detached from the human world as much as possible. Here Roethke becomes the small boy, listening for the voice which will tell him how to begin to be:

> Voice, come out of the silence.
> Say something.
> Appear in the form of a spider
> Or a moth beating the curtain.
>
> Tell me:
> Which is the way I take;

The dark hollows, the moon and the raft do not seem to be able to give answers:

> You will find no comfort here,
> In the kingdom of bang and blab.

'Bang and blab' is the modern world of futile bustle and manic activity. The protagonist of the poem feels rejected by both mother and father:

> The sun was against me,
> The moon would not have me . . .

The cows and birds
Said to me: Die.

The poem is called 'The Lost Son' and it expresses a feeling that
some meaning should have poured out of sources in his home, to
give him an identity, but has failed to do so:

What gliding shape
Beckoned through halls,
Stood poised on the start,
Fell dreamily down?

From the mouths of jugs
Perched on many shelves,
I saw substance flowing
That cold morning.

There is a sense of cold non-being:

I'm cold. I'm cold all over. Rub me in father and mother.
Fear was my father, Father fear.
His look chained the stones.

One can see how the daughter of Otto Plath came to be captivated
by Roethke's poetry — as in her call for her mother to 'eat me'
('Poem for a Birthday'). One can see how she echoes his modes:

. . . Is this the storm's heart? The ground is unstilling itself.
All the windows are burning! What's left of my life?
I want the old rage, the lash of primordial milk!
Goodbye, goodbye, old stones, the time-order is going,
I have married my hands to perpetual agitation,
I run, I run to the whistle of money.

(Roethke)

The enigma is well expressed in these poems, and has to do with a
complex theme. How does one become oneself in the first place?
And how can one fulfil oneself and become whole now in adult life?
The puzzlement centres round the sense that the transformation
must be by something that is *done to one*: yet what is desired is a
growth of being from within, in the context of love. Whatever can
be 'the lash of primordial milk'? The phrase suggests a strange experience of being mothered! The problem is the same as that explored
in Sylvia Plath's 'Poem for a Birthday' and elsewhere. How is love
to be re-experienced, when it seems such an 'impinging' or being-

done-to experience which urges something alien on oneself? 'I have married my hands to perpetual agitation' is echoed in Plath's 'Tulips': 'I have given my name and my day-clothes up to the nurses' and in 'They have swabbed me clear of my loving associations.' The theme of 'The Return' is echoed in her 'Lady Lazarus' and 'Tulips' too. In Roethke's poem in the end what seems to be achieved is a sense of impending light, and a patient waiting:

> Was it light?
> Was it light within?
> Was it light within light?
> Stillness, becoming alive,
> Yet still?
> A lively understandable spirit
> Once entertained you.
> It will come again.
> Be still.
> Wait.

(Cf. Plath: 'I am lost in all this light.')

The influence of these poems of Roethke's on Sylvia Plath (and incidentally on Ted Hughes) is quite uncanny, because what they picked up was this way of talking to oneself, or rather 'to' the regressed libidinal ego:

> Come littlest, come tenderest,
> Come whispering over the small waters,
> Reach me rose, sweet one . . .
>
> The leaves, the leaves become me!
> The tendrils have me!
>> (Roethke)

> O littleblood, little boneless, little skinless . . .
> Grown so wise grown so terrible
> Sucking death's mouldy tits.
>
> Sit on my finger, sing in my ear, o littleblood.
>> (Hughes, 'Littleblood', in *Crow*)

> He won't be got rid of:
> Mumblepaws, teary and sorry,
> Fido Littlesoul, the bowel's familiar.
> A dustbin's enough for him.

> The dark's his bone.
> Call him by any name, he'll come to it.
> (Plath, 'Poem for a Birthday')

The mode and language are strangely evocative: the language of nursery rhyme, and child fantasy is used deliberately to speak of deranged states:

> Where do the roots go?
>   Look down under the leaves.
> Who put the moss there?
>   These stones have been here too long.
> Who stunned the dirt into noise?
>   Ask the mole, he knows.
> I feel the slime of a wet nest.
>   Beware Mother Mildew.
> Nibble again, fish nerves.
>   (Roethke)

> These marrowy tunnels!
> Moley-handed, I eat my way.
> All-mouth licks up the brushes
> And the pots of meat.
> He lives in an old well,
> A stony hole. He's to blame.
> He's a fat sort.
>   (Plath)

> O littleblood, drumming in a cow's skull
> Dancing with a gnat's feet
> With an elephant's nose with a crocodile's tail ...
>   (Hughes, 'Littleblood', in *Crow*)

> These sweeps of light undo me.
> Look, look, the ditch is running white!
> I've more veins than a tree!
> Kiss me, ashes, I'm falling through a dark swirl.
>   (Roethke)

> Give me back my shape. I am ready to construe the days
> I coupled with dust in the shadow of a stone.
> My ankles brighten. Brightness ascends my thighs.
> I am lost, I am lost, in the robes of all this light.
>   (Plath)

The expression in these poems of regression is of a feeling that there is an unborn self, which is either addressed or is made to speak about its hunger to be born. The 'madness' of these poems is valuable, in that it reveals a common predicament, because each of us has some element in the personality which belongs to this sense of being incomplete and unfulfilled. These poems speak of human vulnerability in a way that should, when we understand them, provoke our pity.

There is yet another kind of poetry, however, which seems to come from a desperation which overtakes the poet, when it becomes clear that the hopes to be re-born are not going to materialize. Then, the energy of oral power turns to vengeance or hate, and adopts the postures of defiant contempt and destructive rage, as in some of the poems in Lowell's *Notebooks* and Plath's *Ariel*. And here we need to take a different view from that of Alvarez, who approves the cultivation of psychosis, because the psychotic solution may belong to a total falsification of reality, a complete dissociation from all wisdom. It is possible that by entering into a psychotic delusion (like Sylvia Plath's belief that suicide represented a chance of rebirth) and idolizing that, a writer can follow an inverted or deranged logic, and *define a false path*. This is what Andrew Brink believes Sylvia Plath's poetry did for her (see his essay in *Loss and Symbolic Repair*). It was not that she could not save herself by 'shedding the sicknesses in books' (to adapt a phrase from D. H. Lawrence): it was rather that, coldly and deliberately, she devoted herself, through her poetry, to the very argument that killed her. What can such poetry do for us? If the artist 'cultivates his psychosis', may she not involve us in her madness, and so take us even further from the human insights and positives we need? With Plath the false solutions tend towards the psychotic, as, for instance, in her declaration in 'Lady Lazarus' that she does 'it' – that is, commits suicide every ten years. Or in 'Edge', which seems a beautiful poem at first sight, the assertion that it is natural and 'right' to fold her children back into her body is again suicide.

The last lines, however, give the poem away.

> The moon has nothing to be sad about,
> Staring from her hood of bone . . .

Who is this moon? The mythopoeic answer is – the Mother. What is the Moon-mother doing here, with the assertion she has nothing to be sad about, and the bitter phrase 'her blacks crackle and drag' – evoking a mythical *witch*? And expressing hate – and revenge? 'She is used to this sort of thing' – said with contempt. We cannot answer unless we unravel the psychopathology. The last lines of 'Edge' reveal that behind the image of a perfect, peaceful 'right' suicide *and matricide* there is a seething energy of hatred and revenge. It isn't a question of self-pity: it is rather a question of psychotic delusion. The children are to be killed in the insane delusion that this will bring rebirth, according to the fantasies of schizoid suicide. ('I am too big to go backwards' – she cannot really regress, but, as in 'Poem for a Birthday', all her psychic energy is directed at a rebirth of being and not the false restamping of the inauthentic, 'given', identity offered by conventional psychiatry.)

Besides the impulse to rebirth is that of revenge. The mother's face proved to be devoid of creative response – it is, in her mythology, always blank and stony, bald (and 'the moon is my mother'). When Otto Plath died, Mrs Plath tried to prevent her child daughter from seeing her grief, and Sylvia Plath thus felt that her mother was stony-faced. Her need is to bring a proper emotional response into that face – and her weapons are suicide and matricide.

Yet did not the children have a right to live? And did not Sylvia Plath have a right to live – if only her delusions could have been unravelled? Alas, the fashionable acclaim of the false solutions of hate has tended to push many modern writers, from Dylan Thomas to Anne Sexton, deeper and deeper into falsity. It is clear both from Lowell's poetry, for instance, and his biography that the 'literary' drinking party was a focus of destructiveness, in which hate was given free play:

> something inhuman always rising on us
> . . .
> each day more brutal, oracular and rooted,
> dehydrated and smiling in the fire
> . . .
> hurt when he kicked aside the last dead bottle
> ('Long Summer', p. 24)

In Lowell, this 'false solution' mythology led him into a tired cynicism, as in '1970 New Year':

> By miracle, I left the party half
> an hour behind you, reached home five hours drunker ...

Courtship has

> ... lost half its vice with all its virtue
> Who wants a second life and two more wives?
> Cards will never be dealt us fairly again.
> (Notebook, p. 174)

A knowing, sophisticated, cynical emptiness takes over, and words like 'anger', 'death' and 'love' are used, but without gravity or commitment – or hope.

The participants at the manic mind-blowing simply sit in their own haze of hate.

> the inarticulate mist so thick
> we turned invisible to one another
> across the room; the floor, aslant, shot hulling
> through thunderheads, gun-cotton dipped in pitch ...
> (Notebook, p. 25)

So the poet even comes to rely on authoritarian intervention:

> I have to brace my hand against a wall
> to keep myself from swaying – swaying wall,
> strait jacket, hypodermic, helmeted
> doctors, one crowd, white-smocked, in panic, hit
> stop, bury the runner on the cleated field
> (ibid.)

The heavy drinking evidently belonged to an oral need, and was itself a form of escape from an intolerable reality. The dissociated episodes recurrently included a promising relationship with a new young woman who was going to bring him to spiritual rebirth: confusion of personal and relational reality follows, with outbursts of more destructiveness, so that Lowell had to be locked up.

We have to be careful of applying a strong moralism to poetry, but there can be no doubt that it is impossible to read the work of poets like this without encountering many related difficulties and critical problems. How many poems by Sylvia Plath will endure? Students often begin by being fascinated by her, but a revulsion sets in over her insistent assertiveness, as it does with some of Lowell's poems when he becomes 'incomprehensible and boring', cruel and shallow. They tend towards a kind of sensational journalism and this is, of course, a modern weakness.

At best, however, we must recognize a kind of courage in those who have been willing to reveal some of their most tormented aspects, and this has a universal value, since it exposes the underlying existential problems of our time. When Victor Frankl (as he reports in his *Psychotherapy and Existentialism*, 1964) asked students in Europe whether they had ever experienced a sense of total meaninglessness in life, some 40 per cent put up their hands, whereas when he asked the same question in the USA, this response was given by 80 per cent. Today, I daresay, the result would be different in Europe, where, in France, suicide has become the chief cause of death among young people. Something is wrong with the contemporary Western soul, and these poets give us a clue: it has to do with being, with the failure of love, and it surely has something to do with the lack of an adequate experience of *the mother*, whatever the implications of this may be.

The best poems in the work of the poets under discussion centre around a child spirit that seems to be registering a terrible dread of the world it finds itself in, while also speaking of the joy and mystery of existence. In the symbolism of this, we may perhaps find clues to the troubles of the modern Western consciousness, and its search for a sense of meaning.

TENNESSEE WILLIAMS,
ARTHUR MILLER, AND EDWARD ALBEE

PETER DAVISON

No Western nation has shown itself so sharply divided in its attitude to live, theatre drama as has the United States. It is, *par excellence*, the land of 'Show Biz', a little in decline at the moment, maybe, but for a hundred years, from minstrel shows to musicals, from Broadway to Hollywood, from chautauqua to vaudeville, it has ridden high in vitality, excitement, and sheer panache, supremely self-confident. Yet for decades the performance of plays was banned by law in America – understandable in view of its Puritan foundation. Now, and throughout the twentieth century, the writing and study of drama, the training of actors, and instruction in all aspects of the performing arts have been vigorously encouraged by universities, foundations, and local communities to a degree far beyond that prevailing in Britain. And yet, if it has shaken off that early coolness, the record of American drama in the past four decades seems to fall short of what might be expected from the massive encouragement it has been given. The reasons for this spring as much from the achievements and ethos of Show Biz (whose attractions have too often seduced aspiring dramatists) as from social and historical tradition. Early condemnation, given peculiar force by that of the Continental Congress of 1774, and later suspicion, led to the theatre attempting to justify itself, first by crude chauvinism and scorn for Europe and Europeans; secondly by laying claim to a kind of quasi-educational status. It was almost as if drama had to seem to be other than it was to prove acceptable. That 'educational taint' has been pervasive and long-lasting. Thus, in 1963 Edward Albee's *Who's Afraid of Virginia Woolf?* failed to be awarded the Pulitzer Prize because it did not 'represent in marked fashion the educational value and power of the stage' – a criterion laid down for the Prize. Only when that condition was rescinded was the Pulitzer Prize again awarded to a play – to Albee's *A Delicate Balance*. By far the most successful American 'play' of all time was an adaptation of a novel by a woman to whom theatre was anathema; which was 'educational'; and which was presented in many of its versions with all the stunning resources of nineteenth-century theatre: *Uncle's Tom's Cabin*.

Moreover, American drama has been hamstrung by what ought to be a major strength: innovation. That, however, perhaps inspired by vigorous industrial practice, has been elevated to a dramatic credo, as witnessed by Edward Albee in his Introduction to *Box* and *Quotations from Chairman Mao Tse-tung* (first performed in 1968):

A playwright – unless he is creating escapist romances (an honorable occupation, of course) – has two obligations: first, to make some statement about the condition of 'man' (as it is put) and, second, to make some statement about the nature of the art form with which he is working. In both instances he must attempt change . . , the playwright must try to alter his society [and] : . . the forms within which his precursors have had to work.

What should be a strength can become an end in itself, even a self-indulgent cult.

The overall impression of American theatre drama is that it is subservient to other media and performance arts, which sometimes, as in the creation of modern dance as an expression of the inner self, chiefly through the work of Martha Graham (1893–   ), have influenced developments throughout the world. American drama is more remarkable for interesting, occasionally outstanding, plays than as an art form and so attention here is focused on a few plays by Williams, Miller, and Albee.

Of the three dramatists discussed here, Tennessee Williams (1911–83) is by far the most colourful, varied and prolific in output. Williams took risks in his drama. At first sight those risks may be thought to arise from his dramatization of sexual conflict. He certainly had several brushes with such bodies as the Catholic Legion of Decency (which condemned his film, *Baby Doll*, 1956) and with local officials such as the Boston Police Commissioner and that city's Assistant Censor, who, early in 1941, required cuts in *Battle of Angels* (1940; revised as *Orpheus Descending*, 1957). This, they declared, was a play 'about cheap white trash' with 'Too many lines [having] double meanings'. However, the real risks Williams ran were, as they should be, artistic. Often he over-reaches, but he is never uninteresting and only dull when relatively ordered (as in, for instance, the overvalued *Sweet Bird of Youth*, 1959). But artistic risks are taken at a price. Thus, the Cocalooney Bird of *The Gnädiges Fräulein* was imaginative in conception if disastrous in production, having seven performances in 1966 and twelve in 1974. Williams is particularly associated with the South, but his range is much wider. Although no voice strikes a European as more quintessentially 'American' than that of Mrs Goforth in *The Milk Train Doesn't Stop Here Anymore* (1962), Williams's America is far from being a Protestant Anglo-Saxon America. It is a richly immigrant America dramatized without condescension or special pleading.

Williams has written illuminatingly in notes to his plays or in passing comments within them about his own work and the theatre of his time. In 'The Timeless World of a Play' that precedes printings of *The Rose Tattoo* (1951), he speaks of the 'horror of insincerity, of *not meaning*' that overlays certain social gatherings in America: 'This horror is the only thing, almost, that is left unsaid at such functions . . . Fear and evasion are the two little beasts that chase each other's tails in the revolving wirecage of our nervous world.' It is such fear and evasion, such unspoken horror, to which Williams endeavours to give voice in his drama. The setting of *The Glass Menagerie*, a play which draws on his own early life, is described by Williams as being in one of those huge apartment buildings that are 'always burning with the slow and implacable fires of human desperation'. The results are characters 'bigger than life and twice as unnatural' (as Shannon describes Maxine in *The Night of the Iguana*), and what at the time were unconventional techniques some of which originated in America in the work of Thornton Wilder. Although inclined to 'excess', Williams was not insensitive to the demands of artistic tact when using unconventional techniques. In his Production Note to *The Glass Menagerie* he remarks that these should not permit a play 'to escape its responsibility of dealing with reality, or interpreting experience', but as he has Shannon ask Hannah Jelkes in *The Night of the Iguana*, 'we live on two levels . . . the realistic level and the fantastic level, and which is the real one, really?' Picking up T. S. Eliot's sad truth from *Burnt Norton* (1936), La Madrecita tells the dead Kilroy in *Camino Real* (1953) after describing his heart as made of pure gold and as being as big as a baby's head, 'Rise, ghost! Go! Go bird!

"Humankind cannot bear very much reality."' (The bird is also from *Burnt Norton*.) Then follows a scene typical of Williams's 'fantastical reality'. Kilroy rises from the dead, there is a 'ghostly chase' through the auditorium (for the second time in the play) for the heart of gold, the dried-up town fountain flows with water, Don Quixote stirs from the sleep he has enjoyed from the beginning of the play, and Kilroy joins him as Sancho Panza's replacement as they leave, with hope renewed, for the fearful Terra Incognita that lies outside the run-down seaport at 'the end of the line' on the Royal Route of Life – the Camino Real.

Camino Real is highly imaginative but its fantasy bursts at the seams and there is uncertainty as to whether we are being given characters or stereotypes. *The Rose Tattoo*, with its mystery of the husband's tattoo which is transferred from his chest to his wife's breast at the moment their child is conceived, manages to accommodate fantasy satisfactorily but its sentimental ending is unconvincing. *The Night of the Iguana* is marred by a quasi-chorus of German tourists repeatedly rejoicing in the Luftwaffe's bombing of Britain in 1940, but it otherwise marks a mood of acceptance in Williams's drama, Maxine perhaps speaking for Williams himself:

> We've both reached a point where we've got to settle for something that works for us in our lives – even if it isn't on the highest kind of level.

Ironically, such emotional maturity is inclined to rob Williams's work of that flashing torment that gives his best plays their special character and vitality.

Williams's three masterpieces, all of which burn with the 'slow and implacable fears of human desperation', and all of which are aesthetically controlled, are *The Glass Menagerie*, *A Streetcar Named Desire*, and *Cat on a Hot Tin Roof*. Each achieved enormously long runs when first presented in New York – 561, 855, and 694 performances respectively – and thus artistic and box-office success went hand in hand. Of the three, *The Glass Menagerie* is the most emotionally restrained. The story turns on Tom's hope that a colleague, Jim, will find his sister, the lonely, supremely shy, and partially crippled Laura, attractive. But Jim, though a little better paid than Tom, has also failed and, as it turns out, is hoping to marry another girl. The mother's fine show of Southern style is frustrated,

Laura's hopes are disappointed, so that she returns to the little private world of her collection of glass animals, and Tom abandons the women in an attempt to become a poet, something which, as he explains in a final monologue to the audience, he fails to do. Although the play is about failure, Williams invests his characters, even when most misguided, with warmth and dignity so that their fates involve and touch us. The subject, rather than the story, is concerned with the over-riding importance of charm, illusion, and superficial appearance and their delusory powers. Amanda puts great store by an outworn code of Southern behaviour which she can no longer sustain and she despairs of her daughter's ability to attract a host of 'gentlemen callers'. She can never bring herself to use the word 'crippled' of Laura and rebukes Tom for so doing. Yet Jim had never noticed at school nor during his visit that she was slightly lame. Superficial appearance is rightly exposed for what it is and, in a splendid touch, at the very end of the play, Williams has Amanda refer to Laura as 'an unmarried sister who's crippled and has no job'.

A Streetcar Named Desire takes the superficial gentility of the South a stage further and several degrees lower. Blanche DuBois is at the end of her tether. She cannot come to terms with the loss of the plantation society which she feels to be her true milieu; the family home, Belle Reve, has been broken up; her husband has committed suicide following Blanche's taunts that he is homosexual (a motivation which had to be cut from the film following representations by the Catholic Legion of Decency); and she has been dismissed from her post as a schoolteacher because 'she'd gotten mixed up with' a seventeen-year-old pupil. She has arrived, destitute except for her affectation of breeding and gentility, to live with – and on – her sister, Stella, in a street ironically called Elysian Fields, New Orleans. Stella is married to a Polish-American, Stanley Kowalski, who is virile and direct, unsubtle rather than coarse, and much in love with Stella. To Stanley, Blanche is first and foremost a hypocrite and her loose sexual life poses a threat to the stability of his relationship with Stella. The harshness with which Stanley destroys Blanche (particularly her hopes of marrying his friend, Mitch), is matched by its inevitability and his rape of Blanche during the night when Stella gives birth to their child is dramatically justified. The play can lay claim to being considered a contemporary tragedy; it is powerful, unremitting, devoid of sentimentality, and convincing.

Although Williams's best plays are so concerned with the broken and inadequate, they are enlivened with an acerbic humour, nowhere better displayed than in *Cat on a Hot Tin Roof*. Maggie, the Cat, and her impotent husband, Brick, reveal a mordant wit, especially at the expense of their fecund sister-in-law, Mae, and Brick's aptly named brother, Gooper. Sterility lies at the heart of the play. Brick is haunted by the suicide of his friend, Skipper, around whom hung a suspicion of homosexuality. He cannot make love with his sensuous wife because he believes it was she who forced Skipper to believe he was homosexual. Big Daddy is dying of cancer, a fact cruelly revealed to him by his son when accused by the father of not being able to face realities. The physical and mental pain Big Daddy suffers is compounded by his fear that all he has built up will pass to the Mae and Gooper progeny if Brick cannot father a child. As originally written, the play ends with Big Daddy in agony, his wife in deep uncomprehending sorrow (most movingly dramatized by Williams), and Maggie mendaciously claiming she is pregnant but with only the slightest glimmer of hope that Brick can bring this to pass. Elia Kazan, first director of the play, persuaded Williams to write a more hopeful ending which, ironically, perpetuates the kind of false illusion Williams was so adept at exposing. If the theatre was sometimes unable to present Williams as he wished, film versions were even more seriously emasculated.[1]

The essential, the precise difference between tragedy and pathos, Arthur Miller (1915–) has written, is that tragedy brings not only 'sadness, sympathy, identification and even fear; it also, unlike pathos, brings us knowledge or enlightenment'; that enlightenment, he wrote a month earlier, is the 'discovery of the moral law'.[2] Further, the tragic is open to everyone, it is 'a condition of life, a condition in which the human personality is able to flower and realize itself'. No other modern dramatist has written about the vexed nature of tragedy so simply and directly, *and* has so perfectly justified his stance in the theatre. The choice of the New York Drama Critics' Circle of Miller's *All My Sons* as the best play of 1947 over O'Neill's *The Iceman Cometh* was, with hindsight, a surprising error, but with two of his later plays Miller achieved a tragic intensity and universality equal to O'Neill at his best.

Death of a Salesman (1949), like *All My Sons* – indeed much of Miller's work – owes a superficial debt to Ibsen, in particular to *The Wild Duck* for these two plays, and to *An Enemy of the People* (which Miller adapted in 1950) for *The Crucible* (1953). Ibsen's inspiration goes much deeper in *Death of a Salesman* than the dramatization of false illusions and moral choices. As potential tragedy, Miller's materials are unpropitious. The narrative, and even some of the dialogue, are rather trite. The Salesman, Willy Loman, is a petty self-deceiver, only too willing to stoop to minor crime and to sordid philandering, buying 'love' with silk stockings intended for his hard-pressed wife. Even as a salesman, the lynch-pin of the consumer society, he is a failure. His path is painfully downward and the very machinery of his life – his car and his refrigerator – are breaking down. His legacy to his children is no more than his own false illusions of life, society, family, and self. At the end of the play a little recognition seems to come to Biff, the older son. 'He had the wrong dreams. All, all wrong,' he says after Willy's funeral – a funeral which so many of his supposed friends failed to attend – but his brother, Happy, cannot even bring himself to have that said. The reality is that although Linda, Willy's wife, has made the last payment on their home on the day of the funeral, 'there'll be nobody home. We're free and clear [of debt] . . . We're free,' she sobs, only too aware of the emptiness of such freedom.

Out of this pathetic story of a failed salesman, aptly called Loman, Miller creates a genuine tragedy of the common man, to adapt the title of one of his essays. His technique was developed, wittingly or not, from Ibsen's retrospective exposition. Full understanding of the events of the past come with their climax in the present. In *Death of a Salesman* this prevents Willy's story being simply a downward spiral, depressing and inevitable: inevitability is more than the progression of events. The implication of an early title for the play, 'The Inside of His Head', allows Miller a free-wheeling, though tightly organized, use of time. With magnificent craft, Miller juxtaposes past and present time, place, events, characters, intentions, and dreams, keyed with appropriate music cues. The set was an exploded view of the Loman home. Movement in place could thus be as fluid as movement in time – in the mind, in fact.

Despite the subject matter, the play is often funny, although the humour is bitter and sardonic. Many incidents start comically, even gaily, so the 'downward spiral effect' is completely avoided and the shock of revelation, to Biff and to the audience, comes sharp and final at the end of the play.

After nearly half-a-century, *Death of a Salesman* remains powerful and compelling. Its mechanics are, perhaps, a little obvious now, for it was in the van of that freer dramaturgy that has since become commonplace, but despite that, because it is so well crafted, its technique facilitates rather than hinders the play's tragic effect. Miller's achievement in this play, and surely a lasting achievement, is that he makes the essential link between the tragedy that can afflict the ordinary individual and the society of which he is a member.

As T. S. Eliot showed with poetic drama, costume and the past give superficial advantages to the dramatist who essays that form and much the same initial advantage applies to tragedy. The stylization of language prompts a shift in our responses which seems to make tragedy more acceptable, more 'natural' even. That advantage can be short-lived unless what is at issue is as relevant to the past as to the present. By implication, *The Crucible* draws a parallel between seventeenth-century witch hunts in Massachusetts and those conducted by a committee of the United States Congress two-and-a-half centuries later. The contemporary and continuing strength of Miller's play stems from his insight into how those who experienced the agonies of 1692 learnt to know 'who they were' and it is this process that Miller dramatizes for a generation that had not learnt that essential truth. But possibly Miller's greatest achievement in *The Crucible* is its dramatization of the *fact* of evil. As Dennis Welland has explained: 'In American literature, probably more than in any other, there have always been influences at work to minimize the fact of evil.' Miller, he argued, was the first American dramatist to recognize 'the fact of evil' at work in society: 'The Declaration of Independence may be said to have made evil an unAmerican activity' and American authors 'have generally been quicker to recognize evils than to recognize evil'. Miller dramatized evil at work in society – the society of the twentieth century as much as that of the seventeenth – and it was not surprising that in 1957 he was tried for contempt of Congress and found guilty on two counts, though his convictions were quashed the following year if only on a technicality.

Of Miller's other plays, perhaps the most interesting is *The Price* (1968). This shows a certain acceptance of the 'loss of innocence' as an inevitable state of man. It makes use of Ibsen's technique of retrospective exposition in its purest form (as in *Rosmersholm*). As the characters come to realize the truth of their complex motivation, so the audience's eyes are opened to human capacity for self-deception. The play's resolution, aided by a brilliantly conceived, comic old reprobate of a Jewish furniture-dealer, is a trifle too cosy, so that we are not torn as we ought to be and as we are in Miller's two masterpieces. Nevertheless, *The Price* is moving, effective, and often delightfully comic.

'Edward Albee (1928–), with nice irony, once wrote of how deeply he had been offended when told he was 'a member in good standing of The Theatre of the Absurd'. The absurd theatre, he considered, was 'the theatre uptown – Broadway'. Such a theatre pandered to the public need for self-congratulation and it was a place avowedly in which to relax, to have a good time. The health of a society, he argued, could be 'determined by the art it demands. We have insisted of television and our movies that they not have anything to do with anything, that they be our never-never land.' To Albee, the truly contemporary theatre was where an audience faced 'man's condition as it is'.

Albee's little polemic throws into sharp relief the dilemma of the contemporary dramatist caught between pandering to audiences seeking relaxation in a never-never world (itself a minority audience as compared to film and TV), and dramatizing man's condition as he sees it to a coterie minority of that minority. It is a mark of Albee's achievement that he has resolved this dilemma in a number of plays. In attacking the hollowness he finds in American society he has also proved dramatically effective outside America: the ills he diagnoses are not peculiar to his own society. Albee's prime dramatic strength lies in his marvellous ear for certain kinds of dialogue – for empty chit-chat, lacerating sarcasm, and banality concealing hollow emotions – which he uses to serve his dramatic ends. No one writes with more cruel vitality of what is at heart empty.

His second strength is his fierce, even demonic, urge to expose what he takes to be the falseness of the American Dream, the title of one of his short plays (1961), which does just that. It was, he wrote in a Preface to it:

an examination of the American Scene, an attack on the substitution of artificial for real values in our society, a condemnation of complacency, cruelty, emasculation and vacuity; it is a stand against the fiction that everything in this slipping land of ours is peachy-keen.

Some critics found the play offensive, to which Albee replied in this Preface: 'Is the play offensive? I certainly hope so; it is my intention to offend – as well as amuse and entertain.' Albee can well claim to have 'offended entertainingly' in this and several other plays.

The third characteristic that marks an Albee play is a sense of uncertainty, of doubt, even of terror of the unknown. He has a considerable gift for making what cannot be precisely pinpointed dramatically convincing: Grandma's neatly wrapped boxes in *The American Dream*, Jerry's motivation in *Zoo Story* (1959), the underlying truth of George and Martha's fantasy child in *Who's Afraid of Virginia Woolf?* (1962), the implications of the model and Julian's marriage 'through' Miss Alice in *Tiny Alice* (1964), and, if not quite so successfully, the terror that impels Edna and Harry to seek refuge with Agnes and Tobias in *A Delicate Balance* (1966). Albee is capable, as it were, of dramatizing a fourth dimension and it is a mark of what he can achieve in this respect that an hour of vigorous discussion can prove illuminating and yet leave the 'mystery' inviolate.

For so short a play, *A Zoo Story* is extraordinarily powerful. This is the more remarkable because there are only two characters, one of whom, Jerry, spends a considerable time regaling his unwilling listener, Peter, with the story of his relationship with his dog, a story comic, cruel, and puzzling. Peter, a rather retiring writer of textbooks, is found seated on a bench in Central Park, New York, reading a book. Jerry is returning from a visit to the Zoo and insists on engaging Peter in conversation. Part of the play's effect is a result of the *frisson* most of the audience will recognize from just such unwelcome attempts to make contact. Peter is resentful and fears, with pathetic timidity, that he will lose 'his' park bench. Jerry has a great deal to say but little is about his visit to the Zoo, and the play ends with Jerry impaled on his own knife, now held by Peter. The play has been called more 'melodramatically pretentious' in its conclusion than 'seriously ambiguous' by Walter J. Meserve and considered with cold objectivity that might not seem unjustified, but in performance Albee's skill is such that we become party to Peter's act, even though that act is unwitting and defensive. By means of a combination of realistic and popular dramatic techniques, Albee confronts his audience with its reluctance to become emotionally involved in a concern for others. By this means inaction can be shown as being as dangerous and as violent as action.

Tiny Alice shows considerable skill in its attempt to dramatize an abstraction in the form of the reality or otherwise of Julian's faith. Albee has, with justice, argued that an audience can be assumed to be capable of grasping more complex matters than simple addition or subtraction – they regularly do for Shakespeare – but what remains in the memory of *Tiny Alice* is the ingenuity of the contrivance rather than the force of dramatic illusion.

In *A Delicate Balance* (which perhaps received its Pulitzer Prize in 1967 because *Who's Afraid of Virginia Woolf?* was denied the award in 1963), one ageing couple descends upon another, driven to seek refuge from some unexplained (and undramatized) terror in a neighbouring suburb. With the family with whom they take shelter there is also an alcoholic sister and a daughter who has run home after her fourth marriage has failed. It is a play of wit, interest, and style, but on this occasion the terror is too ill-defined and the assembly of so many neurotics unconvincing. The play lacks the hard edge, the driving compulsion, and the terrifying juxtaposition of hate and love that makes *Who's Afraid of Virginia Woolf?* outstanding. In the latter, the mystery springs from within the play and its characters; in *A Delicate Balance* it is asserted, superimposed.

In *Who's Afraid of Virginia Woolf?* the sterile marriage and lives of George and Martha, long-time members of a New England college community, are contrasted with those of the young, starry-eyed, new arrivals, Nick and Honey. George is a disillusioned member of what is regarded as a *passé* subject, history, who has failed to realize his early promise. His wife is the college president's daughter, older than George, professionally outrageous, and frustrated by his inability to advance himself. Nick represents the new; his biology, according to George, looks forward through genetic engineering to millions upon millions of 'tiny little slicing operations . . . on the underside of the scrotum', an opinion expressed the more bitterly because of George and Martha's inability to produce a child. Both families share an illusion. George and Martha resort to fantasizing that they have a child; Honey had a 'hysterical pregnancy. She blew up, and then she went down'. The action is much taken up with a series of 'blue games for the guests' – Humiliate the Host, Hump the Hostess, Get the Guests: game and fiction in effect take over from a life rendered meaningless through its sterility. At one point, George tells Martha that she has 'ugly talents' and the play dramatizes with raw ferocity what the American – or any other – Dream can be when superficial values have replaced true virtues. The names, George and Martha, are, of course, those of the first President of the United States, George Washington, and his wife. If the play has a weakness it is that we cannot really believe in the efficacy of the exorcism of the last act. ('Exorcism' is the title of the last act and was a working title for the play itself.) Perhaps not even Albee can quite face the logic of an emasculated dream that has become a nightmare.

Walter Meserve has succinctly summed up the achievements of American drama of this period:

> In general, the American theatre did not provide very exciting supporting drama for Miller and Williams . . . Perhaps American drama of the mid-twentieth century will not have more than three plays that might be revived a hundred years hence.

But that is too harsh. American dramatists have had a particularly hard row to hoe. No number of Pulitzer Prizes, Drama Critics' Awards, Obies and Tonies, nor a Theatre Hall of Fame (institutions more diverting than convincing) can persuade one otherwise. That there has been even a handful or two of outstanding plays is a tribute to the art, skill, and persistence of a few dedicated individuals.

NOTES

1. See Maurice Yacowar, *Tennessee Williams and Film* (New York, 1977) for an excellent analysis of fifteen of Williams's films.

2. 'The Nature of Tragedy', *New York Herald Tribune*, 27 March 1949, and 'Tragedy and the Common Man', *New York Times*, 27 February 1949; reprinted in *The Theater Essays of Arthur Miller*, ed. Robert. A. Martin (Penguin Books, New York, 1978), pp. 9–10 and 5.

BLACK WRITERS – JEWISH WRITERS – WOMEN WRITERS

FREDERICK R. KARL

Black, Jewish, and women writers are doomed to be grouped together as a post-war phenomenon in American fiction. In other areas of endeavor – social, economic, political, theoretical – the grouping has fallen apart of its own ill design. One does not speak of black economics, or female social thought, or Jewish theory – even though Hitler once spoke of Jewish physics. And in other literary genres, in drama and poetry, for example, one looks in vain for such groupings; for they hardly exist, although one heard, for a brief time, of black theatre and a black poetic voice. In fiction, however, the phenomenon persists of larger and individual groupings; and this chapter, in part, will demonstrate both the weakness of a fictional gathering together of 'black, Jewish, female' and the misleading nature of the terms themselves.

A relevant question arises why there should have been groups in the first place. It began, of course, in our interest in minority and ethnic cultures and subcultures after the Second World War. Yet while blacks are a large minority and Jews a small one, women are not; blacks are not ethnics, however, since in many instances they represent the very oldest Americans; Jews are ethnics; but clearly women are not. The fit is already misleading. Another source of the groupings came when blacks, Jews, and women, liberated by the war, began to publish in larger numbers, or at least appeared to dominate the literary scene.

Female writers (white) did create a grouping of their own as a spate of novels directly concerned with the reverberations of the women's liberation movement appeared, all within a few years of each other, beginning in the late sixties. This was a legitimate grouping, for a short period of time. But if female writers briefly did have a common subject, black authors did not. For example, nearly all the female authors in this five-year span commonly wrote about separation, divorce, creating an independent life for themselves. Blacks hardly agreed among themselves. Some like Baldwin pursued intensely personal themes, often of one's sexual preferences; others like Morrison and Walker dealt with questions of female identity, amidst black social and political needs. Still others like Ishmael Reed broke with use of standard English to attempt a kind of bebop language which would pass for 'black English'. Alice Walker, in her recent immensely popular *The Color Purple*, has attempted a middle ground between standard and 'black' English.

Among Jewish writers, the divisions are even greater — calling into question not only the validity of grouping Jews with blacks and women, but the valorization of such a term as 'Jewish writers'. As Jews, what do Mailer and Joseph Heller have in common either with each other or with Malamud? and what meaning does the Jewish novel have even for Malamud when he writes *A New Life* (1961) based distinctly on profoundly American pastoral themes, or *The Natural* (1952), which is an archetypal American story of magic, Faust, and baseball?

Heller's distinctive novel is *Catch-22* (1961), and yet except for a kind of New York humor associated with standup comics who plied the Catskill circuit, there is little 'Jewish' about it. Heller's next novel after *Catch-22*, *Something Happened* (1974), was concerned with a Gentile family. Mailer's identification as part of the Jewish group defies description, since neither in subject-matter nor language usage does he suggest any such background. Even Philip Roth, in what is often called the quintessential Jewish work, his collection of stories *Goodbye, Columbus* (1959), is concerned more with clashes of class and caste than with Jewishness. It catches the flavor of suburban life after the Second World War, that quality of posing, upward mobility, ostentatious country club existence, which here happens to be Jewish. And it is played off in class and caste terms against the city poor of Newark, who also happen to be Jewish. Perhaps Mailer's finest fiction is *Why Are We in Vietnam?* (1967), which is about Texas, Lyndon Johnson, and the great white Gentile establishment. Only Bellow, Roth, and Malamud continued to write about Jews, but, as we shall note later, in terms which made their subjects America and Americans rather than Jews and Judaism. Such literary creations are part of a struggle representing not race or religion, or the

Old World, but America, American themes, American temptations.

The vision of all these writers, whatever their individual emphasis, is the matter of America. The language they write in, except for occasional elements of dialect which recall Yiddish or black rural/ inner city life, is American English; and that fact alone pre-empts other distinctions. If we accept that a common language, with minor divergences, draws blacks, Jews, and women together as writers, then distinctions based on color, sex, ethnic affiliation, or religion become secondary, or extraneous. Furthermore, not only language binds them, but a common American heritage – despite the fact that for many Jewish writers ancestors came, mainly, from Eastern Europe. Their history, as a result of schooling, is American history, and their aspirations, reinforced by public school, are part of that upward mobility we associate with American life. Furthermore, their literary and cultural antecedents are Thoreau and Emerson, and large elements of Poe, Hawthorne, Melville, Cooper, and other classic American writers. Saul Bellow (*The Adventures of Augie March*, 1953), James Baldwin (*Go Tell It on the Mountain*, 1953), and Joyce Carol Oates (*them*, 1969) may appear to inhabit different planets, but once we get past obvious superficial differences, they share in America and they write an American version of the *Bildungsroman*.

What, then, remains of our categories? A meaningful question is to ask what certain writers are responding to in American life; then to follow that up with a further question on how their particular situation, as a Jew, black, or woman, has helped to shape their response. Once we recognize that all of them are categories of the genus *American writer*, based on language, history, literary antecedents, and common aspirations, we can make distinctions. Blacks, Jews, and women are indeed different from white American males in their experience and in their perception of and response to that experience. The white American male, mainly Protestant, has, in fact, produced quite a different kind of fiction: what I have elsewhere called the 'Mega-Novel'; that novel like *Gravity's Rainbow* (1973), *The Recognitions* (1955), *JR* (1975), *The Sot-Weed Factor* (1960), *Letters* (1979), and *Lookout Cartridge* (1974) which takes on not a segment of America but America itself. In their hands, the Mega-Novel –

which has length as well as seeming infinitude – attempts to capture the whole; it is the closest we have to a holistic product, the *War and Peace*, *Bleak House*, and *Ulysses* of our generation. Blacks, Jews, and women writers tend to be more compartmentalized, going not after the whole thing but segments. Some of the novelists like Bellow and Oates may seem voracious for experience, but ultimately they do narrow down. What is their development, and what are they after?

For black and Jewish writers, the Second World War was a liberating period, and the post-war era, for several reasons, saw an outpouring of such voices. Women writers in large numbers and pursuing a focused experience came later, when Simone de Beauvoir's *The Second Sex* and then its American epigone, *The Feminine Mystique*, began to take hold in the sixties. For many male writers who had served in the armed forces, the experience with foreign cultures, the subsequent attendance at universities on the G. I. Bill, the growing acquaintanceship with French and German writers, the growth of interest in modernism in literature, music, and art all helped fuel a fiction which broke with the less sophisticated, more issue-oriented novel of the thirties. Another factor is that the 'classic' writers were getting old, or had died, or were losing their power: Wolfe, Fitzgerald, Steinbeck, Hemingway, Faulkner. The latter three were very much alive, and their influence great; but the perception was that their best work was behind them, and this perception proved liberating.

If we have a several-fold development taking place right after the Second World War, we still have to place the increase in black, Jewish, and female writing in perspective. The end of the war opened up writing and the arts as a whole, especially in painting, with the great burst which came to be known as Abstract Expressionism. In poetry, also, there was a virtual renaissance as a consequence of the influence of Whitman, William Carlos Williams, and their distinct American voices. This surge carried into Jewish, black, and female novelists. We must be careful not to extrapolate them from the more general energies nourishing the arts.

The first novels that can be called 'Jewish' in the broadest possible sense are Bellow's first two, *Dangling Man* (1944) and *The Victim* (1947), especially the latter. What creates the Jewish connection in the early novel is the Biblical name of the protagonist, Joseph, which also links him to Kafka's Joseph; above all, his relationship to a whole group of schlemiels, fools, or passive individuals whose sole strength lies in their marginality; the use of a symbolic title which seems to suggest the Jewish condition as marginal, purgatorial, 'dangling' between cultures and countries; and, most importantly, the internalization of all material into an undefined self-consciousness. That latter, often bordering on narcissism – not action or externalized energy – will more than anything else help define the territory which some Jewish writers have carved out.

The enormous success of J. D. Salinger's *The Catcher in the Rye* (1951) and then his saga of the Glass family (*Franny and Zooey*, 1961, along with the stories 'A Perfect Day for Bananafish', 'Raise High the Roof Beam, Carpenter', 'Seymour, An Introduction') suggests that a Jewish sensibility had arrived. But Salinger was far more concerned with mainstream America: Holden Caulfield in the novel is a Huck Finn of sorts, and the Irish–Jewish Glass children partake of American counterfeit, some successful, some doomed, all haunted. Jews and Jewishness are left far behind.

For such writers, the plumbing of the inner life becomes as dramatic as the exploration of externals had been for Hemingway. In *Dangling Man*, Joseph eschews the external world, and instead of energy, there will be 'dangling': a territory between the vigorous and the dead. This will be Bellow's landscape except for *Henderson the Rain King* (1959), whose ebullience and buoyancy suggest how invidious categories can be; for nothing is less a 'Jewish novel' for the Jewish Bellow than *Henderson*.

Implicit in the novel leaning toward a Jewish sensibility is the uneasiness men feel toward women, and the fact that nearly all relationships come to us from the male viewpoint. But we must immediately note that this is also a more general American problem. That uneasiness of men toward women can be found in writers as far from a 'Jewish sensibility' as Styron, Gaddis, Barth, McElroy, Baldwin, and John Williams, whatever the differences among them. Bellow surrounds his passive, dangling, self-serving men by harem-like women; and by women who, incidentally, when they refuse that role become vicious witches. There is little in between.

In still another respect, Bellow helped establish the direction for what would be an outpouring by Jewish novelists: that struggle within the individual as he attempts to save himself from over-indulgence in self and over-regimentation within the society. In the second of two dialogues within *Dangling Man*, Joseph insists on life, not antilife, on humanity, not antihumanity; in the struggle, one finds definition, and perhaps even ceases to dangle. In *The Victim*, three years later, Bellow wrote what appeared to be an intensely Jewish novel, but we find it typical of the 1940s and running parallel to the war and combat novels of the period. The key polemical ideas are suffering, at one end, and one's belief in a transcendent power (by no means God, more often Emerson's transcendental self) at the other. Man lies stretched on a rack in between, and he may gravitate in either direction, toward suffering or toward escape. But despite the Jewish intonation of the novel and the heavy reliance on the Book of Job, Bellow has assayed a form of American existentialism, at the very time it was spreading over the French literary scene. This same influence would find its way into several black writers of the fifties and sixties (Ellison, Baldwin, and Williams, for example).

The Adventures of Augie March (1953) established Bellow as a major novelist at the beginning of the fifties, a position he con-solidated with *Henderson the Rain King* at the end. Two novels could not be more different. In *The Adventures*, Bellow transcends the Jewishness of Augie and the Einhorn family by suggesting a broadly American theme: which is that the individual will can become hostage to the very energies nourishing it. 'I am an American, Chicago-born,' the novel begins, recalling Melville's 'Call Me Ishmael'. But Chicago cannot sustain Augie's energies, and he heads for Mexico to train the American bald eagle. In this, we have an allegory of the decade, for in that eagle Bellow sees all the ambi-guities and ambivalences in Augie himself, in America. The eagle proves cowardly when confronted by an iguana, but Bellow sides with what seems negative capability, letting openness and drift supersede certainties.

The 'black experience' of the fifties was curiously similar, in Ellison's and Baldwin's response to counterfeiting. Ralph Ellison's *Invisible Man* (no 'The') in 1952 (although begun seven years earlier) by its concentration on counterfeiting and forgery of feeling relates to America as much as it does to a specific black experience. Ellison connects the paralysis and enervation of the 1950s with typical American themes, playing off stasis against spatiality and energy. His line of development is a 1950s reflection of the *Bildungsroman* tradition, in this instance of a simpleton who grows up into a realization of how the world really functions, and then, as a result of setbacks, becomes capable of acting on his own condition. Since the narrator is black, his journey has distinctive features of the black experience of rejection and frustration; but his journey is not only a black one. Salinger's Holden Caulfield in a miniature way parallels Ellison's narrator.

In another respect, *Invisible Man* while reflecting America in the 1950s yet distinguishes this experience for the black man. Harlem becomes, for Ellison, a metaphor for instability, disharmony, discontinuity. The sense of disarray here is synesthesiac, the intermixing and muddling of the senses, in which a seemingly stable, orderly society is riven by dissent, deception, invisible forces of subversion and adversariness. To jump to another world, Flannery O'Connor in her major stories and in her novels was also attempting to capture a society and its subcultures as they moved on the edge of the new. Here discontinuity awaited her protagonists; that acute break with tradition and history which threw them into purgatory. For her, the self no longer had a mission when the new invaded. Only indulgence prevailed, and in indulgence she perceived the betrayal of the real self. Yet her vision of self and mission is ironic, and so heavy is the deceit and counterfeit that little is what it seems. Her peacocks are symbols of perfection which have been displaced from the natural world. But she perceives they cannot last, the lovely birds live in a dispossessed, imperfect garden, and no perfect emblem of God can survive such deception of ourselves. The matter of her fiction seems light years away from New York or Chicago Jews and from transplanted black writers; but she is, like them, commenting on the fifties, working through fifties themes.

Malamud's *The Assistant* (1957), his stories in *The Magic Barrel* (1958), and James Baldwin's *Go Tell It on the Mountain* (1953) well accommodate fifties themes while displaying, respectively, Jewish and black experiences. *The Assistant* cuts through layers of artificial responses in order to discover what men live by. It is this exploration of how men live which energizes Malamud's work, not any formal sense of Jewish life. His historical Jewishness is connected to its ethical sense, and how that dimension of behavior can be achieved in lives that must acknowledge other impulses, whether sexual, familial, artistic, or emotional. *The Assistant*, far more than his first novel, *The Natural*, becomes Malamud's quintessential world: a grocery store, a beaten-down owner, his assimilated daughter, the Gentile stranger, the man who first seduces the daughter and then is himself seduced by Judaism. What is unique is that swirling world of post-Holocaust ethics: Jews and Gentiles intermingling in universal suffering, guilt, and penance; that despair which precedes a deepening of ethical belief; the consciousness of miracle which derives from faith in something beyond the self. With this, Malamud is responding to 1950s passivity, moral and ethical ambiguity, counterfeit activities and feelings.

For all its differences of experience, Baldwin's first novel, *Go Tell It on the Mountain* fits into this general mold. Baldwin started out with the need to 'kill' the father, figuratively, literarily, almost physically. His work set off an entire series of challenges and responses which filtered through the fifties and sixties and, as the decades picked up momentum, drew in both black and Jewish writers. Female writers preferred to kill the mother. *Go Tell It*, to begin there, has affinities to both black and white works: Henry Roth's *Call It Sleep* (1934), Farrell's *Studs Lonigan* (1930s on), Wright's *Black Boy* (1945), Delmore Schwartz's *In Dreams Begin Responsibilities* (1938), even Salinger's *The Catcher in the Rye*; later, we find Mario Puzo's *The Fortunate Pilgrim* (1964), then Philip Roth's *Goodbye, Columbus* and *Portnoy's Complaint*. An unlikely brew of novels is held together by a common bind, the American version of the *Bildungsroman*. The basic frame is of a young man (occasionally, a young woman) thrust into an atmosphere in which ethnicity or raciality creates a conflict to be worked out in addition to the usual ones of boyhood and adolescence.

In the American version, the youth may not come through, for race, religion, ethnicity, paternal authority are forms of doom – as they almost are for Baldwin's John Grimes. He struggles through father, race, religious experiences, and his own ambiguous feelings into a kind of process, after hovering near destruction or abulia. But what works, at least temporarily, for John Grimes as he thrashes around in the passionate embrace of the Lord did not work for Baldwin, except in his essays. His later fiction, beginning with *Giovanni's Room* (1956) and continuing through *Another Country* (1962), *Tell Me How Long the Train's Been Gone* (1968) and *Just Above My Head* (1979), lacks the feel for language and the centeredness of *Go Tell It*. He began to explore themes of homosexuality which were meaningful to him, but which he could not literarily communicate, and then in his later novels became strident and didactic about legitimate black frustrations.

Baldwin's essays, however, provide a pivot for the development of black consciousness in the decades after the war. It all started with Baldwin's literary need to throw off the influence of Richard Wright, especially *Native Son*, which Baldwin repudiated in 'Many Thousands Gone', in 1951. Wright, meanwhile, was becoming an icon of black consciousness, and Baldwin was reviled by the black radical left. So, too, was Ellison, who was considered insufficiently black, although *Invisible Man* would prove to be the most enduring work of the post-war black renaissance and possibly of the entire period. Eldridge Cleaver, who had emerged as an essayist of great power in *Soul on Ice*, attacked Baldwin for his alleged hatred of blackness and accused the latter of fearing Wright's masculinity. Cleaver cited Norman Mailer's long essay 'The White Negro', in which the latter had argued for the black stud, among other things. Wright, who had died in 1960, re-entered the late fifties and the sixties as a powerful leader; Baldwin is put down for his homosexuality; Ellison is denigrated as whitey's man. John Williams, in his trenchant *The Man Who Cried I Am* (1967), caught all this, mixing Wright, Baldwin, Malcolm X, King, and others, fathers and sons interwoven.

We find strange alignments, the Jewish Mailer on the side of the more rebellious black critics: Cleaver, Gayle, Killens, Hoyt, all eager to resurrect Wright and dump Baldwin and Ellison. Ellison now entered the fray with a defense called 'The World and the Jug', in which he responded to an article by Irving Howe, called 'Black Boys and Native Sons'. Howe, the outsider to black life, sympathetically describes the black experience as containing unmitigated violence which makes the individual a social victim. Ellison argued that violence is not endemic, that a coherent black culture exists, that one can seek freedom within it, and, finally, that the individual can make choices – black life, accordingly, is neither a trap nor a prison. This was, in fact, almost the last time blacks heated up critically, and what occurred afterward was both unpleasant and unfortunate. Dialogue ended, with blacks and Jews accusing each other of racial and ethnic slurs, and black male writers, except for John Williams, lost much of their direction.

Most Jewish novelists and all female writers kept out of the conflict. William Styron's *The Confessions of Nat Turner* in 1967, although by a non-Jew, opened up all the old wounds and some new ones; but here the conflict is white versus black and it takes on racial overtones outside our purview. John Williams's *The Man Who Cried I Am* in the same year, nicely complementing Harold Cruse's important study *The Crisis of the Negro Intellectual*, was the last large fiction by a black male writer; after that, for a variety of cultural reasons, the mantle was passed to black women: Toni Morrison, Alice Walker, Toni Cade Bambara, as well as the entire decade of white women writers who became prominent in the next decade. Williams's novel attempted to sum it all up, as a roman à clef of the main characters in the racial arena; but more so as a kind of compendium of black fears and frustrations. Williams presents the ultimate in white racism and its effects on blacks, in a way that contrasts with Jewish novelists and their marked avoidance of the Holocaust, Israel, even the larger role of the Jew in America.

No female novelist, black or white, has picked up the passion and urgency of Williams's novel. Jewish novels of the sixties, on the other hand, are inward-turning; moving not onto a world stage, but a personal, sexual one: Roth's *Portnoy* and Bellow's *Herzog*. Yet another novel moved into prominence in the decade, first as a cult novel and then as a vastly popular work, Joseph Heller's *Catch-22* (1961). Heller is Jewish, comes from the Coney Island section of Brooklyn (heavily Jewish), and clearly has something of the wit we associate with Yiddish-speaking standup comedians. His first novel has the caustic, ironic, burlesque quality of Lennie Bruce, the definitive comic of the decade. Is *Catch-22*, then, a Jewish novel? Does it belong with Bellow and Roth, who are more concerned with a Jewish self-consciousness?

Linguistically, it is possible to see Heller's novel as having a 'Jewish' dimension, and that is in his use of litotes for comic purposes. His entire novel is an extended litotes, that form of understatement and irony in which something is expressed by way of the negative of its opposite. One never says 'not many' but 'not a few', creating a dialectical confusion as to how many or how few. 'Catch-22' as a phrase which has entered the language expresses an underlying negative aspect: if you are crazy, you need not fly, but if you do not want to fly, that proves you're not crazy. Since what is stated contrasts with what is suggested, Heller has a linguistic context for the military of the 1940s, the counterfeit of the 1950s, and the defiance of authority which would characterize America of the 1960s.

Bellow's *Herzog* is the other side of the Jewish coin. Bellow turned to the internalized Jew, whose activity consists of researching and writing books, penning letters to world figures, and lying on his back, Oblomov-like in his refusal to do the world's work. Although Herzog is a Jew, and suffers from Jewish guilt, he is located on ground shared by the universal underground man, Oblomov, Camus' Meursault, Ellison's invisible man, Kafka's K. or Joseph K., and Beckett's enervated warriors. While rejecting most technical aspects of modernism, Bellow has turned his protagonist into a modernist amalgam.

Portnoy's Complaint (1969) is also a response to sixties turbulence, an attempt to grapple with a Jewish version of that disorder. But once again we must stress that the Jewish component in Roth has no relationship to religion, race, ethnicity. It is a sense that one is marked, like Cain, as a Jew from birth to death; that one cannot escape a 'Jewish mother'; and that the Jew is always the outsider, most of all when he thinks he is gaining ground in the Gentile world. Once we get past the more sensational aspects, the Roth novel is an updated *Bildungsroman*. Alexander Portnoy must somehow escape his house beautiful to become his own person: the primal theme of growing up fiction. In his document, which is narrated to his analyst, Dr Spielvogel, Portnoy stresses his sexual disturbances, especially his fear of castration, which accompany shame and dread of retribution. He locates himself near Kierkegaard's Abraham and Isaac. He must, in order to discover himself, destroy the father (and mother) in himself; which is to say he must erase his Jewishness and become an American writer. This obsessive need will play a large part in his Zuckerman trilogy (and epilogue): *The Ghost Writer* (1979), *Zuckerman Unbound* (1981), *The Anatomy Lesson* (1983), and *The Prague Orgy* (1985), which constitute the major work of his maturity. The constant in Roth's fiction is the generational conflict which derives from young people's desire to become American, American as exemplified by WASPS.

Portnoy's Complaint proved a cultural turning point for the Jewish writer, writing as a Jew or not. When Portnoy makes his now famous comment about putting the 'Id' back in 'Yid' (and later the 'oi' back in 'Goy'), he is speaking metaphorically about life in America. Sharp dichotomies remain. In a curious way, a good deal of what Roth is getting at has significance for female novelists as well, given the difference in direction of their own interests. But before moving to that decade of writers who limned the female experience, we should note the tremendous contribution of Flannery O'Connor and, to a lesser extent, Carson McCullers. On one hand, O'Connor kept the voice of Faulkner going in American fiction, and, on the other, she carved out her own territory, which differs from Faulkner's. The cornerstone of her fiction rests on her Catholicism in a Protestant South; on her ability to maintain her differences and uniqueness. An early and abiding influence was that of Teilhard de Chardin, whose idea of 'passive diminishment' she identified with. She came to accept an affliction (lupus) which, while determined and unavoidable, was accompanied by a strengthening of will. Thus, she was a battleground of diminishment and response, the affliction leading to a countering achievement not otherwise experienced. This sense of suffering and increase or compensation makes her work far more than Southern or regional, or even uniquely female, as she suggests in her essay 'The Grotesque in Southern Fiction'.

O'Connor established her reputation with her short stories, although her two novels (*Wise Blood*, 1952, *The Violent Bear It Away*, 1960) display her unmistakable themes: the implicit and explicit violence of those who live intensely; lines of hatred and lines of love which are almost indistinguishable; a preoccupation with baptism, damnation, redemption which comes to describe an entire society, not only believers; bizarre, possessed people whom she makes familiar and apparently ordinary. In her two volumes of stories, *A Good Man Is Hard to Find* (1954) and *Everything That Rises Must*

Converge (1965), O'Connor combined a concentration of theme with gem-like prose. In the latter volume, published a year after she died of lupus at thirty-nine, she concentrated on a number of images or symbols which lament the passage of time: the crazy hat of Young Julian's mother in 'Everything That Rises'; the 'artificial nigger', an image of immense desolation emblematic of a waste land; the coffin in 'Judgment Day'; the artificial leg in 'Good Country People'.

In a generation before O'Connor, at the turn of the 1940s, Carson McCullers in *The Heart Is a Lonely Hunter* (1940) and *Reflections in a Golden Eye* (1941) seemed to be mining Faulkner material, but came to define her own ground. Her point of view in her first novel, written at twenty-two, embraces the obsessive need for man to revolt against his own inner isolation, to express himself as fully as possible in a 'wasteful, short-sighted society'. There are stirrings here, a good twenty-five years ahead of its time, of a distinct sensibility – adumbrating those themes of liberation and independence which will limn the 'female experience' of the late 1960s and for the following decade.

We must, before proceeding, distinguish between 'female fiction', an artificial designation, and fiction based on the 'female experience', which does differentiate it from fiction with male protagonists and male sensibilities. To assert that 'female fiction' exists is to suggest that the human experience bifurcates into two distinct streams; so that fear, pity, terror, sympathy, love, not to speak of language itself, are not shared commodities. Since they are, common ground pre-empts differences in the quality and quantity of the given experience. What did appear in the latter part of the 1960s and well into the 1970s was an avalanche of fiction by female writers, some of them black, some Jewish. Thus in creating groups of any kind, we must account for several black and Jewish writers in two areas, and this makes something of a muddle of categories themselves. Further, while black female novelists such as Toni Morrison and Alice Walker are concerned with black life and experiences, few Jewish female novelists – except Cynthia Ozick – write about the 'Jewish experience', or about being Jewish at all. Many of them are indistinguishable from non-Jews in their concern with the felt experience of bondage to male values, and what independence means for women who find themselves approaching Kierkegaard's sense of dread.

If fear and trembling lie in choice, one of the considerable novels of choice is by neither a black nor a Jew, but by Joyce Carol Oates, in *them* (1969, later as *Them*). Yet although it is intensely about a female experience, it is also linked profoundly to American themes of breaking out and reshaping, what goes on in the *Bildungsroman*, male or female. The novel tells of how a young woman, Maureen Wendall, attempts through tremendous odds of both nature and nurture to break a destructive and self-destructive family pattern. Maureen has to learn how to deal with emptiness, and her success or failure is, for Oates, a paradigm of what women must do — that emptiness, for her, defines where women are. Oates demonstrates Maureen's intense hatred of the author's comfortable and secure world, and yet survival depends on her devising strategies to acquire a piece of that world: a husband (any decent man!), her own home and child, a settled and stable existence outside her murderous Wendall background. Almost alone among white female novelists, Oates observes how different 'liberation' is for the lower or working class woman from what it is for those more fortunate.

Toni Morrison, in *Sula* (1973), as well as in *The Bluest Eye* (1970), *Song of Solomon* (1977), and *Tar Baby* (1981), works through many of these lower-class concerns, but with the added dimension of the black woman struggling to assert herself. Unlike Alice Walker's *Meridian* (in *Meridian*, 1976) or her Celie in *The Color Purple* (1982), who function within recognized systems, Sula breaks through all categories and insists on the same prerogatives men obtain: sexual liberation, freedom of movement, indifference to social or familial commitments. Sula disrupts every expectation the black community has for a woman, consciously damning herself in the eyes of others so as to prove to herself what a black woman can do. Morrison's point, by 1973, was not particularly new, although it was something of a radical statement for a black woman, and it foreruns the argument Michele Wallace put together in *Black Macho and the Myth of the Superwoman* (1979); an attempt to do for the black woman what Betty Friedan in *The Feminine Mystique* had done, mainly, for white middle-class women.

This quality also characterizes Joan Didion's fiction (*Run River*,

1963; *Play It As It Lays*, 1970; *A Book of Common Prayer*, 1977) and essays (*Slouching Toward Bethlehem*, 1968; *The White Album*, 1979), which demonstrates many negative aspects of female liberation. Didion focuses on women for whom the idea of liberation and the movement itself have little significance; women who lie outside all activity and are self-serving, narcissistic, anomic. They have already gone over. Such women move in and out of senseless marriages, become involved with men they dislike, and display neuroses like badges. In her minimalist strategies, Didion picks up the anomie of an entire community and society; and her descriptions of wasted women are depictions of a wasted society, one in which all value systems have run down.

Most of the other female novelists listed above are less society-oriented and more attuned to personal needs. The so-called 'me-tooism' or narcissism of the sixties and seventies is revealed in a spate of novels which appeared in the decade from the late sixties. Among them: Judith Rossner's *Looking for Mr Goodbar* (1975) and *Attachments* (1977), Erica Jong's *Fear of Flying* (1973), Marge Piercy's *Small Changes* (1973), Lois Gould's *Such Good Friends* (1970), Marilyn French's *The Women's Room* (1977), Lisa Alther's *Kinflicks* (1976), Alix Kates Shulman's *Memoirs of an ex-Prom Queen* (1972), Maureen Howard's *Before My Time* (1974), Cynthia Buchanan's *Maiden* (1972), and Diane Johnson's *The Shadow Knows* (1974). Added to these should be Alice Walker's *The Color Purple* (1982). Although they differ in narrative strategies, prose styles, qualities of wit and irony, all are linked by common themes of female victimization, the need for women to break through stereotypes held by both men and by themselves, and the difficulty women have in functioning within an essentially patriarchal world. Several of the novels suggest resolutions based on separatism (Lesbian love, female communal life, distinct communities of 'safe houses'), and several chart the disasters which result from what seems an obvious good, liberation.

As we survey blacks, Jews, and women from the heights of the mid-1980s, we discover a growing loss of literary distinction. Blacks have failed to produce any writer of the stature and force of Wright, Ellison, the Baldwin of the fifties and sixties, and Williams in his single sixties novel. The failure of the essay in black hands is perhaps connected to this; for when the novel flourished it was abetted by fine non-fiction from Baldwin, Cleaver, Cruse, and others. There is little sense at this time of a distinct black fictional voice; and while this does not mean assimilation — quite the contrary — it suggests a crisis in black intellectual and creative force as far as the novel is concerned.

Jewish novelists have, also, more or less run their course. Bellow, Malamud, Roth, Heller, Mailer, Doctorow, and others continue to publish, and a few like Heller have moved increasingly into more explicitly Jewish material (*Good as Gold*, 1979; *God Knows*, 1984); but the novelty has worn off. The larger sense of American fiction is now attuned to several difficult and less popular novelists, those I have called Mega-Novelists: Gaddis, Pynchon, McElroy, Barth, among others. The labeling of the 'Jewish novel' was faulty anyway, since the novels always had more of America than of Jews in them, and this as we have noted, was also true of black fiction, despite its intensity and concentration on black life.

As for women novelists, the surge of distinctive voices about the female experience has not abated; but the voices have taken on other sounds and tones in writers like Ann Beattie, Mary Ann Settle, Anne Tyler, Alice Walker, and Bobbie Ann Mason. Furthermore, a good deal of energy — for blacks, Jews, women, and others — has been going into shorter fiction; with a consequent loss of force for the novel, except for those working in the long, Mega-Novel area. Joyce Carol Oates has herself experimented with several forms, writing a series of novels in different genres, with *Bellefleur* (1980) the most wrought. With its emphasis on large emotional patterns, huge passions, life and death elements, it is the kind of fiction which contemporary American women have backed away from.

The black, Jewish, female response to America has been to reflect the country in what is still a common language and a common idiom. With few exceptions, all of these writers overlap in their use of the word, however much they differ from each other in stress and quality. Although we can note many different kinds of fiction in post-war America, they coalesce in their adherence to the pastoral, Jeffersonian tradition, to matters of space and spatiality, to the incoherence and discontinuity of American life, to Americans' reliance on escape and liberation as resolutions of personal dilemmas, to their suspicion of history and frequent rejection of historical precedent, to their deference to determinism and yet Emersonian insistence that the individual must create his own destiny. These are common grounds. Renewal, and all that suggests, creates a bond among American writers; so that inevitably any categorization as blacks, Jews, women is artificial and nonbinding.

AMERICAN INDIAN POETRY
AND THE 'OTHER' TRADITIONS

JEROME ROTHENBERG

> I don't have to go nowhere to see.
> Visions are everywhere.

There is a hidden poetry in America – a range of hidden poetries – as there is elsewhere in the world. It is a poetry outside of literature or rarely represented in those books whose authors claim them as the maps or charters of our literature and hence our culture. For the poetry of which I'm thinking (and poetry is a more apt word for it than literature) is largely, though not wholly, a poetry without books. It is 'oral', carried across generations by the voice, the many, often highly individuated voices of its makers and transmitters. And behind its voices lie different languages and cultures – not only that which is stamped officially *American*. Praised by outsiders for its presumed simplicity, such poetry is often complex, its roots and branches ancient, entangled with the lives of whole peoples and with their perceptions of the world.

I know of no single erm to cover all these poetries. 'Other' is as close as I would come, but that presents as many problems as folk, oral, non-literate, primitive, tribal, and the rest. Such terms, of course, are hardly interchangeable, and the field that they collectively stake out is well beyond the limits of this essay. Ethnic poetry is still another possibility, as are regional and local; and seen from that perspective, the range of the 'other' poetries goes from the hundreds of surviving Native American cultures to those with roots in English-speaking Britain; from immigrant communities with diverse traditions of language and poetry to an Afro-American culture that has profoundly influenced both oral and literate poetry in the United States and elsewhere. As these are a part of the much touted American pluralism, so too are those deliberately alternative traditions and movements – religious, mystical, political, and social – that have come and gone or persisted in America from its beginnings until now. From all these 'other' traditions – including, finally, what we would stake out as our own – there emerges a picture, a map, of a prophetic/visionary poetry that includes, chronologically, the pre-Columbian prophet Chilam Balam and the aboriginal American Indian religions on its far end; New England mystics and utopians, transplanted Shakers, and Black Hoodoo *doctors* towards its center; and the conscious experiments with poetic vision and language from Whitman's time to the present.

The possibilities – here barely stated – are overwhelming: a range and sweep, once we're into it, that presents a world in many ways the match of that presented by our literature as such. That vision as we shape it ties in to changes in our own time such that each new innovation, each dislocation of an old convention, opens the way for new work in the future and for a redefinition of the past. The 1855 *Leaves of Grass*, for example, is a Declaration of Independence from the 'bondage' of British and European conventions that both heralds the 1950s – Charles Olson's 'projective verse' or Allen Ginsberg's *Howl* – and frees us to see and express the structural particularities of archaic and tribal poetries at a similar remove from these conventions. After the Surrealist experiments with 'dream' states and 'automatic' language, we are more attentive to the dreamer traditions – in word and ritual – of aboriginal Australia or native North America. Similarly, the efforts of Dada poets of the 1920s to make use of 'pure sound' link up in our minds with the wordless poetries of pre-literate societies (once thought 'meaningless'), the meditative chants of the East, and certain ritual, magical, and mystical texts of the West. All these probings share the sense of poetry as an act of vision, and as we come to them, we see our works and lives in new relation to those 'others' – often as a part of them ourselves.

Approaching the traditions and poetries of the American Indians in this spirit, it has become clear that the Indians stand apart – in many ways – from the otner hidden traditions in America. Aboriginal or indigenous, essentially autochthonous, they are the keepers of a form of life and thought on this continent that predates by centuries, even millennia, the conquest and naming of America by its European invaders. If it was to the colonizers' advantage to think of the native Americans as small and scattered bands, the facts now at hand paint a very different picture. The Indian cultures not only weren't limited to small bands of hunters and gatherers but ranged from more settled agriculturists to the densely populated city-states of Mexico and South America. (Tenochtitlán (Mexico City) in 1500 was perhaps the largest city in the world.) Like the populations, the number of American cultures and languages was enormous (as many as ten million inhabitants in North America alone, 500 separate languages by the usual counts). Each culture had its own mythology and image-of-the-world, its own ceremonies and gods, its own history, calendars and seasons, ecological niche, sacred mountains and rivers. Even today most of the languages persist as the vehicles for whatever poetry survives, so that those who approach that poetry from the outside can only glimpse the elements in it that can be carried by translation or description. It is different from how one reads – or hears – a 'folk' poetry in English (however particularized the form of English is).

We are in fact not dealing with a folk poetry at all – not as that term is used to designate a 'little' (read: inferior) tradition within a 'great' one. Or if we still want to call it that, then it is *totally* a folk poetry: a people's way of enacting and transmitting its knowledge of the world (human and other-than-human) in which it lives. A tribal poetry as such is often esoteric – within its own culture and in relation to the outside world: 'the province of . . . educated, specialized persons who are privy to the philosophical, mystical, and literary wealth of their own tribe'. (Thus, Paula Gunn Allen, a Native American poet with ties to Laguna and Acoma Pueblos in New Mexico.) Largely but not entirely oral, it retains a solid base in ritual, so that what we would isolate as song or story or dance or music is an inseparable part of a single performative occasion: like Wagner's projection of a primitive *Gesamtkunstwerk* or our own ideas of intermedia, etc. Nor is it fixed in an authoritative single version, but is dynamic, changing, as Victor Turner and others have shown us, in its (oral) transmission within the group and (lest we forget) in response to changes brought or imposed from outside.

All of this it has in common with the great autochthonous poetries everywhere – the flowering on this continent of a vastly old and deeply human resource. Right where we reside – or close to it – is the still living survival of a shamanistic poetry, whose attraction for poets after Whitman and Rimbaud now seems inevitable. If the function of both the poet and the shaman is to fulfill 'the desire to see' (thus, the words of the Iglulik Eskimo initiate, approaching his shaman teacher) or to create 'that emotion which causes to see' (thus: the 'Objectivist' poet, George Oppen), what are we to make of the existence around us of a poetry of vision, not as the work of this or that experimental poet (we who are so often gropers in the dark) but of shaman-poets whose lineage extends into the distant native past?

The work of those seers and singers is so present, so often reported, that we cannot well turn from it as incidental to the world we share. Until recently Iroquois ceremonies enacted dreams or turned them into verbal riddles, word plays to be explicated by whole societies of shamans. Generations of Plains Indian adolescents went to a mountaintop 'to cry for a vision', walking in a state of 'attention' (Black Elk's word) to the minute particulars that Blake saw as the basis of all poetry and all *true* religion. If this is a restricted poet's way for us (though not the way of every poet), it is a more expansive way for them – a hint of that too in the words that Carlos Castaneda gives to the fictive Yaqui shaman, Don Juan Matus: 'Learn to *see*, and then you will know that there is no end to the new worlds for our vision.' Or the very real Pomo shaman, Essie Parrish: 'I don't have to go nowhere to see. Visions are everywhere.'

There is a poetics here and something more – what Paul Radin had in mind when he said that the Pima Indians (and not only the shamans among them) frequently lived in 'a heightened atmosphere' in which they experienced 'reality at white heat'. In such a state, which Blake knew also, the familiar world opens, and the shaman moves through it on all levels, human and other-than-human, in that ecstatic journey which is the mark of his profession. Here enters the idea of a living universe (a 'human universe' in Charles Olson's phrase), with the possibility of transformation/metamorphosis, of living beings who change in reality as they do in language – or, one is tempted to say, *because* they change in language. In the 'Wishing Bone Cycle' of the Swampy Cree oral poet, Jacob Nibènegenesábe, for example, the central figure gains the power of metamorphosis (his own and others') through the wishbone of a snow goose, concerning which the narrator, speaking in the first person, says:

I try to make wishes right
but sometimes it doesn't work.
Once I wished a tree upside down
and its branches
were where the roots should have been!
The squirrels had to ask the moles
'How do we get down there
to get home?'
Then there was the time, I remember now,
I wished a man upside down
and his feet were where his hands
should have been!
In the morning his shoes
had to ask the birds
'How do we fly up there
to get home?'
One time it happened that way.
(English version by Howard A. Norman)

This is an instance – however playful – of what Ezra Pound called
'the undeniable tradition of metamorphosis', and Ernst Cassirer,
speaking of a once universal belief in 'the consanguinity of all forms
of life': 'By a sudden metamorphosis, everything may be turned
into everything. If there is any characteristic and outstanding feature
of the mythical world, any law by which it is governed – it is this
law of metamorphosis.'

Yet the clearest statement I know – and one closer to a native
poetics at its source – comes in the poet Edward Field's recasting of
the words of Nalugiaq, 'an ordinary (Eskimo) woman' (she says),
who learned it from her uncle, Unaraluk the shaman:

In the very earliest time,
when both people and animals lived on earth,
a person could become an animal if he wanted to
and an animal could become a human being . . .
All spoke the same language.
That was the time when words were like magic.
The human mind had mysterious powers.
A word spoken by chance
might have strange consequences,
It would suddenly come alive

and what people wanted to happen could happen –
all you had to do was say it.

The phrase 'come alive' is no fluke here but integral to the tribal/
oral traditions of North America and elsewhere. Poetry or song for
the Indians is, as Kenneth Rexroth pointed out, 'itself a numinous
thing' – a view first articulated to me by Arthur Johnny John at the
Allegany Seneca Reservation (New York), who inquired concerning
the songs I was intending to translate, where they would go and
what their feelings would be 'away from home'. The words of
certain Seneca chants speak of the song as travelling ('it's off in the
distance / it came into the room / it's here in the circle'), and a
chanted Modoc poem puts it in the song's voice: 'I / the song / I
walk there.' It is a familiar enough thing, however far we sometimes
feel from it, as in the well-known Blues verse: 'Woke up this morning, blues all 'round my bed, / Woke up this morning, blues all
'round my bed, / Picked up my pillow, blues all under my head.'
But in the Indian case at least, it is not a trope – not a mere figure of
speech.

What these traditions show us, then, is a genuinely metamorphic
poetry, the work of mythmakers who do not simply transmit a
fixed literature but, like their counterparts elsewhere (poets-of-the-
myth, as Aristotle *literally* called them), change it, orally, in the
telling and performing. For the larger works, the spoken ones in
general, the categories of the folklorists are accurate enough – origin
myths, hero tales, and trickster narratives, presenting, often by de-
formation, the human/animal image on a monumental scale. When
written down – like the Mayan *Popol Vuh* (one of the great surviving
pre-Columbian poems) or Paul Radin's rendering of the Winnebago
trickster cycle – these take on epic or Biblical proportions, even
Rabelaisian ones. If these are images of nature (or of human nature),
they are not only the harmonious and benevolent ones of traditional
song and prayer, but daemonic and dangerous as well. Their visual
projections include the colossal Aztec statue of the fanged goddess
Coatlicue, the Pueblos' variformed Kachina rain gods, the twisted
features of the Iroquois False Faces; and verbally they turn up in
images like those of the Nez Percé, depicting the creator and destroyer god, Coyote: 'Ravening Coyote comes, / red hands, red

mouth, / necklace of eye-balls.' Or again: 'With bloodstained mouth/ comes mad Coyote!'

These are among countless Native American examples of metamorphic/mythic thought and not, let me be quick to add, a home-grown theology of good and evil (God and Devil). As such they take us beyond the popular idea of an Indian religion limited to the celebration of a single, imageless Great Spirit. Great Spirit itself (Lakota: *wakan tanka*) is translated alternatively by terms like Great Mystery or, even, Great Incomprehensibility – a not insignificant resemblance here to André Breton's assertion that the contemporary Surrealist experiment (read: quest) was moving toward a point at which 'the mysteries which are not will give way to the *great Mystery*'. What we have, then, is a problematic metaphysics, an ongoing vision quest that enters language at the level of song ('can this be real / can this be real / this life I am living?'), and, as myth or tale, reveals an extraordinary narrative *realism*. This is not the kind of realism that we speak about in regard to the style of this or that 'realistic' novel or 'realistic' play, but an uncompromising tough-mindedness at the center of thought – the recognition of an inherent ambiguity or ambivalence in both the human and other-than-human worlds. In that vein, a warrior poet composes a death song addressed to his spirit animal: 'Large Bear/You deceive me'; and the Eskimo shaman, Aua, pointing out scenes of hunger and injustice in response to Knud Rasmussen's question about 'the meaning of life', says: 'we explain nothing, we believe nothing, but in what I have just shown you lies our answer to all you ask.'

There is nothing simple or naïve about such a world view – not in the older American cultures and not in our own. Among the Native Americans it develops also into a full-blown comic art, exemplified by a widespread tradition of tricksters and transformers ('absolutely undifferentiated human consciousness,' as Jung once wrote of them, 'god, man, and animal at once') and of ritualized clowning as their projection into sacred acts. (A title I once gave to a Nez Percé narrative – summarizing its contents – is a case in point: 'Coon cons Coyote, Coyote eats Coon, Coyote fights Shit-Men, gets immured in a rock-house, eats his eyes, eats his balls, gets out, cons Bird-Boy for eyes, loses them to the birds & gets them back.') Such a comic view of life makes of the trickster or the (sacred) clown a personification of the grotesque and the ambivalent, with the ritual license to engage in acts 'of gluttony; of eating or drinking filth; of drenching or of being drenched with urine or water; simulating lust, fear, or anger; . . . burlesquing ceremonial; . . . acting or speaking by opposites,' and so on. (Thus, Elsie Clews Parsons' classical description.) Where western artists have been struggling to create (or preserve) such an image, the trickster or clown has persisted in the rapidly occulting native cultures as a kind of Rabelaisian shaman.

Such stances-towards-reality determine the language and forms of poetry or are in turn determined by them. Shamanism and prophecy – with whatever other tools the shaman has at his disposal – are inherently matters of language. The verbal (psychoverbal) techniques of the shaman ('I cure with language,' says the Mazatec shamaness, María Sabina) are close to those that any poet might use, with perhaps this difference: that once forgetting the ends to which those techniques were directed, *we* lose the sense of their values and of our own. For the shaman – as for others whose language works derive from shamanism – his is a language that is something more than language, that begins where normal language fails, 'when people are moved by great forces and ordinary language no longer suffices'. (Thus, the Netsilik Eskimo shaman-poet, Orpingalik.)

In tradition after tradition, the language of the poem or song emerges from the shaman's or quester's vision journey – as its central gift. It is not so much that such songs describe the vision (in fact they rarely do), but that their language is a power in itself or is derived from other power-beings in the dream. So, for example, the Gitksan shaman, Isaac Tens, endures a series of extreme, out-of-the-body experiences (like that 'derangement of the senses' that Rimbaud saw as crucial to the making of the 'absolutely modern' poet-seer), at the end of which he is worked over by a group of older shamans, until (he says):

I began to sing. A chant was coming out of me without my being able to do anything to stop it. Many things appeared to me presently: huge birds and other animals . . . Such visions happen when a man is about to become a shaman; they occur of their own accord. The songs force themselves out complete without any attempt to compose them . . .

The autonomy of such songs should be noted here as an instance of the authorial anonymity that is characteristic of so many of the 'other' traditions. Yet there are also times when individuals stand out as authors and poets in something closer to our sense of it (the aforementioned Orpingalik, for example, or others in the Eskimo tradition); to say nothing of those who, under altered circumstances, become, like Black Elk or María Sabina, collaborators on the books of their own lives as written down by others.

Dream songs or power songs account for a substantial body of traditional Native American poetry. Like the shaman's other language acts these are often in a special language – that of animals and other power-beings, as the deliverers and persons of the song. The Indian song-poems – of whatever kind – are often wordless (a resemblance here to that experimental 'sound poetry' of the West, which is itself a kind of searching for a primal language). More commonly, untranslatable vocables surround the words of a song or invade the words themselves to create what Michael McClure, speaking of his own poetry, calls a 'ghost tantra', composed (he tells us further) in 'beast language'. Archaisms and neologisms are also frequent in the Indian works, and the repetition patterns common to oral poetry not only give the songs – and the spoken narratives – a sense of structure, but serve to hammer home the message and its mysteries.[1]

Still other aspects of these shamanistic languages involve premeditated shifts of *meaning* – like the creation by the Huichol *mara-'akáme* (= shaman) of a language of reversals spoken by the pilgrims on the annual peyote hunt:

'Look,' the mara'akáme [who has dreamed it] says to them, 'it is when you say "good morning", you mean "good evening", everything is backwards . . . You do not shake hands, you shake feet. You hold out your right foot to be shaken by the foot of your companion. You say "good afternoon", yet it is only morning.'

A similar strategy is common to the language of the sacred clowns throughout the Americas (thus, the Crow Indian Crazy Dogs (warrior clowns): 'Talk crosswise: say the opposite of what you mean and make others say the opposite of what they mean in return').

This is the prima materia for a poetics of *displacement*: a poetry that transports us from where we are to where we might be. As such the language turns are more often metaphorical than 'mere' reversals; or something more than that: a distance between the realities brought together that sometimes strains the sense of a comparison. Again the Huichol: 'Sandals are cactus. Fingers are sticks ... Everything is changed ... When one speaks of wood, one really means fish ... When speaking of blowing one's nose, one says, "Give me the honey."' It is the arbitrariness of language itself that confronts us here: a first step in the creation of an other-worldly language (that, say, of the Huichol paradise) beyond our own. And metaphor – if that is what we have or think we have – becomes *transformative*, envisioning, invoking, the strange and *marvelous* (that key word of the Surrealist fathers), 'causing to see'.

From this kind of metaphoric language-making, the shamans and other native ritualists and singers go on to more structured and often more extended forms of visualization. These serve both to disclose the precise physical fact – as in the Pawnee bear song: 'his paw up / to the sun' – and to disclose or to *create* the mental/physical one – as in the Teton Sioux bear song: 'my paw is holy / herbs are everywhere // my paw is holy / everything is holy.' Between these two modes – of placement and displacement – there is probably less separation than we might at first assume. Take, for example, the song-poems of the Yaqui Deer Dancer, in which the other-than-human reality of the Yaquis (called *seyawailo*, or flower world) comes into focus through an iterated/reiterated description of an imaginal geography of flower fawns, flower gardens, flower water, flower bushes, flower ground, etc., along with singular observations of the deer himself: 'under a cholla flower [= sharp-spined cactus] // standing there / to rub your antlers / bending // turning where you stand to rub / your antlers.' Again, on the Papagos' four-day desert journey to the Gulf of California ('the direction of suffering'), to bring back salt and to receive visions and rain, the shaman-poet prepares the other pilgrims by 'throwing words' that re-create scenes of the village life from which they've come and the place-of-vision (and its gods) towards which they're heading. The resulting poem, at which Ruth Underhill's translation only hints, appears from her accompanying description to be an extraordinary display of image, metaphor, and sound – 'a language of roundabout phrases,' she writes, and an oral style of 'panting, on one note, where each syllable stands out separated and accented, like the [monotone] chugging of an engine'. It is by such performances that the shaman-poet, here as elsewhere, directs the communicants to the point where a transformation of sight becomes possible.

Indeed *all* oral poetry is performative – including, as Dennis Tedlock and others have shown, the spoken narratives once thought of as a kind of oral 'prose'. If Mallarmé could have it that 'everything in the world exists in order to end up as a book', it should be as possible to say that everything here exists to end up as a performance. (Mallarmé's last large work, *Le Livre*, was in fact the working journal for a great unrealized performance piece of multiple means.) As performances, the Indian works range from the aforementioned songs and narratives to works of oratory (virtual 'talk poems' in David Antin's recent phrase, or 'chronicle plays' in Constance Rourke's older designation), sound poems and wordless songs, poems chanted by simultaneous choruses (twenty differently worded choruses in one Osage ritual transcribed by Francis LaFlesche), masked rituals and sacred clown dramas, court poetry and court theater among the Aztecs and Mayas, and visual works (also with a performative component) ranging from mnemonic pictographs and 'song-pictures' (thus, Frances Densmore) to pictorial 'calendar counts', ritualized sand-paintings, and the gestural near-poetry of the nineteenth-century Plains Indian sign languages. As what Victor Turner, speaking of ritual in general, described as 'an immense orchestration of genres in all available sensory codes', the longer ritual/performance pieces (if not the shorter excerpts that fill our anthologies) reveal – to the minds of the participants – the capacity of all living beings to move and to perform. Thus Black Elk, seeing the Great Vision of his childhood realized in a newly created ritual called the Horse Dance, says:

> It was so beautiful that nothing anywhere could keep from dancing. The virgins danced, and all the circled horses. The leaves on the trees, the grasses on the hills and in the valleys, the waters in the creeks and in the rivers and the lakes, the four-legged and the two-legged and the wings of the air – all danced together to the music of the stallion's song.

From all of this a vast translated literature has already taken shape

– guided into its present English form by several generations of translators and those native ritualists and singers who were their (often unacknowledged) collaborators. If the native 'poetry' and 'prose' is to that degree no longer 'hidden', it is more than ever a witness to the power of the 'other' traditions and the indigenous American past and present.[2]

As the groundwork for a literature of this continent, that Indian oral poetry dwarfs most of the early Anglo-European works and appears to many of us as the equal of the great American writings of the last two centuries. Its influence during that time – even where distorted by cultural distance and by ideas of 'savagery', noble or otherwise – has been enormous. For an instance of this awareness – or an emblem of it – one might look to Thoreau in the nineteenth century, who carried a sense of the Indian presence as he walked 'the arrowheadiferous sands of Concord' and who spoke the word 'Indian' on his death bed. That presence has reached deep into our own time, where Gary Snyder, among many other poets, felt 'the American Indian [as] the vengeful ghost lurking in the back of the troubled American mind . . . [ready to] claim the next generation as its own'. With the actual hidden traditions (and not only the 'idea of the Indian') now more visible and more alive than earlier generations could have imagined, it has helped to shape a new Indian poetry in the work of native writers like Simon Ortiz, Leslie Silko, and N. Scott Momaday. Its full impact on others – white, black, and red – is yet to be described.

NOTES

1. The centrality in spoken narrative of such repetitions and of other stylistic and paralinguistic features (pitch, timbre, onomatopoeia, tempo shifts, breath junctures, etc.) has been brilliantly described and carried into English ('from oral performance to the printed page') by Dennis Tedlock – our major innovator in the transcription of spoken narrative as poetry. My own experiments with oral song have some features in common.

2. Some idea of the substantial body of American Indian poetry now translated into English can be gleaned from the bibliography to this volume (pp. 700–701). Many of the citations in the present essay come from the several anthologies by Jerome Rothenberg listed therein.

'FORGET ABOUT BEING ORIGINAL':
RECENT AMERICAN POETICS

ERIC MOTTRAM

'A chapter on trends, influences and reactions, giving the reader a notion of what has been happening ... the emphasis needs to be on the way poetry has developed (or 'undeveloped'), on the changing preoccupations of poets, and their sources of strength and weakness.' This is what the editor said he needed: in eight thousand words, including quotations. Immediately the form of response to such an invitation becomes a problem: how to convey the sheer amount of wrestling with language in United States poetry, the extraordinary necessity of writing and performance in resistance against mass existence deteriorating continually into mob consensus. Exposure to creative possibilities in language breaks the monotonies of homogenized national response on a huge scale. It is not a matter of a few romantic rebels and fragmentary individualism. 'American poetry' is a meaningless pair of words since the quantity of writing and the qualities of its variety defy urges towards tight definition and exclusive selectivity. Since roughly 1950, the desire to reshape language, to break rules with new inscription, to expose in performance, publish without waiting for the censorship of that massive juncture of corporation publishing, academic judgement and mass consumption, have resulted in an unprecedented poetic culture. Choice has meaning in the sheer heterogeneity, the massive resistance to homogenization. Inside the nervous disapproval of the so-called Beat Generation poets of the 1950s and 1960s quivered in outrage against the breaking of the assumed privileges of a minority activity. Poetry came out of the classroom, the library and the lonely silence of performance by an isolated reader. The guardians turned round, and the poets were taking no notice; they were speaking, writing and inexpensively publishing for an audience unconvinced by what they had been trained to believe had to be 'poetry'.

In terms of immediate poetics, much of the new poetry undertook inheritances from the 'open forms' of Whitman and Pound – and Pound recognized this necessity in 'The Pact', a poem in *Lustra* (1915) addressed to his predecessor: 'It was you who broke the new wood. / Now is a time for carving. / We have one sap and one root...'.[1] But the new poetics took reinforcements from philosophical and scientific propositions that human artifice surged up within the designs of nature. Created forms emerged in a world essentially formed. Poets released themselves from the production and consumption of fetish objects made under archaic rules in 'traditional' prosody.[2] The essays and interviews presenting Charles Olson, Gary Snyder, Robert Duncan, Robert Creeley and Allen Ginsberg – major and diverse writers with a large production of poetry and poetics – in Egbert Faas's *Towards a New American Poetics* (1978), indicate their consciousness of the essential relationship between poetry and ecology, biology and other cultures besides the immediate capitalist, Christian democracy. This is their sociality of the poetic enterprise. Not surprisingly, it is D. H. Lawrence who repeatedly appears as the respected ancestor, in Olson's word the 'prospective' poet, for forms, criticism of the West, and respect for Native American cultures.

Contemporary American poetry at its finest is inter-cultural, with a very wide range of inventive forms and a large body of substantiating poetics and informational resources. This scene cannot be subdued to a narrative essay. It needs a huge wall chart. What follows is a guide within this *Guide*, citing mainly the poetics of the field, and continuously remembering Gertrude Stein's key: 'The composition in which we live makes the art which we see and hear.' Since there is today no single evaluative basis for judgemental evaluation of poetry, none will be attempted within what is primarily a map. The rest is a long reading process, and as Ezra Pound said, 'there is no substitute for a lifetime'. The energy and seriousness of the poets is obvious. But there is one dangerous omission: a list of records and cassettes through which to hear the poets' voicings. The poetry text today includes the oral and aural as well as the visual; the printed text is a score, to be accompanied at least by a videopoetics, if available.

Basic printed texts here are anthologies and poets' statements – as rapid entrances into the field; but the small and large independent presses which have published the poets warrant an article to themselves, since without their enterprise, poetry would remain static, conventional and safe. Most of the collections cited, however, contain bibliographies.

The most useful guide to the poetics which substantiate the poetry is *Symposium of the Whole: A Range of Discourse Toward an Ethnopoetics*, edited by Jerome and Diane Rothenberg (1983). Ethnopoetics is today's poetics, and an ethnic approach can be made by an investigator from any culture towards any others. The idea of a limiting centre or single point of view is no longer possible: 'the concept of centred structure is in fact the concept of a play based on a fundamental ground, a play constituted on the basis of a fundamental immobility, and a reassuring certitude, which is itself beyond the reach of play'.[3] We no longer wish to be caught in certitude anxiety, and most of the poets to be presented resist the results of that centring, in both politics and religious philosophy. A Brazilian writer on performance, Augusto Boal, refuses Aristotelean tragic theory because it is based on

the *already existing inequalities* . . . justice is already contained in reality itself. Aristotle does not consider the possibility of transforming [them] . . . happiness consists in obeying the laws . . . For those who make the laws, all is well. But what about those who do not make them? Understandably, they rebel.
(*Theatre of the Oppressed*, 1979)

Therefore, 'the coercive system of tragedy' is not a universal. Standing in Brazil, the West is not a centre; there is no single tradition to be glibly referred to and coercively maintained, no infallible 'mainstream', no fixed *arche* and *telos* (origin and end) as the limits of a meaningful sentence, narrative or linearity, within which activity is restricted. But, as Olson wrote in 1962: 'The poetics of such a situation are yet to be found out' (*Maximus Poems IV, V, VI*, 1968). So Rothenberg's 'pre-face' begins:

When the industrial West began to discover – and plunder – 'new' and 'old' worlds beyond its boundaries, an extraordinary countermovement came into being in the West itself. Alongside the official ideologies that shoved European man to the apex of the human pyramid, there were some thinkers and artists who found ways of doing and knowing among other peoples as complex as any in Europe and often virtually erased from European consciousness.

Symposium therefore offers the poetics of the later twentieth-century condition, with 'precedents going back two centuries and more'. Ethnopoetics is

a redefinition of poetry in terms of cultural specifics, with an emphasis on those alternative traditions to which the West gave names like 'pagan', 'gentile', 'tribal', 'oral', and 'ethnic'. In its developed form, it moves toward an exploration of creativity over the fullest human range, pursued with a regard for particularized practice as much as unified theory and further 'defined', as in this book, in the actual discourse.

(Such a recognition is the basis of the most important poetry organization in America, the Committee for International Poetry, with its regular festivals of Indian, Polish, Hungarian, etc., poetry.) Rothenberg, a major poet and performer, rightly emphasizes the radical nature of these propositions: 'a complex redefinition of cultural and intellectual values: a new reading of the poetic past and present which Robert Duncan speaks of as "a symposium of the whole"'. The phrase is in 'Rites of Participation', originally in the poet Clayton Eshleman's *Caterpillar* magazine in 1967 – one of the finest journals of poetry in the 1960s:[4]

The drama of our time is the coming of all men into one fate, 'the dream of everyone, everywhere'. The fate or dream is the fate of more than mankind. Our secret Adam is written now in the script of the primal cell . . . All things have come into their comparisons. But these comparisons are the correspondences that haunted Paracelsus, who saw also that the key to man's nature was hidden in the larger nature. In space this has meant the extension of our 'where' into a world ecology . . . The very form of man has no longer the isolation of a superior paradigm but is involved in its morphology, in the cooperative design of all living things . . . We go now to the once-called primitive – to the bush man, the child, or the ape – not to read what we were but what we are.

Marx's comparative economics and 'world commune', Darwin's comparison of species and 'world family living in evolution', and Frazer's comparative religious rituals and 'world cult' still counter 'imperialist expansions' with the necessity of 'a symposium of the whole' which includes once excluded orders: 'the female, the proletariat, the foreign; the animal and vegetative; the unconscious and the unknown; the criminal and the failure'. Moreover, 'if, as Pound began to see in *The Spirit of Romance*, "All ages are contemporaneous [in the mind]", our time has always been, and the statement that the great drama of our time is the coming of all men into one fate is the statement of a crisis . . . man has awakened to the desire for wholeness in being. "The continuous present", Gertrude Stein called this sense of time and history . . . Man is always in the process of this composition.' That this processual vision is contained in Whitman's essentially processual pre-Civil War poetry, Duncan is well aware,[5] and both his contemporaries – Kenneth Rexroth, Charles Olson, Louis Zukofsky, George Oppen and Charles Reznikoff – and the later generations of Robert Kelly, David Meltzer, Paul Blackburn, Robert Creeley, Allen Ginsberg, Jack Kerouac, Michael McClure and Gary Snyder – are deeply committed to founding a poetics for this enlightened opening. Hence the fusion of their poetry and their poetics into a single complex performance.

What follows here is a method of exploration, with the necessary tools, the apparatus.

Revolution of the Word, edited by Jerome Rothenberg in 1975, is 'a new gathering of American avant-garde poetry 1914–1945' which carefully instances the wide range of poetry through thirty-one poets.

Technicians of the Sacred, edited by Rothenberg in 1968, revised and expanded in 1985, is 'a range of poetries from Africa, America, Asia, Europe & Oceania', with amplificatory 'pre-faces', statements and commentaries. The intention of *Alcheringa*, the brilliant journal edited by Rothenberg and Dennis Tedlock from 1970 onwards, was complementary: to enlarge the understanding of 'poem', to experiment in translation between 'widely divergent cultures', 'to return to complex/"primitive" systems of poetry as (intermedia) performance, etc., & to explore ways of presenting these in translation . . . to combat cultural genocide in all its manifestations'. Some issues included a disc of performed poetry to this end. *Alcheringa*'s fundamental opposition to official United States policy need hardly be mentioned.

America a Prophecy, edited by Rothenberg and George Quasha in 1974, is 'a new reading of American poetry from pre-Columbian times to the present', an attempt to 'map' some of the lines of recovery and discovery, of the old and the new, as they relate specifically to the place we inhabit. A map is a guide to unknown terrain, and American poetry remains largely just that – a vast region of which we're not yet fully conscious.

The New American Poetry 1945–1960, edited by Donald M. Allen in 1960, is a pioneering representation of poetry since the body of work established by Williams, Pound, HD, Stevens, Rexroth, etc., and, in part, developing its proposals, in part innovating beyond it. Allen's divisions seemed sharper to him in 1960 than they actually were, as he has acknowledged, but his groupings had their initial utility: *Origin* and *Black Mountain Review* (journals edited in the 1950s by two fine poets, Cid Corman and Robert Creeley) writers – Olson, Duncan, Creeley, Edward Dorn, Joel Oppenheimer, Jonathan Williams, Denise Levertov, Blackburn, Eigner, etc.; 'San Francisco Renaissance' writers – Brother Antoninus (William Everson), Jack Spicer, Lawrence Ferlinghetti, Philip Lamantia, Lew Welch, etc.; 'Beat Generation' – Ginsberg, Kerouac, Gregory Corso, etc.; 'New York Poets' – John Ashbery, Kenneth Koch, Frank O'Hara, Barbara Guest, James Schuyler, etc.; and a section of uncategorizable poets – Philip Whalen, Snyder, McClure, Meltzer, John Wieners, Gilbert Sorrentino, LeRoi Jones (later Imamu Amiri Baraka). Allen includes vital statements from poets on their poetics, biographical notes, and a bibliography. In 1973, he and Warren Tallman produced *The Poetics of the New American Poetry* – documents from Whitman's letter to Emerson and Fenollosa on the Chinese written character, through to Lawrence, Hart Crane, Lorca and Stein, to the present day.

The Postmoderns: The New American Poetry, edited by Donald Allen and George F. Butterick. The excellent editor of Olson's collected poetry revises Allen's pioneer volume, without substituting for it. The net of inclusion is so wide that the poets are no longer, in some cases, adequately represented, such is the astonishing energy of contemporary American poetry. But this is a useful collection and does loosen the 1960 divisions.

An Anthology of New York Poets, edited by Ron Padgett and David Shapiro in 1970, begins with epigraphs appreciating New York City life from Whitman and Kerouac, and excellently represents twenty-seven poets, including Allen's New Yorkers and many others, with biographies and bibliographies. The preface excludes the possibility of a 'New York School', although the city is seen as 'a fulcrum [the poets] continue to use in order to get as much leverage as possible in literature, a city where they met and continued their lives together, whether they came from Cleveland or Newark or Cincinnati or Providence or Tulsa'. The opening of Ted Berrigan's 'Bean Spasms' can show a poet exhilarated by the city and finding a poetics for the urgencies of a certain kind of New York living:

> in praise of thee
> the ? white dead
> whose eyes know:
> what are they
> of the tiny cloud my brain:
> The City's tough red buttons
> O Mars, red, angry planet candy
> bar, with sky on top,
> 'why, it's young Leander hurrying to his death'
> 'what? what time is it, in New York in these here alps
> City of lovely tender hate
> and beauty making beautiful
> old rhymes? ...

Instead of statements on poetics from each poet, the editors use O'Hara's celebrated essay 'Personism: A Manifesto' which first appeared in LeRoi Jones's magazine *Yugen* in 1959. It carries the poet's characteristic wit and exuberant security – in a word, his urbanity:

> I don't believe in god, so I don't have to make elaborately sounded structures. I hate Vachel Lindsay, always have, I don't even like rhythm, assonance, all that stuff. You just go on your nerve ... I'm not saying that I don't have practically the most lofty ideas of anyone writing today, but what difference does that make? they're just ideas ... But how can you really care if anybody gets it, or gets what it means, or if it improves them. Improves them for what? death? Why hurry them along? Too many poets act like a middle-aged mother trying to get her kids to eat too much cooked meat, and potatoes with drippings [tears] ... And after all, only Whitman and Crane and Williams, of the American poets, are better than the movies ... [Personism] puts the poem squarely between the poet and the person ... The poem is at last between two persons instead of two pages ...

The range of energy and skill in O'Hara's *Selected Poems* (1974) shows his value – or just read 'Ode to Michael Goldberg' ('S Births and Other Births') alongside this airy, skilful occasional poem:

> Lana Turner has collapsed!
> I was trotting along and suddenly
> it started raining and snowing
> and you said it was hailing
> but hailing hits you on the head
> hard so it was really snowing and
> raining and I was in such a hurry
> to meet you but the traffic
> was acting exactly like the sky
> and suddenly I see a headline
> LANA TURNER HAS COLLAPSED!
> there is no snow in Hollywood
> there is no rain in California
> I have been to lots of parties
> and acted perfectly disgraceful
> but I have never actually collapsed
> oh Lana Turner we love you get up

At lease three of the 'Beat Generation' poets were New Yorkers in some sense for part of the time; but the term became useless soon after the publication in 1961 of the key book which first presented their work for study – Thomas Parkinson's *A Casebook on the Beat*. The poetry of Allen Ginsberg, Jack Kerouac and Gregory Corso, for example, extends into careers for which the 1950s term 'beat' is inadequate. Ginsberg, in particular, is now a major, almost official, poet, with an 800-page *Collected Poems 1947–1980* (1985), an exceptional record of highly responsible investigations into the poetics of political, religious and sexual discovery,[6] supported by volumes of letters, journals and interviews (*Allen Verbatim*, 1974), and an important set of texts on writing, *Improvised Poetics* (1972). In this excerpt, the bard speaks finally to the boy in 'Contest of Bards' (1977):

> Each Maple waits our gaze erected tricky branches in the air we breathe.
> Nothing is stupid but thought, & all thought we think's our own.
> My face you've seen palsied bearded White & Changing energies
> from Slavelike lust to snowy emptiness, bald Anger to fishy-eyed
>   prophecy.
> Your voice you've heard naked and hard commanding arrogant, pale
>   dandied

in a fit of Burgundy Pique, Childlike delighted fingers twisting my beard
on Lion coverlets in caves far from the Iron Domed Capitol,
Intelligent deciphering runes yours and mine, dreamed & undreamt.
Plebeian Prince of the Suburb, I return to my eastern office pleased with
  our work.
accident of our causes & Eidolons, Planned Careful in your Dreams and
  in my daylight Frenzies: failed Projections! . . .

John Ashbery's poetry is as individual as Ginsberg's, equally as
critically regarded, and just as difficult to exemplify briefly. His
styles have less range and more concentration on close-meshed syntax
and an intense analysis of modes of interior existence and compositional creativity. 'Rain Moving In' is a poem in *A Wave* (1984):

> The blackboard is erased in the attic
> And the wind turns up the light of the stars,
> Sinewy now. Someone will find out, someone will know.
> And if somewhere on this great planet
> The truth is discovered, a patch of it, dried, glazed by the sun,
> It will just hang on, in its own infamy, humility. No one
> Will be better for it, but things can't get any worse.
> Just keep playing, mastering as you do the step
> Into disorder this one meant. Don't you see
> It's all we can do? Meanwhile, great fires
> Arise, as of haystacks aflame. The dial has been set
> And that's ominous, but all your graciousness in living
> Conspires with it, now that this is our home:
> A place to be from, and have people ask about.

Black Fire, edited by LeRoi Jones and Larry Neal in 1968, provides a
large collection of 'Afro-American Writing', with an opening
section of essays. Being an American work, the range of skills is
phenomenal. Larry Neal speaks for black poets in his 'Afterword':

We have been below-deck stoking the ship's furnaces. Now the ship is
sinking, but where will we swim? . . . most of the book can be read as if it
were a critical re-examination of Western political, social and artistic values
. . . Many of us refuse to accept a truncated Negro history which cuts us off
completely from our African ancestry. To do so is to accept the very racist
assumptions which we abhor . . . The movement is now faced with a serious
crisis. It has postulated a theory of Black Power; and that is good. But it has
failed to evolve a workable ideology . . . This lack of clarity is historical and
is involved with what DuBois called the 'double-consciousness' . . . 'One
ever feels his two-ness – an American, a Negro – two souls, two thoughts,
two unreconciled strivings; two warring ideals in one dark body, whose
dogged strength alone keeps it from being torn asunder' . . . Most con-

temporary black writing of the last few years, the literature of the young, has been aimed at the destruction of the double-consciousness . . . at consolidating the African-American personality.

The New Black Poetry, edited by Clarence Major in 1969, is a useful short collection, and *Black Voices: An Anthology of Afro-American Literature*, edited by Abraham Chapman, 1968, contains a large selection of poetry, from Dunbar to the present day.

Within the Black Crisis in America – since the beginnings of overt revolt and organized resistance to white dominance in the 1950s – the problem of artistic definition has been crucial for any black poet with an ambition beyond quickly versified protest or propaganda. The career of LeRoi Jones/Amiri Baraka has been exemplary as a long career of exploration and invention in poetics. He has edited two important journals – *Yugen* and *Kulchur* – directed the Black Arts Repertory Theatre and written his own excellent plays, and published prose fiction, autobiography, collections of essays which contributed significantly to the black issues, and two essential books on jazz. This extract is from 'In the Tradition', addressed to the outstanding jazz musician, and speaks in 1982 once again for black American potentiality:

> Once again
>   in the tradition
>   in the african american
>   tradition
>   open us
>   yet bind us
>   let all that is positive
>   find
>   us
>   we go into the future
>   carrying a world
>   of blackness
>   yet we have been in the world
>   and we have gained all of what there
>   is and was, since the highest expression
>   of the world, is its total
> & the universal
> is the entire collection
> of particulars
> ours is one particular
> one tradition . . .

Native American Renaissance, edited by Kenneth Lincoln, 1983, and *The Language of the Birds*, edited by David M. Guss, 1985, introduce the energetic resurgence of Native American poetry and other writing. Lincoln offers both range and ethnic contexts, and includes detailed notes and bibliography. Guss's subtitle suggests some of the issues involved: 'Tales, Texts, and Poems of Interspecies Communication'. The power and historical significance of these volumes is matched by two others. First, *The Clouds Threw This Light*, edited by Philip Foss in 1983, is an essential and wonderful collection of 'contemporary Native American poetry', mainly the poets' own choices, and using a range of poetics fully in accordance with the rest of American poetry today. Second, Jerome Rothenberg's pioneering *Shaking the Pumpkin: Traditional Poetry of the Indian North Americans* (1972), whose 'pre-face' opens the problems of translation and the justification for tackling them:

To submit through translation is to begin to accept the 'truth' of an other's language . . . the very nature of 'Indian' and 'white' (words basic to the process I'm describing) is itself a question of language and translation.

'Flowers of Winter: Four Songs' is a poem in Foss by Duane Big Eagle (Osage Sioux):

> Song of the Drowning Man –
> I want to go
> to a place where nothing can hurt me
>
> Song of the New Wife –
> Everything I touch turns to dust,
> his pleasure is a mystery to me.
>
> Song of the Husband –
> My arrows miss the heart of the deer,
> her desire is not equal to mine.
>
> Song of the Newborn –
> I come from the valley of endings,
> there is no place to go but onward.

The World Split Open, edited by Louise Bernikow in 1974, remains the finest collection of women poets (1552–1950) writing in English, but it needs supplementing for the last three decades in America. The introduction is essential, and its conclusion historical and stirring:

Where women have distilled experience into the verbal art form that in so short a space can create for the reader so total a sensation, where women have found language to shape what is in our imaginations, we have made poetry.

We have, from the first, been singers, always.

The epigraph is from one of America's finest poets, Muriel Rukeyser – her 'Käthe Kollwitz' (*The Collected Poems: Muriel Rukeyser*, 1979): 'What would happen if one woman told the truth about her life?/The world would split open.' Elizabeth Janeway condenses some of the implications in her chapter on 'Women's Literature' in the *Harvard Guide to Contemporary American Writing* (edited Daniel Hoffman, 1979), and one useful collection of critical introductions is *Coming To Light: American Women Poets in the Twentieth Century* (1985), edited by Diane Middlebrook and Marilyn Yalom. But in default of a fully representative anthology, we still have a large number of individual volumes by, for instance, Denise Levertov, Adrienne Rich, Diane DiPrima, Diane Wakowski, Barbara Guest, Anne Lauterbach, Diane Ward and Alice Notley.

Anne Waldman is one of the most active and initiating poets in America, an excellent technician and performer, a skilled lecturer on poetics, and an editor of periodicals and collections in the field of poetry. Here is the beginning and the end of the title poem in *Makeup on Empty Space* (1984):

> I am putting makeup on empty space
> all patinas convening on empty space
> rouge blushing on empty space
> I am putting makeup on empty space
> pasting eyelashes on empty space
> painting the eyebrows of empty space
> piling creams on empty space
> painting the phenomenal world
> I am hanging ornaments on empty space . . .
>
> when you are in your anguished head
> when you are not sensible
> when you are insisting on the
> praise from many tongues
> It begins with the root of the tongue
> it begins with the root of the heart
> there is a spinal cord of wind
> singing & moaning in empty space

The L-A-N-G-U-A-G-E Book, edited by Bruce Andrews and Charles Bernstein in 1984, reprints the first three volumes of this magazine, first launched in 1978, and can be used as a representation of the kinds of ideals and practices this latest grouping of American poets affords. Its introduction, 'Repossessing the Word', brings them forward:

> Our project, if it can be summarized at all, has involved exploring the numerous ways that meanings and values can be (and are) realized – revealed – produced in writing. This involves an opening of the field of activity and not its premature foreclosure . . .
>
> The idea that writing should (or could) be stripped of reference is as bothersome and confusing as the assumption that the primary function of words is to refer, one-on-one, to an already constructed world of 'things'. Rather, reference, like the body itself, is one of the horizons of language, whose value is to be found in the writing (the world) before which we find ourselves at any moment. It is the multiple powers and scope of reference (denotative, connotative, associational), not the writers' refusal or fear of it, that threads these essays together.

The politics of the referential issue is summarized, partly, from Ron Silliman's essay 'Disappearance of the Word/Appearance of the World' which 'applies the notion of commodity fetishism to conventional descriptive and narrative forms of writing', in which words 'disappear, become transparent, leaving the picture of a physical world the reader can then consume as if it were a commodity'. The emphasis on language surfaces and structures, partly derived from formalist principles, is itself a controversy for many of the poets so far mentioned in this little guide – Duncan refers to the work as 'really "jerk" poetry' (interview with Michael McClure in *Conjunctions* No. 7, 1985). But in no way can the poetry of Bob Perelman, Barrett Watten, Charles Bernstein, Robert Grenier and Silliman be so dismissed – nor can the principles Andrews and Bernstein offer:

> It is our sense that the project of poetry does not involve turning language into a commodity for consumption; instead, it involves repossessing the sign through close attention to, and active participation in, its production.

The relevant poems can be read in three journals – *Hills* (ed. Bob Perelman), *This* (ed. Barrett Watten), and *Roof* (ed. James Sherry) – and in the first-rate productions of the Tuumba press, edited by Lyn

Hejinian, including work by David Bromige, Ted Greenwald, Michael Palmer, and Carla Harryman. The variety of the poets' procedures is immediately clear in *Legend* (1980), a selection from Bruce Andrews, Charles Bernstein, Ray DiPalma, Steve McCaffery and Ron Silliman. Certain stylistics may be suggested from two excerpts – the first from Charles Bernstein's 'Force of Habit' (*Islets/Irritations*, 1984):

> ... Funny these tulips, inlaid with enameled
> frost, guileless manipulation, altogether
> benched. Target to presuppose umpteen incineration.
> Multipurpose flimsy, albeit unabashed. These
> shames at having truncate what alarms,
> sealed matting to savor
> horn rimmed metrics. Time
> the measured sustenance, becomes
> all more alert to maze like hat
> of bemused facts. I take hat
> in hand, by hand announce
> a sequel logic, steady
> against the line of the shore, pushes
> back as keeps coming, dote on
> pressurized feed grain, wells it shut. Something
> taken, something fleshed on fluorescence
> with parting stem. Springs
> redress, funneled cue not to lost dominance ...

The second is from Bob Perelman's 'Road Tones' (*7 Works*, 1979):

> ... Form is mechanical when the sound
> of its thump does not point
> to a use of chaos, the nine headed
> monster that eats our souls
> with some degree of reciprocity
> in a serious attempt
> to find a solution to the snows
> and winds that snap our bones.
> It remains an open question
> how much special air
> life owes birds of the region.
> There is no way back
> from what is innate.
> Stiff snarls of linguistic soot
> mean space, rejected or filled
> with common emotional biases ...

The poetics are in *Talks* (*Hills* 6/7, Spring 1980), *Writing/Talks* (ed. Perelman, 1985), and *Poetics Journal* (ed. Hejinian and Watten). A useful British introduction is given in *Reality Studios*, Vol. 2, No. 4 (edited by the London poet Ken Edwards), subtitled 'Death of the Referent?'. One of the finest collections of related poetics is certainly *Code of Signals*, edited by Michael Palmer in 1983.

Since the latter is *Io No. 33*, this is the place to draw attention to a brilliant magazine/book series, in the talented hands of Richard Grossinger since 1965, a continuous publishing of information directing poets towards cultural studies in the widest sense, with issues on alchemy, the doctrine of signatures, 'oecology', oneirology, 'mind, memory, psyche'. Each text is substantial, and the series draws on regular resources in poets themselves: Robert Kelly, one of the most distinguished poets in America, Charles Stein, Grossinger himself, McClure, Thomas Meyer, Harvey Bialy (who edited *Io 24*, 'Biopoesis') Paul Metcalf, Theodore Enslin, etc. Poetics here becomes multiple information as nourishment and awareness of conditions. *Io 33* (1984) is 'Nuclear Strategy and the Code of the Warrior'. *Io*, like Rothenberg's collections and *Code of Signals*, provides the necessary onwardgoing *paideuma*, a term Pound found in Leo Frobenius – 'a people's whole congeries of patterned energies, from their "ideas" down to the things they know in their bones, not a *Zeitgeist* before which minds are passive' (Hugh Kenner, *The Pound Era*, 1972). This is what informed Whitman's governing belief in 'vista':

> Past and present and future are not disjoined but joined. The greatest poet forms the consistence of what is to be from what has been and is. He drags the dead out of their coffins and stands them again on their feet . . . he says to the past Rise and walk before me that I may realize you. He learns the lesson . . . he places himself where the future becomes present. ('Preface' to the 1855 *Leaves of Grass*)

Rothenberg's conception of 'vista' brings this sense of scope forward:

> A fully human poetics would include all forms of what Jacques Derrida calls *archécriture* (= primal writing): pictographs and hieroglyphs, aboriginal forms of visual and concrete poetry, sand paintings and earth mappings, gestural and sign languages, counting systems and numerologies, divinational signs made by man or read (as a poetics of natural forms) in the tracks of animals or of stars through the night sky . . . The twentieth century – and with it the attendant modernisms, that have characterized our poetry and art

– is by now winding down. It has been a long haul and a sometimes real adventure, but the work is in no way complete.

Concrete Poetry: A World View, edited by Mary Ellen Solt, 1970, and *An Anthology of Concrete Poetry*, edited by Emmet Williams in 1967, were the first two large-scale collections in this field published in the United States, including major American poets such as Robert Lax, Aram Saroyan, Dick Higgins, Brion Gysin, Al Hansen, Jackson Mac Low and Jonathan Williams. These names immediately suggest the range of 'concrete poetry', the overlap with 'soundtext' poetry, and the large range of methods. Nor have these poets restricted themselves to this field. Richard Kostelanetz introduces his anthology *Imaged Words & Worded Images* (1970) with the problems:

> A new art necessarily demands a new name, and the art of incorporating word within image has recently inspired a spate of new names – 'calligrams', 'concrete poetry', 'ideograms', 'pattern poems', 'concretism'. They all are intended to identify artifacts that are neither word nor image alone but somewhere or something between.

That is, the visual experience of words and signs is at least as primary as the connotative meaning of words. The operative term is *design*. *This Book Is a Movie*, edited by Jerry G. Bowles and Tony Russell in 1971, shows the range developing and links the works to conceptual and information art. By 1979, the expanded area of poetics parallels changes in visual arts, music and post-structuralist critical theories; *SubStance 23/24: Poe/sie//Poetry* (a highly useful journal published at the University of Wisconsin) offers essays on the semiotics of the field. In 1980, the Centre for Twentieth Century Studies at Wisconsin published *Performance in Postmodern Culture* (edited by Michael Benamou and Charles Caramello) to articulate the complex creative relationships between concrete, soundtext and performance poetries, and various forms of oral and visual presentation. In the opening essay Benamou writes:

> The problematic of performance in postmodern culture ranges from questions about shamanism to projections of the human drama playing itself in an expanding universe ... Performance, the unifying mode of the postmodern, is now what matters. From the experiments of the Living Theatre to the sophisticated mixed-mediations of video, performance has changed the scene of the arts, of painting (since Duchamp), of theatre (since Artaud), of poetry (since Olson) ... Notions of orality, tribal reach, and the

global village connecting us with the performance of pre-literate times need redefinition in terms of electronic communication.

In his essay 'Oral and Written Forms' (*Alcheringa*, New Series, Vol. 2, No. 2, 1976, recording the first university gathering in ethnopoetics, at Wisconsin), Benamou draws on early theorists for this field – Marshall McLuhan, Gilles Deleuze and Félix Guattari, and Jacques Derrida, etc. – and then sketches the current positions:

> We are dealing here with two marginalities: the marginality of speech recalling the oral tradition and its supposed mysteries of innocent presence, and a marginality of writing today in the poetics of free play and chance operation: from Mallarmé to Oulipo, from John Cage to Jackson Mac Low ... A cross-over has taken place for the American poet who, grounding his secondary (re-learned) orality on the tribal communitas, is reaching back to primitive graphism; beyond the barbarian order of writing, beyond the civilized order of print; beyond justified margins and typographical conformities, to a non-alignment of voice and writing which is a dialectic essential to marginality; recovering the voice *and* the sign.

A further set of explorations is presented in *The Oral Impulse in Contemporary American Poetry*, a 1975 issue of *Boundary 2* (Vol. III, No. 3), published by the Department of English, State University of New York at Binghamton, with essays by David Antin (the unique exponent of 'talk poems'), George Economou, Barry Alpert, and Rothenberg.

The Poetry Reading, edited by Stephen Vincent and Ellin Zweig, 1981, is 'a contemporary compendium on Language & Performance', an essential gathering of materials on the steady development of poetry readings in the United States since the 1950s, on oral resources, performance conditions, video poetry, discs and cassettes, sound poetry, and so forth. *Poets On Stage* (1978), a special number of *Some* magazine, collects twenty-nine poets' responses to the issues involved in poetry readings.

Talking Poetics from Naropa Institute, Volumes 1 and 2, edited by Anne Waldman and Marilyn Webb, 1978 and 1979, is a large collection based on lectures given at the Institute, in Boulder, Colorado, since 1974. The poets speaking including Duncan, Diane DiPrima, Ted Berrigan, Ginsberg, Dorn, Clark Coolidge, Whalen, Lewis McAdams and Ed Sanders.

These are, then, *some* of the poets and their poetics 'laying bases for new discourse' (Olson, *Human Universe*, 1965), and bringing into 'presentational immediacy' all the possible components of poetry (A. N. Whitehead, *Process and Reality*, 1929). Olson's 'Introduction to Robert Creeley' (*Human Universe*) considers poetry as 're-enactment', with two possibilities. In 'Document',

events do the work . . . the narrator stays out, functions as pressure not as interpreting person, illuminates not by argument or 'creativity' but by master of force (as space is shaper, confining maintaining inside tensions of objects), the art, to make his meanings clear by how he juxtaposes, correlates, and causes to interact whatever events and persons he chooses to set in motion . . . his ego or person is not of the story whatever.

In the opposite process, the narrator is in, 'taking on himself the job of making clear by way of his own person that life *is* preoccupation with itself'. Both 'methodologies' re-enact experience's 'energy and instant' rather than a mimesis of some prior form and assumed repetition of an emotion. What both Olson and Creeley mastered as a method of creating densities of word and rhythm in 'Projective Verse' (1950; in *Human Universe*), Duncan offers as

possibilities of feeling that that would have no fillers . . . [with] breaks and junctures that are part of the utterance . . . the form is always local. So when we talk about finishing we talk about finishing the poem and not finishing the form . . . It is not a homogenization.

Interview with Faas

Gary Snyder speaks to Faas not about 'new forms' but 'a totally new approach to the very ideas of form' – 'the same form is never done twice' – 'every poem as a different solution to a different problem'. The poet makes a human form in a universe of forms. Like Olson and Duncan, he has no intention of simply over-whelming a reader with completion: 'I stop a poem when I feel it has been well enough begun that the reader can carry it from there. That the rest of it is for his mind.' In this way, the 'trap of formal perfectionism' is avoided, and the little totalitarian impositions of 'movements' and 'schools' are obviated. The poet is in process – Albert Cook describes O'Hara as 'a multiple person, who always keeps several steps ahead of himself in the successful tightrope act of never letting multiple turn into less than single' (*Audit* IV, 1964).

Edward Dorn expertly voices a freed poetics such a person can operate:

> The only thing we can hope for is that [the legitimacy of the line] will die of old age as a question ... it's incumbent upon poetic expression to occupy its space in a real way, optically ... I've always thought [Olson's discussion of breath in 'Projective Verse'] was meant to suggest you could get involved physically with the poem in a way that, up to that point, hadn't actually been suggested.
>
> (*Views*, 1980)

For Clark Coolidge 'delight in the process of writing' lies through 'arrangement', rather than 'composition' and 'structure', and the range within that term. He appreciates, therefore, the paintings of Yves Tanguy, 'landscapes without horizon or as a slanting plane, with forms which may be mineral or animal, about to move or frozen, but *placed*', and he quotes another painter, Philip Guston:

> It cannot be a settled, fixed image. It must of necessity be an image which is unsettled, which has not only not made up its mind where to be but must feel as if it's been in so many places all over this canvas, and indeed there's no place for it to settle – except momentarily.

Coolidge then draws in Charlie Parker's 'playing different intervals from a chord', and Merce Cunningham's 'Field Dances': 'body movement [detached] from story framework, so that what you see is the gestures and movements, the possibilities of the body, arranged' (*Talking Poetics at Naropa* 1, 1978). This passage appears on page 5 of his book-length poem *The Maintains* (1974):

> steps also this
> as in the mast of a running suit
> now only in some set tip running
> see court
> wholly from the main dormant
> broadcast rodent
> one shoulders
> an amount of the day of the dope
> used for does not
> fend and right reason
> dulls or to the doodle
> fish ...

David Antin invented 'talk poems' for precise and related reasons:

I see all poetry as some kind of talking/which is some kind of thinking/and because I've never liked the idea of going into a closet to address myself over a typewriter ... I've gotten into the habit of going to some particular place/with something on my mind/ but no particular words in my mouth/looking for a particular occasion to talk to particular people in a way I hope is valuable for all of us. (*Talking*, 1972)

The publication of such a discourse so far has taken two forms, although a third, a videopoetics performance, is possible. A cassette tape, *The Principle of Fit*, was recorded at the Folger Shakespeare library in Washington in 1980, and printed transcriptions, with a newly invented page, have appeared in several volumes as 'notations or scores of oral poems with margins consequently unjustified'. Here is Antin well into a 'poem-talk' entitled 'remembering re-cording representing' (*Talking at the Boundaries*, 1976):

i dont want by any means to knock photographs   one of the things about them that is meaningful is the total conviction of truth we tend to find   in them   which is maybe not the same as finding the truth in them   but it is not entirely different either   possibly because of something about the idea of truth   and the idea of an image   now in a very personal sense   i think i have some understanding of this   when i was a very little boy my father died   i was very young   i think about two   and i have only two images   of his existence   or only two that i can remember   i remember seeing him from the end of a corridor i was passing through   i could see him through the open door of the bathroom and he had one foot up on the bathtub   i think he was shining his shoes ...

Ron Silliman uses a question from Robert Grenier to suggest an alternative artifice: 'Why Imitate Speech?' (*Alcheringa*, New Series, Vol. 1, No. 2, 1975); and in 'On Speech' (*This* No. 1), Grenier returns to the issue which all contemporary poetics confront and within which poems are made; and draws on Barthes' *Writing Degree Zero* (1953):

Words are not, finally, non-referential. For they originate in interactions with the world ... What can be done, however, is to diminish the reference ... By the creation of non-referring structures ... disruption of context ... forcing the meanings in upon themselves until they cancel out or melt ... By effacing one or more elements of referential language (a tactic commonly employed by Russian Futurists), the balance within & between the words shifts, redistributes.

So poetics reaches again into Pound's 'Paideuma': 'the gristly roots or ideas that are in action'. Today's poetry performances expose those roots and their branches, flowers and fruit. The poet's process in American society is therefore bound to be critical, radical and vulnerable. Anne Waldman remembers Charles Olson in action at the Berkeley Poetry Conference of 1965 as an example of the extraordinarily exciting sociality of the truly postmodern occasion, the force of poetry. In fact, even the transcript of Olson's discourse conveys a little of that remarkable occasion (Charles Olson, *Muthologos* Vol. 1, 1979):

> It was incredible to watch a poet seemingly enact his whole life – from infancy to old age – up there in front of you: very scary, but also moving, profound, and totally vulnerable. Up there without props, without a script, every idea of text or presentation tossed to the wind. Not giving you any sort of line, not dishing out some message or propaganda, whatever, just opening up his head in public . . . there's just someone up there doing his or her own music, relating to the audience's energy . . . speaking and moving and being embarrassing not just for himself, but for you, the audience.
> (*Talking Poetics at Naropa*, 1976).

Such an action is far removed from egoism, confessional poetry or the securities of belonging, with every ostentation possible, to a – or even *the* – movement. The exposure of the occasion prevents ego, and may even edge into the metaphysical. As Jackson Mac Low, one of the most inventive performance poets, observes: 'One must assume good will on the part of everybody participating' in what he calls '"eventual verse", composition by event'. For him the merely 'egoic' is obviated by careful methodology:

> The main motive for 'letting in' other things than oneself, randomizing means or other people or the environment, as when performances include long silences . . . you realize there *is* something more than just yourself doing it.
> (*Talking Poetics at Naropa* 1, 1978)

Mac Low's range of method is extraordinary, a lifetime of investigation and achievement usefully summarized in Rothenberg's preface to the *Representative Works: 1938–1985* (1986):

> Mac Low stands, with John Cage, as one of the two major artists bringing systematic chance into our poetic and musical practice . . . the resulting work raises fundamental questions about the nature of poetry & the function of the poet as creator . . . continuing experiments – both beautiful & outrageous –

with a range of composition and performance modes: simultaneities & other group forms, music & language intersections, phonemic sound poems, collage & assemblage, intermedia, high-tec computer work, concrete & visual poetry, acrostics and syllabics . . . [and] he write in prose to clarify his methods & to show their link to ideology.

The basis of that ideology is anarchist & pacifist on its political side, Taoist & Buddhist in its reflection of what he calls 'the world "in general"'.

It is not surprising that in 1976 Ed Sanders, poet, classical scholar and leader of The Fugs group, entitled his poetics *Investigation Poetry*. His gist is: 'Know the new facts early (Olson)', use '*every* bardic skill and metre and method of the last five or six generations' as you invent your own. Further reason for the impossibility of any tidying and judgemental definition of 'American poetry'. The range of confidence and skill is entirely heartening, a fearlessness and a resistance to categorization well in keeping with Allen Ginsberg's well-known statement – in which an attentive reader may hear again the beliefs of Walt Whitman – 'Mind is shapely . . . the message is: widen the area of consciousness.' The exuberant urge to explore and invent has its own politics: 'There are no limits to creativity. There is no end to subversion' (Raoul Vaneigem, *Leaving the Twentieth Century*, 1974).

NOTES

1. Eric Mottram, 'The Pig-headed Father and the Old Wood: An Introduction to the New American Poetry', *London Magazine*, December 1962.

2. Eric Mottram, *Towards Design in Poetry* (1977), Writers Forum, second edition, 1984.

3. Jacques Derrida, *Writing and Difference* (London, 1978), p. 279.

4. Reprinted in *Caterpillar Anthology*, ed. Clayton Eshleman 'New York, 1971).

5. Robert Duncan, 'The Adventure of Whitman's Line', *Convivio: A Journal of Poetics*, No. 1, 1983.

6. Eric Mottram, *The Wild Good and the Heart Ultimately: Ginsberg's Art of Persuasion* (London, 1979).

FOUR DECADES OF CONTEMPORARY
AMERICAN FICTION

EUGENE GOODHEART

We mark time nowadays by decades, not by generations. Considering the contemporary as the period following the Second World War, we experience the embarrassment of four decades of great literary and cultural change, an embarrassment of riches that defies easy reduction to tendencies and trends. Looking backward from 1987, we have the advantage of foreshortening. Who are the writers of the early decades who still loom large and how do they continue to inform the contemporary moment? The major figures still appear to be Saul Bellow (1915–), Bernard Malamud (1914–86), Philip Roth (1933–), Norman Mailer (1923–), Ralph Ellison (1914–), William Styron (1925–), and John Updike (1932–).

The first three writers represent the most considerable literary 'event' of the post-Second World War period, the 'breakthrough' of American Jewish writing onto the main stage of American literature. The novel, more than any other, that signals the event is Bellow's *The Adventures of Augie March* (1953), 'I am an American, Chicago born,' the hero affirms, in order to dispel any expectation that this may be another novel of a Jewish hero enclosed in a claustral *shtetl* psychology. The echo of Mark Twain's great novel in the title suggests that Bellow sees himself in the great tradition of American writing. In tracking Einhorn, one of his larger than life characters ('What would Caesar suffer in this case? What would Machiavelli advise or Ulysses do? What would Einhorn think?'), Bellow or rather Augie finds himself 'not in the center of the labyrinth but on a wide boulevard'. There are, of course, no boulevards in the *shtetl*. Isn't this the achievement of Bellow – to take the Jew off the side-streets and put him on the boulevard of the imagination?

According to editors of an anthology of American Jewish writing, the 'breakthrough' meant not that 'the Jew has caught up with

America. America has at long last caught up with the Jew. His
search for identity is its search. Its quest for spiritual meaning is his
quest.' This is a pleasant fiction, encouraged perhaps by the writers
themselves. Malamud remarks somewhere that the burden of his
work is to show that all men are Jewish. And the narrator of Walker
Percy's (1916–   ) *The Moviegoer* (1961) declares his 'Jewishness by
instinct. We share the same exile.'

But the idea that American writing has finally caught up with the
Jewish writer ignores creative and historical realities. The Jewish
writer had to learn to speak English and he had to learn to speak it
artistically. He also had to overcome his immigrant defensiveness
and his blinding fear of the new country. One need only read the
Yiddish literature written in America in the early twentieth century
(a literature distinguished by sentimentality, self-pity, the absence of
keen observation) to see what was required of the Jewish writer for
him to gain entry into the larger world of American letters.

One enabling condition for the Jewish writer was the breakup of
the tradition that he had brought with him from the old country to
the new country. The breakup freed him to look upon his experience
with detachment and possess it in a new way. There is an often noted
parallel between the new creative power of Jewish writers and that of
Southern writers like Faulkner (1897–1962), Flannery O'Connor
(1925–64) and William Styron who too found imaginative freedom
in the disintegration of Southern tradition.

Qualifications for entry into the mainstream of American writing
did not occur in a historical vacuum. The Second World War served
as a rite of passage for the Jews as well as other ethnic groups. One
of the few benefits of the war was its democratizing effect. *The
Adventures of Augie March* in its picaresque confidence and buoyancy
registers a two-way acceptance of Jews by America and of America
by the Jews. This retrospective view of the significance of *Augie
March* does not square with the view of certain radical intellectuals
at the time, who saw Bellow's affirmativeness as an expression of 'an
age of conformity' (Irving Howe's phrase). Norman Podhoretz,
then in a radical phase, spoke of 'the optimism of American intellectuals' in the Eisenhower era 'as strained and willed as the prose of
Augie March itself'.

This judgement seems to me tendentious and misleading. It is not the philistinism of the Eisenhower era that one hears in Augie's affirmations, but the old American themes of the open road and big river (made famous by Whitman and Twain) in which the self experiences its indeterminacy, its protean freedom to change shape, to assume new roles. Bellow, we know, felt he was breaking from the European-influenced psychology of victimage in his first two novels, *The Dangling Man* (1944) and *The Victim* (1947). Of course, the break was never complete: the old note of entrapment and alienation re-enters *Seize the Day* (1956) and *Herzog* (1964) just as the sense of freedom and possibility persists in *Henderson the Rain King* (1959).

Bellow strikes the note of artistic confidence which enables him and other writers to explore with truth and imagination American and Jewish experience. It makes possible a comically critical view of Jewish family life of the kind we get in Philip Roth's *Goodbye, Columbus* (1959) and *Portnoy's Complaint* (1969), provoking the self-proclaimed spokesmen of the Jewish community to condemn Roth as a traitor to his people. The 'breakthrough' took its toll on Philip Roth. In his recent trilogy and epilogue, *Zuckerman Bound* (1985) (consisting of *The Ghost Writer* (1979), *Zuckerman Unbound* (1981), *The Anatomy Lesson* (1983), and *The Prague Orgy*) Roth records the sufferings of a novelist-celebrity whose life has become a nightmare of unsuccessful expiation for sins of storytelling against family and tribe. Nathan Zuckerman's father challenges his son: 'And how do you think the Gentiles will judge the people in your story, what conclusions do you think they will reach? Have you thought about that?'

If the post-war generation of Jewish writers represents a breakthrough, then it is a mistake to view their work in an exclusively Jewish perspective. Augie's desire for freedom, for protean identity is American and it has its negative as well as its positive aspect.

The negative side of the American desire for a protean freedom is, as Tony Tanner points out in *City of Words* (1971), 'a dread of all conditioning forces to the point of paranoia'. The American (writer as well as non-writer) dislikes plots and systems (the structure of narrative itself): he is suspicious of all 'hidden persuaders'. (The *ne plus ultra* of the paranoid fantasy is Thomas Pynchon's (1937–) *Gravity's Rainbow* (1973), which conceives American reality as an elaborate network of political and technological conspiracy.) Jewish experience, of course, has tended to make the 'paranoia' all too real. Kirby Allbee's anti-semitism in *The Victim* is not merely imaginary. The effect of paranoia is escape into a private realm, not the exercise of political consciousness and imagination.

The radical critique to be made is not of the conformism of American writers, but of their essential indifference to the political life. John Updike (1932–   ) not only admits as much: he sees it as the virtue of realistic fiction: 'We didn't much think of politics . . . We were much more concerned with the private destiny that shaped people.' And in an interview, he asserts: 'You introduce topical material into a novel at your own peril. I am convinced that the life of a nation is reflected, or distorted, by private people and their minute concerns.' The civil rights movement and the war in Viet Nam in the sixties produced a change, an intensification of political consciousness, but these events did not seriously affect the essentially private character of novelistic consciousness in America. For Philip Roth in *The Anatomy Lesson* (1983), the private and the personal are deficiencies, not power. Thus the novelist hero Zuckerman reflects on the destruction of Warsaw during the Second World War in the perspective of his own excruciating, guilt-induced back and neck pains. 'You don't want to represent her Warsaw – it's what her Warsaw represents that you want: suffering that isn't semi-comical, the world of massive historical pain instead of this pain in the neck.' Updike's credo ignores, but Roth–Zuckerman's meditations remind us of, the great nineteenth-century novelists (Tolstoy, Dickens, Dostoevsky, George Eliot) who were able to discover intersections between public events and 'the minute concerns' of private people. It should be said, however, that Roth, despite every intention, does not succeed in overcoming his narcissistic self-preoccupations. All efforts to separate author from character both in the form and the theme of his novels fail. The visit to Eastern Europe provides a larger perspective, but it does not affect the self-obsessions of the protagonist.

In the fifties and the sixties, it is the personal, the private and the domestic that provide the main subject matter of fiction – and in particular marriage or rather the busted marriage. Bellow in *Seize the Day* and in *Herzog*, Updike in *Rabbit, Run* (1960) and *Rabbit*

Redux (1971), Roth in *When She Was Good* (1967), to name the most prominent among an abundance of such novels, explore the oppressions and betrayals that occur within marriage. What is not always clear from the intense investments that the novelists make in their suffering heroes (the autobiographical component is very strong) is the larger sociological, if not political, reality in which marriage itself begins to suffer the consequences of the relaxation of old moral standards, of a new emphasis on personal fulfillment and self-realization. The busted marriage is the price for freedom.

Paradoxically, the breakup and divorce produces its own claustral atmosphere, a preoccupation with the forms of separation, betrayal and self-doubt. Tony Wilhelm of Bellow's *Seize the Day* can think of nothing else. Herzog is distinguished by the intellect of the hero, who finds in his domestic sufferings occasions for cosmic (and comic) speculations about the universe, society, existence, politics in the form of compulsive imaginary letters to world historical figures and ordinary citizens. But for all the daring of his imagination, Herzog remains trapped in his domesticity. Updike's Rabbit Angstrum, in *Rabbit, Run*, the first of a trilogy of Rabbit novels, which include *Rabbit Redux* and *Rabbit Is Rich* (1981), runs from responsibilities on an open road that leads nowhere but to misery. The novel cultivates in the reader the desire for Rabbit to come to rest in a reconciliation with his wife, but then disappoints the desire. After the death of the new baby (by accidental drowning, indirectly caused by Rabbit's second abandonment of his wife), one expects that Rabbit has learned his lesson, but against all expectation he blurts out an accusation against his wife at the funeral of the baby and runs away again. Rabbit needs to transgress the limits: it is his freedom and his suffering. The transgression is a delusive exercise in self-definition. Rabbit tries to establish identity through the friction of transgression only to lose it entirely in the movement of escape.

Writers of the generation of Bellow and Malamud and of Updike and Roth were sufficiently attached to the old superego of eternal marriage to find the broken marriage more suffering than liberation. Yet for all the misery produced by the broken marriage, divorce becomes a rite of passage in American life, perhaps the only path to maturity for the innocent male for whom the initiations that occur in European society are unavailable. The balance of suffering and 'liberation' would change in the late sixties and seventies, and the benefits of liberation would be as much, perhaps more the woman's (that is, the imprisoned housewife's) than the man's.

The political novel of quality is a rarity in contemporary American fiction. E. L. Doctorow's (1931–   ) *The Book of Daniel* (1971) and Robert Coover's (1932–   ) *The Public Burning* (1977) are exceptional attempts to explore the American psyche through an imaginative re-creation of a traumatic event in the life of the American Left: the Rosenberg case. Both novels assume the innocence of the Rosenbergs. The point of view of *The Book of Daniel* is an occasionally bewildering mixture of an objective narrative consciousness and that of the older son of the Isaacsons, the fictional name given to the Rosenbergs. Published in 1971, the novel connects the experiences of the Old Left as embodied by the Isaacsons with those of the New Left as embodied by their son. Doctorow mutes the New Left's repudiation of the Stalinism of the Old Left in order to dramatize the legacy. The point of view of Coover's *The Public Burning* is Richard Nixon's (or Coover's version of Nixon) but the burden of Nixon's narration is self-incriminating. The Rosenbergs speak a noble, idealistic prose that is protected from irony. Nixon speaks the cynical language of the politician (he is keenly aware of all the flaws in the prosecution's case) but he clings to a sincere paranoid view of the world as divided between the American forces of light and the dark forces of the Communist Phantom. There is an ideological tendentiousness in the presentations that the extraordinary skill of both novelists cannot quite redeem. We are made to see the American political psyche as tawdry and corrupt, and Soviet evil as fantasy.

It is fair to say that political novels are generally written by writers on the Left as expressions of disaffection from established authority. The paucity of political novels in America may be a reflection of the weakness of the Left in American life. Occasionally, a political novel gets written that tries untendentiously to encompass the complexity and the contradictions of political struggle. William Styron's *The Confessions of Nat Turner* (1967), written at the time that the Civil Rights Movement was beginning to enter a more militant, even violent phase is a sort of allegory about the necessities and the costs of revolutionary violence. Narrated by Nat Turner, the novel reveals him as a partisan, a man possessed of a vision of truth and justice so fanatical that it denied the humanity of the whites whom he murdered. Like his master Faulkner, Styron seems to share to some extent the imaginative belief that violence liberates the self to new possibilities of experience. But the novel issues not in 'morality', but in tragic contemplation (or meditation, to use Styron's word). We observe the career of Nat Turner's passion with the emotions of pity, terror, admiration. The perspective is a complex, even contradictory, one: tragic consciousness and sympathy for black militancy which excludes tragic consciousness.

It is Norman Mailer who registers most vividly the seismic changes that occurred in the sixties and the seventies. Mailer's first novel *The Naked and the Dead* (1948), published shortly after the Second World War, is, with *From Here to Eternity* (1951) by James Jones (1921–77), one of the two most powerful novels about the Second World War, a superb example of realistic storytelling and depiction. Themes of power and violence in *The Naked and the Dead* emerge in an extravagantly subjective form in Mailer's later work. Indeed, it is still a question of whether and how much he was cause or effect of the turbulent sixties. His career-long ambition has been to revolutionize American consciousness. Gore Vidal has even spoken of him as indirectly responsible for the actions of Charles Manson. Vidal is referring to a transvaluation of values (helped along, if not created, by Mailer) that began to define a portion of American culture during the sixties and the early seventies. The political ferment generated by the Civil Rights Movement and then the war in Viet Nam was accompanied by an exalting of passion over intellect, body over mind, the perverse over the normal, the spontaneous over the habitual, the risks of violence and disaster over the security of our ordinary modes of existence. These are values nurtured in an apocalyptic time, when great change is anticipated and the ordinary rules no longer seem to apply. In his notorious essay 'The White Negro' (written 1957 and reprinted in *Advertisements for Myself on the Way Out*, 1959), Mailer interprets a brutal killing of a storekeeper by a gang of young impoverished hoodlums (reported in the newspapers) as a symbolic anti-bourgeois act. He does not deny the psychopathology of such behavior, but insists in the transvaluative mode that the psychopath 'may be indeed the perverted or dangerous forerunner of a new kind of personality'. And in a powerfully disturbing short story, 'The Time of Her Time' (in *Advertisements*), the Irish hero Sergius O'Shaugnessey brings his Jewish girl friend to orgasm by shouting anti-semitic obscenities at her. Instances such as these exemplify Vidal's accusations.

How seriously should one take these fantasies – or the fantasies of the drug-addicted imagination of William Burroughs (1914–) for that matter? Mailer never says how literally he intends his imaginative adventures. The imagination we know has privileges which resist the reality-testing demands of philistine readers. But in Mailer and in lesser apocalyptists the boundary between imagination and reality is not at all secure. Mailer has wanted the imagination to spill over into reality. He has wanted to be more than a mere writer: indeed, he has even dreamed of being President, or at least an advisor to presidents, though he never got further than a run for mayor of New York. And he himself has shown a proud capacity for acts of violence. (At times he seems more suitable to the role of court jester than that of adviser.) And he was not the only novelist in the sixties who began to explore the relations between fiction and reality.

In a widely quoted essay 'Writing in American Fiction' (1961) Philip Roth expressed the contemporary American novelists' sense of being intimidated by the extravagance of a reality that outdistances their wildest fantasies and in defiance of all the rules of verisimilitude has produced Joseph McCarthy, Roy Cohn, David Shine, Charles Van Doren, and Dwight David Eisenhower. In retrospect, Roth's examples of extravagance seem exaggerated, but he persuasively represented a more general feeling among writers that there were extraordinary stories happening in the world which imaginative writing had to find ways of accommodating. In Truman Capote's (1929–) *In Cold Blood* (1965), Mailer's *Armies of the Night* (1968), Tom Wolfe's *The Electric Kool-Aid Acid Test* (1968), Hunter Thompson's (1939–), *Fear and Loathing in Las Vegas* (1972) and Michael Herr's *Dispatches* (1977), we witness the invention of a paradoxical genre – the non-fiction novel.

It is as if the novelist cannot re-enter the world beyond his private concerns unless he returns to the journalistic origins of his art. (Recent scholarship has documented the emergence of the modern novel in the eighteenth century from journalistic practice.) But what he does not do is abandon his novelistic sensibility in favor of objectivity.

In *Armies of the Night* (1968) Mailer, the author himself, enters the public story as a character, and he can do so, because he himself is already a celebrity, that is, someone with a public persona. *Armies of the Night* is hardly a documentary account of the homefront of the Viet Nam war, the marches and demonstrations: it is rather a psycho-drama of the artist–intellectual's experience of the war and in particular of Norman Mailer.

The focus is not on the preparations for the March on Washington and the thousands of war protesters but rather on Mailer's encounter with another famous writer, the poet Robert Lowell.

So Robert Lowell and Norman Mailer feigned deep conversation. They turned their heads to one another at the empty table, ignoring the potentially acolytic drinkers at either elbow. They projected their elbows out in fact like flying buttresses or old Republicans, they exuded waves of Interruption Repellent from the posture of their backs, and concentrated on their conversation, for indeed tney were the only two men of remotely similar status in the room.

Lowell is the other significant figure in the book not simply because he is a famous poet, the most distinguished of his generation, but because he is the source of a judgement of Mailer's work that rankles: he tells Norman that he and his wife Elizabeth Hardwick believe him to be the best *journalist* in America. *Armies of the Night* is intended as 'proof' that Mailer's 'journalism' imaginatively transcends the facts that it represents. It encompasses political reality through character, plot, episode.

Yet what remains most interesting and most problematic about *Armies of the Night* and Mailer's other work is the powerful impulse toward self-theatricalization, what might be called the celebrity-syndrome that Mailer shares with other famous people in America. (Mailer's more recent *Executioner's Song* (1979), a non-fiction 'novel' about the execution of the murderer Gary Gilmore, is in the self-effacement of the author an exception.) Celebrity is at best a mixed blessing. *Armies of the Night* begins with what Mailer regards as a travesty of the facts of Mailer's performance. (Throughout the book he 'paranoically' complains against journalistic misreporting of the facts.)

Mumbling and spewing obscenities as he staggered about the stage – which he had commandeered by threatening to beat up the previous M.C. – Mailer described in detail his search for a usable privy on the premises. Excretion, in fact, was his preoccupation of the night.

Mailer's own version of the events has him 'composed, illumined by [the] first stages of Emersonian transcendence' as he 'left the men's room'. What matters of course are not the absurd facts of the case (who cares?), but Mailer's equivocations between vainglory and self-irony (transcendence and the men's room) that protect him from being placed in that circle of hell to which American celebrities are normally consigned. The best of Mailer is intimately bound up with a comic awareness (associated with his Jewish origins, though he hardly counts as a significant *American-Jewish* novelist) of the absurdity of his posturings. There is a touching scene in *An American Dream* (1965) in which Deborah Rojak, the existentialist hero's wife sees in him the 'poor peddler from the Lower East Side':

> 'I'm descended from peddlers.'
> 'Don't I know it, honey-one,' said Deborah.
> 'All those poor materialistic grabby little people.'
> 'Well, they never hurt anyone particularly.'

Mailer has been extraordinary, if not unique, in the way he has sought celebrity, so his career may appear to be exceptional. Others, Philip Roth, for example, have had celebrity thrust upon them – in particular, with the publication of *Portnoy's Complaint*, a story about a virtuoso performance of self-abuse and Oedipal guilt. In *Zuckerman Unbound*, a novel that reflects on the novelist's experience of celebrity (the fictional version of *Portnoy* is *Carnovsky*), Roth dramatizes the price of celebrity: intrusions into privacy, threats to the life of his mother, continuous and absurd demands on his time, psychically induced illness. Unlike Mailer, Roth–Zuckerman seems like a very private man. And yet it is hard to resist the feeling that the author of *Portnoy–Carnovsky* has the comedian's exhibitionist impulse, the performer's need for celebrity, one reward for which is a one-night stand with an even greater celebrity, the beautiful actress Caesara O'Shea, mistress of Fidel Castro!

The artist–hero has been the subject of art since the romantic period. In Wordsworth, Shelley, Byron, Goethe and Whitman, to name only a few, the artist–hero is a spiritual presence, an unacknowledged legislator, a revolutionary leader. The contemporary American version is infected with the philistinism of glamour that the media (cinema, television, newspapers and magazines) generate. Even the most gifted and the most distinguished writers find the temptation irresistible. It seems as if it is not enough to be an artist in America; the writer wants fame, fortune, power as well.

What is the role of the novelist–hero in contemporary society? Kurt Vonnegut (1922–) at fifty (in *Breakfast of Champions*, 1973) takes stock midway in his career and has his fictional surrogate Kilgore Trout represent himself as the society jester, the truth-teller: 'I now make my living by being the fool and I am clumsy at it.' The rudeness represents a desire for impact, the effect of which is less truth telling, than a comic (or not so comic) stridency, a forcing of attention, an attempt to capture center stage at all costs. I have already spoken of Mailer's power fantasies. One of Vonnegut's other characters, Eliot Rosewater (*God Bless You, Mr Rosewater*, 1965), reappears in *Breakfast of Champions*, writes a letter to Trout in which he remarks: 'You ought to be President of the US.'

Vonnegut's point of view, unlike that of Mailer or Roth, is cynical, lacking in moral, or for that matter comic, seriousness. In a review of a recent John Irving (1942–) novel, Benjamin DeMott speaks of the inability of contemporary novelists to sustain the noble and the solemn. Jokiness, hokiness, cuteness contaminate even the best fiction. Vonnegut's work seems to me a deadly exemplification of DeMott's observation. So does the recent work of Joseph Heller (1923–).

In his most recent novel, *God Knows* (1984), Heller discovers that God is not an earnest social democrat, but the original comic Jewish novelist. The novel is a tissue of dumb wisecracks. Here is King David on his marriage to Michal: 'Michal, my bride, was not just the daughter but a bona-fide Jewish American Princess . . . I am the first in the Old Testament [*sic*] to be stuck with one.' And here is David again on the comparative merits of the Moses story and his own story: 'Moses has the Ten Commandments, it's true, but I've got much better lines.' Heller has never been able again to make his humor serve a genuine insight into the human situation as he did in his classic *Catch-22* (1961) in which he achieved something like a comically heroic transvaluation of anti-heroism (*Something Happened* (1974) is a heavy labor of banality and *Good as Gold* (1974) has the stridency of *God Knows*). One cause of this stridency, forced wit, bad taste etc. is the inordinate ambition of the contemporary novelist for impact, for celebrity status.

In characterizing the contemporary novelist I have spoken of his varied relation to reality. The vocation of the novelist, as has been the case from the moment of its origin, is realism, whatever the definition. But the novel has also had an aesthetic career, a concern with the forms, structures and language which constitute fiction – and in fact, novelists of a certain persuasion have argued that the business of the novel is not the representation of reality, but the creation of beautiful form or the ludic display of language. John Barth (1930–), John Hawkes (1925–), William Gass (1924–) have in recent years represented this view both fictionally and discursively.

In a brilliant preface to the paperback editions of *In the Heart of the Heart of the Country* (1976) (a collection of short fiction), Gass presents the aesthetic point of view ('serious writing must nowadays be written for the sake of art') as a compensation for the lack of a serious audience. Unlike the dissident East European writer, for example, 'the contemporary writer is in no way a part of the social and political scene'. Not that he is 'muzzled', on the contrary, 'no one fears his bite'. If he composes, it is because of 'a reckless inner need'. And what he writes or what he should write, according to Gass, is a readerless fiction that is sustained only by the language that composes it, 'although a reader now and then lets light fall on them from that other, less real world of common life and pleasant ordinary things'. By describing the social or political condition of his own aestheticism, Gass somewhat compromises it. Would he be able to justify it in a society which muzzles the writer and fears his bite? (The justification for the retreat to the aesthetic in Gass is oddly enough the justification for realism in Updike, who, we might recall, speaks of 'the life of the nation' as reflected, or distorted, by 'private people and their minute concerns'. Updike, the realist, does not care that he is not 'part of the social and political scene'. Gass, the aesthete, sees the alienation from the social and the political as decisive and, it would seem, regrets it.)

The fact is that Gass's 'dream of the ultimate fiction – that animal entity, the made-up syllabic self' is hardly the pure aesthetic thing that he says he wants it to be. Stories like 'The Pedersen Kid' or 'Icicles' are informed with a realist's passion for the detail of experience.

> Big Hans yelled, so I came out. The barn was dark, but the sun burned on the snow . . .
> It was the Pedersen Kid. Hans had put the kid on the kitchen table like you would a ham and started the kettle – Ma was fumbling with the kid's clothes which were stiff with ice. She made a sound like whew from every breath.

As John Gardner (1933–82), Gass's friend and critic, remarks: 'when we read Gass' fiction, especially his early fiction, we see not merely textures but people eating breakfast.' Gass is as much the elegiac poet of nature as he is of art, and his complaint is directed against the urban artifice that constitutes American reality:

> A man in the city has no natural thing by which to measure himself. His parks are potted plants. Nothing can live and remain free where he resides but the pigeon, starling, sparrow, spider, cockroach, mouse, moth, fly and weed, and he laments the existence of even these and makes his plans to poison them.
>
> ('In the Heart of the Heart of the Country')

It is somewhat misleading to quote Gass in order to prove the experiential basis of his fiction, for what Gass achieves is not so much a representation of reality as what John Gardner characterizes with a note of complaint 'the elaboration of texture for its own sake'. Nevertheless, the experiential basis should remind us that what passes for aestheticism in America is often inescapably marked by naturalism. Gass is no Mallarmé.

If one wants an example of the triumph of the aesthetic, the supreme instance is *Lolita* (1958), the masterpiece of Nabokov (1899–1977), an American novel by a writer of European sensibility. *Lolita* is a triumph of style and sensibility, which thoroughly sublimates its perverse subject-matter, the illicit relations between a man and a nymphet, a girl-child: a case of child-abuse, or is it a case of adult abuse? At the same time, the sense of American reality with its motels and shopping malls and the desolation in between is very powerful – at least as powerful as it is in the hands of realists like Updike, Ann Beattie (1947–) and Joan Didion (1934–).

The non-representational 'school' has its problems. How does the novelist free himself from the authority of the past, how does he avoid simply representing (that word again) the work of the past? John Barth has shown an acute awareness of the problem in an essay published in 1967, 'The Literature of Exhaustion', in which he speaks of the writer's sense of 'the used-upness of certain forms or exhaustion of certain possibilities'. Barth's essay is in a sense another version of the arguments made by Walter Jackson Bate (in *The Burden of the Past*, 1970) and Harold Bloom (in *The Anxiety of Influence*, 1973). Barth finds a 'solution' to the problem of exhaustion in the brilliant parasitism (not his word) of Jorge Luis Borges (1899–   ). In his brief fictions, Borges has found a way of reimagining or rather re-viewing the work of the great masters. The self-conscious, ironically intended repetition of an earlier work, may revive the earlier work, the way Barth vulnerably suggests Warhol adds new significance to Campbell Soup ads. Barth never demonstrates to my satisfaction how the repetition of the past (or at least his version of the repetition of the past) revives it. But he does explain at least the motive of his own work in a novel like *The Sot-Weed Factor* (1960), in which he reclaims the eighteenth-century novel as an opportunity for his unique, if not original, art by repeating it self-consciously.

In a recent essay, 'The Literature of Replenishment' (1982), Barth denies the view attributed to him subsequent to the publication of the earlier essay: 'that there is nothing left for contemporary writers but to parody and travesty our great predecessors in our exhausted medium – exactly what some critics deplore as postmodernism.' Instead he claims that what he has always meant is 'a transcension of the antithesis between modern and the pre-modern which would revitalize fiction'. Admirable as this intention is, there is, in my view, little evidence of vitality in the overly long, tedious, scarcely readable *Giles Goat-Boy* (1966) or *Letters* (1979). In his early work, *The Floating Opera* (1956) and *End of the Road* (1958), novels in the realistic mode, Barth showed an extraordinary brilliance and promise that he did not fulfill in his later work. His admiration for Borges, Nabokov and Beckett may have misled him about his own imaginative strengths.

It could be argued that the current hostility to realism among writers (even realists are often embarrassed to declare themselves as such) reflects the reality in which we live. *The Dead Father* (1975) of Donald Barthelme (1931–   ), for example, is pervaded by a surreal violence that has unhappily become part of the daily violence that we experience vicariously through the media, if not personally:

> One day in a wild place far from the city four men in dark suits with shirts and ties and attaché cases containing Uzi submachine guns seized me, saying that I was wrong and would always be wrong and they were not going to hurt me, first with can openers then with corkscrews. Then, splashing iodine on my several wounds, they sped with me on horseback through the gathering gloom.

This, of course, is terrorism – with the extravagant imagination of terrorism. Pick up *The New York Times* on almost any day (we need no longer turn to the yellow tabloids) and one encounters episodes of this kind. For example:

> Mrs Navaretti who was kidnapped Nov. 26 on her way home· from work at the International Training Center here, said she was kept in a tiny room 'without windows and so, so cold'. She said her captors chained her to a wall and cut off her hair, but gave her champagne and cake on Christmas Day.

Pure Barthelme.

Our daily life is what Barthelme describes only in the sense that the images and messages of television and of other media represent our life. They are the violent, stridently forced realizations of possibilities in our lives. Most of us have never been robbed or mugged and fear the possibility only because of the images projected by television and the newspapers. Barthelme differs from the media as conscious parody differs from unconscious parody. Blood in Barthelme is ketchup, skin is papier-mâché, though there may be the threat of something more in the *frisson* provoked by the punishment the Dead Father imagined for triflers:

> On the eighth the trifler is slid naked down a thousand-foot razor blade to the music of Karlheinz Stockhausen. On the ninth day the trifler is sewn together by children . . . On the eleventh day the trifler's stitches are removed by children wearing catcher's mitts on their right and left hands.

Barthelme's anti-realism is the realism of our media-determined and hence 'unreal reality'. (Gore Vidal, whose sense of reality is more traditional, has scornfully dismissed the fiction of Barthelme and Pynchon, among others, as 'plastic fiction'.)

That 'unreal reality' is partly constituted by our language, by the way we speak. Barthelme's realism also lies in his deadly ear for ordinary conversation, that is, for cliché, a power possessed by Flaubert and Joyce to name the greatest of Barthelme's predecessors. The effect of the representation of cliché may be irony — or it may be something beyond irony, an unaccountable fascination. In an early story printed in his first collection of stories, *Come Back, Dr Caligari* (1964), the hero, who is a broadcaster, singles out a word like *nevertheless*, which he repeats endlessly. In its exposure 'to the glare of public inspection the word frequently discloses new properties, unsuspected qualities'. Flaubert has described the aesthetics (a peculiarly modern aesthetics) of the fascination with the banal:

Such a wide gap separates me from the rest of the world that I am often surprised at hearing the simplest and most natural sounding statements. The most ordinary word fills me at times with boundless admiration. Certain gestures, certain inflections of voice fill me with wonder, and certain types of ineptness make me dizzy.

Unlike contemporary French experimental writing, which is invariably accompanied by ideological justification, American experimental writing does not pretend to the status of ideology. Robbe-Grillet, for instance, is openly reflective about the epistemology of his fiction, and he has found his perfect ideological critic in Roland Barthes. Barthelme's fiction is filled with intellectual allusions, even the appearance of intellectual argument which is animated by something like conviction (for instance, the moving passage on Kierkegaard's unfairness to Schlegel in the story with that title), but it is impossible to fix him to an idea. He seeks out 'strange ideas', outrageous combinations, and juxtapositions. The effects are often brilliant, comic, sometimes moving. If there is an ideological bias, he may share the view of the French anti-novelists that the human world lacks depth or transcendence. There is, for instance, no genuine mystery in *The Dead Father*, despite its surreal wildness. Perhaps, though this is only a guess, Barthelme is a latter-day aesthete for whom aesthetic 'purity is often consonant with madness', and 'madness in the pure state offers an alternative to the reign of right reason,' the content of which is rhetoric. But can we be sure, when in 'The Explanation' (the story in which this passage is to be found) he or rather the anonymous character asserts that the content of rhetoric is purity? Everything is turned to nonsense, and one is finally tempted to say that Barthelme's imagination is a parodic simulation of our spirit-alienated world.

All the writers I have discussed, whatever their aesthetic commitments may be, experience a kind of defeat in the face of American reality. It is too extravagant, too vulgar, too powerful, too confusing for the imagination to encompass. The Dickensian–Balzacian–Tolstoyan project of a confident total incorporation of the world is no longer possible. Obliquity, fragmentation are now the necessary aesthetic. There is another view that reality, the world out there, is insubstantial, perhaps radically insubstantial, a big Nothing. In French writing, Nothing is metaphysically reified. The American version is what has been called minimal art, an imagination of self and world, which in its terse economy, its bleak tone, its *will-lessness* represents (the specter of realism once again) the experience of emptiness in the world. In Ann Beattie, for example, the high hopes, the exhilarations of the sixties have produced a kind of 'hangover'. What she gives us in her first novel, *The Chilly Scenes of Winter* (1976) – she had already established a reputation for herself as a short-story writer – is an artful style of desultoriness. The life of a character in Ann Beattie's fiction is represented through uneventful external details:

Charles goes back to bed. He sees that Sam is already in bed in his room. He pulls the covers up over himself and falls asleep. He wakes up at five o'clock when the alarm goes off. He gets up, pushes in the button, and goes back to bed . . .

Nothing happens (as in Joseph Heller's *Something Happened*), but the very fact that Beattie tells her story in the mode of realistic narrative in which events follow one another in a logical consecutive manner (the element of randomness is minimal) preserves a sense of expectation and even promise: something might happen. Nor is the inner life of a character anaesthetically displaced to the external uneventfulness of the character's life. Suffering is the condition of Charles's (the central character's) existence, because then, as his sister

Susan tells him, 'you can be aware of yourself.' Suffering represents the inextinguishable desire for love, happiness, meaning.

Non-teleological narrative (the story that is apparently going nowhere) is a staple of many contemporary American fictions, however diverse the purposes of the fictions are. In Joan Didion's *A Book of Common Prayer* (1977), the heroine Charlotte Douglas lives in a motel in Boca Grande, a Latin American country, beset by revolutionary troubles. On a typical day, she would leave 'Warren sleeping and take the car and drive down the main street of whatever town it was to look for somewhere to spend an hour'. Charlotte belongs to what used to be called the idle rich. Though the form of her life is quite different from the form of the lives of Beattie's or Carver's characters, its essence is the same: an emptiness at the center. The narrator properly wonders: 'Maybe there is no motive role in this narrative.' Joan Didion is not a minimalist writer: *A Book of Common Prayer* possesses a high lyric eloquence that tries perhaps too hard to redeem the banality and emptiness of the lives of the characters. Sometimes the narrative sounds as if it is unfolding to the accompaniment of flamenco music. I interrupt my discussion of the art of Beattie here to show that the minimalist insight into the poverty of experience is shared by writers who are not minimalists.

In the stories of Raymond Carver (1938–　) (he has not written novels, because in his view the novel presupposes what he cannot presuppose: that the world makes sense), there is a terse perfection in the prose that suggests Hemingway: a code of art and of life, minimal as it is. Carver's characters are alcoholic, unemployed, occasionally violent to their spouses and children, victims of passion or circumstance. They are characters on the margins of middle-class life with the values and occupations of the middle class: sales people, teachers, business people, who nevertheless seem always on the brink of *lumpen* existence. They do not quite fall out of the middle class, but the threat of catastrophic failure seems always imminent. They live transient lives in rooms, apartments, and houses which either do not belong to them or to which they do not belong. Neither the utilities nor the furniture can ever be depended on – as if the external world had taken on the emotional uncertainty or inertia of the inner lives of the characters.

Beattie, Carver, and Donald Barthelme's younger brother,

Frederick (1943–), write at a time (it is the mood of the Carter, not the Reagan Administration) when there is a general sense that things have not only gone wrong, but that they will never be right again. America, the land of the future, suddenly seems at the end of its tether. Carver's fiction doesn't explicitly encompass conditions of structural unemployment, incorrigible violence in our cities, the closed frontier and our sense of baffled manifest destiny, but it has superbly caught the mood generated by these conditions.

The breakthrough of the Jewish novelist after the Second World War has been followed by other breakthroughs. Since the sixties we have seen the literary enfranchisement of blacks and women – and in writers like Toni Morrison (1931–) and Alice Walker (1944–), both black women, whose imaginations combine a pioneering realism and a lyric (and in Morrison's case, a Biblical) eloquence. Walker's portrait of the erotic intimacy between two black women in *The Color Purple* (1982) given to us in the illiterate vernacular of one of the women, is stunning in its graphic candor and its complexity of feeling. (The sense of extremity in black lives makes it inconceivable that a black writer would be a minimalist. Minimalism is a luxury only WASP writers can afford.)

Novels by blacks and women were written and published before the sixties. There is no novel by a black writer that compares to Ralph Ellison's *Invisible Man* (1952), and no woman novelist who surpasses Mary McCarthy (1912–) in her discursive and satiric intelligence. But these are isolated achievements and do not constitute a movement or a tradition. *Invisible Man* has as its inspiration American writers like Hemingway (who, on Ellison's own account, taught him accuracy of observation) and Faulkner, and European writers like Dostoevsky and Kafka. Both Ellison and James Baldwin (1924–87) found themselves in conscious rebellion against their precursor Richard Wright whom they believed suffered from a provinciality of imagination, despite the fact that Wright lived many years as an expatriate in Paris and was in contact with international figures like Sartre and Simone de Beauvoir. I will not enter here on the question of the justice of Ellison's view of Wright. What it signifies, however, is Ellison's desire to explore his experience as a human being and a Black with the fullest possible imaginative freedom. The sense of ambiguity of character, situation, role is so deep in *Invisible Man* that it resists any translation into message or ideology.

In the sixties, with the advent of the Civil Rights Movement, Ellison's imaginative freedom seemed inadequate to the needs of the struggle. More than any other writer, James Baldwin came to represent imaginatively and prophetically black aspiration in the sixties. Baldwin was by no means a simple ideologue. Or rather the ideological element in his writing (fiction and non-fiction) was informed by an extraordinary prophetic imagination. Baldwin had inherited the voice of his preacher father in a novel like *Go Tell It on the Mountain* (1953), or a 'sermon' like *The Fire Next Time* (1963). His sensitivity to human suffering, indignity, humiliation came not only from his black experience, but from his homosexual situation as well: see, for instance, his early novel, *Giovanni's Room* (1956). (One might remark in this connection the emergence of homosexual writers, Alfred Chester (1929–71), Hubert Selby (1928–), John Rechy (1934–) and Edmund White (1940–) among others whose work represents the extension of claims to rights and entitlements in the sixties. Gore Vidal (1925–) and Truman Capote (1924–84) have also written about homosexual experience, but they are not single-issue writers and they stand apart from any of the special pleading of single-issue writers.) Compelling as Baldwin's work was in the sixties, its strength was the preacher's strength to move his readers in the presence of scenes of suffering, not in the creation of narrative or characters. Baldwin's 'essays' are more impressive than his fiction.

In describing contemporary American fiction, I have avoided the term 'post-modern', a much abused term in contemporary literary discourse, because it tends to obfuscate rather than clarify the instances that support it. If by post-modern is meant a tendency towards the flattening of character and experience, an undermining of narrative and an exacerbation of the sense of randomness, a destruction of interiority and transcendence, the term may have some relevance to writers like John Barth and Donald Barthelme, but it hardly describes the contemporary scene as a whole.

It is a peculiar frustration of a comprehensive essay of this kind that writers of distinction are omitted from the discussion: William Gaddis (1922–), William Goyen (1915–), Cynthia Ozick

(1928–   ), Don DeLillo (1936–   ), Leslie Epstein (1938–   ),
among others. It is not simply that there is no space to include them:
it is rather that their work for reasons having to do with the vicissitudes of reputation rather than intrinsic merit has not yet been
assimilated into critical consciousness, so that it is difficult to place
them in the discussion.

CONTINUITY OR DISCONTINUITY IN AMERICAN LITERATURE?

SEYMOUR BETSKY

This chapter is addressed to a potential community with a special involvement in, perhaps a sense of urgency about, the status of literature in American culture. It will confine itself to contemporary American fiction: 'serious' novels, bestsellers, and those we identify as formulaic, or genre and sub-genre.

For the first time in American history conglomerates control the publishing industry. Technological innovation, proceeding at its own irresistible momentum, has moved from newspapers, magazines, and the stage, towards the end of the nineteenth century, to radio, film, popular music, present-day journalism, relentless advertising. Above all, TV reigns in its many forms: film, video tapes, cable, satellite. Audio cassettes have invaded literature as well. Electronic publishing can give subscribers novels via computers.

We seem, then, to inhabit a world of technological saturation that calls into question the very habit of reading, especially the reading of fiction. That environment educates with a far greater impact than the many kinds of formal education. Besides, anyone sensitized to the use of language, oral and written, must be deeply concerned about its serious impoverishment, about the debasement of currency. Journalism, even at the level of apparent respectability, politics, business, the criticism of film and of popular music, the world of fashion – all have co-opted the language of serious criticism and writing. How to rescue that language?

These questions invoke the concept of culture, which embodies the country's complex, dynamic vision, what it most deeply believes in and, far more important, lives out. According to that vision, the culture establishes a rough priority among its pursuits, and it rewards with wealth/possessions/property, status/prestige/privilege, and power/influence, those whose activities stand high among those priorities. And the culture employs certain distinctive means to attain its ends, principally modernization/rationalization. Accordingly, it transforms its world, human and non-human.

How, then, does the publishing industry mirror in every significant detail the culture within which it is embedded and lives out its sense of function? The culture assigns the publishing industry to the business sector of the economy. What has been distinctive about American culture, with a slow but increasing velocity in the decades following the Civil War, has been the emergence into unchallengeable power of concentrations, mergers, trusts, oligarchies, cartels, and the like. Alan Trachtenberg, in a book on the complex impact of corporations of those times, *The Incorporation of America: Culture and Society in the Gilded Age*, instances the earliest reaction of those who experienced its effects. 'The system of corporate life,' said Charles Francis Adams, Jr, in 1889, 'is a new power, for which our language contains no name.' And William Dean Howells, at the turn of the century, referred to 'our deeply incorporated civilisation'.

For purposes of convenience, one might use the shorthand phrase, 'Incorporated America' for the corporations, conglomerates, multinationals, takeovers and acquisitions in the present. *Fortune* lists the leading 500 to 1,000 corporations in size and assets, as each offers its goods and services. It provides also the basic categories of related businesses, some thirty in number, among which one finds 'publishing and printing'. *Forbes* follows suit, but adds the leading privately owned firms, among them S. Newhouse & Sons, which owns Random House, Alfred Knopf, Jr, Vintage Paperbacks, Pantheon, the Modern Library, hardback and paperback; and Ballantine Books, a mass-market paperback with some 7.2 per cent of that market.

To begin with, the 'strategy and structure' of corporate publishing resembles that of Incorporated America generally. The phrase comes from two books by Alfred D. Chandler, Jr, *Strategy and Structure: Chapters in the History of American Industrial Enterprise*; and *The Visible Hand: The Managerial Revolution in American Business*. Each follows the process of the rationalization and modernization of American business, starting with the railroads and extending to the present.

Rationalization/modernization now characterizes corporate publishing, the attempt to reduce the cost per unit through continual improvement of product and process and through efficient operation. Indeed, literary and cultural inquiry might now be able to place publishing in the period from the Civil War within an entrepreneurial structure, and see that it was then a commercial enterprise far more attuned to the market place than we may have believed.

For the sake of convenience, we may choose one representative example: Simon & Schuster, whose parent conglomerate is Gulf & Western Industries Inc. According to John Tebbel's authoritative *Between Covers*, the latter owns 'Paramount Pictures, paper and building firms, leisure activities companies, consumer products, natural resources, financial services, and manufacturing'. If we consult the indispensable yearly publication, *The Literary Marketplace*, we can learn, by name, rank and function in roughly hierarchical order, Simon & Schuster's top management and middle management. The Trade Book Division of the latter publishes fiction, as do some of the other groups: Adult Trade Paperback Publishing and Mass Paper. S. & S. has, also, a number of small, independently run subsidiaries which publish fiction: Summit Books, Linden Press, and Wyndham Books. Among its mass-market paperbacks we find Pocket Books, one of the largest. And S. & S. participates in the present-day growth industry in formulaic fiction: women's romances.

S. & S. does not, however, publish many textbooks or scholarly books. The former, as we shall learn, require an investment in the millions, far exceeding that for trade publications. However, Harcourt Brace Jovanovich, a conglomerate with forty acquisitions, publishes a substantial number of textbooks and scholarly works, as well as fiction and other general books, hardback and paperback. According to *Time* magazine, CBS 'sold off its entire educational and professional publishing operations for $500 million to giant Harcourt Brace Jovanovich.' Only a few years ago, H.B.J. had been in the forefront of those publishing fiction. No longer.

The structure and strategy of S. & S. discloses the process of rationalization/modernization characteristic of Incorporated America. Moreover, in the face of our present age of takeovers and acquisitions, conglomerate publishers owning subsidiaries have embarked on a protracted stage of shedding those which fail to return the kind of profit which make them appear desirable for acquisitions. As noted, CBS sold its educational and professional operations to Harcourt Brace Jovanovich. More recently Bertelsmann Verlag, the giant West German publishing empire, owner of the mass-market Bantam Books, acquired Doubleday Inc. (The Literary Guild, the mass-market Dell Books, Dial Press, and Doubleday Bookstores), which has just gone public. Gulf & Western, owners of Simon & Schuster, has in the past four years rid itself of some sixty-five diverse subsidiaries worth more than $4 billion. Will this be the fate of Simon & Schuster? Will other conglomerate-owned subsidiaries submit to the untethered logic of marketplace competitiveness?

In the first place, the goal of publishing, as of Incorporated America, is not only profit but planned profit of a kind commensurate with growth, expansion, stability and maybe continuity. If publishing practice delivers a devastating blow to the continuity of the fiction we respect, so much the worse for such fiction.

Unfortunately, nobody can predict what may, or may not, be a bestseller, only a *potential* one. In practice, then, each corporation 'organizes' democratic numbers in accordance with what it believes that public wants, or can be persuaded it wants. The proof of their calculations is profitable sales. These they trumpet. That their efforts fail more often than they succeed doesn't matter. It is the overwhelming effect on that public by the inferior product that has been so punishing.

Further, each corporation commands all the machinery that helps to arrange the response of the public it addresses. It can place responsibility on shareholders, on the decision-making process itself where responsibility evaporates in the intricacies, or even on the very public it solicits. Those who are heirs to the methods of America's nineteenth-century tycoons, according to Tebbel,

have been far more ruthless and efficient. If publishing did not fit the conventional business pattern they would, by God, be made to fit, and if that meant firing old employees from the top down who had given their lives to the business, it would be done without sentimentality.

Executives in publishing come more and more from concerns outside publishing and act accordingly. The rate of turnovers among executives – the whirl of musical chairs – has multiplied. Those whose performance is no longer satisfactory – their 'track record', in the language of the trade – are dismissed out of hand, however satisfactory that performance in the past or years of service.

'Perhaps the greatest change,' Tebbel writes, '. . . is the imposition of the corporate mentality in a business diametrically opposed to it in the past.' Yet, as Coser, Kashudin and Powell maintain, in *Books: The Craft and Commerce of Publishing* (1982), the editors, as well as others in Trade Book Publishing, embrace the ethos. This should occasion no surprise. The corporation makes available financial security and personal benefits through allocation of resources, and through financial and accounting expertise. Indeed, the common response of editors when asked about the possible disadvantages of their dependent status was 'None', or 'Nothing'. Their sole question was, 'How much money could it make?' Otherwise the book was viewed unfavourably. 'Money and power, the key words of the eighties, have never been consistent with the character of book publishing until now' (Tebbel). Now they are firmly entrenched from top management through the rank and file.

No other business can quite compare with publishing in yet another respect. Tebbel states that

> Books are thrown on the market with little or no preliminary research, a minimum of advertising and promotion in most cases, and are left to sink or swim; the retailer has the privilege of returning what he cannot sell. Nearly eighty percent of published books are financial *failures*. That would ruin most businesses in short order, and the only reason it has not ruined trade publishing is that, *if five books out of a hundred sell in large numbers, ninety-five others can safely make little or no money without bankrupting a publisher*. (Emphasis added)

In other words, a corporate publisher can, in all good conscience, call attention to the 'good' fiction the firm publishes each year. But at what expense, financial and psychic, to writers we respect?

The engine that drives the trade must be the search for the best-seller, or best-selling category, or the blockbuster.

As if these conclusions were not sufficiently sombre, Tebbel describes the boom for textbooks a decade after the Second World War, and quotes *Fortune* as characterizing the textbooks business as 'the fastest-growing, most remunerative and most fiercely competitive branch of book publishing'. By 1958, he comments,

> even though only one percent of American outlays for education were going into books, textbook sales were $280,000,000, with the elementary schools

accounting for $124,000,000; high schools $71,000,000; and colleges and universities $85,000,000. Textbook sales had nearly doubled since the close of the war.

Tebbel tells us that

by far the largest part of the book publishing business is embodied in that great complex of companies and activities producing educational, business, scientific, technical, and reference books and materials . . . seeing only the tip of the publishing iceberg – not more than twenty or twenty-five percent – people believe that publishing is trade books, book-stores, best-selling lists, and reviews . . . to publish a textbook may require an investment of millions *as opposed to a relatively few thousands for a novel or biography.* (Emphasis added)

The future belongs to the 'softcover publishers who have had to be innovative', Tebbel concludes.

They have been tending more and more toward originals designed for their markets, and they have been diversifying through a growing list of categories – romantic fiction, spy novels, thrillers, male adventure books, adult westerns, occult novels, and science fiction, among others. Of these the romance is the most popular, and the only category which has shown a steady growth for more than ten years, although the peak may have been reached.

Kenneth C. Davis informs us that Warner, Pocket Books, Bantam and NAL publish originals in this way. Tebbel comments:

. . . hardcover sales are now concentrated in best-selling blockbusters, while trade paperbacks carry on the book's enduring value and seem to represent the future that hardcover publishing once had.

The accepted word in publishing today is 'aggressive'. But that is an understatement. Incorporated America is fiercely, often lethally, competitive, and America in its fibre perhaps the most competitive of nations.

Not only do corporate publishers contend against each other, even in sales to libraries. Within a given corporation, like S. & S., its smaller units – Summit Books, for example – will compete against the parent company in bidding at an auction for the right to publish a mass-market paperback which it believes might be a bestseller, even though S. & S. owns Pocket Books. Even more, competition among firms knows no limits. The aim is, ultimately, to destroy competing corporations to a point where a 'shakeout' becomes inevitable. One firm, or one mass-market paperback, goes bankrupt, or is absorbed. In a time of takeovers and acquisitions, the predators lie in waiting. Trade publishers know that 80 per cent of the fiction they publish will fail. But so long as they can rescue five or six bestsellers or blockbusters out of ninety-five books sold they can make a profit. Moreover, among the books that fail are many 'good' novels to which publishers can in all good conscience call attention. How to sort them out? And how to stress that the average yearly wage for authors is $5,500, a sum below the poverty level?

For this is the way the culture appraises the publishing industry, placing it among goods and services for numbers. Trade book publishing has sales of about $4 billion annually; all of the publishing about $9.5 billion. It is a service industry of 'entertainment' — of diversion, distraction, relaxation, leisure. The trade uses the terms 'product', 'property' and 'commodity' for what it sells. Fiction, then, competes with other forms of democratized entertainment for numbers. We apply the word entertainment for sports; travel (democratized in the late nineteenth century, but not to the degree of thoroughness in our time); popular music; film; radio; gambling (the 'pointspread' business amounts to some $50 billion annually); and small fragmented pieces of entertainment in newspapers, magazines, and elsewhere; TV; hobbies.

Publishing spews forth fiction in a way which compares with other services in the culture: in quantity; in variety; in 'originality' and 'novelty', hyped by advertising; in built-in obsolescence; in imitations of the success of others; in spotting new trends and manufacturing a demand for them. We know, too, that books are a unique product. Any visit to a large university bookstore, or the New York Public Library, or the Library of Congress tells us so. But fiction publication manages to standardize its product through the categories it publishes, its fiction factories, its novelizations, and its brand-name celebrities. We may even compare a culture's 'durables' with fiction that yields a profit over the years through steady sales and reprints.

As the culture itself exhibits limitlessness and waste in goods and services, so publishing suffocates with a glut. Some 50,000 books are published each year; 5,106 novels in 1985. In 1986, *The New York*

Times Sunday Magazine Section recommended some sixty-seven hardback novels and some forty-seven paperbacks at the year's end. How to receive them? To glut we append waste. Some 40 per cent of the paperbacks are shredded; hundreds of novels remaindered, or returned to bookstores.

Nor can publishing corporations, like Incorporated America, tolerate stasis. Technological innovation has invaded publishing in a way that prompts us to use the phrase 'technological determinism'. We see it in efficient book designing; in the printing and binding of books through the rationalization/modernization of plants which now manufacture books in short-run or long-run terms to suit the respective demands of the market place. Electronic publishing has given publishers the videotext. Laser publishing is the latest invention. Word processors and computers are standard equipment. Many homes will be wired in a two-way system, formed by linking a home television with its own computer to an outside publisher. A subscriber is able to utilize a screen with that base. In this way he or she can read a novel on the home computer. With teletexts, signals are sent over the airwaves, instead of wires. Xerography and radio telephones speed the process of communication. *The New York Times* Sunday Book Review now advertises audio cassettes, enabling the buyer to listen to selected novels, hyped as 'great masterpieces'. The weight of earlier remarks descends near the conclusion of Tebbel's last chapter: 'It is hard for us to think of a time when the electronic age might make the book obsolete, as some economists have predicted.'

What we tend to overlook, yet take for granted, is the *cognitive* nature of the structures and strategies of publishing. Each firm faces the solution of problems – scores of them. The corporation adopts the model, basically, of scientific inquiry for the solution of the practical, the pragmatic, the marketable, the saleable. For the corporation, intelligence and sensibility belong to what, in the best sense of the word, we accept as the function of the I Q.

But the writer of the fiction we respect lives out a different order of function. A novelist at his (or, of course, her) best is a reflective, shaping, exploring, informed, and non-specialist intelligence and sensibility. He conveys as much as possible the wholeness, completeness, and fullness of experience in concrete immediacy. Of its nature such literature eschews generalization, abstractions, concepts, jargon, specialisms to the degree that each fails to provide example after example. It is, to repeat, exploratory. It has nothing to do with solving hard-facted, pragmatic, utilitarian problems. After all, the better writers are the culture's quintessential *individuals*. They are special in almost endless ways. All of them have their own distinctive inheritance.

Bellow's *The Adventures of Augie March* is, in its way, a microcosm of just such an inheritance. In the novel's retrospect, Augie accepts it as his 'fate'. The coherent theme of the novel becomes what he makes of fate so conceived, from a child of nine to a man in his thirties. His technique is a means of coming to terms with each of his experiences. Augie observes, reflects, discriminates, allows his speaking voice release as he addresses the reader, meets with one character after another and judges each, especially the more influential ones, by means of dramatizing each in speech and action. From one, he moves on to another, without abandoning those who continue to play a role in his life. In the end he may seem, ironically, to be trapped. But the novel's ending promises that he will again spring free and continue to elude a predetermined fate.

When the reader or, at the professional level, the critic responds to what a novel offers – a novel from the best to the bestseller – then he brings to it everything he may himself exemplify as a perceptive, sentient, informed, intelligent, and reflective self. Such literature has the effect, in whatever degree, of dislocating momentarily his own vision of experience, his own painfully achieved sense of order. Each of us in the presence of a powerful novel is forced to concentrate, to focus, to bring to a sensitized point that interrogation of the self in the culture, whose continuing goal is to win some measure of coherence in one's world in the face, ultimately, of chaos or death. For lesser novels the response is lesser.

What each critic conveys is a fusion of analysis, interpretation, judgement in a way each finds congenial. By analysis one means a command, implicitly or explicitly, of what we tend to call the 'techniques' each writer uses in the creation of a total, autonomous, imaginative world in full particularity. The critic's job of work is to show that he has been equal to what that work brings into being. Above all, the critic is especially sensitive to the degree the work comes alive, or fails to come alive, through the language.

'Interpretation' concerns what we have come to call the 'intention' of the novel, but, inseparably, the degree to which that intention has been successfully realized in all degrees, or fails of realization. Suffusing the whole, from start to finish, is the overarching control of judgement, or evaluation. These concern the relative significance or insignificance of what a given novel imparts. In most cases what we confront is moral imagination, intelligence, and sensibility.

What makes criticism at its best one of the finest disciplines – a discipline as tough as mathematics, or physics, or molecular biology, or medicine, or psychiatry – is the process of responsiveness which manifests itself in the organized critiques and which evolves, shifts and changes through a lifetime. Responsiveness, then, becomes a way of life.

Yet responsiveness to language has become infinitely harder as language itself has been 'incorporated'. In *The Dean's December*, Saul Bellow's protagonist, Albert Corde, erupts with passion about the articles he had written for *Harper's*: 'Again, the high intention – to prevent the American language idea from being pounded into dust altogether.' The American language has, indeed, been 'pounded into dust'. Some words have lost any meaning we can attach to them: 'goods', 'services', 'entertainment', 'the American dream', 'pluralism', 'good', 'evil', 'love', 'friendship', 'virtue', 'vice': dozens of them. Some of them – again dozens – convey Orwellian 'doublespeak', particularly the language of politics, government and business. Faceless, sapless men and women slash linguistic budgets relentlessly. In the world of publishing they have used the language to place the stamp of Darwinian competitiveness on the industry in the name of 'efficiency'. A good writer must, apparently, be an efficient one. The worlds of fashion, film and TV criticism, of popular song, and of journalism have co-opted the language of serious criticism. Again, dozens of examples: 'aesthetic', 'poetic', 'distinguished', 'original', 'romantic', 'myth', 'archetype', 'significant', 'successfully realized', 'sensitive', 'fantasy', 'gothic', 'serious', 'mainstream'. Words we like to think of as validated in our tradition suffer the same pounding: 'honor', 'courage', 'wisdom', 'loyalty', 'dignity', 'faith', 'pride'. Virtually every discipline or activity can be 'creative', 'imaginative', 'classic'. All products, including fiction, are 'quality-controlled'.

Investigations into literature and cultural inquiry, into this confusion of tongues, this universal flattening and evisceration of discernible meaning, are necessarily long-range. But the active matrix
consists of critic/scholars and writers who regularly carry out first-
hand, independent criticism of fiction, beginning in the present with
novels fresh off the press. What each critic places before an ex-
changing community are succinct or extended written demonstrations that of their nature invite agreement, differences and qualifications.

Out of agreement and disagreement with particular judgements of value a
sense of value in the concrete will define itself, and without this, no amount
of talk about 'values' in the abstract is worth anything.

Over a period of time the more satisfactory, the more convincing,
critiques prevail. At least that is the view, the faith, for literature and
cultural inquiry. Only a compilation of good critical practice for
particular novels will confirm that faith.

The validating community beyond our finest critics is, potentially,
a large one. It includes literary scholars, cultural commentators and
historians of letters; teachers of literature who have practised first-
hand criticism over the years and students who have shown aptitude;
men and women in publishing who refuse to be constricted by
conglomerate standards and who opt for the best, the better, and the
good fiction; men and women in non-literary disciplines willing to
read with us as we have proved abundantly a willingness to read
their works; and the Common Reader, if he or she exists.

In the end we live with a faith that a sufficiently large number of
individuals exist who thirst for novels which corporate publishing
does not provide and who feel suffocated by a cultural environment
of technological determinism, best-selling hype, and hard-sell
advertising. How they may be rallied remains the problem. In the
meantime, the best one can hope for is that local groups at this or
that college and university, or this or that metropolitan centre, or
this or that respected periodical, will each in their own way keep
alive the habit, the discipline, of intelligent reading and discussion.

PART V:
BIBLIOGRAPHY
COMPILED BY PETER DAVISON

CONTINUITY IN DISCONTINUITY
LITERATURE IN THE AMERICAN
SITUATION

WARNER BERTHOFF

The cultural as well as political and institutional history of the United States differs in one clearly documented respect from that of other European and Atlantic nations: it comes down from originating covenants that lack immemorial authority. Whatever privileged standing is claimed for these covenants, they remain vulnerable to the recollection that they were enacted by identifiable persons with identifiable prejudices and life-interests who were addressing the predicaments of a particular historical moment. Accordingly they may always be re-opened, submitted again on any freshly contested issue to point-for-point renegotiation. So in national politics, although the 1787 Constitution and its framers are routinely glorified in public discourse, every actual or alleged historical crisis releases bluff new proposals for reinterpretation and revision, if not for a new constitutional convention to refashion a charter now perceived as antiquated and procedurally inadequate. Characteristically the basic documents, where these survive, contain substantial reminders of their own historical provisionality, as in the counter-prophecy of possible failure underscoring Winthrop's 'city on a hill' peroration in 1630 or the amendment clause – justly valued but too often imprudently invoked – in the Constitution itself.

By the same long-term reckoning – the native Indian patrimony being destroyed root and branch – no North American pre-history intangibly constrains later choices and undertakings. For the culture generally there is no mystery of origins. A definite and memorable past certainly exists, but its acts and assumptions remain at the mercy of present purposes; their intermittent sacralizing by one or another interested party or faction only confirms the fitfulness, at best, of their continuing influence. There is indeed, we may say, a historic continuity in American cultural life, but one of its key principles appears to be a radical disrespect for cultural continuousness as a source of strength and value.

The American art critic Harold Rosenberg, himself an irreverent jack-of-all-critical-trades, had a clear vision of this principled discontinuity, this diachronic radicalism and fragmentation in cultural matters. The explosion of 'action painting' after 1945 crystallized his perception of it, so that Rosenberg first tended to think of it as a distinctively modern (and 'modernist') development. Yet the more he explored it as a determining attitude, the more he had to acknowledge its extension backward across the whole of American history. (It becomes, if we accept the analysis, one more exemplification of Tocqueville's theorem that the peculiar improvisations of American behavior are a forecast of the general human future, however offensive they appear to settled tastes.) In anatomizing this 'tradition of the new', as he named it, Rosenberg understood that it was not simply an affair of ignorance or forgetfulness, the uninstructed disregard of later times for their forerunners' accomplishment. In America that disregard repeatedly proved to have been part and parcel of the accomplishment itself. The 'best examples' of American art, Rosenberg contended, 'consist of individual inventions which do not carry over into the future', in no small part because an indifference to the concept of inaugurating transmittable legacies was as essential to their formation as an indifference to receiving one and passing it forward.

As soon as we propose any such rule important exceptions come promptly to mind. For American writing none looks more consequential than that of Walt Whitman, who offered himself and his book together as generative nourishment for the future and who in time became a recognizable – and recognized – progenitor ('pigheaded father', Ezra Pound would say) of voices as different as Wallace Stevens and Henry Miller, T. S. Eliot and Allen Ginsberg. But the legacy Whitman assembled for his successors is shot through with self-denials. The poem of death that D. H. Lawrence saw all Whitman's work as composing includes, at its acquiescent center, the death, the self-immolation, of the poet's own life-project. 'Who learns my lesson complete' learns first of all that 'it is no lesson'. Its best effect will be to open the field again (the metaphor of another neo-Whitmanian, the San Franciscan Robert Duncan) and leave it

clear for something equally self-engendered and, in turn, self-deny-
ing – in the end it only 'lets down the bars to a good lesson,/And
that to another, and every one to another still.' Whitman's delivered
achievement is thus not finally to be different, historically, from
Homer's or Virgil's, Shakespeare's and Tennyson's. To the ever-
devouring present it, too, will in time be 'gone, dissolv'd utterly like
an exhalation . . ./Pass'd to its charnel vault.' Even in its moment of
triumph the poet's work is only illusorily an object to be acquired
and transmitted for future gain, future Arnoldian acculturations (and
Whitman, examining the Arnold of *Culture and Anarchy*, recognized
at once a national enemy). The true locus of the work's value, for
Whitman, is something that begins disappearing from it the moment
it is printed and bound. The valedictory poem 'So Long' sums the
matter up: 'Camerado, this is no book,/Who touches this touches a
man.'

For Whitman as for Emerson before him, setting out to write his
book not merely as if no one else had ever yet written to sufficient
purpose but as if bookishness of any sort was a trap to the generative
spirit may be seen as making a virtue of historical necessity. If he
found in Emerson's essay 'The Poet' an outline of what he himself
meant to accomplish, he found little else in earlier American literature to help him substantiate it. More uncertainty hangs about
Whitman's original project, the 1855 *Leaves of Grass*, than is
commonly allowed. Even its grandly assertive preface (not, we
discover, a particularly accurate guide to the poetry itself) has its
hesitancies, its self-reservations. If the new master poet should find
himself unready for his imperial task, 'let him merge in the general
run and wait his development'. This, too, masks unstable assumptions. In order to have great poets, Whitman announced – in a
proposition that became the magazine *Poetry*'s cover slogan during
the literary renaissance of 1912 and after, though it seemed to the
brashly contentious young Pound to have got the matter exactly
backwards – you must first have a great audience. That is, you must
be able to trust re-entering that 'general run', the commonwealth of
everyday life and speech, to gain the powers you need.

For Emerson, however, it was just this kind of nourishing environment that America's 'Jacobin manners' could not provide.
'Why is there no genius in the Fine Arts in this country?' Emerson

asked himself at the moment of completing his own first book, the apocalypse-minded *Nature* (1836), and gave as a main answer, 'They are not called out by the genius of the people.' Further, if some such popular genius could be shown to exist, would it in the end be any less harmful to self-fulfillment than either foreign or antique genius, with their distracting perspectives? 'All genius [is] fatal to genius,' Emerson coincidentally declared; 'genius hurts us by its excessive influence, hurts the freedom and inborn faculty of the individual . . .' The undecidability of the whole matter answered to Emerson's own ambivalence about native prospects, starting with his own. A deep-seated fear of inauthenticity, of falseness to some essential frame of self-being, seems the dominant motive. But this in turn was undercut by complementary fears of solipsism and disconnection, above all of a debilitating private indigence.[1] There comes a point in one's march into life, Emerson acknowledged, when self-trust may become indistinguishable from self-deprivation. A single journal sentence in October of 1836 anticipates failure even as it defines the extenuating circumstance. 'The literary man in this country has no critic'; that is, no dialogic 'other' to provoke him to his proper growth. The occasionally strident assertiveness with which in *Nature* and 'The American Scholar' (1837) Emerson proclaimed an end to America's imaginative dependency has this realistic assessment and prognosis as its dark opposite.

A conventional explanation for American-provincial anxieties about inadequate preparation and the want of proper resources was the brevity of the country's 'Civil History' – Emerson's phrase – and the unsettledness and unreadiness of new world undertakings generally. Two and a half centuries past the original English settlements the young Henry James, setting off in the track of Balzac and George Eliot but conscious of peculiar obstacles, could still decry 'our great unendowed, unfurnished, unentertained and unentertaining continent, where we all sit sniffing, as it were, the very earth of our foundations'. James's well-remembered list, in his biography of Hawthorne, of all that was absent from American life and culture, a list compiled by way of commemorating Hawthorne's struggle with the demon of provinciality, had been anticipated by Hawthorne himself and by Fenimore Cooper as each described the special difficulties besetting the vocation of authorship in the United States.

'Poverty of materials' was one such difficulty, Cooper wrote in *Notions of the Americans* (1828). But at least equal to it was the absence of a distinctive authorial tradition. (America, Cooper reminded his readers, is that country which had printers before it had authors.) For Cooper the choice made a century and a half later by James and Pound, Gertrude Stein and Eliot and even, briefly, Robert Frost – to find a world elsewhere to do their work in and have it intelligently received – would have been no more than plain good sense. There is an abundance of everything 'useful and respectable' in American life, Cooper witheringly remarked (himself in France at the time), but the promiscuity of its development and dissemination will indicate 'but one direction to the man of genius'.

Yet any such historical scenario, if we try to match it to actual events, will be rife with contradictions. Cooper and Hawthorne are themselves representative instances. At the moment of directing their energies to literature neither was noticeably embarrassed by a lack of American materials and resources; once on the job, neither wrote as if appealing primarily for European acceptance. That historic accumulation of 'picturesque and gloomy wrong' that Hawthorne congratulated his native land on having so far escaped – this in a preface (to *The Marble Faun*) written on the eve of a national war over the reality of chattel slavery! – was in fact the substance of what his diligent mining of colonial New England records and recollections had repeatedly brought to light, and its impingement on the lives of succeeding generations became one of his richest themes. Also, the recurrent forms of his storytelling borrow from and renew those of the black-browed Puritan forebears he apologized to for his frivolous vocation: the exemplifying moral fable or anecdote, the canvass of spiritual and imaginative 'evidences', the expository divination of the 'types' of human destiny. Cooper too, becoming historian and mythographer of two centuries of North American settlement and expansion, was following in the path not only of Walter Scott's Waverley project but of the chief secular enterprise of American prose in the colonial period: the historiographic chronicling in one new colony after another of new-world community building.

The guild industry of American literary scholarship has, to be sure, a professional stake in demonstrating recurrence and self-propagation in all aspects of the American literary record (a demonstration easier to bring off when the whole grand subject is treated in course-syllabus isolation). An inquiry searching beneath completed texts to discover their full historical origins – where, repeatedly, some European impetus turns up as decisive to renewal – is likely to suggest a different emphasis. (In outlook and practice the major American writers have been, in the main, less parochial than their scholarly guardians.) Yet across palpable gaps and separations in the actual lines of descent, similarities do catch our notice; and if in particular we ask what it is that the writers in question have persistently elected to write *about*, it proves easy enough to show that from the start American literature has held with remarkable tenacity to a concentrated set of imaginative subjects and occasions.

'Theme alone can steady us down', Frost remarked (standing firm against modernism's dream of a wholly self-determined art). If we accept this as belonging to any reasonable methodology for literary historians as well, we find that a very substantial portion of the American writing which survives with imaginative force has attached itself to one – at its strongest to both – of two encompassing themes: (i) the covenants of settlement and community, projected but then in some fashion betrayed and broken in the vicissitudes of new-world history; and (ii) the fortunes of liberated and unsponsored selfhood within a social or else cosmic order that appears to punish success and failure alike with devastating impartiality. We may understand the persistence of these themes as a residue of older religious and sectarian passions. Or we may take them as embodying the anxious self-absorption of a massively triumphant yet fearful entrepreneurial majority. (Both views, in the American context, carry conviction.) Either way, they seem altogether appropriate for a national population which has never yet achieved a steady-state communal identity; a people whose ordinary conduct required Tocqueville, at precisely the onset of America's self-transformation from classical republic to modern imperium, to float a term –'individualism' – unknown at the time except to a small cadre of visionary Saint-Simonians.

Limiting examples to the period following independence and the first surge of the population westward, we can identify a full-scale myth of settlement and its disheartening aftermath not only in Cooper's *The Pioneers* and *The Prairie* in the 1820s but, during the next decade, in James Hall's *Legends of the West*, William Gilmore Simms's frontier romance *Guy Rivers*, Cooper's Templeton (Cooperstown) sequel *Home As Found*, and Caroline Kirkland's sprightly and self-mocking *A New Home – Who'll Follow?*; in popular works like *Mysteries of the Backwoods* (1846) and *Roughing It* (1871) but also, as a formative metaphor and counter-theme, in *Walden* and in Whitman's prophetic verse; and, taken up again though without discernible back-reference, in Willa Cather's Nebraska chronicles (*O Pioneers!*, *My Ántonia*), Faulkner's Yoknapatawpha saga (most notably *Absalom, Absalom!* and *Go Down, Moses*), and, framing the separate 'tales and persons', in *Winesburg, Ohio* and the *Spoon River Anthology*.

But with each of these chronicles of settlement, the theme of selfhood – its prospects, actions, and ultimate vexation – at some point becomes equally compelling. The best, the classic American books almost invariably combine these dominant themes, as with the figural extravagance of *The Great Gatsby*'s closing paragraphs or, awkwardly and incompletely, the master-projects of Hart Crane (*The Bridge*) and William Carlos Williams (*Paterson*). (A casually brilliant early instance is Washington Irving's 'Rip Van Winkle', refashioned from a German original into the first secular American fable of, at once, lighting out for the territory and re-emerging an immigrant and stranger in the place of one's birth. A decade before, in the confessional romance of *Arthur Mervyn* (1799–1800), Charles Brockden Brown singlehandedly projected, though without direct successors, a comparable double myth of, literally, diseased community and enforced estrangement and isolation.) Titles tell us, normally, where the main emphasis is to fall, and the mode of narration normally confirms this emphasis. In Anderson's *Winesburg* an anonymous author-recorder overhears a whole community, one broken before it has properly formed, rehearsing its back-street transformations, its catastrophic secret history; in *The Great Gatsby* a specified first-person witness reconstructs the dream and its consequence, both grotesque, of a spectral alter ego and in the process enters upon his own unappealable American fortune.

When attention shifts to matters of form, and of expressive range, tonality, and purpose, the American bias toward first-person utterance can appear so insistent as to establish a kind of cultural voiceprint. The expressive seductions of this formal mode, in or out of the vernacular, seem irresistible. Even novelists of objective social interchange like James and Dreiser, Edith Wharton, Dos Passos, and Faulkner, Flannery O'Connor and Norman Mailer can come through to us as extruders of visionary monologues. (Over time, Tocqueville prophetically argued, America's democratic–egalitarian society 'turns imagination away from all that is external to man'; its poets 'render passions and ideas rather than persons and acts'.) In both prose fiction and poetry the collective first-person openings of the Declaration of Independence and the federal Constitution – 'we hold these truths', 'we the people' – break up into an infinitude of private impersonation. The work of coercing assent begins with an act of self-projection. 'Call me Ishmael', 'Let me call myself, for the present, William Wilson', 'I celebrate myself', 'I saw the best minds of my generation', 'I am alive – I guess –', 'I am a rather elderly man', 'Here I am, an old man . . .', 'In my younger and more vulnerable years', 'You don't know about me without you have read . . .', 'If you really want to hear about it, the first thing you'll probably want to know is where I was born, and what my lousy childhood was like', 'I am an invisible man', 'I am living at the Villa Borghese', 'It's my lunch hour, so I go/ For a walk', 'What made me take this trip to Africa?', 'In a sense, I am Jacob Horner' – in some such fashion, rather than with 'It is a truth universally acknowledged' or 'The Brangwens had lived for generations on the Marsh Farm', the American literary imagination settles itself, in one text after another, to its chosen tasks.[2]

But for a full historical accounting the question must be: what imaginative gain is there in these recurrences? Does the earlier work prepare the way for the later? Does it make easier or more incisive the discoveries and performative realizations that keep both art and consciousness alive? Does it help secure for them more appreciative audiences? Or must the game be started up again each time, as if only dead reckoning and the dismissal of registered landmarks will bring the writer through to where – 'just go[ing] on nerve', in Frank O'Hara's jaunty formulation – he/she proposes to go? A joke from the complementary disarray of local American topography speaks resignedly to these analytic issues. Somewhere in the unmarked interior – Maine woods, Tennessee knobs and hollows, Minnesota lakes: it doesn't matter where precisely – a traveler asks directions to the next point of interest; after due meditation the reply comes, without surprise: 'Nope, can't get there from here.' To 'get' from one salient achievement to another in American writing can be harder than it looks. (By contrast, French literature after the Renaissance, or Russian after Pushkin, has both the appearance and the creative advantage of an unbroken family argument.) Arguably the continuities proposed by scholarship on the basis, in turn, of Hawthorne's Puritan researches, James's critical reconsideration of Hawthorne's provinciality, and Eliot's insistence on the 'Hawthorne aspect' of James's career have muddied rather than stabilized the business, with each of these authors, of accurate definition and assessment.

In any case the task of linking Roger Williams to Benjamin Franklin (both New Englanders), Franklin to Brockden Brown (both Philadelphians), the New Yorker Irving to either Melville (for travel description) or Mark Twain (for humor), Emily Dickinson to any male or female successor, or Cooper to Fitzgerald to Thomas Pynchon (see my chapter on Fitzgerald and Hemingway, above), is unlikely to yield to merely tabulative – or typological – explanations. Oliver Wendell Holmes, writing Emerson's life in 1884, postulated a direct route from Jonathan Edwards's reconstituted Calvinism in the eighteenth century to Emerson's transcendentalism in the nineteenth, a thesis authoritatively expanded and reinforced by the historian Perry Miller in the 1930s. Given the peculiar durability of the New England character and outlook, this would seem a relatively easy route to mark and keep open; yet in the last twenty years revisionist erosions and new-new-critical frost heaves have pretty well shut it down to ordinary literary–historical traffic. Dr Holmes also identified in Emerson's practice of poetry a technical principle – setting each line to 'the normal respiratory measure' – which would resurface a century later in William Carlos Williams's open metric and Charles Olson's 'projective verse'; typically, however, there is no evidence that either Williams or Olson, at the point of innovation, actually considered the Emersonian precedent or even recognized, after the fact, their kinship with it.

*

Repetition without acknowledgement, renewal without either the advantages or the satisfactions of hereditary fulfillment – the pattern asserts itself so strongly that, beyond circumstantial obstacles, what we might also look for throughout American literary history is some active principle of deterrence, some peremptory inward resistance to any accreditation seen as deriving from past authority or proposed as essential to present and future cultural health. A sense of some such principled resistance and refusal, more dangerous to the commonwealth than mere ignorance of rules, fired Henry James's reaction, in 1865, to the revolutionary poetics of Walt Whitman. (The really damaging consideration, James wrote, is that Mr Whitman's verse does what it does 'on theory, willfully, consciously, arrogantly'.) James himself long afterwards spoke of his brisk review of *Drum Taps* as a 'little atrocity perpetrated ... in the gross impudence of youth', but there is both force and logic in the argument it advances of a necessary sublimation of selfhood and merely personal striving in any art not self-condemned to eccentricity. The same argument, restyled into a quasi-scientific flintiness worthy of Poe, would organize the young Eliot's influential account half a century later of the necessary relations between 'tradition' and 'individual talent'. It is a recognizably American argument, or counter-argument (oddly renewed, in an inside-out way, by recent American-academic speculations about anxieties of influence and a wholly burdensome literary past). The disposition it attacks is presumed to be both deep-rooted and long-lived, an aboriginal if not necessarily unremovable obstruction.

As indeed proves to be the historical case. The first *gran rifiuto* in American letters occurred several years in advance of the settlement of New England; it was the decision by John Cotton of Emmanuel College, Cambridge, not to continue preaching in the erudite and 'oratorious' manner which, according to his first biographer, had made him locally famous as 'another Xenophon, or Musa Attica'. Cotton's spirit 'now savoring of the cross of Christ more than of humane literature' (John Norton, *Abel Being Dead Yet Speaketh*), he rejected an established virtuosity with school rhetoric in favor of the unmediated word and wisdom of God, to the openly expressed disgust of the university wits who had gathered to hear him. It would be stretching matters to say that Cotton's stylistic self-reversal founded a distinctive new-world literary culture, or that it historically determined a similar confrontation in the other Cambridge two and a quarter centuries later between Emerson and certain scandalized auditors of his 'Address' at the Harvard Divinity School. Nevertheless the principle it answered to, a principle splitting open the religious and political culture of the Bay Colony itself within the first decade of its founding, fostered at least two further centuries of invigorating doctrinal conflict and broke down that original cultural consensus into, so far, an endless sequence of contentiously programmatic reconstructions.

The doctrinal name this principle bore in the Puritan 1630s – antinomianism – is awkward to recover, though it retains real diagnostic value. But it was still alive as a fighting term during Emerson's nineteenth-century coming of age, to identify a generalized rejection of models and received lessons that could prove as cramping or narrowing as it was initially exhilarating. ('Beware of Antinomianism', Emerson told himself, as if to acknowledge his own fresh incubation of the old virus.) The unity even in dispute of the original New England culture is, of course, long vanished, and the active 'dissidence or dissent' which, not less than hope of a perfected covenant, fortified Puritan morale now finds expression, where it survives, in sharply altered contexts; but its latter-day dispersion and institutional centerlessness have not seriously weakened its attraction as a pragmatic alternative. To miss the antinomian solution's continuing appeal as a way of addressing modern discontents – paradoxically it works now to produce new secular orthodoxies, like biological Creationism, literary-critical 'deconstruction', a supply-side political economy – is to find oneself unprepared for that recurrent moment in American writing, and in American behavior generally, when the slate is scrubbed clean, established practices and restraints go out the window, and a self-born purity of both intention and execution becomes the only tolerable goal.

It may seem evasively scholastic to attach a seventeenth-century religious term and concept to the description of nineteenth- and twentieth-century cultural patterns. Yet to a degree that may call to mind Islamic attitudes and habituations more than those of the industrialized sister-societies of western Europe, American religiousness has tenaciously resisted marginalization in the power and legitimation struggles of modern mass society. The habit of dissidence, the chronic *ressentiment*, that are a main legacy of post-Puritan sectarianism have on the whole gained force within the national culture from their convergence with modern socio-political displacements and uprootings. In the contexts of secular life, however, this habit of disrespect for continuity-asserting authority, or for anything too fulsomely identified as established and respect-worthy, is probably better described under the secular heading of *populism* – but a populism, in its American manifestation, bent less on defending and restoring social usages overborne in the power conspiracies of modern history than on willing its own self-organized, self-determined, untrammeled and limitless future. (There is such a thing, for example, in the famously socialism-resistant United States, as libertarian-capitalist populism, and no one has proved more adroit than the President it swept into office in 1980 at turning its ahistorical mythology to political advantage.)

What American antinomianism and American populism have in common as cultural universals is above all the dream of an exemption from history, an escape from either continuity or consequence in the cycles of elected experience. This is the real latter-day American dream. The original myth of a new historical beginning – more than that, of a new beginning that would prove the last prefiguration of the great ending promised in Scripture itself – persists, reduced and simplified, in the fantasy of a release from servitude to everything circumstantial and accruent in actual life. The society that, according to subjective need, would make itself over at every moment knows this servitude as its greatest fear: a servitude, or vulnerability, to the mere succession of what happens which (as Charles Ives acutely observed of Hawthorne's narratives), though it is first apprehended as 'something personal', turns ' "national" suddenly at twilight, and universal suddenly at midnight' (*Essays Before a Sonata*). It thus takes hold as the American imagination's defining nightmare. Exemption from history, and the retribution the desire for it inevitably exacts: isn't this the core theme and controlling narrative logic in such books as *Huckleberry Finn* and *The Great Gatsby*, *Tropic of Cancer* and *The Wild Palms*, *Catch-22* and even *Invisible Man*, books in each instance like no other in their first audience's immediate experience but for just that reason all the more classically 'American' in structure and motive?[3]

Yet there is a deflecting temptation in all such theorizing (one confirming, perhaps, the very distemper it seeks to identify and interpret). It is the temptation not simply to cramp the historical data into too narrow an explanatory frame but to misconceive and misrepresent their fundamental mode of existence within actual societies, actual history. All art is more one-sided, as Pasternak said, than people think; and however determined (or self-determining) literary history may appear to hindsight, it is like other kinds of history in being more accident-prone, and more incalculable, than – just at present – either its scholar-guardians or its demystifiers are inclined to allow. The living community of literature is never identical with society as a whole. One of the real lacunae in contemporary literary theory is an orderly understanding, or even a clear exploratory idea, of this jagged relation; an understanding of how, in brief, the sub-society engaged in serious literary production – readers as well as writers – maintains and renews itself and establishes whatever canons of preference contrive to dominate the next era. In particular the volatile mix of popular and esoteric influences at work in anything generously creative tends to escape critical accounting, and does so in roughly the same degree as it surprises established expectations: a paradigm nicely exemplified by the formal originality and, coincidentally, muddled critical reception of *Moby-Dick*, of *Huckleberry Finn*, and of *The Waste Land* (to cite instances of unimpeachable importance).

This elusiveness in the character of the genuinely new and enlivening is something to keep in mind in any effort to calculate future developments – a questionable undertaking at best but, once we pass our first youth, a distressingly natural one. Assumptions persist, for example, that the chief threat to a literature of serious social and moral consequence derives from the vulgarizations of a popular culture backed by the whole weight of modern technocratic programming and possessing now an electronically magnified power to lower standards and subvert imaginative judgement. Yet one may soberly doubt whether in the United States the over-all social framework which – these are Proust's succinct terms for the issue in question – 'supports an art and certifies its authenticity' is any more in hostage now to meretricious excitements and prepossessions than it was in the age (Hawthorne's, Whitman's) of family-magazine sentimentalism and frenzied popular religious revivals, or the age (Dreiser's, Edith Wharton's) of a vaudevillized theater, the yellow press, and the newly invented cinema's narcotic seductions.

In any case complaints about vulgarization are pointless if they rise in the first place from sheer unresponsiveness, or from a self-approving indifference to such unexpected openings to originality and fresh expressive power as materialized around 1960, notwithstanding mountains of dross, in both *nouvelle vague* film-making and the improvised collaborations and adaptations of a mass-marketed popular music: the Beatles, Bob Dylan, Jimi Hendrix, for starters. If a serious art were ever to sustain itself out of this commercialized hurly-burly – as Shakespeare's theater inexplicably arose out of the bear-garden, amusement park, blood-and-gore sensationalism of popular London culture in the 1580s, in combination with an imported humanism and problematic new science – it would doubtless be troublesome and confusing to accommodate critically. It might well be an art not immediately recognized as offering, in its own opportunistic fashion, life-serving refreshment; an art and literature (as Stephen Spender innocently surmised half a century ago, trying to imagine what might succeed the disintegrating culture of bourgeois liberalism) 'of jokes, free association, dream imagery – all the accidents of wit and beauty, childhood and death, which strike us suddenly when we are in the street'; an art as erratic in its contrivances and as desperately salvaged from confusion as may be imagined, yet once again available to the combinatory inventiveness of genius, of intensified local collaboration, or of whatever we think it is that in this year and not some other year brings forth – to everyone's surprise – a genuinely new voice and new word.

That there are serious and possibly unprecedented obstacles to any such happy development, obstacles deriving from those 'new social conditions of culture' described by Alan Trachtenberg above, is no great secret. As of the late 1980s it would seem that the writer who is to make a genuine difference to the whole cultural estate will need 'more than ever' – more even than seemed the case to Henry James, when a century earlier he defined this distinctively American need – 'to be a master'. Perhaps a reversion to tribalization, an escape from adverse circumstance into self-contained enclaves that have given up any effort to speak for the common shared condition – ethnic or feminist enclaves, specialized occupational subgroups converging for self-security upon the workshop concerns that once bound together artisanal communities, even university campuses if all else fails – will continue to support whatever degree of realization remains in prospect for writers of the era ahead. In some such fashion, in recent years, both the most talented younger writers and others less young have managed to find audiences sufficient to keep them going: Toni Morrison as well as Grace Paley and Philip Roth, Brad Leithauser as well as John Ashbery and Adrienne Rich. So with some gallantry (and risk) Frank O'Hara did among the New York painters and dancers as well as fellow poets of the 1950s and 1960s, and so too – well short of his most grandiose ambition but securely enough to compile an indispensable contemporary record – has Norman Mailer, the last American author to think it natural and reasonable to devote himself on something like a national scale to 'making a revolution in the consciousness of our time'.

In all such conjecture the moment of utterance leaves its mark. By common agreement the present moment in American writing is not a grandly distinguished one. In its diminished characterizations, its attenuations of emotion and purpose, its prevailing flatness of idiom, its forced or borrowed ingenuities of design, its despair of imaginative mastery, it might well be compared with the closing years of the last century, when – through the 1880s and 1890s – the generation of Emerson, Melville, and Whitman fell silent, gifted younger talents died insufficiently tested (like Stephen Crane) or were disappointingly realized (like Howells), the art of poetry was the preserve of Edmund Clarence Stedman, Joaquin Miller, James Whitcomb Riley, and a few better tutored but equally conventional college wits and hearties, while figures as masterly as Mark Twain and even Henry James seemed (from some points of view: magazine editors, the book-buying public) to be forgetting year by year how to negotiate a fully compelling art of extended prose fiction. Who then would have predicted what the years between 1900 and 1945 – from

Sister Carrie, The Ambassadors, Three Lives, Personae, North of Boston,
to *The Bridge, The Sound and the Fury, Four Quartets, Notes Toward a
Supreme Fiction, The Iceman Cometh* – were conspiring to bring to
pass?

NOTES

1. An emphasis anticipating Wallace Stevens's obsessive theme of imaginative
'poverty' and also John Berryman's conclusion, under parental remonstrance,
that he lacks 'Inner Resources' (*The Dream Songs*, 14: 'Life, friends, is
boring . . .').

2. The phrases quoted may be recognized as the narrative openings of *Moby-
Dick*, Poe's 'William Wilson', 'Song of Myself', 'Howl', a poem of Emily
Dickinson's, 'Bartleby the Scrivener', 'Gerontion', *The Great Gatsby, Huckle-
berry Finn, The Catcher in the Rye, Invisible Man, Tropic of Cancer*, a poem of
Frank O'Hara's, Bellow's *Henderson the Rain King*, John Barth's *The End of
the Road*, Jane Austen's *Pride and Prejudice* and Lawrence's *The Rainbow*.

3. Isn't this also the imaginative condition argued out in that notably American (and currently undervalued) poem, *Four Quartets*? The mind-set in
question here is one endorsed, if not anchored, in macrohistoric circumstance.
Conceivably American consciousness and the angle of its relation to the
modern world have been affected as much by great historical actions that did
not reach the American shore or were not participated in directly as by those
endured and circumstantially commemorated. Two such events, profoundly
determining on their own ground, are the English civil wars of 1640–60 and,
at the start of the industrial age, the wars of the French Revolution. To have
missed direct engagement in these convulsions and in the hard institutional
and ideological compromises they exacted – an exemption made possible by
extraordinary geopolitical isolation – has at the least made it harder in this
century to outgrow the American propensity to simplistic historical judgements and single-vision solutions.

PART IV

FOR FURTHER READING AND REFERENCE

This bibliography spans a period of nearly four hundred years. The literature of the last half of this period is very considerable and comment upon it vigorous and extensive. This must, perforce, be a highly selective bibliography and thus usually only a selection of an author's work is recorded. Even though a deliberately broad categorization has been adopted – for to separate out, say, the relatively few references to Art or Religion under their own sub-heads would give a false impression of the range of studies available – the reader is nevertheless advised to consult other, relevant sections. This is particularly important for the first two sections. American literary scholars often write with close reference to their society and watertight compartmentalization is impracticable. Particularly significant cross-references are given but these should not be assumed to take account of all relevant titles.

Where it might prove helpful, different publishing dates and titles are given for works published at different times in the United States and United Kingdom. However, these lists are *not* intended to provide a historical publishing record. For exceptions to this, see note preceding *Authors and Works* section, p. 703.

FOR FURTHER READING AND REFERENCE

Historical and Cultural Background

See also, under Authors and Works, Robert Beverley, William Bradford, William Byrd II, John Cotton, J. Hector St J. de Crèvecoeur, Jonathan Edwards, Timothy Flint, Benjamin Franklin, Thomas Jefferson, Sarah Kemble Knight, Abraham Lincoln, Cotton Mather, Thomas Paine, Samuel Sewall, Captain John Smith, George Washington, Michael Wigglesworth, Roger Williams, John·Winthrop, and John Woolman.

Adams, H. *History of the United States of America*, 9 vols., 1889–91
Agee, J. and Evans, W. *Let Us Now Praise Famous Men*, 1941
Ahlstrom, S. E. *A Religious History of the American People*, 1972
Aronowitz, S. *False Promises: The Shaping of American Working Class Consciousness*, 1973
Bailyn, B. *Voyages to the West*, 1986
Baritz, L. *City on a Hill: A History of Ideas and Myths in America*, 1964
Baumol, W. J. and Bowen, W. G. *Performing Arts: The Economic Dilemma: A Study of Problems Common to Theater, Opera, Music, and Drama*, 1966
Beard, C. A. and Beard, M. R. *The Rise of American Civilization*, 2 vols., 1927, rev. 1933–42
Bell, D. *The End of Ideology*, 1965
Blair, W. (ed.) *Native American Humour, 1800–1900*, 2nd edn, 1960
Blum, J. et al. *The National Experience*, 1968
Blum, M. *The Promise of America*, 1965
Boorstin, D. *The Americans: The Colonial Experience*, 1958
    The Americans: The National Experience, 1966
    The Image: A Guide to Pseudo-Events in America, 1964
Boyer, P. S. *Purity in Print: The Vice-Society Movement and Book Censorship in America*, 1968
Bridenbaugh, C. *Cities in the Wilderness: The First Century of Urban Life in America, 1625–1742*, 1938
Brigance, W. N. *A History and Criticism of American Public Address*, 2 vols., 1943
Brogan, H. *Pelican History of the USA*, 1986
Brookeman, C. *American Culture and Society Since the 1930s*, 1984

Brooks, V. W. *The Writer in America*, 1953

Burchard, J. and Bush-Brown, A. *The Architecture of America: A Social and Cultural History*, 1961

Cargill, O. *Intellectual America: Ideas on the March*, 1941

Channing, E. *A History of the United States*, 6 vols., 1905–25

Coben, S. and Ratner, L. (eds.) *The Development of an American Culture*, rev. 1983

Cohen, S. (ed.) *Education in the United States: A Documentary History*, 5 vols., 1974

Commager, H. S. *The American Mind: An Interpretation of American Thought and Character since the 1880s*, 1950

   (ed.) *Immigration and American History*, 1961

Commager, H. S. and Giordanetti, E. *Was America a Mistake? An Eighteenth-Century Controversy*, 1967

Conlin, J. R., *The American Past* [survey] 1990

Croly, H. *The Promise of American Life*, 1910

Curti, M. *The Growth of American Thought*, 1943, 3rd edn, 1964

   Probing our Past, 1955

Davidson, A. *Early American Modernist Painting 1910–1935*, 1981

Davidson, D. *The Attack on Leviathan: Regionalism and Nationalism in the United States*, 1938

Davidson, M. B. *Life in America*, 2 vols., 1951 (pictorial)

DeLeon, D. *The American as Anarchist: Reflections on Indigenous Radicalism*, 1979

Denny, M. and Gilman, W. H. (eds.) *The American Writer and the European Tradition*, 1950

Dickens, Charles *American Notes*, 1843

Eddy, Mary Baker *Science and Health*, 1875 (*with a Key to the Scriptures*, 1883)

Emerson, E. *Puritanism in America*, 1977

Ferguson, R. A. *Law and Letters in American Culture*, 1984

Fleming, D. and Bailyn, B. (eds.) *The Intellectual Migration: Europe and America, 1930–1960*, 1969

Foerster, N. (ed.) *Humanism and America: Essays on the Outlook of Modern Civilization*, 1930

Freeman, J. *An American Testament: A Narrative of Rebels and Romantics*, 1938

Friedman, B. H. *Jackson Pollock: Energy Made Visible, A Biography*, 1972

Fussell, P. *Caste Marks: Style and Status in the USA*, 1984 (also as *Class* for *Caste Marks*)

Gabriel, R. H. *The Course of American Democratic Thought: An Intellectual History since 1815*, 1940, rev. 1956

Galbraith, J. K. *The Affluent Society*, 1958, rev. 1969

   The New Industrial State, 1967

Gorer, G. *The American People*, 1948

Grattan, C. H. (ed.) *The Critique of Humanism: A Symposium*, 1930

Green, M. *The Problem of Boston: Some Readings in Cultural History*, 1966

Greenberg, C. *Art and Culture*, 1961

Griswold, A. W. *The American Cult of Success*, 1934

Hallgren, M. A. *Seeds of Revolt: A Study of American Life and the Temper of the American People during the Depression*, 1933

Handlin, O. *The American People*, 1963

Handlin, O. and Schlesinger, A. M. *et al.* (eds.) *Harvard Guide to American History*, 1954

Hansen, C. *Witchcraft at Salem*, 1969

Harrison, J. R. *The Reactionaries: A Study of the Anti-Democratic Intelligentsia*, 1967

Hobson, A. (ed.) *Remembering America: A Sampler of the WPA American Guide Series*, 1985

Hofstadter, R. *The American Political Tradition*, 1954
    Anti-Intellectualism in American Life, 1963
    Social Darwinism in American Thought, 1860–1915, 1944

Howe, I. *A World More Attractive*, 1963

Jameson, J. F. (ed.) *Original Narratives of Early American History*, 19 vols., 1906–17, repr. 1952–9

Johnson, E. H. (ed) *American Artists on Art: From 1940 to 1980*, 1982

Jones, H. M. *The Age of Energy: Varieties of American Experience, 1865–1915*, 1971

Kittredge, G. L. *The Old Farmer [Robert B. Thomas] and his Almanack: Being some observations on life and manners in New England a hundred years ago*, 1904
    Witchcraft in Old and New England, 1929

Koch, A. *Maddison's 'Advice to my Country'*, 1966

Korshin, P. J. (ed.) *The American Revolution and Eighteenth-Century Culture*, 1984

Larkin, O. *Art and Life in America*, 1949, rev. 1960

Lears, T. J. J. *No Place of Grace: Antimodernism and the Transformation of American Culture, 1880–1920*, 1981

Legman, G. *The Fake [Sexual] Revolt*, 1967

Lehmann-Haupt, H. et al. *The Book in America: A History of the Making and Selling of Books in the United States*, 2nd edn, 1951

Lerner, M. *America as a Civilization: Life and Thought in the United States Today*, 1957

Levin, D. *History as Romantic Art: Bancroft, Prescott, Motley, Parkman*, 1959

Lilienthal, D. E. *Big Business: A New Era*, 1953

Lynd, R. S. and Lynd, H. M. *Middletown*, 1929
    Middletown in Transition, 1937

Lynn, K. S. *The Dream of Success: A Study of the Modern American Imagination*, 1955

Macdonald, D. *Against the American Grain*, 1965

McLanathan, R. *The American Tradition in the Arts*, 1968 (pictorial)

Marchand, R. *Advertising the American Dream: Making Way for Modernity, 1920–1940*, 1986

Marx, L. *The Machine in the Garden: Technology and the Pastoral Ideal in America*, 1964

May, H. F. *The End of American Innocence: A Study of the First Years of Our Own Time, 1912–1917*, 1959

Mercier, L. J. A. *The Challenge of Humanism*, 1933

Mills, C. W. *The Power Elite: On the Ruling Groups in the United States*, 1956
    The Sociological Imagination, 1959
    White Collar, 1951

Morison, S. E. *The Oxford History of the American People*, 1965

Mosier, R. D. *The American Temper: Patterns of Our Intellectual Heritage*, 1952

Mumford, L. *Sticks and Stones*, 1924 (architecture)

Murdock, K. B. *Literature and Theology in Colonial New England*, 1949

Nash, G. N. *The Conservative Intellectual Movement in America*, 1976.

Nevins, A. *The Emergence of Modern America, 1865–1878*, 1927, repr. 1971

Nye, R. B. *The Cultural Life of the New Nation, 1776–1830*, 1960

O'Connor, F. V. (ed.) *Art for the Millions: Essays from the 1930s by Artists and Administrators of the WPA Federal Art Project*, 1975

Parkes, H. B. *The American Experience*, 1955

Parrington, V. L. *Main Currents in American Thought: An Interpretation of American Literature from the Beginnings to 1920*, 3 vols., 1927–30

Pells, R. H. *Radical Visions and American Dreams*, 1973

Pochmann, H. A. *German Culture in America*, 1957

Raffel, N. R. *American Victorians: Explorations in Emotional History*, 1985
    Politicians, Poets, and Con Men: Emotional History in Late Victorian America, 1986

Rembar, C. *The End of Obscenity: The Trials of 'Lady Chatterley', 'Tropic of Cancer', and 'Fanny Hill'*, 1968

Riding, L. and Graves, R. *American Thought, from Puritanism to Pragmatism*, 2nd edn, 1923

Riesman, D. *The Lonely Crowd: A Study of the Changing American Character*, 1950, rev. 1970. (See Lipset, S. M. and Lowenthal, L. (eds.) *Culture and Social Character: The Work of David Riesman Reviewed*, 1961)

Riley, I. W. *American Thought from Puritianism to Pragmatism and Beyond*, 2nd edn, 1923

Rogers, Will *Autobiography*, ed. D. Day, 1949

Rose, A. C. *Transcendentalism as a Social Movement, 1830–1850*, 1981

Rosenberg, H. *The Tradition of the New*, 1959, 1983

Roszak, T. *The Dissenting Academy*, 1967

Rutman, D. B. *American Puritanism, Faith and Practice*, 1970
    Winthrop's Boston: Portrait of a Puritan Town, 1630–1649, 1965

Santayana, G. *Character and Opinion in the United States*, 1920
    The Genteel Tradition at Bay, 1931

Schlesinger, A. M. *The Rise of Modern America, 1865–1951*, 1951
    The Vital Centre: Our Purpose and Perils on the Tightrope of American Liberalism, 1949

Schlesinger, A. M. and Fox, D. R. (eds.) *A History of American Life*, 13 vols., 1927–48

Schlesinger, A. M. and White, M. G. (eds.) *Paths of American Thought*, 1963

Schneider, H. W. *A History of American Philosophy*, 1946, 1963

Seldes, G. *The Years of the Locust: America 1929–1932*, 1933

Smith, J. W. and Jamison, A. L. *Religion in American Life*, 4 vols., 1961

Spencer, B. T. and Jensen, M. (eds.) *Regionalism in America*, 1951

Stearns, H. (ed.) *Civilization in the United States: An Inquiry by Thirty Americans*, 1922, 1971

Steffens, L. *The Shame of the Cities*, 1904

Stokes, A. P. *Church and State in the United States*, 3 vols., 1950

Stone, A. E. (ed.) *The American Autobiography: A Collection of Critical Essays*, 1981

Tallack, D. *Twentieth-Century America: The Intellectual and Cultural Context*, 1991

Terkel, Studs (ed.) *Hard Times: An Oral History of the Great Depression*, 1970

Tocqueville, A. de *Democracy in America*, 1835 (in French), ed. P. Bradley, 2 vols., 1942

Tomlinson, C. *Some Americans: A Personal Record*, 1981

Trachtenberg, A. *Brooklyn Bridge: Fact and Symbol*, 1979

 Democratic Vistas 1860–1880, 1970

 The Incorporation of America: Culture and Society in the Gilded Age, 1987

Trachtenberg, A. with Gross, T. L. *America in Literature*, 2 vols., 1978

Tyron, W. S. (ed.) *A Mirror for Americans: Life and Manners in the United States 1790–1870, as Recorded by American Travelers*, 3 vols., 1952

Viereck, P. *Shame and Glory of the Intellectuals: Babbitt Jr versus the Rediscovery of Values*, 1953

 Wellsprings of a Nation: America before 1801, 1977

White, M. G. *Social Thought in America: The Revolt Against Formalism*, 1949

 Science and Sentiment in America: Philosophical Thought from Jonathan Edwards to John Dewey, 1972

Whyte, W. H. *The Organization Man*, 1956

Williams, R. M. *American Society: A Sociological Interpretation*, 1951

Wright, L. B. *The Elizabethan's America: A Collection of Early Reports by Englishmen in the New World*, 1965

Yates, N. W. *The American Humorist: Conscience of the Twentieth Century*, 1964

Ziff, L. *The American 1980s: The Life and Times of a Lost Generation*, 1966

The Literature

I. HISTORY OF THE LANGUAGE AND LITERATURE

Language

Craigie, W. A. *The Growth of American English*, 1940

Craigie, W. A. and Hulbert, J. R. (eds.) *A Dictionary of English on Historical Principles*, 4 vols., 1938–44

Kapp, G. W. *The English Language in America*, 2 vols., 1925

Laird, C. *Language in America*, 1970

Lloyd, D. J. and Warfel, H. R. *American English in its Cultural Setting*, 1957

Matthews, M. M. *A Dictionary of Americanisms on Historical Principles*, 2 vols., 1951, abridged: *Americanisms: A Dictionary of Selected Americanisms*, 1966

Mencken, H. L. *The American Language*, 4th edn, 1936, with Supplements 1945 and 1948, 1-vol. edn ed. R. I. McDavid, Jr and D. W. Maurer, 1963

Nelson, F. W. *The Structure of American English*, 1958

Nicholson, M. *A Dictionary of American-English Usage*, 1957

Partridge, E. and Clark, J. W. *British and American English Since 1900*, 1951

Simpson, D. *The Politics of American English, 1776–1850*, 1988

Wentworth, H. and Flexner, S. B. *Dictionary of American Slang*, 1960

Literature: General

Aaron, D. *Writers on the Left*, 1979

Aldridge, J. W. *After the Lost Generation: A Critical Study of the Writers of Two Wars*, 1951
  American Literature in an Age of Conformity, 1956

Allen, W. *The Urgent West: The American Dream and Man*, 1969

American Literature in Context, 1. 1620–1830, S. Fender, 1983; *2. 1830–1805*, B. Harding, 1982; *3. 1865–1900*, A. Hook, 1983; *4. 1900–1930*, A. Massa, 1982

The American Reading Public, Daedalus, Winter 1963

Beidler, P. D. *American Literature and the Experience of Vietnam*, 1982

Benamon, M. and Caramello, C. (eds.) *Performance in Postmodern Culture*, 1980

Berthoff, W. *American Literature: Traditions and Talents*, 1960
  The Ferment of Realism, 1884–1919, 1965, rev. 1981

Bier, J. *The Rise and Fall of American Humor*, 1968

Bogardus, R. F. and Hibson, F. *Literature at the Barricades: The American Writer of the 1930s*, 1982

Brooks, Van Wyck *America's Coming of Age*, 1915
  Makers and Finders: A History of the Writer in America, 1800–1915, 5 vols., 1936–52 (1945–52)

Bryan, W. A. *George Washington in American Literature, 1775–1805*, 1952

Budick, E. M. *Fiction and Historical Consciousness*, 1989

Buell, L. *New England Literary Culture: From the Revolution to the Renaissance*, 1986

Burke, W. J. and Howe, W. D. *American Authors and Books, 1640–1940*, 1943, rev. I. R. Weiss, 1962

Calverton, V. F. *The Liberation of American Literature*, 1932

Canby, H. S. *Classic Americans: A Study of Eminent American Writers from Irving to Whitman*, 1931

Carpenter, F. I. *American Literature and the Dream*, 1955

Chametzky, J. *Our Decentralized Literature: Cultural Mediations in Selected Jewish and Southern Writers*, 1986

Channing, W. E. 'Remarks on a National Literature', 1830

Clough, W. O. *The Necessary Earth: Nature and Solitude in American Literature*, 1964

Cook, B. *The Beat Generation*, 1971

Cowley, M. *After the Genteel Tradition: American Writers 1910–1930*, 1937, rev. 1964
    Exile's Return: A Narrative of Ideas, 1934, rev. 1951 subtitled *A Literary Odyssey of the 1920s*
    Think Back on Us [*1930s*], (ed.) H. D. Piper, 1967

Cunliffe, M. *American Literature to 1900*, rev. 1986
    American Literature since 1900, 1975
    The Literature of the United States, 1954, rev. 1970

Elliot, E. *Columbia Literary History of the United States*, 1988

Emerson, E. (ed.) *Major Writers in Early American Literature*, 1972

Feidelson, C. S. *Symbolism and American Literature*, 1953

Feidelson, C. S. and Brodtkorb, P. (eds.) *Interpretations of American Literature*, 1959

Feied, F. *No Pie in the Sky: The Hobo as American Cultural Hero in the Works of Jack London, John Dos Passos, and Jack Kerouac*, 1964

Foerster, N. *Nature in American Literature*, 1923

Franklin, W. *Discoverers, Explorers, Settlers: The Diligent Writers of Early America*, 1979

French, W. *20th Century American Literature*, 1980

Glicksberg, C. I. *The Sexual Revolution in Modern American Literature*, 1971

Green, M. *Re-Appraisals: Some Commonsense Readings in American Literature*, 1965

Hearn, C. R. *The American Dream in the Great Depression*, 1977

Hintz, H. W. *The Quaker Influence in American Literature*, 1940

Homberger, E. *American Writers and Radical Politics, 1900–39*, 1986

Howard, L. *The Connecticut Wits*, 1943
    Literature and the American Tradition, 1960

Howe, I. *The Critical Point: On Literature and Culture*, 1973

Jones, H. M. *The Theory of American Literature*, 1928, 2nd edn, 1965
    O Strange New World, 1964

Jones, H. M. and Ludwig, R. M. *Guide to American Literature and its Backgrounds since 1890*, 4th edn, 1973 (with bibliographies)

Kostelanetz, R. *The End of Intelligent Writing: Literary Politics in America*, 1973

Lawrence, D. H. *Studies in Classic American Literature*, 1923; (1924, without Foreword; as *The Symbolic Meaning*, 1962) (reprinted as originally published in journals 1918–21)

Lawson-Peebles, R. *Landscape and Written Expression in Revolutionary America*, 1988

Leary, L. (ed.) *American Literature to 1900*, 1980

Lease, B. *Anglo-American Encounters: English and the Rise of American Literature*, 1981

Leverenz, D. *The Language of Puritan Feeling*, 1980

Lewis, R. W. B. *The American Adam: Innocence, Tragedy and Tradition in the Nineteenth Century*, 1955

Lewisohn, L. *Expressionism in America*, 1932

Louvre, A. and Walsh, J. *'Tell Me Lies About Vietnam': Cultural Battles for the Meaning of War*, 1988

Lowance, M. I., Jr *The Language of Canaan: Metaphor and Symbol in New England from the Puritans to the Transcendentalists*, 1980

Lynn, K. S. (ed.) *The Comic Tradition in America*, 1957 (1958)

Madden, D. *Proletarian Writers of the Thirties*, 1968

Marder, D. *Exiles at Home: A Story of Literature in Nineteenth-Century America*, 1985

Martin, J. *Harvests of Change: American Literature, 1865–1914*, 1967

Martin, R. E. *American Literature and the Universe of Force*, 1981

Matthiessen, F. O. *American Renaissance: Art and Expression in the Age of Emerson and Whitman*, 1941

Morse, D. *American Romanticism: 1. From Cooper to Hawthorne; 2. From Melville to James*, 1986

Murdock, K. B. *Literature and Theology in Colonial New England*, 1949

Olson, E. *On Value Judgments in the Arts and Other Essays*, 1976

Parkinson, T. (ed.) *A Casebook on the Beat*, 1961

Peach, L. *British Influence on the Birth of American Literature*, 1982

Pizer, D. *Realism and Naturalism in Nineteenth-Century American Literature*, 1966

Poirier, R. *A World Elsewhere: The Place of Style in American Literature*, 1966 (1967)

Quinn, A. H. and Murdock, K. B. *et al. The Literature of the American People: A Historical and Critical Survey*, 1951

Rahv, P. *Literature in America*, 1967

Reynolds, D. S. *Beneath the American Renaissance*, 1989

Rourke, C. *American Humor: A Study of the National Character*, 1931

Simon, M. and Parsons, T. H. (eds.) *Transcendentalism and Its Legacy*, 1966

Spencer, B. T. *The Quest for Nationality: An American Literary Campaign*, 1957

Spiller, R. E. *The Cycle of American Literature: An Essay in Historical Criticism*, 1955, rev. 1967

(ed.) *The American Literary Revolution, 1783–1837*, 1967

Spiller, R. E. and Thorp, W. et al. (eds.) *Literary History of the United States*, 3 vols., 1946–8; 1-vol. edn, 1953; 3rd edn, 2 vols. 1963; 4th edn, 1975; vol. 2 is an annotated bibliography

Stott, W. *Documentary Expression in Thirties America*, 1973

Straumann, H. *American Literature in the Twentieth Century*, 1951

Suvin, D. *Positions and Presuppositions in Science Fiction*, 1987

Tanner, T. *Scenes of Nature, Signs of Men*, 1988

Taylor, G. O. *Studies in Modern American Autobiography*, 1983

Thorp, W. *American Writing in the Twentieth Century*, 1960

Tyler, M. C. *A History of American Literature during the Colonial Period*, 2 vols., 1878, abridged 1962

    The Literary History of the American Revolution, 2 vols., 1897

Walcutt, C. C. *American Literary Naturalism: A Divided Stream*, 1956

Walker, M. *The Literature of the United States of America*, 1983

Walsh, T. J. *American War Literature: 1914 to Vietnam*, 1982

Weimer, D. R. *The City as Metaphor*, 1966

Welland, D. (ed.) *The United States: A Companion to American Studies*, 1974

Wilson, Edmund *Patriotic Gore: Studies in the Literature of the American Civil War*, 1962

Ziff, L. *Literary Democracy*, 1981

Literature: The South

Bradbury, J. M. *The Renaissance in the South: A Critical History of the Literature, 1920–1960*, 1963

Brooks, C. *The Language of the American South*, 1985

Cash, W. J. *The Mind of the South*, 1941

Clark, T. D. *The Emerging South*, 1968

Downs, R. B. *Books that Changed the South*, 1980

Eaton, C. *The Mind of the Old South*, 1964

Gaines, F. P. *The Southern Plantation: A Study of the Development and the Accuracy of a Tradition*, 1924

Gray, R. *The Literature of Memory: Modern Writers of the American South*, 1977

    Writing the South: Ideas of an American Region, 1986

Hobson, F. *Tell About the South: The Southern Rage to Explain*, 1983

Holman, C. H. *The Immoderate Past: The Southern Writer and History*, 1977

    The Roots of Southern Writing: Essays on the Literature of the American South, 1972

Hubbell, J. B. *The South in American Literature, 1607–1900*, 1954

King, R. H. *Southern Renaissance: The Cultural Awakening of the American South, 1930–1955*, 1980

Lawson, L. A. *Another Generation: Southern Fiction since World War II*, 1984

Leary, L. (ed.) *Southern Excursions*, 1971

MacKethan, L. H. *The Dream of Arcady: Place and Time in Southern Literature*, 1980

Marrow, M. *Images of the Southern Writer*, 1985 (pictorial)

Mencken, H. L. 'The Sahara of the Bozart', *Prejudices, Second Series*, 1920

Mixon, W. *Southern Writers and the New South Movement, 1865–1913*, 1980

Rubin, L. D., Jr *The Faraway Country: Writers of the Modern South*, 1963

    The Wary Fugitives: Four Poets and the South, 1978

    William Elliott Shoots a Bear: Essays on the Southern Literary Imagination, 1975

    et al. (eds.) *The History of Southern Literature*, 1985

Rubin, L. D., Jr and Jacobs, R. D. (eds.) *Southern Renascence: The Literature of the Modern South*, 1953

Simpson, L. P. *The Dispossessed Garden: Pastoral and History in Southern Literature*, 1975
    The Man of Letters in New England and the South, 1973
Smedes, S. D. *Memorials of a Southern Planter*, 1981
Sullivan, W. *A Requiem for the Renascence*, 1976
Tate, A. (ed.) *A Southern Vanguard*, 1947
Twelve Southerners *I'll Take My Stand: The South and the Agrarian Tradition*, 1930
Woodward, C. V. *The Burden of Southern History*, 1960

Literature: The Frontier and the West

See also American Indian, Popular Culture; and, under Authors and Works, Timothy Flint and James Hall.

Billington, R. A. *Westward Expansion: A History of the American Frontier*, 1949
    The Far Western Frontier, 1830–1860, 1956
Boynton, P. H. *The Rediscovery of the Frontier*, 1931
Fender, S. *Plotting the Golden West: American Literature and the Rhetoric of the Californian Trail*, 1982
Folsom, J. K. *The American Western Novel*, 1966
Fussell, E. *Frontier: American Literature and the American West*, 1965
Hazard, L. L. *The Frontier in American Literature*, 1927
Jones, H. M. *The Frontier and American Fiction: Four Lectures in the Relationship of Landscape to Literature*, 1956
Klose, N. *Concise Study Guide to the American Frontier*, 1964
Lavender, D. *The Penguin Book of the American West*, 1969
Milton, J. R. *The Novel of the American West*, 1980
Nash, R. *Wilderness and the American Mind*, 1967, rev. 1973
Rusk, R. L. *The Literature of the Middle Western Frontier*, 1925
Smith, H. N. *Virgin Land: The American West as Symbol and Myth*, 1950, 1951; rev. 1970
Turner, F. J. *The Frontier in American History*, 1920; inc. 'The Significance of the Frontier in American History', 1893
Webb, W. P. *The Great Frontier*, 1952
Wright, L. B. *Culture on the Moving Frontier*, 1955
Wyatt, D. *The Fall into Eden: Literature and Imagination in California*, 1986

II. BIBLIOGRAPHIES AND GUIDES

See also Black Literature, American Indian and Women Writers.

There is a copious supply of bibliographies and guides available to the reader of American literature, many of excellent quality. For even the least-known American authors *some* introduction has been published. Thus, Gale

Research, Detroit, has given brief details of over 70,000 authors (not all American) in its *Contemporary Authors* series. In addition to scholarly bibliographies and editions from university presses, commercial publishing houses in the USA have been very active in this area, Gale Research in particular. Its Guides to Information sources (listed in Patterson below) are invaluable and their Dictionaries of Literary Biography offer full-scale, descriptive and critical illustrated articles. An annual cumulative index to all its series, ed. L. Metzger, is published. Bibliographies of individual writers and of genres (not restricted to American authors) have been, and continue to be, published by Whitston (Troy, NY); Appleton-Century-Crofts (Goldentree Bibliographies) now AHM, Arlington Heights, Illinois; Scarecrow Press (Metuchen, NJ); Shoe String Press (Hamden, Conn); and Bruccoli-Clark (Columbia, SC), in addition to those from university presses. Introductions to American authors are published in series by Twayne (New York and Boston and, from 1986, Macmillan, London), some 175 American authors being currently listed; University of Minnesota, Minneapolis (Pamphlets on American Writers, 1959–72); American Book Co. (American Writers series); Sloane and Methuen (American Men of Letters); and Kent State University, Ohio (Serif Series). Useful critical editions and collections of essays are published by Norton (Critical Editions); Macmillan, London (Casebooks); D. C. Heath (Discussions of Literature); Hall (Essays on American Literature); Crowell (Literary Casebooks in American Literature); and Prentice-Hall (Twentieth-Century Views). Useful lists of author bibliographies will be found in Patterson and R. A. Wilson, *Modern Book Collecting*, New York 1980, ch. 10.

The list below is therefore restricted to a few general bibliographies and guides and bibliographies are not normally listed for individual authors in order to conserve space and because they are so readily traceable.

Bibliographies

Altick, R. D. and Wright, A. *Selective Bibliography for the Study of English and American Literature*, 1960, 6th edn, 1979

American Humanities Index [*to periodicals*], quarterly, 1975–

American Literary Scholarship: An Annual, 1963–

Anderson, J. Q. et al. *Southwestern American Literature*, 1979

Basler, R. P. (ed.) *Guide to the Study of the United States: Representative Books Reflecting the Development of American Life and Thought*, 1960, Supplement 1976

Blanck, J. *Bibliography of American Literature*, 6 vols., 1955–73

Bryer, J. R. *Sixteen Modern American Authors: A Survey of Research and Criticism*, 1973 (earlier as *Fifteen . . . Authors*)

Bulletin of Bibliography, quarterly, 1897–

Clarke, I. F. *Tale of the Future*, 3rd edn, 1978 (science fiction)

Eddleman, E. F. (ed.) *American Drama Criticism: Interpretations, 1890–1977*, 2nd edn, 1979, Supplement 1, 1984

Gerstenberger, D. and Hendrick, G. *The American Novel, 1789–1959: A Checklist of Twentieth-Century Criticism*, vol. 1 1961; vol. 2 1960–68, 1970

Gohdes, C. *Bibliographical Guide to the Study of the Literature of the USA*, 1970, 4th edn, 1976

Gross, T. L. and Wertheim, S. *Hawthorne, Melville, Stephen Crane: A Critical Bibliography*, 1971

Havlice, P. P. (ed.) *Index to American Author Bibliographies*, 1971

Holman, C. H. (ed.) *The American Novel through Henry James*, 2nd edn, 1979

Keller, D. H. *Index to Plays in Periodicals*, 1979

Kimball, K. *Ten Modern American Playwrights: An Annotated Bibliography*, 1982

Leary, L. *Articles on American Literature, 1900–1950*, 1954; *1950–1967*, 1970; *1968–1975*, 1979

Levernier, J. A. and Wilmes, D. R. *American Writers before 1800*, 1983

Long, E. H. *American Drama from its Beginnings to the Present*, 1970

MLA International Bibliography of Books and Articles on the Modern Languages and Literatures, annually, 1921–

Myerson, J. (ed.) *The Transcendentalists: A Review of Research and Criticism*, 1984

Nemanic, G. C. *A Bibliographical Guide to Midwestern Literature*, 1981

Nevius, B. (ed.) *The American Novel: Sinclair Lewis to the Present*, 1970

Patterson, M. C. *Literary Research Guide*, MLA 1976, 2nd edn, 1983 (an outstanding, annotated, guide)

Rees, R. A. and Harbert, E. N. (eds.) *Fifteen American Authors before 1900*, 1971

Rubin, L. (ed.) *A Bibliographical Guide to the Study of Southern Literature*, 1969

Sabin, J. et al. *A Dictionary of Books Relating to America from its Discovery to the Present Time*, 29 vols., 1868–1936

Salzman, J. (ed.) *American Studies: An Annotated Bibliography*, 3 vols., 1986
    The Cambridge Handbook of American Literature, 1986

Somer, J. and Cooper, B. E. *American & British Literature 1945–75: An Annotated Bibliography of Contemporary Scholarship*, 1980 (check for defective copies)

Spiller, R. E. *et al.* (ed.) *Literary History of the United States*, vol. 2, Bibliographical Supplement, 4th edn, 1974

Stovall, F. (ed.) *Eight American Authors*, 1956, rev. 1963, 1971

Stratman, C. J. CSV, *Bibliography of the American Theatre, excluding New York City*, 1965

Tanselle, G. T. *Guide to the Study of American Imprints*, 2 vols., 1971

Tate, A. (ed.) *Sixty American Poets, 1896–1944*, rev. 1954

Wertheim, A. F. (ed.) *American Popular Culture: A Historical Bibliography*, 1984. *Year's Work in English Studies*, American literature included since 1954

Guides

Bradbury, M. et al. *Penguin Companion to Literature, vol. 3: United States and Latin American Literature*, 1971

Bradbury, M. and Temperley, H. (eds.) *Introduction to American Studies*, 1981

Hart, J. D. (ed.) *Oxford Companion to American Literature*, 6th edn, 1987

Herzberger, M. J. (ed.), *Reader's Encyclopaedia of American Literature* 1962

Hoffman, D. *Harvard Guide to Contemporary American Writing*, 1979

Jones, H. M. and Ludwig, R. M. *Guide to American Literature and its Background since 1890*, 4th edn, 1972

Kunitz, S. J. and Haycraft, H. (eds.) *American Authors, 1600–1900*, 1938; see also *Twentieth-Century Authors*, 1942; Supp. 1955, 1973; and *World Authors, 1950–70*, ed. J. Wakeman, 1975; Supp. 1970–75, 1980

Scribner's *American Writers*, 4 vols. 1974; 2-vol. Supp. 1979; 2-vol. Supp. 1981 (some 150 Minnesota Pamphlets on American Writers, as revised)

Seymour-Smith, M. 'America' in *Guide to Modern World Literature*, 1 vol. 1973; vol. 1 of 4 1975 rev.; 1 vol. 1985 rev.

III. ANTHOLOGIES

This is but a selection of anthologies published; there is a particularly wide range of paperback drama and poetry collections; see also Journals, American Indian, and Women Writers.

Allen, D. M. and Butterick, G. F. (eds.) *The Postmoderns: The New American Poetry, Revised*, 1982; orig. Allen, D. M. *The New American Poetry, 1945–1960*, 1960

Allen, G. W. *et al.* (eds.) *American Poetry*, 1965

America's Lost Plays, 20 vols., 1940–41; re-issued in 10 vols., 1963–5, with additional vol.

Barksdale, R. and Kinnamon, K. (eds.) *Black Writers of America: A Comprehensive Anthology* , 1972

Baym, N. *et al.* (eds.) *The Norton Anthology of American Literature*, 2 vols., 2nd edn, 1985; shorter 1-vol. edn, 1986

Benét, W. R. and Pearson, N. H. (eds.) *The Oxford Anthology of American Literature*, 2 vols., 1938

Bernikow, L. (ed.) *The World Split Open*, 1974 (women poets 1552–1950)

Best Plays, 1894–1899, 1955; *1899–1909*, 1944; *1909–1919*, 1943; thereafter annually from 1920

Blair, W. (ed.), *Native American Humour, 1800–1900*, 1937

Boatright, M. C. (ed.) *Folk Laughter on the American Frontier*, 1949

Boorstin, D. J. (ed.) *An American Primer*, 2 vols., 1966, 1 vol. 1968 (a fine collection of over 75 documents with scholarly intros.)

Botkin, B. (ed.) *A Treasury of American Folklore*, 1944

Cargill, O. (ed.) *American Literature: A Period Anthology*, 4 vols., rev. edn 1949

Chapman, A. (ed.) *Black Voices: An Anthology of Afro-American Literature*, 1968

Cohen, H. (ed.) *The American Experience*, 1968
   The American Culture, 1968

Corrigan, R. W. (ed.) *New American Plays, I*, 1970 (see Hoffman below)

Ellman, R. and O'Clair, R. (eds.) *The Norton Anthology of Modern Poetry*, 1973

Eshleman, C. (ed.) *A Caterpillar Anthology*, 1971

Federal Theatre Plays: Triple-A Plowed Under, Power, Spirochete, 1938
   One-Third of a Nation, intros. J. Chothia, P. Davison, 1984

Flanagan, J. T. (ed.) *America is West: An Anthology of Middle Western Life and Literature*, 1945

Foley, M. (ed.) *The Best of the Best American Short Stories 1915–1950*, 1952

Gassner, J. (ed.) *25 Best Plays of the Modern American Theatre, 1916–1929*, 1949; *1930–1939*, 1939; *1939–1946*, 1947; *Best American Plays 1945–51*, 1952; *Supp. Vol., 1918–58*, 1961

Gassner, J. and Barnes, C. (eds.) *Fifty Best Plays of the American Theatre, 1787–Present*, 4 vols., 1970

Gassner, J. and Gassner, M. (eds.) *Best Plays of the Early American Theatre*, 1967

Gelpi, A. (ed.) *The Poet in America: 1650 to the Present*, 1973

Hacker, L. M. and Zahler, H. S. (eds.) *The Shaping of the American Tradition*, 2 vols., 1947 (economic aspects)

Haining, P. (ed.) *The Fantastic Pulps*, 1975

Henderson, S. (ed.) *Understanding the New Black Poetry: Black Speech and Black Music as Poetic References*, 1973

Hochfield, G. (ed.) *Selected Writings of the American Transcendentalists*, 1967

Hoffman, W. M. (ed.) *New American Plays, II, III*, 1970 (see Corrigan above)

Jantz, H. S. (ed.) *The First Century of New England Verse*, 1944

Kirk, R. (ed.) *Portable Conservative Reader*, 1982, 1984 (much American material)

Kostelanetz, R. (ed.) *Imaged Words and Worded Images*, 1970

Lincoln, K. (ed.) *Native American Renaissance*, 1983

Locke, A. R. and Gregory, M. (eds.) *Plays of Negro Life: A Source-Book of Native American Drama*, 1927

Matthiessen, F. O. (ed.) *Oxford Book of American Verse*, 1950

Meserole, H. T. (ed.) *Seventeenth-Century American Poetry*, 1968, 1986
   et al. (eds.) *American Literature: Tradition and Innovation*, 2 vols., 1969

Miller, P. (ed.) *The Transcendentalists*, 1950
   (ed.) *The American Transcendentalists*, 1957

Miller, P. and Johnson, T. H. (eds.) *The Puritans*, 1938

Moody, R. (ed.) *Dramas from the American Theatre, 1762–1909*, 1966

Moore, G. (ed.) *American Literature: A Representative Anthology of American Writing from Colonial Times to the Present*, 1964
   Penguin Book of Modern American Verse, 1954, 1959

Moses, M. J. (ed.) *Representative Plays by American Dramatists*, 3 vols., 1918–25, repr. 1964

North, J. (ed.) *New Masses: An Anthology of the Rebel Thirties*, 1969

Padgett, R. and Shapiro, D. (eds.) *An Anthology of New York Poets*, 1970

Parrington, V. L. (ed.) *The Connecticut Wits*, 1926

Philbrick, N. (ed.) *Trumpets Sounding: Propaganda Plays of the American Revolution*, 1972

Proletarian Literature in the United States, intro. by J. Freeman, 1936

Quinn, A. H. (ed.) *Representative American Plays from 1767 to the Present Day*, 7th edn, 1953

Radzinowicz, M. A. (ed.) *American Colonial Prose*, 1984

Rahv, P. (ed.) *Discovery of Europe: The Story of American Experience in the Old World*, 1947

Randall, D. (ed.) *The Black Poets*, 1972

Sandburg, C. (ed.) *The American Songbag*, 1927
  The New American Songbag, 1950

Sitwell, E. (ed.) *The American Genius*, 1951

Turner, D. T. (ed.) *Black Drama in America: An Anthology*, 1971

Untermeyer, L. (ed.) *Modern American Poetry*, enlarged edn, 1962

Vendler, H. (ed.) *The Faber Book of Contemporary American Poetry*, 1987

Weber, B. (ed.) *An Anthology of American Humor*, 1962

IV. LITERARY AND CRITICAL JOURNALS

A large number of literary, critical, and academic journals has been published in America during the past two centuries. Those listed here represent but the tip of a large iceberg and wholly academic journals are excluded. In some instances the names associated with the journals, as editors or contributors, have been noted, as have a few studies and anthologies. Useful bibliographies are: E. E. Chielens *The Literary Journal in America to 1900*, 1975, and *1900–1950*, 1977; and his *American Literary Magazines in the Eighteenth and Nineteenth Centuries*, 1987; see also *The Little Magazine: A History and a Bibliography*, F. J. Hoffman, *et al.*, 1946, repr. 1967; and:

Drewry, J. E. *Concerning the Fourth Estate*, 1942

Goldwater, W. *Radical Periodicals in America, 1890–1950*, 1966

Goodstone, T. (ed.) *The Pulps: Fifty Years of American Popular Culture*, 1970

Leary, L. (ed.) *Articles on American Literature Appearing in Current Periodicals, 1900–1950*, 1954; *1950–1967*, 1970; *1968–1975*, 1979

Mackesy, E. M. *et al. MLA Directory of Periodicals*, 1981

Mott, F. L. *A History of American Magazines*, 5 vols., 1957

Noel, M. *Villains Galore . . . Heyday of the Popular Story Weekly*, 1954

Reed, W. *Little Magazines*, 1963

Riley, S. G. *Magazines of the American South*, 1986

Stratman, C. *American Theatrical Periodicals 1798–1967*, 1970

Tate, A. 'The Function of the Critical Quarterly', *Southern Review*, 1 (1936), 551–9

Taylor, W. F. *A History of American Letters*, 1936
Tebbel, J., *The American Magazine: A Compact History*, 1969
Wish, W. F. *Society and Thought in Modern America*, 2 vols., 2nd edn, 1962

American Literature: A Journal of Literary History, Criticism and Bibliography,
 1929– . Vols. 1–46 (1929–75) repr. with Index, vols. 1–30, 1963
American Mercury, 1924–33. Sinclair Lewis, H. L. Mencken, G. J. Nathan
American Quarterly, 1949–
The Anvil, 1932–5; *The New Anvil*, 1939–40. J. Conroy and C. Johnson
 (eds.). See *Writers in Revolt: The Anvil Anthology*, 1973
The Argonaut, 1877–1907. A. Bierce
Atlantic Monthly, 1857– . W. D. Howells (ed.) 1872–81
Black Mountain Review, 1951–4
Broom, 1921–4. M. Cowley. See H. Loeb, *The Way It Was*, 1959
The Chap-Book, 1894–8. S. Crane, H. Garland, H. James
Commentary, 1945–
Cosmopolitan, 1886–1925. W. D. Howells
The Dial, 1840–44, W. Emerson, M. Fuller; 1880–1929, J. Dewey, S.
 Thayer, T. Veblen; K. Burke, M. Cowley, T. S. Eliot, P. Picasso, E.
 Pound, G. Seldes, William Carlos Williams. Author Index compiled B.
 Zingman, 1975. See G. L. Brown (ed.) *The Dial: Arts and Letters in the
 1920s*, 1981
Dissent, 1954–
The Drama Review, 1955– . First as *Carleton Drama Review*, then *Tulane
 Drama Review*, 1957–67
Esquire, 1933– . F. Scott Fitzgerald, E. Hemingway, N. Mailer
Evergreen Review, 1957–
The Fugitive, 1922–5. J. C. Ransom, A. Tate, D. Davidson. See J. M.
 Bradbury, *The Fugitives: A Critical Account*, 1958; L. Cowan, *The Fugitive
 Group: A Literary History*, 1959
The Galaxy, 1886–78. M. Twain, H. James
The General Magazine and Historical Chronicle, 1741. Benjamin Franklin.
 Facsimile edn, L. N. Richardson, 1938
The Georgia Review, 1947– . *Necessary Fictions: Selected Stories from 'The
 Georgia Review'*, ed. S. W. Lindberg and S. Corey, 1986
Harper's Monthly Magazine, 1850– . W. D. Howells, B. DeVoto
Hound & Horn, 1927–34. R. P. Blackmur, K. Burke, J. Dos Passos, T. S.
 Eliot, A. Tate. L. Greenbaum, *'The Hound & Horn': The History of a
 Literary Quarterly*, 1966; *The Hound & Horn Letters*, ed. M. B. Hamovitch,
 1983
Hudson Review, 1948– . *The Modern Image: Outstanding Stories from the
 'Hudson Review'*, ed. F. Morgan, 1965
Kenyon Review, 1939–70. Index, 1939–63, compiled E. Browne, 1964; J. C.
 Ransom, ed. *The Kenyon Critics*, 1951
The Little Review, 1914–29. M. C. Anderson; H. Crane, T. S. Eliot, J.
 Joyce, E. Pound, William Carlos Williams. Index compiled K. A. Lohf

and E. P. Sheehy, 1961. *The Little Review Anthology*, 1953. See M. Anderson, *My Thirty Years' War*, 1930

The Masses, 1911–17; as *The Liberator*, 1918–24. M. Eastman

The Nation, 1865– . C. Van Doren, J. W. Krutch

New Directions in Prose and Poetry, 1936– . E. Dahlberg, L. Ferlinghetti, A. Ginsberg, K. Rexroth, William Carlos Williams. Index ed. S. Cox, 1980

The New Masses, 1926–48. S. Anderson, G. Hicks, C. Sandburg. '*New Masses': An Anthology of the Rebel Thirties*, 1969; G. Hicks, *Granville Hicks in the New Masses*, ed. J. A. Robins, 1974

New Republic, 1914– . Edmund Wilson

The New Yorker, 1925– . R. Benchley, J. Thurber, Edmund Wilson, A. Woolcott

New York Review of Books, 1963– . R. Lowell, I. Ehrenpreis, R. Ellman, Flannery O'Connor

Partisan Review, 1934– . S. Bellow, M. McCarthy, D. Macdonald, P. Rahv, D. Schwartz, K. Shapiro, L. Trilling, Edmund Wilson. Index vols. 1–31, 1934–83, 1985. *The Partisan Reader . . . 1934–1944*, ed. W. Phillips and P. Rahv, 1946; *Writers and Politics: An Anthology*, ed. E. Kurzweil and W. Phillips, 1983; T. A. Cooney, *The Rise of the New York Intellectuals: 'Partisan Review' and Its Circle 1933–45*, 1986

Poetry, 1912– . Index, 1912–62, compiled E. Wright, 1963. See H. Monroe, *A Poet's Life*, 1938

Prairie Schooner, 1926– . M. Johnson, *The 'Prairie Schooner' Story: A Little Magazine's First 25 Years*, 1955

Quarterly Review of Literature, 1943–

Saturday Evening Post, 1821–

Saturday Review of Literature, 1920– H. S. Canby, M. Cowley

Seven Arts, 1916–17. S. Anderson, Van Wyck Brooks, R. Frost, A. Lowell, Eugene O'Neill, C. Sandburg

Sewanee Review, 1892–

The Southern Review, 1935–42. R. P. Blackmur, C. Brooks, R. P. Warren. *An Anthology of Stories*, ed. C. Brooks and R. P. Warren, 1953

Studies in the American Renaissance, 1977– . Index to vol. 10, 1986

transatlantic review, 1924–5. E. Hemingway (asst. ed.), G. Stein

transition, 1927–38. E. Jolas, H. Crane, J. Joyce, A. MacLeish, E. Paul, G. Stein. Author Index compiled C. L. P. Silet, 1980. See D. McMillan, *'transition': The History of a Literary Era, 1927–1938*, 1976

Yale Review, 1892– . See W. L. Cross (ed. 1911–40), *Connecticut Yankee: An Autobiography*, 1943

V. AMERICAN CRITICS AND CRITICAL THEORY

Included here are one or two critics Canadian by nationality who have been particularly influential in the United States. See also, under Authors and Works: K. Burke, R. Jarrell, A. MacLeish, C. Olson, J. C. Ransom, K. Rexroth, T. Roethke, D. Schwartz, K. Shapiro, S. Sontag, A. Tate, and R. P. Warren.

BIBLIOGRAPHY

Babbit, I. *et al. Criticism in America*, 1924 (see Levin below)

Barnes, A. *On Interpretation*, 1988

Bate, W. J. *The Burden of the Past*, 1970

Beaver, H. *The Great American Masquerade*, 1985

Bercovitch, S. and Jehlen, M. (eds.) *Ideology and Classic American Literature*, 1986.

Blackmur, R. P. *T. S. Eliot*, 1928
  The Double Agent: Essays on Craft and Elucidation, 1935
  From Jordan's Delight, 1937 (poem)
  Language as Gesture: Essays in Poetry, 1952
  Form and Value in Modern Poetry, 1957
  New Criticism in the United States, 1959

Bloom, H. *The Anxiety of Influence: A Theory of Poetry*, 1973
  A Map of Misreading, 1975
  See Fite D., *Harold Bloom: The Rhetoric of Romantic Vision*, 1985

Booth, W. C. *A Rhetoric of Irony*, 1975

Brooks, C. *Modern Poetry and the Tradition*, 1939
  The Well Wrought Urn: Studies in the Structure of Poetry, 1947
  The Hidden God: Studies in Hemingway, Faulkner, Yeats, Eliot, and Warren, 1963.
  American Literature: Mirror, Lens or Prism?, 1967
  A Shaping Joy: Studies in the Writer's Craft, 1972
  The Language of the American South, 1985

Brooks, C. and Warren, R. P. *Understanding Poetry*, 1938, 4th edn, 1976
  Understanding Fiction, 1943
  Modern Rhetoric, 1949

Brooks, C. and Heilman, R. *Understanding Drama*, 1947

Brooks, C. and Wimsatt, W. K. Jr *Literary History: A Short History*, 1957
  See Simpson, L. P. (ed.) *The Possibilities of Order: Cleanth Brooks and his Work*, 1976

Brooks, Van Wyck *America's Coming of Age*, 1915
  Letters and Leadership, 1918
  The Ordeal of Mark Twain, 1920
  The Pilgrimage of Henry James, 1925
  The Flowering of New England, 1815–1865, 1936
  New England, Indian Summer, 1865–1915, 1940
  The Times of Melville and Whitman, 1947
  The Confident Years, 1885–1915, 1952
  The Writer in America, 1953
  See Hoopes, J. *Van Wyck Brooks in Search of American Culture*, 1977; Vitelli, J. R. *Van Wyck Brooks: A Reference Guide*, 1977

Brower, R. A. and Poirier, R. (eds.) *In Defense of Reading: A Reader's Approach to Literary Criticism*, 1962

Conn, P. *Literature in America: An Illustrated History*, 1989

Contemporary Literary Criticism, 1973–   (with cumulative index)

Crane, R. S. *The Languages of Criticism and the Structure of Poetry*, 1953 (ed.) *Critics and Criticism: Ancient and Modern*, 1952, abridged 1953

Curley, D. N. et al. (eds.) *A Library of Literary Criticism: Modern American Literature*, 3 vols, 4th edn, 1969

Elton, W. *A Glossary of the New Criticism*, 1949

Farrell, J. T. *The League of Frightened Philistines*, 1945
Literature and Morality, 1947

Fiedler, L. A. *Collected Essays*, 2 vols. 1971
No! In Thunder: Essays on Myth and Literature, 1960

Fraiberg, L. *Psychoanalysis and American Literary Criticism*, 1960

Fraser, J. *The Name of Action: Critical Essays*, 1985

Frye, N. *Anatomy of Criticism: Four Essays*, 1957
The Critical Path: An Essay on the Social Context of Literary Criticism, 1971
See Krieger, M. (ed.) *Northrop Frye in Modern Criticism*, 1966

Gilbert, J. H. *Writers and Partisans: A History of Literary Radicalism in America*, 1968

Glicksberg, C. I. (ed.) *American Literary Criticism, 1900–1950*, 1951

Goodheart, E. *Culture and the Radical Conscience*, 1973
The Failure of Criticism, 1978

Goodman, Paul, *The Structure of Literature*, 1954
Speaking and Language: Defense of Poetry, 1971

Gunn, G. *The Culture of Criticism and the Criticism of Culture*, 1989

Hirsch, E. D. *Validity in Interpretation*, 1967

Hoffman, F. J. *Freudianism and the Literary Mind*, 1957, rev. 1959

Hyman, S. E. *The Armed Vision: A Study in the Methods of Modern Literary Criticism*, 1948

Jay, G. S. and Miller, D. L. (eds.) *After Strange Texts: The Role of Theory in the Study of Literature*, 1984

Jennings, E. H. (ed.) *Science and Literature: New Lenses for Criticism*, 1970

Jones, H. M. *The Theory of American Literature*, 1948, 1965

Kazin, A. *Contemporaries from the 19th Century to the Present*, rev. 1982

Krieger, M. *The New Apologists for Poetry*, 1956, rev. 1963
Theory of Criticism: A Tradition and its System, 1976

Langer, S. K. *Feeling and Form: A Theory of Art*, 1953

Leary, L. (ed.) *Contemporary Literary Scholarship: A Critical Review*, 1958

Leitch, V. B. *American Literary Criticism from the Thirties to the Eighties*, 1987

Levin, H. *Contexts of Criticism*, 1957
Irving Babbit and the Teaching of Literature, 1961
Memories of the Moderns, 1980

McKeon, K. E. *The Moral Measure of Literature*, 1961

McLuhan, M. *The Literary Criticism of Marshall McLuhan, 1943–1962*, ed. E. McNamara, 1969

Manheim, L. and Manheim E. (eds.) *Hidden Patterns: Studies in Psychoanalytic Literary Criticism*, 1966

Matthiessen, F. O. *The Responsibilities of the Critic*, 1952

Miller, P. *Orthodoxy in Massachusetts, 1630–1650*, 1933, 1959

The New England Mind: The Seventeenth Century, 1939, 1954
The New England Mind: From Colony to Province, 1953, 1961
The Raven and the Whale [*Poe and Melville*], 1956
Errand into the Wilderness, 1947, 1964
The Life of the Mind in America, 1965
Nature's Nation, 1967
Moore, Marianne *Predilections*, 1956
More, P. E. *Benjamin Franklin*, 1900
    Shelburne Essays, 11 vols., 1904–21
    New Shelburne Essays, 4 vols., 1928–36
    A Paul Elmer More Miscellany, ed. A. H. Dakin, 1951
    Shelburne Essays on American Literature, ed. D. Aaron, 1963
    See Shafer, R. *Paul Elmer More and American Criticism*, 1935; Dakin, A.
    H. *Paul Elmer More*, 1960
Parker, H. *Flawed Texts and Verbal Icons*, 1984
Parrington, V. L. *Main Currents in American Thought*, 3 vols., 1927–30
Porter, K. A. *The Days Before*, 1953
Pritchard, J. P. *Criticism in America*, 1956
Rahv, P. *Image and Idea: Twenty Essays on Literary Themes*, 1957
    Literature and the Sixth Sense, 1969
    The Myth and the Powerhouse, 1965
Rathbun, J. W. (ed.) *American Literary Criticism, 1800–1965*, 3 vols., 1979
Rothenburg, J. and D. (eds.) *Symposium of the Whole: A Range of Discourse
    Toward an Ethnopoetics*, 1983
Ruland, R. *The Rediscovery of American Literature: Premises of Critical Taste,
    1900–1940*, 1967
    Theories of American Literature: I. The Native Muse, 1972; *II. A Storied
    Land*, 1976
Shorer, M. *et al. Criticism: The Foundations of Modern Literary Judgment*, 1948
Slote, B. (ed.) *Myth and Symbol*, 1963
Sontag, S. *Against Interpretation and Other Essays*, 1966
    Styles of Radical Will, 1960
Stallman, (ed.) *Critiques and Essays in Criticism, 1920–1948*, 1949
Stedman, E. C. *Victorian Poets*, 1875
    Poets of America, 1885
    The Nature and Elements of Poetry, 1892
    Victorian Anthology, 1895
    American Anthology, 1900
Stovall, F. *The Development of American Literary Criticism*, 1955
Sutton, W. E. *Modern American Criticism*, 1963
Tompkins, J. P. (ed.) *Reader-Response Criticism from Formalism to Structur-
    alism*, 1980
Trilling, L. *Matthew Arnold*, 1932
    E. M. Forster, 1943
    The Liberal Imagination, 1950
    The Opposing Self: Nine Essays in Criticism, 1955

A Gathering of Fugitives, 1956
Freud and the Crisis of Our Culture, 1956
Beyond Culture: Essays on Literature and Learning, 1960
Sincerity and Authenticity, 1972
Mind in the Modern World, 1972
The Uncertain Future of the Humanistic Ideal, 1974
See Anderson, Q. et al. (eds.) *Art, Politics and Will: Essays in Honor of Lionel Trilling*, 1977; Boyer, R. *Lionel Trilling: Negative Capability and the Wisdom of Avoidance*, 1977; Chance, W. M. *Lionel Trilling: Criticism and Politics*, 1980; Shoben, E. J. Jr *Lionel Trilling: Mind and Character*, 1981; Rodder, J. (ed.) *Critical Essays on Lionel Trilling*, 1993

Warren, A. *Rage for Order*, 1948

Webster, G. *The Republic of Letters: A History of Post-War American Literary Opinion*, 1979

Wellek, R. and Warren, A. *Theory of Literature*, 1949

Wilson, E. *Axel's Castle: A Study in the Imaginative Literature of 1870–1930*, 1931
The Triple Thinkers, 1938
The Wound and the Bow, 1941
The Boys in the Back Room: Notes on California Novelists, 1941
Memoirs of Hecate County, 1946, rev. 1960 (novel)
Classics and Commercials: A Literary Chronicle of the Forties, 1950
The Shores of Light: A Literary Chronicle of the Twenties and Thirties, 1952
The Fifties, ed. L. Edel, 1986
The Bit Between My Teeth: A Literary Chronicle of 1950–1965, 1965
See Sherman, P. *Edmund Wilson: A Study of Literary Vocation in Our Time*, 1965; Wain, J. *An Edmund Wilson Celebration*, 1978

Wimsatt, W. K. Jr *Hateful Contraries*, 1965

Wimsatt, W. K. and Beardsley, M. C. *The Verbal Icon: Studies in the Meaning of Poetry*, 1954

Winters, Y. *Primitivism and Decadence*, 1937
Maule's Curse: Seven Studies in the History of American Obscurantism, 1938
The Anatomy of Nonsense, 1943
In Defense of Reason, 1947
The Function of Criticism, 1957
Forms of Discovery: Critical and Historical Essays on the Short Poem in English, 1957
Uncollected Essays and Reviews, ed. Murphy, F., 1957
See Sexton, R. J. *The Complex of Yvor Winters's Criticism*, 1973; Parkinson, T. (ed.) *Hart Crane and Yvor Winters: Their Literary Correspondence*, 1978; Powell, G. *Language and Being in the Poetry of Yvor Winters*, 1980; Davis, D. *Wisdom and Wilderness: The Achievements of Yvor Winters*, 1983

Young, T. D. (ed.) *The New Critics and After*, 1977

Zabel, M. D. *Literary Opinion in America*, rev. 1951; 2nd rev., 2 vols., 1962

VI. POETRY

See also American Critics, Special Groups, Folk and Popular Literature.

Allen, D. M. and Tallman, W. *The Poetics of the New American Poetry*, 1973
Altieri, C. *Enlarging the Temple: New Directions in American Poetry During the 1960s*, 1979
 Self and Sensibility: Contemporary American Poetry, 1984
Alvarez, A. *Stewards of Excellence*, 1958
Baker, C. *The Echoing Green: Romanticism, Modernism, and the Phenomena of Transference in Poetry*, 1984
Beach, J. W. *Obsessive Images: Symbolism in Poetry of the 1930s and 1940s*, 1960
Bloom, H. *Figures of Capable Imagination*, 1976
Bogan, L. *Achievement in American Poetry, 1900–1950*, 1951
Cargas, H. J. *Daniel Berrigan and Contemporary Protest Poetry*, 1972
Christ, C. T. *Victorian and Modern Poetics*, 1985
Ciardi, J. *Mid-Century American Poets*, 1950
Davie, D. *Trying to Explain: Poets on Poetry*, 1979
Dembo, L. S. *Conceptions of Reality in Modern American Poetry*, 1966
Donoghue, D. *Connoisseurs of Chaos: Ideas of Order in Modern American Poetry*, 1965
 (ed.) *Seven American Poets from MacLeish to Nemerov: An Introduction*, 1975
Ehrenpreis, I. (ed.) *American Poetry*, 1965
Engel, B. F. and Julius, P. W. *A New Voice for a New People: Midwestern Poetry 1800–1910*, 1985
Faas, E. *Towards a New American Poetics: Essays and Interviews*, 1978
Feder, L. *Ancient Myth in Modern Poetry*, 1972 (especially for Pound)
Fussell, E. *Lucifer in Harness: American Meter, Metaphor, and Diction*, 1973
Gelpi, A. *A Coherent Splendor: The American Poetic Renaissance 1910–1950*, 1988
Goodman, P. *Speaking and Language: Defence of Poetry*, 1971
Gray, R. *American Poetry of the Twentieth Century*, 1990
Hallberg, R. von *American Poetry and Culture, 1945–1980*, 1985
Haviaras, S. (ed.) *Poet's Voice*, 1978 (recordings of some 130 poems by their authors, 1933–70)
Howard, R. *Alone in America: Essays on the Art of Poetry in the United States since 1950*, 1969
Jackson, R. *Acts of Mind: Conversations with [30] Contemporary Poets*, 1983
Jarrell, R. *Poetry and the Age*, 1953
Kalstone, D. *Five Temperaments: Elizabeth Bishop, Robert Lowell, James Merrill, Adrienne Rich, John Ashbery*, 1977
Kodama, S. *American Poetry and Japanese Culture*, 1985

Kunitz, S. *A Kind of Order, A Kind of Folly*, 1975

Lowell, Amy *Tendencies in Modern American Poetry*, 1917

Malkoff, K. (ed.) *Crowell's Handbook of Contemporary American Poetry*, 1973

Martin, G. and Furbank, P. N. (eds.) *Twentieth-Century Poetry: Critical Essays and Documents*, 1975

Mazzaro, J. (ed.) *Modern American Poetry: Essays in Criticism*, 1970

Mersman, J. F. *Out of the Vietnam Vortex: A Study of Poets and Poetry Against the War*, 1974

Mills, R. J., Jr *Contemporary American Poetry*, 1966

Mottram, E. *Toward Design in Poetry*, 1977, 1984

Nemerov, H. *Poets on Poetry*, 1966

Oberg, A. *Modern American Lyric: Lowell, Berryman, Creeley, and Plath*, 1978

O'Connor, W. van *Sense and Sensibility in Modern Poetry*, 1948

Ostroff, A. (ed.) *The Contemporary Poet as Artist and Critic*, 1964

Owen, G. (ed.) *Modern American Poetry: Essays in Criticism*, 1972

Paz, O. *Children of the Mire: Modern Poetry from Romanticism to the Avant-Garde*, 1971

Pearce, R. H. *The Continuity of American Poetry*, 1961

Pinksy, R. *The Situation of Poetry: Contemporary Poetry and its Tradition*, 1977

Rajan, B. (ed.) *Modern American Poetry*, 1950

Rexroth, K. *American Poetry in the Twentieth Century*, 1971

Rosenthal, M. L. *The New Poets*, 1967

Sanders, E. *Investigating Poetry*, 1976

Simpson, L. *Studies of Dylan Thomas, Allen Ginsberg, Sylvia Plath, and Robert Lowell*, 1979

Southworth, J. G. (ed.) *Some Modern American Poets*, 1950, 1968
  More Modern American Poets, 1954, 1968

Stead, C. K. *The New Poetic*, 1964
  Pound, Yeats, Eliot and the Modernist Movement, 1986

Steinman, L. M. *Made in America: Science, Technology, and American Modernist Poets*, 1987

Sutton, W. *American Free Verse*, 1973

Tate, A. (ed.) *The Language of Poetry*, 1942

Thurley, G. *The American Moment: American Poetry in the Mid-Century*, 1977

Unger, L. (ed.) *Seven Modern American Poets*, 1967

Vendler, H. *Part of Nature, Part of Us: Modern American Poets*, 1980

Waggoner, H. H. *American Poetry from the Puritans to the Present*, 1968, rev. 1984

Walker, R. H. *The Poet and the Gilded Age: Social Themes in Late Nineteenth-Century Verse*, 1963

Weatherhead, A. K. *The Edge of the Image: Marianne Moore, William Carlos Williams, and Some Other Poets*, 1967

White, P. (ed.) *Puritan Poets and Poetics: Seventeenth-Century American Poetry in Theory and Practice*, 1986

Winters, Yvor, *Primitivism and Decadence: A Study of American Experimental Poetry*, 1937

On Modern Poets, 1959

Woodward, K. *At Last, The Real Distinguished Thing*, 1980

VII. NOVEL AND SHORT STORY

See also American Critics, Special Groups, Folk and Popular Literature.

Ahnebrink, L. *The Beginnings of Naturalism in American Fiction, 1891–1903*, 1950, 1961

Aldridge, J. W. *After the Lost Generation: A Critical Study of the Writers of Two Wars*, 1951

 The American Novel and the Way We Live Now, 1983

 (ed.) *Critiques and Essays on Modern Fiction, 1920–1951*, 1952

Allen, D. L. *Science Fiction: An Introduction*, 1973

 Science Fiction Reader's Guide, 1974

Allen, W. *The Modern Novel in Britain and the United States*, 1964

 The English and American Novel from the Twenties to Our Time, 1986

Baumbach, J. *Landscape of Nightmare: Studies in the Contemporary American Novel*, 1965

Beaver, H. *Figures in the Carpet: Irony in the American Novel*, 1962

Bewley, M. *The Complex Fate: Hawthorne, Henry James, and Some Other American Writers*, 1952

 The Eccentric Design, 1959

Blake, N. M. *Novelists' America: Fiction as History, 1910–1940*, 1969

Blotner, J. *The Modern American Political Novel, 1900–1960*, 1966

Booth, W. *The Rhetoric of Fiction*, 1961

Brace, G. W. *The Stuff of Fiction*, 1969

Bradbury, M. *The Modern American Novel*, 1983

Bradbury, M. and Palmer, D. (eds.) *The American Novel in the Nineteen Twenties*, 1971

Bryant, J. H. *The Open Decision: The Contemporary American Novel and its Intellectual Background*, 1970

Chase, R. *The American Novel and its Tradition*, 1957 (1958)

Clareson, T. D. *Some Kind of Paradise: The Emergence of American Science Fiction*, 1985

Clark, R. *History, Ideology and Myth in American Fiction, 1823–52*, 1984

Cooperman, S. *World War I and the American Novel*, 1967

Cowie, A. *The Rise of the American Novel*, 1948

Edel, L. *The Modern Psychological Novel*, 1959, 1964

Fiedler, L. *An End to Innocence*, 1952

 Love and Death in the American Novel, 1960 (1961); rev. 1966

Fisher, P. *Hard Facts: Setting and Form in the American Novel*, 1985

Frederick, J. T. *The Darkened Sky: Nineteenth-Century American Novelists and Religion*, 1969

French, W. *The Social Novel at the End of an Era*, 1966

Frohock, W. M. *The Novel of Violence in America: 1920–1950*, 1950: rev. 1957

Galloway, D. *The Absurd Hero in American Fiction*, 1966, rev. 1981

Geismar, M. *Writers in Crisis: The American Novel Between Two Wars*, 1942
    Rebels and Ancestors, 1953 (Crane to Dreiser)

Gelfant, B. H. *The American City Novel 1900–1950*, 1954

Gerlach, J. *Toward the End: Closure and Structure in the American Short Story*,
    1985

Goodheart, E. *The Failure of Criticism*, 1978
    The Skeptic Disposition in Contemporary Criticism, 1985

Gray, R. *American Fiction: New Readings*, 1983

Harris, C. B. *Contemporary American Novelists of the Absurd*, 1971

Hart, J. D. *The Popular Book: A History of America's Literary Taste*, 1950

Hassan, I. *Radical Innocence: Studies in the Contemporary American Novel*, 1961

Hicks, G. *The Great Tradition: An Interpretation of American Literature Since
    the Civil War*, 1935, rev. 1968

Hicks, J. *In the Singer's Temple: Prose Fictions of Barthelme, Gaines, Brautigan,
    Piercy, Kersey, and Kosinski*, 1981

Hilfer, T. *American Fiction Since 1940*, 1992

Hoffman, D. G. *Form and Fable in American Fiction*, 1961

Hoffman, F. J. *The Modern Novel in America, 1900–1950*, 1951

Howe, I. *Politics and the Novel*, 1967

Howells, W. D. *Criticism and Fiction*, 1891

Hoyt, C. (ed.) *Minor American Novelists*, 1970 (includes N. West)

Karl, F. R. *American Fictions, 1940–1980*, 1982

Kaul, A. N. *The American Vision: Actual and Ideal Society in Nineteenth-
    Century Fiction*, 1963

Kazin, A. *On Native Grounds: An Interpretation of Modern American Prose
    Literature*, 1942, rev. 1956
    *Bright Book of Life: American Novelists and Storytellers from Hemingway to
    Mailer*, 1973

Kerr, H. et al. (eds.) *The Haunted Dusk: American Supernatural Fiction 1820–
    1920*, 1983

Klein, M. *After Alienation: American Novels in Mid-Century*, 1970

Klinkowitz, J. *Literary Disruptions: The Making of a Post-Contemporary
    American Fiction*, 1975, rev. 1980
    The Practice of Fiction in America, 1980

Lee, B. *American Fiction 1865–1940*, 1988

Lehan, R. *A Dangerous Crossing: French Literary Existentialism and the Modern
    American Novel*, 1973

Leisy, E. E. *The American Historical Novel*, 1950

Levin, H. *The Power of Blackness: Hawthorne, Poe, and Melville*, 1958
    Symbolism and Fiction, 1956

Litz, A. W. (ed.) *Modern American Fiction: Essays in Criticism*, 1963

Long, E. *The American Dream and the Popular Novel*, 1985 (Updike, Bellow,
    Steinbeck, Mailer)

McMurty, J. *Victorian Life and Victorian Fiction*, 1986

Malin, I. (ed.) *Psychoanalysis and American Fiction*, 1965

Mangione, J. *The Dream and the Deal: The Federal Writers' Project, 1935–1943*, 1972

Meeter, G. *Bernard Malamud and Philip Roth: A Critical Essay*, 1968

Mellard, J. M. *The Exploded Form: The Modernist Novel in America*, 1980

Millgate, M. *American Social Fiction: James to Cozzens*, 1964

Mizener, A. *Twelve Great American Novels*, 1967

Munson, G. B. *Style and Form in American Prose*, 1929

Nadeau, R. L. *Readings from the New Book on Nature: Physics and Metaphysics in the Modern Novel*, 1981

Nelson, G. B. *Ten Versions of America*, 1972

O'Brien, E. J. *The Advance of the American Short Story*, 1931

O'Connor, W. V. *Seven Modern American Novelists*, 1964

O'Faolain, S. *The Vanishing Hero: Studies of Novelists of the Twenties*, 1957

Patee, F. L. *The Development of the American Short Story: An Historical Survey*, 1923, 1966

Peden, W. *The American Short Story: Front Line in the National Defense of Literature*, 1964
    The American Short Story: Continuity and Change, 1940–1975, 1975

Perkins, G. (ed.) *The Theory of the American Novel*, 1970

Pizer, D. *Realism and Naturalism in Nineteenth-Century American Literature*, 1966

Porte, J. *The Romance in America*, 1969

Quinn, A. H. *American Fiction*, 1936

Rideout, W. B. *The Radical Novel in the United States, 1900–1954*, 1956

Rubin, L. D. and Moore, J. R. (eds.) *The Idea of an American Novel*, 1961

Schneider, R. *Five Novelists of the Progressive Era*, 1965

Stafford, W. T. *Books Speaking to Books: A Contextual Approach to American Fiction*, 1981

Stewart, J. L. *The Burden of Time: The Fugitives and Agrarians*, 1965

Stuckey, W. J. *The Pulitzer Prize Novels: A Critical Backward Look*, 1966

Tanner, T. *City of Words: American Fiction, 1950–1970*, 1971

Taylor, G. O. *The Passages of Thought: Psychological Representation in the American Novel, 1870–1900*, 1969

Taylor, W. F. *The Economic Novel in America*, 1942

Van Doren, C. *The American Novel, 1789–1939*, 1940

Voss, A. *The American Short Story: A Critical Survey*, 1975

Watkins, F. C. *In Time and Place: Some Opinions of American Fiction*, 1977

West, R. B., Jr *The Short Story in America, 1900–1950*, 1952, 1968

VIII. DRAMA

See also Black Literature, Women Writers.

Bentley, E. *The Theatre of Commitment, and Other Essays on Drama in our Society*, 1967
    What Is Theatre? Incorporating the Dramatic Event and Other Reviews, 1944–1967, 1968

Thirty Years of Treason: Excerpts from the Hearings before the House Committee on Un-American Activities, 1938–1968, 1971

Bigsby, C. W. E. *A Critical Introduction to Twentieth-Century American Drama: I. 1900–1940; II. Williams, Miller, Albee; III. Beyond Broadway*, 1982–5

Bogard, T. et al. *American Drama* The Revels History of Drama in English, vol. 8, 1977

Bordman, G. *The Oxford Companion to the American Theatre*, 1984

Boyd, A. K. *The Interchange of Plays Between London and New York, 1910–39*, 1948

Broussard, L. *American Drama: Contemporary Allegory from Eugene O'Neill to Tennessee Williams*, 1962

Brustein, R. *Seasons of Discontent: Dramatic Opinions 1959–1965*, 1965.
    The Culture Watch: Essays on Theatre and Society, 1969–1974, 1975

Clurman, H. *The Fervent Years: The Story of the Group Theatre in the Thirties*, 1945; rev. 1957; rev. again 1975
    The Divine Pastime: Theatre Essays, 1974

Cohn, R. *Dialogue in American Drama*, 1971
    New American Dramatists, 1960–1980, 1982

Deutsch, H. and Hanau, S. *The Provincetown: A Study of the Theatre*, 1931

Dukore, B. F. *American Dramatists, 1918–1945*, 1984

Dunlop, W. *History of the American Theatre*, 2 vols., 1832, repr. 1963

Dusenbury, W. L. *The Theme of Loneliness in Modern American Drama*, 1960

Engel, L. *The American Musical Theater*, rev. 1975

Flanagan, H. *Arena: The History of the Federal Theatre*, 1940

Flexnor, E. *American Playwrights, 1918–1938*, 1938

Freedman, M. *American Drama in Social Context*, 1971

Goldstein, M. *The Political Stage: American Drama and Theater after the Great Depression*, 1974

Gottfried, M. *A Theatre Divided: The Post-War American Stage*, 1967

Grimsted, D. *Melodrama Unveiled: Theater and Culture, 1800–1850*, 1968

Harris, N. *Humbug: The Art of P. T. Barnum*, 1973

Hartman, J. G. *The Development of American Social Comedy, 1787–1936*, 1939, 1971

Heilman, R. B. *The Iceman, the Arsonist, and the Troubled Agent: Tragedy and Melodrama on the Modern Stage*, 1973

Hethmon, R. H. (ed.) *Strasberg at the Actors Studio: Tape-Recorded Sessions*, 1966

Hodge, F. *Yankee Theatre: The Image of America on the Stage, 1825–1850*, 1964

Houseman, J. *Run-Through*, 1972

Hughes, C. *Plays, Politics, and Polemics*, 1973

Kervan, A. B. (ed.) *The Modern American Theater*, 1967

Kolin, P. C. *American Playwrights since 1945*, 1989

Krutch, J. W. *The American Drama Since 1918: An Informal History*, 1939, rev. 1957

Little, S. W. *Off-Broadway: The Prophetic Theater*, 1972

McArthur, B. *Actors and American Culture, 1880–1920*, 1984

McConachie, B. A. and Friedman, D. (eds.) *Theatre for Working-Class Audiences in the United States, 1830–1930*, 1985

Mathews, J. DeH. *The Federal Theatre, 1935–1939*, 1967

Matlaw, M. (ed.) *American Popular Entertainment*, 1979

Mersand, J. E. *The American Drama Since 1930*, 1951

Meserve, W. J. *American Drama to 1900*, 1980

    Heralds of Promise: The Drama of the American People During the Age of Jackson, 1829–1849, 1986

Munk, E. (ed.) *Stanislavski and America*, 1966

Murphy, B. *American Realism and American Drama: 1880–1940*, 1987

O'Connor, J. and Brown, L. *Free, Adult, Uncensored: The Living History of the Federal Theatre Project*, 1980 (pictorial)

Poggi, J. *Theater in America: The Impact of Economic Forces, 1870–1967*, 1968

Porter, T. E. *Myth and Modern American Drama*, 1969

Quinn, A. H. *A History of the American Drama from the Beginning to the Civil War*, rev. 1943

    A History of the American Drama from the Civil War to the Present Day, rev. 1937

Salem, J. M. (ed.) *A Guide to Critical Reviews, Part 1, American Drama 1909–1969*, 2nd edn, 1979

Seilhamer, G. O. *History of the American Theatre before the Revolution*, 3 vols., 1888–91; repr. 1968, intro. by N. Philbrick

Seller, M. S. *Ethnic Theatre in the United States*, 1983

Shank, T. *American Alternative Theatre*, 1982

Sievers, W. D. *Freud on Broadway: A History of Psycho-Analysis and the American Drama*, 1955

Taubman, H. *The Making of the American Theatre*, 1967 (pictorial)

Taylor, K. M. *People's Theater in America [since the 1930s] Documents by the People Who Do It*, 1972

Taylor, W. E. (ed.) *Modern American Drama: Essays in Criticism*, 1968

Toll, R. C. *Blacking Up: The Minstrel Show in Nineteenth-Century America*, 1974

    On With the Show: The First Century of Show Business in America, 1976

Williams, H. B. (ed.) *The American Theatre: A Sum of its Parts*, 1971

Wilson, G. B. *Three Hundred Years of American Drama and Theatre*, 1973

IX. SPECIAL INTEREST GROUPS

Literature is literature but, quite apart from the user's convenience, the attention given in recent decades to the literature of those with particular interests demands separate listing. These are fast-developing areas and a number of specialized bibliographies have been published (e.g. by Gale Research, Detroit) and those should be consulted to take further the modest selection of titles given here. The special number of *Daedalus*, Spring 1961, *Ethnic Groups in American Life*, is worth noting.

Black Literature

See also, under Authors and Works, W. E. DuBois, John Woolman.

Abramson, D. *Negro Playwrights in the American Theatre, 1925–1959,* 1969
    The American Negro Writer and His Roots, 1960
Arata, E. S. and Rotoli, N. J. *Black American Playwrights, 1800 to the Present,* 1976
Baker, H. A. *The Journey Back: Issues in Black Literature and Criticism,* 1980
Bigsby, C. W. E. (ed.) *The Black American Writer, 1. Fiction; 2. Poetry and Drama,* 1969
Bone, R. *The Negro Novel in America,* 1965
Brawley, B. G. *The Negro in Literature and Art in the United States,* 1918; rev. as *The Negro Genius,* 1937, 1966
Brown, S. *The Negro in American Fiction,* 1937
Chametzky, J. *Black Writers Redefine the Struggle,* 1989
Craig, E. Q. *Black Drama of the Federal Theatre Era,* 1980
Cruse, H. *The Crisis of the Negro Intellectual,* 1967
Davis, A. P. *From the Dark Tower: Afro-American Writers 1900 to 1960,* 1974
Douglass, Frederick *Autobiography,* 1845, as *My Bondage and My Freedom,* 1855, with intro. by P. S. Foner, 1969; as *Life and Times of Frederick Douglass,* 1822; see *Narrative of the Life of Frederick Douglass, An American Slave,* ed. B. Quarles, 1960; ed. H. A. Baker, 1982
Elkins, S. *Slavery: A Problem in American Institutional and Intellectual Life,* 1959
Fisher, D. and Stepto, R. B. (eds.) *Afro-American Literature: The Reconstruction of Instruction,* 1979
Ford, N. A. *The Contemporary Negro Novel: A Study in Race Relations,* 1936
Gates, H. L., Jr (ed.) *Black Literature and Literary Theory,* 1984
Gayle, A., Jr (ed.) *Black Expression: Essays by and about Black Americans in the Creative Arts,* 1969
    The Black Aesthetic, 1971
Gibson, D. B. (ed.) *Five Black Writers: Essays on Richard Wright, Ralph Ellison, James Baldwin, Langston Hughes, and LeRoi Jones,* 1970
Gross, S. and Hardy, J. E. (ed.) *Images of the Negro in American Literature,* 1966
Hemenway, R. (ed.) *The Black Novelist,* 1970
Hill, H. (ed.) *Anger and Beyond: The Negro Writer in the United States,* 1966
    The Theater of Black Americans, 2 vols., 1980
Howe, I. 'Black Boys and Native Sons', *Dissent,* 10 (1963), 353–68; repr. in his *A World More Attractive,* 1963
Inge, M. T. et al. (eds.) *Black American Writers: Bibliographical Essays,* 2 vols., 1978
Levine, L. W. *Black Culture and Black Consciousness: Afro-American Folk Thought from Slavery to Freedom,* 1977
Loggins, V. *The Negro Author, his Development in America,* 1931, 1964

Margolies, E. *Native Sons: A Critical Study of Twentieth-Century Negro American Authors*, 1968

Mays, B. E. *The Negro's God as Reflected in His Literature*, 1938, 1968

Mitchell, L. *Black Drama*, 1967

Myrdal, G. *An American Dilemma*, 1944

Oak, V. V. *The Negro Newspaper*, 1948

Ostendorf, B. *Black Literature in White America*, 1982

Payne, L. *Black Novelists and the Southern Literary Tradition*, 1981

Peavy, C. D. *Afro-American Literature and Culture Since World War II*, 1979

Popkin, M. (ed.) *Library of Literary Criticism: Modern Black Writers*, 1978

Redding, J. S. *To Make a Poet Black*, 1939, 1968

    Drumvoices: The Mission of Afro-American Poetry, A Critical History, 1976

Sherman, J. R. *Invisible Poets: Afro-Americans of the Nineteenth Century*, 1974

Starke, C. J. *Black Portraiture in American Fiction: Stock Characters, Archetypes, and Individuals*, 1971

Wagner, J. *Black Poets of the United States from Paul Laurence Dunbar to Langston Hughes*, trans. from French edn 1963 by K. Douglas, 1973

Wallace, M. *Black Masks and the Myth of the Superwoman*, 1979

Washington, T. Booker *Up From Slavery: An Autobiography*, 1901; with intro. by L. R. Harlan, 1986

Welsch, E. K. *The Negro in America: A Research Guide*, 1965

Whelchel, L. H., Jr *My Chains Fell Off: William Wells Brown, Fugitive and Abolitionist*, 1985

Whitlow, R. *Black American Literature: A Critical History with a 1520-title Bibliography*, 1973

Young, J. O. *Black Writers of the Thirties*, 1973

American Indian

A useful bibliography is: Marken, J. W. (ed.) *American Indian: Language and Literature*, 1978

Astrov, M. *The Winged Serpent*, 1946; repr. as *American Indian Prose and Poetry*, 1962

Barbeau, M. *Medicine-Men on the North Pacific Coast*, National Museum of Canada Bulletin 152, 1958

Bierhorst, J. *Four Masterworks of American Indian Literature*, 1974
    Cantares Mexicanos: Songs of the Aztecs, 1985

Brinton, D. G. *Aboriginal American Authors and their Productions*, 1890
    Myths of the New World: A Treatise on the Symbolism and Mythology of the Red Race of America, 1876, 1969

Brown, D. *Bury My Heart at Wounded Knee: An Indian History of the American West*, 1971

Chapman, A. *Literature of the American Indians: Views and Interpretations*, 1975

Cronyn, G. W. *The Path of the Rainbow*, 1918; repr. as *American Indian Poetry: An Anthology of Songs and Chants*, 1972

Densmore, F. *Chippewa Music* and *Teton Sioux Music*, Bureau of American Ethnology Bulletins, 45 and 53, 61, 1910, 1913, 1918

Edmonson, M. S. *The Book of Counsel: The Popol Vuh of the Quiché Maya of Guatemala*, 1971

Eggan, F. *The American Indian: Perspectives for the Study of Social Change*, 1966

Estrada, A. *María Sabina: Her Life and Chants*, 1981

Fiedler, L. A. *The Return of the Vanishing American*, 1968

Fleck, R. F. *Henry Thoreau and John Muir among the Indians*, 1986

Fletcher, A. C. *The Hako: A Pawnee Ceremony*, 1904

Goetz, D. and Morley, S. G. *Popol Vuh: The Sacred Book of the Ancient Quiché Maya*, 1950

Kroeber, K. (ed.) *Traditional American Indian Literature: Texts and Interpretations*, 1981

Matthews, W. *The Night Chant, a Navaho Ceremony*, 1902

Myerhoff, B. G. *Peyote Hunt: The Sacred Journey of the Huichol Indians*, 1974

Neihardt, J. G. *Black Elk Speaks: Being the Life Story of a Holy Man of the Oglala Sioux*, 1961

Norman, H. A. *The Wishing Bone Cycle: Narrative Poems from the Swampy Cree Indians*, 1972, 1982

Olson, C. *Human Universe*, 1967

Pearce, R. H. *The Savages of America: A Study of the Indian and the Idea of Civilization*, 1953; rev. as *Savages and Civilization*, 1965

Radin, P. *The Trickster: A Study in American Indian Mythology*, 1956, 1972

Rothenberg, J. *Technicians of the Sacred: A Range of Poetries from Africa, America, Asia, Europe, and Oceania*, 1968, 1985
    Shaking the Pumpkin: Traditional Poetry of the Indian North Americas, 1972, 1986

Rothenberg J. and Rothenberg, D. *Symposium of the Whole: A Range of Discourse toward an Ethnopoetics*, 1983

Rothenberg, J. and Quasha, G. *America a Prophecy: A New Reading of American Poetry from Pre-Columbian Times to the Present*, 1973

Roys, R. L. *The Book of Chilam Balam of Chumayel*, 1933, 1967

Schubnell, M. *N. Scott Momaday: The Cultural and Literary Background*, 1986

Snyder, G. *Earth House Hold*, 1969

Swann, B. *Smoothing the Ground: Essays on Native American Oral Literature*, 1983

Tedlock, D. *Finding the Center: Narrative Poetry of the Zuni Indians*, 1972
    Popol Vuh, 1985

Tedlock, D. and Tedlock B. *Teachings from the American Earth: Indian Religion and Philosophy*, 1975

Thompson, S. *Tales of the North American Indians*, 1929

Turner, F. W. (ed.) *Viking North American Indian Reader*, 1974 (1977)

Underhill, R. M. *Red Man's America: A History of the Indians in the United States*, 1953

Singing for Power: The Song Magic of the Papago Indians of Southern Arizona, 1968

Velie, A. R. *Four American Indian Literary Masters*, 1982 (Momaday, Welch, Silko, Vizenor)

Washburn, W. E. (ed.) *The American Indian and the United States*, 4 vols, 1979

Jewish Writers and Literature

See the Guide to Information Sources, Nadel, I. B. *Jewish Writers of North America*, 1981.

Fiedler, L. A. *The Jew in the American Novel*, 1959

Fisch, H. *The Dual Image: The Figure of the Jew in English and American Literature*, 1971

Fried, L. *et al.* (eds.) *Handbook of American-Jewish Literature*, 1988

Guttmann, A. *The Jewish Writer in America: Assimilation and the Crisis of Identity*, 1971

Liptzin, S. *The Jew in American Literature*, 1966

Malin, I. *Jews and Americans*, 1965

    (ed.) *Contemporary American-Jewish Literature: Critical Essays*, 1975

Morsand, J. *Traditions in American Literature: A Study of Jewish Characters and Authors*, 1939

Pinsker, S. *The Schlemiel as Metaphor*, 1971 (especially for Bellow)

Roth, P. 'Writing about Jews', *Commentary*, 36 (1963) 445–52

Schulz, M. F. *Radical Sophistication: Studies in Contemporary Jewish-American Novels*, 1969

Walden, D. *Twentieth-Century American-Jewish Fiction Writers*, 1984

Wisse, R. *The Schlemiel as Modern Hero*, 1971

Women Writers: Women in Literature

Agress, L. *The Feminine Irony*, 1978

Auchinloss, L. *Pioneers and Caretakers: A Study of Nine American Women Novelists*, 1965

Barolini, H. *The Dream Book: An Anthology of Writing by Italian American Women*, 1985.

Borden, K. W. and Rinn, F. J. (eds.) *Feminist Literary Criticism: A Symposium*, 1974

Brown, C. and Olson, K. (eds.) *Feminist Criticism: Essays on Theory, Poetry, and Prose*, 1978

Brown, J. *Feminist Drama: Definition and Critical Analysis*, 1979

Chinoy, H. K. and Jenkins, L. W. (eds.) *Women in American Theater*, 1981

Cornillon, S. K. (ed.) *Images of Women in Fiction: Feminist Perspectives*, 1972

Deegan, D. Y. *The Stereotype of the Single Women in American Novels: A Social Study with Implications for the Education of Women*, 1951

Donovan, J. *New England Local Color Literature: A Women's Tradition*, 1983
    (ed.) *Feminist Literary Criticism*, 1975
Duncker, P. *Sisters and Strangers: An Introduction to Contemporary Feminist Fiction*, 1986
Friedan, B. *The Feminine Mystique*, 1953
Gelfant, B. H. *Women Writing in America: Voices in Collage*, 1985
Gilbert, S. and Gubar, S. *The Norton Anthology of Literature by Women*, 1981
Guy, P. A. *Women's Poetry Index [of anthologies, 1945–1982]*, 1985
Hallissy, M. *Venemous Woman: Fear of the Female in Literature*, 1988
Harris, S. K. *Nineteenth-Century American Women's Novels*, 1990
Homans, M. *Women Writers and Poetic Identity*, 1981
Huf, L. *A Portrait of the Artist as a Young Woman: The Writer as Heroine in American Literature*, 1983
Kauffman, L. (ed.) *Feminism and Institutions*, 1989
    Gender and Theory, 1989
Kessler, C. F. (ed.) *Daring to Dream: Utopian Fiction by United States Women Writers, 1836–1919*, 1984 (anthology)
Keyssar, H. *Feminist Theatre: An Introduction to Plays by Contemporary British and American Women*, 1984
Leavitt, D. L. *Feminist Theater Groups*, 1980
Maniero, L. and Faust, L. L. *American Women Writers: A Critical Reference Guide from Colonial Times to the Present*, 4 vols., 1979
Millett, K. *Sexual Politics*, 1971
Newton, J. and Rosenfelt, D. *Feminist Criticism and Social Change*, 1986
Rendall, J. *The Origins of Modern Feminism: Women in Britain, France and the United States, 1780–1860*, 1985
Roller, J. M. *The Politics of the Feminist Novel*, 1986
Spacks, P. M. (ed.) *Contemporary Women Novelists*, 1977
Todd, J. *A Dictionary of British and American Women Writers, 1660–1800*, 1985
Walker, C. *The Nightingale's Burden: Women Poets and American Culture, before 1900*, 1983
Warren, J. W. *The American Narcissus: Individualism and Women in Nineteenth-Century American Fiction*, 1984

X. POPULAR CULTURE, FOLK LITERATURE AND THE
MASS MEDIA

There is a vast literature devoted to popular culture and the mass media. This brief selection does no more than recognize the importance of these aspects in making a full study of the literary arts of the United States. A useful handbook is that edited by Ithiel de Sola Pool, *et al. Handbook of Communication*, 1973.

Popular Culture

Bode, C. *The Half-World of American Culture*, 1965

Davison, P., Shils, E. and Meyersohn, R. (eds.) *Literary Taste, Culture and Mass Communication*, 14 vols. 1978–80

Gans, H. J. *Popular Culture and High Culture: An Analysis and Evaluation of Taste*, 1974

Inge, M. T. *Handbook of American Popular Culture*, 1981

Innis, H. A. *The Bias of Communication*, 1951

Levine, L. W. *Highbrow/Lowbrow: The Emergence of Cultural Hierarchy in America*, 1988

Lowenthal, L. *Literature, Popular Culture and Society*, 1968
    Literature and Mass Culture: Communication in Society, 1983

McLuhan, Marshall, *The Mechanical Bride*, 1951
    The Gutenberg Galaxy, 1962
    Understanding Media: The Extensions of Man, 1964
    See Miller, J. *McLuhan*, 1971; Stearn, G. E. (ed.) *McLuhan Hot and Cool*, 1968

Mass Culture and Mass Media, Daedalus, 1960, published as *Culture for the Millions?*, ed. N. Jacobs

Nye, R. B. *The Unembarrassed Muse: The Popular Arts in America*, 1970

Packard, V. *The Hidden Persuaders*, 1957

Rosenberg, B. and White, D. M. (eds.) *Mass Culture: The Popular Arts in America*, 1957

Russell, J. and Gablick, S. *Popular Art Redefined*, 1969

Schiller, H. I. *Mass Communication and American Empire*, 1970

Seldes, G. V. *The Seven Lively Arts*, 1928
    The Great Audience, 1950
    The Public Arts, 1956

Ulanov, B. *The Two Worlds of American Art: The Private and the Popular*, 1967

Warshow, R. *The Immediate Experience: Movies, Comics, Theatre and other Aspects of Popular Culture*, 1962

White, D. M. (ed.) *Popular Culture in America*, 1970

White, D. H. and Abel, R. *The Funnies: An American Idiom*, 1963

Wilder, A. *The American Popular Song*, 1972

Film

Alexander, W. *Film on the Left: American Documentary Film from 1931–1942*, 1981

Bluem, A. W. *Documentary and American Television: Form, Function, Method*, 1965

Campbell, R. *Cinema Strikes Back: Radical Filmmaking in the United States, 1930–1942*, 1982

Davis, P. and Neve, B. (eds.) *Cinema, Politics, and Society in America*, 1981

French, P. *Westerns: Aspects of a Movie Genre*, 1977

French, W. (ed.) *The South and Film*, 1981

Gomery, D. *The Hollywood Studio System*, 1986

Jacobs, L. *The Rise of the American Film: A Critical History*, 1939

Kael, P. *Kiss, Kiss, Bang, Bang*, 1968

Knight, A. *The Liveliest Art*, 1959

McCann, G. *Woody Allen: New Yorker*, 1990

MacDonald, D. *On Movies*, 1981

Miller, G. *Screening the Novel: Rediscovered American Fiction in Film*, 1980.

Nash, J. R. and Ross, S. R. *The Motion Picture Guide 1913–1984*, 12 vols., 1985

O'Connor, J. E. and Jackson, M. A. (eds.) *American History/American Film: Interpreting the Hollywood Image*, 1979

Quart, L. and Austin, A. *American Film and Society since 1945*, 1984

Roffman, P. and Purdy, J. *The Hollywood Social Problem Film . . . from the Depression to the Fifties*, 1981

Ross, H. *Film as Literature, Literature as Film*, 1987

Ross, L. *Picture*, 1953 (filming *The Red Badge of Courage*)

Sarris, A. *The American Cinema: Directors and Directions, 1929–1968*, 1968

Spatz, T. *Hollywood in Fiction: Some Versions of the American Myth*, 1969

Walker, A. *Stardom: The Hollywood Phenomenon*, 1970

Welles, Orson *The Citizen Kane Book*, 1971 (includes P. Kael, 'Raising Kane')

Folk Literature

Blair, W. *Folklore in America: A Legendary History of our Humorous Heroes*, 1944

Boatright, M. C. (ed.) *Folk Laughter on the American Frontier*, 1949

Dorson, R. *American Folklore*, 1959

Flanagan, J. T. and Hudson A. P. (eds.) *Folklore in American Literature*, 1958

Lomax, A. *The Folk Songs of North America*, 1960

Thomas, H. N. *From Folklore to Fiction*, 1989

Thompson, S. *The Folktale*, 1946

Journalism and Magazines

Brasch, W. M. *Black English and the Mass Media*, 1981

Cook, R. J. *Muckrakers: Crusading Journalists who Changed America*, 1972 (includes Upton Sinclair)

Hollowell, J. *Fact and Fiction: The New Journalism and the Non-Fiction Novel*, 1977

Johnson, M. L. *The New Journalism: The Underground Press, The Artists of Nonfiction, and Changes in the Established Media*, 1971

Mott, F. L. *A History of American Magazines*, 5 vols., 1930–68
    American Journalism, rev. 1962

The News in America, 1952

Peterson, T. *Magazines in the Twentieth Century*, 1956, rev. 1964

Wilson, C. P. *The Labor of Words: Literary Professionalism in the Progressive Era*, 1985 (journalism)

Wood, J. P. *Magazines in the United States: Their Social and Economic Influence*, 1949

Popular Literature

Hackett, A. P. *Seventy Years of Best Sellers 1895–1965*, 3rd edn, 1967

Hart, J. D. *The Popular Book: A History of America's Literary Taste*, 1950

Holtsmark, E. B. *Tarzan and Tradition: Classical Myth in Popular Literature*, 1981

Inge, M. T. (ed.) *Handbook of American Popular Literature*, 1988

Lyles, W. *Putting Dell on the Map: A History of Dell Paperbacks*, 1983

Miner, M. M. *Insatiable Appetites: Twentieth-Century American Women's Bestsellers*, 1984

Mott, F. L. *Golden Multitudes: The Story of Best Sellers in the United States*, 1947

Roberts, T. J. *An Aesthetics of Junk Fiction*, 1990

Radio and Television

Amg, I. *Watching Dallas: Soap Opera and the Melodramatic Imagination*, 1985

Barnouw, E. *History of Broadcasting in the United States*, 3 vols., 1966–70

Koch, H. *The Panic Broadcast*, with script by H. Cantril, 1970 (Orson Welles's *Invasion from Mars*, 1938)

Rose, B. G. (ed.) *TV Genres*, 1985

AUTHORS AND WORKS

Only the more important works are listed individually. Dates are of first publication except for plays, for which first performance is usually given; place of publication is only given if this might be of particular interest in the cases of certain authors. Much work is being done on the preparation of scholarly editions of all important American authors and for many there is a particularly large body of critical writing which shows no sign of abating. These lists are, therefore, highly selective and cannot be quickly overtaken by events. To conserve space, bibliographies of individual writers are not listed: see note preceding Bibliographies and Guides (p. 680).

ADAMS, HENRY BROOKS (1838–1918): Historian; ed. of *North American Review; The Life of Albert Gallatin*, 1879; *Democracy: An American Novel*, 1880; *John Randolph*, 1882; *Esther*, 1884; *The History of the United States During the Administrations of Thomas Jefferson and James Madison*, 9 vols., 1889–91, abridged in 2 vols. by H. Agar as *The Formative Years*, 1948; *The Memoirs of Marau Taaroa, Last Queen of Tahiti*, 1893, rev. 1901; *Mont-Saint-Michel and Chartres: A Study of Thirteenth-Century Unity*, 1904, 1913; *The Education of Henry Adams: A Study of Twentieth-Century Multiplicity*, 1907, 1918; *The Degradation of the Democratic Dogma*, 1920 (essays); *Letters, 1861–1865*, ed. W. C. Ford, 2 vols., 1920; *Letters, 1858–1915*, ed. W. C. Ford, 2 vols., 1930–38; *Henry Adams and His Friends: A Collection of his Unpublished Letters*, ed. H. D. Cater, 1947; *Selected Letters*, ed. N. Arvin, 1951.

See:
E. N. Harbert (ed.), *Critical Essays on Henry Adams*, 1981
G. Hochfield, *Henry Adams: An Interpretation and Introduction*, 1962
W. H. Jordy, *Henry Adams: Scientific Historian*, 1952
H. Kaplan, *Power and Order: Henry Adams and the Naturalistic Tradition in American Fiction*, 1981
J. C. Levenson, *The Mind and Art of Henry Adams*, 1957
E. Samuels, *The Young Henry Adams*, 1948; *Henry Adams: The Middle Years*, 1958; *Henry Adams: The Major Phase*, 1964

ALBEE, EDWARD (b. 1928): Dramatist; *Zoo Story*, 1959; *The Death of Bessie Smith*, 1960; *The Sandbox*, 1960; *The American Dream*, 1961; *Who's Afraid of Virginia Woolf?*, 1962; *Tiny Alice*, 1964; *A Delicate Balance*, 1966; *Box, and Quotations from Chairman Mao Tse-tung, Two Interrelated Plays*, 1968; *All*

Over, 1971; *Seascape*, 1975; *Listening*, and *Counting the Ways*, 1977; *The Lady from Dubuque*, 1980.

See:

R. E. Amacher, *Edward Albee*, 1969; rev. 1981
C. W. E. Bigsby, *Albee*, 1969
    (ed.), *Edward Albee: A Collection of Critical Essays*, 1975
G. Debusscher, *Edward Albee: Tradition and Renewal*, trans. A. W. Williams, 1967
G. McCarthy, *Edward Albee*, 1986
A. Paolucci, *From Tension to Tonic: The Plays of Edward Albee*, 1972
M. E. Rutenberg, *Edward Albee: Playwright in Protest*, 1969

ALCOTT, LOUISA MAY (1832–88): Children's author; *Little Women*, 1868–9.

See:

K. S. Anthony, *Louisa May Alcott*, 1938
Horn Book Magazine, Special Issue, October 1968
J. A. Marsella, *The Promise of Destiny: Children and Women in the Short Stories of Louisa May Alcott*, 1983
M. B. Stern, *Louisa May Alcott*, 1950, 1971; biography
C. Strickland, *Victorian Domesticity: Families in the Life and Art of Louisa May Alcott*, 1985

ANDERSON, MAXWELL (1888–1959): Dramatist; *What Price Glory* (with Laurence Stallings), 1924; *Saturday's Children*, 1927; *Elizabeth the Queen*, 1930; *Winterset*, 1935; *The Eve of St Mark*, 1942; *Joan of Lorraine*, 1946; *Anne of the Thousand Days*, 1948; screenplays inc. *All Quiet on the Western Front*, 1930; Collection: *Eleven Verse Plays, 1929–1939*, 1940.

See:

M. D. Bailey, *Maxwell Anderson, the Playwright as Prophet*, 1957
B. H. Clark, *Maxwell Anderson: The Man and His Plays*, 1933
A. S. Shivers, *Maxwell Anderson*, 1976

ANDERSON, SHERWOOD (1876–1941): Novelist, short-story writer; *Marching Men*, 1917; *Winesburg, Ohio*, 1919; *Poor White*, 1920; *Horses and Men*, 1923; *Dark Laughter*, 1925; Autobiographies: *A Story Teller's Story*, 1924, 1968; *Notebook*, 1926; *Tar: A Midwest Childhood*, 1926, 1969; *Memoirs*, 1942, 1969; *Reader*: ed. P. Rosenfeld, 1947; *Portable Sherwood Anderson*, ed. H. Gregory, 1949, rev. 1972 (1977); *Short Stories*, ed. M. Geismar, 1962.

See:

D. A. Anderson (ed.), *Sherwood Anderson: An Introduction and Interpretation*, 1967
    (ed.), *Critical Essays*, 1981

R. Burbank, *Sherwood Anderson*, 1964
I. Howe, *Sherwood Anderson*, 1951, 1966
J. Schevill, *Sherwood Anderson: His Life and Work*, 1951
W. Sutton, *The Road to Winesburg*, 1972
B. Weber, *Sherwood Anderson*, 1964
R. L. White (ed.), *The Achievement of Sherwood Anderson*, 1966

BALDWIN, JAMES (1924–87): Novelist, essayist, playwright; *Go Tell It on the Mountain*, 1953; *Giovanni's Room*, 1956; *Another Country*, 1962; *Tell Me How Long the Train's Been Gone*, 1968; *Just Above My Head*, 1979; stories: *Going to Meet the Man*, 1965; plays: *The Amen Corner*, 1950, 1964; *Blues for Mr Charlie*, 1964; non-fiction: *Notes of a Native Son*, 1955; *Nobody Knows My Name*, 1961; *The Fire Next Time*, 1963; *A Rap on Race* (with M. Mead), 1971; *The Devil Finds Work*, 1976.

See:

F. M. Eckman, *The Furious Passage of James Baldwin*, 1966
F. L. and N. V. Standley (eds.), *Critical Essays*, 1981
W. J. Weatherby, *Squaring Off: Mailer vs. Baldwin*, 1977

BARTH, JOHN (b. 1930): Novelist and short-story writer; *The Floating Opera*, 1956; *End of the Road*, 1958; *The Sot-Weed Factor*, 1960 (see Ebenezer Cook); *Giles Goat-Boy; or, The Revised New Syllabus*, 1966; stories: *Lost in the Funhouse*, 1968; *Letters*, 1979; essay: 'The Literature of Exhaustion', *Atlantic Monthly*, 220, 1967.

See:

J. J. Waldmeir (ed.), *Critical Essays*, 1980

BARTHELME, DONALD (1931–89): Novelist and short-story writer; *Snow White*, 1967; stories: *Come Back, Dr Caligari*, 1964; *Unspeakable Practices, Unnatural Acts*, 1968; *City Life*, 1970; *The Dead Father*, 1975.

See:

M. Couturier and R. Durand, *Donald Barthelme*, 1982

BEHRMAN, SAMUEL NATHANIEL (1893–1973): Dramatist and novelist; *Serena Blandish; or, The Difficulty of Getting Married* (based on Enid Bagnold's novel), 1929; *Biography*, 1932; *Rain from Heaven*, 1934; *End of Summer*, 1936; *No Time for Comedy*, 1939; *Jacobowsky and the Colonel* (based on Franz Werfel's play), 1944; autobiography: *People in a Diary*, 1972 (as *Tribulations and Laughter*, 1972).

See:

K. T. Reed, *S. N. Behrman*, 1975

BELASCO, DAVID (1859–1931): Dramatist, actor, and producer noted for scenic innovation; *Madame Butterfly* (with L. Long), 1900; *The Girl of the Golden West*, 1905; *The Return of Peter Grimm*, 1911; all in *Six Plays*, ed. M. J. Moses, 1929.

See:

L.-L. Marker, *David Belasco: Naturalism in the American Theatre*, 1975

BELLOW, SAUL (b. 1915): Novelist, b. Quebec, educated USA; *Dangling Man*, 1944; *The Victim*, 1947; *The Adventures of Augie March*, 1953; *Seize the Day: with Three Short Stories and a One-Act Play*, 1956; *Henderson the Rain King*, 1959; *Herzog*, 1964, *Criticism and Text*, ed. I. Howe, 1974; *Mosby's Memoirs and Other Stories*, 1968; *Mr Sammler's Planet*, 1970; *Humboldt's Gift*, 1975; *The Dean's December*, 1982; stories: *Him with His Foot in His Mouth*, 1984; non-fiction: *Recent American Fiction* (lecture), 1963; *To Jerusalem and Back*, 1976; *Portable Saul Bellow*, ed. G. Josipovici, 1974 (1977).

See:

A. Bezanker, 'The Odyssey of Saul Bellow', *Yale Review*, 58, 1969, 359–71
M. Bradbury, *Saul Bellow*, 1986
J. Braham, *A Sort of Columbus: The American Voyages of Saul Bellow's Fiction*, 1984
H. Cixous-Berger, 'Situation de Saul Bellow', *Lettres Nouvelles*, March/April 1967, 130–45
S. B. Cohen, *Saul Bellow's Enigmatic Laughter*, 1974
D. Fuchs, *Saul Bellow: Vision and Revision*, 1983
I. Malin, *Saul Bellow and the Critics*, 1957
J. Newman, *Saul Bellow and History*, 1984
K. M. Opdahl, *The Novels of Saul Bellow*, 1967
E. Rovit, *Saul Bellow: A Collection of Critical Essays*, 1975
T. Tanner, *Saul Bellow*, 1965

BERRYMAN, JOHN (1914–72): Poet; *Selected Poems 1938–1968*, 1972; *Henry's Fate and Other Poems*, 1972; essays and reviews: *The Freedom of the Poet*, 1976; critical biography: *Stephen Crane*, 1950, 1962.

See:

G. Q. Arpin, *The Poetry of John Berryman*, 1978
J. Conarroe, *John Berryman: An Introduction to the Poetry*, 1977
J. Haffenden, *John Berryman: A Critical Commentary*, 1980
    Life, 1982

BEVERLEY, ROBERT (c. 1673–1722): Historian, b. Virginia, educated England, ran family plantation in Virginia and was elected to Virginia House of Burgesses; *The History and Present State of Virginia*, London 1705, rev. 1722; ed. L. B. Wright, 1947.

BIERCE, AMBROSE (1842–1914?): Short-story writer and journalist who disappeared during civil war in Mexico; *Tales of Soldiers and Civilians*, 1891, as *In the Midst of Life*, 1898; *Beetles in Amber*, poem, 1892; *Can Such Things Be?*, 1893; non-fiction: *The Cynic's Word Book*, 1906, as *The Devil's Dictionary*, 1911; *Wright it Right*, essay, 1909; *Collected Writings*, ed. C. Fadiman, 1946; *Complete Short Stories*, ed. E. J. Hopkins, 1970; L. I. Berkove (ed.), *Skepticism and Dissent: Selected Journalism from 1898–1901*, 1980; *The Enlarged Devil's Dictionary*, ed. E. J. Hopkins and J. M. Myers, 1967 (1983).

See:

M. E. Grenander, *Ambrose Bierce*, 1971
R. O'Connor, *A Biography*, 1967 (1968)
R. A. Wiggins, *Ambrose Bierce*, 1964

BISHOP, ELIZABETH (1911–79): Poet; *Selected Poems*, 1967; *Complete Poems*, 1969.

See:

A. Stevenson, *Elizabeth Bishop*, 1966
World Literature Today, Special Issue, 51 (1977)

BRACKENRIDGE, HUGH HENRY (1748–1816): Editor and author, b. Scotland, educated Princeton; *A Poem on the Rising Glory of America*, 1772; novel: *Modern Chivalry*, serialized 1792–1815, ed. L. Leary, 1965.

See:

C. M. Newlin, *Life and Writings of Hugh Henry Brackenridge*, 1932

BRADFORD, WILLIAM (1590–1657): Pilgrim Father and governor of Plymouth colony, being re-elected thirty times; *History of Plimmouth Plantation*, unpublished until 1856, ed. S. E. Morison, 1952.

See:

B. Smith, *Bradford of Plymouth*, 1951

BRADSTREET, ANNE (c. 1612–72): Poet; *The Tenth Muse Lately Sprung Up in America*, London 1650; *Complete Works*, ed. J. R. McElrath, Jr, and A. P. Robb, 1981; Selection: A. P. Amore, ed., *A Woman's Inner World: Selected Poetry and Prose*, 1983

See:

John Berryman, *Homage to Mistress Bradstreet*, poem, 1956
J. Piercy, *Anne Bradstreet*, 1965
A. Stanford, *Anne Bradstreet: The Worldly Philosopher*, 1974
E. W. White, *Anne Bradstreet: The Tenth Muse*, 1978

BRAUTIGAN, RICHARD (b. 1935): Novelist and poet; *A Confederate General from Big Sur*, 1964; *Trout Fishing in America*, 1967; *In Watermelon Sugar*, 1968; collected poems: *The Pill versus the Springhill Mining Disaster*, 1968.

See:
M. Chénetier, *Richard Brautigan*, 1983

BROWN, CHARLES BROCKDEN (1771–1810): Novelist, journalist, essayist, founder (with Elihu Smith) of Society for the Attainment of Useful Knowledge; *Wieland*, 1798; *Ormond*, 1799; *Arthur Mervyn*, 1799; *Edgar Huntley*, 1799; *Clara Howard*, 1801 (in England as *Philip Stanley*); *Jane Talbot*, 1801; *The Novels*, 6 vols., 1887, 1868; *Works*, ed. S. J. Krause and S. W. Reid, proj. 8 vols., 1969–

See:
D. L. Clark, *Charles Brockden Brown: Pioneer Voice of America*, 1952
D. A. Ringe, *Charles Brockden Brown*, 1966
H. R. Warfel, *Charles Brockden Brown: American Gothic Novelist*, 1949

BRYANT, WILLIAM CULLEN (1794–1878: Lawyer, journalist, editor, political campaigner (especially for Lincoln); *Poetical Works*, 2 vols., ed. P. Godwin, 1883; *Prose Writings*, 2 vols., ed. P. Godwin, 1884; representative selections, *William Cullen Bryant*, 1935.

See:
A. F. McLean, *William Cullen Bryant*, 1964

BUCK, PEARL SYDENSTRICKER (1892–1973): Novelist, Nobel Prize 1938; *The Good Earth*, 1931; *Sons*, 1932; *The Mother*, 1933; *A House Divided*, 1935; trans. from Chinese: *All Men Are Brothers*, 1933.

See:
P. Doyle, *Pearl S. Buck*, 1965

BULLINS, ED (b. 1935): Dramatist; *The Electric Nigger*, 1968; *Goin' a Buffalo*, 1968; *The Theme is Blackness: 'Corner' and Other Plays*, 1972.

BURKE, KENNETH DUVA (b. 1897): Poet, music and literary critic, short-story writer; *Counter-Statement*, 1931, rev. 1953; *Permanence and Change: Anatomy of Purpose*, 1935, rev. 1954; *Attitudes Toward History*, 1937; *The Philosophy of Literary Form: Studies in Symbolic Action*, 1941; *A Grammar of Motives*, 1945; *A Rhetoric of Motives*, 1950; *A Rhetoric of Religion*, 1961; *Language as Symbolic Action: Essays on Life, Literature, and Method*, 1966; *Collected Poems, 1915–1967*, 1968; selections: *Perspectives of Incongruity*, and *Terms of Order*, ed. S. E. Hyman, 1964.

See:

G. E. Henderson, *Kenneth Burke: Literature and Language as Symbolic Action*, 1989

G. Knox, *Critical Moments: Kenneth Burke's Categories and Critiques*, 1957

W. H. Rueckert, *Kenneth Burke and the Drama of Human Relations*, 1963
  Critical Responses to Kenneth Burke, 1924–1966, 1969

BURROUGHS, WILLIAM (b. 1914): Novelist; *Naked Lunch*, Paris 1959, New York 1962; *The Soft Machine*, Paris 1961, New York 1966; *The Ticket that Exploded*, Paris 1962, New York 1967; *Nova Express*, New York 1964; *The Job*, interview on working methods, 1970.

See:

D. Lodge, 'Objections to William Burroughs', *Critical Quarterly*, 8 (1966), 203–12

E. Mottram, *William Burroughs: The Algebra of Need*, 1970

BYRD II, WILLIAM (1674–1744): Virginian landowner and lawyer, educated England, elected to Virginia House of Representatives and Council of State, twice represented Virginia in London; declined to publish in his lifetime; *The Westover Manuscripts*, 1841; *Prose Works*, ed. L. B. Wright, 1966; *The London Diary, 1717–1721, and Other Writings*, ed. L. B. Wright and M. Tinling, 1958.

See:

P. Marambaud, *William Byrd of Westover*, 1970

CALDWELL, ERSKINE (1903–87): Novelist and short-story writer; *Tobacco Road*, 1932; *God's Little Acre*, 1933; *Journeyman*, 1935; *Georgia Boy*, 1943; *Complete Stories*, 1953; autobiography: *Call It Experience: The Years of Learning How to Write*, 1951; biography of his father: *Deep South*, 1968; *Writing in America*, 1967.

See:

S. MacDonald (ed.), *Critical Essays on Erskine Caldwell*, 1981

CAPOTE, TRUMAN (1924–84): Novelist; *Breakfast at Tiffany's: A Short Novel and Three Stories*, 1958; *In Cold Blood*, 1965; *Selected Writings*, 1963.

CATHER, WILLA SIBERT (1873–1947): Novelist and short-story writer; *April Twilights*, poems, 1903, enlarged 1933; *Alexander's Bridge*, 1912; *O Pioneers!*, 1913; *The Song of the Lark*, 1915; *My Antonia*, 1918; *One of Ours*, 1922; *A Lost Lady*, 1923; *The Professor's House*, 1925; *My Mortal Enemy*, 1926; *Death Comes for the Archbishop*, 1927; *Shadows on the Rock*, 1931; *Lucy Gayheart*, 1935; *Sapphira and the Slave Girl*, 1940; stories: *The Troll Garden*, 1905; *Youth and the Bright Medusa*, 1920; *Obscure Destinies*, 1932; *Collected Short*

Fiction, 1892–1912, ed. V. Faulkner, 1965; *Uncle Valentine and Other Stories: Uncollected Fiction, 1915–29*, ed. B. Slote, 1973; essays etc.: *Not Under Forty*, 1936; *On Writing: Critical Studies on Writing as an Art*, ed. S. Tennant, 1949; *The Kingdom of Art: Willa Cather's First Principles and Critical Principles, 1893–1896*, ed. B. Slote, 1966; *The World and the Parish: Willa Cather's Critical Articles and Reviews, 1893–1902*, ed. W. M. Curtin, 2 vols., 1970.

See:

M. Arnold, *Willa Cather's Short Fiction*, 1984
M. R. Bennett, *The World of Willa Cather*, 1951, rev. 1961
E. and L. Bloom, *Willa Cather's Gift of Sympathy*, 1962
P. Gerber, *Willa Cather*, 1975
R. Giannone, *Music in Willa Cather's Fiction*, 1968
E. Lewis, *Willa Cather Living: A Personal Record*, 1953
J. Murphy (ed.), *Five Essays on Willa Cather*, 1974
    (ed.), *Critical Essays on Willa Cather*, 1984
S. O'Brien, *Willa Cather: The Emerging Voice*, 1987
P. Robinson, *Willa: The Life of Willa Cather*, 1983
W. Schroeter (ed.), *Willa Cather and Her Critics*, 1967
E. S. Sergeant, *Willa Cather: A Memoir*, 1953
B. Slote and V. Faulkner (eds.), *The Art of Willa Cather*, 1974
D. Van Ghent, *Willa Cather*, 1964
J. Woodress, *Willa Cather: Her Life and Art*, 1970

CHOPIN, KATE (1851–1904): Novelist and short-story writer; *At Fault*, 1890; *The Awakening*, 1899; stories: *Bayou Folk*, 1894; *A Night in Acadie*, 1897; *Complete Works*, ed. P. Seyersted, 2 vols., 1969; *The Awakening and Selected Stories*, ed. B. H. Solomon, 1976.

See:

C. Arnavon, intro. to *Edna*, French title of *The Awakening*, Paris 1953
L. Leary, intro. to *The Awakening and Other Stories*, 1970
W. Martin (ed.), *New Essays on 'The Awakening'*, 1988
P. Seyersted, *Kate Chopin: A Critical Biography*, 1969

CONNELLY, MARC (1890–1980): journalist, dramatist, novelist; *Merton of the Movies*, with George S. Kaufman, 1922; *The Green Pastures: A Fable*, adapted from R. Bradford, *Ol' Man Adam an' His Children*, 1930; memoirs: *Voices Off-Stage*, 1968.

See:

P. T. Nolan, *Marc Connelly*, 1969

COOK, EBENEZER (1670–c.1732): Hudibrastic poet; *The Sot-Weed Factor; or, A Voyage to Maryland*, 1708.

See:

J. Barth, *The Sot-Weed Factor*, (novel) 1960

P. E. Diser, 'The Historical Ebenezer Cook', *Critique*, 10 (1968), 48–59

COOPER, JAMES FENIMORE (1789–1851): Novelist; *The Spy*, 1821; *The Pioneers*, 1823; *The Pilot*, 1823; *Lionel Lincoln*, 1825; *The Last of the Mohicans*, 1826; *The Prairie*, 1827; trilogy: *The Bravo*, 1831; *The Heidenmauer*, 1832; *The Headsman*, 1833; *Homeward Bound*, 1838, and sequel: *Home As Found*, 1838; *The Pathfinder*, 1840; *The Deerslayer*, 1841; trilogy: *Satanstoe*, 1845; *The Chainbearer*, 1845; *The Redskins*, 1846; *The Crater*, 1847; *The Ways of the Hour*, 1850; essays: *A Letter to His Countrymen*, 1834; *Notions of the Americans*, 1836; *The American Democrat*, 1838; *Novels*, 32 vols., 1859–61; *Works*, 33 vols., 1895–6; *Letters and Journals*, ed. J. F. Beard, 6 vols., 1960–68.

See:

M. Bewley, 'Form in Fenimore Cooper's Novels', in *The Eccentric Design*, 1959

M. Cunningham (ed.), *James Fenimore Cooper: A Reappraisal*, 1954

G. Dekker, *James Fenimore Cooper: The American Scott*, 1957

G. Dekker and J. P. McWilliams (eds.), *Fenimore Cooper: Critical Heritage*, 1985

W. Fields (ed.), *James Fenimore Cooper: A Collection of Critical Essays*, 1979

J. Grossman, *James Fenimore Cooper*, 1949

K. S. House, *Cooper's Americans*, 1965

D. H. Lawrence, *Studies in Classic American Literature*, 1923, 1961

T. Philbrick, *James Fenimore Cooper and the Development of American Sea Fiction*, 1961

Y. Winters, 'Fenimore Cooper, or the Ruins of Time', in *Maule's Curse*, 1938

COTTON, JOHN (1584–1652): Theologian, Dean of Emmanuel College, Cambridge, England; migrated to Bay Colony 1633; *God's Promise to His Plantation*, 1630; *An Abstract of the Lawes of New England*, 1641; *The Bloudy Tenent Washed and Made White in the Bloud of the Lambe*, 1647 – see Roger Williams; *The Way of Congregational Churches Cleared*, 1648; selection: *John Cotton on the Churches of New England*, ed. L. Ziff, 1968.

See:

E. H. Emerson, *John Cotton*, 1965

J. Norton, *Abel Being Dead Yet Speaketh*, London 1658, Boston 1834 (first American biography)

L. Ziff, *The Career of John Cotton: Puritanism and the American Experience*, 1962

COZZENS, JAMES GOULD (1903–78): Novelist; *SS San Pedro*, 1931; *The Last*

Adam, 1933 – in England as *A Cure of Flesh: Men and Brethren*, 1936; *Ask Me Tomorrow*, 1940; *The Just and the Unjust*, 1942; *Guard of Honor*, 1948; *By Love Possessed*, 1957; *Morning, Noon, and Night*, 1968.

See:
F. Bracher, *The Novels of James Gould Cozzens*, 1959
G. Hicks, *James Gould Cozzens*, 1968
D. E. S. Maxwell, *Cozzens*, 1954
H. J. Mooney, *James Gould Cozzens: Novelist of Intellect*, 1963

CRANE, HART (1899–1932): Poet; *White Buildings*, 1926; *The Bridge*, 1930; *Complete Poems and Selected Letters and Prose* (ed.) B. Weber, 1946.

See:
R. W. Butterfield, *The Broken Arc: A Study of Hart Crane*, 1969
L. S. Dembo, *Hart Crane's Sanskrit Charge: A Study of The Bridge*, 1961
A. Hanley, *Hart Crane's Holy Vision: 'White Buildings'*, 1981
P. Horton, *Hart Crane: The Life of an American Poet*, 1937, 1957
H. A. Leibowitz, *Hart Crane: An Introduction to the Poetry*, 1968
R. W. B. Lewis, *The Poetry of Hart Crane*, 1967
H. N. Nilsen, *Hart Crane's Divided Vision*, 1980
A. Trachtenberg (ed.), *Hart Crane: A Collection of Critical Essays*, 1981
J. Unterecker, *Voyages: A Life of Hart Crane*, 1969

CRANE, STEPHEN (1871–1900): Novelist, poet and short-story writer; *Maggie: A Girl of the Streets*, 1893; *The Red Badge of Courage*, 1895; *George's Mother*, 1896; *The Third Violet*, 1897; *Moran of the Lady Letty*, 1898; *Active Service*, 1899; *The O'Ruddy*, 1903, unfinished, completed Robert Barr; poetry: *The Black Riders*, 1895; *War is Kind*, 1899; *Poems*, ed. J. Katz, 1966; stories and sketches: *The Little Regiment*, 1896; *The Open Boat*, 1898; *The Monster*, 1899; *Wounds in the Rain*, 1899; *Whilhomville Stories*, 1900; *Last Words*, 1902; non-fiction: *Notebook*, 1969; *Letters*, ed. R. W. Stallman and L. Gilkes, 1960; *Works*, ed. F. Bowers, 10 vols., 1969–75; *Portable Stephen Crane*, ed. J. Katz, 1969 (1977)

See:
M. Bassan (ed.), *Stephen Crane: A Collection of Critical Essays*, 1967
T. Beer, *Stephen Crane*, 1923
J. Berryman, *Stephen Crane*, 1950, 1962
E. H. Cady, *Stephen Crane*, 1962
D. G. Hoffman, *The Poetry of Stephen Crane*, 1957
J. Katz (ed.), *Stephen Crane in Transition*, 1972
M. LaFrance, *A Reading of Stephen Crane*, 1971
C. K. Linson, *My Stephen Crane*, ed. E. H. Cady, 1958
E. Solomon, *Stephen Crane: From Parody to Realism*, 1966
R. W. Stallman, *Stephen Crane*, 1968
R. M. Weatherford (ed.), *Stephen Crane: The Critical Heritage*, 1973

CREELEY, ROBERT WHITE (b. 1926): Poet, novelist, short-story writer; *Divisions and Other Early Poems*, 1969; *Selected Poems*, 1972; *Later: New Poems*, 1979; novel: *The Island*, 1963; stories, *The Gold Diggers*, 1954, 1965.

See:

D. Allen (ed.), *Contexts of Poetry: Interviews, 1961–1971*, 1973
G. F. Butterick (ed.), *Charles Olson and Robert Creeley: The Complete Correspondence*, 2 vols., 1980
C. D. Edelberg, *Robert Creeley's Poetry: A Critical Introduction*, 1978
A. C. Ford, *Robert Creeley*, 1978

CRÈVECOEUR, J. H. St J. de (1735–1813): b. Normandy, educated in part in England, fought against British in Canada and then migrated to America, naturalized 1764; imprisoned by British, returned to France 1780, then again in 1783 to America where he served as French Consul until 1790 before retiring to Europe. *Letters from an American Farmer*, 1782 (in French), ed. W. B. Blake, 1957; *Sketches of Eighteenth-Century America*, ed. H. L. Bourdin, et al., 1925; both, ed. A. E. Stone, 1981.

See:

G. W. Allen and R. Asselineau, *St John de Crèvecoeur: The Life of an American Farmer*, 1988
T. Philbrick, *St John de Crèvecoeur*, 1968

CUMMINGS, EDWARD ESTLIN (1894–1962): Poet and painter; *Complete Poems*, 2 vols., 1968; *Etcetera: The Unpublished Poems*, ed. G. J. Firmage et al., 1984; plays: *Him*, 1928; *Santa Claus*, 1946; prose: *The Enormous Room*, 1922; collections of drawings and paintings include *CIOPW*, 1933.

See:

N. Friedeman, *E. E. Cummings: The Art of His Poetry*, 1960
   e.e.cummings: The Growth of a Writer, 1964
B. A. Marks, *E. E. Cummings*, 1964
C. Norman, *The Magic-Maker: E. E. Cummings*, 1958
R. E. Wegner, *The Poetry and Prose of E. E. Cummings*, 1965

DAHLBERG, EDWARD (1900–1977): Autobiographical author; *Bottom Dogs*, intro. by D. H. Lawrence, 1930; *From Flushing to Calvary*, 1932; *Those Who Perish*, 1934; *Do These Bones Live?*, 1941; *The Flea of Sodom*, 1950; *Because I Was Flesh*, 1964; non-fiction: *The Sorrows of Priapus*, 1957; *Aims for Oblivion*, 1964; *Reasons of the Heart*, 1965; *The Carnal Myth*, 1968; poetry: *Cipango's Hinder Door*, 1966; *Edward Dahlberg Reader*, ed. P. Carroll, 1967.

See:

H. Billings, *Edward Dahlberg: American Ishmael of Letters*, 1968

DANA, RICHARD HENRY, JR (1815–82): *Two Years Before the Mast: A Personal Narrative of Life at Sea*, 1840; *An Autobiographical Sketch*, 1953; *Journal*, ed. R. F. Lucid, 3 vols., 1968.

See:

H. W. L. Dana, *The Dana Saga*, 1941

DICKEY, JAMES (b. 1923): Poet and novelist; poetry: *Into the Stone*, 1960; *Drowning with Others*, 1962; *Helmets*, 1964; *Buckdancer's Choice*, 1965; *Poems 1957–1967*, 1967; *The Zodiac*, 1976; *The Strength of Fields*, 1979; *The Early Motion*, 1981; *The Central Motion: Poems, 1968–1979*, 1983; novel: *Deliverance*, 1970; essays: *The Suspect in Poetry*, 1964; *Babel to Byzantium: Poets and Poetry Now*, 1968.

See:

N. Bowers, *James Dickey: The Poet as Pitchman*, 1985
R. J. Calhoun, *James Dickey: The Expansive Imagination*, 1973
B. Weigl and T. R. Hummer (eds.), *The Imagination as Glory: The Poetry of James Dickey*, 1984

DICKINSON, EMILY (1830–86): Poet; *The Poems*, ed. T. H. Johnson, 3 vols., 1955; *Complete Poems*, ed. T. H. Johnson, 1 vol., 1958; selections: *Choice of Emily Dickinson's Verse*, ed. Ted Hughes, 1968; *Selected Poems*, ed. James Reeves, 1959; *Letters*, ed. T. H. Johnson and T. Ward, 3 vols., 1958; *Manuscript Books*, ed. R. W. Franklin, 2 vols., 1981.

See:

C. A. Anderson, *Emily Dickinson's Poetry: Stairway for Surprise*, 1960
C. R. and C. F. Blake, *The Recognition of Emily Dickinson*, 1964
R. V. Chase, *Emily Dickinson*, 1951
J. F. Diehl, *Dickinson and the Romantic Imagination*, 1981
J. D. Eberwein, *Dickinson: Strategies of Limitation*, 1985
A. J. Gelpi, *Emily Dickinson: The Mind of the Poet*, 1965
C. Griffith, *The Long Shadow in Emily Dickinson's Tragic Poetry*, 1964.
S. Juhasz, *The Undiscovered Continent: Emily Dickinson and the Space of the Mind*, 1983
   (ed.), *Feminist Critics Read Emily Dickinson*, 1983
B. Lindberg-Seyersted, *The Voice of the Poet: Aspects of Style in the Poetry of Emily Dickinson*, 1968
R. Miller, *The Poetry of Emily Dickinson*, 1965
B. A. C. Mossberg, *Emily Dickinson: When a Daughter is a Writer*, 1983
D. Porter, *The Art of Emily Dickinson's Early Poetry*, 1966
   Dickinson: The Modern Idiom, 1981
B. L. St Armand, *Emily Dickinson and Her Culture: The Soul's Society*, 1985
R. B. Sewall, *The Life of Emily Dickinson*, 2 vols., 1974
   (ed.), *Emily Dickinson*, 1963

DIDION, JOAN (b. 1934): Novelist and essayist; *Run River*, 1963; *Play It As It Lays*, 1970; *A Book of Common Prayer*, 1977; essays: *Slouching Toward Bethlehem*, 1968; *The White Album*, 1979.

DOCTOROW, EDGAR LAURENCE (b. 1931): Novelist; *The Book of Daniel*, 1971.

See:
P. Levine, *E. L. Doctorow*, London 1985

DONLEAVY, JAMES PATRICK (b. 1926): Novelist; *The Ginger Man*, Paris 1955; London 1956, New York 1958 (expurgated); London 1963, New York 1965 (unexpurgated); *Fairy Tales of New York*, 1961; *A Singular Man*, New York 1963, London 1964; *Meet My Maker the Mad Molecule*, New York 1964, London 1965; *The Saddest Summer of Samuel S.*, New York 1966, London 1967; *The Beastly Beatitudes of Balthazar B.*, New York 1968, London 1969; *The Onion Eaters*, 1971; *A Fairy Tale of New York*, 1973; *The Destinies of Darcy Dancer, Gentleman*, 1977; *Schultz*, 1979; *The Plays of J. P. Donleavy*, New York 1972, Harmondsworth, 1974.

See:
J. P. Mastinton, *J. P. Donleavy: The Style of his Sadness*, 1975

DOS PASSOS, JOHN (= John R. Madison) (1896–1970): Novelist and social historian; *One Man's Initiation – 1917*, 1920; *Three Soldiers*, 1921; *Manhattan Transfer*, 1925; trilogy, *USA*, 1938 = *The 42nd Parallel*, 1930, 1919, 1932, and *The Big Money*, 1936; trilogy, *District of Columbia*, 1952 = *Adventures of a Young Man*, 1939, *Number One*, 1943, and *The Grand Design*, 1949; *Most Likely to Succeed*, 1954; *The Great Days*, 1957; *Midcentury*, 1961; *Century's Ebb*, 1975; non-fiction: *Chosen Country* (autobiographical), 1951; *Mr Wilson's War*, 1963; *The Best Times: An Informal Memoir*, 1966; *The Fourteenth Chronicle: Letters and Diaries of John Dos Passos*, ed. T. Ludington, 1973; selection: *The World in a Glass*, ed. K. Lynn, 1966.

See:
A. Belkind (ed.), *Dos Passos, The Critics, and the Writer's Intention*, 1971
J. D. Brantley, *The Fiction of John Dos Passos*, 1968
R. G. Davis, *John Dos Passos*, 1962
M. Landsberg, *Dos Passos's Path to 'USA': A Political Biography 1912–1936*, 1971
T. Ludington, *John Dos Passos: A Twentieth-Century Odyssey*, 1980
B. Maine (ed.), *Dos Passos: The Critical Heritage*, 1988
J. Rohrkemper, *John Dos Passos: A Reference Guide*, 1980
R. C. Rosen, *John Dos Passos: Politics and the Writer*, 1981
J.-P. Sartre, 'John Dos Passos', in *Literary and Philosophical Essays*, 1956

DREISER, THEODORE (1871–1945): Novelist, short-story writer, poet, editor, playwright; novels: *Sister Carrie*, 1900 (expurgated), 1981 (complete); *Jennie Gerhardt*, 1911; *The Financier*, 1912; *The Titan, 1914; The 'Genius'*, 1915; *An American Tragedy*, 1925; *The Bulwark*, 1946; *The Stoic*, 1947; story collections: *Free and Other Stories*, 1918; *Chains*, 1927; *A Gallery of Women*, 2 vols., 1929; *The Best Short Stories*, ed. H. Fast, 1947; poetry: *Moods, Cadenced and Declaimed*, 1926, rev. 1928; *Plays of the Natural and Supernatural*, 1916; non-fiction: *Tragic America*, 1931; *America Is Worth Saving*, 1941; *Letters*, ed. R. H. Elias, 3 vols., 1959.

See:
H. Dreiser, *My Life with Dreiser*, 1951
R. H. Elias, *Theodore Dreiser: Apostle of Nature*, 1949, rev. 1970
W. M. Frohock, *Theodore Dreiser*, 1972
P. Gerber, *Theodore Dreiser*, 1963
A. Kazin and C. Shapiro (eds.), *The Stature of Theodore Dreiser: A Critical Survey of the Man and His Work*, 1955
R. Kennell, *Theodore Dreiser and the Soviet Union, 1927–1945*, 1969
R. D. Lehan, *Theodore Dreiser: His World and His Novels*, 1969
J. Lydenberg (ed.), *Dreiser: A Collection of Critical Essays*, 1971
J. McAleer, *Theodore Dreiser: An Introduction and Interpretation*, 1968
F. O. Matthiessen, *Theodore Dreiser*, 1951
E. Moers, *Two Dreisers*, 1969
C. Shapiro, *Theodore Dreiser: Our Bitter Patriot*, 1962
    Guide to Theodore Dreiser, 1969
W. A. Swanberg, *Dreiser*, 1965
R. P. Warren, *Homage to Theodore Dreiser*, 1972

DUBOIS, WILLIAM EDWARD BURGHARDT (1868–1963): Sociologist and author, founder of National Association for the Advancement of Colored People; editor of *Crisis*; became Ghanaian citizen and died in Ghana. *The Philadelphia Negro*, 1899; *The Souls of Black Folk*, 1903, 1953; *Black Reconstruction*, 1935, 1955; novel trilogy, *The Black Flame*, 1957–61; poetry: *Darkwater: Voices from Within the Veil*, 1920, 1964; autobiography: *Dusk of Dawn*, 1940, 1968; selections: *An ABC of Color*, 1963; *Black Titan*, by eds. of *Freedomways*, 1970

See:
F. L. Broderick, *W. E. B. DuBois: Negro Leader in a Time of Crisis*, 1959
M. Marabte, *W. E. B. DuBois: Black Radical Democrat*, 1987
W. M. Tuttle (ed.), *W. E. B. DuBois*, 1973

DUNCAN, ROBERT (b. 1919): Poet; *Selected Poems 1942–1950*, 1959; *The Years as Catches: First Poems 1939–46*, 1966; *Derivations: Selected Poems 1950–56*, 1968; *The First Decade: Selected Poems 1940–1950*, 1968.

See:

R. J. Bertholf and I. W. Reid (eds.), *Robert Duncan: Scales of the Marvellous*, 1979

DUNLAP, WILLIAM (1766–1839): Dramatist, theatre manager, founder of National Academy of Design; *André*, 1798; *A Trip to Niagara; or, Travellers in America*, 1828; *Four Plays* (additional to these), ed. J. Mates, 1976; *Diary*, 3 vols., ed. D. C. Barck, 1930; repr. as *Diary of a Dramatist, 1766–1839*, 1969; *History of the American Theatre*, 2 vols., 1832; as 1 vol., 1963.

See:

R. H. Canary, *William Dunlap*, 1970
O. S. Coad, *William Dunlap: A Study of His Life and Works and His Place in Contemporary Culture*, 1917, 1962

EDWARDS, JONATHAN (1703–58). Minister and missionary, scientist and theologian; first scientific essay, 'On Insects', written when 11; appointed President of New Jersey College (later Princeton) but died following smallpox inoculation three months after taking up office. *A Narrative of Surprising Conversions*, 1736; *A Faithful Narrative of the Surprising Work of God*, 1737 (important also in Europe); *A Treatise Concerning Religious Affections*, 1746; *A Farewell Sermon*, 1751; *A Careful and Strict Enquiry into . . . Freedom of Will*, 1754; *The Great Christian Doctrine of Original Sin Defended*, 1758; *Two Dissertations: 1. Concerning the End for which God Created the World; 2. The Nature of True Virtue*, 1765; *Works:* ed. E. Williams and E. Parsons, 10 vols., 1847, 1968; ed. P. Miller et al., 1957– ; *Representative Selections*, ed. C. H. Faust and T. H. Johnson, 1935, rev. 1962.

See:

E. M. Griffin, *Jonathan Edwards*, 1971
D. Levin (ed.), *Jonathan Edwards: A Profile*, 1969
P. Miller, *Jonathan Edwards*, 1949
O. E. Winslow, *Jonathan Edwards, 1703–1758*, 1940, 1961

ELIOT, THOMAS STEARNS (1888–1965): Poet and critic. (This volume is concerned only with Eliot's work until 1930; see also Vol. 7, pp. 529–30.) *Prufrock and Other Observations*, London 1917; *Poems*, Richmond, Surrey, 1919; *Ara vos prec (vos as vas)*, London 1920 – as *Poems*, New York, 1920, with slightly different contents and order; *The Waste Land*, in *Criterion* and *Dial* 1922, New York 1922, Richmond, Surrey, 1923, facsimile and transcript. ed. V. Eliot, London 1971; *Poems 1909–1925*, London 1925, New York [1932]; *Journey of the Magi*, London and New York 1927; *A Song for Simeon*, London 1928; *Animula*, London 1929; *Ash Wednesday*, London and New York, 1930; *Marina*, London 1930; see also *Poems Written in Early Youth*, Stockholm 1950, London and New York 1967; *Collected Poems 1909–1962*,

London and New York 1963; prose: *Ezra Pound, His Metric and Poetry*, New York 1917; *The Sacred Wood*, London 1920, New York 1921; *Homage to John Dryden*, London 1924; *Shakespeare and the Stoicism of Seneca*, London 1927; *For Lancelot Andrewes*, London 1928, Garden City, NY, 1929; *Dante*, London 1929; essays and introductions (dates when first published, titles as in essay collections): 'Andrew Marvell', 1922; 'Seneca in Elizabethan Translation', 1927; 'Wilkie Collins and Dickens', 1928; 'A Dialogue on Dramatic Poetry', 1928; 'Preface', E. A. Mowrer, *This American World*, London 1928; 'Tradition and Experiment in Present-Day Literature', 1929; 'Arnold and Pater', 1930; 'Baudelaire', 1930; 'Religion without Humanism', in *Humanism and America*, ed. N. Foerster, New York 1930; 'Introduction', G. Wilson Knight, *The Wheel of Fire*, 1930; Eliot ed. *Criterion* 1922–39, frequently contributing thereto.

See:

C. Aiken, 'Divers Realists', 1917; repr. in his *Scepticisms*, 1919

G. Clarke (ed.), *T. S. Eliot: Critical Assessments*, 4 vols., 1990

C. B. Cox and A. P. Hinchcliffe (eds.), *T. S. Eliot – 'The Waste Land': A Casebook*, 1968

N. Gish, *Time in the Poetry of T. S. Eliot*, 1981

L. Gordon, *Eliot's Early Years*, 1977

M. Grant (ed.), *T. S. Eliot: The Critical Heritage*, 2 vols., 1982

H. Kenner, *The Invisible Poet*, 1959

F. R. Leavis, in *New Bearings in English Poetry*, 1932, rev. 1950

R. March and M. J. Tambimuttu (eds.), *T. S. Eliot: A Symposium*, 1948

J. D. Margolis, *T. S. Eliot's Intellectual Development, 1922–39*, 1972

M. Martin, *A Half-Century of Eliot Criticism . . . 1916–1965*, 1972

F. O. Matthiessen, *The Achievement of T. S. Eliot*, 1935; rev. C. L. Barber 1958

D. E. S. Maxwell, *The Poetry of T. S. Eliot*, 1952

J. Middleton Murry, 'The "Classical" Revival', *Adelphi*, 3 (February, March 1926), 585–95, 648–53

A. Oras, *The Critical Ideas of T. S. Eliot*, 1932

E. Pound, 'T. S. Eliot', 1917; reprinted in *The Literary Essays of Ezra Pound*, 1954

J. C. Ransom, 'Waste Lands' in *Modern Essays*, Second Series, ed. C. Morley, 1924

I. A. Richards, in *Science and Poetry*, 1926
    'On Mr Eliot's Poetry' in *Principles of Literary Criticism* 1926; 2nd edn, 1930

L. Riding and R. Graves, in *A Survey of Modernist Poetry*, 1927

E. Sigg, *The American T. S. Eliot*, 1990

G. Smith, Jr, *T. S. Eliot's Poetry and Plays: A Study in Sources and Meaning*, 1956, rev. 1960 and 1974

B. C. Southam, *T. S. Eliot – 'Prufrock', 'Gerontion', 'Ash Wednesday' & Other Shorter Poems: A Casebook*, 1978

A. Tate, Critique of *Ash Wednesday*, *Hound & Horn*, 4 1932; repr. in *Reactionary Essays*, 1936

L. Unger (ed.), *T. S. Eliot: A Selected Critique*, 1948

G. Williamson, *The Talent of T. S. Eliot*, 1929

E. Wilson, 'T. S. Eliot' in *Axel's Castle*, 1931; earlier version, *New Republic*, 60, 13 November 1929

ELLISON, RALPH (b. 1914): Novelist; *Invisible Man*, 1952, rev. 1961; *Noble Savage I*, 1960; essays: *Shadow and Act*, 1964 (incl. 'The World and the Jug').

See:

J. Hersey (ed.), *Ralph Ellison: A Collection of Critical Essays*, 1974

R. G. O'Meally, *The Craft of Ralph Ellison*, 1980
(ed.), *New Essays on 'Invisible Man'*, 1988

EMERSON, RALPH WALDO (1803–82): Philosopher, poet; lapsed Unitarian minister; *Nature*, 1836; 'American Scholar' and 'Divinity School' addresses, 1837, 1838; *Essays*, two series, 1841, 1844; *Poems*, 1844; *Representative Men*, 1850; *English Traits*, 1856; *The Conduct of Life*, 1860; *May-Day and Other Pieces*, 1867; *Society and Solitude*, 1870; *Letters and Social Aims*, 1876; *Lectures and Biographical Sketches*, 1884; *Natural History of the Intellect*, 1893; *Works*, ed. E. W. Emerson, 12 vols., 1903–4; *Journals*, ed. E. W. Emerson and W. E. Forbes, 10 vols., 1909–14; *Journals and Miscellaneous Notebooks*, 16 vols., ed. W. H. Gilman, 1960–82 (vol. 15); *Letters*, ed. R. L. Rusk, 6 vols., 1939; *Emerson in His Journals*, ed. J. Porte, 1982; *Essays and Lectures*, ed. J. Porte, 1983; selections: *Portable Emerson*, ed. M. Van Doren, 1946, rev. C. Bode and M. Cowley, 1981; *Emerson: A Modern Anthology*, ed. A. Kazin and D. Aaron, 1959.

See:

G. W. Allen, *Waldo Emerson*, 1981

J. Bishop, *Emerson on the Soul*, 1964

K. W. Cameron, *Emerson the Essayist*, 1945

M. Cowan, *City of the West*, 1967

V. C. Hopkins, *Spires of Form: A Study of Emerson's Aesthetic Theory*, 1951

W. M. Konvitz and S. Whicher, *Emerson: A Collection of Critical Essays*, 1962

L. Leary, *Ralph Waldo Emerson: An Interpretative Essay*, 1980

C. R. Metzger, *Emerson and Greenough: Transcendental Pioneers of an American Esthetic*, 1954

J. Miles, *Ralph Waldo Emerson*, 1964

P. L. Nicoloff, *Emerson on Race and History*, 1961

J. Porte, *Emerson and Thoreau*, 1965
Representative Man: Ralph Waldo Emerson in His Time, 1979

D. Porter, *Emerson and Literary Change*, 1978

P. Sherman, *Emerson's Angle of Vision: Man and Nature in American Experience*, 1952

D. Van Leer, *Emerson's Epistemology: The Argument of Essays*, 1986

S. E. Whicher, *Freedom and Fate: An Inner Life of Ralph Waldo Emerson*, 1953

FARRELL, JAMES THOMAS (1904–79): Novelist, short-story writer, critic (for which see 'American Critics'); Studs Lonigan trilogy: *Young Lonigan*, 1932, *The Young Manhood of Studs Lonigan*, 1934, and *Judgment Day*, 1935; *The Short Stories*, 1937; *Selected Essays*, ed. L. Wolf, 1964.

See:

E. M. Branch, *James T. Farrell*, 1971

FAULKNER, WILLIAM CUTHBERT (1897–1962): Novelist, short-story writer, poet, Nobel Prize, 1949; novels: *Soldier's Pay*, 1926; *Mosquitoes*, 1927; *Sartoris*, 1929; *The Sound and the Fury*, 1929; *As I Lay Dying*, 1930; *Sanctuary*, 1931; *Light in August*, 1932; *Pylon*, 1935; *Absalom, Absalom!*, 1936; *The Unvanquished*, 1938; *The Wild Palms*, 1939; *The Hamlet*, 1940; *Go Down, Moses*, 1942; *Intruder in the Dust*, 1948; *Requiem for a Nun*, 1951; *A Fable*, 1954; *The Town*, 1957; *The Mansion*, 1959; *The Reivers*, 1962; stories: *These 13*, 1931; *Doctor Martino and Other Stories*, 1934; *Knight's Gambit*, 1949; *Collected Stories*, 1950; *Big Woods*, 1955; poetry: *The Marble Faun*, 1924; *A Green Bough*, 1933; *Selected Letters*, ed. J. Blotner, 1977; unfilmed screenplay, 'Battle Cry', in *Faulkner: A Comprehensive Guide to the Brodsky Collection*, vol. 4, ed. L. D. Brodsky and R. W. Hamblin, 1985; *Portable Faulkner*, ed. M. Cowley, 1946 (1977).

See:

R. P. Adams, *Faulkner: Myth and Motion*, 1968

M. Bachman, *Faulkner: The Major Years*, 1966

J. Bassett (ed.), *William Faulkner: The Critical Heritage*, 1975

W. Beck, *Faulkner's Essays*, 1976

    Man in Motion: Faulkner's Trilogy, 1961

G. Bedell, *Kierkegaard and Faulkner*, 1972

A. Bleikasten, *The Most Splendid Failure: Faulkner's 'The Sound and the Fury'*, 1976

J. L. Blotner, *Faulkner: A Biography*, 2 vols., 1974

R. H. Brodhead (ed.), *Faulkner: New Perspectives*, 1983

C. Brooks, *William Faulkner: First Encounters*, 1983

    William Faulkner: Toward Yoknapatawpha and Beyond, 1978

    William Faulkner: The Yoknapatawpha Country, 1963

P. R. Broughton, *William Faulkner: The Actual and the Abstract*, 1974

M. Cowley (ed.), *The Faulkner–Cowley File: Letters and Memories, 1944–1962*, 1966

T. M. Davis, *Faulkner's 'Negro'*, 1983

M. Gresset and P. Samway (eds.), *Faulkner and Idealism: Perspectives from Paris*, 1983

F. Hoffman and O. Vickery (ed.), *Three Decades of Criticism*, 1960

I. Howe, *William Faulkner: A Critical Study*, 1952, rev. 1962

J. T. Irwin, *Doubling and Incest/Repetition and Revenge*, 1975

M. Jehlen, *Class and Character in Faulkner's South*, 1976

L. Jenkins, *Faulkner and Black–White Relations: A Psychoanalytic Approach*, 1981

D. M. Kartiganer, *The Fragile Thread: The Meaning of Form in Faulkner's Novels*, 1979

B. F. Kawin, *Faulkner and Film*, 1977

A. F. Kinney, *Faulkner's Narrative Poetics*, 1978

R. Kirk and M. Klotz, *Faulkner's People: A Complete Guide and Index to Characters in the Fiction of William Faulkner*, 1963

M. Kreiswirth, *William Faulkner: The Making of a Novelist*, 1984

L. G. Levins, *Faulkner's Heroic Design: The Yoknapatawpha Novels*, 1976

J. T. Matthews, *The Play of Faulkner's Language*, 1982

J. B. Meriwether, *The Literary Career of William Faulkner*, 1961

M. Millgate, *The Achievement of William Faulkner*, 1966, 1990

D. Minter, *William Faulkner: His Life and Work*, 1980

G. L. Mortimer, *Faulkner's Rhetoric of Loss: A Study in Perception and Meaning*, 1983

C. H. Nilon, *Faulkner and the Negro*, 1965

S. Page, *Faulkner's Women: Characterization and Meaning*, 1972

R. D. Parker, *Faulkner and the Novelistic Imagination*, 1983

C. Peavy, *Go Slow Now: Faulkner and the Race Question*, 1971

J. Pikoulis, *The Art of William Faulkner*, 1982

L. H. Powers, *Faulkner's Yoknapatawpha Comedy*, 1980

M. Putzel, *Genius of Place: William Faulkner's Triumphant Beginnings*, 1983

J. W. Reed, *Faulkner's Narrative*, 1973

H. M. Ruppersburg, *Voice and Eye in Faulkner's Fiction*, 1983

D. M. Schmitter (ed.), *William Faulkner: A Collection of Criticism*, 1973

J. L. Sensibar, *The Origins of Faulkner's Art*, 1984

W. J. Slatoff, *Quest for Failure: A Study of William Faulkner*, 1960, 1972

G. L. Stonum, *Faulkner's Career: An Internal Literary History*, 1979

E. J. Sundquist, *Faulkner: The House Divided*, 1983

P. Swiggart, *The Art of Faulkner's Novels*, 1962

W. Taylor, *Faulkner's Search for a South*, 1983

L. Thompson, *William Faulkner: An Introduction and Interpretation*, 1963

O. Vickery, *The Novels of William Faulkner*, 1959, rev. 1964

H. Waggoner, *William Faulkner: From Jefferson to the World*, 1966

R. P. Warren (ed.), *A Collection of Critical Essays*, 1966

D. Williams, *Faulkner's Women: The Myth and the Muse*, 1977

J. B. Wittenberg, *Faulkner: The Transfiguration of Biography*, 1979

FITZGERALD, F. SCOTT (1896–1940): Novelist and short-story writer; *This

Side of Paradise, 1920; The Beautiful and Damned, 1922; The Great Gatsby, 1925; Tender Is the Night, 1934; The Last Tycoon, ed. E. Wilson, 1941; The Crack-Up, ed. E. Wilson, 1945; Stories, ed. M. Cowley, 1951; stories and essays: Afternoons of an Author, ed. A. Mizener, 1957; Letters, ed. A. Turnbull, 1963; selection: Portable Scott Fitzgerald, ed. D. Parker, 1945.

See:
M. J. Bruccoli, The Composition of 'Tender is the Night', 1963
M. J. Bruccoli and R. Layman (eds.), Fitzgerald/Hemingway Annual, 1969–
J. Callahan, The Illusions of a Nation: Myth and History in the Novels of F. Scott Fitzgerald, 1972
K. Eble, F. Scott Fitzgerald, New York 1963; rev. 1985
    (ed.), F. Scott Fitzgerald: A Collection of Criticism, 1973
R. A. Gallo, Scott Fitzgerald, 1984
J. A. Higgins, F. Scott Fitzgerald: A Study of the Stories, 1971
A. Kazin (ed.), F. Scott Fitzgerald: The Man and His Work, 1951
R. Lehan, F. Scott Fitzgerald and the Craft of Fiction, 1966
A. Le Vot, F. Scott Fitzgerald, trans. W. Byron, 1984 (biography)
N. Milford, Zelda, 1970
J. E. Miller, Jr., The Fictional Technique of F. Scott Fitzgerald, 1957, rev. as F. Scott Fitzgerald: His Art and Technique, 1964
A. Mizener, The Far Side of Paradise: A Biography of F. Scott Fitzgerald, 1951, rev. 1965
    (ed.), F. Scott Fitzgerald: A Collection of Critical Essays, 1963
J. M. Pair, Borrowed Time: The Philosophy and Fiction of F. Scott Fitzgerald, 1988
S. Perosa, The Art of F. Scott Fitzgerald, 1965
H. D. Piper, F. Scott Fitzgerald: A Critical Portrait, 1965
C. Shain, F. Scott Fitzgerald, 1961
R. Sklar, F. Scott Fitzgerald: The Last Laocoön, 1967

FLINT, TIMOTHY (1780–1840): Congregational minister and novelist; Francis Berrian, or, The Mexican Patriot, 1826; Recollections of the Last Ten Years [in the West], 1826.

FRANKLIN, BENJAMIN (1706–90): Printer (as he is described on his tombstone), scientist, diplomat; Do-Good Papers, 1722; A Dissertation on Liberty and Necessity, Pleasure and Pain, 1725; Causes of American Discontent Before 1768, 1768; Remarks Concerning the Savages of North America, 1784; Autobiography [1731–59], published 1868; annual: Poor Richard's Almanack, 1732–58; Writings, ed. A. H. Smyth, 10 vols., 1905–7; Papers, ed. L. W. Labaree et al., 1959–83 (vol. 23); Representative Selections, ed. F. L. Mott and C. E. Jorgensen, 1936, 1962; Autobiographical Writings, ed. C. Van Doren, 1945; The Autobiography . . . A Genetic Text, ed. J. A. Leo Lemay and P. M. Zall, 1981.

See:

A. O. Aldridge, *Benjamin Franklin: Philosopher and Man*, 1965
R. E. Amacher, *Benjamin Franklin*, 1962
I. B. Cohen (ed.), *Benjamin Franklin: His Contribution to the American Tradition*, 1953
P. W. Connor, *Poor Richard's Politicks*, 1965
T. Hornberger, *Benjamin Franklin*, 1962
C. Van Doren, *Benjamin Franklin*, 1938 (biography)

FRENEAU, PHILIP (1752–1832): Poet, journalist, blockade-runner (1780); founded and edited *National Gazette* (1791–3) which supported Jefferson; *The Poems*, 1786; *Miscellaneous Works*, 1788; selections: *Poems*, ed. H. H. Clark, 1929, 1960; *Letters on Various Interesting and Important Subjects*, ed. H. H. Clark, 1943.

See:

M. W. Bowden, *Philip Freneau*, 1976
L. Leary, *That Rascal Freneau*, 1941
P. M. Marsh, *Philip Freneau, Poet and Journalist*, 1967
  The Works of Philip Freneau: A Critical Study, 1968

FROST, ROBERT (1874–1963): Poet; *The Complete Poems*, 1949; *In the Clearing*, 1962; *Selected Prose*, ed. H. Cox and E. C. Lathem, 1977; *Selected Letters*, ed. L. Thompson, 1964.

See:

E. Barry, *Robert Frost on Writing*, 1973
R. Brewer, *The Poetry of Robert Frost*, 1963
J. M. Cox (ed.), *Robert Frost: A Collection of Critical Essays*, 1963
S. Cox, *A Swing of Birches: A Portrait of Robert Frost*, 1957
P. Gerber, *Robert Frost*, 1966; rev. 1982
E. C. Lathem (ed.), *Interviews with Robert Frost*, 1966
J. L. Potter, *Robert Frost Handbook*, 1980
W. H. Pritchard, *Frost: A Literary Life Reconsidered*, 1984
R. D. Sell, *Robert Frost: Four Studies*, 1980
D. Smythe, *Robert Frost Speaks*, 1965
L. Thompson and R. H. Winnick, *Robert Frost*, 3 vols., 1966–77; as 1 vol. by E. C. Lathem and R. H. Winnick, 1981 (biography)

FULLER, MARGARET (1810–50): Transcendentalist critic; *Writings*, ed. M. Wade, 1941; *Memoirs*, ed. R. W. Emerson et al., 2 vols., 1852.

See:

J. W. Howe, *Margaret Fuller*, 1883
P. Miller (ed.), *Margaret Fuller: An American Romantic*, 1963

M. B. Stern, *The Life of Margaret Fuller*, 1942

M. M. O. Urbanski, *Margaret Fuller's 'Women in the Nineteenth Century': A Literary Study of Form and Content, of Sources and Influence*, 1980

M. Wade, *Margaret Fuller: Whetstone of Genius*, 1940

GARLAND, HAMLIN (1860–1940): Novelist and short-story writer; *Main-Travelled Roads: Six Mississippi Stories*, 1981; essays: *Crumbling Idols*, 1894, 1960; *Works*, 45 vols., 1890–1939; *Diaries*, ed. D. Pizer, 1968.

See:

J. Holloway, *Hamlin Garland: A Biography*, 1960

D. Pizer, *Hamlin Garland's Early Work and Career*, 1960

GINSBERG, ALLEN (b. 1926): Poet; *Howl and Other Poems*, 1956; *Kaddish and Other Poems, 1958–60*, 1961; *Reality Sandwiches*, 1963; *Airplane Dreams*, 1968; *Ankor-Wat*, 1968; *Planet News, 1961–1967*, 1968; *The Fall of America: Poems in These States*, 1972; *Mind Breaths: Poems 1972–1977*, 1977; *Mostly Sitting Haiku*, 1979; *Collected Poems 1947–1980*, 1985; *Improvised Poetics*, 1972; *Allen Verbatim: Lectures on Poetry, Politics, Consciousness*, ed. G. Ball, 1974.

See:

J. Kramer, *Allen Ginsberg in America*, 1969

E. Lucie-Smith, *Mystery in The Universe: Notes on an Interview with Allen Ginsberg*, 1965

T. F. Merrill, *Allen Ginsberg*, 1969

E. Mottram, *Allen Ginsberg in the Sixties*, 1972

P. Portugés, *The Visionary Poetics of Allen Ginsberg*, 1978

GLASGOW, ELLEN (1873–1945): Novelist; *The Voice of the People*, 1900; *The Battle-Ground*, 1902; *Deliverance*, 1904; *Virginia*, 1913; *Barren Ground*, 1925; *The Romantic Comedians*, 1926; *Vein of Iron*, 1935; *In This Our Life*, 1941; *Collected Stories*, ed. R. K. Meeker, 1963; criticism: *A Certain Measure*, 1943, 1969; autobiography: *The Woman Within*, 1954; *Letters*, ed. B. Rouse, 1958.

See:

L. Auchinloss, *Ellen Glasgow*, 1964

F. P. W. McDowell, *Ellen Glasgow and the Ironic Art of Fiction*, 1960

J. R. Raper, *From the Sunken Garden: The Fiction of Ellen Glasgow, 1916–1945*, 1980

L. W. Wagner, *Ellen Glasgow: Beyond Convention*, 1982

HALL, JAMES (1793–1868): Lawyer and journalist; *Letters from the West*, 1828; *The Legends of the West*, 1832; *Sketches of History, Life and Manners in the West*, 2 vols., 1834–5.

See:

J. T. Flanagan, *James Hall: Literary Pioneer of the Ohio Valley*, 1950

HANSBERRY, LORRAINE (1930–65): Dramatist, *A Raisin in the Sun*, 1959; *The Sign in Sidney Brustein's Window*, 1964; *To Be Young, Gifted and Black*, 1969; *Les Blancs* (adapted by R. Nemiroff), 1970; also: *The Movement: Documentary of a Struggle for Equality*, 1964 (as *A Matter of Colour*, 1965).

See:
Freedomways, Special Issue, 19, 1979

HARRIS, JOEL CHANDLER (1848–1908): Novelist, short-story writer; *Uncle Remus, His Songs and His Sayings*, 1880; ed. R. Hemenway, 1982; *The Complete Tales of Uncle Remus*, ed. R. Chase, 1955.

See:
R. B. Bickley, *Joel Chandler Harris*, 1978
    (ed.) *Critical Essays on Joel Chandler Harris*, 1981
S. B. Brookes, *Joel Chandler Harris: Folklorist*, 1950
P. M. Cousins, *Joel Chandler Harris: A Biography*, 1968
J. C. Harris, (ed.) *Life and Letters*, 1918
S. Ives, *The Phonology of the Uncle Remus Stories*, 1954

HARTE, BRET (1836–1902): Short-story writer: *The Luck of Roaring Camp and Other Sketches*, 1870; *Writings*, 20 vols. 1896–1914; *Works*, 25 vols. 1914; *Letters*, ed. G. B. Harte, 1926; *Representative Selections*, ed. J. B. Harrison, 1941; *Harte's 'The Outcasts of Poker Flat' and Other Tales*, ed. W. Stegner, 1961.

See:
M. Duckett, *Mark Twain and Bret Harte*, 1964
R. O'Connor, *Bret Harte: A Biography*, 1966
G. R. Stewart, Jr, *Bret Harte: Argonaut and Exile*, 1931

HAWTHORNE, NATHANIEL (1804–1864): Novelist and short-story writer; novels: *The Scarlet Letter*, 1850; *The House of the Seven Gables*, 1851; *The Blithedale Romance*, 1852; *The Marble Faun*, 1860; stories: *Twice-Told Tales*, 1837; *Mosses from an Old Manse*, 1846; *The Snow-Image, and Other Twice-Told Tales*, 1851; *Letters to William Ticknor, 1851–64*, 1910; *Love Letters*, 1907; *Works*, ed. W. Charvat et al., 14 vols. projected, 1963–80; *Portable Nathaniel Hawthorne*, ed. M. Cowley, 1948.

See:
N. Arvin, *Life of Nathaniel Hawthorne*, 1929
M. Bewley, *The Eccentric Design*, 1959
B. B. Cohen (ed.), *The Recognition of Nathaniel Hawthorne: Selected Criticism since 1828*, 1969
F. C. Crews, *The Sins of the Fathers: Hawthorne's Psychological Themes*, 1966
J. D. Crowley (ed.), *Hawthorne: The Critical Heritage*, 1970

E. H. Davidson, *Hawthorne's Last Phase*, 1949

L. DeSalvo, *Nathaniel Hawthorne* (a feminist critique), 1987

M. J. Elder, *Nathaniel Hawthorne: Transcendental Symbolist*, 1969

G. C. Erlich, *Family Themes and Hawthorne's Fiction*, 1985

D. H. Fogle, *Hawthorne's Fiction: The Light and the Dark*, 1952
    Hawthorne's Imagery, 1969

L. S. Hall, *Hawthorne, Critic of Society*, 1944

Henry James, *Hawthorne*, 1879; with intro. by T. Tanner, 1967

C. D. Johnson, *The Productive Tension of Hawthorne's Art*, 1981

A. N. Kaul (ed.), *Hawthorne: A Collection of Critical Essays*, 1966

D. H. Lawrence, *Studies in Classic American Literature*, New York 1923,
    London 1924; as *The Symbolic Meaning*, ed. A. Arnold, 1962

R. B. Male, *Hawthorne's Tragic Vision*, 1957

T. Martin, *Nathaniel Hawthorne*, 1964, rev. 1983

J. Normand, *Nathaniel Hawthorne: An Approach to an Analysis of Artistic
    Creation*, trans. D. Coltman, 1970

R. H. Pearce (ed.), *Hawthorne Centenary Essays*, 1964

R. Stewart, *Nathaniel Hawthorne*, 1948

A. Turner, *Nathaniel Hawthorne: A Biography*, 1980

M. Van Doren, *Nathaniel Hawthorne: A Critical Biography*, 1949

E. Wagenknecht, *Nathaniel Hawthorne: Man and Writer*, 1961

H. Waggoner, *Hawthorne: A Critical Study*, 1963

HELLER, JOSEPH (b. 1923): Novelist: *Catch-22*, 1961; *Something Happened*,
1974; *Good as Gold*, 1979; *God Knows*, 1984; play: *We Bombed in New
Haven*, 1968.

See:

D. Seed, *Joseph Heller: Against the Grain*, 1989

HELLMAN, LILLIAN (1906–84): Dramatist; *The Children's Hour*, 1934; *The
Little Foxes*, 1939; *Watch on the Rhine*, 1941; *Another Part of the Forest*, 1946;
Toys in the Attic, 1960; *Collected Plays*, 1972; autobiography: *An Unfinished
Woman*, 1969.

See:

J. H. Adler, *Lillian Hellman*, 1969

K. Lederer, *Lillian Hellman*, 1979

R. Moody, *Lillian Hellman Playwright*, 1972

W. Wright, *Lillian Hellman: The Woman Who Made the Legend*, 1986 (as
    Lillian Hellman: The Image, The Woman, 1987)

HEMINGWAY, ERNEST (1899–1961): Novelist and short-story writer, Nobel
Prize, 1954; novels: *The Torrents of Spring*, 1926; *The Sun Also Rises*, 1926,
published in England as *Fiesta*; *A Farewell to Arms*, 1929; *To Have and to
Have Not*, 1937; *For Whom the Bell Tolls*, 1940; *Across the River and into the*

Trees, 1950; *The Old Man and the Sea*, 1952; *Islands in the Stream*, 1970; stories: *Men without Women*, 1927; *Winner Take Nothing*, 1933; *The Fifth Column and the First Forty-nine Stories*, 1938; *African Stories: The Stories, Their Sources, Their Critics*, ed. J. M. Howell, 1969; non-fiction: *Death in the Afternoon*, 1932; *A Moveable Feast*, 1964; *By-Line Ernest Hemingway: Selected Articles and Dispatches*, ed. W. White, 1967; selections: *Portable Hemingway*, ed. M. Cowley, 1944, (as *Essential Hemingway*, 1947) *Hemingway Reader*, ed. C. Poore, 1953.

See:

J. Atkins, *The Art of Ernest Hemingway*, 1952
C. Baker, *Ernest Hemingway: A Life Story*, 1969
    Ernest Hemingway: The Writer as Artist, 1952
    Ernest Hemingway: Critique of Four Novels, 1962
    (ed.) *Hemingway and His Critics: An International Anthology*, 1961
S. Baker *Ernest Hemingway*, 1967
J. Benson, *Hemingway: The Writer's Art of Self-Defense*, 1969
M. J. Bruccoli and R. Layman, (eds.), *The Fitzgerald–Hemingway Annual*, 1969–
C. Fenton, *The Apprenticeship of Ernest Hemingway*, 1954
S. Grebstein, *Hemingway's Craft*, 1973
L. Gurko, *Ernest Hemingway and the Pursuit of Heroism*, 1968
R. Hovey, *Hemingway: The Inward Terrain*, 1968
F. H. Laurence, *Hemingway and the Movies*, 1982
A. R. Lee (ed.), *Ernest Hemingway: New Critical Essays*, 1983
K. S. Lynn, *Hemingway*, 1987
J. McCaffery (ed.), *Ernest Hemingway: The Man and His Work*, 1950
J. Meyers, *Ernest Hemingway: The Critical Heritage*, 1982
M. Reynolds, *The Young Hemingway*, 1986
L. Ross, *Portrait of Hemingway*, 1961; *New Yorker* articles 1950
E. Rovit, *Ernest Hemingway*, 1963; rev. G. Brenner, 1986
R. O. Stephens, *Hemingway's Nonfiction: The Public Voice*, 1968
A. Waldhorn, *A Reader's Guide to Ernest Hemingway*, 1972
    (ed.) *Ernest Hemingway: A Collection of Criticism*, 1973
R. P. Weeks, *Hemingway: A Collection of Critical Essays*, 1962
W. Williams, *The Tragic Art of Ernest Hemingway*, 1981
P. Young, *Ernest Hemingway: A Reconsideration*, 1966

HOLMES, OLIVER WENDELL (1809–94): Professor and Dean of Harvard Medical School, author; *Elsie Venner*, 1860–61; *The Guardian Angel*, 1867; *A Mortal Antipathy*, 1885; *The Autocrat of the Breakfast Table*, 1857–8; *The Professor at the Breakfast Table*, 1860; *The Poet at the Breakfast Table*, 1872; biography: *Ralph Waldo Emerson*, 1885; *Complete Works* (with J. T. Morris's *Life and Letters*), 15 vols., 1896; *Poetical Works*, ed. H. E. Scudder, 1895; *Representative Selections*, ed. S. I. Hayakawa and H. M. Jones, 1939

See:

M. A. De W. Howe, *Holmes of the Breakfast Table*, 1939

C. P. Obendorf, *The Psychiatric Novels of Oliver Wendell Holmes*, 1943, abridged 1946

M. R. Small, *Oliver Wendell Holmes*, 1962

E. M. Tilton, *Amiable Autocrat: A Biography of Oliver Wendell Holmes*, 1947

HOWARD, SIDNEY (1891–1939): Dramatist; *They Knew What They Wanted*, 1924; *The Late Christopher Bean*, 1932; *Alien Corn*, 1933.

See:

S. H. White, *Sidney Howard*, 1977

HOWELLS, WILLIAM DEAN (1837–1920): Novelist, critic, essayist, playwright, journalist and editor of *Atlantic*, 1871–81; *A Chance Acquaintance*, 1873; *Private Theatricals*, 1875–6 – as *Mrs Farrell*, 1921; *A Modern Instance*, 1882; *The Rise of Silas Lapham*, 1885; *Indian Summer*, 1886; *The Minister's Charge*, 1887; *A Hazard of New Fortunes*, 1890; *The Landlord at Lion's Head*, 1897; *The Kentons*, 1902; *Complete Plays*, ed. W. J. Meserve, 1960; *Selected Edition*, in projected 41 vols., ed. E. H. Cady, 1968–   ; *Selected Writings*, ed. H. S. Commager, 1950.

See:

W. Alexander, *William Dean Howells: The Realist as Humanist*, 1981

G. N. Bennett, *William Dean Howells: The Development of a Novelist*, 1959

E. H. Cady, *The Road to Realism*, 1956; *The Realist at War*, 1958 (biography)

E. Carter, *Howells and the Age of Realism*, 1966

K. E. Eble, *William Dean Howells: A Century of Criticism*, 1962

W. M. Gibson, *William Dean Howells*, 1967

C. M. Kirk, *W. D. Howells and [Visual] Art in His Time*, 1965

W. McMurray, *The Literary Realism of William Dean Howells*, 1967

E. Prioleau, *The Circle of Eros: Sexuality in the Work of William Dean Howells*, 1983

HUGHES, LANGSTON (1902–67): Poet, story-writer, and dramatist; poetry: *Weary Blues*, 1926; *Selected Poems*, 1959; novels: *Not Without Laughter*, 1930; *Tambourines to Glory*, 1958, (1969); stories: *The Ways of White Folks*, 1935; *Simple Speaks His Mind*, 1950; *Laughing to Keep from Crying*, 1952; *Simple Takes a Wife*, 1953; *The Best of Simple*, 1957; *Something in Common and Other Stories*, 1963; plays: *Mulatto*, 1935 (revised), 1939 (original version); *The Prodigal Son*, 1965; *Five Plays*, ed. W. Smalley, 1963; autobiographies: *The Big Sea*, 1940; *I Wonder as I Wander*, 1956; selection: *The Langston Hughes Reader*, 1958.

See:

J. A. Emanuel, *Langston Hughes*, 1967

T. B. O'Daniel (ed.), *Langston Hughes, Black Genius: A Critical Evaluation*, 1971

A. Rampersad, *The Life of Langston Hughes*, 2 vols., 1988

INGE, WILLIAM (1913–73): Dramatist and novelist; *Come Back, Little Sheba*, 1950; *Picnic*, 1953; *Bus Stop*, 1955; *The Dark at the Top of the Stairs*, 1957; *Four Plays*, 1958, (1960); novel: *My Son is a Spendid Driver*, 1971.

See:

R. B. Shuman, *William Inge*, 1965

IRVING, WASHINGTON (1783–1859): Short-story writer and historian; *A History of New-York*, 1809; *The Sketch Book of Geoffrey Crayon, Gent.*, (inc. 'The Legend of Sleepy Hollow' and 'Rip Van Winkle'), 1819–20; *The Crayon Miscellany* (inc. 'A Tour on the Prairies'), 1835; *Complete Writings*, ed. H. A. Pochmann et al., 28 vols. 1969–

See:

M. W. Bowden, *Washington Irving*, 1981

S. Brodwin, *The Old and New World Romanticism of Washington Irving*, 1986

Van Wyck Brooks, *The World of Washington Irving*, 1944 (1945)

W. L. Hedges, *Washington Irving: An American Study*, 1965

L. Leary, *Washington Irving*, 1963.

A. B. Myers (ed.), *Washington Irving: A Tribute*, 1972.

S. T. Williams, *The Life of Washington Irving*, 2 vols., 1935

JAMES, HENRY (1843–1916): Novelist, playwright, critic; settled in England 1876; naturalized British 1915; *Roderick Hudson*, 1876; *The American* 1877; *The Europeans*, 1878; *Daisy Miller*, 1879; *Washington Square*, 1880; *The Portrait of a Lady*, 1881; *The Bostonians*, 1886; *The Princess Casamassima*, 1886; *The Reverberator*, 1888; *The Tragic Muse*, 1890; *The Spoils of Poynton*, 1897; *What Maisie Knew*, 1897; *The Awkward Age*, 1899; *The Sacred Fount*, 1901; *The Wings of the Dove*, 1902; *The Ambassadors*, 1903; *The Golden Bowl*, 1904; *The Outcry*, 1911; *The Ivory Tower*, 1917; *The Sense of the Past*, 1917; stories: *The Aspern Papers*, 1888; *The Real Thing*, 1892; *In the Cage*, 1898; *The Turn of the Screw*, 1898; *Complete Tales*, ed. L. Edel, 12 vols., 1962–4; *The Tales*, ed. M. Aziz, 1973–83 (vol. 2); *Complete Plays*, ed. L. Edel, 1949; critical writings: *French Poets and Novelists*, 1878; *Hawthorne*, 1879; *Partial Portraits*, 1888; *Notes on Novelists*, 1914; *The Art of the Novel* (prefaces), ed. R. P. Blackmur, 1934; *The Scenic Art*, ed. A. Wade, 1948; *The Art of Fiction and Other Essays*, ed. M. Roberts, 1948; *The House of Fiction*, ed. L. Edel, 1957; *Selected Literary Criticism*, ed. M. Shapira, 1964; autobiographical writings: *The American Scene*, 1907; *A Small Boy and Others*, 1913; *Notes of a Son and Brother*, 1914; *The Middle Years*, 1917; collected as *Henry James: An*

Autobiography, ed. F. W. Dupée, 1956; *Letters*, ed. P. Lubbock, 2 vols., 1920; *Letters*, ed. L. Edel, 1975– ; *Selected Letters*, ed. L. Edel, 1956; *Notebooks*, ed. F. O. Matthiessen and K. B. Murdock, 1947; selections: *Portable Henry James*, ed. M. D. Zabel, 1951, rev. L. H. Powers, 1968.

See:

J. W. Beach, *The Method of Henry James*, 1918, 1954
A. Berland, *Culture and Conduct in the Novels of Henry James*, 1981
R. P. Blackmur, *Studies in Henry James*, 1982
O. Cargill, *The Novels of Henry James*, 1961
S. Chatman, *The Later Style of Henry James*, 1972
S. B. Daughtery, *The Literary Criticism of Henry James*, 1981
F. W. Dupée, *Henry James*, 1951, 1956
L. Edel, *Henry James*, 5 vols., 1953–72 (biography)
    (ed.) *Henry James: A Collection of Critical Essays*, 1963
L. Edel and G. N. Ray (eds.), *Henry James and H. G. Wells*, 1958
D. M. Fogle, *Henry James and the Structure of the Romantic Imagination*, 1981
R. L. Gale, *A Henry James Encyclopaedia*, 1989
R. Gard, *Henry James: The Critical Heritage*, 1968
M. Geismar, *Henry James and his Cult*, 1964
A. Habegger, *Henry James and the 'Woman Business'*, 1990
C. G. Hoffman, *The Short Novels of Henry James*, 1957
P. Horne, *Henry James and Revision*, 1990
M. Jacobson, *Henry James and the Mass Market*, 1984
D. Jefferson, *Henry James and the Modern Reader*, 1964
V. Jones, *James the Critic*, 1985
D. Krook, *The Ordeal of Consciousness in Henry James*, 1962
F. R. Leavis, *The Great Tradition*, 1948
R. E. Long, *Henry James: The Early Novels*, 1983
F. O. Matthiessen, *Henry James: The Major Phase*, 1944
W. Morris, *The Territory Ahead*, 1958
N. Page (ed.), *Henry James: Interviews and Recollections*, 1984
R. Poirier, *The Comic Sense of Henry James*, 1960
E. Pound, 'Henry James', repr. in *Literary Essays*, intro. by T. S. Eliot, 1954
S. G. Putt, *Reader's Guide to Henry James*, 1966
J. C. Rowe, *The Theoretical Dimensions of Henry James*, 1985
P. Sicker, *Love and the Quest for Identity in the Fiction of Henry James*, 1980
S. Spender, in *The Destructive Element*, 1935
T. Tanner, *Henry James*, 2 vols., 1979
    (ed.), *Henry James: Modern Judgements*, 1968
J. A. Ward, *The Search for Form: Studies in the Structure of James's Fiction*, 1967

JARRELL, RANDALL (1914–65): Poet, novelist, critic; *The Complete Poems*, 1969 (1971); novel: *Pictures from an Institution*, 1954; criticism: *Poetry and the Age*, 1953; *A Sad Heart at the Supermarket*, 1962; *The Third Book of Criticism*, 1969;

letters etc.: *An Autobiographical and Literary Selection*, ed. M. Jarrell, 1986.

See:

R. Lowell *et al.* (eds.), *Randal Jarrell 1914–1965*, 1967

B. Quinn, *Randall Jarrell*, 1981

K. Shapiro, *Randall Jarrell*, 1967

JEFFERSON, THOMAS (1743–1826): Legislator, diplomat, third President of the USA (1801–9); drafted Declaration of Independence, 1776; *Notes on the State of Virginia*, 1784–5; *Autobiography*, 1820; *Portable Thomas Jefferson*, ed. M. D. Peterson, 1975.

See:

C. L. Becker (ed.), *The Declaration of Independence: A Study in the History of Political Ideas*, 1942

D. J. Boorstin, *The Lost World of Thomas Jefferson*, 1948

C. G. Bowers, *Jefferson and Hamilton: The Struggle for Democracy in America*, 1925.

L. W. Levy, *Jefferson and Civil Liberties: The Darker Side*, 1963

N. Schachner, *Thomas Jefferson: A Biography*, 2 vols., 1951

JEWETT, SARAH ORNE (1849–1909): Novelist and short-story writer; novels: *Deephaven*, 1877; *A Country Doctor*, 1884; *A Marsh Island*, 1885; *The Tory Lover*, 1901; stories: *A White Heron*, 1888; *The King of Folly Island*, 1888; *A Native of Winby*, 1893; *The Country of the Pointed Firs*, 1896; poems: *Verses*, 1916; *Letters*, ed. R. Cory, 2nd edn., 1967; works: *Stories and Tales*, 7 vols., 1910; *The Best Stories*, ed. Willa Cather, 2 vols., 1925 – as *The Country of the Pointed Firs and Other Stories*, 1 vol., 1956.

See:

F. Bishop, *The Sense of the Past in Sarah Orne Jewett*, 1959

R. Cary, *Sarah Orne Jewett*, 1962

J. E. Frost, *Sarah Orne Jewett*, 1960

F. O. Matthiessen, *Sarah Orne Jewett*, 1929

M. F. Thorp, *Sarah Orne Jewett*, 1966

P. D. Westbrook, *Acres of Flint*, 1951, rev. 1981

JONES, LEROI (b. 1934), from 1968 known as IMAMU AMIRI BARAKA ('Imamu' dropped after 1974): Dramatist, poet, novelist, essayist; plays: *Dutchman, The Slave, The Toilet*, 1964; *The Motion of History*, 1977; poetry: *Preface to a Twenty Volume Suicide Note*, 1961; *The Dead Lecturer*, 1964; *Black Art*, 1964; *Selected Poetry*, 1979; novel: *The System of Dante's Hell*, 1965 (1968); non-fiction: *Blues People . . . Negro Music in White America* 1963 (as *Negro Music in White America*, 1965); *Home: Social Essays*, 1966 (1968); *Selected Plays and Prose*, 1979; *Autobiography*, 1984.

See:

K. W. Bentson, *Baraka: The Renegade and the Mask*, 1976

(ed), *Imamu A. Baraka: A Collection of Critical Essays*, 1978
L. W. Brown, *Amiri Baraka*, 1980
T. H. Hudson, *From LeRoi Jones to Amiri Baraka: The Literary Works*, 1973
W. Sollors, *Amiri Baraka/LeRoi Jones: The Quest for a Populist Modernism*, 1978

KEROUAC, JACK (1922–69): Autobiographical novelist; *The Town and the City*, 1950; *On the Road*, 1957; *The Subterraneous*, 1958; *The Dharma Bums*, 1958, *Doctor Sax*, 1959; *Big Sur*, 1962; *Desolation Angels*, 1965; *Sartori in Paris*, 1966; *Vanity of Duluoz: An Adventurous Education, 1935–46*, 1968; poetry: *Mexico City Blues*, 1959; travel: *Lonesome Traveller*, 1960.

See:
A. Charters, *Kerouac: A Biography*, 1973
T. Clark, *Jack Kerouac*, 1984
R. A. Hipkiss, *Jack Kerouac: Prophet of the New Romanticism*, 1976
D. McNally, *Desolate Angel: Jack Kerouac, the Beat Generation, and America*, 1979

KNIGHT, SARAH KEMBLE (1666–1727): Married a sea captain and engaged in business, farming and teaching – Benjamin Franklin was possibly taught by her; *Journal [1704–5]*, 1825, 1970; ed. G. P. Winship 1920.

KUNITZ, STANLEY JASSPON (b. 1905): Poet, editor, translator; head of poetry section of Library of Congress; *Intellectual Things*, 1930; *Passport to the War*, 1944; *Selected Poems, 1928–1958*, 1958; essays: *A Kind of Order, A Kind of Folly*, 1975; see also Guides (p. 683).

See:
M. Hénault, *Stanley Kunitz*, 1980

LARDNER, RING WILMER (1885–1933): Short-story writer, journalist; *Works*, 4 vols., 1925; *Collected Short Stories*, 1941; parodic autobiography: *The Story of a Wonder Man: Being the Autobiography of Ring Lardner*, 1927; *Portable Ring Lardner*, ed. G. Seldes, 1946; *Ring Lardner Reader*, ed. M. Geismar, 1963; *Best of Ring Lardner*, 1984.

See:
W. R. Patrick, *Ring Lardner*, 1963

LEWIS, HARRY SINCLAIR (1885–1951): Novelist, Nobel Prize, 1930; *Babbitt*, 1922; *Main Street*, 1920; selected essays etc.: H. E. Maule and M. H. Cane (eds.), *The Man from Main Street*, 1953; letters: H. Smith (ed.), *From Main Street to Stockholm*, 1952.

See:

D. J. Dooley, *The Art of Sinclair Lewis*, 1967
S. Grebstein, *Sinclair Lewis*, 1962
J. Lundquist, *Guide to Sinclair Lewis*, 1970
M. Shorer, *Sinclair Lewis: An American Life*, 1961
    (ed.), *Sinclair Lewis: A Collection of Critical Essays*, 1962

LINCOLN, ABRAHAM (1809–65): (Sixteenth President of the United States: *First Inaugural Address*, 1861; *Emancipation Proclamation*, 1862; *Gettysburg Address*, 1863; *Second Inaugural Address*, 1865; all but the first are in D. J. Boorstin (ed.), *An American Primer*, 1966, with individual introductions; *Speeches and Writings*, ed. R. P. Basler, 1946.

See:

L. Dunning, *Lincoln's Funnybone*, 1942
B. P. Thomas, *Abraham Lincoln: A Biography*, 1952
M. Van Doren, *Life and Writings*, 1940

LONDON, JACK (John Griffith) (1876–1916): Novelist, short-story writer, social polemicist; novels: *The Call of the Wild*, 1903; *The Sea-Wolf*, 1904; *The Game*, 1905; *White Fang*, 1906; *The Iron Heel*, 1907; *Martin Eden*, 1909; *Burning Daylight*, 1910; *The Assassination Bureau, Ltd*, completed by R. Fish, 1963; stories: *The God of His Fathers and Other Stories*, 1901; *The Faith of Men and Other Stories*, 1904; *Tales of the Fish Patrol*, 1905; *Moon-Face and Other Stories*, 1906; *The Cruise of the Snark*, 1911; *South Sea Tales*, 1911; *The Valley of the Moon*, 1913; *Jerry of the Islands*, 1917; *Michael, Brother of Jerry*, 1917; non-fiction: *The People of the Abyss*, 1903; *The War of the Classes*, 1905; *John Barleycorn* (autobiographical), 1913; *Human Drift*, 1917; *Letters*, ed. K. Hendricks and I. Shepard, 1965; P. S. Foner (ed.), *Jack London, American Rebel: A Collection of His Social Writings*, 1947, 1964; K. Hendricks and I. Shepard (eds.), *Jack London Reports: War Correspondence*, etc., 1970; works: Fitzroy Edn, ed. I. O. Evans, 1963–7; Bodley Head Edn, ed. A. C. Marshall, 4 vols., 1963–8; there are many collections of the stories.

See:

E. Labor, *Jack London*, 1974
Joan London, *Jack London and His Times*, 1939, rev. 1968
R. O'Connor, *Jack London: A Biography*, 1964
G. Orwell, intro. to *Love of Life and Other Stories*, 1946; repr. in *Collected Essays, Journalism and Letters*, ed. S. Orwell and I. Angus, Vol. IV, item 7, 1968
A. Sinclair, *Jack: A Biography of Jack London*, 1977
F. Walker, *Jack London and the Klondike: The Genesis of an American Writer*, 1966

LONGFELLOW, HENRY WADSWORTH (1807–82): Poet; *Evangeline, A Tale of*

Acadie, 1847; *The Song of Hiawatha*, 1855; *Poetical and Prose Works*, 14 vols. 1886–91; *Letters*, ed. A. Hilen, 2 vols., 1967; *Representative Selections* [*of Poetry*], ed. O. Shepard, 1934.

See:

N. Arvin, *Longfellow: His Life and Work*, 1934
E. Wagenknecht, *Longfellow: A Full-Length Portrait*, 1955
C. B. Williams, *Henry Wadsworth Longfellow*, 1964.

LOWELL, AMY (1874–1925): Poet and critic; *Complete Poetical Works*, 1955; biography: *John Keats*, 1925; criticism: *Tendencies in Modern American Poetry*, 1917; *A Critical Fable*, verse, 1922.

See:

R. Benvenuto, *Amy Lowell*, 1985
S. F. Damon, *Amy Lowell*, 1935
H. Gregory, *Amy Lowell*, 1958

LOWELL, JAMES RUSSELL (1819–91): Professor of Modern Languages, Harvard, diplomat, journalist, critic, poet, humorist; *Conversations on Some of the Old Poets*, 1845; *Among My Books*, 1870, 1876; poetry: *A Year's Life and Other Poems*, 1841; *A Fable for Critics*, 2 vols., 1848; *Ode Recited at the Harvard Commemoration*, 1865; *The Cathedral*, 1870; humour: *Biglow Papers*, First Series, 1848; Second Series 1867; non-fiction: *The Anti-Slavery Papers*, ed. W. B. Parker, 2 vols., 1902; *Complete Writings*, ed. C. E. Norton, 16 vols., 1904, 1974; *Representative Selections*, ed. H. H. Clark and N. Foerster, 1947.

See:

R. C. Beatty, *James Russell Lowell*, 1942
M. B. Duberman, *James Russell Lowell*, 1966
L. Howard, *Victorian Knight-Errant: A Study of the Early Literary Career of James Russell Lowell*, 1952
C. McGlinchee, *James Russell Lowell*, 1967

LOWELL, ROBERT (1917–77): Poet; *Land of Unlikeness*, 1944; *Lord Weary's Castle*, 1946; *Poems 1938–1949*, 1950; *The Mills of the Kavanaughs*, 1951; *Life Studies*, 1959; *Imitations*, 1961 (1971); *For the Union Dead*, 1964 (1965); *Near the Ocean*, 1967; *Prometheus Bound*, 1967 (1970); *Notebook 1967–68*, 1969; enlarged 1970; *The Dolphin*, 1973; *History*, 1973; *Day by Day*, 1977 (1978); *Selected Poems*, 1976, rev. 1977; plays: *Phaedra and Figaro*, free translation, 1961; *The Old Glory*, three plays, 1965 (1966); *The Oresteia*, 1979; selection: *The Achievement of Robert Lowell*, ed. W. J. Martz.

See:

S. G. Axelrod, *Robert Lowell: Life and Art*, 1978
V. M. Bell, *Robert Lowell: Nihilist as Hero*, 1983

P. Cooper, *The Autobiographical Myth of Robert Lowell*, 1970

P. Cosgrave, *The Public Poetry of Robert Lowell*, 1970

R. J. Fein, *Robert Lowell*, 1970, rev. 1979

I. Hamilton, *Robert Lowell: A Biography*, 1982

J. Mazarro, *The Poetic Themes of Robert Lowell*, 1965

T. Parkinson (ed.), *Robert Lowell: A Collection of Critical Essays*, 1968

B. Raffel, *Robert Lowell*, 1981

M. Rudmen, *Robert Lowell: An Introduction to his Poetry*, 1983

L. Simpson, *A Revolution in Taste*, 1979

H. B. Staples, *Robert Lowell: The First Twenty Years*, 1962

S. I. Yenser, *Circle to Circle: Structures in the Poetry of Robert Lowell*, 1975

MCCULLERS, CARSON (1917–67): novelist and short-story writer; *The Heart Is a Lonely Hunter*, 1940; *Reflections in a Golden Eye*, 1941; *The Member of the Wedding*, 1946 (dramatized 1950); *Clock without Hands*, 1961; stories: *The Ballad of the Sad Café and Collected Short Stories*, 1952; play: *The Square Root of Wonderful*, 1958.

See:

V. S. Carr, *The Lonely Hunter: A Biography*, 1975

D. Edmunds, *Carson McCullers*, 1969

O. Evans, *Carson McCullers: Her Life and Work*, 1965

M. B. McDowell, *Carson McCullers*, 1980

MACLEISH, ARCHIBALD (1892–1982): Poet, critic, dramatist and one-time librarian to Congress and editor of *Fortune*; *Collected Poems 1917–1952*, 1952; *The Human Season: Selected Poems 1926–1972*, 1972; plays: *Panic*, 1935; *The Fall of the City*, 1937; *Air Raid*, 1938; *JB*, 1958; *Herakles*, 1965; non-fiction: *A Time to Speak: The Selected Prose*, 1941; *A Time to Act: Selected Addresses*, 1943; *The American Story: Ten Broadcasts*, published 1944; *Poetry and Opinion: The Pisan Cantos of Ezra Pound*, 1950; *Poetry and Experience*, 1960; *The Dialogues of Archibald MacLeish and Mark Van Doren*, ed. W. V. Bush, 1962.

See:

S. L. Falk, *Archibald MacLeish*, 1965

G. Smith, *Archibald MacLeish*, 1971

MAILER, NORMAN (b. 1923): Novelist, short-story writer, polemicist; novels: *The Naked and the Dead*, 1948; *Barbary Shore*, 1951; *The Deer Park*, 1955 (dramatized 1967); *The Time of Her Time*, 1959; *An American Dream*, 1965; *Why Are We in Vietnam?*, 1967; *Ancient Evenings*, 1983; stories: *Advertisements for Myself on the Way Out*, with autobiography, 1959; *The Short Fiction*, 1969; poetry: *Deaths for the Ladies and Other Disasters*, 1962; non-fiction: *The Presidential Papers*, 1963; *Cannibals and Christians*, with a short story, 1966; *The Idol and the Octopus*, 1968; *The Armies of the Night: History as a Novel, the Novel as History*, 1968; *Marilyn: A Biography*, 1973; *The Executioner's Song*, 1979; selection: *The Essential Mailer*, 1982.

See:
J. Bailey, *Norman Mailer: Quick-Change Artist*, 1979
L. Braudy (ed.), *Norman Mailer: A Collection of Critical Essays*, 1972
R. Foster, *Norman Mailer*, 1968
D. L. Kaufmann, *Norman Mailer: The Countdown*, 1969
B. H. Leeds, *The Structured Vision of Norman Mailer*, 1969
P. Manso, *Mailer*, 1985 (1986)
R. Merrill, *Norman Mailer*, 1978

MALAMUD, BERNARD (1914–86): Novelist, short-story writer; novels: *The Natural*, 1952; *The Assistant*, 1957; *New Life*, 1961; *The Fixer*, 1966; *Pictures of Fidelman: An Exhibition*, 1969; *The Tenants*, 1971; *Dubin's Lives*, 1979; stories: *The Magic Barrel*, 1958; *Idiots First*, 1963; *Rembrandt's Hat*, 1973; selection: *A Malamud Reader*, intro. by P. Rahv, 1967.

See:
I. Alter, *The Good Man's Dilemma: Social Criticism in the Fiction of Bernard Malamud*, 1981
J. and J. Field (eds.), *Bernard Malamud and the Critics*, 1970
S. J. Hershinow, *Bernard Malamud*, 1980
S. Richman, *Bernard Malamud*, 1966

MAMET, DAVID (b. 1947): Dramatist; *American Buffalo*, 1975; *A Life in the Theatre*, 1977; *The Water Engine*, 1977; *Sexual Perversity in Chicago* and *The Duck Variations*, 1978; *Lakeboat*, 1981; *Edmond*, 1983; *Glengarry, Glen Ross*, 1983.

See:
C. W. E. Bigsby, *David Mamet*, 1985
D. Carroll, *David Mamet*, 1987

MASTERS, EDGAR LEE (1868–1950): Poet and biographer; *Spoon River Anthology*, 1915, with additional poems, 1941, dramatized 1963; biographies: *Lincoln, the Man*, 1931; *Walt Whitman*, 1937; *Mark Twin*, 1938; prose: *The Sangamon [River]*, 1942; autobiography: *Across Spoon River*, 1936.

See:
K. Flaccus, *The Vermont Background of Edgar Lee Masters*, 1955
J. T. Flanagan, *Edgar Lee Masters: The Spoon River Poet and his Critics*, 1974

MATHER, COTTON (1663–1728): Grandson of John Cotton (q.v.), Puritan minister, prolific author and publisher; opposed 'spectre evidence' in Salem witchcraft trials; his interest in science – he campaigned for inoculation against smallpox – led to his election to Royal Society, London; *Memorable Providences Relating to Witchrafts and Possessions*, 1689; *The Present State of New England*, 1690; *Political Fables*, circulated 1692–3; *Wonders of the Invisible World*, 1693; *Magnalia Christi Americana; or, The Ecclesiastical History of New-England*, 1702; *Bonifacius. An Essay upon the Good*, 1710; *Manuductio ad Ministerium*, 1726; *Selected Letters*, ed. K. Silverman, 1971; *Selections*, ed. K. B. Murdock, 1926, 1960.

See:

R. P. and L. Boas, *Cotton Mather: Keeper of the Puritan Conscience*, 1928, 1964

M. R. Breitweiser, *Cotton Mather and Benjamin Franklin*, 1985

A. P. Marvin, *The Life and Times of Cotton Mather*, 1892, 1973

MELVILLE, HERMAN (1819–91): Novelist, short-story writer, poet; novels: *Typee*, 1846; *Omoo*, 1847; *Mardi*, 1849; *Redburn: His First Voyage*, 1849; *White-Jacket*, 1850; *Moby-Dick*, 1851; *Pierre; or, The Ambiguities*, 1852; *Israel Potter*, 1855; *The Confidence-Man: His Masquerade*, 1857; *Billy Budd*, 1924, *A Genetic Text*, ed. H. Hayford and M. Sealts, Jr, 1962; stories: *Piazza Tales*, 1856; poetry: *Battle-Pieces*, 1866; *Clarel*, 1876; *John Marr and Other Sailors*, 1888; *Timoleon*, 1891; *Letters*, ed. M. R. Davis and W. H. Gilman, 1960; *Works*, 16 vols., (London 1922–4) 1963; *Writings*, ed. H. Hayford et al., 15 vols., 1968– ; selection: *Portable Herman Melville*, ed. J. Leyda, 1957.

See:

G. W. Allen, *Melville and His World*, 1971 (illustrated)

N. Arvin, *Herman Melville*, 1950, 1957

W. Berthoff, *The Example of Melville*, 1962

W. B. Billingham, *An Artist in the Rigging: The Early Work of Herman Melville*, 1972; *Melville's Short Fiction 1853–1856*, 1977; *Melville's Later Novels*, 1986

M. Bowen, *The Long Encounter: Self and Experience in the Writings of Herman Melville*, 1980

W. G. Branch, *Herman Melville: The Critical Heritage*, 1985

P. Brodtkorb, Jr, *Ishmael's White World: A Phenomenological Reading of Moby Dick*, 1965

R. Chase (ed.), *Melville: A Collection of Critical Essays*, 1962

E. A. Dryden, *Melville's Thematics of Form: The Great Art of Telling the Truth*, 1968

R. M. Fogle, *Melville's Shorter Tales*, 1960

H. B. Franklin, *The Wake of the God: Melville's Mythology*, 1963

J. W. Herbert, Jr, *Marquesan Encounters: Melville and the Meaning of Civilization*, 1980

L. Howard, *Herman Melville: A Biography*, 1951

A. R. Humphreys, *Herman Melville*, 1962

C. L. Karcher, *Shadow over the Promised Land: Slavery, Race and Violence in Melville's America*, 1980

J. Leyda, *The Melville Log: A Documentary Life*, 1969

J. E. Miller, *A Reader's Guide to Herman Melville*, 1962

J. Mushabac, *Melville's Humor*, 1981

C. Olson, *Call Me Ishmael*, 1947

M. M. Sealts, *Melville as Lecturer*, 1957

W. E. Sedgwick, *Herman Melville: The Tragedy of Mind*, 1944 (1945)

R. A. Sherrill, *The Prophetic Melville: Experience, Transcendance and Tragedy*, 1979

H. P. Vincent, *The Trying-Out of Moby Dick*, 1949

MENCKEN, HENRY LOUIS (1880–1956): Columnist, editor, critic; *Book of Prefaces*, 1917; *The American Language*, 1919, rev. 1921–48; *Prejudices*, Six Series, 1919–27; *A Mencken Chrestomathy*, 1949 (his own selection).

See:

C. Bode, *Mencken*, 1969

F. Hobson, *Serpent in Eden: H. L. Mencken and the South*, 1974

E. A. Martin, *H. L. Mencken and the Debunkers*, 1984

MILLER, ARTHUR (b. 1915): Dramatist; *The Golden Years*, 1940; produced (by BBC) 1987; *All My Sons*, 1947; *Death of a Salesman*, 1949; *The Crucible*, 1953; *A View from the Bridge*, in one act 1955; in two acts 1956; *After the Fall*, 1964; *Incident at Vichy*, 1964; *The Price*, 1968; *The Creation of the World and Other Business*, 1972, rev. as *Up from Paradise*, 1974; *The Archbishop's Ceiling*, 1977; *The American Clock*, adapted from Studs Terkel's *Hard Times*, 1980; *Collected Plays*, 1957 (1958); *The Theater Essays*, ed. R. A. Martin, 1978; novels: *Focus*, 1945; *The Misfits*, 1961 (originally a short story; filmed 1961); autobiography; *Timebends*, 1987; *Portable Arthur Miller*, ed. H. Clurman, 1971 (1977).

See:

N. Carson, *Arthur Miller*, 1982

J. H. Ferras (ed.), *Twentieth-Century Interpretations of 'The Crucible'*, 1972

A. P. Foulkes, *Literature and Propaganda*, 1983 (for *The Crucible*)

J. Goode, *The Story of 'The Misfits'*, 1963

S. Haftel, *Arthur Miller: The Burning Glass*, 1965

R. Hogan, *Arthur Miller*, 1964

L. Moss, *Arthur Miller*, 1964; rev. 1980

E. Murray, *Arthur Miller: Dramatist*, 1967

D. Welland, *Miller the Playwright*, 1961, 3rd edn 1985

S. White, *Guide to Arthur Miller*, 1970

MILLER, HENRY (1891–1980): Autobiographical novelist; *Tropic of Cancer*, 1934; *Black Spring*, 1936; *Tropic of Capricorn*, 1939; *The Colossus of Maroussi*,

1941; trilogy: *Sexus*, 1949, *Plexus*, 1953, *Nexus*, 1960; *Big Sur and the Oranges of Hieronymus Bosch*, 1957; *My Life and Times*, with B. Smith, 1971; selections: *Henry Miller Reader*, ed. L. Durrell, 1959, 1972; *Henry Miller on Writing*, ed. T. Moore, 1964; *Genius and Lust*, ed. N. Mailer, 1976.

See:

I. Hassan, *The Literature of Silence: Henry Miller and Samuel Beckett*, 1967
L. H. Lewis, *Henry Miller: The Major Writings*, 1986
E. Mitchell (ed.), *Henry Miller: Three Decades of Criticism*, 1971
J. Nelson, *Form and Image in the Fiction of Henry Miller*, 1970
G. Orwell, 'Inside the Whale' in book of that title, 1940
A. Perlès, *My Friend Henry Miller: An Intimate Biography*, 1955
A. Perlès and L. Durrell, *Art and Outrage*, 1959
G. Wickes (ed.), *Henry Miller and the Critics*, 1963

MITCHELL, MARGARET (1900–1949): Novelist; *Gone With the Wind*, 1936.

See:

F. Farr, *Margaret Mitchell of Atlanta*, 1966
A. G. Jones, *Tomorrow is Another Day*, 1981

MOORE, MARIANNE (1887–1972): Poet and essayist; *Complete Poems*, 1967, 1984; essays: *Predilections*, 1955; *A Marianne Moore Reader*, 1961.

See:

B. Costello, *Marianne Moore: Imaginary Possessions*, 1981
J. Garrigue, *Marianne Moore*, 1965
M. Holley, *The Poetry of Marianne Moore*, 1988

MOWATT (RITCHIE), ANNA CORA (1819–70): Actress and dramatist; *Fashion*, 1845; *Armand, The Child of the People*, 1847; *Autobiography of an Actress; or, Eight Years on the Stage*, 1854.

See:

E. W. Barnes, *The Lady of Fashion* (in England as *Anna Cora*), 1954

NABAKOV, VLADIMIR (1899–1977): Novelist and short-story writer; *Bend Sinister*, 1947; *Lolita*, Paris 1955, 1958; *Pnin*, 1957; *Pale Fire*, 1962; a number of novels written in Russian in the 1920s and 1930s have been translated into English, mainly by the author; stories: *Nabokov's Dozen*, 1958; *Nabokov's Quartet*, 1967; *Lectures on Literature*, 1980; *Lectures on Russian Literature*, ed. F. Bowers, 1981; autobiography: *Inconclusive Evidence*, 1951, rev. as *Speak Memory: An Autobiography Revisited*, 1980; selection: *Nabokov's Congeries*, ed. P. Stegner, 1968.

See:

L. S. Dembo, *Nabakov: The Man and his Work*, 1968
A. Levy, *Vladimir Nabokov*, 1984
L. Maddox, *Nabokov's Novels in English*, 1984
E. Pifer, *Nabokov and the Novel*, 1980
D. Rampton, *Vladimir Nabokov*, 1984
P. Stegner, *Escape into Aesthetics: The Art of Vladimir Nabokov*, 1967

NORRIS, FRANK (1870–1902): Novelist and short-story writer; *Moran of the Lady Letty*, 1898; *McTeague*, 1899; *Blix*, 1899; *A Man's Woman*, 1900; proposed trilogy: *The Octopus*, 1901, *The Pit*, 1903, the final novel, 'The Wolf', was not written; *Vandover and the Brute*, 1914; stories: *A Deal in Wheat*, 1903; *The Third Circle*, 1909; essays: *The Responsibilities of the Novelist*, 1903; *Literary Criticism*, ed. D. Pizer, 1964; *Letters*, ed. F. Walker, 1956; *Collected Writings*, 10 vols, 1928, 1967.

See:

W. B. Dillingham, *Frank Norris: Instinct and Art*, 1969
W. French, *Frank Norris*, 1962
E. Marchand, *Frank Norris: A Study*, 1942
D. Pizer, *The Novels of Frank Norris*, 1966
F. D. Walker, *Frank Norris: A Biography*, 1932

O'CONNOR, FLANNERY (1925–64): Novelist, short-story writer; novels: *Wise Blood*, 1952; *The Violent Bear It Away*, 1960; stories: *A Good Man Is Hard to Find*, 1955; *Everything That Rises Must Converge*, 1965; *Complete Stories*, 1971.

See:

F. Asals, *Flannery O'Connor: The Imagination of Extremity*, 1983
R. Coles, *Flannery O'Connor's South*, 1980
R. Drake, *Flannery O'Connor*, 1966
L. V. Driskell, *The Eternal Crossroads: The Art of Flannery O'Connor*, 1971
M. J. Friedman and L. A. Lawson (eds.), *The Added Dimension: The Art and Mind of Flannery O'Connor*, 1977
M. B. Gentry, *Flannery O'Connor's Religion of the Grotesque*, 1986
J. Hendin, *The World of Flannery O'Connor*, 1970
S. E. Hyman, *Flannery O'Connor*, 1966
C. W. Martin, *The True Country: Themes in the Fiction of Flannery O'Connor*, 1968

ODETS, CLIFFORD (1906–63): Dramatist and screenwriter; *Waiting for Lefty*, 1935; *Awake and Sing!*, 1935; *Till the Day I Die*, 1935; *Golden Boy*, 1937; *The Flowering Peach*, 1954; *Six Plays*, 1939.

See:

H. Cantor, *Clifford Odets: Playwright – Poet*, 1978

M. Mendelsohn, *Clifford Odets, Human Dramatist*, 1969
E. Murray, *Clifford Odets: The Thirties and After*, 1968
R. B. Shuman, *Clifford Odets*, 1962
G. Weales, *Odets the Playwright*, 1985

OLSON, CHARLES (1910–70): Poet and critic; *The Maximus Poems*, 1960; *The Maximus Poems, IV, V, VI*, 1968; *The Maximus Poems, Volume Three*, ed. C. Boer and G. F. Butterick, 1975; essays: *Human Universe and Other Essays*, 1965 (inc. 'Projective Verse', 1950); *Letters for 'Origin'* (journal ed. C. Corman) *1950–1956*, 1969; *Causal Mythology*, 1969; letters: *Charles Olson and Robert Creeley: The Complete Correspondence*, ed. G. F. Butterick, 2 vols., 1980; *Selected Writings*, ed. R. Creeley, 1966.

See:
G. F. Butterick, *A Guide to the 'Maximus Poems'*, 1978
D. Byrd, *Charles Olson's 'Maximus'*, 1980
P. Christensen, *Charles Olson: Call Him Ishmael*, 1979
P. Sherman, *Olson's Push: Origin, Black Mountain, and Recent American Poetry*, 1978

O'NEILL, EUGENE (1888–1953): Dramatist; Nobel Prize 1936; *Bound East for Cardiff*, 1916; *Before Breakfast*, 1916; *The Moon of the Caribbees*, 1918; *Beyond the Horizon*, 1920; *Anna Christie*, 1921 (as *Chris*, 1920); *The Emperor Jones*, 1920; *The Hairy Ape*, 1922; *Welded*, 1924; *All God's Chillun Got Wings*, 1924; *Desire Under the Elms*, 1924; *The Great God Brown*, 1926; *Lazarus Laughed*, 1927; *Strange Interlude*, 1928; *Dynamo*, 1929; *Mourning Becomes Electra*, 1931; *Ah! Wilderness*, 1933; *Days Without End*, 1934; *The Iceman Cometh*, 1946; *A Moon for the Misbegotten*, 1947; *Long Day's Journey into Night*, 1956; *A Touch of the Poet*, 1957; *Hughie*, 1964; *More Stately Mansions*, 1962; *Lost Plays of Eugene O'Neill*, 1950; *Ten 'Lost' Plays*, 1964 (1965), *Poems 1912–1944*, ed. D. C. Gallup, 1980.

See:
D. Alexander, *The Tempering of Eugene O'Neill*, 1962
N. Berlin, *Eugene O'Neill*, 1982
T. Bogard, *Contour in Time*, 1972, rev. 1988
O. Cargill et al. (eds.), *O'Neill and his Plays*, 1961
J. Chothia, *Forging a Language*, 1979
B. H. Clark, *Eugene O'Neill: The Man and his Plays*, 1929
E. A. Engel, *The Haunted Heroes of Eugene O'Neill*, 1953
D. Falk, *Eugene O'Neill and the Tragic Tension*, 1958, 1981
V. Floyd (ed.), *Eugene O'Neill at Work: Newly Released Ideas for Plays*, 1981
J. Gassner (ed.), *O'Neill: A Collection of Critical Essays*, 1961
A. and B. Gelb, *O'Neill*, 1962
C. Leech, *O'Neill*, 1963
J. Y. Miller, *Eugene O'Neill and the American Critic*, 1973

L. Sheaffer, *O'Neill: Son and Playwright*, 1968

    O'Neill: Son and Artist, 1973

R. D. Skinner, *Eugene O'Neill: A Poet's Quest*, 1935

T. Tiusanen, *Eugene O'Neill's Scenic Images*, 1968

E. Törnqvist, *A Drama of Souls: Studies in O'Neill's Supernaturalistic Technique*, 1968, 1969

PAINE, THOMAS (1737–1809): Political activist, born in England, emigrated to America at Franklin's persuasion but from 1787 was active in French revolutionary politics and came near to being guillotined; his books were burned in England and on his return to America in 1802 he was virtually rejected; *Common Sense*, 1776; *The American Crisis*, 13 pamphlets, 1776–83; *The Rights of Man*, 1791–2 (dedicated to Washington), ed. with intro. by H. Collins, 1969; *The Age of Reason*, 1794, 1796; *Letter to George Washington*, 1796; *Complete Writings*, ed. P. S. Foner, 2 vols., 1945.

See:

A. O. Aldridge, *Man of Reason: The Life of Thomas Paine*, 1959

D. F. Hawke, *Paine*, 1974

W. E. Woodward, *Thomas Paine: America's Godfather*, 1945

PARKMAN, FRANCIS (1823–93): Historian; *The Oregon Trail*, 1849; *Parkman Reader*, ed. S. E. Morison, 1955.

See:

H. Doughty, *Francis Parkman*, 1962

O. A. Pease, *Francis Parkman's History: The Historian as Literary Artist*, 1953

PERCY, WALKER (b. 1916): Novelist and essayist; *The Moviegoer*, 1961; *The Last Gentleman*, 1967; *Love in the Ruins*, 1971; *Launcelot*, 1977; *The Second Coming*, 1980.

See:

W. R. Allen, *Walker Percy: A Southern Wayfarer*, 1986

R. Coles, *Walker Percy: Am American Search*, 1978

M. Luschei, *The Sovereign Wayfarer: Walker Percy's Diagnosis of the Malaise*, 1972

P. L. Poteat, *Walker Percy and the Old Modern Age*, 1984

J. Tharpe (ed.), *Walker Percy: Art and Ethics*, 1980

PHILIPSON, MORRIS (b. 1926): Philosopher, novelist, Director of Chicago University Press (since 1967); *Outline of Jungian Aesthetics*, 1963; *Six Stunning Paradoxes*, 1968; ed. with P. J. Gudel, *Aesthetics Today*, 1961; novels: *Bourgeois Anonymous*, 1964; *The Wallpaper Fox*, 1987; *Secret Understandings*, 1983; *A Man in Charge*, 1987; *Somebody Else's Life*, 1987.

PLATH, SYLVIA (1932–63): Poet; *The Colossus and Other Poems*, 1960; as *The Colossus*, 1967; *Ariel*, 1965; *Crossing the Water*, 1971; *Winter Trees*, 1971; *Crystal Gazer and Other Poems*, 1971; *Collected Poems*, ed. Ted Hughes, 1981; novel: *The Bell Jar*, 1963 (under pseudonym, Victoria Lucas), 1966; *Journals*, ed. Ted Hughes and F. McCullough, 1982; prose; *Johnny Panic and the Bible of Dreams*, intro. by Ted Hughes, 1979.

See:

E. Aird, *Sylvia Plath: Her Life and Work*, 1973
A. Alvarez, *The Savage God*, 1971
C. K. Barnard, *Sylvia Plath*, 1978
S. Bassnett, *Sylvia Plath*, 1986
A. Brink, *Loss and Symbolic Repair*, 1977
M. L. Broe, *Protean Poetic: The Poetry of Sylvia Plath*, 1980
L. K. Bundtzen, *Plath's Incarnation: Woman and the Creative Process*, 1983
E. Butscher (ed.), *Sylvia Plath, the Woman and the Work*, 1977
D. Holbrook, *Sylvia Plath: Poetry and Existence*, 1976
J. Kroll, *Chapters in a Mythology: The Poetry of Sylvia Plath*, 1976
B. Kyle, *Sylvia Plath: A Dramatic Portrait*, London 1976; New York 1977 (a play)
G. Lane (ed.), *Sylvia Plath: New Views on the Poetry*, 1979
I. Melander, *The Poetry of Sylvia Plath: A Study of Themes*, 1970
C. Newman (ed.), *The Art of Sylvia Plath*, 1970
J. Rosenblatt, *Sylvia Plath: The Poetry of Initiation*, 1979
N. H. Steiner, *A Closer Look at Ariel: A Memory of Sylvia Plath*, 1973
A. Stevenson, *Bitter Fame: A Life of Sylvia Plath*, 1989
M. D. Uroff, *Sylvia Plath and Ted Hughes*, 1979
L. W. Wagner-Martin, *Sylvia Plath: A Biography*, 1987
    (ed.), *Sylvia Plath: The Critical Heritage*, 1988

POE, EDGAR ALLAN (1809–49): Poet, short-story writer, critic; *Complete Works*, 17 vols., ed. J. A. Harrison, 1902; *Collected Works*, ed. T. O. Mabbott, 1969– ; *Complete Poems*, 1959; *The Poems*, ed. F. Stovall, 1965; *Poetry and Tales*, ed. P. F. Quinn, 1984; *Essays and Reviews*, ed. G. R. Thompson, 1984; *Literary Criticism*, ed. R. L. Hough, 1965; *Letters*, 2 vols., ed. J. W. Ostrom, 1948, enlarged 1966; *Works*, 10 vols., 1908, 1981; *Select Prose and Poetry*, ed. W. H. Auden, 1950; *Portable Edgar Allan Poe*, ed. P. V. D. Stern, 1945 (1977); *Representative Selections*, ed. M. Alterton and H. Craig, 1962; *Selected Writings*, ed. D. Galloway, 1967.

See:

J. Alexander, *Affidavits of Genius: Edgar Allan Poe and the French Critics, 1847–1924*, 1971
H. Allen, *Israfel: The Life and Times of Edgar Allan Poe*, 2 vols. 1926; 1 vol. 1934 M. Allen, *Poe and the British Magazine Tradition*, 1969
K. Campbell, *The Mind of Poe and Other Studies*, 1933

E. W. Carlson (ed.), *The Recognition of Edgar Allan Poe: Selected Criticism since 1829*, 1966

E. H. Davidson, *Poe: A Critical Study*, 1957

R. L. Gale, *Plots and Characters in the Fiction and Poetry of Edgar Allan Poe*, 1970

D. Hoffman, *Poe Poe Poe Poe Poe Poe Poe*, 1972

W. L. Howarth (ed.), *Twentieth-Century Interpretations of Poe's Tales*, 1971

R. D. Jacobs, *Poe: Journalist and Critic*, 1969

S. P. Moss, *Poe's Literary Battles*, 1963

A. H. Quinn, *Edgar Allan Poe: A Critical Biography*, 1941

P. F. Quinn, *The French Face of Edgar Poe*, 1957

G. Rans, *Edgar Allan Poe*, 1965

R. Regan (ed.), *Poe: A Collection of Critical Essays*, 1967

F. Stovall, *Edgar Poe the Poet*, 1969

J. Symons, *The Tell-Tale Heart*, 1978 (biography)

G. R. Thompson, *Poe's Fiction: Romantic Irony in the Gothic Tales*, 1973

E. Wagenknecht, *Edgar Allan Poe: Man Behind the Legend*, 1963

I. M. Walker, *Edgar Allan Poe: The Critical Heritage*, 1986

PORTER, KATHERINE ANNE (1890–1980): Novelist, story-writer, essayist; *Flowering Judas*, 1930; *Pale Horse, Pale Rider: Ten Short Novels*, 1939; *The Leaning Tower*, 1944; *Ship of Fools*, 1962; *Collected Stories*, 1964; essays: *What Price Marriage*, 1927; *The Days Before*, 1952; *Collected Essays and Occasional Writings*, 1970.

See:

L. Hartley and G. Core (eds.), *Katherine Anne Porter: A Critical Symposium*, 1969

G. Hendrick, *Katherine Anne Porter*, 1965

M. M. Liberman, *Katherine Anne Porter's Fiction*, 1971

J. Mooney, *The Fiction and Criticism of Katherine Anne Porter*, 1957; rev. 1962

W. L. Nance, *Katherine Anne Porter and the Art of Rejection*, 1964

D. H. Unrue, *Truth and Vision in Katherine Anne Porter's Fiction*, 1985

POUND, EZRA LOOMIS (1885–1972): Poet and critic. (This volume is concerned only with Pound's work until 1930; see also Vol. 7.) *A Lume Spento*, 1908; *A Quinzaine for this Yule*, 1908; *Personae*, 1909 – independent of later volumes including this title; *Exultations*, 1909; *Provença*, 1910; *Canzoni* 1911; *The Sonnets and Ballate of Guido Cavalcanti*, 1912; *Ripostes*, London 1912, Boston 1913; *Personae and Exultations*, 1913; *Cathay*, 1915; ed. *Catholic Anthology 1914–1915*, 1915; *Lustra of Ezra Pound*, 1916; *Quia pauper amavi*, 1918; *Umbra*, 1920; *Hugh Selwyn Mauberley*, 1920; *Poems 1918–1921*, 1921; *Personae: The Collected Poems*, 1926; *Selected Poems*, intro. T. S. Eliot, 1928; *A Draft of Cantos 17–27*, 1928; *A Draft of XXX Cantos*, Paris 1930, London 1933; *Collected Early Verse*, ed. M. J. King, 1977; prose: *The Spirit of Romance*, 1910, rev. 1953; *Gaudier-Brzeska, A Memoir*, 1916; *Pavannes and*

Divisions, 1918; *Instigations*, 1920; *Antheil and the Treatise on Harmony*, 1924;
Selected Prose 1909–1965, ed. W. Cookson, 1972; *Selected Letters*, ed. D. D.
Paige, 1951.

See:

R. Aldington, *Ezra Pound v. T. S. Eliot: A Lecture*, 1954 (written about
   1940)
I. F. A. Bell, *Critic as Scientist: The Modernistic Poetics of Ezra Pound*, 1981
   (ed.), *Ezra Pound: Tactics for Reading*, 1983
P. Brooker, *A Student's Guide to the Selected Poems*, 1979
R. Bush, *The Genesis of Ezra Pound's Cantos*, 1976
W. Cookson, *A Guide to the Cantos of Ezra Pound*, 1985
G. Davenport, *Cities on Hills: A Study of [Cantos] I–XXX*, 1983
T. S. Eliot, *Ezra Pound, His Metric and His Poetry*, 1917
G. S. Fraser, *Ezra Pound*, 1960
B. Frogelman, *Shapes of Power: The Development of Ezra Pound's Poetic
   Sequences*, 1988
P. Grover (ed.), *The London Years, 1908–1920*, 1978
D. Hoffman (ed.), *Ezra Pound and William Carlos Williams*, 1983
E. Homberger, *Ezra Pound: The Critical Heritage*, 1972
M. A. Kayman, *The Modernism of Ezra Pound*, 1986
H. Kenner, *The Poetry of Ezra Pound*, 1951
   The Pound Era, 1972
F. R. Leavis, *New Bearings in English Poetry*, 1932
Wyndham Lewis, *Time and Western Man*, 1927
B. Lingberg-Seyersted (ed.), *Pound/Ford: The Story of a Literary Friendship*, 1982
P. Russell (ed.), *A Collection of Essays to be Presented to Ezra Pound, 1907–
   1941*, 1951
C. K. Stead, *Pound, Yeats, Eliot and the Modernist Movement*, 1986
N. Stock, *The Life of Ezra Pound*, 1970
H. Zinnes (ed.), *Ezra Pound and the Visual Arts*, 1980

PYNCHON, THOMAS (b. 1937): Novelist; *V.*, 1963; *The Crying of Lot 49*,
1966; *Gravity's Rainbow*, 1973.

See:

P. L. Cooper, *Signs and Symptoms: Thomas Pynchon and the Contemporary
   World*, 1983
D. Cowart, *Thomas Pynchon: The Art of Allusion*, 1980
D. Seed, *The Fictional Labyrinths of Thomas Pynchon*, 1988
J. O. Stark, *Pynchon's Fictions: Thomas Pynchon and the Literature of Informa-
   tion*, 1980

RANSOM, JOHN CROWE (1888–1974): Poet, critic, and founder of *Kenyon
Review* (ed. 1939–61); *Selected Poems*, 1945, 1963; essays and criticism: *God
Without Thunder*, 1930; *The World's Body*, 1938; *The New Criticism*, 1941;

ed. *The Kenyon Critics*, 1967; selections: *Poems and Essays*, 1955; *Letters*, 1984.

See:
K. F. Knight, *The Poetry of John Crowe Ransom*, 1964
J. E. Magner, Jr, *John Crowe Ransom: Critical Principles and Preoccupations*, 1971
T. H. Parsons, *John Crowe Ransom*, 1969
T. D. Young, *John Crowe Ransom: Critical Essays and a Bibliography*, 1968
   Gentleman in a Dustcoat: A Biography, 1976

REXROTH, KENNETH (1905–82): Poet and critic; *Collected Shorter Poems*, 1966; *Collected Longer Poems*, 1968; *New Poems*, 1974; essays: *Bird in the Bush*, 1959; *Assays*, 1962; *The Alternative Society: Essays from the Other World*, 1970; *An Autobiographical Novel*, 1966; *A Kenneth Rexroth Reader*, ed. E. Mottram, 1970.

See:
M. Gibson, *Kenneth Rexroth*, 1972

RICE, ELMER (1892–1967): Dramatist; *On Trial*, 1914; *The Adding Machine*, 1923; *Street Scene*, 1929; *We the People*, 1933; *Judgment Day*, 1934; *Dream Girl*, 1945; *Seven Plays*, 1950; *Three Plays*, 1965; novel: *A Voyage to Purilia*, 1930; non-dramatic: *Minority Report: An Autobiography*, 1954, 1963; *The Living Theatre*, 1959, 1960.

See:
F. Durham, *Elmer Rice*, 1970
R. Hogan, *The Independence of Elmer Rice*, 1965

RICH, ADRIENNE CECILE (b. 1929): Poet; *Selected Poems*, 1967; *Poems Selected and New, 1950–1974*, 1975; *The Dream of a Common Language: Poems 1974–1977*, 1978.

See:
B. C. and A. Gelpi (eds.), *Adrienne Rich's Poetry*, 1975
C. Keyes, *The Aesthetics of Power: The Poetry of Adrienne Rich*, 1986

RILEY, JAMES WHITCOMB (1849–1916): Journalist and poet; *Homestead Edition of the Poems and Prose Sketches*, 16 vols., 1897–1914; *Letters*, 1930.

See:
R. Crowder, *Those Innocent Years: The Legacy and Inheritance of a Hero of the Victorian Era, James Whitcomb Riley*, 1957
J. C. Nolan, *James Whitcomb Riley, Hoosier Poet*, 1941

ROETHKE, THEODORE (1908–63): Poet; *Words for the Wind: The Collected*

Verse (London 1957), 1958; *The Collected Poems*, 1968; *On the Poet and his Craft: Selected Prose*, ed. R. J. Mills, 1965; *Selected Letters*, ed. R. J. Mills, 1968; *The Notebooks*, ed. D. Wagoner, 1970.

See:
R. A. Blessing, *Theodore Roethke's Dynamic Vision*, 1974
N. Bowers, *Theodore Roethke: The Journey from I to Otherwise*, 1982
L. R. Bryant, *Theodore Roethke: Poetry of the Earth . . . Poetry of the Spirit*, 1981
K. Malkoff, *Theodore Roethke: Introduction to the Poetry*, 1966
J. Parini, *Theodore Roethke, An American Romantic*, 1979
A. Seager, *The Glass House: The Life of Theodore Roethke*, 1968
A. Stein (ed.), *Theodore Roethke: Essays on the Poetry*, 1965
R. Sullivan, *Theodore Roethke: The Garden Master*, 1975
H. Williams, '*The Edge is What I Have*': *Theodore Roethke and After*, 1977
G. Wolff, *Theodore Roethke*, 1981

ROTH, PHILIP (b. 1933): Novelist; *Goodbye, Columbus*, 1959; *Letting Go*, 1962; *When She Was Good*, 1967; *Portnoy's Complaint*, 1969; *My Life As a Man*, 1974; *The Ghost Writer*, 1979; *Zuckerman Unbound*, 1981; *The Anatomy Lesson*, 1983; *The Prague Orgy*, 1985; *Zuckerman Bound*, 1985.

See:
J. P. Jones and G. A. Nance, *Philip Roth*, 1981
H. Lee, *Philip Roth*, 1982

SALINGER, JEROME DAVID (b. 1919): Novelist, short-story writer; novel: *The Catcher in the Rye*, 1951; stories: *For Esmé with Love and Squalor*, in USA as *Nine Stories*, 1953; *Franny and Zooey*, 1961; *Raise High the Roof Beam, Carpenters* and *Seymour: An Introduction*, 1963.

See:
W. F. Belcher and J. W. Lee (eds.), *J. D. Salinger and the Critics*, 1962
W. French, *J. D. Salinger*, 1963, rev. 1976
F. L. Gwynn and J. L. Blotner, *The Fiction of J. D. Salinger*, 1958
M. Laser and N. Fruman (eds.), *Studies in J. D. Salinger*, 1963

SANDBURG, CARL (1878–1967): Poet and biographer; *Complete Poems*, 1950; novel: *Remembrance Rock*, 1948; biography (of Lincoln): *The Prairie Years*, 2 vols., 1926, *The War Years*, 4 vols., 1939; autobiography: *Always the Young Strangers*, 1953; *Letters*, ed. H. Mitgang, 1968.

See:
R. Crowder, *Carl Sandburg*, 1964
K. W. Detzer, *Carl Sandburg: A Study in Personality and Background*, 1941

SAROYAN, WILLIAM (1908–81): Dramatist; *My Heart's in the Highlands*,

1939; *The Time of Your Life*, 1939; stories: *The Daring Young Man on the Flying Trapeze*, 1934; novel: *The Human Comedy*, 1943, rev. 1971; autobiography: *Places Where I've Done Time*, 1972 (1973); *William Saroyan Reader*, 1958; *Best Stories*, 1942.

See:

H. R. Floan, *William Saroyan*, 1966
E. H. Foster, *William Saroyan*, 1984

SCHULBERG, BUDD (1914–86). Novelist, screenwriter, producer; *What Makes Sammy Run?*, 1941; *The Disenchanted*, 1950 (loosely related to Scott Fitzgerald's life); screenplays include *On the Waterfront*, 1954.

See:

J. Spatz, *Hollywood in Fiction*, 1969

SCHWARTZ, DELMORE (1913–66): Poet, short-story writer, critic; *In Dreams Begin Responsibilities* (stories and poems), 1938; *Shenandoah* (verse play), 1941; stories: *The World is a Wedding*, 1948; *Summer Knowledge: New and Selected Poems, 1938–1958*, 1959; *What is to be Given* (poems), ed. D. Dunn, 1978; *Selected Essays*, ed. D. A. Dike and D. H. Zucker, 1970.

See:

J. Atlas, *Delmore Schwartz: The Life of an American Poet*, 1977
R. McDougall, *Delmore Schwartz*, 1974

SEWALL, SAMUEL (1652–1730): Businessman and judge (including service at Salem witchcraft trials); *The Revolution in New England Justified*, with Edward Rawson, 1691; *The Selling of Joseph*, 1700 (on slavery), ed. S. Kaplan, 1969; *Diary, 1674–1729*, 1878–82, ed. T. H. Halsey, 2 vols., 1973.

See:

T. B. Strandness, *Samuel Sewall: A Puritan Portrait*, 1968
O. E. Winslow, *Samuel Sewall of Boston*, 1964.

SEXTON, ANNE (1928–74): Poet; *Complete Poems*, ed. L. G. Sexton, 1981; *Anne Sexton: A Self-Portrait in Letters*, ed. L. G. Sexton and L. Ames, 1977.

See:

J. D. McClatchy (ed.), *Anne Sexton: The Artist and Her Critics*, 1978

SHAPIRO, KARL JAY (b. 1913): Poet, critic, editor of *Poetry*, 1950–56, and *Prairie Schooner; Collected Poems, 1940–1977*, 1978; prose poem and autobiography: *The Bourgeois Poet*, 1958, 1964; essays: *English Prosody and Modern Poetry*, 1947, 1969; *Beyond Criticism*, 1953; *In Defense of Ignorance*, 1960; *To Abolish Children and Other Essays*, 1968; *The Poetry Wreck*, 1975.

See:
J. Reino, *Karl Shapiro*, 1981

SHEPARD, SAM (b. 1943): Dramatist and actor; *Cowboys*, 1964; *Chicago*, 1965; *Icarus's Mother*, 1965; *Red Cross*, 1966; *Melodrama Play*, 1966; *La Turista*, 1967; *The Tooth of Crime*, 1972; *Angel City*, 1976; *Buried Child*, 1978; *Curse of the Starving Class*, 1978; *True West*, 1980; *Chicago and Other Plays*, 1981; *Fool for Love*, 1982; *Motel Chronicles*, 1983, *Seven Plays*, ed. R. Gilman, 1981.

See:
L. Hart, *Sam Shepard's Metaphorical Stages*, 1986
C. Rosen, *Sam Shepard*, 1986

SIMMS, WILLIAM GILMORE (1806–70): Novelist, poet, editor; *Martin Faber*, 1833; *Guy Rivers: A Tale of Georgia*, 1834; *The Yemassee*, 1835; *Works*, 20 vols., 1853–9; *Writings*, 24 vols. projected, 1969–.

See:
J. V. Ridgely, *William Gilmore Simms*, 1962
W. P. Trent, *William Gilmore Simms*, 1892 (biography)

SIMON, NEIL (b. 1937): Dramatist: *Come Blow Your Horn*, 1960; *Barefoot in the Park*, 1964; *The Odd Couple*, 1965; *Plaza Suite*, 1968; *Last of the Red Hot Lovers*, 1969; *The Sunshine Boys*, 1972; collection: *The Comedy of Neil Simon*, 1971 (seven plays with intro. by Simon).

See:
R. K. Johnson, *Neil Simon*, 1983
E. M. McGovern, *Not-So-Simple Neil Simon: A Critical Study*, 1978

SINCLAIR, UPTON (1878–1968): Novelist: *Manasias*, 1904, rev. as *Theirs be the Guilt*, 1959; *The Jungle*, 1906; *The Moneychangers*, 1908; *Oil!*, 1927; *World's End*, 1940 (series of 11 novels); *Autobiography*, 1962; *My Lifetime in Letters* (written to him), 1960; *An Upton Sinclair Anthology*, ed. I. O. Evans with intro. by Sinclair, 1934.

See:
F. Dell, *Upton Sinclair: A Study in Social Protest*, 1927
S. G. Putt, in *Scholars of the Heart*, 1962
W. Rideout, in *The Radical Novel in the United States, 1900–1954*, 1956

SMITH, CAPTAIN JOHN (1580–1631): Traveller (especially in Eastern Europe), arrived in Virginia in 1605 and helped found Jamestown; Pocahontas allegedly saved his life when he was ambushed by Indians in 1607; returned to England in 1609 and made an expedition to New England (which he named) in 1614; *A True Relation of such occurrences as hath hapned in Virginia*, 1608; *A Map of Virginia. With a Description of the Countrey*, 1612; *A Description of New England*, 1618; *Travels and Works*, ed. W. Arber, 2 vols., 1910; selection: *Captain John Smith's America*, ed. J. Lankford, 1967.

See:
P. L. Barbour, *The Three Worlds of Captain John Smith*, 1964
E. H. Emerson, *Captain John Smith*, 1971
B. Smith, *Captain John Smith*, 1953

SONTAG, SUSAN (b. 1933): Critic, novelist; novels: *The Benefactor*, 1963; *Death Kit*, 1967; non-fiction: *Against Interpretation*, 1965, 1981; *Trip to Hanoi*, 1969; *Styles of Radical Will*, 1969; *On Photography*, 1980; *Under the Sign of Saturn*, 1980; *A Susan Sontag Reader*, 1983.

STEIN, GERTRUDE (1874–1946): Novelist, poet; novels: *Three Lives*, 1909; *Tender Buttons*, 1914; *Geography and Plays*, 1922; *The Making of Americans*, 1925; non-fiction: *Autobiography*, 1933; *Lectures in America*, 1935; *Picasso*, 1939; *Paris France*, 1940; *Wars I have Seen*, 1945; *Writings and Lectures, 1911–45*, ed. P. Meyorowitz, 1967; *Selected Writings*, ed. C. Van Vechten, 1946; *Yale Edition of the Unpublished Writings*, 8 vols., 1951–8; *The Yale Gertrude Stein*, 1980.

See:
J. M. Brinnin, *The Third Rose: Gertrude Stein and Her World*, 1959.
J. L. Doane, *Science and Narrative: The Early Novels of Gertrude Stein*, 1986
E. Fuller (ed.), *Leo Stein [her brother]: Journey into the Self*, 1950
S. Neuman (ed.), *Gertrude Stein and the Making of Literature*, 1988
B. L. Reid, *Art by Subtraction: A Dissenting Opinion of Gertrude Stein*, 1958
A. Stewart, *Gertrude Stein and the Present*, 1967
D. Sutherland, *Gertrude Stein: A Biography of her Work*, 1951
Alice B. Toklas, *What is Remembered*, 1963
J. L. Walker, *The Making of a Modernist*, 1984

STEINBECK, JOHN (1902–68): Novelist, Nobel Prize 1962; *Tortilla Flat*, 1935; *In Dubious Battle*, 1936; *Of Mice and Men*, 1937; *The Grapes of Wrath*, 1939; *The Moon is Down*, 1942; *Cannery Row*, 1945; *East of Eden*, 1952; *The Winter of Our Discontent*, 1961; non-fiction: *Sea of Cortez*, with E. F. Ricketts, 1941; war reports: *Once There was a War*, 1958; *Portable Steinbeck*, ed. P. Covici, Jr, 1971.

See:
W. French, *Film Guide to 'The Grapes of Wrath'*, 1973,
    John Steinbeck, 1961, rev. 1975
T. Kiernan, *The Intricate Muse*, 1979
H. Levant, *The Novels of John Steinbeck: A Critical Study*, 1974

P. Lisca, *John Steinbeck: Nature and Myth*, 1978
P. McCarthy, *John Steinbeck*, 1980
F. W. Watt, *Steinbeck*, 1962

STEVENS, WALLACE (1879–1955): Poet; *Harmonium*, 1923; *Ideas of Order*, 1935; *Owl's Clover*, 1936; *The Man with the Blue Guitar*, 1937; *Notes Towards a Supreme Fiction*, 1942; *Parts of a World*, 1942; *Transport to a Summer*, 1947; *The Auroras of Autumn*, 1950; *Collected Poems*, 1954; *The Rock*, 1955; *Opus Posthumus*, poems and essays, ed. S. F. Morse, 1957; *On Extended Wings: Wallace Stevens' Longer Poems*, 1969; essays: *The Necessary Angel: Essays on Reality and the Imagination*, 1951; *Letters*, ed. H. Stevens, 1966; selection: *The Palm at the End of the Mind*, ed. H. Stevens, 1985.

See:
J. Baird, *The Dome and the Rock: Structure in the Poetry of Wallace Stevens*, 1968
L. Beckett, *Wallace Stevens*, 1979
M. Boroff (ed), *Wallace Stevens: A Collection of Critical Essays*, 1963
R. Buttel, *Wallace Stevens: The Meaning of 'Harmonium'*, 1967
F. Doggett, *Stevens' Poetry of Thought*, 1966
C. Doyle, *Wallace Stevens: The Critical Heritage*, 1985
J. J. Enck, *Wallace Stevens: Images and Judgements*, 1964
A. Gelpi, *Wallace Stevens: The Poetics of Modernism*, 1986
F. Kermode, *Wallace Stevens*, 1960
A. W. Litz, *Introspective Voyager: The Poetic Development of Wallace Stevens*, 1972
R. S. Patke, *The Long Poems of Wallace Stevens*, 1986
R. H. Pearce and J. H. Miller (eds), *The Act of Mind: Essays on the Poetry of Wallace Stevens*, 1966
R. Rehder, *The Poetry of Wallace Stevens*, 1986
W. Van O'Connor, *The Shaping Spirit: A Study of Wallace Stevens*, 1950
H. W. Wells, *Introduction to Wallace Stevens*, 1964

STOWE, HARRIET BEECHER (1811–96): Novelist and reformer; *Uncle Tom's Cabin*, 1852; *Key to Uncle Tom's Cabin*, 1853; *Dred: A Tale of the Great Dismal Swamp*, 1856.

See:
J. R. Adams, *Harriet Beecher Stowe*, 1963
H. Birdoff, *The World's Greatest Hit: Uncle Tom's Cabin* [in the theatre], 1947
A. C. Crozier, *The Novels of Harriet Beecher Stowe*, 1969
T. R. Hovet *The Master Narrative*, 1989
E. J. Sundquist (ed.), *New Essays on 'Uncle Tom's Cabin'*, 1987
E. Wagenknecht, *Harriet Beecher Stowe: The Known and the Unknown*, 1965

STYRON, WILLIAM (b. 1925): Novelist; *Lie Down in Darkness*, 1951; *The*

Long March, 1953; *Set this House on Fire*, 1960; *The Confessions of Nat Turner*, 1967; *Sophie's Choice*, 1979.

See:

J. H. Clarke (ed.), *William Styron's Nat Turner: Ten Black Writers Respond*, 1968

R. H. Fossum, *William Styron*, 1968

R. C. Mackin, *William Styron*, 1969

R. K. Morris (ed.), *The Achievement of William Styron*, 1981

TATE, ALLEN (1899–1979): Poet, novelist, critic; *Collected Poems, 1919–1976*, 1978; novel: *The Fathers*, 1938; essays: *Reactionary Essays on Poetry and Ideas*, 1936; *Reason in Madness: Critical Essays*, 1941; *On the Limits of Poetry: Selected Essays, 1928–1948*, 1948; *The Hovering Fly and Other Essays*, 1948; *The Forlorn Demon: Didactic and Critical Essays*, 1953; *The Man of Letters in the Modern World: Selected Essays, 1928–1955*, 1955; *Collected Essays*, 1959; *Essays of Four Decades*, 1968; *Memoirs and Opinions, 1926–1974*, 1975.

See:

R. S. Dupree, *Allen Tate and the Augustinian Imagination: A Study of the Poetry*, 1983

R. Squires, *Allen Tate: A Literary Biography*, 1971

J. C. Stewart, *The Burden of Time: The Fugitives and Agrarians*, 1965

TAYLOR, EDWARD (*c.* 1644–1729): Dissenting schoolmaster; migrated to Boston, Mass., 1668; graduated from Harvard and became minister at Westfield, Mass., where he wrote his poetry which he did not wish published; the poetry was not printed until 1939. *Poems*, ed. D. E. Stanford, with intro. by L. L. Martz, 1960; reprinted with intro. by Stanford, 1963; *Diary*, ed. F. W. Murphy, 1964.

See:

N. S. Grabo, *Edward Taylor*, 1961

K. E. Rowe, *Saint and Singer: Edward Taylor's Typology and the Poetics of Meditation*, 1986

THOREAU, HENRY DAVID (1817–62): Naturalist, poet, essayist; *A Week on the Concord and Merrimack Rivers*, 1849; 'Resistance to Civil Government', 1849, reprinted as 'Civil Disobedience' in *A Yankee in Canada, with Anti-Slavery and Reform Papers*, 1866; *Walden; or, Life in the Woods*, 1854, annotated edn ed. P. V. D. Stern, 1970; *The Maine Woods*, 1863; *Cape Cod*, 1865; *The Writings*, 20 vols, 1906; *Collected Poems*, ed. C. Bode, 1964; *Correspondence*, ed. C. Bode and W. Harding, 1957; *Portable Thoreau*, ed. C. Bode, 1947 (1977).

See:

S. Cavell, *The Sense of 'Walden'*, 1972

F. Garber, *Thoreau's Redemptive Imagination*, 1977

W. Harding, *The Thoreau Handbook*, 1959
   The Days of Henry Thoreau, 1965

J. W. Krutch, *Henry David Thoreau*, 1948

C. R. Metzger, *Thoreau and Whitman*, 1961

F. Ochlschlaeger and G. Hendrick (eds.), *Toward the Making of Thoreau's Modern Reputation*, 1980

S. Paul, *The Shores of America: Thoreau's Inward Exploration*, 1958

R. Ruland (ed.), *Walden: A Collection of Critical Essays*, 1967

E. Wagenknecht, *Henry David Thoreau: What Manner of Man?*, 1981

THURBER, JAMES (1894–1961): Humorist (particularly associated with *New Yorker*) and children's writer; *Is Sex Necessary?*, with E. B. White, 1929; *Let Your Mind Alone*, 1937; collections include: *The Owl in the Attic and Other Perplexities*, 1931; *The Seal in tthe Bedroom and Other Predicaments*, 1932; *My Life and Hard Times*, 1933; *Fables for our Times*, 1940, 1956; *Thurber Carnival*, 1945; *The Beast in Me and Other Animals*, 1949; *Thurber Country*, 1953; autobiography: *The Years with Ross* [editor of 'New Yorker'], 1959 (1984).

See:

C. M. Kenney, *Thurber's Anatomy of Confusion*, 1984

R. E. Morseberger, *James Thurber*, 1964

TWAIN, MARK (SAMUEL LANGHORNE CLEMENS) (1835–1910): Novelist, humorist; novels: *The Gilded Age*, with C. D. Warner, 1873; *The Adventures of Tom Sawyer*, 1876; *The Prince and the Pauper*, 1882; *The Adventures of Huckleberry Finn*, 1885; *A Connecticut Yankee in King Arthur's Court*, 1889; *Tom Sawyer Abroad*, 1894; *The Tragedy of Pudd'nhead Wilson*, 1894; *A Double-Barrelled Detective Story*, 1902; *The Mysterious Stranger*, 1916; travel: *The Innocents Abroad*, 1869; *Roughing It*, 1872; *Europe and Elsewhere*, 1923; essays: *Christian Science*, 1907; *Is Shakespeare Dead?*, 1909; autobiography: *Life on the Mississippi*, 1883; *Autobiography*, ed. C. Neider, 1959; *Notebooks and Journals*, ed. F. A. Anderson, et al., 1975– ; *Letters*, ed. A. B. Paine, 2 vols, 1917; *Writings*, ed. A. B. Paine, 37 vols., 1922–5; *Works*, ed. J. C. Gerber, et al., 24 vols. projected, 1969– ; selections: *Portable Mark Twain*, ed. B. DeVoto, 1946 (1977); *Satires and Burlesques*, ed. F. R. Rogers, 1967.

See:

H. G. Baetzhold, *Mark Twain and John Bull: The British Connection*, 1970

G. C. Bellamy, *Mark Twain as a Literary Artist*, 1950

W. Blair, *Mark Twain and Huck Finn*, 1960

G. A. Cardwell (ed.), *Discussions of Mark Twain*, 1963

J. M. Cox, *Mark Twain: The Fate of Humor*, 1966

S. de S. Davis and P. D. Betdler, (eds), *The Mythologizing of Mark Twain*, 1984

B. DeVoto, *Mark Twain at Work*, 1942
   Mark Twain's America, 1932
M. Duckett, *Mark Twain and Bret Harte*, 1964
W. M. Gibson, *The Art of Mark Twain*, 1976
J. Kaplan, *Mr Clemens and Mark Twain: A Biography*, 1966
L. Leary (ed.), *A Casebook on Mark Twain's Wound*, 1962
K. S. Lynn, *Mark Twain and Southwestern Humor*, 1960
A. L. Scott, *Mark Twain at Large*, 1969
   (ed.), *Mark Twain: Selected Criticism*, 1955
H. N. Smith, *Mark Twain: The Development of a Writer*, 1962
   (ed.), *Mark Twain: A Collection of Critical Essays*, 1963
R. A. Wiggins, *Mark Twain: Jackleg Novelist*, 1964

UPDIKE, JOHN HOYER (b. 1932): Novelist, poet; *Rabbit, Run*, 1960; *The Centaur*, 1963; *Couples*, 1968; *Rabbit Redux*, 1971; *Rabbit Is Rich*, 1981; *Roger's Version*, 1986; *Rabbit at Rest*, 1990; stories: *Pigeon Feathers and Other Stories*, 1962; *Olinger Stories*, 1964; *The Music School*, 1966; poetry: *The Carpentered Hen and Other Tame Creatures*, 1958; non-fiction: *Bech: A Book*, 1970.

See:

A. and K. Hamilton, *The Elements of John Updike*, 1969
G. W. Hunt, *John Updike and Three Secret Things: Sex, Religion, and Art*, 1980
C. T. Samuels, *John Updike*, 1969
S. H. Uphaus, *John Updike*, 1980

WARD, ARTEMUS (Charles Farrar Browne) (1834–67): Humorist, journalist; *Artemus Ward: His Book*, 1862; *Artemus Ward: His Travels*, 1865; *Artemus Ward in London*, 1867; *Complete Works*, ed. T. W. Robertson and E. P. Hingston, 1903; *Selected Works*, ed. A. J. Nock, 1912, 1924.

See:

J. P. Pullen, *Comic Relief: The Life and Laughter of Artemus Ward*, 1984
D. C. Seitz, *Artemus Ward . . .: A Biography and a Bibliography*, 1919

WARREN, ROBERT PENN (1905–89): Novelist, poet, critic, playwright; novels: *Night Rider*, 1939; *At Heaven's Gate*, 1943; *All the King's Men*, 1946; *World Enough and Time*, 1950; *Band of Angels*, 1955; *The Cave*, 1959; *Wilderness: A Tale of the Civil War*, 1961; *Flood: A Romance of Our Time*, 1964; *Meet Me in the Green Glen*, 1971; *A Place to Come To*, 1977; short stories: *The Circus in the Attic*, 1947; poetry: *New and Selected Poems, 1923–1985*, 1985; essays and non-fiction: *John Brown: The Making of a Martyr*, 1929; *Segregation: The Inner Conflict in the South*, 1956; *Selected Essays*, 1958; *The Legacy of the Civil War*, 1961; *Who Speaks for the Negro?*, 1965; *A Plea in Mitigation: Modern Poetry and the End of an Era*, 1966; *Homage to Theodore Dreiser*, 1971; *Democracy and Poetry*, 1975; *A Collection of Critical Essays*, ed. J. L. Longley,

1965; with Cleanth Brooks: *Understanding Poetry*, 1938, 4th edn 1976; *Understanding Fiction*, 1943; *Fundamentals of Good Writing*, 1950.

See:

C. Bedient, *In the Heart's Last Kingdom: Robert Penn Warren's Major Poetry*, 1984

C. H. Bohner, *Robert Penn Warren*, 1964; rev. 1981

L. Casper, *Robert Penn Warren: The Dark and Bloody Ground*, 1960

W. B. Clark (ed.), *Critical Essays on Robert Penn Warren*, 1981

J. H. Justus, *The Achievement of Robert Penn Warren*, 1981

J. L. Longley, (ed.), *Robert Penn Warren: A Collection of Critical Essays*, 1965

N. Nakadate, (ed.), *Robert Penn Warren: Critical Perspectives*, 1981

H. Ruppersburg, *Robert Penn Warren and the American Imagination*, 1990

K. Snipes, *Robert Penn Warren*, 1984

V. H. Strandberg, *The Poetic Vision of Robert Penn Warren*, 1977

F. C. Watkins and J. T. Hiers, (eds.), *Robert Warren Talking: Interviews 1950–1978*, 1980

WASHINGTON, GEORGE (1732–99): C.-in-C., Continental Army, American War of Independence; First President of USA (1789–97); *First Inaugural Address*, 1789, and *Farewell Address*, 1796, reprinted with intros. in *An American Primer*, ed. D. J. Boorstin, 1966; selection: *The George Washington Papers*, ed. F. Donovan, 1968.

See:

R. Harwell, *Washington*, 1968

WELTY, EUDORA (b. 1909): Novelist, short-story writer: *The Robber Bridegroom*, 1942; *Delta Wedding*, 1946; *The Ponder Heart*, 1954; *Losing Battles*, 1970; *The Optimist's Daughter*, 1972; stories: *A Curtain of Green*, 1941; *The Wide Net and Other Stories*, 1943; *The Golden Apples*, 1949; *Short Stories*, 1950; *The Bride of Innisfallen and Other Stories*, 1955; *The Collected Stories of Eudora Welty*, 1980.

See:

A. Appel, *A Season of Dreams: The Fiction of Eudora Welty*, 1965

J. A. Bryant, Jr, *Eudora Welty*, 1964

A. J. Devlin, *Eudora Welty's Chronicle: A Story of Mississippi Life*, 1983

E. Evans, *Eudora Welty*, 1981

R. M. V. Kieft, *Eudora Welty*, 1962

M. Kreyling, *Eudora Welty's Achievement of Order*, 1980

J. L. Randisi, *A Tissue of Lies: Eudora Welty and Southern Romance*, 1982

WEST, NATHANAEL (Nathan Weinstein) (1903–40): Novelist; *The Dream Life of Balso Snell*, 1931; *Miss Lonelyhearts*, 1933; *A Cool Million*, 1934; *The Day of the Locust*, 1939; *Collected Works*, 1 vol., ed. A. Ross, 1957.

See:

V. Comerchero, *Nathanael West: The Ironic Prophet*, 1964

S. E. Hyman, *Nathanael West*, 1962

D. Madden, (ed.), *Nathanael West: The Cheaters and the Cheated*, 1973

I. Malin, *Nathanael West's Novels*, 1972

J. Martin, *Nathanael West: The Art of His Life*, 1970.
    (ed.) *Nathanael West: A Collection of Critical Essays*, 1971

R. Reid, *The Fiction of Nathanael West: No Redeemer, No Promised Land*, 1967

WHARTON, EDITH (1862–1937): Novelist, short-story writer; *The Valley of Decision*, 1902; *The House of Mirth*, 1905; *The Fruit of the Tree*, 1907; *Ethan Frome*, 1911; *The Reef*, 1912; *The Custom of the Country*, 1913; *Summer*, 1917; *The Marne*, 1918; *The Age of Innocence*, 1920; *Old New York*, 1924; *Twilight Sleep*, 1927; *The Children*, 1928; *Hudson River Bracketed*, 1929; *The Gods Arrive*, 1932; *The Buccaneers*, 1938; stories: *Collected Short Stories*, 2 vols, ed. R. W. B. Lewis, 1968; non-fiction: *The Decoration of Houses*, 1897; *Italian Villas and Their Gardens*, 1904; *Fighting France: From Dunkerque to Belfort*, 1915; *French Ways and Their Meaning*, 1919; *The Writing of Fiction*, 1925; autobiography: *A Backward Glance*, 1934; *The Constable Edith Wharton*, 4 vols., ed. M. Millgate, 1966; *Edith Wharton Reader*, ed. L. Auchinloss, 1965.

See:

E. Ammons, *Edith Wharton's Argument with America*, 1980

L. Auchinloss, *Edith Wharton*, 1961

M. Bell, *Edith Wharton and Henry James: The Story of their Friendship*, 1965

D. Holbrook, *Edith Wharton and the Unsatisfactory Man*, 1991

I. Howe, (ed.), *Edith Wharton: A Collection of Critical Essays*, 1962

G. Kellogg, *The Two Lives of Edith Wharton: The Woman and her Work*, 1965

M. Lyde, *Edith Wharton: Convention and Morality in the Work of a Novelist*, 1959

C. M. Rae, *Edith Wharton's New York Quartet*, 1984

G. Walton, *Edith Wharton: A Critical Interpretation*, 1970

WHITMAN, WALT (1819–92): Poet: *Leaves of Grass*, 1855; *Whitman's Manuscripts: 'Leaves of Grass' (1860)*, ed. F. Bowers, 1955; *Facsimile Edition of the 1860 Text*, ed. J. E. Miller, Jr, 1961; *Walt Whitman's Blue Book*, ed. A. Golden, 1968; *Correspondence*, ed. E. H. Miller, 5 vols., 1961–9; *Collected Writings*, 18 vols. projected, ed. G. W. Allen and S. Bradley, 1961– ; *Complete Poetry and Prose*, intro. by M. Cowley, 1948; *Poetry and Prose*, ed. L. Untermeyer, 1949; selections: *Portable Walt Whitman*, ed. M. Van Doren, 1945, (1977); *Poems*, ed. G. W. Allen and C. T. Davis, 1955 (with critical notes).

See:

G. W. Allen, *Walt Whitman Handbook*, 1946
    The Solitary Singer, 1955; 3rd edn 1967 (biography)
    Walt Whitman: As Man, Poet, and Legend, 1961; rev. 1969
R. Asselineau, *The Evolution of Walt Whitman*, Paris 1954; 1960–62
J. Beaver, *Walt Whitman – Poet of Science*, 1951
R. Chase, *Walt Whitman Reconsidered*, 1955
D. Donoghue, in *Connoisseurs of Chaos*, 1965
W. Eitner, *Walt Whitman's Western Jaunt*, 1981
J. Kaplan, *Walt Whitman: A Life*, 1980
J. P. Krieg, (ed.), *Walt Whitman: Here and Now*, 1985
R. W. B. Lewis, (ed.), *The Presence of Walt Whitman*, 1962
E. H. Miller, *Walt Whitman's Poetry: A Psychological Journey*, 1969
E. W. Miller, *Walt Whitman's Poetry*, 1968
S. T. Musgrove, *T. S. Eliot and Walt Whitman*, 1952
R. H. Pearce, (ed.), *Whitman: A Collection of Critical Essays*, 1962
J. Perlman and E. Folsom, eds., *Walt Whitman: The Measure of his Song*, 1981
F. Schyberg, *Walt Whitman*, (Copenhagen 1933), trans. E. A. Allen, 1951
H. J. Waskow, *Whitman: Explorations in Form*, 1966
P. Zweig, *Walt Whitman: The Making of a Poet*, 1985

WHITTIER, JOHN GREENLEAF (1807–92): Journalist, politician, reformist (especially for abolition of slavery), essayist and poet; poetry: *Legends of New England*, 1831; *Voices of Freedom*, 1846 (anti-slavery poems); *Home Ballads*, 1860; *Snow-Bound*, 1866; *The Pennsylvania Pilgrim*, 1872; *The Writings*, 7 vols, ed. H. E. Scudder, 1888–9; selection of poetry: *Whittier*, ed. D. Hall, 1960; prose: *Justice and Expediency*, 1833 (abolitionist pamphlet); *Whittier on Writers and Writing*, ed. E. H. Cady and H. H. Clark, 1950.

See:

L. Leary, *John Greenleaf Whittier*, 1961
J. B. Pickard, *John Greenleaf Whittier*, 1961
E. Wagenknecht, *John Greenleaf Whittier: A Portrait in Paradox*, 1967

WIGGLESWORTH, MICHAEL (1631–1705): Minister and physician; *Day of Doom*, 1662, ed. K. B. Murdock, 1929; *Diary . . . 1653–1657*, ed. E. S. Morgan, 1965.

WILDER, THORNTON (1897–1975): Dramatist, novelist; plays: *The Happy Journey to Trenton and Camden*, 1936 (published 1931 with *The Long Christmas Dinner* and *Pullman Car Hiawatha*); *Our Town*, 1938; *The Merchant of Yonkers*, 1938, rev. as *The Matchmaker*, 1955; *The Skin of Our Teeth*, 1942; *The Alcestiad*, 1977; *Three Plays*, 1957; novels: *The Cabala*, 1926; *The Bridge of San Luis Rey*, 1927; *The Woman of Andros*, 1930; *Heaven's My Destination*, 1934; *The Ides of March*, 1948.

See:

R. Burbank, *Thornton Wilder*, 1961
M. Goldstein, *The Art of Thornton Wilder*, 1965
R. H. Goldstone, *Thornton Wilder: An Intimate Portrait*, 1975
B. Grebanier, *Thornton Wilder*, 1965
D. Haberman, *The Plays of Thornton Wilder*, 1967
M. C. Kuner, *Thornton Wilder: The Bright and the Dark*, 1972
H. Papajewski, *Thornton Wilder*, 1968
L. Simon, *Thornton Wilder: His Work*, 1979

WILLIAMS, ROGER (*c.* 1603–83): Dissenter, unordained minister; migrated to Massachusetts 1630, banished 1635, founded Providence Plantation 1636, granted charter for Rhode Island in 1643 by Cromwell; *A Key into the [Indian] Language of America*, 1643, ed. J. J. Teunissen and E. J. Hinz, 1973; *The Bloudy Tenent of Persecution, for Cause of Conscience Discussed*, 1644; *The Bloudy Tenent yet more Bloudy*, 1652 (in response to John Cotton's defence of theocracy: *The Bloudy Tenent Washed and Made White in the Bloude of the Lambe*, 1647); *George Fox Digg'd Out of His Burrowes*, 1676; *Writings*, 1866–74, 1963.

See:

S. H. Brockunier, *The Irrepressible Democrat: Roger Williams*, 1940
H. Chupack, *Roger Williams*, 1969
J. E. Ernst, *Roger Williams: New England Firebrand*, 1932, 1969
P. Miller, (ed.), *Roger Williams: His Contribution to the American Tradition*, 1953, 1962

WILLIAMS, TENNESSEE (1911–83): Dramatist; *The Glass Menagerie*, 1944; *A Streetcar Named Desire*, 1947; *The Rose Tattoo*, 1951; *Camino Real*, 1953; *Cat on a Hot Tin Roof*, 1955; *Baby Doll* (film), 1956; *Orpheus Descending*, 1957 (revised version of *Battle of Angels*, 1940); *Suddenly Last Summer*, 1958; *Sweet Bird of Youth*, 1959; *The Night of the Iguana*, 1961; *The Milk Train Doesn't Stop Here Anymore*, 1962; *The Gnädiges Fräulein*, 1966; stories: *Collected Stories*, ed. Gore Vidal, 1986; poetry: *In the Winter of Cities*, 1956, enl. 1964; *Letters to D. Windham, 1940–1965*, ed. D. Windham, 1976.

See:

R. Boxhill, *Tennessee Williams*, 1986
S. L. Falk, *Tennessee Williams*, 1961, rev. 1978
C. R. Hughes, *Tennessee Williams: A Biography*, 1978
R. F. Leavitt (ed.), *The World of Tennessee Williams*, 1978
B. Nelson, *Tennessee Williams: The Man and his Work*, 1961
D. Rader, *Tennessee Williams: An Intimate Memoir*, 1986
D. Spoto, *The Kindness of Strangers: The Life of Tennessee Williams*, 1985
J. L. Tharpe, *Tennessee Williams: A Tribute*, 1977
N. Tischler, *Tennessee Williams: Rebellious Puritan*, 1961

G. Weales, *Tennessee Williams*, 1965
M. Yacowar, *Tennessee Williams and Film*, 1977

WILLIAMS, WILLIAM CARLOS (1883–1963): Poet, novelist, short-story writer, essayist; poetry: *Paterson*, 5 books, 1946–58, complete 1963; *Collected Earlier Poems*, 1951; *Collected Later Poems*, 1950, rev. 1963; *Journey to Love*, 1955; *Pictures from Brueghel and Other Poems*, 1963; novel trilogy: *White Mule*, 1937, *In the Morning*, 1940, *The Build-Up*, 1952; stories and documentaries: *The Knife of the Times and Other Stories*, 1932; *Life Along the Passaic River*, 1938; *Make Light of It*, 1950; *The Farmers' Daughters*, 1951; essays etc.: *The Great American Novel*, 1923; *In the American Grain*, 1925; *Selected Essays*, 1954; collected drama: *Many Loves and Other Plays*, 1961; autobiographies and biography: *Autobiography*, 1951; *I Wanted to Write a Poem*, ed. E. Heal, 1958; *Yes Mrs Williams: A Personal Record of My Mother*, 1959; *Reader*, ed. M. L. Rosenthal, 1966; *Selected Poems*, ed. C. Tomlinson, 1976.

See:
C. Doyle, *William Carlos Williams and the American Poem*, 1982
B. Duffey, *A Poetry of Presence: The Writing of William Carlos Williams*, 1986
J. Guimond, *The Art of William Carlos Williams*, 1969
V. Koch, *William Carlos Williams*, 1950
C. J. MacGowan, *William Carlos Williams's Early Poetry: The Visual Arts Background*, 1984
P. Mariani, *William Carlos Williams: A New World Naked*, 1981 (biography)
J. H. Miller, (ed.), *William Carlos Williams: A Collection of Critical Essays*, 1966
A. Ostrom, *The Poetic World of William Carlos Williams*, 1966
L. W. Wagner, *The Poems of William Carlos Williams: A Critical Study*, 1964
M. Weaver, *William Carlos Williams: The American Background*, 1977
T. R. Whitaker, *William Carlos Williams*, 1968

WINTHROP, JOHN (1588–1649): Governor of Massachusetts Bay Colony; 'A Modell of Christian Charity', 1630 ('City upon a Hill' lay sermon), in *An American Primer*, ed. D. J. Boorstin, 1966, with intro.; *History of New England 1630–1649*, ed. J. K. Hosmer, 2 vols., 1908.

WOLFE, THOMAS (1900–1938): Novelist; *Look Homeward, Angel*, 1929; *Of Time and the River*, 1935; *The Web and the Rock*, 1939; *You Can't Go Home Again*, 1940; *The Short Novels*, ed. C. H. Holman, 1961; stories: *From Death to Morning*, 1935; *The Hills Beyond*, 1941; plays: *Gentlemen of the Press*, 1942; *Mannerhouse*, 1948; *Welcome to Our City*, 1957; non-fiction: *The Story of a Novel* [*Look Homeward, Angel*], 1936; *A Western Journal*, 1951; *Letters to his Mother*, ed. J. S. Terry, 1943; *The Letters*, ed. E. Nowell, 1956; selection: *Portable Thomas Wolfe*, ed. M. Geismar, 1946.

See:

E. Evans, *Thomas Wolfe*, 1983

L. F. Field (ed.), *Thomas Wolfe: Three Decades of Criticism*, 1968

C. H. Holman, *The Loneliness at the Core: Studies in Thomas Wolfe*, 1975

P. Hansford Johnson, *The Art of Thomas Wolfe*, 1963

R. S. Kennedy, *The Window of Memory: The Literary Career of Thomas Wolfe*, 1962

E. Nowell, *Thomas Wolfe: A Biography*, 1960

P. Reeves, *Thomas Wolfe's Albatross: Race and Nationality in America*, 1969

L. D. Rubin, Jr, *Thomas Wolfe: The Weather of his Youth*, 1955

A. Turnbull, *Thomas Wolfe*, 1967

WOLFE, TOM (b. 1931): 'Non-fiction novelist', novelist and critic; *The Kandy-Kolored Tangerine-Flake Streamline Baby*, 1965; *The Electric Kool-Aid Acid Test*, 1968; *The Mid-Atlantic Man*, 1969; *Radical Chic & Mau-Mauing the Flak Catchers*, 1970; *The Right Stuff*, 1979; *In Our Time*, 1980; *From Bauhaus to Our House*, 1981; ed. with E. W. Johnson, *The New Journalism* (anthology), 1975; novel: *Bonfire of the Vanities*, 1987.

WOOLMAN, JOHN (1720–72): Preacher; *Some Considerations on the Keeping of Negroes*, Pt 1 1754; Pt 2 1762; *A Plea for the Poor*, 1793; *The Journal and Major Essays of John Woolman*, ed. P. Moulton, 1971.

See:

P. Rosenblatt, *John Woolman*, 1969

WRIGHT, RICHARD (1908–60): Novelist, short-story writer; *Native Son*, 1940; *The Outsider*, 1953; *The Long Dream*, 1958; *Lawd Today*, 1963; stories: *Uncle Tom's Children*, 1938; rev. 1940; *Eight Men*, 1961; non-fiction: *The God that Failed*, 1950; *Black Power*, 1954; *The Color Curtain*, 1956; *Pagan Spain*, 1957; autobiography: *Black Boy*, 1945.

See:

R. A. Bone, *Richard Wright*, 1969

R. Fabre, *The World of Richard Wright*, 1985

R. Felgar, *Richard Wright*, 1980

A. Gayle, *Richard Wright: Ordeal of a Native Son*, 1980

K. Kinnamon, *The Emergence of Richard Wright: A Study in Literature and Society*, 1972

D. McCall, *The Example of Richard Wright*, 1969

E. Margolies, *The Art of Richard Wright*, 1969

C. Webb, *Richard Wright: A Biography*, 1968

ACKNOWLEDGEMENTS

For permission to print copyright material, acknowledgements are made as follows:

JOHN ASHBERY: To Viking Penguin Inc. and Carcanet Press Ltd for 'Rain Moving In' from *A Wave*. Copyright © 1983 by John Ashbery.

CHARLES BERNSTEIN: To Sun & Moon Press for 'Force of Habit', © Charles Bernstein, 1983 (from *Islets/Irritations*, New York: Jordan Davies, 1983).

EMILY DICKINSON: To Little, Brown & Company for lines from Poems 269, 419 from *The Complete Poems of Emily Dickinson*, edited by Thomas H. Johnson. Copyright 1935 by Martha Dickinson Bianchi; Copyright © renewed 1963 by Mary L. Hampson. To the publishers and the Trustees of Amherst College for extracts from *The Poems of Emily Dickinson*, edited by Thomas H. Johnson, Cambridge, Mass.: The Belknap Press of Harvard University Press, Copyright 1951, © 1955, 1979, 1983 by the President and Fellows of Harvard College. A version of this chapter first appeared in *Sewanee Review*, 1983.

T. S. ELIOT: To Harcourt Brace Jovanovich, Inc., and Faber & Faber Ltd for an extract from 'Ash-Wednesday' from *Collected Poems 1909–1962*.

ROBERT FROST: To Jonathan Cape Ltd and Henry Holt & Company, Inc., for extracts from 'A Servant to Servant', 'Two Look at Two', 'Home Burial', 'The Black Cottage', 'Stars', 'An Old Man's Winter Night', 'Come In', 'The Vantage Point' and 'Storm Fear' from *The Poetry of Robert Frost*, edited by Edward Connery Lathem; and extracts from *The Selected Letters of Robert Frost*, edited by L. Thompson.

ALLEN GINSBERG: To Penguin Books Ltd, and Harper & Row, Publishers, Inc. for ten specified lines from 'Contest of Bards' from *Collected Poems 1947–1980* (Viking Books, 1985), Copyright © Allen Ginsberg, 1984.

TED HUGHES: To Faber & Faber Ltd and Harper & Row, Publishers, Inc., for four lines from 'Littleblood' (in *Crow*) from *New Selected Poems*, Copyright © 1971 by Ted Hughes.

RANDALL JARRELL: To Faber & Faber Ltd for 'Some Lines from Whitman' from *Poetry and the Age*.

LEROI JONES: To The Sterling Lord Agency, Inc., for 'In the Tradition' by LeRoi Jones (Amiri Baraka), Copyright © 1980 by Amiri Baraka.

ROBERT LOWELL: To Faber & Faber Ltd and Farrar, Straus & Giroux, Inc., for extracts from *Poems 1938–49*, © 1972, 1974, 1975 by Robert Lowell, *For the Union Dead*, © 1960, 1964 by Robert Lowell, and *Notebook*, © 1967, 1968, 1969 by Robert Lowell.

FRANK O'HARA: To City Lights Books for 'Poem' from *Selected Poems*, © 1964 by Frank O'Hara; to Alfred A. Knopf, Inc. for 'Personism: A Manifesto' from *The Collected Poems of Frank O'Hara*, edited by Donald Allen.

EUGENE O'NEILL: To Jonathan Cape Ltd, the Executors of the Eugene O'Neill Estate, and the Collection of American Literature, The Beinecke Rare Book and Manuscript Library, Yale University, for extracts from *Desire Under the Elms* and *The Iceman Cometh*.

BOB PERELMAN: To The Figures for 'Road Tones' (1978).

SYLVIA PLATH: To Olwyn Hughes, Faber & Faber Ltd and Harper & Row, Publishers, Inc. for forty-seven lines of poetry from 'Poems for a Birthday', copyright © 1960 by Ted Hughes, 'The Night Dances', copyright © 1965 by the Estate of Sylvia Plath, and 'Edge', copyright © 1963 by Ted Hughes, from *The Collected Poems of Sylvia Plath* edited by Ted Hughes.

EZRA POUND: To Faber & Faber Ltd and New Directions Publishing Corporation for extracts from Ezra Pound: *Selected Letters 1907–1941*, edited by D. D. Paige and Ezra Pound, Copyright 1950 by Ezra Pound; *The Cantos of Ezra Pound*, Copyright 1934 by Ezra Pound; and *Personae*, Copyright 1926 by Ezra Pound.

THEODORE ROETHKE: To Faber & Faber Ltd and Doubleday & Company Inc. for excerpts from 'The Lost Son', 'The Shape of the Fire', 'The Long Alley', copyright 1947 by Theodore Roethke; and excerpts from 'Meditation at Oyster River', copyright © 1960 by Beatrice Roethke as executrix of the Estate of Theodore Roethke. All from *The Collected Poems of Theodore Roethke*.

ANNE SEXTON: To The Sterling Lord Agency, Inc. for 'Wanting to Die' from *Live or Die* (Houghton Mifflin Co., 1966), Copyright © 1966 by Anne Sexton.

ACKNOWLEDGEMENTS

WALLACE STEVENS: To Alfred A. Knopf, Inc., and Faber & Faber Ltd for excerpts from *The Collected Poems of Wallace Stevens*.

ANNE WALDMAN: To the publishers and the author for 'Makeup on Empty Space', which first appeared in *Makeup on Empty Space* (The Toothpaste Press, 1984), Copyright © 1984 by Anne Waldman.

WILLIAM CARLOS WILLIAMS: To Penguin Books Ltd and New Directions Publishing Corporation for *Paterson*, copyright © W. C. Williams, 1946, 1948, 1949, 1951, 1958; copyright © Florence Williams, 1963; to New Directions Publishing Corporation and Carcanet Press Ltd for 'The Red Wheelbarrow', 'The Widow's Lament in Springtime' from *Collected Earlier Poems*, Copyright 1938 by New Directions Publishing Corporation.

The publishers regret that their attempts to contact the copyright holders of works by Ted Berrigan and Duane Big Eagle, and the holder of US rights in Randall Jarrell's work, have been unsuccessful. Due acknowledgement will gladly be made in later editions if the relevant information is forthcoming.

NOTES ON CONTRIBUTORS

John W. Aldridge is Professor of English at the University of Michigan. He has written several volumes of literary criticism, among them *After the Lost Generation* and *The American Novel and the Way We Live Now*; a novel, *The Party at Cranton*; and social commentary, *In the Country of the Young*.

Harold Beaver was Professor of American Literature at the University of Amsterdam and visiting professor at the University of Denver. He has edited Melville and Poe for the Penguin English Library. His books include *Huckleberry Finn* and collected essays, *The Great American Masquerade*.

Pearl K. Bell, a writer who lives in Cambridge, Massachusetts, was formerly the book critic for *The New Leader* and the fiction critic for *Commentary*.

Alwyn Berland is Professor Emeritus and former Dean of Humanities at McMaster University. He is the author of *Culture and Conduct in the Novels of Henry James*, and has completed a study of William Faulkner, being published in 1992.

Warner Berthoff is Henry B. and Anne M. Cabot Professor of English and American Literature at Harvard University. His books include *The Example of Melville, The Ferment of Realism, Hart Crane* and *American Trajectories: Authors and Readings 1790–1970*.

Seymour Betsky (d. 1987) held the Chair in American Literature at the University of Utrecht, the Netherlands. He has published in *Scrutiny*, the Sewanee Review, *Essays in Criticism*, and *Universities Quarterly*.

T. A. Birrell was Professor of English and American Literature at the University of Nymegen, the Netherlands. He is editor of *English Studies* and his books include *The Library of John Morris, Engelse Letterkunde, Amerikaanse Letterkunde, Shakespeare Stuk voor Stuk*, and *English Monarchs and their Books*.

Hugh Brogan is a Professor of History at the University of Essex. His books include *The Life of Arthur Ransome* and the *Penguin History of the United States of America*.

Jean Chothia is a fellow of Selwyn College and University Lecturer in

English and American Literature, Cambridge. She is the author of *Forging a Language: A Study of the Plays of Eugene O'Neill* and *Directors in Perspective: Andre Antoine* (1991).

Donald Davie, the English poet, was Professor of English at Vanderbilt University, Tennessee, returning to England for good in 1988 after twenty years teaching in the USA. His books include many volumes of poetry, and also *Articulate Energy, Ezra Pound, A Gathered Church*, and *These the Companions: Recollections*.

Peter Davison was formerly a Fellow of the Shakespeare Institute and Professor of English and American Literature, University of Kent. He is now Visiting Professor, De Montfort University and President of the Bibliographical Society. His 20-volume edition of Orwell works, is due in 1994. He has published fifteen books and editions, mainly of drama.

Lillian Feder is Distinguished Professor of English, Classical, and Comparative Literature at the Graduate School, City of University of New York. She is the author of *The Meridian Handbook of Classical Literature, Ancient Myth in Modern Poetry*, and *Madness in Literature*.

Wayne Fields is Professor of English at Washington University. He has written on nineteenth-century American literature and politics and is the author of *What The River Knows, The Past Leads a Life of Its Own* and *A Union of Words* (1993).

Philip Fisher is Professor of English at Harvard University. He is the author of *Making and Effacing Art: Modern American Art in a Culture of Museums* and *Hard Facts*. He has recently edited the collection *New American Studies* and is at work on a philosophical and literary study of the passions.

John Fraser is Munro Professor of English at Dalhousie University. He is the author of *Violence in the Arts, America and the Patrons of Chivalry*, and *The Name of Action: Critical Essays*. In 1990 he gave the Alexander lectures at the University of Toronto.

Blanche Gelfant is the Robert E. Maxwell Professor in the Arts and Sciences at Dartmouth College. Her publications on twentieth-century fiction and writers include *The American City Novel, 1890–1950* and *Women Writing in America: Voices in Collage* and a forthcoming book on cross-cultural literary criticism.

Richard Gooder is a Fellow of Clare College, Cambridge, and an editor of *The Cambridge Quarterly*. He has recently published on Shakespeare, Emily Dickinson, Henry James, Mark Twain and Frank O'Hara.

Eugene Goodheart is Edytha Macy Gross Professor of Humanities at Brandeis University. He is the author of books of literary and cultural criticism, among them *Culture and the Radical Conscience, The Failure of Criticism*, and *The Skeptical Disposition in Contemporary Criticism*.

Fred Hobson is Professor English and co-editor of the *Southern Literary Journal* at the University of North Carolina at Chapel Hill. He is the author of *Serpent in Eden: H. L. Mencken and the South, Tell about the South: The Southern Rage to Explain* and *The Southern Writer in the Postmodern World*.

David Holbrook is an Emeritus Fellow of Downing College, Cambridge. His books include *Sylvia Plath: Poetry and Existence*, and *Lost Bearings in English Poetry*. Recent studies include *The Skeleton in the Wardrobe* on C. S. Lewis and *Where D. H. Lawrence was Wrong About Women*. His latest novel *Even if They Fail*, and his *Selected Poems* were published in 1980.

Randall Jarrell (1914–65) taught literature mainly at the University of N. Carolina, Greensboro. His books include *Kipling, Auden & Co., Poetry and the Age*, and *The Third Book of Criticism*, as well as volumes of poems, a novel, children's books, and a translation of Goethe's *Faust, Part 1*.

Frederick R. Karl is Professor of English at New York University. He is the author of *Joseph Conrad: The Three Lives, American Fictions: 1940–1980, Modern and Modernism: The Sovereignty of the Artist, 1885–1925*. He is the general editor of the *Collected Letters of Joseph Conrad* (in 8 volumes).

L. C. Knights (d. 1997) was King Edward VII Professor of English Literature Emeritus in the University of Cambridge. One of the first editors of *Scrutiny*, his books include *Drama and Society in the Age of Jonson, Public Voices: Literature and Politics, with Special Reference to the Seventeenth Century, Some Shakespearean Themes*, and volumes of critical essays.

Townsend Ludington is Cary C. Boshamer Professor of English and American Studies at the University of N. Carolina, Chapel Hill. He has edited *The Fourteenth Chronicle: Letters and Diaries of John Dos Passos*, and his books about American literature and culture include *John Dos Passos: A Twentieth Century Odyssey*, and *Marsden Hartley: The Biography of an American Artist*.

Susan Manning is University Assistant Lecturer in the Faculty of English at Cambridge, and Fellow of Newnham College. She has recently published a book on American and Scottish Literature. *The Puritan-Provincial Vision*, and is currently working on *The Art of Pleasure*.

Michael Millgate is Professor of English at the University of Toronto. His books on American literature include *American Social Fiction* and *The Achievement of William Faulkner*. He is also author of *Thomas Hardy: A Biography*, and *Testamentary Acts: Browning, Tennyson, James, Hardy*.

Eric Mottram is Professor of English and American Literature at King's College, University of London. He is the author of *William Burroughs: The Algebra of Need, William Faulkner: A Profile, Towards Design in Poetry*, and books on Kenneth Rexroth, Allen Ginsberg and Paul Bowles; he co-edited *The Avenel Companion to English and American Literature*, Vol. 2, and is the author of a dozen books of poetry.

Joel Porte is the Ernest I. White Professor of American Studies and Humane Letters at Cornell University. His books include *The Romance in America, Representative Man: Ralph Waldo Emerson In His Time*, and *In Respect to Egotism: Studies in American Romantic Writing*.

William H. Pritchard is Henry Clay Folger Professor of English at Amherst College. His books include *Seeing Through Everything: English Writers 1918– 1940, Lives of the Modern Poets, Frost: A Literary Life Reconsidered*, and *Randall Jarrell: A Literary Life*.

Jerome Rothenberg is Professor of Literature and Visual Arts at the University of California, San Diego. A co-founder and editor of the journal, *Alcheringa*, his over forty books of poetry and seven anthologies include *Technicians of the Sacred, Shaking the Pumbpkin, America a Prophecy*, and *New Selected Poems 1970–1985*.

Richard Ruland is Professor of English and American Literature at Washington University, St Louis, Missouri. His books include *The Rediscovery of American Literature: Premises of Critical Taste, 1900–1940*, two collections with commentary of theories of American Literature, *The Native Muse* and *A Storied Land*, and – with Malcolm Bradbury –*From Puritanism to Postmodernism: A History of American Literature*.

Charles Tomlinson is Emeritus Professor of English at the University of Bristol. A poet, artist and teacher, his most recent books are *Collected Poems, The Door in the Wall* and *Poetry Metamorphosis*. *Eden* contains a selection of his graphics.

Alan Trachtenberg is Neil Gray, Jr. Professor of American Studies and English at Yale University. He is the author of *Brooklyn Bridge: Fact and Symbol, The Incorporation of America: Culture and Society in the Gilded Age*, and *Reading American Photographs: Images as History Creative Experiment*

Frank Whitehead was Reader in English and Education at the University of Sheffield. He is the author of *The Disappearing Dais* and co-author of the Schools Council Research Study *Children and Their Books*.

INDEX

READ MORE IN PENGUIN

In every corner of the world, on every subject under the sun, Penguin represents quality and variety – the very best in publishing today.

For complete information about books available from Penguin – including Puffins, Penguin Classics and Arkana – and how to order them, write to us at the appropriate address below. Please note that for copyright reasons the selection of books varies from country to country.

In the United Kingdom: Please write to *Dept. EP, Penguin Books Ltd, Bath Road, Harmondsworth, West Drayton, Middlesex UB7 ODA*

In the United States: Please write to *Consumer Sales, Penguin Putnam Inc., P.O. Box 12289 Dept. B, Newark, New Jersey 07101-5289*. VISA and MasterCard holders call 1-800-788-6262 to order Penguin titles

In Canada: Please write to *Penguin Books Canada Ltd, 10 Alcorn Avenue, Suite 300, Toronto, Ontario M4V 3B2*

In Australia: Please write to *Penguin Books Australia Ltd, P.O. Box 257, Ringwood, Victoria 3134*

In New Zealand: Please write to *Penguin Books (NZ) Ltd, Private Bag 102902, North Shore Mail Centre, Auckland 10*

In India: Please write to *Penguin Books India Pvt Ltd, 11 Community Centre, Panchsheel Park, New Delhi 110017*

In the Netherlands: Please write to *Penguin Books Netherlands bv, Postbus 3507, NL-1001 AH Amsterdam*

In Germany: Please write to *Penguin Books Deutschland GmbH, Metzlerstrasse 26, 60594 Frankfurt am Main*

In Spain: Please write to *Penguin Books S. A., Bravo Murillo 19, 1° B, 28015 Madrid*

In Italy: Please write to *Penguin Italia s.r.l., Via Benedetto Croce 2, 20094 Corsico, Milano*

In France: Please write to *Penguin France, Le Carré Wilson, 62 rue Benjamin Baillaud, 31500 Toulouse*

In Japan: Please write to *Penguin Books Japan Ltd, Kaneko Building, 2-3-25 Koraku, Bunkyo-Ku, Tokyo 112*

In South Africa: Please write to *Penguin Books South Africa (Pty) Ltd, Private Bag X14, Parkview, 2122 Johannesburg*

READ MORE IN PENGUIN

LITERARY CRITICISM

The Practice of Writing David Lodge

This lively collection examines the work of authors ranging from the two Amises to Nabokov and Pinter; the links between private lives and published works; and the different techniques required in novels, stage plays and screenplays. 'These essays, so easy in manner, so well-built and informative, offer a fine blend of creative writing and criticism' *Sunday Times*

A Lover's Discourse Roland Barthes

'May be the most detailed, painstaking anatomy of desire we are ever likely to see or need again ... The book is an ecstatic celebration of love and language ... readers interested in either or both ... will enjoy savouring its rich and dark delights' *Washington Post*

The New Pelican Guide to English Literature Edited by Boris Ford

The indispensable critical guide to English and American literature in nine volumes, erudite yet accessible. From the ages of Chaucer and Shakespeare, via Georgian satirists and Victorian social critics, to the leading writers of the twentieth century, all literary life is here.

The Structure of Complex Words William Empson

'Twentieth-century England's greatest critic after T. S. Eliot, but whereas Eliot was the high priest, Empson was the *enfant terrible* ... *The Structure of Complex Words* is one of the linguistic masterpieces of the epoch, finding in the feel and tone of our speech whole sedimented social histories' *Guardian*

Vamps and Tramps Camille Paglia

'Paglia is a genuinely unconventional thinker ... Taken as a whole, the book gives an exceptionally interesting perspective on the last thirty years of intellectual life in America, and is, in its wacky way, a celebration of passion and the pursuit of truth' *Sunday Telegraph*

READ MORE IN PENGUIN

A CHOICE OF CLASSICS

READ MORE IN PENGUIN

A CHOICE OF CLASSICS

READ MORE IN PENGUIN

New Pelican Guide to English Literature

Edited by Boris Ford

'The best and most lively general survey of English literature available to schools, students and general readers' – *The Times Educational Supplement*

Authoritative, stimulating and accessible, the original seven volume *Pelican Guide to English Literature* has earned itself a distinguished reputation. Now enlarged to ten volumes and a readers' guide, this popular series has been wholly revised and updated.

What this work sets out to offer is a guide to the history and traditions of English literature, a contour-map of the literary scene. Each volume includes these standard features:

   (i)   An account of the social context of literature in each period.

  (ii)   A general survey of the literature itself.

 (iii)   A series of critical essays on individual writers and their works – each written by an authority in their field.

 (iv)   Full appendices including short author biographies, listings of standard editions of authors' works, critical commentaries and titles for further study and reference.

The *Guide* consists of the following volumes:

   1.   Medieval Literature
       Part One: Chaucer and the Alliterative Tradition
       Part Two: The European Inheritance
   2.   The Age of Shakespeare
   3.   From Donne to Marvell
   4.   From Dryden to Johnson
   5.   From Blake to Byron
   6.   From Dickens to Hardy
   7.   From James to Eliot
   8.   From Orwell to Naipaul
   9.   American Literature

and

A Guide for Readers